THE
YELLOWLEGS

THE
YELLOWLEGS

THE STORY OF THE UNITED STATES CAVALRY

RICHARD WORMSER

FRONTLINE
BOOKS

THE YELLOWLEGS
The Story of the United States Cavalry

This edition published in Great Britain in 2018 by Frontline Books,
an imprint of Pen & Sword Books Ltd, Yorkshire – Philadelphia.

First published by Doubleday & Company Inc., New York, 1966.

Copyright © Richard Wormser
ISBN: 978 1 52674 234 6

Typeset in 10/12.5 pt Palatino
Printed and bound by TJ International, Padstow, Cornwall

Pen & Sword Books Ltd incorporates the imprints of Pen & Sword Archaeology, Air World
Books, Atlas, Aviation, Battleground, Discovery, Family History, History, Maritime, Military,
Naval, Politics, Social History, Transport, True Crime, Claymore Press, Frontline Books,
Praetorian Press, Seaforth Publishing and White Owl

For a complete list of Pen & Sword titles please contact:

PEN & SWORD BOOKS LTD
47 Church Street, Barnsley, South Yorkshire, S70 2AS, UK.
E-mail: enquiries@pen-and-sword.co.uk
Website: www.pen-and-sword.co.uk

Or

PEN AND SWORD BOOKS,
1950 Lawrence Roadd, Havertown, PA 19083, USA
E-mail: Uspen-and-sword@casematepublishers.com
Website: www.penandswordbooks.com

Contents

Introduction

Probably no phase of American history can awaken such loud and bitter disputes as that part played in it by the United States Cavalry, the Yellowlegs, the men who counted their numbers in sabers: "There were present three officers and eighteen men of the First Dragoons: twenty-one sabers in all; and seventeen men and an officer of the Eighth Infantry; eighteen rifles."

This is a quotation from a report of Lieutenant, later Major General, P. St. George Cooke to Colonel, later Major General, Stephen Watts Kearny. Writers of regimental and other cavalry annals, no enemies of clichés, always call the former the Grand Old Man and the latter the Father of the Cavalry. So, the description should be accurate.

It isn't. The saber was never a frontier weapon; in the years from the Civil War till the final Massacre at Broken Knee, cavalrymen invariably left their swords behind when they took to the field. It is possible that they still carried them when Cooke was a lieutenant; certainly, his son-in-law, J.E.B. Stuart, was astounded in his first anti-Indian battle by the order to draw saber and charge.

The charge failed, and the cavalrymen dropped off their horses and used their carbines as they should have; because the post-revolutionary cavalryman was a mounted infantryman, a horseman who used his mount to get to the fighting, then got down and shot it out from ground cover.

The first two regiments of United States Cavalry (after the Legions of the Revolution) were called Dragoons. The next was called Mounted Rifles. Then, in 1855, the War Department changed the 1st and 2nd Dragoons to the 1st and 2nd U.S. Cavalry; the Mounted Rifles became the 3rd, and the 1st and 2nd Cavalry – six years later – became the 4th and 5th.

A Dragoon does what a mounted rifleman does, except he uses a shorter gun, a carbine, to do it with. A cavalry outfit, on the other hand, is supposed – by classical definition, which never holds when the bullets are real – to be held in reserve behind the infantry when a battle starts. Then, when the foot soldiers have their enemy counterparts on the run, the cavalry flanks and completes the rout.

It is obvious that there never was an Indian tribe on the Plains who would hold still for this sort of treatment; and when the Indians made a stand in the mountains or woods, there was always a rock or a tree to hide behind while the Yellowlegs thundered by.

However, during the Revolution – and occasionally during the Civil War – classical cavalry tactics were used. How effective they were is disputed; many highly reputable students of the Civil War claim that J.E.B. Stuart could have tipped the scales for the South in several battles if, after using his horsemen as brilliant scouts and flank protectors, he had ordered them into formation to charge infantry.

In the Revolution, one British cavalry officer was so enraged by the failure of Francis Marion and Light-Horse Harry Lee to stand and be killed as a good hussar should that he sent over a message challenging the Yankees to a fixed duel. The reply was that this would be done, twenty riders against twenty riders, after which the Englishman thought better of the whole thing.

In three wars – 1812, 1898, and 1917 – no American horse action counted at all. Roosevelt's Rough Riders – so called because they were in Roosevelt's regiment, though commanded by Colonel Leonard Wood – never took their horses to Cuba with them, nor did the Buffalo Soldiers of the 9th Cavalry, who rescued the elite regiment after it had stuck itself on San Juan Hill.

After the war, the Rough Riders returned to Long Island, picked up their mounts, and rode them up Fifth Avenue triumphantly, for the first cavalry action of the fracas. Fifth Avenue is in New York, and the only enemies encountered were politicians who planned on ruining Theodore Roosevelt's career by kicking him into the vice-presidency two years later.

The Yellowlegs were brave, dashing, and Lord knows, hard-working: besides carrying out all the other duties of a soldier, they had the horses and gear to care for.

They profoundly changed the course of American history; they opened up the Santa Fe trail, they eventually drove the Cheyenne and Sioux out of the Plains, and no names were more feared by the enemy than those of Marion and Lee in the Revolution and Stuart and Sheridan in the War between the States.

But they suffered – the leaders, that is – from a strange two-headedness. They wanted to be cavalrymen, beaux sabreurs, in situations that called for gunmen, carbineers.

Custer, who wore the two stars of a major general within four years of leaving West Point, failed utterly at Little Big Horn; Cooke, as tough an Indian fighter as the Army ever put into the West, was pulled out of the field and sent on recruiting duty after one disastrous battle against the Confederacy.

It is probable that Cooke could have handled Sitting Bull without trouble, that Custer could have overtaken Stuart at the Peninsula. Indians needed frontier methods; Stuart's men could have been defeated by an officer with wartime dash, rather than Regular Army caution.

A mounted rifleman or a Dragoon was not a cavalryman, and a cavalryman was not at his best fighting dismounted.

But the Army never learned. When the last horse soldiers were dismounted, in the years just before Hitler marched into Poland, a new cavalry maneuver was being taught.

Instead of charging with the saber overhead, ready to slash, cadets and recruits were now instructed to hold the blade straight in front of them, ready to pierce.

But there hadn't been a genuine U.S. Cavalry charge in seventy years.

There were just tough, hard-riding, hard-shooting, leather-tailed dragoons, underpaid, underfed, and overworked. If there hadn't been, this would now be one of three English-speaking countries on this continent, none of them as important as Mexico. The Yellowlegs didn't win big battles – that must be done by the infantry – but the horse soldiers set the battle up so it could be won.

From the time Light-House Harry Lee went south with his Legion after Valley Forge till the end of the nineteenth century, when his great grandson, Fitzhugh Lee, Jr., reported for duty as a shavetail Yellowleg, the United States needed the horse soldiers.

List of Maps

Chapter 1

Washington's Best Boy

Henry Lee was only three years out of the College of New Jersey at Princeton when he joined General Washington's army. The childless Washington was notoriously fond of young men to replace the son he never had; Harry Lee had other qualifications.

He was a close relative of Richard Henry Lee, whose prestige in Virginia matched that of the general, and whose background was as similar as anyone's could be to the rich Washington's. Washington, in fact, had been born about ten miles from Stratford, home of the Lees.

Richard Henry Lee and his brother, Francis Lightfoot Lee, had both signed the Declaration of Independence. Also, tradition has it, Washington had at one time courted Harry Lee's mother.

The general made rather a pet of the young Virginian; and he never had cause to regret it. But Harry Lee had not joined the Revolution to carry the general's pen and inkhorn; he soon established himself as an excellent scout and – very important to the impoverished Continental Army – forager. Harry Lee's original commission had been in the Virginia cavalry, but when he was transferred to the Continental forces, he must have been attached to the general staff; General Washington and the Congress did not commission any cavalry until the war had been on a good two years, though four message-riding state groups had some vague Continental standing.

The Revolution was, during that period, largely a matter of the northern colonies, or states as they were beginning to think of themselves. This may, in large part, account for the acquiescence of the Massachusetts leaders to the high appointment of so many Southerners; the southern agriculturists were not nearly so angry with England's oppressive mercantile policy as were the northern merchants and processors, and southern heroes were needed to inspire the South.

Not only was the revolutionary government northern oriented, the early fighting was, too. And in the New England states, cavalry would have been

1

of little use; the battles were in the wilderness, where the best, sometimes the only, trails were waterways.

Washington was skeptical of the use of cavalry, anyway. He had been a colonel in Braddock's campaign against the French and Indians in 1755 and had experienced that Englishman's embarrassment at trying to provide fodder for his column.

It must be remembered that even without horse soldiers, an army in those days required huge amounts of hay and grain, when it was not waterborne. The artillery was, of course, horse-drawn – but so were the ambulances, the supply wagons, everything including the officers.

Toward the end of 1776 the war had moved as far south as New York, where the Continentals underwent a smashing defeat on Long Island. That appendage of New York is flat, sandy, and even then, was highly cultivated; cavalry could have thrived and probably turned the day for the Americans. But there was no cavalry; Harry Lee and the general's second cousin, William Washington, were used as scouts, but they had left their Virginia horse troops back home.

The British and the Hessians did have cavalry, and Banastre Tarleton was promoted to brigadier general for his work in the northern campaigns. The Hessian horsemen, however, do not seem to have been much of a factor; practically every British order commands, pleads with, or requests field commanders to find mounts for Baron von Riedesel's dragoons. Most of the British and German mounts had died on the transports.

Escaping from Long Island, Washington fought his way across Westchester County and into New Jersey. He had not only lost a battle; he had lost most of the prestige the Continental Army had, and most of the confidence the central states had held in him. The New Jersey and Maryland time-expired men went home; the New Jersey militia refused to answer a call to arms.

Washington took Trenton and then struck at Princeton. Neither Harry Lee nor William Washington seems to have been with him at the latter battle; when the British were routed, the general himself picked up a troop of Philadelphia light horse and harassed the British rear, which was covered by troops from the 16th and 17th (British) Light Dragoons.

The pursuit was successful until the Dragoons halted, dismounted, and turned their carbines on the Americans. Washington called off the pursuit; it is quite possible that he learned a lesson about Dragoons and mounted riflemen there on the red soil of New Jersey.

Incidentally, the British commander, Mawhood, went into the Battle of Princeton on a light pony, his two favorite spaniels trotting on either side of him.

At Princeton General Washington noted that he took two brass guns but was unable to carry them away because of the lack of horses.

Congress had authorized three thousand light horse troops in the last week of 1776, but it had also authorized more than seventy thousand other recruits; this was a paper army, to be paid in paper – worthless Continentals – and few Federal horse were sworn in. Note that only "light horse" were authorized; the United States never considered having heavy, or armored, horse soldiers, which were already outmoded except for parade.

The winter went on with light fighting; by spring Washington had cleared the enemy out of Jersey and was marching on Pennsylvania. His orders for the march show a "Sub. (altern) and twelve light horse" heading the column, and cavalry: "a troop of horse 150 yds. in the rear of all the rest."

It is not entirely clear whether these were Continental troops or militia; if the latter, they were probably Pennsylvanians.

As the column moved on Philadelphia, Lord Howe faced them with a strong force of troops fresh out from England. The British attack was delayed because of the condition of the Light Dragoon horses after a trip in transports across the Atlantic. At least they were alive – more than three hundred had died – and when recovered they took part in a foray at Elkton, Maryland, from which – British sources claim – the Philadelphia Horse fled. This would lead us to believe that the troop of horse with Washington had, indeed, been militia.

By September, however, some Federal Dragoons had been organized and put under the command of Count Casimir Pulaski. Thereafter, they are seldom mentioned in the dispatches and reports; it can be presumed that the European general handled them in the European way, and thus lessened their efficiency. As the Army was to find out sixty years later – and continue to find out until the Sioux surrendered at almost the end of the nineteenth century – an American cavalryman could not drill in the European manner and still find time to fight. European methods depended on an enemy who knew the rules and on indoor bivouacs (commandeered barns and stables in which the horses could shelter in bad weather).

In December Washington went into winter quarters in Valley Forge. Harry Lee was now a Continental, rather than a Virginia officer, and beginning to prove himself invaluable in the miserable winter of Valley Forge. There is no use repeating here the sad, weary story of the footsteps in the snow. The enemy ceased to be England, King George, or taxation without representation; it became, simply, winter, starvation, and death from exposure.

Harry Lee turned twenty-two that January of 1778. George Washington became forty-six the next month. Forty-six is not old, nowadays; perhaps it wasn't old then. But twenty-two is young any way you look at it. Harry Lee, together with Anthony Wayne and Allan McLane, took it upon himself to forage. That the army survived the winter, that the United States survived at all, is almost completely dependent on those three men and their followers. To the north and east there was still some Continental Army, but at least two of its generals thought the war was lost, and one of them was to desert to the British before very long.

Wayne, not yet called "Mad Anthony", earned the nickname of the Drover by stealing a huge herd of cattle, almost all the cattle in New Jersey, and driving them into a camp too famished to cheer.

Allan McLane, captain of Philadelphia militia light horse, was later to be known as Harry Lee's best and most active troop commander; he served with Harry Lee all through the war.

Harry Lee proved himself a good thief during that horrible time; maybe not as good a one as McLane, but second to no one else at Valley Forge. He took Delaware as his particular province, perhaps because McLane expected to return there after the war and didn't want to start neighborhood feuds. Lee stole cattle and chickens, eggs and blankets, and outshone all others in his procurement of hay and other fodder; necessary, bulky, and of supreme importance to George Washington, once field officer of Braddock's hayless expedition, more often a gentleman stock farmer.

In other words, Harry Lee proved, at Valley Forge, that he could take a cavalry outfit and keep it fed and mounted under the most adverse conditions.

He did more. He bounced back from his fatigue, every night he was in camp, and proved himself ready to divert the harrassed general with gentle talk of the port bottle and the sack decanter, of well-bred horses and cotillions back in the Old Dominion, of all the joys of the gentle life in Tidewater Virginia that the neighbors could look forward to enjoying after the war.

Their homes were about fifteen miles apart, and one topic they certainly didn't discuss was the ownership of Mount Vernon; a Lee had married Lawrence Washington's widow, and claimed that George, only a half-brother of Lawrence, had not inherited the home; the widow had. On at least one occasion, George Washington is known to have paid rent to the Lees, and the two families were socially stiff with each other over the matter. No doubt, George Washington thought of Harry Lee as his mother's, rather than his father's, son; but even if he didn't, Virginians are famous for feuding with their kissing kin, while the kissing continues.

It became the general's habit to send for Harry Lee each night when the dispatches to Congress were written – dreary, sad work – and the orders for the next day given.

In the spring Henry Lee was promoted to major and made the head of Lee's Legion, a mixed force of horsemen and footmen, depending on how successful it was in stealing horses. He was under orders to keep his foot and horse separate, but he never did. His men, icidentally, wore smart green jackets and doeskin breeches, rather than the blue-and-bluff of other Continentals.

Light-Horse Harry Lee had moved into the pages of history.

At the Battle of Stony Point, back up on the Hudson in early summer, he had used his troops as scouts, and had stolen information – Allan McLane was particularly useful – with the same ease that he had stolen forage in Delaware. McLane's men hid in the trees around the fort and came out to stop farmers and deserters for questioning.

But this wasn't cavalry work; this was an assignment for Mounted Scouts. Dash in, count troops, memorize redoubts and bastions, get out again, and ride at the gallop if there is a shot fired at you in anger. The infantry saying that no one ever saw a dead cavalryman was being born.

Mad Anthony Wayne had been the hero of Stony Point; his troops were light infantrymen. The principal weapon was the bayonet, with the ax secondary; most of the Continentals didn't even load their guns. Once the fighting started, the horse soldiers could rest. They didn't feel very gallant about it.

As Washington Irving was to write: "Stony Point piqued his (Harry Lee's) emulation."

While on the scout, setting up Stony Point for Wayne, Lee and his men had noticed another British fort, which might well have been called Swampy Point but was, in fact, called Paulus or Powles Hook.

New Yorkers who want to see it can just glance across the North River; it is now part of Jersey City, a low blunt projection into the Hudson. Sandy itself, it was backed by tidal marsh, with a single, perfunctorily filled road connecting it to firm mainland. At first glance it seemed a proposition for Yankee gunboats, rather than Dragoons.

But Lee and his sturdy McLane had a plan. They dismounted their Dragoons to form a right wing, borrowed a hundred Virginians from General Woodford to make – with two small companies of Marylanders – a left wing. Unfortunately, Woodford sent a major who was senior to Harry Lee, and not of a mind to take orders from a junior; so half the Virginians went home again.

Nevertheless, Lee struck at the fort and took it, gloriously, if on foot. He killed fifty Britishers and Hessians and captured another hundred and fifty; he had matched or outshone Mad Anthony's accomplishment. Only two Americans were killed, three wounded.

This was to be another strike-and-run battle. Paulus Hook was in the heart of the British strength; it could not be held. Lee had arranged for boats to take his victors to safety, but when they got to the rendezvous,

5

Captain Péyton, First Company, Lee's Legion, had gotten tired of waiting – there are more polite ways of putting it, but they are not as accurate – and gone home.

Lee and his men were worn out from charging through swamps; there wasn't a speck of dry powder amongst them.

Major General the Earl of Stirling – a sort of Benedict Arnold in reverse – had three hundred men at New Bridge, holding them as a reserve in case Lee got into trouble. Lee sent word to the Earl to bring his men along now and marched his force north toward the Bridge by sheer force of personality.

Call it luck – it seems more the result of Harry Lee's dash and his possession of that peculiar quality called glamour – but Captain Catlett of Virginia reappeared at this moment, with fifty of the men the militia major had taken away before the battle. They had dry powder, and Lee split them to cover his rear; he was moving in three wornout columns.

Just in time, for minutes later a column of New Jersey Tories struck at the wornout raiders. They were rebuffed, and Lee got away without further casualties.

The Virginia major had Harry Lee court-martialed for insubordination, thus setting up a pattern that was to be repeated in the careers of many of the cavalry heroes of the future.

Major Lee was acquitted with high honors, and the publicity did him no harm. His Legion began to be known as Lee's Light Horse, and he as Light-Horse Harry Lee, and the American public, shaken by defeat after defeat, finally had a hero to pin its hopes to – a young, dashing hero who would be a lieutenant colonel before he was twenty-five.

That was the last battle of 1779. The army soon went into winter quarters in New Jersey, with Lee's Legion posted at Monmouth. The foraging started again; Harry Lee notes that he levied two hundred cattle from Salem and fifty from Cape May. They were honorable foragers, it seems; Allan McLane recorded paying six hundred shrinking Continental dollars for a pair of boots.

Spring came with the Revolution still alive, and Washington sent his young neighbor south with his Legion and his lieutenant colonel's commission, but not before Lee had a good chance to show what the Legion could do as real cavalry; in the battle of Morristown they made a stand and threw Mathews' British troops back into the main body of Baron Wilhelm von Knyphausen's army and were generally credited with saving the day for the Continentals.

In other words, Harry Lee got to lead his troops in a real cavalry maneuver; one in which they stood, waiting, while the infantry stormed the enemy, mostly with bayonets, because the unrifled muskets of the day were so inaccurate; the British didn't even bother to teach their rank and file to aim.

When the enemy foot soldiers were routed – and men routed by the bayonet run fast and in terror – the horsemen came around the flanks and charged them with sabers – and this is the only use sabers ever had. They were valueless against ground troops standing firm. Any kind of a firearm aimed by any kind of a soldier can hit a horse and rider; and a bayonet-armed foot soldier, standing firm, can at once wound a horse so badly that the rider is too busy staying in the saddle to slash.

Remember that the bayoneteer has the advantage of reach; he can pierce a horse's head or breast before the sabreur can get anywhere near him. But in a rout, or the beginnings of a retreat, the horseman has all the advantage.

Harry Lee was a gentleman; well-bred, gently reared, educated with the best of his day. But he was a soldier, and to be a soldier a man has to take some pleasure in killing. Cavalry-charging routed enemies can be a heady experience; perhaps the headiest in the world. It is highly superior to lurking amongst the trees, grabbing commercial-minded farmers as they go or come from an enemy fort, and extracting information from them. In a few minutes it gives all the thrill of weeks of raiding enemy hayricks and ammunition dumps and supply piles.

In the West there is a saying: "Don't try and rope cows off a horse that's been raced in company." The same thing could apply to horse soldiers: "Don't try and make a mounted rifleman out of an officer who's led a cavalry charge."

In any event, Harry Lee led his Legion south, into cavalry country. William Washington was there, too, now also wearing lieutenant colonel's insignia; there were Continental and militia leaders named Buford and Lincoln; and above all there was Tarleton of the British 17th Dragoons, a hard-riding, pitiless outfit that ate Yankee (which included Southern) Dragoons for breakfast.

Francis Marion was there, too, the Swamp Fox, of whom considerably more later. To this day as many Southern boys are named Francis M., after Marion as are named Robert E., after Harry Lee's son. But then, Harry Lee wrote the book – the two-volume *Memoirs of the War in the Southern Department* – and it is to be expected that a Lee of Virginia would go out of his way to praise a rival.

Nathanael Greene of Rhode Island had just taken over the command in the Southern District from English-born Horatio Gates who had successively plotted to replace Washington with himself and then lost nearly all of his army to Cornwallis. The old problem of prestige was uppermost again; Greene needed a victory in order to recruit men, and he needed men in order to win a battle.

It was a time for what was called "partisan" action; in other words, for small quick forays; light infantry and Dragoon tactics. Nothing else was possible; the "army" turned over by Gates consisted of ninety cavalrymen, sixty artillerymen, and less than fifteen hundred foot soldiers. About half of these patriots were properly clothed and equipped. There was food for a few days, and little chance of getting more; Tarleton and William Washington had stripped the countryside bare.

When in doubt, attack. Greene was a Dragoon-type general; he detached William Washington, with his sixty men and two hundred mounted militia, against a force of two hundred and fifty Tories. Washington rode forty miles in a day and capped the drive by wiping out the enemy without any loss to his own men.

At this point Harry Lee marched his Legion into Greene's headquarters and Revolutionary prestige began building again.

The Legion, just then, was a little less than three hundred men, of whom about a third were mounted. But they counted for much more than their numbers would indicate. The young man who had talked horse all through the long nights at Valley Forge was not just a talker; his horses were superb, and superbly tended; his Legion could move faster than any force Tarleton had; Harry Lee had taught his mounts to carry double, so that no man had to walk all of any march. This, of course, was against General Washington's orders to keep horse and foot separate. Foot soldiers who vault behind cavalrymen when speed is needed were called *voltigeurs.* Later Congress authorized a small force of voltigeurs but did not authorize any Dragoons to work with them; this was after the Revolution, when the country tried to get along with as small an army as possible, depending on militia in case of war.

There was no sense in keeping a force like the Legion in the starving camp. Greene dispatched Lee to Francis Marion with orders to take Georgetown, South Carolina.

The attack was not a complete success. Light-Horse Harry and the Swamp Fox seem to have clashed temperamentally; it was a little like asking the leading actress of Broadway to collaborate with her Hollywood counterpart: Who, then, is First Lady? The Dragoons captured the British commander of Georgetown but were unable to breach the walls of the fort there; so, they paroled their prisoner and got out.

But the thought that these ragamuffins – a British term, but actually Lee kept his Legion neatly and beautifully uniformed in green – were on the loose disturbed Cornwallis, and that was very much to the good. He had the larger, the better-equipped, the better-trained force; how then could Greene send expeditions around the country? Why didn't he keep his force all in one spot, fearful of attack from the stronger enemy?

Tarleton, in his memoirs, thought that Greene didn't know how very much stronger Cornwallis' army was. In view of Greene's record, and especially in view of the reputation that had preceded Lee's Legion, it is dubious if Greene would have kept Light-Horse Harry at heel if King George and all his Guards had been in the Carolinas.

Greene had split his force; Lee's Legion remained with him, and William Washington went with General Dan'l Morgan, over toward Cowpens. So, Harry Lee was not in the battle there that was so decisive; Washington commanded the cavalry at Cowpens and used them classically.

Heading the British horse was General Sir Banastre Tarleton, chief opponent to Colonel Washington, Harry Lee, and Francis Marion all through the war in the south. He was only a little older than Lee, about twenty-six at the time of Cowpens, and nobody in the South ever names his son Banastre; Tarleton was a good cavalryman, perhaps better than either Lee or Marion, but he was ruthless.

Like Lee's, his immediate command was mixed horse and foot and was called a Legion; he also had under him, most of the time, the British 17th Dragoons and sometimes the 16th. The Legion itself was Tory, American Loyalists, with a scattering of British officers.

At Cowpens he was not only horse commander, but over-all general, mustering about eleven hundred effectives, of which half was his Legion, fifty were from the 17th, and the rest were mostly British Regulars, infantrymen.

Dan Morgan had about the same number of men to throw against Tarleton, but they were not nearly so well trained, armed, or clothed. Under Morgan, William Washington had only about eighty dragoons, plus thirty mounted militia from South Carolina and Georgia.

Harry Lee, in his *Memoirs,* has criticized Morgan for standing at Cowpens, a battle site more useful to the cavalry than to the infantrymen.

Morgan himself later defended his choice of terrain in a curious way; he claimed that he had to line up his infantry in such a way that the notorious Tarleton could surround them with his cavalry, or they would have deserted: "When men are forced to fight, they will sell their lives dearly."

Lee did not believe Morgan was telling the truth, but we are discussing cavalry as cavalry here, not as the writers of memoirs. Morgan's feelings were backed up by his actions; he threw his weakest and most unreliable men in front, to meet Tarleton's first blows, and put his veterans behind them.

Sharpshooters did cover the front line, but they were under orders to wait till the British were in close range, shoot the officers, and then drop back to the strong second line.

The Dragoons held the rear, augmented by the Georgia mounted militia, who had been issued sabers for the occasion. This was the classic position for cavalry, to be held in reserve ready to harass a routed enemy. This showed optimism on Morgan's part; Tarleton could not be expected to run.

The British were thrown into a completely classic formation, with the foot soldiers of Tarleton's Legion holding the center of the front line – remember, this was nearly half his foot force – flanked by light infantry and then by Dragoons.

In reserve, Tarleton held a regiment of Highlanders and the cavalry part of his Legion, thus making the unusual distinction – for American fighting – between Dragoons and cavalry.

His first move was to ride forward, with his command party, to size up the situation. This brought him within sight of the sharpshooters behind their trees.

They probably were not dressed in the proper uniforms; Tarleton decided to wave them out of the way with a toss of his British hand; he ordered his Legion cavalry to ride around and wipe them out.

The marksmen had their orders and they obeyed them. They let the green-jacketed horsemen come within fifty yards of their sights, fired, and knocked fifteen Legionnaires out of the saddle. Then they ran back, through the weak first line of militiamen, and joined the strong second line of Continentals.

Tarleton bellowed at his cavalry to pursue the marksmen – who were not routed but were retreating and firing as they did so – but his Legion declined, and went back into reserve, all two hundred of them.

Tarleton had a disobeyed order in his craw. If his cavalry wouldn't change, his infantry had to. He ordered the whole line forward.

This is where Morgan's weak front line earned their pay. They fired and ran toward the flanks, to take cover behind the second line, which was now augmented by the sharpshooters.

The British Dragoons pursued them, happily and conventionally. Tarleton's heavy Legion infantry stormed the second line, traditionally just a reserve, not up to the calibre of front-line men.

They ran into the heavy fire of the second line, faltered, came on again and again, for half an hour, at tremendous cost to the Britishers and the Tories, and with few casualties for the Americans, firing from fixed and chosen positions. Meanwhile, the happy Dragoons charged around the right flank of the American line, pursuing what they thought was the routed main line.

Suddenly William Washington led his cavalry around the flank and confronted the Dragoons with sabers; Colonel Washington had ordered his men not to fire their single-shot pistols. The Dragoons pulled rein and ran.

Again, Tarleton – a cavalryman himself – saw his horse routed and retaliated by ordering infantry to do what cavalry couldn't or wouldn't; he pulled the Scotties out of reserve and sent them to turn the right flank of the Yankees.

Major John Eager Howard, holding that right flank, ordered his Continentals to wheel and face the flank, but they misunderstood him, and neatly – without fear or haste – marched to the rear instead.

Finding out what had happened, Morgan decided to take advantage of it. He ordered Howard to find a firm position, anchor his men as the second line had been anchored, and hold fire till the British broke through to him.

Meanwhile, Colonel Washington was having a fine, fine day. He and his cavalry had ridden over a hill that concealed most of the British force from Morgan's sight and had seen that the English were in absolute confusion. Washington sent word to Morgan to lay one round among the British, and then charged, hitting the British flank and tearing it open.

Morgan could see now. He told his Continentals to fix bayonets, and charge.

Pinned between blades, the footmen of Tarleton's Legion and the lobsterbacks of the Royal Fusiliers surrendered, throwing down their arms.

Tarleton was not there. He was in the rear of his troops, trying to persuade what remained of his two hundred Dragoons to charge. They declined. The argument was still going on when Washington, leaving the infantry to guard the prisoners, charged the reserve position.

There were less than a hundred and fifty of Tarleton's Legion Dragoons left. Washington drove them into a flying retreat and followed it up with a rout in which he was nearly killed twice.

The third attempt was made by Tarleton himself, with a saber, and for a minute two cavalry commanders dueled on horseback, a rare enough thing in any war.

Tarleton wounded Washington's horse, finally, and escaped, leaving a hundred of his men dead, more than twice that many wounded, and six hundred able-bodied, uninjured Tories, and Britishers in a prison stockade.

Not very big numbers, as later wars counted their hurts. But an equal force of Americans had routed and almost wiped out trained Britishers and the dreaded Tarleton Legion.

Furthermore, the Battle of Cowpens had had classic features usually absent from Harry Lee and Francis Marion's forays; the European troops had been beaten in a game of their own rules.

Morgan had gone into the battle afraid his men would desert a losing war; he came out of it with the Revolutionary cause triumphant, and fence-sitters all over the country climbing down on the Continental side.

This was in late January.

Tarleton's fleeing Dragoons ran straight for Cornwallis' main army and told him what had happened.

Morgan headed for Greene, and the main column of the Continentals. He had won a battle, but he had also soiled the British escutcheon; he knew that Cornwallis would do anything to wipe out the small force that had destroyed Tarleton's brigade.

Colonel Andrew Pickens, who had commanded the horse militia under William Washington, gathered up the American wounded; there were only sixty of them, and about a dozen dead; no price at all to pay for the terrible casualties the British had suffered.

Cornwallis thought he had learned a lesson: he who would triumph in America should travel light. So, he spent two days destroying the impedimenta of his army; he burned most of the wagons, threw out the heavy gear necessary to European dignity, and then moved after Morgan.

But Morgan had had very little gear to start with. His militia, and most of his Continentals were accustomed to traveling with one blanket, a pouch of parched corn, a flask of spruce beer (probably very useful to disguise the taste of swamp water) and some ammunition. What else they needed they got off the country.

By the time Cornwallis got through making ready to hurry, Morgan had hurried. He crossed two rivers, the Broad and the Catawba, and figured he was way ahead of Cornwallis; so he sent the useful Pickens off with the prisoners, to be delivered to a permanent stockade, and threw the rest of his troops into a rest camp.

Greene, apprised of this, worried. He ordered all prisoners, those from Cowpens included, sent north to Virginia, and he recalled Lee's Legion from its unsatisfactory alliance with Francis Marion. Then he himself rode for Morgan's camp, through Tory infested country.

The danger to Morgan was not so strong as it might have been. Cornwallis had figured that if he were Morgan, he would go north; so, he went that way, making the distance between him and Morgan greater every day, fatiguing his own troops while Morgan's were getting stronger.

When Cornwallis realized his mistake and came south again, it was too late. The Catawba River had flooded, and Morgan was on the wrong – from the British point of view – side.

It was almost as though Cowpens had changed the side the elements were on. Nature was now beginning to believe in the Revolutionary cause.

Greene, who had been so successful in the tangled North, now went back to northern tactics, and started building boats.

Cornwallis, when the river went down, feinted with his heavier infantry, sending them toward the safest ford, and then tried to cross elsewhere with his cavalry and light infantry.

This was at Cowan's Ford, where American sentries were heavy. The English formed into columns of four and probably beat drums and blew bugles as they marched into the river.

The American sentinels sat on the river bank and mowed the British troops down. Horses were swept off their feet, three generals being dismounted this way. But the light infantry of the British Guards brigade did cross and drove off the sentries.

By which time, Morgan had taken his main body far away. The delaying fight by the sentries had given him plenty of time.

There were American casualties, though. General William Davidson of the North Carolina militia was killed at the ford, and his men scattered. Many of them rendezvoused at a tavern up the road, where Tarleton, finally across the river, found them. He charged, with the remnants of his once proud Legion, and the militiamen fired a few rounds, and fled.

Tarleton claimed a great victory, a strong revenge for Cowpens. But a British officer, not of the Tarleton Legion, later reported that he was there, and that Cowpens had been avenged by the death of about ten American militiamen.

That was very early in February. About two weeks later Lee's Legion got its crack at Tarleton; the intervening time had been taken up by large movements of troops on both sides.

As time passed and the British didn't attack, Greene's army became bolder and bolder. Harry Lee, William Washington, and Colonel William Campbell – who had relieved Pickens as commander of the Virginia militia – forayed daily, sniping at British vedettes, burning British stores and – worse – foraging ahead of the British so that there was nothing to commandeer when Cornwallis' hungry men went looking.

The tactic was good – the shortness of Cornwallis' temper was well known. Early in March, Cornwallis decided to move in force against the slippery Americans, force them to stand and fight.

A small patrol of Virginians got the news first and sent word to General Otho Williams of Maryland when Cornwallis' outriders were only two miles from Campbell's men, who held the left flank.

Harry Lee and Washington rode to Campbell's support at once. The heavier part of the Continental army pulled out, away from the oncoming Cornwallis.

The three cavalry outfits slowed the British down successfully, but Tarleton slipped past them and raced Williams for the ford by the mill at High Rock on Reedy Fork.

Williams got his van to the ford just as Tarleton did; Harry Lee, who was over-all commander of the cavalry, closed in on Tarleton's rear, and they had the British dragoon in a pincers.

But the main British Army was right behind Lee. Williams gave Light-Horse Harry a couple of light infantry battalions to help his horsemen and lent his own efforts to getting his main army across the ford safely.

Harry Lee laid his infantry out to face Tarleton, then concealed his sharpshooters in the thick brush above and behind them. He hid his horsemen over the crest of the hill – a repetition of Cowpens, without the weak front line, which probably would not have fooled Tarleton a second time.

Cornwallis threw Webster's brigade – crack troops, all British except for a few Hessians – at the ford. The sharpshooters caught them crossing, and they retreated.

Brigadier James Webster rallied them, but by then Lee had moved his flanks back of his horsemen, and the sharpshooters concentrated the center of the line.

Then Harry Lee retreated slowly, for about five miles.

By this time Williams had gotten his corps into a tight camp; Cornwallis gave up and retreated.

It wasn't a victory for the Americans, but it was as nice a rearguard action as light cavalry could stage.

Losses were about even, but without Light-Horse Harry, Greene could have lost half of his army to the heavier-armed and trained British. Henry Lee had proved his value and versatility again.

In the next ten days three thousand men were raised in the Middle South and started to augment Greene's force. Almost as many were raised in the Carolinas and southern Virginia.

The popularity of the Revolution, the hope in American hearts that it might succeed, had been reborn at Cowpens. Lee and Washington and Campbell proved on Reedy Fork that the Cowpens had not been a fluke. The American force began to be stronger than the British in the crucial Carolinas.

Of the four thousand men, more or less, that Greene had under arms a week or so after Reedy Fork, only about a hundred and fifty or sixty were cavalry; half from Lee's Legion, half under the command of William Washington. The infantry were about half untried, and many of the veterans were enlisted under peculiar militia contracts that enabled them to go home when they wanted to.

Greene, in camp near Guilford Courthouse, went in for a period of training; Lee went back to his old game – the one at which he was always happiest – of scouting for news and supplies.

He was out with both his foot and horse when he met – who else? – Tarleton, leading what was left of his Dragoons; some of the survivors of Cowpens and Reedy Fork had been detached to convoy wounded and sick out of the battle zone. With the British cavalry were a considerable number of light infantry and some Hessian marksmen.

Lee retreated slowly, luring Tarleton on until the Britisher thought he had the Legion pinned down in a deep cut road. Then Light-Horse Harry charged.

Tarleton's detachment broke and ran clear back to the main column of Cornwallis' army. Lee skirmished a bit with them there, and then turned and galloped as fast as he could back to Greene with the news of Cornwallis' movements, which was what he had been sent out to do in the first place.

Humiliating Banastre Tarleton was Harry Lee's avocation, not his main job, at the time. But a man doesn't get to be known as Light-Horse Harry because of his strict obedience to all orders.

Dan'l Morgan had retired after Cowpens. Even at the battle he was very ill with sciatica and malaria and a few other things. Now, however, he wrote to Greene at Guilford and gave him advice about the next battle, when, but not if, it was joined; Cornwallis was far from defeated.

The advice was sound: don't trust your militia, put some good men behind them and on the flanks, so they won't run away.

Greene took the old man's word. As Cornwallis approached Guilford, they would face, first, the North Carolina militia, an untried and untrusted force; this would be backed up by the Virginia militia, who would, in turn, be in front of the guns of the Continentals and the Maryland militia.

The left flank was held by Lee's Legion, augmented by extra infantry and the right flank by Colonel Washington's men, similarly strengthened. Any fair weather soldier who wanted to run away would have to do it to the front, toward Cornwallis. Lee and Washington both held their cavalry behind their infantry, classically.

Cornwallis came on. Greene went among the Carolinians holding the front line and told them what Morgan had told his front line at Cowpens – loose a couple of rounds at the lobsterbacks, and you can slide back of the front.

Which is what they did, and all they did, scampering to safety behind the Virginians when each man had fired two shots. They weren't cowards, but they weren't very well trained, and their muzzleloaders were slow to load and quick to heat.

But some of them had found out that fighting was fun; they drifted over to the left flank and – as it were – re-enlisted for a second time, with Lee's Legion.

Their scampering had had the effect of driving the strong British vanguard in between the hidden sharpshooters.

The British swung to the American left and came up in heavy force against Harry Lee's light flank guard. Lee retreated, fighting all the way, until he had dragged the Hessians and some British troops out of the main battle. Then he made his stand on a hill, far south of the main battlefield and had, to all purposes, a private war all his own.

Washington's cavalry was left to cover the British rout, as Greene's main body charged and broke the ranks of the King's men. If Lee had been able to stand and help, Cornwallis' army would have been destroyed, most experts agree; but Greene had not planned it that way; this was his main force, not a detachment as at Cowpens, and he didn't want to risk a defeat that would really mean the end of the Revolution.

Lee's men, fighting among trees in the fashion they loved, held the Hessians to a standstill; the rest of both forces milled around the battlefield indecisively.

Finally, Greene decided to retreat, still going on the principal that he couldn't risk losing the only army the Americans had in the southern field. Greene marched back to his old camp.

Harry Lee kept on fighting until Cornwallis sent out Tarleton – who must have been willing to go – to rescue the Hessians from Lee's Legion. Then Lee gave the order, and the Legion melted away, to re-form back with Greene and the main army.

Cornwallis had won a victory, in the European sense; that is, he occupied the ground where the battle had been fought. But more than five hundred, over a fourth of his army, were casualties; while the Americans had only a little more than half that many dead and wounded, which made it a victory in the American sense. It is a nice thing when both sides can figure they won; it doesn't often happen.

The field that Cornwallis had won was a dreary one. The battle was followed by drenching rain; and the nearest food available to the British was two hundred miles away, on the North Carolina coast.

General Greene sent his army surgeons back under flag of truce to help tend the many British wounded; but when this was done and Cornwallis headed for the shore and his supplies at Wilmington, the American general sent another kind of party out: Lee's Legion and a regiment of Virginians to harass the moving column and see that they couldn't forage.

This was Lee's forte; for three weeks he rode wildly around the British Army, pinning their scouts in closely, forcing the British belts to tighten a notch a day. If he had had a stronger force, Light-Horse Harry could have prevented the Cornwallis men from ever reaching Wilmington, and they would have starved to death on the Cape Fear River, where they had built a necessary bridge over which to escape. Lee got his Legion to the bridge, but it was too heavily guarded to attack.

Cornwalh's gave up the South. He refitted his people at Wilmington and headed back for the Middle Atlantic states, where Washington was waiting for him; so was a town named Yorktown, where Cornwallis would surrender to George Washington in the fall.

But it was still spring in North Carolina, and there was still a British Army in South Carolina. Greene let Cornwallis go into Virginia, and headed south to search out the British there, under a colonel named Rawdon, sometimes called "Lord" Rawdon because his elevation to the peerage, two years later, was already anticipated by his English colleagues.

Francis Marion was already in the southern Carolina country, on the Pee Dee River. Greene sent word to him and to Pickens, who was also engaged in harassing Rawdon, that he was coming, and then took stock of his own situation.

Greene also sent Light-Horse Harry, his Legion, and a company of Maryland Continentals to Marion. But Lee was ordered not to go in a straight line; first he was to march down the Cape Fear, feinting at Wilmington in order to keep Cornwallis off guard.

News that Lee's Legion was on the way to the coast hastened Cornwallis' scuttling for Virginia, and Harry Lee was free to cooperate once more with the Swamp Fox, Francis Marion.

Lee's men were in high spirits; he reports that they not only had ample food, but plenty of rum.

This time there seems to have been no prima donna trouble between Light-Horse Harry and the Swamp Fox. Together they surrounded Fort Watson, a well-built, sturdy little British fort on the Santee River, downstream from Lord Rawdon's headquarters at Camden, South Carolina.

Having surrounded the fort, the light cavalrymen had no idea of how to breech it; they had no artillery, no engineer companies, and the fort stood on solid rock, arising from a level plain.

Time was important. Marion's spies had found out that the commander of Fort Watson was out with a heavy detachment, looking for the Swamp Fox. He might return at any moment, to find his quarry pinned down on the flat between the fort and the column of searchers.

A South Carolinian, Colonel Maham, took over, in a very un-light horse way. He had his men fell logs in the nearby forest and build a tall platform just at rifle range from the fort. This he manned with sharpshooters; the tower was tall enough to command the fort.

While the marksmen pinned the garrison down, Lee and Marion and their axmen charged the stockade, cut their way in, and captured the garrison of over a hundred men. The engagement cost them two dead Americans, a few wounded.

Rawdon's communication line was cut, his already small army was made smaller, and Light-Horse Harry had advertised his arrival in South Carolina, always a sobering bit of news to Tories.

Greene, meanwhile, was camped about a mile from Camden; he had too light a force to attempt to assault the British headquarters and was waiting for Lee and Marion to join him. While he waited he sent William Washington out foraging, with quite a bit of success; the besiegers dined on beef nightly.

But neither Lee nor Marion was on his way to the general; they had heard that Colonel Watson, whose fort they had just captured, had as many as five hundred men out with him looking for the Swamp Fox, so they went looking for the lookers.

Rawdon, learning how weak Greene's army was – the only cavalry in the American command was Washington's, and less than sixty of them were mounted – proceeded to attack.

The battle was at Hobkirk's Hill and was inconclusive. That reliable veteran, William Washington, alternately covered himself and his Dragoons with glory, and made serious blunders, one of which was stopping to make prisoners of a bunch of British noncombatants – sick men, wounded, convalescents. Fifty of these he mounted behind his troopers, slowing the Dragoons down so that they couldn't complete the circuit of Rawdon's army that Greene had ordered.

When Washington heard the English attacking and about to capture Greene's guns, he dumped the passengers off the cantles of his saddles, and rode to the rescue, hooked the cavalry horses to the guns, and brought them to safety.

After the inconclusive battle, the Dragoons returned to bring off the wounded. While doing so they were attacked by a party of New York cavalry, whom they drove off the field.

As with Cornwallis, Greene lost the field and came close to winning the day; that is, the British casualties were much higher than the American. But, as so often happened, the Americans suffered heavy desertions among the militia, who often used the smoke of battle as a cover under which to return to civilian life.

This time General Greene had not taken old Dan Morgan's advice and pinned his militia in the front line, where they had to go through the British bayonets to get away.

Now Greene decided to go looking for Light-Horse Harry Lee and Swamp Fox Marion, who were still hunting Watson, who was still hunting them.

Watson won; he eluded Marion and Lee, slipped past Greene, and joined Rawdon in Camden. So did a Major McArthur, with almost four hundred Dragoons.

Rawdon and Watson now had a fine, big army, larger than all the American forces south of Virginia. They moved this massive force against Marion and Lee, who were besieging a fort called Motte, about forty miles due south of Camden, across the Congaree River.

Light-Horse Harry and Francis Marion had attacked Fort Motte because it was the principal depot between Charleston and Camden, and therefore essential to Rawdon if he were to get supplies from the coast; and like all the British in the South, he was in constant need of food and fodder.

Motte had not always been a fort; it had started life as the residence, a combination of mansion and farmhouse, of a lady named Rebecca Motte, a torrid partisan of the Revolutionary cause even before the British had taken over her house and forced her to move in with a neighbor.

The British had then fortified the house; the gallant cavalrymen had proposed to get it back for Mrs. Motte. They were going at it in the classic Corps of Engineer fashion – trenches and offsets and tunnels – when their pickets reported Lord Rawdon's approach.

Regretfully, the cavaliers told Mrs. Motte they had failed to retake her home. She replied that, since she couldn't have the mansion, the British shouldn't either, and suggested that the cavalry shoot a few burning arrows at it before departing.

The house started burning, the British garrison surrendered, and Mrs. Motte invited all the officers involved, both British and American, to join her, in her borrowed quarters, in what one of the Britishers later described as a "sumptuous" dinner. Light-Horse Harry long remembered that Mrs. Motte's conversation was filled with "ease, vivacity, and good sense." While the officers were enjoying all this, the enlisted British, under the command of their captors, put out the fire.

Then Greene arrived, and ordered the horsemen on the foray again; he sent Marion to the coast to attack Georgetown and ordered Harry Lee and his Legion to Fort Granby; the rest of the army would follow the Legion at a necessarily slower pace.

Lee got to Fort Granby the next day. It was a tough, strong wooden fort, with mounted guns, ditches, everything necessary to stave off light troops.

But Harry Lee and his men had always been expert at getting information; on the march they had learned that Major Maxwell, who commanded Granby, was the most notorious looter ever to come out of Maryland. Lee used his brains. He had a couple of artillery guns with him; he fired these at Fort Granby, had his men parade to show his strength – which was much smaller than Maxwell's, but could be made to look larger by circling – and then sent a white flag with a message that all private property would be respected if the garrison surrendered; otherwise Granby would be burned as Motte had been, and this time there would be no fire fighting.

Tory Maxwell apparently didn't feel like conducting a fire sale; he surrendered and drove bravely out the gate with two wagons full of his "personal property."

Lee and his men sent the garrison off after their commander, under parole to go to Charleston and refrain from further fighting; then they tallied up their own loot: salt, guns – both personal and artillery – and quite a bit of liquor.

Greene, as usual, was not far from the fighting. He commended Harry Lee, undoubtedly helped to sample the captured stores, and then took stock. The British were just about out of the Carolinas. Posts remained at Charleston, Savannah, a place called Ninety-Six, and Georgetown. In Georgia there was only one British garrison, at Augusta.

Greene could forget Georgetown; he'd sent Francis Marion to handle that. He would take Ninety-Six, and the Legion, Pickens' light infantry, and some militia under a Major Eaton would handle Augusta.

Bee-line, it is seventy miles from Fort Granby to Augusta; by the trails and roads of that day, it was probably closer to a hundred. Lee's column made the march in three days, fast for any outfit except that of Light-Horse Harry.

He was almost at Augusta when he heard that there was a delightful amount of ammunition, other military stores – including more rum – stored at a fort twelve miles below Augusta in anticipation of the annual day when the King gave presents to his loyal Indians as payment for continued loyalty. So, Lee told Eaton – who had the amazing first name of Pinketham – to keep the rest of the column marching on Augusta. Then he told the infantry part of the Legion to climb on the cantles of the Dragoons, and they moved out.

On the way they picked up some local militia. Lee posted these on one side of the rich fort, with a few Legionnaires, and had them feint an attack, and then run, as though deserting. The garrison poured out to pursue these Sunday soldiers, and Lee poured in on the other side. He and the Legion were not disappointed in the prize they won.

They remounted, and headed for Augusta again, being rejoined on the road by the Legion men who had led the fake retreat; it had been no trouble for them to outwit the pursuing garrison.

There were two forts guarding Augusta, Cornwallis and Grierson; the latter was the smaller, and was attacked first. The garrison deserted and attempted to make a run for Fort Cornwallis. It would not have been much of a fight at all, except for the fact that most of the British were local Tories; they were slaughtered by their former neighbors, the Georgia militia. Major Eaton was also killed at Fort Grierson.

Then the Americans surrounded Fort Cornwallis, which was heavily garrisoned by Tories and King's Indians, Creeks who were not about to get their annual gift from their monarch.

The garrison fought fiercely, driving off all attempts of the besiegers to approach by the ditch and offset method. Lee remembered Colonel Maham and his tower, and had his men build one like it; though under heavy fire, they completed the job, hauled some of their heavy guns to the top, raked the fort and knocked its heavy guns out of action. Colonel Browne of the Tories held out for several days, and then surrendered.

Now there was only Ninety-Six left in all the interior south, and Greene was marching on it. Light-Horse Harry started for there, forty-one miles away.

This was on June 6, or perhaps the next day. Greene had gotten to Ninety-Six on May 21, while Lee was gathering in the Indian gifts; Greene's army arrived the next day.

His engineer officer, Thaddeus Kosciusko, at once started paralleling – the ditch and turn method that Lee and Marion had had to learn at a half dozen forts. Briefly, the idea is to dig a trench at an angle down which the garrison cannot fire, and then to dig another one in the opposite direction, until your men and your ditches breech the fortress walls.

He started too close to the strongest part of the fort, the star redoubt. The British mounted three guns, straddled the working party, and sent out a sally to kill the workers and capture their tools.

The Polish officer started again, farther away. Greene covered the workers with artillery fire, and sent another outfit to build a Maham tower.

The British re-enforced their parapets and ripped off their wooden roofs before they could be set on fire. This, according to one British officer, left the men exposed to "all the pernicious effects of the night air."

Things were at a stalemate when Harry Lee arrived. The engineering skill that the light horseman had had to acquire told him that Kosciusko was approaching from the wrong side; the fort got its water from the other, the west side, and without water would soon have to surrender.

This was a curious matter; Harry Lee had never served in the waterless west, nor had any of the other officers, but it seems strange that nobody had noticed that the fort and an auxiliary stockade were connected with a covered way which straddled a runlet, obviously the water supply.

Light-Horse Harry borrowed one gun to cover him and put his Legion to work digging. In five days he had made the English begin to feel thirst; they dug a well inside the fort but did not hit water.

Then a rider came in with disastrous news; Lord Rawdon with all his army was on his way to relieve Ninety-Six. Time was running out for Greene's inferior force. A squad of the Legion tried to burn through the stockade and were driven away by heavy fire.

On the seventeenth a British dispatch rider tricked his way through the siege lines and got into the stockade. The cheers that rose told the Americans that Rawdon must be close by.

Greene had to attack at once or pull off in failure. He split his force in two, with Lee, his Legion, and some light troops under Kirkwood to take the west side; Campbell of Virginia attacked on the east. On the eighteenth they charged. The Legion almost at once took the stockade that defended the water supply and breached the main stockade.

But on the east the Star Redoubt was bitterly defended. Campbell's Virginians and Maryland Continentals fought hard and were about to break through into the fort when New York and New Jersey Tories sallied, caught the axmen from the rear, and used their bayonets to such good advantage that the Continentals retreated to Kosciusko's trenches; the attack had failed.

Greene got away from there only a day before Rawdon arrived. The American casualties were almost a hundred and fifty, including the usual missing; the British lost only ninety, with none missing. There is little doubt that if Harry Lee had been present at the beginning of the siege, the Tories would have been draughted out successfully.

On the retreat – rout would be justified – from Ninety-Six, Lee and his Legion rode rearguard. As always, the Loyalists pursuing Harry Lee did so on empty stomachs, riding starving horses. Greene pulled ahead, and got his men rested.

Rawdon got re-enforcements from the coast and forted up in Orangeburg. Washington and Marion brought their cavalry up to join Greene; so did General Thomas Sumter, a cavalry leader who had been around the South during most of Greene's actions, but who seldom seemed to be where he was needed. Such as now. General Greene had all the horse of William Washington, Light-Horse Harry Lee, Swamp Fox Marion, and Sumter; but Orangeburg was so situated that horse troops were useless. In addition, the American troops were almost as badly off as the British; they had covered a lot of distance in very bad heat, on very poor rations – rice and frogs mostly.

The infantry rested for six weeks, but Rawdon, seeing that Greene was not going to attack, sallied toward Charleston with a strong force, and Greene sent Lee, Sumter, and Marion after him. They couldn't keep Lord Rawdon from the coast, but they took a hundred and fifty of his men prisoners and captured more than that of his horse.

Then Harry Lee rode back to Greene, leaving Marion and Sumter garrisoning and guarding captured ferries.

Rawdon sailed for England almost at once; he had had enough of the South.

He had left Colonel Stuart in command; that officer now moved to Eutaw Springs, in order to shorten his logistic line from Charleston; in so doing, he put two wide rivers between him and Greene, and probably felt safe.

General Greene recalled his cavalry and moved out in a wide circle to get at Stuart. The two armies were about equal in numbers, and most of the militia that had planned on deserting Greene had already done so.

Greene had one big advantage: Lee's horse, William Washington's horse, Marion's horse had Stuart surrounded; they were back at what they did best, harassment and foraging, and Stuart led his command in complete ignorance; his scouts could not get out of camp, or if they did, had to run so fast from the mounted scouts that they had time to learn nothing.

As always, the King's troops were hungry. Believing it safe, a party of unarmed men was sent out to gather sweet potatoes. Rumors reached Stuart that the potato pickers were in danger, and while he didn't believe it, he sent out his horse – about fifty men, under Major John Coffin – to patrol around them.

Coffin ran into the Legion, heading most of Greene's army; William Washington brought up the rear. Coffin charged, and while the Legion infantry held him engaged, Lee's cavalry rode around to his rear. More than a hundred foot soldiers were with Major Coffin; almost all of those not killed were captured; his cavalry took flight. The big party of sweet potato men were also taken.

Now Stuart drew up a formal line of battle. He threw all of his heavy infantry into a single line, and placed his few horse, his light infantry and his grenadiers on the flanks and slightly to the rear.

Greene stopped on the other side of some woods, facing the British, and threw his militia into a front line, his regulars of infantry into a second line, the Legion on the right flank, some South Carolina cavalry and light infantry on the left, and all the rest of the horse to the rear, under William Washington, to be aided by Kirkwood's light infantry.

The British had several times as much artillery as did the Americans; but the Continentals had the cavalry.

This was in September; the war was almost won. The militia worked through the woods like veterans, like Continentals or Legionnaires; Greene later said they would have done credit to the Prussian Army.

The Legion, seeing the center holding, tried to outflank the British and got into a heavy battle forward of the line; this left Pickens and Marion to hold the flank, and they weren't up to it.

Wade Hampton – grandfather of the Confederate leader – held the South Carolina men on the flank opposite the Legion and rallied them into attack after attack. Soon he had a separate war on his side, as the Legion did on the other.

Greene took personal charge of the center. He had not yet used his best infantry, the Continentals; and William Washington's cavalry was still in reserve, with the valuable Kirkwood and his light infantry.

With Captain Michael Rudulph in the lead, the Legion infantry now completed their flanking movement; on the British right, Howard of Maryland came up to help the flaming Wade Hampton, and the enflankment was completed. The British center started to drop back.

Now William Washington made the classic move, under Greene's orders; he brought his horse around and forward to pursue a broken enemy.

If there hadn't been a shrub oak thicket in the way, the maneuver would have succeeded. But while Washington's Horse were skirting the impenetrable brush, Stuart sent up re-enforcements to the fleeing center of his forces, and Washington had to lead his men right across their fire.

William Washington's horse was shot out from under him; he couldn't get free of his stirrups and was captured. Half his men were killed or taken, not a one of them escaped some sort of wound, and they had just about run out of officers when Hampton showed up, rallied them, and charged the enemy.

It didn't work; the British on that front were no longer routed – but it held them until Kirkwood could bring up his light infantry to the rescue of their old comrades of the horse.

Major Marjoribanks of the 19th rallied the British and they stood firm on a ridge, though the rest of their army had fled.

Most of the Americans pursued the main body of troops under Stuart and were doing well enough until they reached the British camp; there a British officer took a good party of men into a strong brick house and made a stand while Stuart went off to rally his fleeing troops.

The Americans could have taken the brick house and they certainly could have kept Stuart on the run, but the British camp was full of grog; the Continentals behaved like militia, and the militia behaved like themselves, after their good start in the battle.

The Legion held firm and disciplined, and Kirkwood's infantry wanted to avenge their friends of Washington's Horse. Lee's foot soldiers helped them, and they grabbed Britishers for shields and fought their way to the very bricks of the walls. Greene ordered up a gun to breach the walls, but the garrison shot the gunners.

Stuart had rallied his men; he started to bring them back to the brick house to relieve the siege. But there had been three hours of fighting under the Carolina sun; hard fighting. The Americans withdrew into the shadow of the woods; the British, technically victors because they held the field, did not pursue.

Most of the ranking officers were dead, wounded or captured; of the American forces, Harry Lee was one of two unharmed regimental commanders. Casualties were heavy on both sides, but there was a significant change in the statistics: this time the Americans reported only eight men missing, the British more than four hundred. The war was ending, in other words; men do not desert a side they think is winning.

That was Eutaw Springs. It virtually marked the end of hostilities in the Carolinas and Georgia. The British pulled back to Charleston, where they could do little damage, but could at least eat. In many respects, Eutaw Springs was one of the biggest cavalry engagements of the Continental Army. How did the horse soldiers do?

Not too well. If Washington's men had been trained as mounted infantry, they would have had weapons to fight on foot; they would have dismounted at the blackjack thicket, and gone through it with carbine and sword, leaving their mounts with horseholders. Kirkwood, coming up with light infantry, traveled slower, but did more damage when he got there; mounted infantry would have been as fast as cavalry, as deadly as light infantry.

Lee's Legion was only partly mounted, and after the first charge, fought as irregulars, not as cavalry; Marion's horse did not play as big a part in the battle as his foot.

Wade Hampton led several mounted cavalry charges, but the last one, against Marjoribanks, was repulsed so severely that one of Hampton's captains thought he was the only man left alive in the outfit. He was wrong, but the casualties were heavy.

After Eutaw Springs, Greene put Hampton in charge of a force to take Harry Lee's usual position after a battle, between the enemy and Greene's recuperating army; he sent Lee and Marion to cut the road to Charleston.

But the British troops in Charleston had gotten word of Stuart's troubles, and were on the march. Stuart did not wait to rest up; he headed for Charleston at once and met his relievers almost under the eyes of the Legions, who were in no condition to attack the army that had just fought a draw with their own forces, especially now that it was re-enforced. They had to let the British go into camp at Moncks Corner.

Greene, apprised of this, started after them, but then decided that his men were in too bad shape to march through the dry lands; he headed back for the battlefield, where the British had abandoned their wounded.

The war was ending in the north. Eutaw Springs was fought on September 8; Cornwallis surrendered on October 19. Before a generation had passed it was America's habit to think that the Revolution ended at Yorktown; but in the South it lingered on, in sporadic fighting. There were still Tories out in great numbers.

Lee's Legion and the rest of the cavalry were led by Greene against Dorchester, nor far from the British stronghold at Charleston. Because the American commander-in-chief was at the head of the besiegers, the King's commander thought the whole Revolutionary Army was marching on him and panicked into a quick surrender.

But there were still more than three thousand British and Tories in Charleston itself. The command had descended from Lord Rawdon through Colonel Stuart – wounded at Eutaw Springs – to a major.

William Washington was back in the field; Kirkwood had received an honorable discharge, and his infantry were turned over to Washington, to make up a legion similar to Light-Horse Harry's.

Washington got close enough to Charleston to camp. Greene turned over enough men to Harry Lee to bring the Legion up to what was probably the greatest strength it ever had – about seven hundred men – and told him to take Charleston.

Marion and his Legion went along. The temperamental clashes between the two great foragers that had made it impossible for them to work together early in the war were long forgotten; the Legions and their leaders had been through too much together.

Lee almost took Charleston, but his second column, under a Major Hamilton, dallied on the way, and he had to back off because of being too badly outnumbered.

Mad Anthony Wayne arrived in the south with a number of Continentals, including some cavalry. Greene turned over the dilatory Sumter's command to the heroic and dashing Wade Hampton.

The British had a choice of starving in Charleston or foraging. It was a rough choice, with such veterans as Lee's and Marion's Legions, Hampton's mounted infantry, and Mad Anthony Wayne prowling around the watery city.

In the middle of December, the British gave up and sailed for home, and Light-Horse Harry's war was over.

He went back to Virginia, married the heir to the senior branch of the Lees, and thus became master of Stratford. He helped write the Constitution, he served in Congress, he was Governor of Virginia; he wrote his fine *Memoirs of the War in the Southern Department*; he had children. His wife died, and he married again; he was fifty when Robert E. was born.

He fought Thomas Jefferson every chance he got; not with light horse and a Legion, but in politics. The free-riding ranger matured into a conservative and rather stem man. When a rebellion was mounted against Hamilton's tax laws, General Washington called on his old comrade and sent Light-Horse Harry out as a general to put down the moonshiners.

Years later Harry Lee's son married Martha Washington's granddaughter; it would have pleased both Light-Horse Harry and his general.

Chapter 2

The Swamp Fox

Francis Marion of South Carolina was a much older man than Harry Lee; he was, in fact, the same age as George Washington.

The Revolution was not his first war; he had taken the field against the Cherokees in 1761, which makes him a colleague with most of the other great cavalry leaders of the United States – the Indian fighters. Even Light-Horse Harry, as we have seen, took a small turn at it by stealing the supplies and gifts the King meant for the Creeks.

The Five Civilized Nations – Cherokees, Creeks, Choctaws, Seminoles, and the Chickasaw – never cared for the English until the Revolution, when they joined the King in killing Americans. The Indian attitude was probably justified, but it explains why the Dragoons finally had to move most of the tribes to Oklahoma; they had been at war with the white Southerners for over a hundred years.

The Cherokee Rebellion, in which Marion wet his saber – or fired his carbine – opened when the tribe rose in Tennessee and surrounded Fort Loudoun, up near the Virginia border, not far from Knoxville. That garrison surrendered, on promises of safe-conduct; when they marched out, the Cherokees slaughtered them, and the war was on. The twenty-nine-year-old Francis Marion received a lieutenant's commission.

It was a bitter war; there was plenty of right on both sides. The Cherokees were still hunters in those days; they turned to agriculture later. A hunting economy needs huge room to survive; the immigrants pouring into the South from Scotland, Ireland, and England wanted – needed – farms. They cut up the South with plows, they drove the game out of the hereditary Cherokee hunting grounds. They harassed the Cherokees into a rage; the massacre of the garrison at Fort Loudoun drove the whites to fury.

At Echota, near the Cherokee capital, the invading militia were stalled at a narrow pass, defended by the Cherokees. Lieutenant Marion offered to clear the defile; he took a party of thirty men, and in a very short time twenty-one of them were dead.

Francis Marion had found out that war is real. Fifteen years later, in another and harder war, he was to apply the lesson, fight for five or six years, and come out alive.

The Cherokee Insurrection was put down, unsatisfactorily; the whole problem of the Civilized Nations dragged on for years. But Lieutenant Marion was released and went home to South Carolina. He dabbled in politics and was elected to the Provincial Congress of his colony. When the Revolution started, he raised a company of militia and enrolled them under Colonel William Moultrie.

Captain Marion and his company were in on the capture of two of the British forts that guarded the entrance to Charleston Harbor: Fort Johnson, which they took almost before the British governor knew the war was on, and later, Fort Moultrie. These were amphibious operations, the forts were built on low, sandy islands.

By the time they moved against Fort Sullivan, Marion had been raised to major.

The South Carolina militia had proved so unreliable – the farther south the Revolution went, the less unreasonable the King seemed to the citizens – that Moultrie's Second Regiment of Foot and several other outfits had reformed as "provincial troops." Their makeup was peculiarly aristocratic. The officers were all volunteer gentlemen, the other ranks all mercenaries. As could be expected, the aim of the Provincials was more to gain glory than to win the war.

In 1779, having taken most of the defenses of Charleston – which remained a British stronghold until the end of the Revolution – Marion was with the troops that besieged Savannah from the land; a French fleet covered the sea, and demanded that the British surrender – within twenty-four hours!

Naturally, the garrison used their day of truce fully; by the time the ultimatum was refused, the British were so well entrenched that the attack failed.

The next year Charleston was retaken by the British; Marion, who was supposed to be there, was on sick leave with a broken ankle, and was not captured.

The war, as we have already seen, was moving south; previously what Southern Continentals there were had gone north to help General Washington, and the southern militia had been unreliable and inactive.

Now that the real fighting had begun in his homeland, Francis Marion got sick of fighting like a gentleman; the gentlemanly fiasco at Savannah had shocked him, and there is no doubt that his own disastrous gallantry when he was a lieutenant against the Cherokees had taught him a lesson.

Near Williamsburg, in his home state, a band of marauders had formed to foray out of the swamps, harass the Loyalists, and retreat before the King's revenge could be mounted. This wasn't chivalrous, but it was effective. The marauders needed a leader, and Marion went to join them. Governor John Rutledge gave him a commission as a brigadier general, State of South Carolina; if Marion ever joined the Continental Army, it isn't recorded.

His "brigade" consisted of thirty men, but he saw to it that each man had a good rifle – worth twenty smooth bores – and a good horse. Unlike Harry Lee, he didn't bother to uniform his Legion, as it later came to be known, after Lee's. In fact, the men were frequently sent home to sleep in their own beds and eat their wives' cooking, and to pose as innocent fanners, no hard thing to do in the divided South. While in the swamps, they lived for the most part on sweet potatoes and an occasional hunk of beef, carved off the stringy hide of some runaway animal.

After he had armed and mounted his men, Francis Marion led them in a series of raids on sawmills. The plundered saws were beaten into sabers, which must have been left in the swamps when the marauders went home; a farmer can have a rifle, and certainly a horse, but the British would have shot as a traitor anyone caught wearing a cavalry sword.

General Horatio Gates was still in command of the Southern Department when Marion took to the swamps; a few days after the South Carolinian went under cover, the American Army suffered one of its worst defeats of the war, the Battle of Camden.

The American losses there were so heavy that Gates, reorganizing his forces, put four Maryland regiments into one battalion and all the rest of his infantrymen into another; he also had two guns; William Washington, lieutenant colonel of cavalry, had less than a full troop riding behind him.

Marion called his new brigade together and sallied out of the swamps; he tracked down a force of ninety British and Tory soldiers escorting a larger number of American prisoners to the stockade at Charleston.

The raiders struck. Tradition in the South says that they waited until the Tories and the lobsterbacks were drunk, but more reliable sources say it was simply a dawn attack upon surprised and sleepy guards. Nineteenth-century historians were inclined to attribute teetotalism to their heroes, alcoholism to their enemies; there seems little hope now of piercing through to the truth. The success was complete; the guards were taken prisoners, the prisoners set free. But only half of them went back to fighting; the rest went home and studied war no more.

Cornwallis was beginning to be annoyed. He sent Tarleton out after the man the South was beginning to call the Swamp Fox. Tarleton was the best the British had to offer; and he was not inclined to underestimate an enemy. He augmented his Tory force with a strong company of British Regulars.

They succeeded in almost surrounding Marion's Brigade; the Tories cut off his rear, the Regulars his van, and bad terrain flanked him. But bad terrain was Marion's terrain; his men simply melted through the swamps and brush, cached their swords, and went back to being farmers. About sixty of them ate and then rejoined their general at his muggy headquarters.

Of course, this wasn't cavalry work; it was marauding and raiding and sniping and harassing. Except for the charge on the prison train, Marion's men could well have left their sabers to the sawmills.

But the knowledge that the Swamp Fox and his brigade were out on the countryside discouraged a number of lukewarms from joining the Tories, and the sabers may have done their bit in drawing recruits to the Brigade and to the Revolutionary cause in the South.

Marion's chief camp – he had others and maintained a mobility that was highly distressing to the orderly British – was on the Pee Dee River, on a high and dry location surrounded by swamp. Here occurred an incident so widely repeated that it might have happened; at any rate, it was a great American tradition until well into the twentieth century.

The story goes as follows: A young British officer was sent out to treat with Marion about the exchange of prisoners. Blindfolded, the Englishman was conducted to the camp on the Pee Dee; here he was courteously received by Brigadier General Marion, and invited to dinner, which, when served, turned out to be nothing but roasted potatoes on a slab of bark.

According to the nineteenth-century prose, the officer cried: "Surely, General, this is not your ordinary fare!"

Whereupon Marion allegedly answered, "Indeed it is, and we are fortunate on this occasion, entertaining company, to have more than our usual allowance."

The officer, the legend continues, concluded his errand, returned to British headquarters, and resigned his commission, saying that such men could not, and should not, be conquered.

The above account is from Lossing's *Centennial History of the United States*, published in 1876; Glazier's *Heroes of Three Wars*, published a little later, has the English officer also asking if the Brigadiers do not draw "noble pay" and being assured that they do not earn a cent. Earlier histories of the sort that should have gloried in this sort of story, fail to mention the incident; it is included because it typifies the hold that cavalry has always had on the American imagination – a legendary concept that kept the cavalry poor: troopers didn't need comfort.

Another Marion tradition, and one that seems to have a good deal more solid base to it – at least the British officers are named – concerns one Major

McIlraith, a British cavalryman who sent a message to the Swamp Fox that his hit-and-run tactics were ungentlemanly and unmilitary, and that he should stand and fight.

Marion answered that he'd be glad to send twenty of his picked men against twenty of McIlraith's, the encounter to take place in open ground at an agreed-upon hour. McIlraith accepted the challenge, then backed out an hour before the duel was to begin.

When Greene succeeded Gage in the command of the South, he sent Harry Lee to work with Marion. But they could not work together and split their commands again until the brilliant action against Fort Watson. By now both guerrilla leaders were covered with so much glory there was no room for jealousy, and their common exploits have already been related in the story of Light-Horse Harry.

Marion, to finish his biography, was forty-nine when Cornwallis surrendered; the Swamp Fox retired from the field and tried to rebuild his plantation in St. John's Parish, South Carolina. His neighbors elected him a state senator, and the state Senate voted him thanks and a gold medal. In 1784 he got more substantial rewards – command of a fort in Charleston Harbor and a salary of five hundred pounds a year.

Now he was over fifty and a bachelor; he married a wealthy lady, retired to the country, and lived another eleven years, quietly dying in 1795.

Harry Lee, like William Washington and Thomas Sumter, commanded a Legion, mixed foot and horse; Francis Marion, on the other hand, seemed to make a big point of having all his effectives mounted. But he was leading true Irregulars; his troopers returned home as often as they could – where there were farmhands or sons to tend the horses, and wives to cook for them – and when in camp were waited on by slave body servants.

Both methods, that of the Legion and that of the Swamp Brigade, underlined a weakness of cavalry that was to plague the Yellowlegs as long as the horse remained a means of military transport: a man cannot take care of a horse; a weapon; himself; his camp duties of foraging, digging, water-hauling and so on; and still fight. Lee had two men or more to a horse, Marion had servants or family to aid his men in grooming and housekeeping; either way worked, but the horse soldier of the prairies had no help but his own; the cavalry trooper who fought the Sioux and the Apache led the most miserable life of any man in the U.S. Army, as we shall see.

In any event, the Revolution ended, and the cavalry had played a big part in at least the southern part of it. Lee and Marion are legendary figures; William Washington is almost completely forgotten, which is too bad; Sumter seems to be a good man to forget, though the fort named after him is well-remembered.

Chapter 3

Eclipse for the Horse Soldiers

For the next fifty years after the Revolution there was seldom any U.S. Cavalry. There was a multitude of reasons for this lack. One of them was geographical and real: the new country felt that future wars would menace it only from three sources: Spanish Florida, British Canada, and the sea. The last, of course, was not cavalry ground, but neither were the other two; the horse soldiers had played no Revolutionary part in the North, and the Florida border was too densely overgrown to allow the sort of maneuvers that Lee and Marion had found so successful elsewhere in the southern states.

The second reason for the temporary demise of the cavalry was personal. The new government knew no one better to consult on the question of a standing army than General George Washington; and Washington had always been opposed to horse soldiers. To his old objection about the difficulty of obtaining forage – pretty well demolished by Harry Lee – he now added another one, which the Americans were to share for many years. The general wrote to Alexander Hamilton – who had been put at the head of a committee to investigate the need for a standing army – that any kind of professional army was "dangerous to the liberties of the country." Soldiers on horseback, probably because of their glamour, were particularly dangerous.

However, General Washington went on, some sort of army was necessary to "awe the Indians," protect trade, and impress Canada and Florida. He recommended four regiments of infantry and one of artillery, and posed the idea that, in the long run, a strong navy might be the only thing the country needed.

Speculation after nearly two hundred years is fruitless; but it is interesting to wonder if Washington's attitude toward cavalry would have been the same if Lee and Marion had not both retired to marry wealthy women and build up country estates, making themselves unavailable for duty.

The states did not want a professional army at all, emotionally; financially they did not see how they could pay, as individual states, for the militia necessary to patrol the borders, and they were against a professional class of military men, who might – and usually did, in other countries – turn into dictators. Again, as in Washington's case they felt that the cavalry was glamorous enough to be particularly appealing to the public mind. Also, cavalry is more expensive to equip and maintain than infantry. When Hamilton turned in his report to Congress, he recommended that a regiment of dragoons be included in the small standing army. But Congress struck that clause out, apparently for financial reasons.

Fear of military coups, financial lacks, and geography were only part of the story, however. Despite the poor showing of militia in the Revolution, the belief persisted in American hearts – and does to this day – that any male American can, at a moment's notice, jump to arms and do a better job of fighting than professional soldiers can do. Every American seems to believe, in his heart, that he can ride a horse and shoot a gun, especially if he has never tried to do either. Perhaps with modern techniques of spacecraft and guided missiles and atomic submarines, reality will drive this dream to death, but if a war calling for armed horsemen were to start, the citizenry would still be surprised at how long it takes to learn to be a cavalryman. The mounted branch suffered little by being excluded from the early Regular Army; by 1791 the standing Federal troops numbered about a thousand, though many more had been authorized. Meanwhile, the Indians were harassing the western border of the young country, which had pushed over the Appalachians into the Northwest Territory, now Ohio, Indiana, Illinois, Michigan, Wisconsin, and the eastern part of Minnesota.

In 1792 Mad Anthony Wayne, the Drover of Valley Forge, became commander-in-chief of the Army, with the rank of major general. He at once reorganized the regiments into a Legion, similar to the Revolutionary ones: a composite of all arms, each sub-legion – there were four – to include a troop of dragoons along with two regiments of infantry and a battalion of (unmounted) riflemen, together with a battery or company of artillery.

There is no record that dragoons were ever enlisted. When Wayne moved out against the Indians in the summer of 1794, he took along fourteen hundred "mounted militia," who were not cavalry, but frontiersmen carrying their own guns and hunting knives instead of sabers.

In August he faced the Indian confederation at Fallen Timbers and routed them with the bayonet. Then he sent his horsemen in pursuit of the fleeing hostiles; they did well in keeping the Indians on the run, but this was the classic role of cavalry – pursuing an enemy that the infantry had started fleeing – and sabers would have been useful, for one of the few times in the long history of Indian fighting.

In 1796 the Legion type of reorganization was dropped. The new Army included two companies of light dragoons, who were dispatched to the "Southwest," that is, Mississippi.

Two years later, President John Adams and his Secretary of War, James McHenry, alarmed by the possibility of war with France, asked Congress for a regiment of infantry, one of artillery, and one of cavalry. The cavalry part of the request was denied at once. The artillery regiment was authorized, and, instead of a regiment of infantry, Congress authorized the founding of the U.S. Marine Corps, according to official records of the Army; according to the history of the Marines, as published by the Corps itself, it has been in existence since 1775.

The threat of war with France grew larger, and Congress authorized a Provisional Army, to serve during the emergency only. This was to include a regiment of cavalry and twelve of infantry. The Provisional Army was never completely raised, and the part of it that was enlisted never got out of training camp; the trouble with France was settled on the high seas, by the Navy and by privateers.

Thomas Jefferson was elected President in 1800, to succeed John Adams. He was much more opposed to a strong army than were Adams or Washington; he cut back both the Army and the Navy, and completely abolished the cavalry a year after taking office.

The arms of the United States continued in this diminished form until the War of 1812. When the Shawnees rose in 1811, under Tecumseh, General William Henry Harrison added mounted militiamen to his force of Regulars and Territorial infantry. At the Battle of Tippecanoe – which gave Harrison enough fame to later elect him President – his mounted frontiersmen put on a charge that routed Tecumseh and his men. But the horsemen were again fighting with knives, as they did in the only mounted charge of the War of 1812, when Richard M. Johnson, later Vice-President of the United States, commanded a thousand Kentucky horsemen at the Battle of the Thames, between Lakes Erie and Huron. The enemy was once more Tecumseh, with about twenty-five hundred tribesmen and less than a thousand British and Candian troops. The American commander was again Harrison, and instead of a line-to-line infantry attack – which was never very useful against a predominantly Indian foe – he ordered the mounted Kentuckians to charge.

Johnson split his force into two equal bands of five hundred each and sent them off; he couldn't lead them because Harrison needed him to plan further strategy.

He wasn't needed on the charge. The wild frontiersmen struck at the Indians fiercely; the tribesmen ran into thick woods, thinking themselves safe from the horse charge; the Kentuckians dropped off their horses, fired one round into the woods, and continued the charge on foot, brandishing their hunting knives.

They killed Tecumseh, and just about ended the land, or British-and-Indian phase of the war. The Northern Confederation of Indians – led by the Shawnees – dissolved, and Lake Erie fell entirely into American hands.

The Creeks, far to the south, revolted before they heard of Tecumseh's defeat and death; Andrew Jackson put them down with an infantry bayonet charge.

The Kentuckians had never spent much time arguing whether they were dragoons or cavalrymen; their method of attack may be called the stab-and-scalp; it was never to be included in any manual of training for the cavalry.

The war ended in 1815; at once Congress moved to reduce the Army from more than thirty thousand men to less than ten thousand. The last phase of the war had seen two regiments of light dragoons authorized; now there were to be none. The Army was divided into two departments, Northern and Southern.

The Louisiana Purchase, in 1803, had doubled the size of the United States and most of the territory added was good horse-maneuver ground: more lightly wooded than the old East, and nicely watered and grassed. While the men going west were horsemen, they were even more violently against the idea of professional soldiers than were the stay-at-homes. Mounted militia could be raised in a day against Indians; and the European threats from Spain, France, and England were ended. No U.S. Cavalry was needed, the people felt. In fact, the Army itself shrank pitifully in the years following the War of 1812; by 1821 it was down to six thousand officers and men.

Outside factors were moving to strip the saber from the cavalryman, when and if he was to return to the American scene. Gunsmiths and ordnance officers all over Europe were working to design, first, a muzzle loader that could be rifled and still fire in a hurry; and second, a breech loader that could be fired even faster.

The old British soldier used a muzzle-loaded, smoothbored musket that was so inaccurate, as noted earlier, that his officers did not bother to teach him marksmanship; British orders were to point the gun vaguely at the enemy and pull the trigger. There were riflemen, here and there, as we have seen; but in order to load a rifle from the muzzle, the powder, then the patch, and then the ball had to be dropped down, and the whole rammed home with enough force either to wrap the patch around the ball – so it would fit the grooving – or to expand the ball itself. Neither process was fast, and during the moments of loading, a sabreur on horseback had the foot soldier at his mercy. So, infantrymen, whether riflemen or musketeers, were dependent for a large part of battle-time on their bayonets, which could fight off a saber-bearing horseman until the foot soldier started to retreat. Against any kind of rapid-fire, the horseman was better off to dismount and fire-fight himself, if he had a rapid loading gun.

Breech-loading was not to become really feasible until 1846, when Houiller of Paris invented the first metallic cartridge, which not only loaded fast, but sealed the chamber in the rear against expanding gas. Meanwhile, Claude Minié, an officer in the French Army, had developed the "Minnie ball," which was no more a ball than was his name pronounced in two syllables; it was a true bullet, in the modern sense, whose base expanded on discharge to meet the grooves and lands of the rifling. Thus, it was small enough to load quickly from the muzzle, and accurate enough to pick off an enemy at some distance.

Samuel Colt invented and produced his revolver – a terrific arm for cavalry sergeants and officers – in time for the Seminole War of 1837 and the Texas War of Independence in 1836. The Army, however, did not think of using it till after the Mexican War had ended in 1847, though some officers supplied themselves with the repeating hand gun.

When the Battalion of Mounted Rangers was authorized by Congress in 1832, the horse soldiers were to take the field with smoothbore carbines and sabers.

The day of the true cavalryman had passed, if it ever really existed in North America. The Legionnaires – Lee, Marion, William Washington, and the others – while they had, on occasion, fulfilled the cavalry function of charging broken infantry, had really been most effective as foragers and anti-foragers – witness Lee's feeding of the camp at Valley Forge and Marion's forbidding food to Cornwallis' southern column.

The new cavalry started life first as Mounted Rangers, and then as Dragoons; the old – and mostly non-existent – horse troops occasionally recommended to Congress, less often authorized by that body, and hardly ever actually mounted and put into the field, had always been called dragoons, or even light dragoons. It is a curiosity of language that nothing actually called United States Cavalry was ever commissioned until the repeating rifle had made dictionary cavalry a thing of the past.

Chapter 4

The Trail Guards Appear

The scene now moves West, past even the Louisiana Purchase, to New Mexico, which, after the Mexican Revolution, had become a step-child of Mexico. This was in 1821.

Until that time, Spanish law had forbidden anyone but Spanish citizens from trading in Spanish territory. American Army explorers – Benjamin Bonneville, John C. Frémont, and especially Zebulon Pike – had penetrated deep into Spanish land. Pike was courteously imprisoned and shipped to Mexico in 1807; Frémont skirted north of New Mexico and ended up in California, where government was so weak that it only protested mildly at the intrusion; and Bonneville, Paris-born, disguised himself and his men as Canadian trappers, harmless to the Spanish government, and a familiar breed around Taos, where many French-Canadians wintered.

Later, Captain Bonneville, in a letter to Washington Irving, said that dragoons were absolutely necessary to patrol the Santa Fe Trail; he also urged that the United States government build and operate a trading post above New Mexico on the Arkansas; this would keep the Indians quiet, he said, as hostiles never attacked traders who supplied them with the things they needed to piece out their meager economy.

The captain went on at some length, pointing out that many of the most dangerous tribes did not have any concept of horse breeding, never keeping brood mares, and therefore had to get along by stealing from each other, the Mexicans, and the Trail; a trading post that exchanged horses – presumably for buffalo hides and other furs – together with the constant threat of reprisal from the dragoons – would end a lot of Plains warfare.

Some of the fur trappers who wintered in New Mexico were from the United States, and Americans settled in California, changing their citizenship and swearing fealty to the Spanish throne and the Catholic Church. But their numbers were few, and their intentions were not commercial; Spain did not seem to care about the fur trade but death was often inflicted on anyone who encroached on the Spanish monopoly of selling to the northern province.

The new republic of Mexico did not feel this way. Mexicans had suffered more from Spanish high prices and Spanish scarcity than had the gringo traders denied the field; they welcomed traders of any nationality or religion.

There were two trails to Santa Fe, capital of New Mexico: the Chihuahua trace, through El Paso (now Ciudad Juárez) and the road from Franklin or Independence, Missouri, that was to come down in history as *the* Santa Fe Trail.

It was the more practical way to reach Santa Fe. Chihuahua was and is a high mountain city, five hundred miles from the Gulf of Mexico over desert and mountains; the road to the Gulf of California was impossible; the Sierra Madre Occidental is as rough a chain of mountains as can be found.

But from Missouri the trader's train went easily across the rolling plains of Kansas and eastern Colorado, had a little trouble at Raton Pass – wagons needed an extra team – and then had no trouble getting to goods-starved Sante Fe.

There was a catch, however. The Santa Fe Trail lay right across the territory of the Comanches, Shawnees, Arapahoes, Utes, and almost any other hostile tribe that could be named. The Apaches sometimes came that far north, and the Sioux often wandered that far south.

Politicians nowadays are fond of extolling the virtues of the early pioneers. Those rugged individuals, they proclaim, didn't wait for government handouts or Federal assistance; they struck off across the wilds and settled a country with their bare hands.

The truth is that the merchants of St. Louis and Independence did not just ask for Federal aid; they screamed for the Army to come and protect their profits.

Thomas Hart Benton, Senator from Missouri, father-in-law of explorer John C. Frémont, was an influential man in Washington. The Army sent out infantry to cover the Santa Fe Trail, escort the traders, fight off the hostiles. Infantry was all the Army had.

In the summer of 1827 Fort Leavenworth, close to the eastern end of the trail, was built and named after its builder, Brigadier General Henry Leavenworth.

Here, in 1830, reported Stephen Watts Kearny, major of the 3rd Infantry, and his bride. Though the major was a New Jersey man, he accepted a pair of Negro slaves from his St. Louis stepfather-in-law. The wife served as Mrs. Kearny's maid; the husband attended the major, and followed him on horseback, certainly caring for both horses. This arrangement, reminiscent of Francis Marion and his men, seemed to Kearny the only possible way of life for a horse soldier. There were no enlisted horse soldiers.

The Santa Fe trade had grown from fifteen thousand dollars a year in 1822 to a hundred and twenty thousand dollars; it was no longer competing with the Chihauhua trade, but Missourians were taking their goods on from Santa Fe to the rich mines at Chihuahua.

The clamor of the traders for protection had resulted in several treaty-making expeditions, but the peace between the Indians and the traders was no more substantial than the smoke from the pipes that had sealed it.

The year before, 1829, the Army had sent out Major Bennet Riley – for whom the Cavalry School was to be named – and four companies of the 6th Infantry from Fort Leavenworth. The escort kept up with the train as far as the Arkansas, turned back, and then heard that the traders had been attacked and lost a man; so Riley took his soldiers back, and got the wagons into Mexican territory safely. But his report stated that the march was too hard for foot soldiers, that they did not have the mobility to choose their battleground; they ought to be mounted. No further escort was furnished the merchants of the Santa Fe Trail till the horse soldiers came into being.

It was not Riley's report so much as Congressional economy that eliminated infantry coverage of the caravans. Congressmen from all over the United States protested against paying four companies of troops to protect a trade that only amounted to two hundred thousand a year, and benefited chiefly one state, Missouri, which had less than two percent of the population of the country.

A mounted soldier, it was obvious, could cover much more line of march than a man on foot; he could range out as a scout, and if he discovered hostiles, he could choose his field of battle away from the wagons and the civilians; in this situation, a horseman was the equivalent of a dozen or more pedestrians. Forage was less of a problem than in other military situations, as the worst of the hostiles were horse Indians, and only went on the raiding path when the grass was good.

To digress for a moment, the Black Hawk War was just over. This was a brief campaign, mostly remembered because Abraham Lincoln served as a captain in it; most of the troops involved were Illinois militia, though any Regular Army men around were ordered to serve as aides or advisers to the militia generals, and some outfits of Regular infantry were sent to help out.

The militia were all mounted. P. St. George Cooke, of whom very much more later, got into the war; it was his finding that there wouldn't have been a war at all if the militia had not pushed the Indians around senselessly; and also, that a mounted man – and the Western militiaman would not go to war without a horse – was a nuisance unless he had had several months' training with the saber.

However, Major Henry Dodge raised a battalion of mounted miners in the Black Hawk War and managed to get a good deal of use out of them. Even Cooke admitted that this one militia outfit was capable.

In Illinois, and elsewhere, a man who volunteered to fight Indians or other enemies of the United States, and who brought a horse to the fray, called himself a "ranger." The title has always been popular with the American tongue; it has meant almost as many things as there have been decades in our history. Even today, there is about as much difference between a Texas Ranger and a Ranger-naturalist in the National Park Service as there was between Rogers' Rangers in the Revolution and a horse-owning Illinois farmer.

Probably to overcome the taxpayers' aversion to mounting professional soldiers, the first outfit of horse soldiers, established in 1832, were called the Battalion of Mounted Rangers. They were an elite corps, enlisted for one year only, each man to furnish his own horse and arms and to be paid a dollar a day, which was considerably more than that of a private soldier, or even a first sergeant.

This outfit did not last long. The Rangers were all officers, in their own opinion, and above any kind of labor; they did not take orders easily and seem to have been unfavorable toward drilling.

The Rangers were dissolved, and the 1st Regiment of Dragoons organized. Some of the old Rangers passed into this outfit, usually as lieutenants; the rest of the officers were taken from the infantry, and the men were recruited from all over the United States and its Territories. Later, most of the privates of the Army and many of the non-coms were to be foreigners; but the big immigration was yet to come, in the '40s.

Dodge was made colonel and Kearny lieutenant colonel of what was called an "elite" regiment. Cooke, then a lieutenant, was sent out on enlistment duty, an adventure which provoked the literary excesses that always hid immediately under his military hide. He was then twenty-four years old and had been out of West Point six years.

The regiment mustered at Jefferson Barracks, near St. Louis. Nothing was waiting for them; no stables, no uniforms, few horses. Some of the old Ranger spirit persisted; the men complained that Kearny was too tough, Dodge too soft. Cooke, back from recruiting, gave the recruits enough hours of dismounted drill a day to keep them tired.

The troopers were then ordered to build barracks and stables. They hadn't enlisted for this; they had enlisted to be men on horseback, cavaliers, gentlemen, not common laborers. There was a rash of desertions, of malingering, of dark mutterings in the corners of such buildings as had been provided for them.

The regiment mustered through the summer; in October enough horses arrived for three companies. They were all colors; it was decided to break them into six groups, and assign each group to a company by color, a system the Cavalry was to follow pretty much to the end. However, the original colors were not only bay, iron-gray, black and chestnut (or sorrel). There were also white and cream-colored mounts, which were later dropped from remount purchase orders, as being too conspicuous on the plains. The first horses were bought off farms and out of sales barns all over the country, usually by recruiting officers.

Now the men had mounted drill, dismounted drill, carpentry, and ordinary housekeeping duties as well as grooming to fill their days. It was too much. There were always some men on sick call, as well as some absent on regimental duties; there were officers' horses and ambulance horses and some of the sergeants were entitled to have their horses groomed by a trooper. It was a rare day when a man did not have two mounts to clean up after, water and groom – an hour above the knees, an hour below is the required time to keep a horse healthy. It took longer when there were no stables; fall in Missouri is no time to picket a horse. Nevertheless, when an inspector general came through in November, he found the troopers and their few horses in good shape.

Whereupon the regiment – what there was of it – was ordered to march five hundred miles to Fort Gibson on the Arkansas. The reasons were political. The Dragoons had been raised to serve in the Territories – Missouri was a state. The dreaded professional soldiers-on-horseback had to be removed; to keep them where they were was an insult to the Missouri militia, which numbered thousands, at least on paper.

The men moved out, toward the Indian Territory, which was to be their own headquarters. They had been enlisted to fight Indians, hadn't they?

Kearny didn't accompany the Dragoons on the dismal march; Dodge commanded them and sent his lieutenant colonel out to drum up more recruits, muster them at Jefferson Barracks, and follow to Gibson.

Kearny and others raised enough men for six more companies – the term troop was not to be official for years – and then the lieutenant colonel rejoined his regiment.

This was in late spring 1834. Congress was in the process of authorizing a second regiment of Dragoons, but the first was not up to strength; men and horses thronged the sick list, and by now a trooper was lucky if he didn't have three or four horses a day to care for. Dismounted drill had fallen off.

Not the least of a Dragoon's daily chore was the care of his uniform. The Army was button-mad. There were twenty gilt buttons on a dress blouse, and seventeen on a field tunic. All of these had to be shined for inspection, retreat, and so on and so forth.

Incidentally, the Dragoons were Yellowlegs from the day of their formation; the yellow stripes down their outseams were three-quarters of an inch wide, they wore yellow spurs, and for dress a yellow or orange silk net was tied on one hip; why, history does not state.

Before leaving the subject of uniform – by saying that that of the Dragoons was impossible for prairie service, and an absolute killer on a cross-country foot march – the report of the Military Committee inspecting West Point in that year of 1834 may shed some light on why the horse soldiers were treated as they were:

"The committee found fault only with the shape of the buttons used in the cadet's uniform. They are too large and most inconvenient. When the belt, owing to the size of the cadets, comes to pass over one of them, either a most unseemly protrusion is created, or a hole made through the belt, which entirely destroys the uniformity. It is considered that bullet buttons could be advantageously replaced by flat, or nearly flat, buttons."

After the committee happily reported that the "military duties of the cadets (were) found not to be oppressive," the chairman, Achille Murat, went on to philosophize: "However dangerous standing armies are to a nation's liberty in time of peace, they nevertheless possess immense advantages in time of war … Officers of infantry and cavalry can easily be recruited from the rank and file of the army; but the engineers, the staff, and the artillery require men educated for these professions."

The report concludes that engineers and artillerymen can be assigned, in times of peace, to the infantry and cavalry, and then used in their "professions in wartime."

Cooke was a West Pointer; Kearny, who was not, depended quite a bit on the young man's ideas. Cooke felt, as we have seen, that many months were required to make a cavalryman; certainly, it would take longer to make a cavalry officer.

But they were up against the old American tradition that any man can ride a horse and aim a gun. And perhaps, in that day, any farm boy could. But there is a terrible difference between shooting at a hawk or a deer and shooting at an Indian who is shooting back; and there is perhaps a greater difference between riding a horse all day and then putting him in a stable and tending that same horse on a three-week patrol. If a farm horse broke down from overwork or chill or because forage was scarce, his chores could be postponed for a day or even more; if a cavalry mount gave out while in pursuit of, contact with, or flight from hostile Indians, his rider was likely to be dead and the horse himself captured by Sioux or eaten by Apaches.

In addition, there is a gap between sergeants and officers, a gap of function. The sergeant, if he is a good one, sees that the men keep themselves and their horses in good condition, making an efficient weapon of the outfit; the officer determines where and how that weapon should be pointed.

42

The very gap in pay between top kicks and second lieutenants precluded there being any strategists or even tacticians in the Regular Army. When top enlisted pay was twenty-five dollars a month, a newly hatched shavetail got fifteen hundred, if mounted, fourteen hundred if dismounted, a year. That wasn't great pay, even in the fat dollars of those years, but it could attract young men of intelligence; enlisted pay could only appeal to men who wanted to leave real responsibility behind with their civilian clothes.

Of course, conditions changed rapidly in wartime, and many a patriot enlisted as a private and ended up wearing shoulder straps, sometimes with eagles or stars on them.

Ready or not, the 1st Dragoons went on their first anti-Indian expedition in June of 1834. On the fifteenth of that month Colonel Dodge led a patrol out against the Comanches and the Pawnee Picts, neither of whom had yet come under any kind of government control.

The cavalry went as an advance party; six days after they moved out, General Henry Leavenworth followed them with the 7th Infantry and some other people, including the painter George Catlin and Carl Beyrich, a German naturalist.

The expedition was supposed to have started with the first good grass, about May 1; general confusion held it up. Fort Gibson was left under the command of Kearny who had returned from recruiting.

A secondary intention of the strong patrol was to impress the Osages and the Kiowas, who were fighting each other. The very size of the column was expected to do that; most Indians had seen no more than a few white men in their entire lives.

The late start almost wrecked the cavalry before they got going. It turned dreadfully hot – 105 degrees in the shade – with the killing, humid heat of the Mississippi Valley. The troopers presumably unbuttoned and then discarded their heavy blouses; military reports seldom mention such things, which can be held against the commander by superiors who would have allowed the same thing. But none of the uniform was made for this heat. A man – and the officers suffered as much as the troopers – either had to expose his skin to the blistering sun or suffer excessive and unnecessary dehydration from sweating.

Bad water, copiously drunk by these newcomers to the prairies, took its toll. After eighty miles the expedition ground to a halt, half the men down with fever, dysentery, heat exhaustion, sunstroke. Kearny came up with the rest of the Dragoons and was told off, with a Surgeon Hailer to set up a sick camp. It was both medical and veterinary; the good grass of May was long gone, and the horses that did not have heat staggers were starving.

But it was necessary to carry out at least part of the original intention. Leavenworth sent Dodge on with what troopers could ride and what horses could carry them, to impress the Osages and the Kiowas. About two hundred men moved out behind their colonel.

But at that, the cavalry had proved itself; it was in better shape than the infantry; sufficiently so to prove that mounted troops were essential for Western use.

Moving southwest, Dodge came to brush country, called the Cross Timbers, possibly after the almost-forgotten battle site of Tecumseh's war, twenty years before and a thousand miles to the northeast. This had originally been blackjack oak and other scrub timber. But the Indians had burned it out, repeatedly, to drive game toward them; it had gone into dense undergrowth. The horsemen got down and cut paths with their firewood axes and proved that sabers were useful; they could be swung through light brush, as machetes.

Behind Dodge, Leavenworth moved what effectives he could, slowly and painfully. He himself came down with a fever – probably typhoid – but tried buffalo hunting anyway, and, on July 21, was thrown and died. Dodge, out ahead, was now in command of the whole column, though he didn't know it.

Kearny was moving his sick camp forward all the time, enlarging it as he overtook more invalids. When he reached the site of Leavenworth's death, on the edge of the Cross Timbers, he took command. His assumption wasn't disputed; the only other officers on their feet in the whole column – including Dodge's advance party – were Dodge, a major, and two lieutenants. Dr. Haile was frightfully ill, and Kearny was commander and doctor both, the surgeon giving him instructions from his pallet.

Dodge pushed on, through the Kiowa-Osage country, and managed to keep his men in enough order so that the warring Indians were impressed; they agreed to come into Gibson in the early fall to parlay.

Then the colonel turned back, to find out from Kearny that Leavenworth was dead. Dodge took command and led what effectives there were back to Fort Gibson, leaving Kearny to nurse the ailing men and horses along at a slower rate.

Orginally it was planned to have the lieutenant colonel go riding through to Fort Leavenworth with his invalids, but by the time he got back to Gibson – August 24 – everyone was too sick to go farther. Which probably saved some lives; the temperature continued to climb, reaching 114 degrees one miserable day.

As it was, this first encounter of the Dragoons with the Indians of the West – the true, final West, as against the old Northwest and Southwest frontiers on the Great Lakes and the Mississippi – cost the lives of almost ninety men of a regiment authorized at six hundred and sixty, and not nearly up to strength when the campaign started. This without hostilities.

But the results were spectacularly successful. Eight days after Kearny brought his sick detachment into the fort, the Kiowas and the Osages started coming in to treat for peace. Other tribes followed suit; when the Five Civilized Nations were moved from the Southeast to Indian Territory, the Dragoons at once made a show of strength, and continued to make it till the Cherokees, the Creeks, the Seminoles, and – less rebellious – the Choctaws and Chickasaws settled down in their new and rather disappointing country.

The pony soldiers were in the West to stay. They were beginning to learn how to deal with this new and treacherous country; if they had only learned one thing, not to miss the May grass, it was something. But they had learned more, about dressing for summer heat, about carrying grain for troop horses, perhaps about not depending on buffalo-staled water.

Which brings up perhaps the most controversial point about the Dragoons in the West. Why did they use such heavy horses? The lighter ponies of the Sioux and Cheyenne and other Plains tribes could outrun them, apparently do it on cottonwood bark if they had to; the troop horses had to be grained and given more careful grooming than a washdown under the saddle and a roll on the prairie.

The Apache do not enter into this matter. Despite romanticists, the Apache – as good riders as the world has ever seen – did not keep horses in the Sioux or European sense. An Apache prided himself on horse stealing – often a one-man activity, rather than a group affair as with the Sioux – and the horse on which he outran the Dragoons was often one he'd gotten only the night before.

When an Apache had ridden his horse to death, he ate as much of the animal as he had time for, and went on afoot, until he could steal another horse, or mule. The latter were preferred – they tasted better to Apache palates.

On the other hand, the Sioux were not only horsemen, but horse lovers, and so were other Plains tribes. But they did not cut loose from a base, as the troopers had to, and go off on three- and four-week forays. They were followed by their villages, with large remudas of remounts and with corn, dragged on travois by dogs or packed on the backs of squaws.

The Spanish and the Mexican travelers used the remuda system, too – anywhere from six to a dozen horses to a rider. Later on, the cowboys, miners, and ranchers of the West were to scorn the Army riders, as slow and elaborate travelers; but the cowboy, particularly, used a remuda when working cattle, and did not count on a good roping horse as a trail mount. When the big cattle drives started, an hour and a half to two hours was considered a day's work for a pony; then he was thrown back into the remuda and replaced with a fresh animal.

The heavy troop horse was a necessity if he was to work day after day for several weeks. Grain was a necessity if the horse was to carry his rider, carbine, picket line, pistol and so on all through a day whose late afternoon might involve a charge. A horse must graze at least half of every twenty-four hours – or eat hay as roughage when he is in camp or fort – but grass alone will not carry a hard working animal, not even the rich burr clover of California.

It is hard to see why the Dragoons did not use remudas, at least on the prairies and plains where the unburdened horses could be herded off to one side of the trail to find fresh grass. Horse wrangling was considered a lower occupation than cattle driving, but the Army has never minded assigning menial work to its enlisted men.

The horses bought for the Army were all Eastern; later they were to be called "American" horses to distinguish them from New Mexican, Texan, and Californian stock. Morgan blood was highly esteemed; any kind of Standardbred came next, with part Thoroughbred in third place. To achieve the size necessary to carry a trooper, his saddle, slicker, ammunition, canteen, bedding, and so on, these animals had to be about fifteen hands three inches tall, and sturdy; to gain that size, the horse raisers who hoped to sell to the Army grain-fed their colts almost from birth, and the resultant remounts never could get along without oats or barley. The more grain a horse carried, the larger he had to be. Each horse on patrol carried a few days' grain for himself, and a few days' food for his trooper, as well as enough ammunition to get through a pretty extensive fight.

Civilian herders were employed to bring along mule trains carrying food, grain and extra ammunition; they were guarded, usually by a single platoon. Another platoon could have guarded a remuda, so that each horse would have every other day in which to graze, barebacked.

No argument so far advanced explains why this wasn't done. Perhaps it was the lingering fear of soldiers-on-horseback; maybe a two-horse man was considered more likely to get full of pride and join in a coup d'etat than a one-horse man.

At any rate, the cavalry never had more than one horse assigned to a trooper, unless he was driving an ambulance or other wheeled vehicle.

Chapter 5

Sabers on the Prairie

In the fall Kearny was ordered to take slightly more than a hundred of the 1st Dragoons – three companies, officially – and strike northeast, toward where the Des Moines River joins the Mississippi. This is now Iowa; it was then called Michigan Territory. The new fort was to be called Des Moines, but it was more than a hundred miles down the Des Moines River from the present city; and it wasn't on that river at all.

Southeast Iowa is pretty country, rolling, with nice woods along the rivers. But the powers that – according to every private – hate soldiers had picked a swampy spot for the new fort, miserable, without a view, cold in winter and soggy in summer and without any military value that Colonel Kearny and his officers could discern.

Orders were orders. The barracks and stables had been started – badly – by the Quartermaster's Department, but never finished. Kearny was ill and most of his men were in even worse condition. They were Dragoons, learning a new trade the hard way. Once again, they had been told to be carpenters or perish. Kearny put them to work, asking the War Department only that they be furnished double rations, which they were, on paper; most of the supplies never arrived.

Winter broke early that year; by November Kearny had his horses and men under cover, but the Dragoon-built buildings were drafty and constantly damp.

The War Department then sent in a number of recruits, together with their horses. The frost-bitten Dragoons – still sick from the past summer's excessive heat – got out the saws and the hammers again.

To the colonel's other troubles were added a number of indifferent and untrainable officers. They had taken their commissions – often through political influence – to reap glory, not work. Drill, when there was time for it, was left to the sergeants; and at that time, when literacy was not required

47

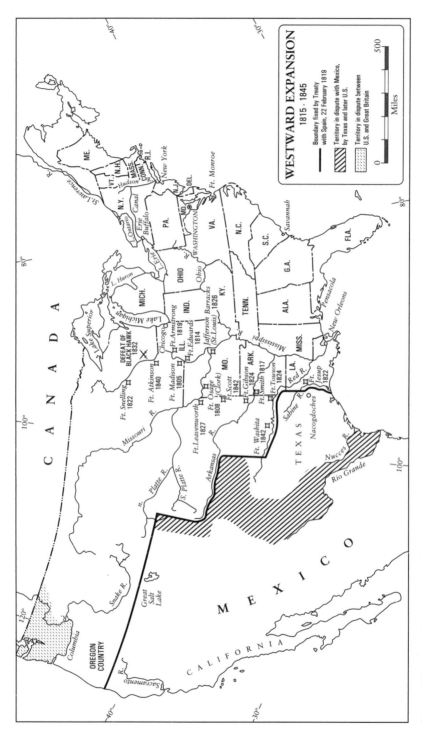

Map 1 Westward Expansion, 1815-1845

of a soldier, anyone who could read and write a little was good enough to be a sergeant.

As for the construction, it was a day when an officer and a gentleman would never admit that he had ever worked with his hands, though many of the officers had probably been farmers' sons and could have supervised construction if they had deigned to. No manual of mounted drill or cavalry tactics had yet been written; the officers probably knew the dismounted drill well enough, but most of them were not inclined to stand on a freezing, soggy parade ground and see it carried out.

There was a newly founded town near the fort, calling itself Nashville. Most of the inhabitants decided to get through the winter by selling liquor to the troopers.

Kearny had had this trouble before, back when he was in the infantry as commandant of Fort Towson on the Red River, in southeast Arkansas. He ordered his troops out, now, and attempted to destroy every drop of whiskey in Nashville. The settlers then produced a civilian authority – someone on the order of a justice of the peace – who found two of the Dragoons guilty of destroying property. Kearny refused to turn them over to the jackleg court, and wrote a full report to the War Department, taking the blame, and saying that the Dragoons had been under his orders.

His stock rose with the men. The colonel was tough, but he was as tough on himself as he was on them; maybe worse. The veterans of the sick camp of the Cross Timbers told the recruits how the Old Man had been just about the last Dragoon on his feet, and how he had nursed them when even the surgeon was flat on his back. Somehow, they got through the winter.

In the spring Kearny received a new lieutenant, Albert M. Lea, class of 1831, West Point, and assigned him to command Company I, whose captain was off on remount duty. Lea took hold at once. He found his stables inadequate; so he set up a small, hand-run mill, and made cutting lumber a disciplinary measure. Company I's troopers straightened up and began to act like soldiers; but before they did, Lea had enough lumber to get all his horses under proper cover. Kearny was so delighted with the lieutenant that he gave the captain of another company – Nathan Boone, son of Daniel – leave and put Albert Lea in charge of both troops.

Kearny wanted to get out of Fort Des Moines for the summer, both because he felt that the bivouac was the best place to train Dragoons and because the summer climate at the fort was unbearable. He applied to the War Department for permission to make a patrol, showing the flag to some of the northern Plains Indians. The letter crossed one from the War Department, telling him that it had never been the intention to make his present location a permanent one; he was to move up the Des Moines to the junction of the Raccoon – pretty much present-day Des Moines – and set up a fort there.

In June he moved out, with a hundred and fifty Dragoons, a doctor, and several Indians, together with a squaw man to interpret.

The Army hadn't told him to go directly up the river; he took about eight hundred miles to go less than a hundred and fifty. He covered most of present Iowa, cut over into Minnesota, and impressed a band of Sioux under Chief Wabasha, as well as some wandering Sacs. The country traversed was not hostile; there were numerous Indian bands, but they were small and not inclined to dispute the right of free passage to three companies of Dragoons. Wabasha and the Sacs signed treaties with Kearny.

Then the major led his Dragoons across country till they cut the Des Moines River; they followed it south to the junction where they were to build a fort. But Kearny had had enough of cavalrymen as carpenters; he ruled the site unfavorable, and took the direct route home, having gone nearly eleven hundred miles without losing a man or a horse.

Considering the patrol of the summer before, it was almost a miraculous ride. The Dragoons had learned how to live in the Western plains. Little is said in the contemporary accounts about this second column of patrol put out by the Dragoons, but it is safe to speculate that they wore simpler clothing this time. Gold mesh nets on the hip and seventeen-button blouses had failed to impress the inhabitants of the Indian Territory and would have done no more for the denizens of what was now called Wisconsin Territory.

Kearny went into winter quarters at old Fort Des Moines. Miserable as it was, it existed, which made it highly superior to an empty point without stables and barracks. The garrison had probably spent the summer improving the fort, because Kearny's family joined him that fall.

While Kearny was out seeing the Sacs and a band of Sioux and other small groups of Indians, Colonel Dodge had taken a patrol out from Fort Leavenworth to strike much farther northwest than any body of undisguised American soldiers had ever been. The summer before the Dragoons had impressed the Indians along the eastern stretch of the Santa Fe Trail; now they swung around to show themselves on the western end, before the Trail struck south and crossed the Arkansas into what was still Mexico – now southern Colorado.

Most of the bands of Indians Dodge met at first were peaceful, and, in any event, not strong enough to stand up against a hundred and twenty Dragoons – Dodge's three companies were not up to the muster of Kearny's three.

But the Arikaras had been augmenting their hunting-maize economy with a good deal of piracy, practiced on anyone, white or red, who ventured their way. Most of the whites had been Canadians, but the Indians took no chances that the Yellowlegs were not English; they got out of the way.

Dodge pursued them and learned at once that troop horses could never catch Indians who didn't want to be caught. But the fugitives were subject to curiosity; they came in and parlayed with Colonel Dodge, committed a little light pilfering against any Dragoon careless enough to leave gear loose on the prairie, and then rode out, promising love and fealty to the Great White Father, promises which they didn't mean and which Dodge probably didn't believe.

Then the three companies went on, through the country to the Southern Cheyenne, to Bent's Fort on the Santa Fe Trail. Here they could look south, across the river, into New Mexico, where traders were busily selling whiskey to the Cheyennes and some Arapahoes, a trade forbidden north of the water, in United States Territory. It was all as noisy, gay, and dusty as Tijuana during Prohibition days.

Charles Bent and Ceran St. Vrain entertained Colonel Dodge and his officers in the fort.

The enlisted Dragoons, of course, crossed the river to join the border-town orgy. Though one sergeant wrote in his diary that he was shocked by the drunken nakedness of the Indian men, women, and children, he also mentions the aborigines' liberality with the whiskey they had just purchased so dearly – at least one buffalo skin for a drink of alcohol flavored with water, chewing tobacco, and red pepper. It sounds like a professional private's ideal Saturday night, and perhaps was; the column seems to have reached Bent's Fort on Friday night, August 7, in that year of 1835.

By Monday there were enough Arapahoes at the fort for Colonel Dodge to make a speech, distribute medals, and prepare to return to Leavenworth. The colonel was probably not convinced of the value of the speeches and the medals; Cooke, who was with him, recorded his skepticism.

Before the Dragoons left Bent, young William Bent came in from the Red River, where Dodge had patrolled the summer before. The colonel was overjoyed to learn that the Comanches, who had promised him to be peaceful, still were. He turned his three companies toward home, proud of them and of himself.

But down the valley of the Arkansas the scouts recognized a big encampment of Cheyennes, surrounded by freshly stolen Comanche ponies. The peace that the Dragoons were to bring to the prairies seemed tenuous; Dodge kept his mouth shut and told the Cheyennes they had missed a big parlay at Bent's Fort, but that he had left gifts for them there.

At this point a number of Pawnees and Arikaras arrived in the Cheyenne camp, discharging their single-shot firearms as they came in, to show

51

that they were peaceful. The noise did not panic the summer-hardened Dragoons.

Probably Dodge's, and possibly Kearny's, patrols of that summer did not do as much to pacify the Indians as the Army thought; there was a widespread coalition and realignment among the Plains tribes going on that had nothing to do with seeing the Dragoons and their flags; things were peaceful until the war chiefs found out who was on whose side.

But another future enemy was impressed. The fifteen-year-old Republic of Mexico was having trouble with Texas, where a number of United States families – mostly led by Moses Austin of Connecticut – had been induced to settle.

Mexico has always had trouble with its northern provinces. The Mexican personality has an emotional attachment to the central valley and is reluctant to live very far away from the capital of the republic; the governments of Mexico and of Baja California are still devising lures to get that northeast state settled to its capacity.

The Anglo-Texans were in constant dispute with the central government. For one thing, they wanted Negro slavery, to which Mexico was opposed; for another they wanted statehood, which Mexico felt should be withheld until the population of Texas had increased.

Stephen Fuller Austin, son of the founder, eventually declared Texas a Mexican state and a slave-holding one, without the consent of the Mexican government. He was thrown into prison, released in 1835, and a Texas War of Independence became certain.

The part that the United States would play in this was by no means predetermined. There was never any doubt that Texas would be slave country; the Congress was evenly balanced, and if the big Mexican state joined the Union, that balance would be destroyed. A bitter battle was going on in the Congress over the matter of slavery in the District of Columbia; it seemed certain that a request for an appropriation to aid a slave-holding country – even if Texas remained independent – would cause a furor.

Andrew Jackson, a Southerner, was finishing his two terms as President; he would be succeeded by Martin Van Buren of New York.

The authorization of a second regiment of Dragoons was partly inspired by the threat of Texas-Mexican trouble, but more largely by another uprising of one of the Five Civilized Tribes, this time the Seminoles in Florida.

This bloomed into a full-scale war in 1836. In the same year Henry Dodge resigned from the Army to accept a Territorial Governorship, and Kearny became colonel of the 1st Dragoons.

The 2nd Dragoons were formed, and at once shipped to Florida. No one in that swampy war behaved very gloriously except the Seminoles; they numbered a few more than three thousand, of whom about a third were warriors. In the six years that the war lasted, more than fifteen hundred soldiers and many civilians were killed. The Army estimated that hunting Seminoles cost the government twenty million dollars.

The object of the Seminole War was to remove the Seminoles from Florida. There are still Seminoles in Florida.

The 2nd, first as Dragoons and then as the 2nd Cavalry, served honorably and well in the West and in the Civil War; it seems best to forget their start. The swamp-dwelling Seminoles were no target for cavalry, anyway; mostly the Dragoons acted as escorts for officers meeting with the Indians to treat, and as scouts or messengers. After the war, the 2nd was dismounted as an economy measure.

Back to the 1st; Stephen Watts Kearny was now in command. He was to shape the U.S. Cavalry into what it would be for the rest of its horseback life. His twenty-two-year-old nephew, Philip, having inherited a million dollars from a grandfather, and thus being free of his father's desire to make him into a lawyer, joined the Dragoons as a lieutenant in 1837, was seasoned in the West, and then sent to France with two other officers to write the first *Cavalry Manual*, an idea of the colonel's.

Phil Kearny and his fellow first lieutenants studied cavalry tactics at Saumur for a while; then he got permission from Secretary of War, Joel Roberts Poinsett, to go help the French fight Arabs in Algeria. He was offered a lieutenant colonelcy by the French government but returned to the United States. He became a general in the Civil War, and had a fort named after him: Fort Phil Kearny in Montana. In this he was more fortunate than his uncle. Fort Kearny in Nebraska, named after Stephen Watts Kearny, had become Kearney by 1864, when the journalist Eugene W. Ware served there; it was still Kearny in the 1855 edition of *Lippincott's Gazetteer*.

Inserting the "e" into the name seems irresistible. The name of P. St. George Cooke, who was to become Colonel Kearny's right-hand man, suffers an opposite fate; it loses the "e" that Kearny gains. There is a range called Cook's Mountains in southern New Mexico, and an organization of Latter-Day Saints has erected monuments to the Mormon Battalion, which Cooke commanded, all along the battalion's route of march; according to the plates, the Saints were commanded by "Captain Cook." Cooke was a lieutenant colonel at the time.

Stephen Watts Kearny came from a family of wealth in Newark, New Jersey. He was the fifteenth child of his parents; this may have had something to do with the fact that there was not the opposition to his military career that the family made about Phil's.

His father had been a Loyalist in the Revolution, but by the time the War of 1812 started, Stephen had been an ensign in the New York Militia for a year; he then, at nineteen, took a commission as first lieutenant in the U.S. Army. He served through the war, officially in Colonel Winfield Scott's 2nd Infantry, but after being wounded and captured by the British at Queenston Heights, he was exchanged and assigned to recruiting duty.

He came out of the war a captain, went back to the 2nd, then was transferred, in 1819, to the 6th Infantry and went west, as far as Council Bluffs. From then on, except for the short tour in New York just before the 1st Dragoons were organized, Kearny was a man of the West; on September 5, 1830, in St. Louis, he married Mary Radford, step-daughter of General William Clark, former Governor of Missouri Territory.

But he was, of course, an infantryman of the West; there was no cavalry. Often, he had been a waterborne infantryman – he had been down the Mississippi by boat, and had worked his way up the Missouri, occasionally riding the commercial ships that were freighting supplies up and furs down the Big Muddy.

He had been to the Yellowstone; he had fought Indians and made treaties with Indians. He was thoroughly convinced of the necessity of horse soldiers to handle the vast and valuable territory west of the junction of the Kaw and Missouri rivers.

Dodge had political ambitions and wanted his soldiers to like him, an attitude that weakened his effectiveness; so really it was Kearny who formed the 1st Dragoons, and thus founded the United States Cavalry.

In 1837 he published, through the War Department, a carbine manual for the use of Dragoons. But there was not yet any sort of manual of mounted drill, and this lack may well have enabled Kearny and the 1st Dragoons to get as much done as they did.

For when the Cavalry really shaped up – say, in the years after the Civil War – there was a firm policy that horseback riders off the farm did not make good recruits. The drillmasters – sergeants or officers – wanted their troopers to ride Army style, or not at all. Non-riders were preferred.

They remained non-riders more times than is believable. At best, the cavalrymen were only supposed to have four and a half hours of mounted drill a week according to General Orders. (This was in 1879, but they seldom varied.) But the exceptions were numerous – men were told off for construction and repair work, for gardening – the Cavalry was nearly obsolescent before vegetables became part of government issues, and even vegetable seeds had to be paid for out of company funds – as officers' servants, as KPs, as guards, and so on and so forth, meaning they missed equitation classes.

Kearny must have passed up an awful lot of the fooforaw and nonsense, the elaborate ceremonies raising and lowering the flag, the rigid stamping around a parade ground by men who would never meet a uniformed enemy, in order to turn out the 1st Dragoons the way they were. And he must have allowed the men to ride at ease, which was, of course, what they would do when they left their forts to engage in their business of impressing what Indians they could and fighting those they couldn't impress.

Their numbers impressed Indians; their carbines impressed them; quite possibly the size and well-being of their horses did. But formation drill would only look silly to a Sioux or an Apache unless it could be sold as some sort of particularly efficacious war dance, and there is absolutely no record of this sort of propaganda.

The Dragoons must have had some of the informality of Harry Lee's old Legion, or even of Francis Marion's Irregulars. In the years between 1836 and the Mexican War of 1846 they kept the peace from Louisiana to Michigan, built three forts, added a few structures to Fort Leavenworth, and kept the Santa Fe Trail open. But their strength was not authorized over six hundred and sixty officers and men, and they were seldom up to strength.

Reviewed, in 1837, by General Edmund P. Gaines, he reported them as one of the finest military outfits he had ever seen. But considering that they had to cover the whole west half of the Mississippi Valley – Kearny seldom sent them across the river, believing that they belonged where the Indians were – and had to garrison or help garrison a dozen posts; close order drill, which took up about half of the infantry's time in the form of parades, retreats, guard mounts, assemblies, must have been omitted from the Dragoon's life; it was not omitted from that of the Dragoons' successors, the Cavalrymen. Target practice was not important; the manual of arms was. If a carbine was handled smartly, in other words, it didn't matter if it could shoot an enemy.

Enemies were not lacking in the ten years before the Mexican War. In 1839 the Cherokees, newly removed to Indian Territory, began rumbling ominously, which was curious, because there was a garrison of Dragoons at Fort Wayne, in the country assigned to the Cherokee Nation.

Kearny led two hundred and fifty Dragoons out of Leavenworth, nearly the whole garrison there, and made a forced march to Fort Wayne, I.T. He found his men there in a deplorable state; he replaced them with some of the crack Leavenworth horsemen, and marched the rest of his command back to the Kansas post, where he could bring the backsliders up to regimental standards.

It was a daring, typically Dragoon, move. In the first place, he counted on terrific speed to get back to Leavenworth before hostiles found out it was virtually unguarded; in the second place, the expedition was not only not authorized by any superior, it was unfinanced by the Quartermaster; Kearny bought the supplies for the three hundred mile march out of his own pocket.

The Dragoons were only away from Leavenworth nine days, including the time spent at Fort Wayne; they must have moved at about forty miles a day, almost twice what was usually expected of horsemen on a protracted trip.

A month before that Kearny had taken two hundred of his troopers north to the Oto country, ridden in among more than a thousand armed Indians – not all of them but many of them drunk – refused to talk until all Indian arms had been laid down, and ridden away again, leaving peace behind by the sheer force of his personality, and his obvious willingness to use his Dragoons if he had to.

In an 1842 clash with the Seminoles who were being shipped out from Florida, his report notes that a Seminole boy "continued to struggle though surrounded by flashing sabers" and also recounts his orders that, if it came to a fight, the Dragoons were to "put their sabers well in." Since this, too, was protracted patrol, rather than a foray out of a post, it seems that the Dragoons were still carrying their swords out against the Indians. Of course, there were no repeating carbines yet, and the Colt revolver, invented in 1836, was not issued, although some officers had purchased them; when the Indians got breech-loading repeating rifles the sabers would be confined to the parade ground.

Also, in 1842, the 2nd Dragoons were dismounted and made into a rifle regiment. They were to get their horses back two years later; the dismounting had been an economy measure following the Seminole War, the remounting was in preparation for the almost certain Mexican War; both candidates for the presidency in the campaign of 1844, James Knox Polk and Henry Clay, promised to annex Texas if elected, and Mexico had sworn to fight if that happened.

Until it happened, the 1st Dragoons were pretty much on the side of the Mexicans in that the regiment had the protection of the Santa Fe Trail as one of its prime duties, and the merchants who used the Trail were often Mexican citizens, though not always by birth: one was named Magoffin and had been born in Kentucky, and a group of brothers were named Spiegelberg and had started life as Prussian Jews.

But Don Antonio José Chávez was Mexican enough, and when he was attacked by bandits with peculiar commissions from the Republic of Texas, the Dragoons took out after his murderer, one "Captain" McDaniel, and ran him and his men down on the Trail, as they headed for Missouri. McDaniel and his brother were hanged, and their gang imprisoned.

Despite the anti-Mexican feeling, this did not prejudice the Texans against Kearny and his Dragoons; what happened next did. There is a good deal of doubt that President Mirabeau Lamar or any other Texas official ever commissioned McDaniel; but Jacob Snively was most certainly a Texas general, or at least a colonel.

With about a hundred and fifty men under his command, Snively marched north to prey on the Santa Fe Trail; his orders read that he was to seize all of New Mexico and annex it to Texas, but it is dubious if he ever intended that grand scheme.

The Arkansas River, west of 100 degrees longitude, was the border between Mexico and the United States; east of that point, both north and south banks were American.

The plan was to camp just west and south of the corner, on Mexican soil, and wait for the big annual caravan from Independence to Santa Fe. The trade was rumored to be particularly rich that year.

The Dragoons, as the Texans knew, would escort the wagons as far as the river, and then turn back, unlicensed to cross into Mexican New Mexico. The Texas camp was located opposite Chouteau's Island, a landmark that marked the international corner.

But the Arkansas, like most Western rivers, was undependable. Cooke and his Dragoons did not turn back when they hit the river but came on across and told the Texans that they were east of the 100-degree point.

Snively objected; Cooke, under orders from Kearny not to start a war – which the raid would have done – disarmed the Texans and sent them out on the prairie with only enough guns to kill game.

Some of the men went across the trail to Missouri, as being the safer route; but Snively and a hundred of his troops headed south for Texas. And on the way they had several fire-fights with Indians, producing weapons they had concealed from the Dragoons, and others which were the property of men not present at the disarming, but losing several Texians, as they were then called, to the hostiles.

As a result, Cooke – and Kearny because Cooke was his junior officer – became hated in Texas; later on, when they brushed with Frémont in California and were called East to testify before the Senate, the Texas senators sided with Frémont's friends, damaging Cooke's career; Kearny died shortly after the hearing.

In 1842 Kearny was promoted; he remained as Colonel of the 1st Dragoons, but also became commanding officer of the Third Military Department, still as a colonel, but with headquarters at Jefferson Barracks, outside St. Louis, instead of at Leavenworth.

That was in the fall of 1843. Next spring the colonel was back at Leavenworth presiding over the court-martial of St. George Cooke, demanded by the Texans. The court found Cooke had done nothing "harsh and unbecoming" in the gobbledegook language of the charge and returned him to duty.

A year later the colonel led five companies of the 1st Dragoons on one of its most famous expeditions – a march toward Oregon, then disputed between the United States and Britain.

The foray had a secondary purpose – to show strength to the hostile and wild tribes of Indians who were menacing the increasingly important Oregon Trail.

Kearny was not well; as a matter of fact, he had only a little more than three years to live. Nobody who survived that first westward march of the Dragoons from St. Louis to Indian Territory ever recovered entirely; most of them had malaria the rest of their lives, a disease Kearny seems to have missed. But he had various digestive troubles that would probably now be diagnosed as ulcers.

Nevertheless, the Commanding Officer of the Third Military Department ordered the Colonel of the 1st Dragoons to become commander of the Oregon expedition. Kearny, as all three men, obeyed joyously.

It was an experiment in living off the country. While the Dragoons did herd some cattle and a few sheep along to get them started, the colonel planned on living off the country, by killing buffalo and other game.

This was a much larger column than went out on routine patrol – nearly three hundred men, mostly Dragoons, the rest artillerists, civilian guides, teamsters, and a few infantry officers from the Third Department staff.

It was almost as large as a wartime command could expect to be; war with Mexico and possibly with Great Britain and Canada was now so imminent that Kearny wanted the Dragoons prepared for it.

The expedition was an Oregon one only in name; it went only as far as the western end of South Pass, almost three hundred miles past Fort Laramie, or about two-thirds of the way across present Wyoming. A third of Wyoming and all of Idaho lay between them and present Oregon; it was even farther to the disputed territory that is now the State of Washington. But Cooke romantically recorded that they were on the "mountain edge of Oregon"; in that time, all the Northwest was called "Oregon country."

The point was that the Dragoons had proved they could move in force against the British if they had to. Despite their name, Fort Laramie, and its neighbor and rival Fort Platte, had never seen American troops; they were privately owned fur trading posts. Bonneville had been through this country, of course, but disguised as a trapper; technically Captain Bonneville had been on leave when he made his exploration of the fur country and California. He had played the part of a fur trader to the hilt, even going into bankruptcy along with several rival traders, though his expedition had the sanction of the Army.

The trip was a disappointment to Phil Kearny, who had returned to the regiment as captain of Company F: there was no fighting. But numerous bands of Pawnees, Sioux, and other potential enemies were passed and contacted and impressed; that was the purpose of the expedition to begin with; the artillery guns, always impressive to Indians and perhaps even more so to the Hudson's Bay Company, had been brought along for their shock value, rather than with the thought that some fort would have to be breached. One of them was fired, for the delectation of some emigrants, on the Fourth of July.

Grass proved a problem; there were so many emigrants on the Oregon Trail that the Dragoons had to leave the trace and forage off to the side to find graze. But there was plenty of game, and the troopers enjoyed the change from the horrible government issue bacon and salt pork and pickled beef.

Near Fort Laramie, Colonel Kearny parlayed with a large body of Sioux, and got their chiefs' promise of peace. There is little doubt that the strong emigration was worrying the Sioux; the Dragoons were a warning of what would happen and who would cause it to happen if the Indians turned hostile.

Having crossed the Continental Divide, the column turned and went back to Fort Laramie, then south to Bent's Fort on the Santa Fe Trail, stopping to parlay with the Cheyenne on the way.

Bent's Fort was almost on the Mexican (New Mexican) border. Charles Bent and his partner Ceran St. Vrain were happily astounded to see such a large detachment of the United States Army; war with Mexico was expected at any moment. The traders entertained the officers at a sumptuous dinner; no doubt the troopers found entertainment of their own, as they had on their first visit to the fort.

Hungover or not, Kearny marched the Dragoons out the next day, having reprovisioned at Bent's Fort from rice and hardtack cached there three years before by the Army, which had now proved that dry provisions would keep indefinitely in the arid Western air.

Kearny was in a hurry to get back to Leavenworth and resume contact with his superiors; he had accomplished everything the Oregon expedition was supposed to accomplish. But he let St. George Cooke and a surveyor take shots at the site of Cooke's argument with Snively and his Texans. This proved that Jackson's Grove, as Cooke had named the Texas camp, was in the United States, as Cooke had claimed. It was a sort of moral victory for the Dragoons and their captain and the court-martial which Kearny had presided over, but it did nothing to pacify Texas, of course.

Ninety-nine days after they left Fort Leavenworth the Dragoons rode in again. They had gone twenty-two hundred miles, according to a measuring device on one of the wagon wheels; they had not lost a man, and they were returning in good health – though there had been a day of alkali sickness along the way and other temporary ailments.

The Dragoons had ridden out of Leavenworth leather-hard; they returned pure rawhide. This was the twelfth year of their existence, eleven years after they had made their first tragic patrol, under General Leavenworth and Colonel Dodge, and they had proved what they could do; actually, they had proved that only mounted troops could keep the peace in the West.

But Congress had still only authorized two regiments of mounted men. The 2nd Dragoons were again mounted and standing by down around the Brazos and Nueces rivers. Bonneville, reinstated in the Army after his Western explorations had caused him to overstay his leave, was in command of a company, and later of a battalion, or squadron.

Kearny sent his report off to Washington; General Winfield Scott, who headed the Army, seemed to agree with him. There were two major points: the first was that the whiskey and arms smuggling to the Indians would not be controlled until the Indian country – meaning the West then and from then on – was under martial law. This raised a legal point that was never resolved; organized territories could not be kept under perpetual martial law any more than states could, but could not the Indian lands be called unorganized territories until the hostiles were put down?

The second point that Kearny made was that heavy cavalry patrols – two or three times a year – would be more efficient in keeping the hostiles down than a line of forts at remote points. Scott's endorsement went on the document.

There is little doubt that the patrol method would have settled the West sooner. Not to belabor a point, it would have meant that the Dragoons would have been relieved of carpentry and maintenance and all the rest of the housekeeping chores that would mire them down for the next fifty years.

Unfortunately, Frémont, with the heavy senatorial backing of his father-in-law, Thomas Hart Benton, favored forts. Frémont was a curious man, a mixture of scholar and adventurer, of brooder and charger. He seemed to see the "line of remote forts" as ideal for expeditions to explore the new country, record its geography and botany and mineralogy; light patrols, not to impress the Indians but to find out what the United States had in the way of new country, could move from fort to fort, replacing supplies and resting.

Frémont and his ideas were to prevail; Frémont was to become an implacable enemy of Kearny and of Cooke who tried to carry out Kearny's ideas after Kearny died. Perhaps if Kearny had lived things would have been different. The Kearny family and its connections had immense wealth and influence in New Jersey and in New York, and through marriage they were strong in Missouri, Benton's state.

But Cooke was a poor man, the son of a small-town doctor, and his only influence had been earned in the military field. Frémont and the Texans tarnished his bright record, and the horse soldiers were condemned to a life in which almost anything came before horse-soldiering.

Curiously, the concept of housekeeping troops was never mentioned after the first third of the nineteenth century; now it is the rule. Units of the present U.S. Army as small as regiments have their "combat teams," and their service of supply that keep the combat teams out in the field; as early as World War I there were construction battalions and combat battalions, clearly separated.

The Army of the middle 1800s had a fine source of labor; the potato famine in Ireland, depression in England, the revolutions in the German states had sent all kinds of hard-working immigrants into the Eastern ports, where they found such grinding unemployment that it was a matter of enlist or starve.

The ranks of the Army became more and more foreign; and many of these men would have, surely, preferred work they knew – construction, cooking, gardening, wood and hay cutting – to being molded into Dragoons. But a private was a private in those days, and no differentiation was made below the rank of corporal. Certain men – horseshoers, called farriers; blacksmiths, other than horseshoers; and wagoners were paid as corporals. A hospital steward was a sergeant or even first sergeant as to pay, though his assistants were just privates drawn from the ranks; and an ordnance sergeant was higher paid than a sergeant major.

But no provision was made to pay or instruct cooks; each company told one man off, and he was expected to fulfill all his other duties, too. Each company also chose a barber, who shaved and cut the hair of his company mates on his own time – the men paid him a few pennies a month out of their pay, which was usually seven dollars for a private.

And the farriers and corporal-blacksmiths had to drill. Which would have been fair enough – many a commander has turned a charge by putting guns in the hands of his specialists and the fighting records of such outfits as the Seabees are well-known – if the drill had anything to do with the cavalry job of slogging out onto the plains and over the mountains and reminding the Indians that Uncle Sam was watching them. But it didn't. The big drill of the day was parade on foot, around and about and in and out on the parade ground, while the band played and the officers watched and had their daily monotony relieved.

The year of 1846 – De Voto's Year of Decision – started for Stephen Watts Kearny with fort building. Eight years before he had recommended that a fort be built up the Missouri from Leavenworth. In view of his report at the end of the Oregon expedition, he might have changed his mind by 1846, though what was to be known as "Old" Fort Kearny was not in a remote location; it was less than a hundred miles from Fort Leavenworth and controlled the Oregon Trail in much the way that the older fort straddled the Santa Fe Trail.

Kearny had just returned to Leavenworth in May – had been in the fort only a few hours as a matter of fact – when he received dispatches from Washington. The United States had been at war with Mexico for thirteen days. Colonel Kearny was to be general commanding one of the three Armies that were to fight the war, the Army of the West. The Governor of Missouri had already been asked to raise volunteers to bring the Department of the West up to wartime strength. The objective of the Army of the West was Santa Fe.

A week or so later he received a second dispatch. He was to add a thousand mounted Missourians to his command; he was to raise a force among the Mormons, which was not to exceed a third of all the men he had under arms (lest the Mormons turn their guns on the United States); and as soon as he moved out toward Santa Fe, he was to become a Brevet Brigadier General, which meant he would still receive colonel's pay but could fly his own one-star flag over his tent and at the head of his column.

Missouri was wildly in favor of this war; company upon company of mounted men rode into Leavenworth and was sworn into the 1st Missouri Mounted Volunteers, Colonel Alexander W. Doniphan commanding.

Doniphan was a good man, a very good man. But his men were wild frontiersmen who – the old militia story – had enlisted to fight, not to take orders, drill, or dig latrines. There were only three hundred 1st Dragoons on hand; some of the regiment had been detailed to help piece out the understrengthed 2nd Dragoons with General Zachary Taylor's Army of Observation down in the southeast corner of Texas.

Now Kearny received orders to send St. George Cooke and Captain Edwin V. Sumner to General John E. Wool's Army of Occupation which was striking south from San Antonio toward Chihuahua or Parras.

Brigadier General Brooke had taken over Brevet Brigadier Kearny's job as commander of the Department of the West, and therefore was highest ranking officer around. Kearny protested so loudly to Brooke that he was allowed to keep both Cooke and Sumner and their men. When the Dragoons started their march along the Santa Fe Trail, they numbered about four hundred, including a St. Louis volunteer outfit named the LaClede Rangers, who were attached to the Regular Army, rather than to the Missouri Militia. Together with that militia, Kearny had about fifteen hundred horsemen, less than a hundred infantry and some artillery moving toward Santa Fe by July. Captain James Allen of the 1st Dragoons was up at Council Bluffs, dickering with Brigham Young about raising the Mormon Battalion. Missouri was enrolling the 2nd Mounted Volunteers under a loud-mouthed politician named Sterling Price.

Ahead of them the Dragoons and their dubious auxiliaries could count on having a New Mexican Army of about five thousand men, who would be fighting on their own rocky, mountainous, almost impassable terrain.

The Dragoons, according to a member of a St. Louis Artillery Battery, left Leavenworth as rearguard, led by their colonel; they arrived at Bent's Fort leading the Army of the West. It is possible that Kearny had heard Dan'l Morgan's advice about how to make militia operate: put your toughest troops behind them and they'll go toward the enemy.

At any rate, Doniphan's Missourians proved, by the time they got to Santa Fe, that they were real soldiers, eager to meet the enemy, reasonably willing to be disciplined, reluctantly willing to do manual labor; which is really all that was ever needed in frontier soldiers. Militia often did prove perfectly adequate; more often, of course, it failed as in the Revolution, the War of 1812, the Black Hawk War, and – outstandingly – the Seminole War.

But when the wars were over, each time, the former militiamen were voters, and the Regulars were not; the officers considered it improper to vote in an election involving their Commander-in-Chief, the President, and those of the enlisted men who were not foreigners were often without true homes, illiterate, or under false names. And the militia had a habit – understandable – of coming out of a war hating the Regulars who had been their non-coms and drill officers; so the Congressmen whom the ex-militiamen and their neighbors elected continued to starve the Army and treat the Army private as though he were a cretinous ruffian.

There was really no trouble between Leavenworth and Santa Fe. Governor Armijo of New Mexico put up a token front at Glorieta Pass – Apache Canyon – just east of the capital of his province, and then fled, for reasons that are more the story of St. George Cooke than of S.W. Kearny.

Kearny marched into Santa Fe amid the cheers of the populace, who were heartily sick of a Mexican government that sent little but tax-collectors over the long road from Mexico City.

By now the Santa Feans had gotten used to gringos; there were the traders – Magoffin, several other Kentuckians and Missourians; Spiegelberg and several other Prussian Jews, whom the Spanish population thought of as Americans – and the mule and ox drivers of the Santa Fe Trail. The former paid better wages than the impractical Mexican traders, and the latter were inclined to give a man a few pesos for watching his team while he broke his thirst after a ride, whereas Mexican government officers gave a sword-whipping if the mount was not watched.

The American flag was hoisted over the old Palace of the Governors, and Kearny, in due process, announced New Mexico as a United States possession, forever free of the yoke of Mexican taxation. Armijo fled south, and Kearny made plans to move on California.

Dispatches had already told him this would soon be in American hands; Commodores Robert F. Stockton and John D. Sloat of the Navy and Captain John C. Frémont of the Topographical Corps were there and had flown the American flag over Monterey and other cities. When the news reached Santa Fe, the New Mexicans tolled the church bells while the soldiers fired in the air.

Sterling Price's 2nd Missouri Mounted had almost reached Santa Fe by the time Kearny moved out. They were deemed capable of keeping the peace in a peaceful capital and were left to garrison Santa Fe. The Mormon Battalion was also nearly in, minus their commander, Allen, who had died back in Kansas. Kearny turned the Mormons over to Cooke, with instructions to follow Kearny and the Dragoons to California, building a wagon road as he went.

Doniphan was dispatched south to Mexico, to rendezvous with General Wool. The LaClede Rangers still wanted to be attached to the Dragoons, and by now considered themselves Regulars; they were very contemptuous of the other Missouri Militia.

But horses were scarce; Kearny had his five companies of Dragoons mounted on mules, which were stronger and more prevalent than New Mexico horses. A hundred LaClede Rangers volunteered to become California Rangers, but they had to be left with the garrison.

The mules the Dragoons rode were not, according to Cooke, the best in the West; he describes one of them as having been his acquaintance for thirteen years in the Dragoons. But they would have to do.

As the Dragoons marched south for the Jornada del Muerto, and eventually, the Coast, they were dressed in blue-flannel breeches and shirts; they were armed with a carbine, two pistols, a bowie knife, and a hunting knife apiece. The sabers had been left behind, perhaps at Leavenworth, if not along the Santa Fe Trail.

They left Santa Fe on September 22, following the Rio Grande south, planning to find forage for their mounts along the river. This was not an unknown trace, but the Chihuahua Trail, older than the Santa Fe. The farmers along the valley, however, knew hardship when they saw it; they dickered hard for their corn, and many a Dragoon "lost control" of his reins, and let his starving mount wander into some unchartered corn field. It is recorded that General Kearny, when he found out about this, made the Dragoon pay for the corn eaten, but it is not written whether the rate of pay was the farmer's or the Army's.

Kearny had been this way before, on an exploration trip. He knew the Jornada del Muerto was before him. This part of the trail – the name means single day's journey of the dead man – actually took about three days; it traversed country where the Rio Grande went down into a gorge impassable for travelers, who had to cross a waterless, forageless desert high above the water table.

But before they got to the Jornada, the Dragoons were in trouble. This was in the Pueblo country that stretches approximately from Santa Fe down along the river through Isleta Pueblo, near Los Lunas. The peaceful Pueblo Indians had never even been Indians in the Spanish-Mexican definition, but New Mexicans, citizens found living in the country when the Spanish conquered. Though they had no written language, they had most other characteristics of rural civilization – farming, both dry and irrigated; town government; permanent homes; and a formalized religion which the very Catholic Spanish themselves had to recognize after the Pueblo Revolt of 1680-93. Each pueblo had an officer who could speak for the entire village on temporal matters, such as selling corn and supplies and horses. Kearny anticipated no trouble in their valley country.

But other Indians were on the loose. The Navajos – classed in Spanish as *indios bravos*, wild Indians – got ahead of the column and raided the pueblos so steadily that when the Dragoons arrived, there was little to buy; fields had been burned, storage bins emptied, livestock run off.

Kearny sent word back to Santa Fe for Doniphan to postpone his march to Mexico long enough to raid into the Navajo country. As Quantrell was to claim and Sherman to prove less than twenty years later, when you raid the homeland of volunteer troops, the soldiers want to go home and protect their families. The Navajo raids lessened.

Near Socorro the five companies of Dragoons met Kit Carson, temporarily a lieutenant in the Army, riding for the East, where he was to take dispatches to President Polk, telling him that the Navy, with some assistance from California Irregulars, had taken California. Frémont, the dispatches said, was governor of California. Kearny considered this. Ahead of him the Jornada still threatened; past it the lesser-known deserts of what is now Arizona – then part of New Mexico – were reputed to be terrible going.

The fewer horses a column had to feed, the better the chance of getting through. Obviously, troops were not immediately needed in California; and if they were, a regiment was coming around by boat from New York.

Kearny selected his best mounts, put two companies of Dragoons on them, and sent the other three companies back to Santa Fe to add themselves to Doniphan's expedition against the Navajos and, eventually, to the aid of Wool in Chihuahua.

He also dispatched Tom Fitzpatrick, his mountain man guide, to take Kit Carson's dispatches to Washington, and ordered Carson to turn around and guide the Dragoons to the Coast.

Poor Carson! He had planned on going through Taos, his home, with a stopover to see his family; he'd been in the field with Frémont for over a year.

But he knew the trail, and Broken Hand, as the Indians called Fitzpatrick, didn't; it made sense, and Carson obeyed. Which was to involve him in a Congressional hearing, a fate no man envies today, nor did then.

For Kearny was marching toward what was to be his worst enemy, John Frémont, a romantic with dreams of iron; a fighter for things that didn't matter; a man full of whims, the crossing of which caused him to substitute venom for his habitual charm. Kit Carson would be involved, too, and so – more disastrously – would be St. George Cooke. But now they were all three going down the Rio Grande, headed for the Jornada.

They got through; the men parched a little corn to eat on the way, filled their canteens, traveled by night, and came out south of the Jornada in only slightly worse condition than when they went in.

The mules were tough, the Dragoons just as tough. In all probability the Regulars didn't even find this very hard duty; it was better than building forts or mounting retreat, and probably not much harder than some of the traverses they had made the year before on the Oregon expedition.

South of the Jornada they had some clashes with "Navajos," who were probably Apaches; the country was south of the usual Navajo raiding area, but just right for those other Athapascans, the Mescalero Apaches.

They left the Rio Grande somewhere around Las Cruces, and struck west for the Gila, crossing into present-day Arizona. Several of the officers kept diaries – Emory, and Johnston, Dr. Griffin, and sometimes Turner – and they mention the fact that rations were meager, the nights cold, and the two brass howitzers cumbersome, but they don't get very excited about it. They had water – they stuck to the Gila wherever possible – and were better off than on many routine Dragoon patrols. They were Regulars, doing routine duty, losing a few mules at it, but moving out, in the cavalry phrase.

When they got to the Pima and Maricopa country, they fared better; those unwarlike Indians were willing to feed them for nothing, though when they found out that Kearny insisted the government pay, they made a great and laughing business of chaffering. To the delight of the diarist-officers, the Indians laughed as hard when they were bested in a deal as when Kearny's quartermasters were. But these ancient and most practiced of the desert-dwellers were farmers, not stockmen or hunters. They had no horses or mules to sell or lend or give away. Mules and horses were just bait for the Apaches in that country.

The Dragoons went on westward; by now it was not uncommon for one man to pull a mule while another soldier pushed. Their general had lost his horse, and was riding a mule, too, when the mule could carry him; when he couldn't, Kearny led and pulled.

Where the Gila falls into the Colorado – approximately present-day Yuma – they received more news from California. There were signs of an encampment of men, with a remuda of about a thousand horses.

The footsore Dragoons were ready to buy horses, steal horses, fight for horses. Kit Carson scouted, and made a guess that these were not part of an Army coming up from central Mexico to retake California, but instead were Californians, either soldiers or horse thieves.

The cavalrymen didn't care. They wanted something better than worn-out mules to throw their saddles on. Carson went out again and brought in the strangers. They were apparently Californians, as he had guessed; what they were really doing there has never been learned. They were also about as accomplished liars as the widely-traveled Kearny had ever met. But they handed over some half-broken horses along with their windy and wild tales of what they were doing, where they had come from, and the conditions of things in California.

While the Dragoons happily risked their necks – and the seats of their worn-out uniforms – teaching some fear of the United States Army to the remounts, Kearny and his officers tried to make truth out of the herders' lies by repeated questioning, getting the Mexican-Californians apart when they could, and checking one liar's story against another.

It began to be clear that the situation in California had deteriorated, to use a modern military expression for having blown up completely. California was no longer ruled by "Governor" Frémont under the protection of the Navy. The revolt had spread, successfully, as far north as Santa Barbara, perhaps farther.

Lieutenant William H. Emory, tired of questioning men who changed their stories every version, tried scouting on his own. He encountered another Spanish-speaking man, who claimed to be out herding horses. But it was a strange place to graze stock; the Mexican turned out to be a courier for the Mexican Army. His dispatches confirmed the fact that the peaceful conquest of California had only been an interlude.

Kearny lacked details, but he knew he was needed over on the Coast. In the last week of November, he and his half-dead mules, his wild remounts, his empty commissary, and his detail of a hundred and twenty-five nearly naked men forded the Colorado and were in present-day California.

Today, in a gas-filled car, with an iced thermos on the back seat, and the paving beautifully maintained on the road, the way from Yuma westward – once the watered area of Winterhaven is passed – is a shock. This is not the mesquite-covered desert of southern Arizona, it is not the cactus-and-rock country, which can be mean – everything the Dragoons met back there had torn a shred of uniform and usually a little skin away – but is at least picturesque. This is nothing. Yellow sand, occasionally white sand,

and sometimes brown sand for variety covers the country, and bounces the sun back to burn the underside of a deeply tanned man's chin.

The Dragoons staggered across it. It was fifty-four miles to the first well. They dug that out and ate horse, without salt. Emory reported that it wasn't even very good horse, poor and tough.

In the Imperial Valley they turned north, skirting what is now the Salton Sea – then an alkali sink – and striking into the mountains, toward the Palomar country. Eight days after they crossed the river, they came out at Warner's Ranch, looking so desperate that Juan José Warner's vaqueros took the cattle to the hills. It might have been a wise precaution. Seven Dragoons are reported to have eaten a whole sheep in a single sitting.

Warner – a naturalized Mexican citizen from the East – was not at home. His foreman and an Englishman named Stokes, who ranched nearby, confirmed the rumors, however; California had risen, Stockton had gone to sea, Frémont might still be governor of California, but had no one to govern.

Not to make a mystery out of events so long past, what had happened was that the Californians, though apparently as anxious as the New Mexicans to get out from under the rule of a capital so inaccessible to the province, did not like being treated as cowardly scum; but the Navy and Marine officers there had no respect for the dark-skinned Californians, and showed it.

Stockton was so sure there was no fight in the vaqueros and rancheros that he told off Frémont to raise a command of a thousand Anglos – practically all there were in California – which Stockton would send to help Taylor take Mexico City.

Los Angeles, largest town in the territory, was put under the command of Marine Lieutenant Archibald Gillespie, who treated the people like "gooks," long the Marine Corps word for anyone who isn't a white Anglo-Saxon, preferably Protestant.

Marines are brave, fearless, sometimes bloodthirsty; but being tactful has never been a prerequisite to membership in the Corps. Gillespie, who was in California as some sort of personal envoy from President Polk – himself a self-named War Hawk – had not had the sense or the patience to see that there were two precisely divided groups in Los Angeles – highly respectful *gente de razon* and the lowest sort of ruffians. He had treated all of them alike and had achieved something that nothing else could have achieved: an alliance between the aristocrats and the gutter rats. They ran Gillespie and his small command out of town. He marched to San Pedro, the port of Los Angeles, and stowed his men safely aboard the *Vandalia*, a merchant ship.

Stockton had put into Yerba Buena, now part of San Francisco. He got word that the garrison at Monterey was about to fall, sailed there, and put marines ashore as re-enforcements; it was there that he also learned that this was not an isolated attack, but part of a revolution working its way northward; so, he sailed on to San Pedro. Before he got there, Captain William Mervine, USN, sailed in on the USS *Savannah* and announced that nothing could stop the United States Navy. He ranked Gillespie, who had found out that Mexicans could fight, and would probably have rather waited for more re-enforcements; but Mervine ordered the small garrison off the *Vandalia,* added it to his Marines and shore-party sailors, and augmented it with a strange and wonderful outfit called Fauntleroy's Dragoons.

Reading about the Navy-Marine activities in the taking of California is like reviewing the script of an old Keystone Kops comedy. Fauntleroy's rank and title was Purser in the Navy; apparently, he was a sort of chief steward or yeoman or paymaster. In the taking of Monterey he had been put ashore with a bunch of sailors, marines, and waterfront characters whom he had mounted; the Navy lovingly called them Fauntleroy's Dragoons.

They had been present at the bloodless surrender of Monterey; they had also gone cross-country to take San Juan but had found Frémont already in possession of it.

Apparently, Mervine felt that all this cavalry experience had made the Purser into an artilleryman; he had Purser Fauntleroy land two guns from the *Vandalia* and cover the rear of the little column that started out from San Pedro to Los Angeles. The column got about twelve miles, camped for the night, was harassed all night by vaqueros, and in the morning was driven back to San Pedro.

Stockton arrived, and decided that everyone should go south to San Diego, retake that town, and strike north from there.

A month later he was still trying to organize a shore party to retake Los Angeles; he had lost touch with Frémont and gone to Monterey to get word from that prima donna.

About which time Kearny came off the desert at Warner's and sent word to San Diego that he was on his way, but his Dragoons were in sad shape from the desert crossing; would Stockton send clothes, ammunition, boots, and a little help?

Stockton, unaccountably, said he couldn't just at the moment.

Kearny, meanwhile, heard there was a Mexican Army remuda of horses and mules at Aguanga, north of Warner's on the road to Los Angeles. He sent some Dragoons there to take them, while he and the rest of the column went south down the Valle de San José to Santa Ysabel, where Stokes ranched. There the detachment rejoined the main body with the captured animals, some of which were highly usable; the rest, half broken and wild, were turned out.

Stockton had caught up with his chores by then, and sent Gillespie, a handful of volunteers, Lieutenant Edward F. Beale, and ten sailors to bring the Dragoons in. Kearny added them to his exhausted column and turned west to go through the Witch Creek country to the coast.

But Gillespie had been seen leaving San Diego with his small force; and the half-neutral Californians hated the Marine personally. Andres Pico, a gentleman and a professional soldier, rode out after Gillespie, only half believing that any United States force in San Diego County was not under siege at the harbor.

It had been raining for several days; the Dragoons were miserable, Gillespie and his men were miserable, but so were the riders of Andres Pico. They got as far as the ranchería of San Pasqual and took shelter in some Indian huts.

Kearny knew that Pico lay across his trail; but he had too few men, horses, supplies to do anything but attack; he couldn't surround the Californians, and there seemed little use in backing up and trying one of the other trails through the mountainous country.

What followed was the Battle of San Pasqual. It was only a small skirmish by almost any military standards, and there is no real account of what happened, but it was bloody.

Anybody who has been out in the rain of San Diego County's mountains for several days can understand the exhausted state that Dr. Griffin, Gillespie, Emory, and Kearny himself were in when they tried to tell what happened at San Pasqual. Kearny's biographer, Clarke, favors the version Beale gave to Commodore Samuel F. Du Pont in San Diego.

The valley in which San Pasqual lies is narrow; the hills on either side are impassable, covered with chaparral so dense that a man can only cut a few feet through before he has to stop and sharpen his blade. There was nothing to do but charge; and nothing to charge with but half-broken, exhausted Dragoon mounts and some half-mounted sailors. Kearny ordered a charge, anyway, and there was enough surprise in it to rout the Californians and drive them out of the ranchería. The Indians, as they had previously announced, remained completely neutral.

What happened next will never be completely explained. The Dragoons, possibly exalted at the idea that they were, for once, acting as real cavalry, continued the charge too long and drove the routed caballeros into a main body of insurgents, who joined their fellow-Californians in the fight.

Or, perhaps, Gillespie's volunteers and sailors did not push ahead fast enough to back up the Dragoons, who had been advance guard. If so, they could hardly be blamed; a cavalry charge was nothing they knew anything about.

At any rate, the skirmish was short and disastrous. Nineteen of the United States column were killed and fifteen wounded. Kearny was one of the wounded, and so was Gillespie, which proves that the Navy detachment got into the fight at least part of the time.

The column got through to the San Bernardo Ranch, and took up a position on high ground, but they lost their mounts and supplies doing it. They had fought their way to within twenty miles of the coast.

An Indian dropped the strict neutrality imposed by his tribal spokesman to go to San Diego and tell Stockton that Kearny was in trouble; the commodore at once dispatched a relief party.

But Kearny couldn't know this, nor that Stokes, the Englishman from Santa Ysabel, had also gone into San Diego with the news. Kearny was on the ground at San Bernardo, badly wounded; Dr. Griffin was saving what he could of the wounded – three more were to die within a week – it was raining, cold, and dark. It was noisy, too. The hill was surrounded by howling wolves – they may have been coyotes, but no matter – who had smelled the wounded and the dead.

Beale and Kit Carson, together with another of the neutral Indians, sneaked out of camp, on Kearny's orders, to take the word to Stockton. It took them two days to get into town – which wasn't bad, considering that they were moving through hostile country, and had about thirty miles to go to the besieged cantonment on San Diego Bay.

Stockton had already acted with reasonable promptness, sending out over two hundred of his Marines and shore-party sailors. It took them two days to get to San Bernardo, which seems slow, especially as they later made the return trip, carrying the wounded, in half that time. Pico, who had been besieging the camp, pulled his men out when he got word of the size of the re-enforcements.

The Dragoons had reached the Pacific. Kearny had fulfilled his mission and done it remarkably well. New Mexico and California had always been isolated from each other, though the latter territory had been settled by the Spanish for over a hundred years, New Mexico for more than two hundred. The Dragoons had broken that isolation on horse – more often mule – back. St. George Cooke was coming behind them with the Mormon Battalion to end the separation forever with the first wagon road built from Santa Fe to the Coast.

Kearny had carried out his mission, but his troubles were just starting. The wound that Pico's men had given him would seem trivial after the political battle he was about to wage with Frémont and Sockton.

Chapter 6

Across the Rio Grande

Meanwhile, the 2nd Dragoons, together with about half of the 1st, had gotten into the main current of the Mexican War, down in Texas and the northeastern states of Mexico. They were part of General Zachary Taylor's so-called "Army of Observation," which lay just above the Rio Grande, around the present towns of Brownsville and Point Ysabel. This was back in early April, eight months before Kearny met Pico at San Pasqual. Taylor had his Regulars build a fort, later called Fort Brown, after which Brownsville is named.

The Mexican soldiers were infiltrating in force north of the river; the cavalry were excused from the hated building operations to throw out small patrols. This was duty that the Dragoons were used to, not very different from moving about the plains to keep the Indians under control.

The first men to die in the war were members of a cavalry patrol that got trapped near the building Fort Brown; every man was either captured or slaughtered.

Less than two weeks later Taylor routed the famous Mexican cavalry at the Battle of Palo Alto, but he did it with infantry and artillery. The troopers had to wait till the Battle of Resaca de la Palma – Dry Palm River – the next day. The Mexicans were defiladed by the natural trench that the dry river bed made; pools of standing water and thickets of cactus, called *mottes* in that country, made a second line of embankments.

The so-called "flying artillery" – horse-drawn field guns – were the pride of the Army. They had been the stars of the Battle of Palo Alto yesterday, but had seen their commander, Major Samuel Ringgold, killed. Now Lieutenant Randolph Ridgely took them galloping down the road to the Resaca, while two regiments of infantry started squirming through the mottes in support.

Ridgely came smack up against a battery of Mexican artillery already trail-down the road and ready to fire. He pulled back, and the Dragoons

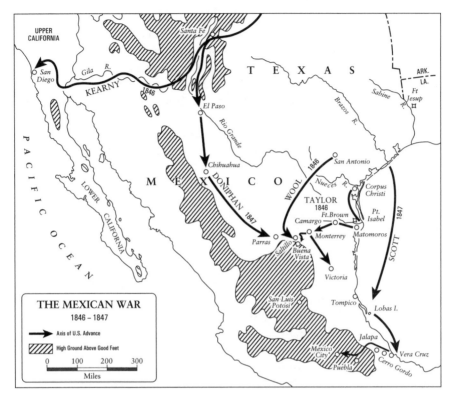

Map 2 The Mexican War, 1846-1847

went in, drove the Mexican cannoneers from their guns, and went past them; turned, and re-formed, only to find the artillerists back at their posts.

But they had given the foot soldiers enough time to get out of the cactus and charge, and the road was open. Ridgely had unlimbered his own guns by now, and the Mexicans were routed.

The Dragoons pursued the fleeing *soldados,* but with little success, due to the thickness of the cactus and chaparral.

It was, perhaps, a good thing that "Rough and Ready" Taylor had never gone to West Point, where the books would have taught him that cavalry should never, never charge artillery. It was all wrong, but it worked, though some of Taylor's educated staff officers never quite recovered from hearing him give Captain Charles A. May the order to charge.

There was no question who had won the action at Resaca; Mexican losses exceeded a thousand before the routed army reached the Rio Grande, where drowning raised the toll. The Americans had thirty-three dead and less than a hundred wounded.

The pursuit in Mexico proper – as against disputed Texas – was held up for ten days while boats were procured or built to take the North Americans across the Rio Grande, which was in full spring water.

But on the day of the battle, news had reached Washington about the wiping out of the cavalry patrol more than two weeks before. President Polk at once drafted a declaration of war. Congress passed it four days later, on May 13, and followed it up with a generous contribution to double the strength of the Army (by raising the number of men in each company), purchase Naval and merchant vessels to fight or transport troops, and add a third mounted regiment to the Regulars.

This was to be called the 1st Mounted Riflemen, instead of the 3rd Dragoons. Like the Dragoons when first mustered, it was to be a regiment of the elite; perhaps it would be more accurate to compare it to the Mounted Rangers. The "elite" concept was not badly chosen, because this was wartime, and young men of some background and learning could be expected to enlist to fight, where they would never have signed up for the life of barracks building, yard policing and slum-gullion eating that was the routine of the peacetime soldier.

It is dubious if Taylor knew there was a war on when he crossed into Mexico; he was not the man to wait on Congressional papers. On the south side he ordered his Dragoons to strike south, and look for the enemy, who had disappeared in the last ten days. Taylor was mad; he had asked the War Department for pontoon boats a year before but had never gotten them.

The horse soldiers patrolled sixty miles into the State of Tamaulipas without encountering resistance, water, or forage in any noticeable quantities. They rode back to the river and reported to Taylor that no great force could subsist in the arid country south of the border.

President Polk had talked about a "quick" war. Taylor had found out differently on the Rio. He lay over through May, June, and July, training the Militia and Volunteer regiments that were pouring into Matamoros, and collecting wagons and boats to move upriver, where there was a better road into the interior – it was to be a railroad right-of-way some day – from Camargo to Monterrey.

It had started to rain, which was good news for the Dragoons and the artillery and the teamsters of the Quartermaster Corps, all of whom had been wondering, after the Dragoon patrol south of Matamoros, whether they were going to find any forage in any part of Mexico. But the rain was hard on the Volunteers and the Militia, who had not had the Regulars' hard-won experience in taking care of themselves. By the time U.S. Quartermaster General Thomas S. Jesup had sent Taylor enough flat-bottomed boats to go up the Rio Grande, only six thousand men were in condition to go; disease had crippled Taylor's large force.

Two-thirds of his effectives were Regulars. The dearly loved American theory that militia could be substituted for a standing army had been disproved again.

On September 17 Taylor reached Monterrey, most important of the North Mexican cities, and started storming against a Mexican garrison that outnumbered his Army by a thousand or more men.

The Battle of Monterrey was the worst sort of dismounted fighting, house-to-house; and the houses were built Mexican style, flush and almost blind to the street, with tough adobe walls and iron grilles on the few small windows. The Mexicans were hard, and the Mexican Army was used to almost continuous action against revolutionary and counterrevolutionary guerrillas. It took a full week to blast the defenders off rooftops and out from behind 'dobe walls, and herd them into the central plaza of Monterrey.

With a long line of supply and communication to hold behind him and no clear idea of just what he was expected to do in Mexico, Taylor was glad to get the city on any terms; he signed an eight-week armistice with General Pedro de Ampudia and permitted the Mexican soldiers to march out of town. It is hard to see how he could have taken them prisoner, since they outnumbered his entire force.

But President Polk was outraged, and the Commanding General of the Army, Winfield Scott, ordered Taylor to redeem himself by taking the "High Road to the capital of Mexico," an order that Secretary of War William L. Marcy at once softened to "if you think it possible and practical."

Taylor didn't. By now he knew Mexico as well as Scott knew Pennsylvania Avenue. He advised an assault from the sea, via Veracruz, the route Cortes had used in his original capture of the Aztec capital.

Scott finally agreed. He himself would lead the assault. Meanwhile he would go to Camargo to see what troops he could rob Taylor of.

Taylor spent the time taking Ciudad Victoria and Saltillo, and General Wool had a force of about two thousand men marching on Parras, from which he would be able to supply Taylor. Northern New Mexico was pretty well secured, except for Chihuahua, which was not considered a major military objective because of its mountainous isolation.

Scott stripped Taylor of most of his forces, leaving him only Volunteer Infantry, and two battalions of Dragoons. Five other companies of Dragoons were ordered to join the Veracruz expedition, which already had the new Mounted Rifles.

Scott specifically asked for Phil Kearny's company, the Gray Horse Troop of the 1st Dragoons (troop was not to become the official name of a cavalry company until several years after the Civil War, though it was sometimes used unofficially, as was squadron for battalion).

Phil Kearny was again in command of Company F. But this was not the old Company F that he had once drilled into excellence. Most of the troopers of that outfit had finished their enlistments and left the Army; the rest had been dispersed among other companies. Phil took over a paper command.

This was fine with him. He drew money from the War Department to buy a hundred and twenty horses and to pay the same number of recruits a hundred dollars apiece to enlist, and took off for Illinois, where he felt both the horses and men would be of the highest quality.

Philip Kearny was always a good captain for a trooper to serve under. When he had originally joined the 1st Dragoons, his men had resented serving under a "dude shoulderstrap," as one of them wrote home about him. But the captain was a millionaire. He bought saddles, food, uniforms, equipment out of his own pocket. He was a hard drillmaster, but the nasty chores of building and digging and yard-birding were usually spared his company since his troopers were in demand for show occasions because of their smart appearance.

Since Phil's first tour with the Dragoons, his father had died and left him a second fortune. This was a mixed blessing for the young captain; he had trouble serving with troops; time after time generals' ladies with unmarried sisters or nieces had their husbands put in for Phil Kearny as an aide. But he had married in 1841, which removed some of that sort of trouble. His wife, Diana Bullitt of Louisville, Kentucky, was a relative of the Clark family of Lewis and Clark and other fame, as was his Uncle Stephen's wife.

Now that he was to have a second Company F, the wealthy captain again spared nothing, including his own pocket-book. He added a hundred dollars of his own money to the government enlistment bonus, and issued a stalwart call for "dauntless patriots" to enlist in a company that would have the finest equipment, saddles, uniforms – all paid for by their captain. He probably paid more for his horses than the government remount price, too. When Company F passed through New Orleans, a reporter wrote that the beautifully equipped, beautifully uniformed troopers were mounted on matched grays. All this took time. Before the Gray Horse Troop reached the Mexican front, the Dragoons had had plenty of trouble.

Phil Kearny and his troop arrived in Camargo on October 1. Monterrey, Saltillo, and Ciudad Victoria were already taken, and the Dragoons were spending their time patrolling and drilling while Taylor waited for Scott, who did not arrive at Camargo until New Year's Eve. Taylor was down in Ciudad Victoria at the time, securing his lines, the armistice with Ampudia having ended. He had two companies of Dragoons with him, under Captain May, who had been brevetted at both Palo Alto and Resaca and could now call himself Lieutenant Colonel.

Scott sent Taylor a dispatch asking him to come up to the border to plan strategy, then, without waiting for an answer, ordered Taylor stripped of all his Regulars except May's command of two hundred and fifty Dragoons. This left Taylor confronting a Mexican Army that outnumbered his seventy-five hundred amateurs three to one. Scott and his column sailed for Veracruz, which was under Naval siege till they could get there.

Phil Kearny was delighted to be going off with what looked like the column that would see the most fighting. But his excellent drilling and equipping worked against him; Winfield Scott planned on using the Gray Horse Troop as a personal bodyguard, which meant that in a battle his Dragoons would serve as messengers, orderlies, and dog robbers.

Taylor, having sent an angry note to Scott about being stripped of his troops, went about doing what he could. The General, Santa Anna, who had lost to Texas in 1836, had returned from political exile – Mexican generals are almost always politicians as well, and were then, too – and relieved Ampudia of his command. He made his headquarters at San Luis Potosí and re-enforced that city. If Taylor had ever intended to attack there, he changed his mind; the final battle of the north was to be at Buena Vista, but there was a good deal of shifting before that.

May and his 2nd Dragoons reconnoitered steadily to obtain the information that made Taylor pick Buena Vista. So did Major Solon Borland and a company of 1st Dragoons, who had come down from San Antonio with General Wool, crossed the Rio Grande at Presidio Rio Grande, which seems to be present Del Rio, and then, instead of going west to Chihuahua, marched south to Monclova and Parras, putting Wool in Taylor's field of operations. This change of plans was made by constant correspondence between Wool and Taylor; Washington concurred that nothing much would be gained by taking Chihuahua.

In the middle of January, Wool, who was at Buena Vista, sent Borland and his Dragoons out on reconnaissance, feeling for Santa Anna's army, rumored to be marching from San Luis Potosí. Then he sent a Major Gaines and a Captain Clay out to re-enforce the patrol; strengthened, Borland decided to go on from Encarnación, the original limit of his scout, to Salado, where the outfit camped for the night at a hacienda.

Santa Anna had his cavalry on the move, too, and he had many more horse soldiers than did Wool and Taylor; in all, the Mexicans had fifteen regiments of Regulars against the North Americans' two Dragoon and one Mounted Rifle detachments.

General Miñon with fifteen hundred cavalrymen, according to Mexican sources, and two thousand by American reporters, surrounded the hacienda at Salado in the night. There was no use resisting; Borland surrendered, and his whole command was taken prisoner and shipped to Mexico City.

The Mexicans reported that they had taken over eighty men; Taylor reported to the War Department that the number was seventy, including officers.

It is not clear whether Miñon knew that the Dragoons were at Salado, or just stumbled on them, but their capture warned Taylor that the battle was going to break soon; this was confirmed in a few days when a small patrol of Kentucky Volunteers were also caught out on patrol and shipped to the Mexican capital.

Taylor was then at Agua Nueva. A month after Borland was taken, Colonel May and some of his 2nd Dragoons rode in from the same patrol that Borland had been sent on; they had finally pinpointed Santa Anna's position; he was at Encarnación and Miñon's horse soldiers were nearby.

Aqua Nueva was open on the left flank. Taylor started at once to fall back on Buena Vista, a hacienda twelve miles away. The move was not rear-guarded by the Dragoons, but by Colonel Archibald Yell of Arkansas and his regiment of Volunteer Cavalry.

Everything went off beautifully. Almost all the military stores had been moved before Yell's pickets charged into camp ahead of Miñon's outriders. The Arkansawyers set fire to what was left, and hightailed it for Buena Vista, arriving lathered but safe at daybreak.

Santa Anna was getting to Agua Nueva by then. He had made a brilliant night march, planning to surprise the enemy; now he found himself with an exhausted army and an empty camp to capture. He let his men fill their canteens, then pushed them on. He still had a chance, if Miñon was holding the Americans out in the open.

But Taylor split his forces. He had taken the smaller part for himself and gone into Saltillo, ready to defend that city; Wool had the far greater part of the United States force lined up at a place called Angostura.

Angostura means narrow; the battlefield was, and furthermore Wool's position was guarded front and rear by deep barrancas, almost canyons, which made the use of cavalry almost impossible to the Mexican general.

Wool had put Captain John M. Washington's battery on the road itself. (This was regular Field Artillery, not Dragoon field guns.) On the high ground to either side he placed his volunteers. The Dragoons, with two more batteries of artillery and two regiments of volunteer and militia infantry were kept in reserve on a ridge behind the left flank. Two of the state outfits, Kentucky and Tennessee, were horse soldiers, but as the Mexicans approached, they were dismounted and used as infantry.

Taylor had, without much difficulty, turned Miñon from Saltillo, where he arrived as Santa Anna was maneuvering his twenty thousand troops into position to attack. The Mexican general sent over a flag of truce and a note: Taylor was outnumbered four to one and would be given an hour to surrender.

Old Rough and Ready declined at once. About a hundred of the 2nd Dragoons had been left to guard Saltillo.

The day at Angostura was spent maneuvering, both armies trying to outflank each other. Taylor took Lieutenant Braxton Bragg's battery out of reserve and sent it to support Washington's guns; but three of these were sent up on the heights.

Night fell without serious engagement; the Mexicans had succeeded in their flanking movement, but the Americans had improved their entrenchments. Taylor, satisfied that there would be no major attack during the night, went back to Saltillo. He returned before morning, bringing the Dragoons and a regiment of Mississippi militia with him.

Daylight saw the Santa Anna forces thronging into the barranca in huge numbers. Lieutenant O'Brien of Washington's battery brought a 12-pound howitzer around till he had the small canyon enfiladed; then he swept the attackers with shrapnel, very successfully.

Santa Anna was heavy with cavalry, many of them lancers; he sent them against the American infantry repeatedly. The militia – the 2nd Kentucky and the 2nd Illinois were notable exceptions – were routed; Taylor threw the Dragoons from Saltillo in to hold ground that had been deserted by several regiments. With aid from the artillery, they stood fast until officers – largely Regulars – could rally some of the fleeing State troops.

The Mississippi regiment that had come from Saltillo with the Dragoons and Taylor had gotten there too late to see their fellow State troops routed; they held fast, the Mexican charge was temporarily rolled back, and Taylor had time to reconsider.

Torrejon's cavalry, a thousand strong, ran into the fleeing dismounted State cavalrymen in the hacienda proper; a tangled mess ensued in the narrow alley that separated the ranch buildings.

May and his Dragoons charged into this, probably mad enough not to care whether they struck at their own troops or Torrejon's; the latter cut loose, and fled through a gorge in the mountains, with two guns that May had brought with him heaving shells after them long after they were out of range.

The tide was turning. The Mississippi riflemen turned a charge by a crack brigade of Mexican lancers. The Americans now started advancing; the Militia and Volunteers got back into the fray; and the right wing of Santa Anna's army was almost severed from the body. Santa Anna sent an envoy to ask what Taylor's demands would be.

General Taylor sent General Wool across the lines under the white flag. But Santa Anna would not see him, claiming that a Mexican officer had pretended to be an envoy from him in order to escape capture.

Miñon had left Saltillo – he never made a serious attempt at that city, not knowing how heavily it was garrisoned, if at all – and attacked the rear of

Taylor's forces. But there was still a howitzer at Saltillo. Captain Shover brought it down the road at a gallop to attack Miñon's rear; another gun hit the Mexicans from the front; and Miñon led his cavalry out of the fight and into the hills.

Taylor worked all through that night to repel another attack by Santa Anna, but the Mexican troops were through. They were used to quick maneuvering and living off the country; Taylor, on the other hand, had spent weeks building up his supplies, and his men were well fed and watered. A truce was arranged to exchange prisoners, and the Mexican Army headed south, the 2nd Dragoons harassing their rear as long as was feasible.

May received another brevet for the Battle of Buena Vista and could now be called a full colonel by his friends. He was still paid as a captain, however, though he commanded two hundred and fifty Dragoons. A like command in the State forces rated the shoulder straps, pay, and appurtenances of a brigadier general.

After Buena Vista the war in northern Mexico was about over. Taylor's orders from Scott were simply to hold on.

Doniphan took Chihuahua, after a brisk skirmish, in the same week that Santa Anna lost at Buena Vista. In the spring he joined Wool at Saltillo, and was sent home, his triumphant regiment no longer needed; they were discharged in June in New Orleans, having marched three thousand miles, pretty much a military record. It is too bad that they had never had an opportunity to face the enemy when the issue was historically critical; they were good cavalrymen.

Chapter 7

Montezuma Country

Scott landed just south of Veracruz about a week after Taylor routed Santa Anna. He had part of the 2nd Dragoons, most of the 1st Dragoons, and the Mounted Rifles with him. The Rifles, however, were no longer mounted; most of their horses had died at sea – from seasickness, because horses cannot vomit, or from pneumonia as a result of being put in slings to prevent injury and thus unable to breathe properly. All of Phil Kearny's beautiful grays came through all right, though, and Company F became Scott's guard of honor.

Taking Veracruz was made easier by the fact that revolt had broken out in Mexico City – several generals wanted to rule Mexico and each had a following – and no troops could be sent to add to the five thousand who garrisoned the port.

Most of the Dragoons – outside of Kearny's troop – were under Brigadier General David E. Twiggs, commanding one of three armies under Scott. Twiggs had been the first colonel of the 2nd Dragoons, back in the disastrous Seminole War, when horse soldiers had found themselves building and paddling pirogues and rafts. He had still been colonel when the 2nd were trained as lancers in 1841, and when they were dismounted and made into a rifle regiment in 1842. Now their colonel was William S. Harney, who had been lieutenant colonel since the regiment was first formed. The dismounted Mounted Rifles were under Colonel Persifor Smith.

Scott besieged Veracruz for four days, bombarding the city with both naval and artillery guns until the garrison surrendered. Scott allowed the garrison to march out with honors, confiscated their arms, and made the usual speech about being there to liberate the Mexican people from their wicked rulers and not to war on them. Since the Mexican War was the United States' first war on foreign territory, this may have been the first time that an American officer announced that we were friends of the people whose government we were attacking; if so, a number of generals, admirals, and politicians owe a plagiaristic debt to Winfield Scott.

Scott had been a little slow. Santa Anna – temporarily turning over the presidency of Mexico – had come south after his defeat by Taylor, raised a new army, and was waiting for the gringos at Cerro Gordo, thirty miles from Veracruz.

It was not a very good site for a battle, but it was the best Santa Anna could find. There was no water; but he had plenty of labor among his troops, who have been estimated at any figure between eighty-five and a hundred and ten thousand men. He had some of them dig a three-mile ditch to bring water down to the proposed battleground, and he had others throw up trenches and build artillery positions.

The pre-battle preparations are almost classic examples of the difference between United States and Mexican Army methods. Scott planned to fight the battle without his Dragoons or his Volunteer horse, because he had a thirty-mile supply line through hostile country to defend; the horse soldiers would patrol it in force, making sure that supplies of food and ammunition came in a steady stream to the combatants.

Santa Anna, on the other hand, apparently raised his large army first, and then had random thoughts about feeding them. After they were laboring on the earth works with empty bellies, he made arrangements with a merchant in Jalapa to sell him food, making himself personally responsible, and then drove a herd of cattle into the hard-digging camp in time to put some beef into his half-starved workmen-soldiers.

The Mexicans had the larger force of cavalry; at Cerro Gordo there were fifteen hundred of them. The Americans, with their careful logistics, could have used more. When the main body of United States troops clashed with Santa Anna, there were sure to be skirmishes and raids on the supply line if a patrol in force and density was not maintained, and that sort of patrol could not be done by anyone else nearly as well as by the Dragoons.

Scott was apparently not a follower of old Dan'l Morgan; he put Twiggs's division, all Regulars, at the forefront of his march; part of General Worth's Volunteer infantry followed.

Twiggs marched up the National Road – Carretera Nacional – without incident, using what Dragoons he could to reconnoiter for information as to the strength of the enemy. The reports, garnered from natives rather than by sight, varied from two thousand up to thirteen thousand. When he got to Plan del Rio, where the road twists from a northwesterly to a southwesterly direction, his outriders contacted the enemy, and found Santa Anna well entrenched by natural bluffs, the gorge of the River of the Plain (Rio del Plan), the bluffs of Cerro Gordo (Fat Hill), and Telegraph Hill (el Atalaya). Atalaya was so steep that Santa Anna didn't bother to garrison it.

Twiggs stopped and spent two days sizing up the situation. Scott came up from Veracruz with more accurate information, presumably gathered from deserters and traitors, concerning the size of Santa Anna's new army. It was decided that Santa Anna's left flank, with the undefended Telegraph Hill as its anchor, was the weakest point in the Mexican line.

Scott's army carried what were then called Topographical Engineers. Under their direction a road was cut up the back of the hill until it came within sight of the Mexican lines. When the diggers were fired on, Scott called them off.

Twiggs led the attack with his division. Santa Anna at once sent a heavy force against Atalaya; a detachment held him off till the 7th Infantry and the Mounted Rifles – having no horses they were useless for patrol and reconnaissance – could come up, followed by the 1st Artillery. The Rifles drove Santa Anna back down the hill, the guns unlimbered and chased them with shrapnel. Then the dismounted Rifles turned themselves into an outfit of snipers; from the shelter of rocks and brush they used their rifles – by far the longest range and most accurate shoulder arms on either side – to drive back every attempt of the Mexicans to come up the hill. Santa Anna shelled their position from Cerro Gordo, but they were too scattered to be hurt much.

That night heavy artillery was snaked by hand to the top of Atalaya. The next day the Rifles, the 7th Infantry and part of the 3rd charged down Atalaya and up the front of Cerro Gordo.

Meanwhile, Twiggs had sent the rest of his force up the back of that thick hill. The two arms of the pincers closed at the very summit, and the Mexicans fled toward Jalapa.

This took care of the center and the left of the Mexican Army. General Pillow tried to take the right wing with his Volunteers; when they found themselves under enemy artillery fire, they broke and ran.

So did Santa Anna. At Orizaba, on the other arm of the National Highway from Veracruz to Mexico City, he rallied three thousand men and started leading another army, his third since the first of the year. It was now late April.

Scott took Jalapa without trouble from the Mexicans, but with the Volunteer trouble that had plagued every American war up till then. Three thousand of his men, seven regiments, had only a few weeks more to go before their enlistments ran out. He had expected replacements, but Washington – Secretary Marcy – had diverted them to Taylor. There was nothing to do but send the Volunteers to Veracruz, from where they could sail to New Orleans for a victor's discharge.

Scott fretted; the time to take a country was during the confusion following a big and successful battle. But his force was now too small to risk the danger of a full battle.

Nevertheless, he sent General Worth forward toward Puebla with a force that was largely infantry, augmented by just enough cavalry to provide pickets. Scott followed this up with artillery under Colonel Garland.

This artillery outfit, under escort from the 6th Infantry, was the first to contact Santa Anna's new army. The Mexican general had succeeded in mustering enough troops to put on a general harassment of supply lines and movement – guerrilla warfare.

By capturing Garland's guns, Santa Anna hoped to inspire the people of Puebla, where the two arms of the National Road meet, to resist Worth's advance. But Garland's guns drove the guerrillas off.

If he had been truly President of Mexico, as he claimed he was, Santa Anna could have driven Worth, and then Garland, and then Scott back to the sea. But the people did not trust Santa Anna. He led his cavalry against the Americans. But Worth had been re-enforced by two regiments under Quitman; the odds were too great. Santa Anna's infantry and artillery, following behind to watch his charge, retreated, and the general could do nothing but turn his horse column and follow. Worth took Puebla by treaty.

Scott made another pronunciamento at Jalapa. Now the United States had intervened in Mexico in order to put down a monarchical plot. Maybe he put ideas into Santa Anna's head; up in the capital that one-legged general made himself dictator of Mexico.

During the battle of Cerro Gordo and after it the Mounted Rifles had managed to capture enough Mexican troop horses to mount two companies. The rest of the regiment was still foot-slogging. It would have been a wonderful chance to try the old Legion system of Harry Lee, the combination in one tactical force of foot and horse soldiers, so that two men shared the housekeeping and horse-tending chores, but neither General Scott nor Colonel Sumner seems to have been a student of history.

Phil Kearny's troop escorted Scott into Puebla and stood at attention behind him while he made his second pronunciamento.

In August Scott moved out on the last leg of his conquest, the eighty-four miles from Puebla to Mexico City. He had about ten thousand men; Santa Anna had raised an army of twenty-five thousand. Scott decided to cut loose from his long base line to Veracruz. He called in the Dragoons and assigned them to his first division, under General Twiggs. Twiggs formed them into a brigade under Colonel Harney and they moved out on August 7, closely followed by the rest of the first division.

Persifor Smith, the original colonel of the 2nd Dragoons, commanded the infantry brigade that marched right behind the horse soldiers; he was now a brigadier.

Harney's outfit rode cautiously; Puebla is only a little more than eighty miles from the capital, the country is mountainous, and there was every reason to expect strong resistance.

But Santa Anna knew his people; the capital of Mexico and the valley in which the capital lies are much more important to the Mexicans than foreigners realize. The Dictator-General could inspire the people to the defense of that valley much more easily than he could order volunteers out to fight in the Province of Puebla.

The city faced its attacker in a mood that was almost gay. The artillery guns were festooned with flowers, the roofs of the houses were covered with spectators, it was a sort of fiesta with guns.

The main body of Santa Anna's troops were held in the city, ready to defend the causeways that Scott would have to cross to gain access to the capital. It had been raining – battle weather – and the lakes and swamps were full; there were only the narrow Aztec-built bridges to attack on.

Two divisions, one infantry under Valencia and the other made up of four thousand cavalrymen under Alvarez, went out to harass the approaching army.

The Dragoons led Scott over the ridge and down into the central valley of Mexico. Intelligence contacted a number of Mexicans who were willing to guide the United States forces; Scott learned that the best way into the city, between the lakes of Tezcuco and Chalco was also the best-defended; Alvarez and his crack horsemen were at Chalco, Valencia with an infantry force as large as Alvarez's cavalry was at Tezcuco, and the ground between them was heavily barricaded.

Scott decided to swing to the south and attack through Mexicalcingo. But there were strong defenses here, too; his motive seems to have been the brave but expensive one of "being sure of getting a good fight" there.

Worth had had his cavalry out scouting. He advised going even farther south and then coming up through the Pedregal, a lava bed on the edge of the city and the present home of the university.

Scott was by now quarreling with Worth, as he had quarreled with Taylor and with Secretary Marcy, and almost everyone else. As a result, the record is marred; Worth reported that his division was leading the whole army; Scott, that his subordinate was only making a feint.

Santa Anna had swung his harassing forces to the south when he heard of the United States troop movements. The Dragoons ran into Alvarez's cavalry, but shrugged them off; the Mexican horse commander refused to take advantage of the passes and defiles that Scott's heavily bagged column had to go through, and charged in a valley, where the Americans' heavier and more accurate fire power gave them great advantage over horse troops that were largely armed with lances and smooth bores.

If Scott was quarrelsome, so was Santa Anna. He and Valencia got themselves embroiled in an argument; Valencia refused to take orders from his commanding general, and swung down on the advancing army, determined to crush Scott before the Americans could engage with Santa Anna. If he succeeded, Valencia would be the biggest man in Mexico; if he failed, he couldn't be in much more trouble with the Dictator than he already was.

Dragoon picket detachments were out ahead of the main force of Worth's division. Two reconnaissance parties, under Captains Lee and Thornton contacted Valencia. Just which Lee this was is not clear; it was not Robert E. – Light-Horse Harry's son was a colonel of engineers and on Scott's staff. While Lee drove the Mexican pickets back to their main body, Thornton, whose capture above Brownsville had started the war, was killed. Captain Lee reported that Valencia's infantry were no great threat to the advance of the Army; Worth pushed on.

Santa Anna was on his way out from Mexico City with about six thousand men; he no longer had faith in Valencia and wanted to take over the harassing defense himself. One of Valencia's subordinates, General Frontera, had pulled out such cavalry as were attached to Valencia's infantry division and was leading them with pretty good effect at San Geronimo against General Bennet Riley's brigade, when Frontera was killed.

It had been raining; now it began to pour. The American Army struggled across the Pedregal, were thrown back once, then came on again. Santa Anna left the field for Churubusco, pretty well satisfied that he had lost the battle, and Valencia's division with it, but not entirely certain; the weather was so bad that the confusion had mounted into chaos.

The Americans rested as well they could that night, and in the morning moved on Churubusco, where Santa Anna had set up his headquarters. Scott has been severely criticized for attacking Churubusco, which guarded a road into the capital he did not need to use. But if we consider that Santa Anna had raised three distinct armies against the United States, putting him personally out of the fight was more important than the taking of any particular stronghold or road. If that was Scott's aim, it was a wise one.

The day before had not seen a battle so much as several separate battles. The cavalry had fought dismounted or been held in reserve; Santa Anna was a cavalry-minded man, and his earthworks and bastions had been designed to prevent mounted attacks. Dismounted troopers figured chiefly in the taking of San Antonio but detachments were also present at Padierna and Contreras.

The Mounted Rifles, mounted or dismounted, had been glad to fight on foot; they were learning that their long rifles were clumsy in the saddle; the dragoon carbine (which is redundant, since dragoon means carbine) was the proper piece for a horse soldier.

Now the Battle of Churubusco was to be joined and was to engage all of both armies. Scott's staff estimated that Santa Anna had about thirty thousand troops assembled behind barriers of cactus, maguey (the thorny tequila plant), canals, and newly dug trenches. The Mexican artillery covered every road. In addition, all of Mexico City was behind the Santa Anna forces; men could be brought up in force if needed; and due to the constant revolutions of nearly forty years, most Mexican men had had some military experience.

The estimate of troops in the line was probably high by about five thousand men; everything else was not exaggerated. One artillery outfit consisted of two hundred and fifty American deserters, who called themselves Los San Patricios, and claimed that they were Irish Catholics who had changed sides because they could not fight their co-religionists. If captured, the Saint Patricks were due to be shot for desertion; so they would fight to the death.

Phil Kearny went to Scott just before the battle started and asked to be relieved from headquarters duty. Realizing that the future of any officer depended on his battle record, the general told the young millionaire to take his crack Gray Horse Troop and join Harney's Cavalry Brigade. Harney put the troop in the line, which was constantly growing and shrinking as patrols were ordered out; Scott and their divisional commander Worth were taking no chances on fighting in ignorance.

Satisfied that there were no soft points to Santa Anna's defense, Scott threw the 6th Infantry into the battle first. They waded a twenty-foot ditch brim-full of water, and flung themselves at the convent of San Pablo, which was built of heavy stone, screened by stalled freight cars and garrisoned by General Rincón with seven guns and more than a thousand men.

The defenders poured artillery fire at the 6th, but the foot soldiers kept going; the rest of Twiggs's division was behind them.

Meanwhile, the Dragoons, the Rifles, and Worth's infantry pushed their way up the main road to the north and the capital, called Carretera San Antonio, and perhaps the modern Calle Piño Suarez. The other two divisions were set out to try flanking Santa Anna and coming up behind Churubusco.

This last attempt was defeated by Santa Anna's lancers, who charged the American brigades and forced them directly against the main line of infantry-in-depth that Santa Anna had counted on to decimate the United States forces.

They nearly did. The Americans broke, rallied, broke and rallied again; the San Patricios brought their guns to bear, but the stalled trains made as good cover for the attackers as they did for the troops who had stalled them there. Some of the gringo infantry got across the river; numbers of Santa Anna's reserve broke and ran for the city.

The Dragoons pursued them until they had overrun a battery of Rincón's heavy guns, stationed at the north end of the bridge. Together with infantrymen from their division, the troopers brought the guns around to bear on the convent, diverting the garrison from firing on the assault from the south. The garrison surrendered – one San Patricio pulling down the white flag as fast as another would put it up – and the horse soldiers continued routing the fleeing reserves.

This was saber work – slashing and thrusting at broken infantry. Phil Kearny and his troop were in the forefront of it, Kearny riding in the manner he had learned in Algeria: pistol in one hand, saber in the other, reins in his teeth.

The Dragoons were way ahead of the main line of advancing Americans; Scott and Worth's bugler sounded the recall; Harney's headquarters trumpeters took it up and galloped forward to pass it on to the Dragoons.

But there was too much noise up in the front, where Kearny and the troopers were charging a battery at San Antonio de Abad, forcing fleeing infantry into the guns as shields for the horsemen. Perhaps Phil Kearny, wearied by months of guard-of-honoring, was not willing to obey the trumpets; certainly, there must have been enough noise to dim them, if not drown them out completely. Later he admitted that he had heard the order, but that it was not the kind of order he cared to obey; that is, he said: "I was sure it was not for me."

But most of his followers – they were not all from his troop – dropped out and reined back to Harney and brigade headquarters. By the time Phil Kearny got to the gates of San Antonio and the pill boxes guarding it, only about a dozen troopers were following him.

Then he hit a ditch, filled with routed Mexicans. It was too wide to jump, and too full to ride through. He jumped off his horse and charged on foot. The artillery in the pillbox fired into the crowd; the sentries tried to take aim at the dismounted Dragoons, who had formed into a circle, and were trying desperately to keep the mob off them with their sabers.

They didn't succeed; as a man was killed, the one behind him used the body for a shield. Sabers stuck in bodies and were carried away; the thing degenerated into a mob fight, with the Dragoons having their arms and most of their clothes torn away from them.

Kearny got loose, ran for an abandoned Dragoon horse, scrambled into the saddle and swung his spurs home. The animal moved out at a tired shamble, completely exhausted by the charge that had gotten him this far from the front line of the battle.

The Mexican loaded with grape and fired point-blank at the escaping officer. Phil Kearny was hit in the left arm, but he managed to get away; so did some of the other Dragoons who had followed him to San Antonio.

Army surgeons amputated Phil Kearny's arm that night. Any other officer would have felt that his military career was over. But Kearny was used to riding with his reins in his teeth. He was promoted to rank of major for his bravery, shipped home, asked for six months' disability leave, and then went on recruiting service for a while.

Santa Anna and at least one member of Scott's staff felt that if the recall had not been sounded, and if Scott had allowed Worth to send the infantry into the gap that Phil Kearny and his Dragoons opened up, Mexico City could have been carried on that day of the 20th of August, 1847.

It was an American victory at Churubusco. Scott recorded that he had killed or wounded four thousand Mexicans and captured another three thousand, including eight generals. Also he had taken thirty-seven artillery pieces, and a number of small arms. For this, he said, he had paid with a hundred and thirty-nine dead and less than nine hundred wounded. But he neglected to list his missing.

Santa Anna got away again and asked for an armistice. Scott has been very much criticized for granting it, but his orders from Washington seem to make it clear that he had been ordered to subdue Mexico as peacefully as possible; the United States did not want to seize Mexico proper, but only New Mexico and California, which the republic to the south didn't seem too determined to hold anyway. In any event, a two-weeks' armistice was granted.

Santa Anna used it to recruit and reform his fourth army of the year, and to strengthen the defenses of the capital, especially the Palace of Chapultepec.

Actually, the cease-fire held for more than two weeks; Santa Anna stalled for three or four days as to the terms, giving himself as much time as possible. The chief clerk of the War Department, Nicholas Trist, had been in Mexico almost since the landing at Veracruz, trying to make a peace settlement; Scott had had the usual Scott-tvpe arguments with the man who was Marcy's emissary. With the two jealous American chiefs bickering, Santa Anna was in a good position to slow things down.

But, eventually, Scott grew angry at the constant rumors of fortification that were being brought him; and the Mexican congress became enraged because Santa Anna had let a small army (compared to theirs) reprovision itself, almost three hundred miles from the sea-coast.

It is believed that some of the rumors reaching Scott were sent directly by Santa Anna. Whether this is true or not will never be known, as it was not the fashion in those days for spies and traitors to write their memoirs. In any event, Scott believed that El Molino de Key (the King's Mill), near Chapultepec Palace, was an artillery foundry. He ordered Worth and his 1st Division to take it on the night the armistice was called off.

Worth seems to have always had better information than the commander-in-chief. He reported that the Molino was a lot stronger than it looked, built of heavy stone and strongly garrisoned. One of the nearby buildings was called the Casamata, or casemate, and was not the harmless storage shed it looked.

Scott finally gave Worth's division some re-enforcement and told him he could take the King's Mill by daylight.

Worth made the attack with thirty-five hundred men and several artillery pieces. The Mexican garrison remained silent under the preliminary bombardment; but when the charge was made, they let loose with artillery and rifle fire, and the attackers were thrown back. In all, three or four charges were made, before the garrison broke and ran; they would not have gone then, except that Alvarez, hovering on the flank with four thousand of his cavalrymen, failed to attack the engaged Americans.

Sumner had been holding some of the Dragoons mounted in reserve; he brought them in and crossed the bridge under fire from the casemate and shoved the retreating forces along until an artillery piece could be brought up to shell them.

From the other direction, Santa Anna came up with re-enforcements; seeing this, Brigadier General Gideon Pillow, acting without instructions from Scott, came to Worth's aid, and the Mill and casemate were taken.

In the taking the Mounted Rifles lost enough men and captured enough horses to become a fully horse-borne outfit again.

Worth wanted to go on and take the Castle of Chapultepec, but Scott had ruled that it was a harmless piece of Mexican property; Pillow would not go past the Molino against Scott's orders, and Worth did not dare make the assault with what was left of his division; he had had almost eight hundred casualties, between a fourth and fifth of his whole force. It must be remembered that the command had included about half of all the effectives the United States had in and around the capital.

Examination of the captured site revealed no foundry, only a few old moulds; four guns were captured, and about seven hundred prisoners. Mexican losses had been heavy, but there were plenty of Mexicans left; and the city went wild at what it judged to be a Mexican victory.

Again, Scott stalled. Santa Anna took out a cavalry patrol personally and found out what was needed to re-enforce the city; Scott gave him time to do this, and then decided that the best way into the capital was through the west, commanded by Chapultepec, instead of from the south, which Harney and most of his Dragoons had been keeping more or less open.

The west flank of the battlefield was the cavalry ground; here Alvarez and his army of lancers faced a small force of Dragoons, re-enforced with light infantry.

Chapultepec was not a cavalry battle; artillery and bayonet carried the first part of the fight; then, when the garrison had been driven out into the open, Worth's division of Regulars took the main gate of the capital with bitter house-to-house fighting.

The castle fell, and the city was open to the United States. Phil Kearny was invalided, but the beautiful matched dappled gray troop horses he had bought for his company furnished a guard of honor for Scott the next morning when the general rode from the castle to the Zocalo which is the center of the city. With the fall of the capital, Mexican government collapsed; during the triumphal march to the Zocalo, a shot was fired at Worth, and riots broke out in all the central part of the capital.

Scott had artillery guns trained down the streets leading from the Zocalo and loaded with grape and cannister, the anti-personnel ammunition of the time. The riots broke up.

General Scott named Brigadier General John A. Quitman military governor of Mexico. Santa Anna left government and went out in the countryside on his endless round of mending his political fences and raising another army.

The central valley was in complete disorder. The Dragoons settled down to what they always did best – patrolling hostile country, showing the flag. It was not too different from patrolling Indian country, except that the food was better, the sergeants had trouble keeping their troopers away from the tequila, and the scenery was more varied.

They had little trouble; there was a businesslike air about the platoons as they trotted through the suburbs and towns. There were skirmishes in Cordoba and Orizaba between rival groups of Mexican insurgents; the Dragoons broke up the fighting and imposed military law.

Squabbles over the terms of a peace treaty made Washington at one point order Scott to resume fighting; but he continued negotiations, and the Treaty of Guadalupe Hidalgo was signed on February 2, 1848, about five months after the fall of Chapultepec. The following August the last United States troops left Mexico.

Congress at once started reducing the size of the Army, though the war had increased the size of the Southwest tremendously, and more troops than ever were needed to patrol the new land, much of it Apache country.

The 3rd Dragoons were dissolved, but the Mounted Rifles were kept in the Regular establishment, the only wartime regiment to be retained. The Rifles were at once ordered to Oregon.

However, the enlistment law read that Regulars who had fought in the war could end their enlistments and so many of the Rifles took advantage of this that the regiment had to wait at Leavenworth until early May of 1849, recruiting and drilling new troopers. Then the Rifles started out on the two thousand mile ride to the Northwest coast. The 1st and 2nd Dragoons took over the new Southwest, the old Santa Fe Trail, and the sudden surge of gold-seekers to California through Indian country.

Peace was a word on paper in Washington.

Chapter 8

Kearny and the Prima Donna

Nine months before Mexico fell, Stephen Watts Kearny had reached San Diego, with the two companies of 1st Dragoons that he had felt were all he needed after learning from Kit Carson that Stockton and Frémont had California well in hand.

He had found out differently at Warner's Ranch and Santa Ysabel, and the lesson had been driven home at San Pasqual. Now he trailed into San Diego, battered, his command virtually dismounted, exhausted, and half-naked. He himself was wounded and weak from starvation and loss of blood. Three of his officers were dead.

John C. Frémont was now governor of California only on paper. Also, on paper, he was now a lieutenant colonel. Stockton had promoted him from his old rank, Captain of Topographical Engineers, U.S. Army, to be commander of a battalion of California Volunteers, U.S. Navy, which was surely the strangest promotion in United States military history.

There was a commission for Frémont as Lieutenant Colonel, Mounted Rifles, but it had not yet reached him. Kearny's orders from Secretary of War Marcy had been to conquer California and set up a military government, as he had in New Mexico. Unfortunately, Commodore Stockton's orders from Secretary of the Navy John Mason had read almost the same way. The men held the same rank, the lowest flag or general rank in each service.

If California had actually been under the United States flag, it is probable that Kearny would have left Frémont in control. They were old friends, and Colonel Kearny had received favors from the powerful Senator Benton, Frémont's father-in-law.

But Frémont and the Navy and Marine Lieutenant Archibald Gillespie, had made the Californians feel that life under the gringos would be impossible; revolt ran up and down the coast.

Kearny recuperated while writing out a long report to the War Department; he was lavish in praise of the aid Stockton had sent him before and after San Pasqual. Then he proceeded to do what his orders – countersigned by President Polk – said to do: take charge of all U.S. military forces in California.

Stockton refused to turn over his naval and Marine shore parties.

Kearny sent a message to Frémont, who was marching on Los Angeles to report to him.

Frémont was back in the Army; his Mounted Rifle commission had reached California. Presumably he still held the other Army (or California militia) commission that the Navy had given him. But, though he was clearly back in the Army, he refused to obey Brigadier General Kearny, Commanding General, Army of the West.

Kearny bided his time. St. George Cooke was on the way with his Mormon Battalion. Though the Battalion of Saints, when last heard from at Santa Fe, had been a ragged, mutinous bunch of civilians, Kearny knew Philip St. George Cooke, Captain of the 1st Dragoons and Lieutenant Colonel of the Mormon Battalion. The Saints would be soldiers when they finished their thousand-mile march, and they would be soldiers loyal to Cooke.

While Kearny waited, Commodore Stockton, who must have had boyhood dreams of being a cavalryman, mounted his sailors and tried to teach them how to be dragoons. Kearny finally helped him in this amphibious venture.

Frémont had gotten himself besieged in Los Angeles; Kearny proposed to Stockton that they march to his defense. The commodore was reluctant to do this, though by combining the naval and Army forces, they would have a column of six hundred men with several fieldpieces. The Mormon Battalion was still out on the desert.

After several delays, orders and counterorders, the expedition started for Los Angeles, something over a hundred miles north of San Diego. The Dragoons went on foot; they had been offered horses but felt that none of them were worth dragging along.

Kearny was in command, but Stockton called himself "commander-in-chief." The small army seemed to have as many heads as the Navy whip had tails.

This same whip, according to report, came out at San Luis Rey, where some of the sailors broached a barrel of mission wine and got thoroughly out of hand. Kearny, according to Navy Commander Samuel Du Pont, took the cat-o'-nine-tails out of the petty officer's hand and cut it to pieces with his pocket knife; the sailors were now under Army command, and the Army didn't use such brutal punishments. The march was ponderous; cattle were being driven along for food and made considerable trouble.

At San Gabriel, east of Los Angeles (presumably the column had gone the long way around to avoid hostile country), the Californians attacked, under Flores and Andres Pico. The column went into a square, baggage in the middle, the Dragoons in the front, facing the enemy. "Went" is the right word; whether Stockton or Kearny was commanding has never been satisfactorily determined. The unmounted Dragoons were under a Captain Turner.

Enemy snipers peppered the square with little effect. Then the Califomians tried a favorite local tactic; they stampeded a bunch of wild horses toward the square, which was moving slowly forward. The broomtails broke around the halted square and then scattered out on the land, wild and free again.

In order to avoid conflict, Kearny and Stockton agreed that the infantry was all Army and the artillery all Navy. Stockton got his guns across the river, covered by the Dragoons and some sailors, unlimbered and began to feel for the range.

The Dragoons, re-enforced by sailors, continued forward; Stockton got the range and his shots began to fall home against the enemy, who forayed, first against the Marines on the right flank, then against the sailors on the left.

Both flank attacks were turned off; they had, however, given the Dragoons time to start charging the heights where the main body of Californians still were sniping down.

The charge gained momentum, the combat forces from the rest of the column followed the Dragoons up the hill, and the Californians broke and fled. The unmounted Dragoons could not pursue, of course; the column went into camp for the night, placing their animals below the banks of the river for protection from sniping or theft. San Gabriel cost the United States two dead and nine wounded.

The next day the march was resumed. Early in the morning a Californian rode in under a white flag and reported that Frémont and his California Battalion had left Los Angeles and were now near the San Fernando Mission.

Kearny – or Stockton – led on to Los Angeles anyway. At a place called La Mesa they fought a brief skirmish, which developed into an artillery duel with the Californians. Routed, the enemy – who had already divided themselves into Mexicans and Californians – ran into Frémont. He granted them amnesty, in his capacity as governor of California. Kearny and Stockton reoccupied Los Angeles. Then Kearny went back to San Diego, to await Cooke and the Mormon Battalion.

It is interesting to read Stockton's report on the Battles of San Gabriel and La Mesa: "I have thus truly exhibited to you, sir, sailors (who were principally armed with boarding pikes, carbines and pistols, having no more than 200 bayonets in the whole division) victorious over an equal number of the best horsemen in the world, well mounted and well armed with carbines, pistols and lances."

This not only disregards Kearny's two companies of dismounted Dragoons; it overlooks Gillespie's Volunteers, who were mounted as rifles; and does not even mention Stockton's own work with the artillery, which probably turned both battles.

Tons of paper have been covered with arguments and dissections of the trouble between Kearny and Stockton, and between Kearny and Frémont. It is not really a cavalry matter, though Kearny and Cooke were Dragoons, and their opponent Frémont was, at least on paper, a Mounted Rifleman. He was never to serve with his regiment.

It is matter for speculation, however, if Kearny and Cooke's defeat of Frémont's ambition to be governor of California did not affect the future of the cavalry. Thomas Hart Benton was as powerful a man as there was in the Senate; and he never forgot. When Kearny was up for promotion to major general, Benton conducted a one-man filibuster that lasted almost two weeks; and his hatred of Kearny may well have been carried over to the Dragoons in general. At any rate, after the war Congress ordered the 3rd Dragoons disbanded, and never again authorized a Dragoon regiment other than the 1st and 2nd. When what were to be the 4th and 5th Cavalry were authorized in 1855 – after events in the West had proved that the two Dragoon and one Mounted Rifle regiments were hopelessly inadequate to keep the peace there – they were called the 1st and 2nd Cavalry.

At any event, with the Pueblo of Los Angeles retaken, and Frémont put in command of it, the coast quieted down.

A few days later St. George Cooke marched his Mormon Battalion into San Diego. They were ragged and battered but Cooke had made them into soldiers, and they not only didn't resent this, they were fiercely loyal to their gentile commander.

Cooke was always a hothead; he urged Kearny to throw Fremont into jail for mutiny. His former colonel and present general quieted him down, and put him in command of San Luis Rey, up whose river all kinds of trouble had been going on.

Commodore W. Branford Shubrick arrived and took over from Stockton. With him was Richard Mason, who had succeeded to the command of the 1st Dragoons when Kearny was promoted to brigadier. Eventually Kearny made Mason governor of California, without argument from Shubrick; by now instructions from Washington were clear, and the interservice squabble was over.

Not so the trouble between Kearny and Frémont. Ordered to muster his Volunteers into the Army, Frémont read them the order in a desultory way, then informed Cooke that they had declined to be mustered – though the officers at least seemed willing enough; and that he could not disband them, because there were no U.S. troops available to keep the peace. He disregarded the Mormon Battalion because he believed, as he later testified, that all Mormons were traitors to their country. He signed his letter as governor, which he definitely was not; Mason had brought orders from the President that Kearny was governor as long as he stayed in California, and that Mason was to succeed him when he left.

The same orders stated that Frémont was not to be kept in California any longer than was necessary, but was to return to Washington as soon as possible. This was not a dismissal, but an act of courtesy on the part of the administration to Senator Benton's daughter Jessie, who wanted her hero home.

Gillespie was also ordered to Washington to report to the U.S. Marine Corps Commandant.

Frémont rode north to Monterey from Los Angeles, and in an interview with Kearny grossly insulted Mason, who was present as the man who would be governor after Kearny went about his military duties. At the same time Frémont offered to resign from the U.S. Army; Kearny refused to accept the resignation and sent word to Cooke to take over Los Angeles.

Cooke took Kearny's Dragoons and four companies of his own Mormons and went north and took over Frémont's command. About the same time Frémont, having thought things over, apologized to Kearny, and started south. Kearny sent Mason after him as inspector general, with written orders to make Frémont obey.

The orders were needed. Cooke had found blank insubordination at Frémont's post of San Gabriel, where a captain of Volunteers refused to acknowledge the Army's command over the Volunteers and withheld some artillery Cooke needed. The volatile Cooke for once did not lose his temper. He reported that Frémont's man, a Captain Owens, was completely ignorant of military law and procedure. Cooke was right to go softly; many of the California Volunteers were Missourians who had recently rioted against the Mormons in their state, and were ready to riot again; if he had insisted on Owens giving up his post to the Mormon Battalion, he might have had a civil war on his hands, with only the weary remnant of the 1st Dragoons to go between two forces, each much more numerous than the troopers.

Cooke was hotheaded, but fiercely intelligent; Frémont was hotheaded, but the best that could be said for him was that he was brave. He had served well as an explorer, dealing with rough mountain men; he was lost in the discipline of the Army, as lost as a spoiled child on the first day of school.

When the Pathfinder returned from Monterey to find Cooke firmly entrenched at Los Angeles, he refused to call on Cooke; later he testified that a Lieutenant Colonel of Mounted Rifles did not make duty calls on a Captain of Dragoons (Cooke's substantive rank was actually major by then); Frémont did not recognize Cooke's lieutenant colonelcy because it was only Mormon.

Mason got into the Pueblo, as Los Angeles was usually then called, a few days after Frémont. He ordered Frémont to report to him when he got there; Frémont announced himself insulted because Cooke was present.

Mason ordered all of Frémont's records and a band of horses that Frémont was holding out in the valley turned over to him. Frémont furnished a few papers, said the rest of his appointments and expenditure accounts had been sent to Washington, and ignored the order about the horses. When Mason repeated the order, Frémont went to his headquarters, and spoke so insolently that Mason threatened to put him in irons. Frémont challenged him to a duel. Kearny heard about the matter and forbade the two colonels to shoot at each other with the double-barreled shotguns they had chosen as weapons.

A regiment of New York Volunteers had arrived by sea; the California Volunteers were disbanded. Frémont, however, remained in California, getting up a band of men with whom – as an officer of the Topographical Engineers – he proposed to take up his explorations again. And as an officer of Mounted Rifles, he also asked to be shipped to join his regiment in Mexico.

It doesn't seem possible to be an officer in two branches of the Army at once; Kearny apparently felt the silliness of this, and ordered Frémont to turn his surveying equipment over to Lieutenant Henry W. Halleck, who was an engineer, a West Pointer, and a future Civil War General-in-Chief.

Kearny turned California over to Mason, as his orders had read, allowed Cooke to resign as commandant in the south and commander of the Mormons, and to become a simple Dragoon officer again.

Then, with a rather large party of officers, Kearny started back east for Leavenworth, ordering Frémont to accompany him. Cooke went along as Kearny's aide; all the other Dragoons were left in California.

Frémont took with him the surveyors who did not want to stay in California; each night they camped apart from Kearny and his headquarters. Both parties reached Fort Leavenworth late in August, just about the time that Scott was taking Contreras and Churubusco. Kearny told Frémont to pay his men anything the Army owed them and then to put himself in arrest and report to the War Department in Washington, to be court-martialed for insubordination.

The war was over by the time the court-martial started in late 1847, though the peace treaty was not signed until early the next year.

On October 31, 1848, the founder of the Dragoons, Stephen Watts Kearny, died in his bed in St. Louis. In the interim, a court-martial had found Frémont guilty, though President Polk suspended the sentence and allowed the Pathfinder to resign from the Army. Kearny and Cooke had been the principal witnesses against him.

Before he died, Kearny had been brevetted major general, despite Benton's thirteen-day filibuster, and had served in Mexico as commander and military governor at Veracruz, in the army of occupation. It was there that he caught the yellow fever – old yellow jack – that eventually caused his death. General William O. Butler, who had succeeded Scott in the Mexican command, had Kearny brought to the healthier climate of Mexico City and then shipped home to receive his brevet, but the general never recovered.

The cavalry branch of the Regular Army was only sixteen years old. But the youngster had shape and form and muscle, and all of these derived from Stephen Watts Kearny. The cavalry might have been a better branch if its founder had studied the methods of Light-Horse Harry Lee but that is a matter of opinion.

And if there had not been a Kearny, bold, decisive, and firm, Congress might have dissolved the horse soldier branch of the service altogether after the Mexican War; but the Kearny-trained Dragoons and the Mounted Rifles had proved themselves in both foreign war and frontier patrol.

Chapter 9

The Dragon Slayer

When Philip St. George Cooke had been promoted from captain to major he had been transferred, on paper, from the 1st to the 2nd Dragoons, though he really was serving on Kearny's staff. In the small postwar Army he found himself lieutenant colonel of the 2nd, and its virtual commander; the service was now so undermanned that the colonels of regiment mostly were needed in Washington to do staff work, and Colonel Harney was seldom with the 2nd.

St. George Cooke – he was never called Philip – was born near Leesburg, Virginia, on June 13, 1809. Despite the name of the nearby town, this was not the Tidewater Virginia of Harry Lee and the Washingtons; this is the corner where Maryland and West Virginia come together with the Old Dominion. The location was to be important to Cooke in 1861: of the three states that now form the area, Maryland did not secede from the Union, Virginia did, and West Virginia then seceded from Virginia to remain with the North.

The Cookes were a good family in the Virginia sense, colonial stock. St. George Cooke's grandfather had been a judge and had a plantation in Bermuda, which is why the boy was named St. George. The family has a theory that he was never named Philip, that the West Point office gave him the name out of confusion with another officer named Philip St. George Cocke, but since Cocke was five years after Cooke at the Academy, the reverse is more likely true. His father, Dr. Stephen Cooke, died when the boy was thirteen and in a boarding school. His mother wrote him that the money had just about run out, and to leave school and get a job. Instead St. George wrote to his older brothers, who in turn wrote to various congressmen, and he received an appointment to the Military Academy at West Point. He entered when he was fourteen.

For most of its history the age of admission to West Point has been fixed by Congress; usually it has been "between the ages of seventeen and twenty-two," the present reading. But apparently for a short period the issue was left open; P. St. George Cooke, who was graduated and commissioned at eighteen, is not the youngest graduate in the Academy's history.

There was no Cavalry in 1827, and Second Lieutenant Cooke was assigned to the infantry. He went to the Black Hawk War with the 6th Infantry, arriving a little before his regiment; he was promptly offered the job of adjutant to one of the numerous militia generals who cluttered up the theater of war, declined, and joined his regiment, for which he served as adjutant. It was in that war that he first gained his absolute loathing for amateur soldiers.

When the Mounted Rangers Battalion – a dollar a day and bring your own horse and gun – proved impractical, Cooke was sent to Tennessee to recruit for the Regiment of Dragoons that was to become the 1st Dragoons. This was to be an elite regiment – the Army loved that word elite – in which each man was to have the rank and privileges of a West Point cadet, and pay of eight dollars a month, somewhat more than infantry privates got.

Cooke managed to recruit quite a number of Dragoons. They had to be of decent families and of American citizenship, unusual even in the pre-immigration wave. The young lieutenant noted in his journal that the men he persuaded to join would have time in which to regret their action, which indicates that he didn't have much faith in the "elite" promise.

Cooke was a literary man. One of his nephews was a poet, another a novelist, his brother was a constitutional lawyer. The professional soldier kept journals all his life; they have been lost, but he published two books based on them: *Scenes and Adventures in the Army, or Romances of Military Life*, and *The Conquest of New Mexico and California*. He also published *New Cavalry Tactics* in 1884.

Think of an adjective, and some historian has applied it to P. St. George Cooke. Bernard De Voto, for instance, called him: romantic, hard-bitten, a martinet, a gourmet, a West Point precisian, a splendid officer, very intelligent, a Virginian on the most generous scale, and a few other things.

He could be tactful, as when he held his tongue about Frémont at Los Angeles. He could be ingenious, as when he talked the Texans into not attacking the Santa Fe Trail train.

He was a tall man; one of his lieutenants is reported to have said that he had served under Cooke for some time before he noticed that the senior officer was only "a foot or so taller than most men." He is reputed to have had the most steely gaze ever seen on an Army officer, which is probably an exaggeration. Early in his career he started picking up all the diseases a man on active duty could get – malaria, chronic dysentery, a few others – but he served in the Army until he was sixty-four, when mandatory retirement applied.

100

His life spanned the history of the active cavalry. Harry Lee's Continental Legion was before his time, and Pershing's Mexican chase of Villa was after; but he recruited the first Dragoons and when he died the Massacre of Wounded Knee was over, and the horses were never ridden into battle again, except just before and during Pershing's "hot pursuit" in 1917, as noted.

He was Kearny's man. Kearny selected him as a recruiting officer, Kearny came to his aid when his hot tongue got him in trouble with other officers, one of them his lieutenant colonel, Richard Mason, when Cooke was only a captain. Kearny consistently used Cooke when the job seemed impossible – once he sent him to cross a deep river with two companies of Dragoons and only one small canoe – or when what was needed was unusual ingenuity. He was Kearny's spearhead officer and his ambassador and when Lieutenant Andrew Jackson Smith whipped the Mormon Battalion into near-mutiny and nearer exhaustion, Kearny turned the battalion over to Cooke, with total success.

From the time Texas came into the Union, Cooke always had two enemies in the Senate; after he testified against Frémont, he had a third, Benton; and for a year Frémont himself was in the Senate. But Cooke stayed in the Army and took his chances with the body that determined military expenditures and confirmed Presidential appointments, promotions, brevets, and other honors.

He had a son, John Cooke, who became a general in the Confederacy. His daughter Flora was married to no smaller rebel than J.E.B. Stuart. But Cooke remained in the Union Army, where he had the dubious experience of serving under a man who had once been his very junior aide.

He had violent dislikes, one of them being militia, of which he held the lowest opinion since old Dan'l Morgan's time. In New Mexico in 1846 he enjoyed – or suffered – the longest drunk a man ever underwent in the name of patriotism and government service. He was a cavalryman in the old style, the hard-riding Indian fighter; but in his spare time he studied law, and was admitted to the Virginia bar in 1835 and, fifteen years later, to that of the United States Supreme Court. When the Army retired him, he practiced corporation law in Detroit for his remaining twenty-one years.

The Black Hawk War over, young Lieutenant Cooke started out on his enlisting tour. The campaign against the Sac and Fox had shown him the futility of militia; his opinion of the temporary soldiers fell even lower when he met up with one of their generals, in plain clothes, a military man to the core, he assured Cooke. The general – the West Pointer did not inscribe his name for posterity – offered to help Cooke in his recruitment.

But first they must have a drink. The general led the way to an inn. Those were the days when bartenders set a bottle down, and later judged how much had been drunk out of it; the tavernkeeper placed two bottles in front of Cooke and the general. Cooke reached for one.

"Don't drink that," the general roared. "Try this bottle. It's three weeks old."

Cooke survived the recruiting journey, brought in enough men to satisfy Kearny, who was then head of recruiting for the entire Army, and went on duty with the 1st Dragoons when they were organized and Kearny was made their lieutenant colonel.

Cooke went along on the terrible Dodge-Leavenworth expedition into the Pawnee Pict country, and recorded his impressions of it. He picked up one of his lifelong ailments there.

He was on almost all of the 1st Dragoon patrols and expeditions of the early years. He had his fight with Richard Mason in 1839 – the same Mason by whose side he was later to battle Frémont – and Kearny sent him off on recruiting duty again so that Colonel Mason could forget his anger at the lanky captain.

The 2nd Dragoons were rounding up Seminoles and shipping them west; the 1st Dragoons found themselves on the receiving end out in Indian Territory. About three hundred Indians – this was in 1842 – decided to move into Cherokee land, near Fort Gibson. The 1st went out to stop them.

Nacklematha, the Seminole chief, promised to turn back; then did not move. Kearny ordered Cooke and his company to lead a saber charge, one of the few that were ever made by United States horse soldiers against unrouted Indians.

It was only mildly successful. The Indians gave up their stand and moved, but only a small number were rounded up; the rest of them escaped across the Illinois River, which meant they were moving in the wrong direction, east when they had been ordered to move south.

Kearny told Cooke to take two companies and go after them. The river was in flood, it was getting dark, and the only transport Cooke could find was a small canoe or dugout. *"But I had faith"* Cooke wrote in his journal. He also wrote that if he had stopped to think it over, he probably would have told Colonel Kearny that the job couldn't be done.

It was a wild scene. The cutbanks of the flooded Illinois were too high and too steep to ride down; the troopers, harassed by their fierce captain, dismounted, stampeded their horses over the edge of the bank, and then jumped in after them, grabbing stirrup leathers and reins and forcing the swimming animals to drag them over.

Since swimming was not a common accomplishment among enlisted men in those days, and probably not among officers either, it was a wonder that no one drowned. But they didn't; in half an hour Cooke had three-quarters of his men and half his horses over, which seemed to be enough.

He quit when he was ahead and went after the Seminoles in the old Legion manner, with a dismounted man trotting at the stirrup leather of every other mounted soldier.

It is a good way to move; a horse can go as fast with a man dragging from his leather as he can without him, and the man arrives at the battleground almost as fresh as if he'd ridden. The horse carries the weight and the dismounted man's body does just enough work to keep the blood circulating.

No mention is made of the other quarter of the men left behind. Presumably they spent the night rounding up the horses which had not been kicked into the river. Cooke and his men, dripping wet, charged a thicket where the Seminoles were supposed to be hiding; but all they flushed were a bunch of rabbits.

However, the next day they did find the errant Indians, and herded them back across the Illinois and turned them south away from the Cherokees. The only casualty in the whole affair was one Seminole who got slashed by a Dragoon saber. Kearny announced himself pleased with Captain Cooke.

Cooke was with the 1st Dragoons when they started patrolling the Santa Fe Trail. Then the outfit moved back to Jefferson Barracks, where he promptly got into another fight with a fellow officer; this time he picked an equal, another captain named Trenor.

Kearny reprimanded Cooke – with a wink, his biographers say – and then wrote a friend that nobody really liked Trenor, and that Cooke was "a gentlemanly clever fellow" with faults. The philosophic colonel added: "Who has not?"

But it seemed wise to get the stiff-necked captain out of barracks. The Santa Fe traders, very influential in St. Louis, wanted help. Cooke went out with four companies to Fort Leavenworth and the Trail; Captain Nathan Boone – old Dan Boone's son – was sent out from Fort Gibson to join Cooke's command and re-enforce it.

The commands had come together, with Cooke as commandant, when the famous clash with Snively's Texans occurred. It has been described earlier in this book; briefly, Cooke persuaded the Texas Invincibles, as they called themselves, that they had invaded the United States when they thought they were in Mexico (New Mexico, or course), disarmed them and sent them home, since the Republic of Texas did not want a war with the United States.

Too much importance cannot be placed on this incident; three years later Texas was to join the Union as a full state with two United States Senators; and every man elected from the Lone Star State took his seat in the Senate with anger toward P. St. George Cooke; he was never forgiven.

By the time Texas had come into the Union, Cooke had found out he was in the right that day along the Arkansas; he had had an Army surveyor locate the spot where the argument took place, and had found out he had, in truth, been in the United States. At the time he wasn't sure; he was only doing what he had been ordered to do, postpone a war between Texas and Mexico until the United States was ready for one.

By the time the Mexican War started, the 1st Dragoons were considered the best regiment in the Army, and Cooke one of the 1st's best officers. But at that point he was a long way from the war. He and Captain Edwin Vose Sumner – called "Bull" because of his bass voice – had their companies way up north around the headwaters of the Mississippi, where they had been exploring and showing their crack troops to the Canadian border; war with Canada over Oregon was still a strong possibility.

The two captains hurried south, anxious to go to Mexico and engage in the battles that make military promotion and distinction. But Colonel Kearny had other ideas; he demanded from his superiors that the companies be attached to his expedition which was to march on and conquer Santa Fe and New Mexico.

Cooke was disappointed; the eyes of the country were on Taylor and Wool, not on Kearny and the 1st Dragoons. But he had no choice. He and Sumner and their companies marched out of Leavenworth a week after Kearny, hurrying to catch up.

Two weeks later, he wrote: *"The howls of wolves, in which I ever took a singular pleasure, swelling upon the night breeze, set my pen in motion"* a sample of the literary effulgence in which he usually indulged. He went on to complain about the Kansas weather, which was hot, dusty, and full of flies during the day, and thunderous and wet at night.

They had left Fort Leavenworth on July 6; they caught up with Kearny on July 31, having averaged twenty-eight miles a day. By then they had passed the scene of Cooke's clash with the Texas Invincibles; he noted the sardonic fact that he was now riding to the aid of Texas. They had also passed Chouteau's Island in the Arkansas, where, as an infantryman, young Cooke had led thirty foot soldiers against five hundred Comanches (whom he called savage Scythians) and routed them.

The next day Kearny sent for Cooke and told the captain that he was to go ahead of the Army of the West under a white flag to negotiate for the peaceful capture of Santa Fe. The general was emphatic; he had waited for Cooke particularly, though there were senior officers available.

It is always a temptation to quote St. George Cooke directly: "At a plaintive complaint, that I went to plant the olive, which he would reap a laurel, the general endeavored to gloss the barren field of toil."

In other words, Cooke was afraid that he would be diverted from the chance of ever getting into a fight, and come out of the war in the same grade he went in. When Kearny's attempts to "gloss the barren field" failed, the general confided in his junior. Even if Cooke succeeded, and New Mexico fell without a fight, the Army of the West was going to go on to California, and surely there would be battles there.

Cooke agreed to go on the mission of peace; actually, it is hard to see how a captain could have refused to obey the orders of an acting brigadier general who was also colonel of his regiment.

He was to start out from Bent's Fort, which they were then approaching, together with a gentleman known in those parts as Don Santiago and in his native Kentucky as Mr. James Magoffin. Magoffin was a very big trader on the Santa Fe and Chihuahua trails; he was also the founder of present-day El Paso. He had been back in Washington the month before and had gone with Senator Benton to the White House, where he had talked long and to the point with President Polk.

Time has not unshrouded a certain mystery about that talk, and about Cooke's and Magoffin's later meeting with Governor Armijo of New Mexico. It is usually supposed that Armijo was bribed not to pit the Mexican Army of New Mexico and the New Mexican militia against the Army of the West; but whether he was given fifty thousand or thirty-five thousand dollars, and whether Magoffin brought government funds West to do the job or advanced them out of his own pocket is not known, and probably never will be. Some historians deny the bribe at all and say that Armijo was simply persuaded that his badly armed soldiers didn't have a chance. Most of the evidence leads to the conclusion that there was a bribe of thirty-five thousand dollars, advanced by Magoffin. In any event, Cooke and Don Santiago met at Bent's Fort and left from there on the second of August.

Their preparations for the three-hundred-mile trip were simple. Cooke bought or commandeered a pack mule and loaded it with the possibles for a trip; Magoffin sought out a "private" nook where he and the captain could drink a pitcher of iced punch promised by the Bents. He found the nook, an upstairs storeroom in the big fort, but to the annoyance of the ambassadors, a lanky straggler from Pike County, Missouri, edged into the small room with them, eyes fixed on the beaded pitcher. However, Cooke noted, the aroma from the pitcher softened their hearts and they fraternized with the intruder. The protracted patriotic drunk had started.

Magoffin and a Señor Gonzales went ahead; Cooke followed with twelve troopers from his company. Magoffin was in his private coach, Gonzales apparently in a mule-drawn wagon, the troopers were on horseback, and Magoffin's servants herded Cooke's pack mule and extra horses for their master.

The first day or so they passed through various detachments of the Army that Kearny had sent ahead; Cooke camped with a captain of infantry who had bought a bottle of molasses to disguise the flavor of the alkali creek by which they camped. He did not see Magoffin that night, or if so, he didn't note it. The don had one of his vaqueros, a certain Juan, out on the prowl; Magoffin's well-stocked coach was out of brandy!

He had not run out of other things. On the third day he and Cooke lunched together and the captain noted at some length a speech that Magoffin made to his own private, beloved corkscrew, which, he told Gonzales and Cooke, he had carried for eight years. The speech was to the effect that the corkscrew had cost him a thousand, perhaps five thousand dollars in its lifetime, but he didn't care; Don Santiago loved the precious tool all the more.

They continued south, sometimes in a party, sometimes separating so that the troopers could take advantage of horse trails where the wheels couldn't go. Whenever they met, Cooke made a note of the generosity of Magoffin whose "provision of wine defied all human exigencies." Water for the horses – and the enlisted men – was harder to come by.

At Las Vegas Cooke and Magoffin visited the mayor, or alcalde, who provided whiskey; Magoffin was well-known to him.

The travelers separated again, to remeet at Tecolote, where Cooke, returning from buying supplies for his camp, was handed a bottle of aguardiente by Magoffin. He found it strong. Señor Gonzales also imbibed, and then made a speech to some of his fellow countrymen about the glories of living under the American flag.

By the eleventh they had crossed the Pecos, and Don Santiago had captured a turtle and made soup out of it. This proved too much for Cooke's chronic disorders; he dosed himself with opium, and the next day turned his horse over to be led and rode in Magoffin's carriage.

His health got worse. Don Santiago Magoffin treated him – with wine, of course – and he got some sleep.

They came to Glorieta Pass-Apache Canyon, the narrow, deep gut that guards Santa Fe from eastern attack. The aching, ailing captain was still a Dragoon. He reported the Pass looked impregnable, but that he had figured a way to flank it.

That night he was alone; his escort had ridden ahead to wait at the first source of water. They missed a little stream or spring, by which he slept a few miles short of Santa Fe. During the night, he noted, he awoke and drank some wine that Magoffin had kindly supplied.

Afterward there is silence in Cooke's account. He tells what Santa Fe looked like, and that his escort of twelve troopers were somewhat afraid in the midst of Armijo's numerous army; he comments on the excellence of New Mexican baking, and on his belief that no one but a Mexican can make a drinkable chocolate; he tells of official receptions, and of the food he couldn't eat and the whiskey he couldn't drink.

But all he says about his arrangements with Armijo are that he made two official calls on the Governor and General of Nuevo Mejico. He does mention that the governor was strong in avarice but mentions it in connection with the bribes Armijo would be able to collect if the Santa Fe Trail was under United States guard all the way, and thus attractive to rich caravans from the States to New Mexico and Chihuahua.

Armijo sent a commissioner back with Cooke, an Englishman named Dr. Conolly. Don Santiago Magoffin was to go on to Chihuahua, where he was arrested but treated decently because he served excellent dinners and copious drink to his officer-captors. Cooke, who was not there, calculated that the Don's expenditure of champagne alone was 3392 bottles.

Cooke and Conolly got back to Kearny and the Army of the West at Tecolote. Kearny had been administering the oath of allegiance to the United States at every town he passed through; there had been no trouble so far with the New Mexicans, who were under constant attack from Apaches, and anxious to see if the United States would give them stronger anti-Indian guard than Armijo had done.

At San Miguel the *alcalde* refused to sign this oath; Cooke seems to have admired him for his stand. He refers to the New Mexicans as "great mass reared in real slavery, called peonism, but still imbued by nature with enough patriotism to resent this outrage" of being forced to swear allegiance to a conqueror. When Kearny couldn't persuade the local officials to change flags, he forced them, to Cooke's disgust. He didn't think this was a very good "first lesson in liberty."

At the Pecos ruins – which had inspired Cooke, while with Magoffin, to deep religious and historical reflections – Kearny's column halted. They kept getting word, through captured natives, that Armijo had heavily re-enforced Apache Canyon. Cooke slept, and in the morning commanded the advance guard. Since Kearny had not told him to take the flanking route that Cooke had spied out, he concluded that the general had gotten word in the night that the canyon wouldn't be defended.

It is too bad that Cooke did not record what his bypass was; it was probably Cañada de los Alamos, but we cannot be sure. More than fifteen years later a Texas Army was to suffer a defeat there from the Union because they did not understand the management of the narrow canyon.

Leading his Dragoons, Cooke found only some timbers laid across the pass; Armijo had, indeed, brought his army out there, and then had told them it was useless to resist the Army of the West, and had fled south to Socorro to get away from the war.

The occupation of Santa Fe is more Kearny's story than Cooke's; the captain commanded the guard the first night, with fifty Dragoons, and had considerably more trouble with drunken Missouri volunteers than he did

107

with New Mexicans. His health must have improved, for him to lead an advance guard all day and then patrol the streets all night.

Cooke liked Santa Fe, which was unusual among gringos of the day; nine years later *Lippincott's Gazetteer* was to report: "on the whole, the appearance of Santa Fe is very uninviting, and the population is exceedingly depraved." But the literary captain, who spoke what he called schoolbook Spanish, was amused at how quickly and easily the Dragoons and Missouri Volunteers communicated with the New Mexicans, and particularly enchanted with one of the officers with whom he shared quarters, who spent a long period every morning telling their Ute slave maid how to make his bed – in English, of which she had not a word.

Kearny informed Cooke that the captain was to command a column which would try to get to California by the little-known Gila River route; the main Army – Cooke always wrote it "army," the quotation marks indicating that he thought it much too small for the conquest assigned to it – would go by what was called the Old Spanish Trail, north into what is now Wyoming and Colorado. This was the route by which Frémont had returned from his Second Expedition in 1843, and Kearny would have the use of Frémont's notes. It was known that no wagons could be used on this trail; it was feared that Cooke would not find a wagon route, either.

Reports came in that a Mexican Army was on its way to Santa Fe up the Rio Grande. On August 27, a week after they had taken over Santa Fe, Cooke marched out with half his Dragoons – probably twenty-five men – to try and find grazing where the troop and other horses could be brought back to strength; there was little forage around Santa Fe.

He camped on the Galisteo and recorded that he caught a slight cold. Four days later he was back at Santa Fe, his horses in better shape. He received orders to stand by, night and day, ready to march south on an hour's notice.

But the whole Dragoon column moved out, Cooke with one party, Kearny with the main body, heading south. The rumors about a Mexican attack from that source had subsided, and the principal objective of the move – to the lower country around the Keres pueblos of Santo Domingo, Cochiti and San Felipe – was to get the horses into shape for the crossing to California.

Forage remained a difficulty; the Dragoons were worried about their horses. The northern route was abandoned because of the lateness of the season and the danger of snow.

New arrangements were made. Doniphan would go to General Wool in Chihuahua as the 1st Mounted Missouri Volunteers could leave the garrisoning of Santa Fe to Price's 2nd Missouris. All five of the Dragoon companies would try the Gila River route; the Mormon Battalion would follow them when it got to Santa Fe in October.

Then the plans were changed again. There would not be enough grass on the Gila; the Dragoons would have to make a long loop down through Sonora.

The Dragoons bought corn, stalks and all, from the Spanish and the Pueblo Indians but the horses continued to lose weight. The conquest of California became a dreary prospect. It snowed on the Sangre de Cristos above Santa Fe and rained on the horse camps farther south.

Cooke worried about the horses, he worried about his Dragoons, who were shabby and underfed, he worried about his future. This far from the theater of war, he mused, the best he could hope for was a place in the "appendix of history."

On September 26 they moved out for good and found grass at last; Cooke now worried about the scarcity of fire wood. The next day Cooke and his company were late in getting started because of a runaway mule; then they broke a wagon pole. They caught up with the column at Bernalillo, and Cooke found this Rio Abajo country more habitable than that around Santa Fe. But that night they hit another grassless camp.

As they moved through the present Sandoval and Bernalillo counties, the Army tried desperately to exchange the worn-out wagon mules for fresher ones, with little success. In a footnote Cooke apologized for mentioning every tree he passed, saying that only someone who had been there could appreciate what a welcome sight any kind of greenery and promise of fuel was. At Valencia he paid two reales for a small stick.

The next day a message came from Price, who had arrived at Santa Fe; he reported that James Allen, who had been lieutenant colonel in charge of the Mormon Battalion, was dead, and that Lieutenant Andrew Jackson Smith had taken over the Battalion of Saints.

Kearny sent for his favorite captain: Cooke was to return to Santa Fe and take over the Mormons. The general "very kindly" allowed Cooke to keep three of his Dragoons.

Cooke was also to take new orders to Doniphan; the Missouri colonel was to foray against the Navajos before leaving for the Chihuahua theater of war.

The Mormon Battalion was not Cavalry, and it was not an outfit of Regulars. But from its birth to its dismissal in California, it was always commanded by officers of the 1st Dragoons – Allen, Smith, and then Cooke – and should be part of the history of that regiment.

Chapter 10

Footnote to the Horse Officers

The battalion was the idea of that rather strange President, Polk. The Latter-Day Saints had been run out of Missouri and Illinois; they had just wintered at Council Bluffs on the Nebraska coast of Iowa. They were determined to leave the United States and found a republic someplace in Spanish country, where they could follow their religion.

They would not – and Brigham Young must have known this – have been allowed in or near any of the Mexican settlements, but the Indians had kept the Spanish out of a good deal of the territory that Spain and then Mexico had claimed.

The Saints were definitely inimical to the United States. Polk had some idea that a Mormon army might land on the back of the troops he sent to attack and conquer New Mexico and California. Also, here were men already in the West and anxious to go farther. He ordered Colonel Kearny at Leavenworth to recruit a battalion of five hundred men and use them in the Army of the West.

For once Kearny didn't send Cooke; he had other plans for his favorite subordinate. He sent Captain James W. Allen, 1st Dragoons, to winter quarters at Council Bluffs. Allen was persuasive; the church would receive cash money it badly needed, the recruited Saints would be discharged in California – which was then Brigham Young's most probable goal – and would each be issued a musket to take away with him after his year's enlistment was up.

The men turned over to the Dragoon captain by the Prophet were not choice. The able-bodied and young were kept to help the Mormon migration; the feeble, the old, and the immature were somehow palmed off on Captain Allen.

He marched them to Leavenworth and either drilled them or didn't; Cooke later said they had had no drill at all. But before the march to Santa Fe had hardly started Allen died, and First Lieutenant Andrew Jackson

Smith appointed himself lieutenant colonel, the temporary rank Allen had held.

The self-appointment was not popular. The Mormons had wanted one of their own officers to succeed Allen; probably Jefferson Hunt, Captain of A Company. But Smith persuaded them that only a Regular officer would be able to certify their pay and held the command.

The march from Leavenworth to Santa Fe was not very successful. A horde of dependents straggled along, Smith tried to make a reputation by hurrying too fast, the doctor was a Missourian and thus suspect of being a poisoner of Saints, a belief that has been handed down in Mormon legendry. They were hit by a tornado and almost parched to death on the Cimarron cutoff, which they, alone of Kearny's army took. They arrived in Santa Fe more than half starved, about as naked as they were hungry, and ready to murder Smith and the doctor Sanderson.

Leaving his baggage on the Rio Abajo with two of the Dragoons Kearny had "kindly" left him, Cooke and his trumpeter rode back to Santa Fe to take over the scarecrow battalion.

At Otero's ranch on the Rio Grande – somewhere around Valencia – he swapped his hardy but unmanageable brown pony for a mule. He did so with regret and a good deal of typical Cooke literary flamboyance, though the pony's last action in the Dragoons consisted of backing into an irrigation canal and thoroughly wetting both himself and his captain.

But in all their discussions Kearny's staff had agreed that no horse could endure the hardships of the Gila Trail; mules are hardier and expend their energy more calmly and thriftily. The mules seem to have been of only slightly higher quality than those on which Kearny and his Dragoons rode west from Santa Fe.

Cooke was to grow fond of the mule he got from Señor Otero; at night on the trek to California, he would personally feed corn to the mount, and once threatened to shoot a wagon mule who tried to share the colonel's mule's mess.

He slept over at Algodones and then rode into Santa Fe. The command of which he was now to be lieutenant colonel had not yet arrived, so he went about acting as his own commissary of subsistence, in the title of the day.

He found the Quartermaster's Department penniless, without supplies, and unable to buy any from the disaffected New Mexicans. Cooke felt that mismanagement was evident; the principal merchants of Santa Fe were accustomed to accept notes on St. Louis banks, and the United States credit should have been good.

He noted mildly that: "The consequence seems almost fatal to my expedition." In other words, he didn't think that it would be easy to traverse more than a thousand miles, mostly desert, without food for the five hundred men he expected to command. The lack of mules worried him more than anything else.

By now he had received further orders from Kearny: the battalion was not only to march from Santa Fe to San Diego, it was to build a wagon road as it went. This was almost three hundred years after the Spaniards had first entered New Mexico; it was more than two hundred years since Santa Fe had been built; it was seventy-seven years since Padre Serra founded the San Diego Mission; and in all those years no one had gotten a wagon from one Holy City to the other.

Five days after Cooke got to Santa Fe his command straggled in. He was not encouraged. He had never liked militia or Volunteer troops; these were as undisciplined as any he had ever seen. The women stragglers were an unbearable nuisance; the recruits were often too old, too feeble or too young; their clothing was scanty; they could not be paid; and their mules were utterly used up.

What mules Cooke had been able to procure were hungry and breaking down every day from the lack of forage at Santa Fe. He had to hurry. He lined up the troops and invalided eighty-six of them, with two officers; these were ordered to take all the women and go north to what is now Pueblo, Colorado, where there was an advance party of the Mormon migration. Five of the remaining officers offered to purchase transportation to California for their wives, and the Dragoon officer reluctantly consented. He does not mention it in his journal, but Mormon accounts say that Captain Hunt's sons also accompanied the battalion to San Diego.

Cooke bullied some rations out of the Quartermaster: sixty days' supplies of flour, sugar, coffee, and salt (he did not seem to know that the Mormons didn't use coffee) and twenty days' worth of salt pork. He also procured pack saddles and some oxen and beef cattle.

Five days after the Saints came into Santa Fe they were on the move again, if only to Agua Fria, six miles out, where there was some grass. Following them there that night, Cooke found there were not enough picket pins to secure the mules at night; he broke up an old wagon and made pins out of the metal parts.

At Galisteo, Lieutenant Smith joined the battalion in his new capacity as assistant Commissary of Subsistence, which seems an awful comedown from being commanding colonel; the preliminary "assistant" must have been a humbling measure of discipline, since no mention of a full Commissary is ever made.

Lieutenant George Stoneman also joined on, and was titled Acting Assistant Quartermaster; actually, he was Cooke's aide. This officer had just graduated from the Point in the class of 1846, at the age of twenty-three;

this was his first assignment. In the Civil War he was to be Chief of Cavalry of the Union Army, and Cooke's superior.

Cooke had always felt that the practice of "nooning" – eating a heavy meal and grazing the animals – in the middle of the day was wrong. He did not allow it here. The animals were watered in the Galisteo River and marched on, a process that took an hour and a half to accomplish. They lost several cattle that day; the animals just fell down with bleeding feet and refused to move. Cooke had them rolled out of the trail and went on.

The third or fourth day out George Stoneman proved valuable; the young officer talked a rancher into exchanging fifteen good mules for thirty worn-out ones. Cooke himself bought corn; Smith might have been sulking.

It began to rain. Cooke still had his cold. There was no fuel. Cooke spent the cold nights bawling out his Mormon captains about taking better care of mules and mustering their men more promptly; he broke a first sergeant down to private. The battalion was beginning to respect their new colonel.

By November 2 they were moving out at a better clip, though Cooke had had to send several empty wagons with worn-out oxen back to Santa Fe. Guides arrived, sent back by Kearny; and three hundred sheep were added to the supply train; small ones, however. The next day they were in better sheep country; Cooke ordered Smith to buy some of the larger animals at the same price paid for the small ones, and if there was trouble, just to take them. He noted: *"He got them."*

The battalion was now beginning to do roadwork, improving the track left by Kearny's column. They found they could not only make a respectable hike every day but could work as they went. Anything, the Mormon diary-keepers report, was better than crossing Colonel Cooke.

The ground got worse, but the country was richer in game. By November 9, three weeks after leaving Santa Fe, the guides reported that there were no mules who could possibly last to California. Cooke noted that the whole thing was impossible. So, he sent back to Santa Fe fifty-five more Saints who were too feeble to go on. He sent enough supplies to see them through, barely, rejoicing that he had gotten rid of eighteen hundred pounds of dead weight, and could increase the fresh meat allowance for his survivors. He had hired Mexican herders to drive the cattle and some extra mules, and had dropped off ten wagons, without teams, for the Army of Occupation to pick up.

There were true accounts of Navajo raids all around, and false rumors of a north-coming Mexican Army.

Things were picking up; much of the baggage was now being carried by pack mules and some of the oxen had been persuaded to carry packs, too, after performing "antics that were perfectly ludicrous."

Tent poles had been abandoned; the men sheltered themselves by putting pegs in the muzzles of their muskets and holding up their tents this way; at the lower height, the tents spread farther and sheltered more men. This was November in middle New Mexico and cold.

They left the Rio Grande and headed west to miss the Jornada del Muerto. Cooke increased the dry rations to lighten the load and reported that it speeded up their progress. The guides took them north again and disclosed that none of the men who were supposed to show Cooke the road to California had ever been more than forty miles from the Rio Grande.

Cooke struck out in a generally southwest course. Sometimes they camped dry, sometimes they found water – a spring he discovered was called Cooke's Spring on early maps and then, of course, became Cook's – and sometimes they dug wells. There was no more talk of mutiny among the Mormons; they had found out that the colonel, though harsh, had no more against Mormons than he did against any other militia or Volunteers, and would bawl out ex-Colonel Smith as quickly as he would anyone else.

Near the present line between Arizona and New Mexico – they had gone down into what was then Sonora – the battalion fought its only battle, one against hordes of feral bulls. They had had previous encounters with small numbers of these animals, who had been abandoned by ranchers as the Apache troubles got worse and worse in that country. Cooke himself had had more or less peaceful encounters with the Apaches, whom he did not care for; they seemed brutal and debased and their language was hideous.

The Apaches, to the literary Dragoon, were Parthian, where the Comanches had been Scythian. Either the curriculum at West Point was considerably more classical than Congress knew – Colonel Cooke carried a library with him – or the fourteen-year-old boy had been severely educated before he went to the Academy. Parthians, to save modern readers the trouble of seeking out reference books, were bow-and-arrow Turkomans of the old Persian empire; Scythians were steppes dwellers famed for their savagery.

Mexicans and friendly Indians were encountered who told the interpreters that there was a big garrison at Tucson which was preparing to fight. Foster, one of the interpreters, was sent into Tucson to dicker. Later a corporal's guard of the Mexican army was taken; the corporal turned out to be the son of the Tucson commandant, and he said Foster had been taken prisoner. Then the interpreter was returned to Cooke by a commissioner, who was told that if the garrison surrendered a few weapons as a token, the battalion would not wipe them out.

But when they got to Tucson the garrison had marched out. Cooke left a note for the commandant, pointing out that he had not come as an enemy of the people of New Mexico (of which Arizona was a part) but as a better friend than the Mexicans who supplied arms and ammunition to the Indians who made life around Tucson almost unendurable. Then he got what supplies he could and marched on.

On the Gila he picked up Kearny's trail and followed it along the river. He made a map as he went, and the ordinarily modest Dragoon later noted that his map, made by sight, almost exactly coincided with that of Emory in Kearny's command; and Lieutenant Emory was a Topographical Engineer with the finest of instruments.

He marched the battalion into Pima country, and was enchanted with those farming Indians, who gave the column any supplies available, and seemed reluctant to take pay for it. He found the Pima girls "of all ages and pretty," naked above the waist, and called it a "gladdening sight."

Between the Pimas and the land of the Maricopas a dispatch reached him from Kearny, who had gotten to Warner's Ranch and had found out that the Stockton-Frémont conquest of California had blown up; the battalion was badly needed on the Coast. Cooke pushed the weary Mormons on, still making roads as they went; he was now to hurry, but not to abandon the wagons.

The desert, on either side of the Colorado, is the worst in North America. They followed the Gila River, and so had water and some forage, but after the Salt River – which Cooke called the Saline – comes in, the Gila is brackish. When they had to leave the river because of bends or bad footing, the sand was exhausting.

Two of the wagons had been built so that they could be used as pontoons. Young George Stoneman told his commander that he had had some experience with boating; he was told to take the pontoons off their running gear and ferry the supplies to the mouth of the Gila.

He arrived, but with an empty boat; the river had gone down to three or four inches in places, and Stoneman had had to cache the supplies. Parties of mules were sent back to recover the precious food, but without much success.

The mules were failing, the Mormons were exhausted. Where the Gila joins the Colorado, Cooke camped for the night, and sent a guide across to fire the rushes on the other side, in order to make the next day's roadbuilding easier.

The pontoons were more useful here; but it took an hour and a half for each crossing, and little could be carried at a time. Once the boat carrying Stoneman got away from its polesman and started down to the Gulf of California. Cooke, on muleback, swept off his hat and called to his lieutenant to "give my regards to the folks" at the mouth of the Colorado, but there wasn't much other humor in the day's work.

The colonel was determined to get everyone over that day; Kearny's dispatch had him worried, and there was no forage on the east bank. He decided to drive the wagons through the water, which was about four feet deep, with ice in the backwaters; this was mid-January. Several mules were drowned.

115

Riding the back trail, Cooke found the Mormons, especially Company C, had about given up. He stormed and raged, and they rallied.

When he had two thirds of the battalion over he started the march away from the west bank, leaving the rest of his men to struggle with the sheep, most of whom are still in the river.

Camp was made fifteen miles from the river, where there was some desert forage, mesquite beans and what Cooke called *tornia,* which was probably *tornillo,* or screwbean mesquite. They were still in the alluvial sand, but having terrible trouble getting water; the sides of the two wells they tried to dig collapsed just as they hit moisture.

One of the officer's wives had a washtub; when her wagon came up, Cooke asked for it to line a well; the lady refused, to his amazement. He commandeered the valuable article, and finally got a well going by punching holes in the lady's contribution.

The guides, who had apparently been reconnoitering, reported that the next well was completely dry; and it was a night and two days away. Cooke wrote down that he was full of despair, and then ordered a beef slaughtered to strengthen his men, who had had one of the most exhausting days in history.

Stoneman and some men went ahead to see if they could improve the dry well, the Pozo Mocho – literally Dishonored Well; the battalion camped dry. The best that could be done with the Pozo was to get a gill of water per man; while it was being doled out, another dispatch came, telling of Kearny's trouble – defeat or victory – at San Pasqual.

They staggered on, up the bed of San Felipe Creek, which was dry. When they found grass, it was alkali growth or so rank that it didn't nourish the mules, who were dying at the rate of about eight a day. Twenty-one mules abandoned by Kearny were picked up; in that desert country they had hardly recuperated since being turned out.

They had crossed the Colorado on the eleventh; on the eighteenth they came to a dead, grinding halt. They had reached the Narrows of San Felipe Creek – Cooke called it San Philippi – and the wagons could go no farther; a sheer rock barrier higher than a man's head was across the steep-walled canyon.

Most of the road tools had been lost crossing the river. Cooke went to the head of the stalled train, started tearing at the wall as an example, got a pebble out, then a larger rock, the Mormons took heart from his example, and started swinging at the rock with axes.

The first wagon was taken to pieces and passed over the workmen's heads, the second had only to be broken down into running gear and body, and each part was passed up on its side. The last two wagons were driven up and through, mules attached and cargo aboard.

The wagon road to the coast from Santa Fe was finished; there was only one bad ridge left to cross, and that could be done by hitching ropes to help the mules. On the twenty-first the battalion was at Warner's Ranch.

The local Indians were engaged in inter-tribal warfare; Cooke's column went with some of them to furnish cover while some battle-killed braves were buried, then went across the Valle de San Jose, and down the San Luis Rey River to the Mission; the battalion got its first glimpse of the Pacific.

On January 30, 1847, the Mormons were in the Presidio of San Diego, hearing Colonel Cooke read a fulsome Order of the Day, praising them for what they had done, and ending up by promising them that he would now teach them how to drill.

The wagon road was open; and Frémont's ambitious quasi-insurrection was over. The Mormons were loyal to Cooke and Cooke was loyal to his general, and the President's orders would be carried out; the Army would rule California.

The rest of the California story was Kearny's; Cooke carried out his orders, went East to testify at Frémont's trial and then resumed his normal career as major of the 2nd Dragoons.

In California Cooke observed with amazement the ranchero method of traveling – at a dead run, with a remuda of remounts driven alongside. His only observation was that this was too expensive for the Cavalry. After twenty years in the Army a man can be pardoned if he gets cynical about some things, especially Congressional appropriations committees.

Two sequels to the story of the Mormon Battalion are worth adding: The peace treaty with Mexico did not recognize the value of the wagon road cut by the Battalion of Saints; after the treaty was signed, Washington had to send an ambassador, James Gadsden, to purchase, for ten million dollars, the right-of-way and its adjacent land.

And two veterans of the battalion were in the party of carpenters that discovered gold in Sutter's Mill on January 24, 1848 and started the California Gold Rush.

Chapter 11

The Time of the Paper Peace

The last skirmish the 2nd Dragoons had in Mexico was on September 13, 1847; thereafter the patrol records of the Army of Occupation mention only the Mounted Rifles among the regular cavalry. They were aided by the Texas Rangers. After that date the Army list of engagements shows parts of the 2nd fighting Indians in Nebraska, Texas, and five times in New Mexico.

The 1st Dragoons and the 2nd now had the hugely expanded West to police. The 3rd Dragoons were disbanded, the Mounted Rifles were stuck back in the states trying to recruit somewhere near to strength.

California, Oregon, New Mexico, what are now Arizona, Nevada, Washington, Utah, part of Colorado, Montana, and Wyoming had been added to the old West, which had been too big for the Army to handle before the war. In addition, the removal of the threat of war with England and Mexico was an inducement to settlers to try moving toward the new lands; and this movement was an inducement to the Indian tribes to go on the warpath.

But the worst hazard to patrolling the new West was desertion. The news of the gold strike in California was electrifying; and why should a man shovel out horse stalls for a few dollars a month when he could become a millionaire with the same amount of shoveling in a California sand bank?

Desertion had been a problem during the Mexican War, especially among the Regulars. There were about as many desertions charged to the U.S. Army – as separate from the state troops – as there had been enlisted men at the beginning of the war. This, of course, does not mean that every professional private and noncom deserted; in wartime the companies were doubled in personnel, so that the same number of officers and experienced noncoms commanded twice as many men.

It must have been a shock to a patriotic young man to find himself among a cadre of hard-bitten troopers, settled in their ways and used to getting along on a handful of beans a day. What the Mexicans call *mordido* and the gringos the chisel was frequently applied; old Joe so-and-so always gets so many pennies a month from each trooper for shaving the boys, old Hank is paid to raise us a few fresh vegetables, Monk expects something for cooking, and so on.

And the customs. You can't sit there; everybody knows that that is old Spike's favorite nail keg. The young patriots frequently deserted for the purpose of joining a more easygoing Militia or Volunteer outfit.

After the war, the desertion problem got worse. Many men enlisted only to get free transportation to the gold fields; troops could simply not be kept in Oregon or New Mexico and especially not in California itself. Congress voted extra pay for duty on the coast, and then added the Territory of New Mexico to the bonus zone. It didn't stop desertion, but it helped.

Legally the combined strength of the two Dragoon regiments was about thirteen hundred officers and men; but they never came up to strength. The Mounted Rifles were allowed almost eight hundred personnel, when and if they could get into the field.

There were almost forty-five hundred people allowed in the eight infantry regiments, but they were not much help in patrolling the rising Indian trouble. There were thirty-two new forts to be built at once, mostly to protect the booming traffic along the Santa Fe and Oregon Trails and on Cooke's wagon road. After 1847 the official Army list of engagements does not list anything but Dragoon fights except in Texas, Nebraska, and once in New Mexico until 1853, when the infantry, done with its building program, began to get out into the field again.

Infantry was not a good patrol weapon, anyway. Although it is perfectly true that a foot outfit will make more miles a day, after the first few days, than a mounted one, it cannot cover the country as well. The very height of a mounted man gives him more scope; and it is easy to have a trooper explore up a side canyon and then trot to catch up with the walking column; this is almost impossible with foot troops.

If the remuda system of traveling was impossible, the Legion method would not have been. If the officers, sergeants, a few scouts, and half of each platoon had been mounted and the riflemen on foot, the patrols could have moved just as fast, and the two hours of grooming every day that were added to the numerous trooper's chores could have been split up. But a horse outfit was a horse outfit and an infantry regiment mounted no one but the officers, who supplied their own chargers.

Generals Scott and Taylor were still very much in the picture. Both of them tried for the Whig nomination for President; Taylor got it, which must have salved the old wound of having his crack troops taken away by Scott in Mexico.

Scott remained as General-in-Chief, commandant of the whole Army. He was also Commander of the Eastern Division, with about one-fifth of the Army under him to man the forts of the Atlantic Coast and the Great Lakes. Florida was in the Western Division, weirdly, as was all the West except the Pacific Coast. Zachary Taylor commanded the Western Division until politics took him out of the Army; Persifor Smith, colonel of the Mounted Rifles, was in command of the Pacific Division, with the brevet of Brigadier General.

Taylor and Scott may have had their difficulties, but the new President was still a soldier; as soon as Taylor took office in 1849, his General-in-Chief asked that the Army be doubled in size. Taylor concurred, and ordered his Secretary of War, George W. Crawford, to make a study of the situation.

Crawford was a tactful man. With Benton still powerful in the Senate, with the two Texas Senators hating the Dragoons because of Cooke, with Frémont about to take office as a junior, short-term Senator, there was no use asking outright for more Dragoons, which was what was needed.

Instead, he asked that all companies be raised to a strength of seventy-four privates, instead of fifty in the Dragoons and forty-two in the Infantry, sixty-four in the Mounted Rifles. He also got permission to mount some of the Infantry outfits serving in Texas against the Comanches, thus; getting the vote from the Lone Star delegation.

So, in the summer of 1850, the Army went from about ten to almost thirteen thousand men.

It wasn't enough. Scott was never happy with the mounted infantrymen; they didn't get either enough dismounted drill or enough equitation to satisfy him. Looking back, it is hard to see how dismounted drill could be of much use against Indians, which was the principal purpose of an Army stationed four-fifths in the West; but without it it is hard to impress on recruits that they are now in the Army and must obey all orders, no matter how pointless they sound. An officer under fire does not have time to explain his motives to his men, though many a miliftia commander had tried just that.

Between the Mexican and the Civil Wars, the picture along the frontier changed for the worse. The Northern Plains tribes had never given serious trouble before, mostly because their territory hadn't been bothered; now they began to chafe at the sight of settlers and coast-bound miners intruding on their buffalo ranges. The Apaches, Navajos, and Comanches in the Southwest had never stopped giving trouble; the Lipans in Texas – cousins to the Navajos and Apaches – went on the warpath; many of the Eastern tribes that had been moved into Indian Territory didn't like it there. The tiny Army did its best. The Dragoons and the Mounted Rifles patrolled constantly, though the small size of their detachments created an illusion among the Indians that there were more members of any given tribe than there were white men in the whole world. The Infantry held down – in a random year – almost a hundred and forty posts.

On July 9, 1850, Taylor died of typhus, shortly after the Army was expanded. Vice-President Millard Fillmore succeeded him as Chief Executive, and Fillmore was from New York, more interested in the industrial East than the expanding West. Franklin Pierce succeeded Fillmore in 1853, and though the new President was from New Hampshire, he had served in the Mexican War as a Brigadier of Volunteers. He appointed another veteran, Jefferson Davis, as Secretary of War. Davis was not only a veteran; he had seen his service in the 1st Dragoons.

The Army got two more horse regiments. Benton and Frémont had left the Senate, so perhaps it was to assuage the Texans that the new outfits were called Cavalry instead of Dragoons, though their purpose was to fight Indians and not to charge formal troops, as Cavalry is intended to do. There is a possibility that the change in names was promoted by Jeff Davis, so that he could pick officers for the Cavalry by geography instead of Dragoon seniority.

This was to be the status of the horse soldiers until the Civil War, when the 1st Dragoons became 1st Cavalry, 2nd Dragoons 2nd Cavalry, Mounted Rifles the 3rd Cavalry, and the 1st and 2nd Cavalry became the 4th and 5th.

In the 1850s the official Army register lists twenty-two so called "wars" and thirty-seven "engagements" in which casualties occurred. Most of these were Indian troubles, of course; two were not. Both of the non-Indian troubles were assigned to the 2nd Dragoons; they kept the peace in the Bleeding Kansas election of 1856 and they put down a Mormon war in 1857.

First, however, there was plenty of Indian trouble. St. George Cooke, after testifying for a week in the trial of Frémont for insubordination, was excused and went back to St. Louis; Company K, 1st Dragoons, which he had commanded, had had its paperwork completely fouled up and Major Cooke, anxious to join the 2nd, wanted to clean up the mess.

After he had the accounts straightened out the War Department held him at Jefferson Barracks, largely because Frémont and Benton were accusing the Administration of spiriting an important witness away. When he finally joined the 2nd in Mexico City, the hour of glory was long over; it was April of '48.

But he did have the new experience of taking command of a regiment; his superiors Colonel Harney and Lieutenant Colonel Fauntleroy – not the same man as the Navy Purser who had commanded the California Dragoons – were both absent, and the major was ranking officer.

The duties were peaceful. Two months later the Army of Occupation moved to the coast; Cooke commanded the brigade of cavalry that rode rearguard to Veracruz.

He was ill again. He applied for and got two months' sick leave. Convalescent, he was appointed head of recruiting for the Cavalry. He was headquartered in Pennsylvania – first Philadelphia and then Carlisle Barracks for four long years.

In 1852 the exile from the West ended. Harney was serving as a general and old Nathan Boone, who had replaced Fauntleroy as lieutenant colonel, unaccountably left his post. Captain May, who had been brevetted three times at three different battles in Mexico, held the command until Cooke could get there.

He took over command at Fort Mason, near the San Saba River, northwest of San Antonio. He got action almost at once; the Lipans and the Caddos started shooting at each other, the Lipans struck down a small wagon train in the course of the feud, and Persifor Smith, acting as Commanding General of the Department of Texas, ordered Cooke out against the Lipans.

The 2nd Dragoons were scattered. At least three companies were in New Mexico, and there were detachments in California, the northern Mississippi Valley, and elsewhere.

Cooke took out two companies of Dragoons and two of the recently mounted companies of the 8th Infantry. The Dragoons had only two rounds of pistol ammunition apiece; the Mounted Infantry had impossibly bad horses, and worse riders.

At Fort Terrett, at the headwaters of the Llano, he received reconnaissance reports that Manuel, the leader of the warpath Lipans, was on the St. James River. He studied the map.

If Manuel – or Emanuel – was where he was supposed to be, an attack would send him retreating along the San Pedro or the Nueces. Apaches never stood up to force; they considered it foolhardy. They weren't cowards, just sensible; since they knew the horse-soldiers would pursue them, they would pull back and snipe, causing great damage to the military personnel, but never giving up a life to hold ground which they considered worthless.

So, Cooke deployed the Dragoons to make a frontal attack and the Mounted Infantry to set up a trap. It was a sort of pincers movement, with the lower jaw of the pincers remaining fixed while the upper jaw ground down.

The Lipans moved back as they were supposed to, the Dragoons pursuing relentlessly, if cautiously, with much picketing. Cooke, who had seen the Mounted Infantry, got extra-cautious; he borrowed reserves from Terrett under Captain James Longstreet and personally led them to back up the Mounted Infantry.

He was too late. The novice riders on their poor horses let the Lipans through while parleying with Manuel for surrender.

Company G, 2nd Dragoons, went in pursuit and engaged a small part of the Indians; the Dragoons took eighteen prisoners and captured a hundred ponies, but it was only a rearguard action; Manuel and the main body of Lipans got away.

Coming up, Cooke burned the abandoned Indian lodges, bawled out the officer who had let the Lipans through, and went back to headquarters at Fort Mason.

Service in Texas was not the happiest way of life for the officer who had turned back the Texas Invincibles. Cooke reported to Harney that attempts had been made on his life in the little town of San Saba, near Fort Mason; Harney transferred him to the part of the regiment serving in New Mexico, about as anti-Texas country as could be found.

Old Boone resigned, and Cooke went back to Leavenworth to be made lieutenant colonel; he took the opportunity to visit his family in St. Louis. When he got back to New Mexico, he found that the Apaches had made life in the Rio Grande Valley unbearable. The Jicarillas were harassing the Rio Arriba, in the north, the Mescaleros and others were out in the Rio Abajo, below. Since the Apaches and Comanches and Utes had already made all New Mexico but the Rio Valley untenable – they had gotten wilder and wilder while the Mexicans and Americans fought each other elsewhere – this almost meant giving up the big territory.

Cooke sent a patrol out against the Jicarilla Apaches, who had just murdered a family of Anglo settlers. The small detachment – thirty men – made contact, fought, and then were pinned down; Cooke had to organize a relief party.

The long New Mexico winter settled in, and hostilities were over till the end of March, when the Jicarillas reappeared, this time accompanied by a good many Ute allies.

All other Indians – except perhaps the Piutes – have always looked down on the Utes, but they knew how to fight. The Apache-Ute party hit the mail coach, under Dragoon escort, not far from Taos and Jailed thirty of the soldiers, half of the party.

Cooke organized a strong party to go after the warriors: a company of 2nd Dragoons, a detachment of 1st Dragoons, some artillerymen working as dismounted riflemen, and a group of Taos Pueblo scouts.

Kit Carson, who was serving as Jicarilla agent, responsible for issuing government rations to them and keeping them off the warpath, went along with the column. They headed into the rough country above Taos, still largely impassable.

Carson should have known better; or perhaps the threat to American domination of the country was so severe that delay would have seen it destroyed. The beginning of April is spring only on the calendar in those altitudes of between eight and thirteen thousand feet. Of course, it was too early for there to be any grass; and when the column wasn't fording icy creeks, it was marching across windswept and waterless mesas. Two days after they started, they did get some forage at a small Spanish town; then they pushed on and two days after that picked up the Indian trail; it led into deep snow fields.

That afternoon the Taos scouts suddenly stumbled into the Jicarilla camp. A fire fight started between the two groups of Indians, and Cooke pressed forward to help his scouts.

The Jicarillas were forted up in a narrow canyon; a good, unfrozen stream ran from them to the Army; they could not be sieged out of there.

Cooke used a dramatic, almost unprecedented tactic. He threw a line of sharpshooters behind the front line of Taos scouts, and ordered both lines prone. Then he ordered the 2nd Dragoon company to charge over the skirmishers' backs, as soon as the sharpshooters could get all the Jicarillas pinned down behind their boulders.

It worked. The troopers rode right through the Apaches, and dismounted on a rise that commanded the hostiles' rear. They had hardly opened fire with their carbines when the Indians broke, rushed to the right and into a charge by dismounted Dragoons and the artillerymen.

The Apaches milled around in confusion, in a bad cross fire; the soldiers who had been kept in the saddle were busy securing the hostiles' ponies. The Apaches took to the hills as night fell.

Cooke at once burned the Jicarillas' winter stores and their lodges. There was little doubt that the Dragoons had broken up the mountain stronghold from which the Jicarillas had forayed out on the Rio Arriba.

But if it was still winter, it was late winter. The Apaches could get through to spring only by raiding the small villages of the Upper Rio. They might even be forced to storm Taos itself for stores. This was not only a war camp that had been hit, but winter quarters for the warriors' wives and children, too; the Jicarillas would be desperate. The next day re-enforcements arrived; Major Carleton and another company of the 1st Dragoons. Cooke pushed the pursuit of the Jicarillas, and finally wore them down; they came off the mountains into Chama Valley and dispersed into small harmless family groups. Cooke rested his horses at Chama, before the march back to Taos and Cantonment Burgwin, near there.

Later in the spring, and farther south, Cooke sent out a detachment to start harrying the Mescalero Apaches, then took the field himself with re-enforcements.

It was late May, about a hundred miles farther south than the Jicarilla campaign, and the altitudes weren't as high, but it snowed on the column, anyway. One trumpeter later told the chronicler of the 2nd Dragoons that he slept under three blankets and eight inches of snow. The column never actually contacted the Apaches, and it lost all its pack mules and most of the troop horses, but Cooke had found out with the Jicarillas that you didn't have to shoot Apaches to beat them; you merely had to prove that you could keep them moving until their women and children began to starve. There were Apache peace overtures in June; then, later in the summer, Utes and both bands of eastern Apaches took the warpath again, and so did Cooke, harrying and harassing steadily.

By the fall – this was still 1854 – he had shown the Army how. Harney ordered him north to quell Sioux trouble, and Cooke left the Dragoons in northern New Mexico with an aggressive policy that put the Mescaleros, Utes and Jicarillas all on reservations in 1855.

But by then Cooke was in the field in Nebraska against the Brulé Sioux; he had four companies of 2nd Dragoons with him. This was open prairie; the harassment method wouldn't work. Cooke showed the flag all summer, without serious incident; the sight of the four company patrol would have been enough to make the Sioux cautious. Then the Army picked up information that the Cheyennes were allying themselves with the hostile Sioux, and big trouble could be expected soon. In late August Harney joined Cooke with six companies of infantry, some of them mounted, and a company of artillery.

They located the Sioux and planned an encircling movement. Cooke left his tents standing and made a night march around the Sioux encampment; at dawn Harney would attack and force the Brulés into Cooke's ambush. Cooke led two companies of Dragoons; the artillerymen, acting as riflemen; and a company of mounted infantry.

The tactic nearly worked; but, as in Texas, the mounted infantrymen stumbled, and the Sioux got through them. Nevertheless, eighty-six hostile braves were killed, and the Army captured a number of squaws and horses. Harney had the troops build a small fort near the site of the battle as a reminder that the white man was on the Plains to stay. The fort was garrisoned with infantry; the five horse regiments had to keep moving, out of Leavenworth at first, then out of Fort Riley, which in time was to become the big cavalry school of the nation. It was built where two rivers met in Kansas, and Cooke moved his headquarters there.

Before he left Leavenworth, the 1st Cavalry moved in. With them was a first lieutenant named J.E.B. Stuart. Before the 2nd Dragoons moved to Riley, young Stuart and Cooke's daughter Flora had a chance to meet and get engaged. They were married at Riley in the fall.

Cooke's son John R. Cooke was also in the Army now, though as an infantry officer. And the Civil War was coming on. It affected St. George Cooke personally in 1856; the 2nd Dragoons were ordered out to keep the peace in the election that was to put the adjective "Bleeding" before the name of Kansas for years. Briefly, the dispute was whether Kansas would come into the Union as slave or free. The balance of Congress depended on it; the old Mason-Dixon line, extended, passed almost through the north border of the Territory.

Missouri was slave, and Missouri borders Kansas on the east. The other three borders were Territorial; this resulted in different tactics being used by the Southern and Northern strategists. The Abolitionists raised big sums of money to move New England and other Free State families into Kansas; the pro-slavery forces armed Missouri riffraff to show up in Kansas on election day and vote, then to return to Missouri.

It must be remembered that Jefferson Davis was Secretary of War. When the Kansas state legislature was moved near Riley – with the expulsion of its pro-slavery members as part of the move – Davis declared that the new capital was on the military reservation, and ordered Cooke to tear the town down. The Dragoons carried out the order; it probably never occurred to Davis that Cooke might not; the colonel was a soldier, and he was a Virginian.

Sumner at Leavenworth was a soldier, too, but he was a Bostonian. Nevertheless, Davis ordered both colonels to obey the orders of the Territorial Governor and to use their regiments in cases of anti-slavery insurrection. He added that they were to avoid bloodshed, if possible.

In the spring of '56, a gang of Missourians crossed into Kansas and assaulted the town of Lawrence. John Brown, the half-crazed Abolitionist with the numerous sons, took four of his boys and retaliated by killing five pro-slavery men in cold blood.

The Territorial Governor – pro-South – called out Sumner and his 1st Cavalry. Sumner did what he could, but with no recognized courts, there wasn't much use arresting anyone; and there were more professional criminals and hoodlums in the Territory than there were soldiers. He lined the 1st Cavalry up along the Missouri border to try and stop the horde of gangsters hired by the pro-slavery people and the gun-runners hired by the Abolitionists from coming into Kansas and making the situation worse.

This left the law-and-order patrol up to Cooke and the 2nd Dragoons. The governor appointed by President Buchanan had set up his capital at Lecompton; he called for help. Cooke galloped down there with a hundred and thirty-four troopers and a field gun.

The governor may have been trying to be impartial; most of the outlaws around Lecompton were pro-slave Missourians. But when Cooke got there the Territorial Secretary was in charge, and he was biased; he told Cooke there was no trouble and held him in check. That afternoon the governor, Shannon, returned, and conferred with the colonel.

Cooke told him what Sumner had already learned; that without speedy and fair trials, arrests were useless. This apparently didn't please Shannon; Cooke took his troops back to Fort Riley.

Two months later he received direct, Army orders, to go back to Lecompton; this time the threat was being made by James H. Lane's Jayhawkers, who were the striking arm of the Abolitionists.

Woodson, the Territorial Secretary, was acting as governor; Shannon had quit. Woodson ordered Cooke to surround Lane and his men and hold them under the muzzles till a marshal could arrest the leader. Cooke remarked that if you point a gun, you might have to fire it, and these were American citizens.

But his orders to place his troops at Woodson's disposal were clear. He cordoned off the Jayhawkers. Then it was found that the U.S. Marshall did not have a deputy brave enough to face Lane. The trouble subsided.

Woodson's next order was flatly refused by Cooke; a Virginian of the leanings of his son-in-law Stuart might have found it reasonable. It was to march on Topeka, a Free State stronghold, and disarm the inhabitants. Apparently, the Missourian border hounds would do the rest. The Department of the West – Persifor Smith of Pennsylvania – backed Cooke up, and Topeka continued to be armed against the hordes that threatened it.

There was uneasy peace for a month. Then Cooke had to take his men out against Free Staters – an armed, organized body of them, outnumbering the squadron that Cooke had with him by two-to-one. They were marching on Lecompton, determined to free a number of Abolitionist prisoners that Woodson was holding without trial.

The Dragoon who had talked Snively into turning back to Texas called on his eloquence again. He promised that the acting-governor had promised that if the Free State army dispersed, the prisoners would be released on the next day.

In Cooke's own words: "there was one flag yet." The trouble broke up. But when the threatening guns were gone, Woodson tried to hedge the promise which had been backed by Cooke's promise. Cooke had held his rather famous temper long enough. He sent a full platoon of armed troopers to call on the governor. The prisoners were released.

President Buchanan sent a new governor out, John Geary, and Woodson was no longer in command. Geary seems to have been sincere in his efforts to be impartial; he turned the 2nd Dragoons out to garrison Lawrence, always an anti-slavery town.

Cooke found the three hundred men of Lawrence in a state of siege; they had armed their homes as well as they could against the threat of two thousand more or less organized Border Ruffians marching on them.

Cooke re-enforced them with seven companies of Dragoons and a battery of field artillery. He himself was determined to arrest Lane if the Free State leader showed up; Cooke had decided that the Jayhawk leader was the focus of most of the trouble.

But Lane, if he was in Lawrence, stayed out from under the eyes of the tall Dragoon. Governor Geary and Cooke rode out on the road to Franklin, from which the Missourians were marching. The colonel estimated there were twenty-five hundred of the insurgents, complete with artillery. Governor Geary made a speech; then Cooke made one. The old tongue didn't fail; as he modestly reported to Jefferson Davis, Americans had been educated to respect national authority.

That was the last attempt of the pro-slavery forces to win Kansas by arms; Cooke sent out patrols to break up the Jayhawkers. He was reasonably successful, making several large confiscations of arms.

Cold weather ended the trouble; the Dragoons went back to Riley, the 1st Cavalry left two companies with the governor and went back to Leavenworth and winter quarters.

Cooke had been in frightful health all during the Bleeding Kansas campaign. A trooper reporting to the 2nd Dragoon headquarters after duty with the companies in New Mexico said that the colonel had always been thin, but not as slight as he now appeared.

It was during that winter in quarters that Cooke wrote a letter that summed up the weakness in his professional beliefs which has astounded all the students of Cavalry since.

The letter – an official one, sent through channels all the way up to General-in-Chief Winfield Scott – stated that the armament of the 2nd Dragoons was terrible, which it was; of the six companies at Riley three had an outmoded brand of carbine, two had what Cooke called "an incompatible" supply of Sharps carbines, and the third had the old musketoon. In battle, and even before battle, these arms would get mixed up, so that one trooper couldn't use another's ammunition.

Fair enough. But Cooke went on to say that Dragoons didn't need shoulder arms at all; they now had Colt's six-shooters, and that was enough.

"I favor sharp sabers," the colonel went on, pointing out that he had probably had as much wilderness and Indian fighting as any officer in the Army. He probably had; this commission would be thirty years old in the spring. He went on to say that he had only seen companies of Dragoons fight on foot once, and that that was when a mounted charge had already dispersed the enemy. He said that this was in the Rocky Mountains, so the enemy was presumably Indian; Cooke never had to fire on the Mexican Army.

There was a lot of right on Cooke's side. The repeating rifle was not yet a fact, and the metallic cartridge was still giving trouble. Indians didn't carry bayonets and their lance work was no threat against six-shooters.

Amazingly, Scott, who had seen the Mounted Rifles on foot in Mexico, who had used dismounted horse soldiers to secure the capital of that country, listened, and told Cooke to turn in his carbines.

But history, remote from Fort Riley, did not listen. Before the start of the Civil War, four years later, repeating rifles – made for sport, but widely used in that war – were a fact and a dependable metallic cartridge was a fact.

St. George Cooke, having enrolled at West Point when he was a child, was still only middle-aged – forty-seven – when he wrote the letter. But thirty years is a long time, and when that thirty years has been accomplished on a constantly more elevated level, a man is inclined to think that the methods that made him a success are the methods that should be followed till eternity. If Cooke had thought more progressively, if Scott had not listened to Cooke, the Civil War would have been different.

There was still campaigning left for the beau sabreur. In the summer of 1857 Cooke and Sumner had all their troops out in the field, showing the Indians and the two parties on Kansas that crime would not pay.

Fort Riley was not deserted, however; the officers' families, the wives and laundresses of Suds Row, and about twenty-five infantry-men were still there when rumors came in that the southern Cheyennes were mounting a massive raid on the post. Cooke was near Lawrence again when he got the word. He struck camp and was on the road in an hour with what he called "a hundred sabers," meaning that all members of his column were Dragoons. Then he force-marched to Fort Riley – ninety-eight miles in less than twenty-eight hours!

This is undoubtedly a record, not for miles per hour – less than four – but for continuous marching in heat and over country where there was frequently no road.

The Cheyennes didn't appear. The Dragoons rested for a month, and then went on another "expedition," to Utah. The so-called Mormon war was about to start, and St. George was called on to command the Cavalry against his former troops. Whether James Buchanan and Jefferson Davis really believed that the Mormons in Utah were in a state of insurrection is difficult to determine. The President may have felt that giving the North and the South a common enemy would prevent war between the two regions; and maybe Jefferson Davis felt that sending the U.S. Army West would be a help if there was a war; and maybe one or both of them believed the hysterical anti-Mormon charges that Brigham Young was about to undermine the United States government.

Young was not only president of the Church and spiritual leader of the Latter-Day Saints; he was also Territorial Governor of Utah. The appointment of the governors of the various Territories was, of course, the privilege of the President and one of his most valuable political tools; the jobs went to big contributors to the campaign funds, to party hacks who needed to be raised in the public eye, and so on.

Buchanan appointed a new governor, secretary, and judges to Utah Territory. Brigham Young warned him that these gentiles would not be able to keep order.

How many Mormons had settled in Utah will never be satisfactorily answered. The census listed eleven thousand for 1850, forty thousand for 1860. The size and wildness of the country, the lack of cooperation between the Mormon administration and that of the United States government make it certain that not everybody was counted. The Territorial government itself – Brigham Young in 1850 – claimed many more inhabitants than the Census Bureau allowed, and said Utah had enough people to be admitted as a state. If nobody knew how many Mormons there were in Utah, the number of non-Mormons was even more of a mystery.

The trouble the Mormons had had in Illinois and Missouri and elsewhere was not caused by the fact that the Saints believed in polygamy. They had been run out of places long before the announcement or even the suspicion of that fact got abroad. It was because the Church of Latter-Day Saints was such a tight, all-embracing organization. A community that had a majority of Mormons would not tolerate gentiles holding political office; Mormons would not deal with non-Mormon stores; a public school system would not receive Mormon support. Mormons tithed to the Church and felt their tax obligations were ended; the Church would supply police, schools, municipal and state government. This was intolerable to the United States. When Buchanan sent out Territorial and Federal judges, the Mormons not only failed to honor them, they went into court and insulted the dignitaries.

Not all the wrong was on the Saints' side. Some of the judges were peculiar choices, to say the least. One of them was a professional gambler who lived in concubinage (in the phrase of the day) and announced publicly he had only come to Utah to make money.

Secretary of War Davis ordered Colonel Harney, commander of the 2nd Dragoons, to take all the troops he could spare from the Jayhawker trouble into Utah and put down the "insurrection."

Harney was busy; he sent two regiments of infantry off before he could start himself, and then had to report to Leavenworth to replace the commander of the Department, Persifor Smith. Albert Sidney Johnston, colonel of the 2nd Cavalry took command of the expedition, acting as general; Colonel Edmund B. Alexander of the 10th Infantry commanded the troops under Johnston. The 2nd Dragoons were also ordered to Utah, but Cooke was busy in Kansas, and the rest of the 2nd was held up to bodyguard the new Governor of Utah.

Johnston was late arriving, too; he had been on duty in Washington. When he got to Leavenworth and found Alexander had already started, he followed him with what troops he could muster; he would have preferred to wait for the Dragoons – every commander in the expedition was a cavalryman except Alexander – but he could not leave the infantry to go it alone.

Alexander had taken off from Leavenworth on July 18. The last of his troops were under way two months later, on September 17, and Cooke complained that that was too soon; he had hardly any time at all to outfit for a winter march over the Rockies. This was as late as the foray against the Jicarillas had been early, through the same sort of country, and farther north. Fifty troopers deserted.

The first week was terrible; forage was practically non-existent, the wagon mules staggered on the slick mud – it was, of course, raining – and on a single day twenty wagon tongues broke.

Cooke, with one eye on the sky, pushed hard; he managed to make twenty-one miles a day. He commandeered corn off a small wagon train headed for the Mormon country and fed it to his animals. But mules died, and the men ate their rations – largely bacon – half raw; the rain had ruined the few buffalo chips that were the only fuel available. One of the troopers got lockjaw and died and was buried with full military honors. There were ten days in the first month when it didn't rain and the column rejoiced.

But after that first month the snow started. A week later the column made it into Fort Laramie, where Cooke's orders stated that he could winter.

But he didn't. There was news at the fort that made it seem imperative that he get on to Utah. A week after he'd left Leavenworth Alexander's infantry column had gone over the caprock into the Mormon basin; the Nauvoo Legion – Mormon army – had raided the supply train, burned fifty wagons, and run off five hundred head of cattle.

There was really no way for infantry to protect what supplies they had left; it would take Cavalry patrols to fend off the numerous and expert Mormon horse soldiers.

The Dragoons condemned their worst horses, left their sickest men – and eighteen laundresses who had accompanied them this far – rested three days at Fort Laramie and shoved on.

Meanwhile, Johnston had caught up with Alexander and taken charge; the column had moved deeper into the inter-mountain area to a stone fort owned by mountainman Jim Bridger, who was guiding the outfit for a major's pay and perquisites. They went into winter quarters.

131

Cooke's Dragoons were not resting. They were going through snow and once through what Cooke described as "frozen fog." Their horses were starving, though they were herded at night instead of being picketed, and were led every other hour on the march, under blankets. The colonel recorded one night when the mules were so tired they wouldn't graze when herded out, but stood, "crying piteously."

Of a hundred and forty-four horses that started from Fort Laramie, Cooke noted, he lost all but ten before he reached Fort Bridger; he also lost a great many sabers, which the men had to pile into a wagon and abandon.

The Dragoons – though dismounted – were still Dragoons; Johnston assigned them the task of guarding the animal herd: wagon horses, oxen, mules.

Cooke's temper was going. He told Johnston that he wanted the infantrymen to relieve his troopers on the herd guard duty; after all, the snow was too deep for horse patrols, even if there had been troop horses available.

Johnston ordered Alexander to give Cooke a little help; Cooke didn't think it was enough and got a dispatch off to Harney. Harney told him that Johnston was in command, and not to go over Johnston's head again.

The troops in winter quarters didn't have it so bad; there seems to have been more whiskey available than at almost any other time in the history of the Regulars. Cooke got hold of some of it, and offered it as prizes in a target practice, he seems to have been determined that his Dragoons, at least, would not come out of the snow completely demoralized.

The Mormon war fizzled out when the snow melted. Brigham Young and Governor Alfred Gumming came to a peace settlement that seemed to save everyone's face, including Colonel Johnston's; Young had specified that the military would have no hand in the settling of the dispute, but Johnston held out for a triumphal march through Salt Lake City and got it.

Horses were apparently procured for the Dragoons, because on June 15 they *rode* out of Fort Bridger on a reconnaissance, with the owner of the fort along as guide. Where the horses came from is not recorded, but possibly they were from the Mormons as part of the peace settlement.

The day before, Cooke had been made a full colonel with command of the 2nd Dragoons. It was thirty-five years, minus a month, since he had entered West Point. He was forty-nine years and one day old when the new commission reached him.

With the Dragoons leading, the whole Army of Utah marched from Fort Bridger to Salt Lake City; Cooke got enough ahead of the column to halt for a day and hold a regimental drill.

On the June 26 Albert Sidney Johnston led his men into Salt Lake City for the triumphal march that meant so much to him.

The march was made without an audience. The Mormon capital had been abandoned; the Saints were saving their faces in their own way. One account says that Colonel Cooke – whose Dragoons brought up the rear of the parade – rode all the way bareheaded in honor of his old Mormon Battalion, but his trumpeter, Drown, didn't mention it.

Cooke's mood was apparently vile. He noted that, after leaving Salt Lake City, Johnston marched the column on, apparently looking for "the most complete desert to be found" before camping.

On July 4, Colonel Cooke, annoyed at the racket, arrested a whole tentful of officers – many of them not Dragoons – for celebrating Independence Day. A month after that he applied for sixty days leave, with the option of asking for another nine months.

The leave was approved, and he went east to Washington, and then to New York to see Winfield Scott, still the General-in-Chief of the Army.

Scott and Cooke talked Army: What else? The old gentleman gave his consent for Cooke to translate the Cavalry tactics handbook then current in France, and to bring up to date the system of cavalry management that Phil Kearny had brought back from Europe before the Mexican War. Before his leave was over Cooke had started on the book.

He was to remain in the Army until 1873 and to live until 1895, but the days of his glory ended when he brought the Dragoons into Fort Bridger. He'd never asked anything of fate but a chance to lead his Dragoons; now fate seemed determined to make a buffoon of him.

He went to Europe to observe a war in Spain that ended before he could get there. He wrote a book of tactics for the Cavalry that was based on the assumption that the United States would never have a horse soldier force larger than a brigade, just before the Civil War was to bring tens of thousands of cavalry out on the field. The same book was based on the movement in battle of close-packed ranks of horsemen; this became suicidal as soon as repeating weapons were available, and was, indeed, foolhardy when written, for rifled artillery was already in use.

He fought in only one battle in the Civil War, and then had the humiliating experience of riding after his own son-in-law and failing to catch him. This was not Cooke's fault, but he spent the rest of his war on various boards or in recruiting duty.

After the war he was sent West again as a Department Commander, a general but a desk officer. Then he went back on recruiting duty and served out the time till his sixty-fourth birthday.

It doesn't seem fair; for thirty odd years he was as good an officer as the Army had. Worst of all, three of his four children deserted him and the United States for the Confederacy. His daughter Flora was Mrs. J.E.B. Stuart; his son John became a Confederate brigadier; his daughter Maria

133

was married to Dr. Charles Brewer, who became Surgeon General of the Confederacy. Only his daughter Julia married a Union soldier, Jacob Sharpe of New York, who rose to be Brigadier General of Volunteers, U.S.A.

Cooke himself, of course, stayed with the Union. His reasons make a good ending to his story, except for the necessary brief mention of him later in the Battle of the Peninsula: "At fourteen years of age I was severed from Virginia; the National government adopted me ... gave me an education and a profession ... I owe Virginia little, my country much."

In the West there has long been a standard description of a good man: He minds his business and he pays his bills.

It will do for St. George Cooke.

Chapter 12

The Rising Son-in-Law

Of the cavalry situation in the Union Army at the beginning of the Civil War, it can only be said that it was non-existent. After the fiasco of the first battle, called Bull Run, George B. McClellan was given the command of the Army of the Potomac, to protect Washington.

McClellan had been a Dragoon; as a captain he had been sent to Europe in the mid-'50s, just as Phil Kearny had been ten years before, to learn what he could about the management of horse troops.

He had brought back the McClellan saddle, a lightweight Hungarian tree, covered with leather or rawhide, with hooks, loops, and slots on it to which could be attached everything a cavalryman could need. It was a good saddle in that it weighed very little, allowed for circulation of air under the rider and over the horse blanket, and did not chafe the horse's back if properly blanketed. The officer's version, called the Military saddle, was padded, and had skirts to keep the rider's legs free from sweat; the enlisted man's didn't.

But a new saddle – and the issues covered with rawhide soon split and tortured their troopers – was not the answer to an Army that had five regiments of cavalry, numbering less than three thousand effectives at most times, and needed tens of thousands of men.

George McClellan had been a horse soldier, but he had quit, and risen to be the president of a large railroad. In that position of power, he had hired another ex-officer, Ambrose Burnside, who had also quit the Dragoons, but had failed in business. He brought Burnside back into the Army with him. To the five regiments of Cavalry – the names Dragoon and Mounted Rifle now died forever – the Army added a 6th Cavalry. To these were added regiment upon regiment of state troops, Militia and Volunteer, bringing their own horses or calling on the United States to supply them.

The old illusion about Americans – that they can all ride a horse, aim a gun and play poker – was back in force. Many of the new state troops could – literally – not mount a horse successfully. Others could get on but fell off again if the horse went any place.

And some were crack riders but had devoted all their regimental time to fancy parade drill, with marksmanship completely neglected. Of course, there were three or four of the Sunday soldier outfits who were as good, perhaps better, than anything the Regular Army had. But the reason they were good was that each trooper was an educated, literate, usually successful man; these did not remain privates, but were drained off to officer in other regiments.

The armament of the trooper was frightful. Though Cooke had recommended, and Scott had endorsed, the revolver, the side arm of issue was a horse pistol, about a foot long, muzzle-loaded and single fire. Its recoil would knock a careless trooper out of the saddle.

The six-shooter available at the start of the war in 1861 was muzzle-loaded, too. The barrel acted as a loading tube, and the chamber was revolved behind it until all six shots were ready. Then the chamber could be taken out, another put in, and a second set of six prepared. In this way a soldier with an extra chamber in his possession could fire twelve times in the space of time needed to load a horse pistol once. The issue carbine of the time jammed more often than not.

The saber was still a heavy European model, exhausting to wield and annoying to ride with. The cavalry troopers soon learned to strap it under their legs, and to leave it on the saddle when they dismounted to fight.

Cooke had recommended a new, light saber that could be locked on the carbine as a bayonet. Few were available. McClellan had been a cavalryman and given it up. Light-Horse Harry Lee's son had been a cavalryman and risen to being a full colonel of a regiment. And he had Cooke's son-in-law, J.E.B. Stuart. He used him.

The obvious advantage to the South lay in the fact that it was still farming and planting country; people got around on horses. The North was more highly industrialized than it knew; while the politicians still talked about the sacred American farmer, they were, in the North, more often than not talking to the farmer's son, who worked in a factory and got around in streetcars and on trains. When the South sent a volunteer cavalry outfit to the front, it sent a group of experienced horsemen.

The less obvious advantage was that the Cavalry officers – Dragoon is heard for the last time – were so predominantly Southern that the five regiments of Regulars were stripped. Sumner stayed with the Union, of course, but was at once made a general, and spent his war more concerned with massed infantry than with rapid movements of horse soldiers.

George Stoneman, who at twenty-three had been Cooke's aide in the Mormon Battalion, was made McClellan's cavalry commander. He insisted on having Cooke in his command; St. George Cooke, now a brigadier general, was suspect because of his Virginian background, the desertion of his family to the Southern cause, and, possibly, the impatient and irascible disposition bestowed on his ailing body by the terrible Mormon expedition.

Irvin McDowell took the field first, not McClellan. Brigadier General McDowell had just been promoted from major. He was operating under the orders of General-in-Chief Scott, now seventy-five years old, but neither senile nor stupid.

Scott saw the war as a simple problem of logistics. He wanted to put a naval blockade along the Atlantic coast of the South and a gunboat blockade along the Mississippi River; then he would mass his troops and move slowly south, fighting a starving Confederacy as he went. The South had a fourth as many white men as the North, and the Southern Negroes could be counted on not to work their masters' fields very diligently if the slaveowners and white overseers were away at battle.

There was nothing dashing about this plan; the newspapers ridiculed it. They wanted copy, and a blockade was not dramatic.

Another force entered in; under the law, the Militia were only enlisted for three months. If they were not used in that time they would go home, and the painful training of citizens would have to start all over again. Scott told McDowell to go ahead; the three months were almost up.

Bull Run was about twenty miles south of Washington. General P.G.T. Beauregard had about twenty thousand troops there, near a town called Manassas. (This was the Southern name for the battle; the Confederacy named battles after the nearest town; the Union, in general, but not always, after the nearest body of water. Likewise, the Southern Army of Northern Virginia opposed the Northern Army of the Potomac.)

McDowell had thirty-five thousand troops; he had another eighteen thousand to the west, in the Shenandoah Valley, pinning down a Confederate force under General Joseph E. Johnston, who had been a lieutenant colonel under Cooke on the Mormon expedition of a few years before.

Beauregard was badly outnumbered; but he had J.E.B. Stuart, then a colonel. The young officer moved his cavalry beautifully; they formed a screen through which Northern pickets could not reconnoitre, and Beauregard had his men set and ready while McDowell and his Militia were straggling down the road from Washington. By the time he was in a position to try and flank the Southern forces, they had moved away and out.

The opposing forces stumbled into each other rather than charged. Thomas Jonathan Jackson, an instructor at Virginia Military Institute, commanded a brigade and used it as a rallying point for the Confederate units with such effect that he was nicknamed Stonewall from that day on. The Union Militia and Volunteers very largely dissolved at the sight and feel and sound of fire; McDowell, like all Regulars of the day, had never commanded more than a few hundred men and tried to use the tactics that were fine for small units; he rode around the battle line, sending platoons and squads and occasionally a company forward, and lost the effect of mass that his superior numbers gave him.

The North was thrown back and the battle ended inconclusively, with Southern cavalry playing the traditional role of harassing the fleeing troops. McDowell was relieved, and McClellan given the command. Bull Run was not big nor important; but it proved a few things. The best thing it did for the North was to indicate which regiments were good and which needed more training; and as a result Lincoln, against the law, asked, the next day, for a half million men to enlist for three *years* or the duration of the war. Congress promptly amended the law to make the call-up legal, and the North was on its way to having a real Army.

For the South, the victory, of course, was heartening, but the South didn't need heartening; the old cavalier spirit rode high there, and any Southerner could lick twenty Yankee peddlers and ribbon clerks. But the South, at once, realized that its cavalry was an important arm, and J.E.B. Stuart an important man. Cavalry wouldn't win the war; but it would back up and speed up infantry attacks.

The North was not to find this out until Phil Sheridan came east in 1864. For the time being the Army of the Potomac treated cavalry as part of the infantry; there was no Cavalry Division or Corps, and the single Cavalry regiment assigned to each division was split up into little detachments to scout for infantry brigades, to gallop with messages, to guard wagon trains.

But Jefferson Davis – one-time junior officer of Dragoons – at once ordered his cavalry of Northern Virginia to be formed into a division; later it was raised to a corps. James Ewell Brown Stuart was promoted to brigadier general; he was twenty-eight years old.

McClellan took over the Army of the Potomac. Old General Winfield Scott retired and Lincoln offered McClellan the job of General-in-Chief. Little Mac took it, but kept the Army of the Potomac, too; really more work than one man could handle. He set about training his new, massive, Army. Response to Lincoln's call for Volunteers had been generously met; now there were five hundred and sixty regiments of Infantry, almost ninety of Cavalry, and ample field artillery. The Regular Army, however, was still less than twenty thousand men. Lieutenants and captains, U.S. Army, were serving as colonels and even generals of Volunteers.

A Congressional Committee on the Conduct of the War held an investigation and decided that no man who had not been an abolitionist before the start of the war should be given command. At once this eliminated all the Regular officers – who were expected to be impartial and apolitical.

While McClellan trained his new Army, the war went on in the West. Albert Sidney Johnston, former Union cavalry colonel, was the general in command of the Southern forces there. A West Pointer who had quit the Army and then come back at the start of the war – specifying that he not be given a command larger than a regiment – was beginning to look like quite a general on the Union side. His name on the Army records was U.S. Grant; he had been born with the first name of Hiram.

The War in the West was not really western at all, in the terms of where the Cavalry had been. This was the West of the Cumberland, Tennessee, and Mississippi rivers.

Like the war in the Northern Theater of the Revolution, this was largely a matter of waterways. The Navy had a Flag Officer and a full captain there; gunboats did much of the artillery work, flatboats moved lots of troops.

In the summer fighting started up again for the Army of the Potomac, General George B. McClellan commanding, General George Stoneman cavalry chief. This would be the Peninsular Campaign, General Joseph E. Johnston commanding the Confederates. McDowell was still in the field, holding an army off to one side; J.B. Johnston headed the Confederate forces, J.E.B. Stuart commanding the cavalry brigade.

Cooke was in charge and command of the so-called Cavalry Reserve behind McClellan's army; he was under the direct command of Fitz-John Porter. Porter, in turn, was under John Pope; an attenuated line of command that seemed to get weaker as it got higher.

Stuart patrolled and patrolled before the fighting started; he was as superb as Harry Lee had been at keeping his general supplied with information and at the same time harassing the enemy logistics. McClellan, never very decisive, was a long time getting into position again at Manassas, where he wanted to fight. When he was all lined up there, Joe Johnston at once fell back nearer Richmond, where *he* wanted to fight.

As the campaign opened, Cooke had had a large imposing force in his Cavalry Reserve; but Union policy being against massive cavalry strikes, he lost his men by platoons, companies and squadrons, until there were barely five hundred left "under his hand," as the Mexicans would put it; the rest of the men he theoretically commanded were guarding wagon trains, running errands, picketing as videttes or riding escort for infantry generals, and even colonels.

The Virginians call the country between the James and the York rivers the Peninsula; it is really a Mesopotamia, but no matter. It was the direct route to Richmond, and McClellan – and Lincoln – wanted Richmond, where the only Southern ordnance factory lay. They wanted it even more for morale purposes; if the Confederate capital fell, Northern support of the war would become more nearly unanimous.

The United States Navy swept the two rivers; the *Merrimac,* renamed the CSS *Virginia,* had too deep a draft to leave the sea, and the Southern sailors scuttled her.

McClellan had a good chance at Richmond; his column could be supplied by water from the rear. J.B. Johnston fell back behind Yorktown, which he could not defend against naval fire.

Stuart covered Johnston's withdrawal; it really was not a retreat. The Virginia cavalier didn't have it all his own way. Union cavalry – the 5th Regulars were involved – broke up Colonel Wickham's 4th Virginia Cavalry; then Colonel William H. Emory and a regiment of Pennsylvania horse soldiers got behind Stuart and made the position of his brigade dangerous. This was the Emory who had been major of 1st Cavalry out West when Stuart was a lieutenant in that outfit.

Stuart slipped down to the beach and got away. This was on May 4, 1862. On May 9 Stuart wrote to his wife. Since he was the most important cavalryman of the early part of the war – as Phil Sheridan of the Union was the most important in the second half – the letter is worth reproducing.

So much has been written about Stuart – call him Jeb, though he never signed himself that way – that he seems unreal. A man who rode into battle wearing an ostrich plume, sided by his personal banjo player; a man who never took a drink; a man who searched his soul before switching from being a Methodist to being an Episcopalian, and then made the switch only because he was on a Western post where the only service was Episcopal; a man who had his wife constantly searching for tailor-made cloaks and special hats while the war raged through Virginia; he sounds like the invention of some screenwriter frustrated because the movie camera wasn't invented yet.

Then you read his letters, and it's all there: the love of fighting, the piety, the vanity; in the cavalry word, the *dash*:

Hd. Qu's in the Saddle
May 9th, 1862

My Darling Wife-
Blessed be God that giveth *us* the victory. The battle of Wmsburg* was fought and won on the 5th. A glorious affair, brilliantly achieved by the rear portion (Longstreet's) of our army. On the 4th my Brigade distinguished itself, and on the 5th by its attitude and maneuvering under constant fire prevented the enemy's leaving the woods for the open ground – thus narrowing his artillery scope of fire. I consider the most brilliant feat of the 5th to have been a dash of the *Stuart* Horse Artillery to the front. Coming suddenly under a galling fire from the woods, from a reinforcement of the enemy, they wheeled

into action sustaining in the most brilliant manner the fortunes of the day till the Inf'y could come to their support, and all the time under a continuous Inf'y fire of 200 yards or less distance. For *myself* I have only to say that if you had seen your husband you would have been proud of him. I was not out of fire the whole day. The day before (4th) the Cavalry made several charges – and Lawrence Williams told the bearer of a flag of truce that I came within an ace of capturing my father-in-law. Our Cavalry charged their Cavalry handsomely and, even they were entirely routed – their artillery captured, the Cav flag of the enemy was captured – but the 4th Va Cavalry lost its standard bearer and flag. Col Wickham was wounded on the 4th and Major Paine, severly wounded on the 5th. Robertson is sick in Richmond. The Floyd County Militia in Pelham's battery behaved in the most handsome style astounding every one beyond measure – I only got them as I passed through Richmond. The 3rd Va Cavalry (Col Goode) is now in my Brigade and made a handsome charge. We were without rations & therefore had to withdraw that night from the field, leaving our wounded with the ladies at Wmsburg – the enemy was driven from the field entirely

God bless you—

Yours,
J.E.B. Stuart.

* *Williamsburg.*

The italics are Stuart's: *us, I, Stuart, myself.* Brilliant or brilliantly is used three times as is handsome or handsomely. There is a preoccupation with flags, but that was common in those days.

The rest of the month petered out as McClellan crept toward Richmond, not able to bring himself to attack. The South, of course, could win by doing nothing; the only demand of the Confederacy had been to be allowed to separate itself from the Union.

McClellan had three corps so close to Richmond that the campfires could be seen in the city. J.B. Johnston suddenly lashed out at a division of one of them, Casey's, in the front line. Longstreet led the Confederates in the fight which threw the Union back two miles, killed a third of the Southern men involved, and salvaged sixty-four hundred of the valued Union rifles and ten fieldpieces. The cavalry were not involved in this; Stuart was at Johnston's headquarters, writing some more of his letters.

The battle was inconclusive; both sides could be said to have won; but Joe Johnston was wounded, and Robert E. Lee, military adviser to President Jefferson Davis, came out to take command.

141

Lee had new ideas about defending Richmond; mainly they involved digging trenches and keeping Stonewall Jackson west in the Shenandoah to neutralize the three small armies there: Banks', Shields', and that commanded by John C. Frémont, again trying for glory.

Jackson had a reputation. He not only tied down the three generals assigned to him, he frightened Washington, and Lincoln's War Department ordered McDowell to stay between the capital and Stonewall, instead of marching on Richmond. McClellan postponed trying to take the Confederate capital until McDowell re-enforced him.

Lee sent for Stuart. He needed information. He wanted to bring Jackson down the valley to come up behind McClellan's, specifically Fitz-John Porter's, rear. To do this he had to know just how Porter had his forces disposed. Stuart would please take out a patrol in force and gain this intelligence; while out, he would also destroy the enemy's wagon trains. But he was to return promptly and not hazard his command unnecessarily. In other words, fry the egg but don't crack the shell.

Lee never bothered to be specific with Jeb Stuart again. He just told him what he wanted where, and let the cavalier go do it.

Stuart drew a selected force of twelve hundred officers and men from his brigade and added two field guns. He always treated artillery – the *Stuart Horse Artillery* – as a natural accompaniment to cavalry, though field guns would seem to be an unnecessary impediment to a reconnaissance.

Immediately under Brigadier General Stuart rode two colonels – W.H.F. Lee, called Rooney, and Fitzhugh Lee, called Fitz. The former was Robert E.'s son, the latter his nephew. Another son, Custis – George Washington Custis – was aide to President Davis. Light-Horse Harry, who had done so much to found the Republic, had left a line of descendants who were doing their best to dissolve it, but they were just as gallant troopers as he had been.

The column moved out, Stuart wrote later, without flags or glitter. It went in column of fours, the standard formation for Dragoon-type fighting; if the troopers had to drop down and fight dismounted, every fourth man grabbed the other three horses in his file and took them to the rear. With the fieldpieces, the column stretched for a half a mile; when the columns of four had to break into twos because of the narrowness of the country lanes, it was a mile from Stuart to his rear pickets.

As they went out of camp Sweeney, Stuart's personal banjo player, and the rest of the general's party sang *Kathleen Mavourneen*. Apparently you had to have a good voice to be in Jeb Stuart's personal detachment, though what Von Borcke's German accent made of the Irish names has been lost to us.

They covered twenty-two miles from early morning to dark and camped cold, without cooking fires. The next day, by middle morning, they were behind Porter's rearguard; then they contacted some of Cooke's cavalry, near Hanover Courthouse.

The blue horse soldiers they ran into were Regulars, about a hundred 5th Cavalrymen. This was Fitz Lee's old regiment; Stuart sent Fitz out to ride on the other side of the Regulars and contain them.

The detachment of the 5th was under a Lieutenant Leib. Seeing himself outnumbered, and flanked, he withdrew slowly and without disorder toward the main body, under Captain Royall. At first, they moved east and Stuart kept contact with them; but when Leib swung south, the Confederates let him go; since their reconnaissance mission was still farther east.

Fitz Lee had gotten himself into a swamp; this was a miserable part of Virginia, dank and humid and overgrown with briery bushes. One straying sergeant of the 5th was taken prisoner. Stuart's patrol was not through with the 5th Cavalry; Leib had sent gallopers to Royall, who brought up another two companies. The Regulars were now two hundred, and probably did not know that the Southerners outnumbered them six to one; it was still early in the war, and it was difficult for any officer of the old cavalry to believe that horse soldiers came in four and five figures.

Rooney Lee and the 9th Virginia Cavalry had the advance guard. They overrode a 5th Cavalry Picket without pausing, fighting as they moved. The Yankee resistance was overcome at one of the numerous creeks – Totopotomoy – that moved sluggishly across the Peninsula, and the way widened out enough for Stuart to throw out flank videttes.

Then the woods closed in on them again, the flankers rode back in to the main body. Royall, who had gotten ahead of the Confederates, attacked with a head-on saber charge.

Captain Latane had the lead in Rooney Lee's 9th Virginia. He ordered his company to countercharge; almost at once he was killed and Royall badly wounded. The troopers on both sides were using pistol and saber indiscriminately; it is reported that many a man cut off his own mount's ear. The Regulars fell back to open country, tried to re-form and were ridden down by sheer numbers; Rooney Lee had as many men in his second squadron as their whole force, and Fitz Lee brought up his regiment to support his cousin's. The Regulars broke, fighting as they went, back to their camp and through it. Several of the Stuart riders dropped off to burn the camp.

Some of the 5th found themselves prisoners after the fight, but most of them got away singly or in little knots. Lieutenant Byrnes, a junior officer in the 5th, reported to his Union superiors that Stuart was being supported by several regiments of infantry, probably because the Southern general had covered the Lee regiments' flanks with dismounted troopers.

That afternoon the three reports – Leib's original one, Royall's just before the skirmish, and Byrnes's post-mortem – reached St. George Cooke.

Cooke had some Regulars, the 1st Cavalry, formerly the 1st Dragoons, and some of the 5th and 6th Cavalry. He sent them out at once, with an outfit of – of all things – Pennsylvania *Lancers.* They proceeded cautiously. Several misguided souls had confirmed young Byrnes about the infantry support that Stuart had with him. Actually, of course, he had none.

It was now ten o'clock at night, in swamp country. This was not Cooke's part of Virginia, and even if it had been, he hadn't been home for years. Stuart had all sorts of local men to guide him; some of them officers or men in his outfit, aided by Volunteers; Cooke was in hostile country, and if any of the locals had volunteered as guides, he would have been a fool to trust them through the swamps. Stuart held up at the former 5th Cavalry camp. Scouts reported back in; he now knew everything he needed to know about Fitz-John Porter's corps.

Cooke may have stayed with the Union and thus incurred his son-in-law's anger, but Stuart did not think the old brigadier was either stupid or cowardly. St. George Cooke would be forming in his rear, the Cavalier was sure. Probably, for all his excellent intelligence work, Stuart did not believe that the Cavalry Reserve had been as drained as it was.

Stuart decided to go ahead. For one thing, it was the unexpected thing to do; though he would have to ride clear around McClellan's force, cutting across lines of supply and observation, the troops ahead would not be expecting him. If he turned back he would be doing the only thing anyone could believe he would and this would play right into Cooke's strength. He moved his men out, happily observing the confidence they had in him, as he led them "apparently, into the very jaws of the enemy." Rooney Lee's regiment came first, the Jeff Davis Legion of Mississippians followed, guarding the fieldpieces. (There were a number of Volunteer Legions in the Southern Army, possibly as tribute to Robert E. Lee's father. But they were not the effective, mixed foot-horse outfits that Harry Lee's Legion had been.)

The resistance they expected did not develop all through the night and the next day. Mostly they encountered weakly guarded supply trains; they took the guards prisoner and upset the wagons that were supposed to supply McClellan's army.

The ground was so soggy and cut by creeks that they were almost a mounted navy. At one point they burned two schooners that had sailed up the Pamunkey.

Then they marched on the Tunstall Station of the York River Railroad. They captured two squads of infantry, cut the telegraph wires, burned the station and a bridge, but not before a Union train thundered through under their muzzles.

The word had gone ahead of them; at White House Plantation, which belonged to Rooney Lee when he was home, a Union quartermaster colonel armed his clerks and drovers and laborers and added them to his six hundred guards.

Stuart bypassed White House. If he had not, Rooney Lee would have had the bitter experience that many Confederates were to have in the next few years: burning his own home to keep the Union from using it as a strongpoint.

They had moved out of Magruder's army at dawn of the 11th; at nine o'clock on the night of June 13 they made their second camp, near a Union hospital. Here they rested for three and a half hours; probably no man got more than an hour's sleep. They had captured plenty of food, and a number of horses; the troopers remounted themselves and put the prisoners on tired troop horses or on U.S. mules.

Of course, Stuart had pickets out to cover his rear. They reported that the Lancers, completely foundered, had camped four miles back.

It was time to move out again. The trumpets probably did not blow to horse; sound would travel four miles to the Pennsylvanians. With plenty of captured livestock, the artillery was double-teamed.

The next problem was crossing the Chickahominy, which was and is called a river, but deserves that name only in floodtime; usually it is a slow moving black water creek. But this was June, late spring, and the water was going to the sea from back-country Virginia; Rooney Lee tried swimming his horse, and demonstrated that it wouldn't do for the cavalry, and was out of the question for the field guns.

Stuart was pinned down. If the Volunteers were camped behind him, the Regulars were not far away, and Regulars could be counted on to have husbanded their horses better than the Lancers. The rear was cut off; and not charm, strategy nor prayers would cause the waters of the Chickahominy to go down. But he only had about thirty miles more to go to safety, so Stuart sent off a non-com galloper to ask Lee to attack the front of McClellan's left wing while the reconnaissance column sneaked by the rear.

Lee must have been startled to learn where his patrol column was. But he and Stuart understood each other. Having sent the message, Stuart prepared to cross the water, certain that his general would cooperate. The column moved a mile downstream and began rebuilding a burnt bridge by tearing down a nearby warehouse.

His men were fresh; hadn't they had a three-and-a-half-hour camp? Those who weren't working on the bridge led the horses over by walking on the first planks while the unburdened animals swam.

Finally, there was enough decking for the guns to get over, and just in time; as Fitz Lee, herding the rearguard, got across, the Lancers arrived on the other bank and began shooting. Fitz Lee took time to burn the bridge, and they were rolling again, away free.

They had to cross the snakelike Chickahominy again, but at a place that was wide enough to give them a shallow ford. There was no further pursuit

Twenty miles from Richmond Stuart halted, told his men to bivouac, and rode on, with a single orderly, to report to Lee.

The mission was not a complete success. Four troopers were missing – lost or captured as stragglers – Captain Latane was dead, and on the second crossing of the Chickahominy an artillery limber had been lost.

The whole ride was about a hundred miles. In that kind of country, it would have been a good distance just to cover in four days of peacetime; fighting and fording it was amazing.

It gave Lee just the information he wanted; he sent at once to Jackson and told Stonewall how and where to move against Porter. It replenished Stuart's supplies and badly dented those of the Union.

And it finished St. George Cooke's career as a combat officer. When the Seven Days' Battle ended – the fight that Lee made based on Stuart's information – the brigadier was taken from the field and used only as a desk officer. At the end of the war he was breveted major general, which may have tickled his always sardonic mind.

There has never been as hashed-over a war as that between the States. There are still arguments as to whether Cooke was indecisive, or even lukewarm about capturing his daughter's husband; one point of view says that he was held back by Porter, who later proved to be no great asset to the Union, and was removed from the Army, not just from combat as Cook was.

Cooke was put in charge of Army Reserve until a post farther from the fighting front could be found for him. The story of cavalry in the United States had ceased to focus on Cooke and found a new hero in his son-in-law, J.E.B. Stuart.

Chapter 13

Stuart Writes a Poem

Lee now knew that Porter's right flank was, in the military phrase, in the air; unfortified, untrenched. To remove McClellan's army as a threat to Richmond, Porter was the man to attack, and his right flank the place to do it. Jackson was up in the northeast, with about twenty thousand men, probably less than more; the records of how many Confederates were in a command at any one time are seldom clear.

If Jackson could move swiftly and secretly, he could damage Porter irreparably from the rear, while Lee's strength – about sixty thousand me – could hit from the front and probably cause McClellan to depart from Richmond.

But moving that many men secretly is a problem.

Lee sent for Stuart. General Jackson had said he could be in position by June 25; Lee had advised him to take another day. The attack would be on the 26th; on the 25th Stuart and half his brigade would be out on Jackson's road, ready to meet him and screen his advance. While Stuart did that, the other half of his brigade would be under the command of Magruder, to protect Richmond in case of emergencies.

About two thousand troopers rode out behind Jeb Stuart and his musical headquarters group. This time they were within their own lines; they clattered across the Chickahominy on a bridge. They rode up to Ashland Station, and found Jackson late; he should have been out of there by morning, but he was just coming in at sundown.

Stuart reported to Stonewall and placed his column at that general's disposal, as ordered by Lee.

He was to screen Jackson's march into position against Porter and otherwise carry out General Jackson's orders.

Screening was an important function of the cavalry in the Civil War. By riding between a moving body of troops and the enemy in as much force as possible, the troopers could engage any patrols in fire fights or charges,

147

and send them back to their generals, if possible, as ignorant as when they went out.

In previous wars this had been done but was not of so great importance. The small bodies of troops engaged in the two wars against England could be judged by the size of the dust clouds they sent up, or even by reading their tracks after they had passed. Screening hadn't been really possible in the Mexican War, because all the troop movements were in Mexico, and a Mexican scout could easily find out how many men had passed by asking the inhabitants. Also, the Mexican Army had, for the most part, fought from fixed positions, and therefore had no choice but to face as many troops as the Americans could throw against them.

But in the Civil War, it was important for a general to know if two thousand or twenty thousand men were moving against him; and scouting was really the only way to determine this (though an occasional observation balloon, inflated with hot air, was used).

The North, already at a disadvantage from the counterintelligence point of view in that it had to fight in enemy territory, increased this disadvantage by not having sufficient cavalry to screen its movements in the early years of the war.

Stuart reported in to Stonewall Jackson, then, and returned to his column's bivouac, taking none of his officers into his confidence about the interview, and never, thereafter, recording anything about it.

Thomas Jonathan Jackson was the exact opposite of a dashing cavalryman. A poor boy, he'd had to educate himself; his appointment to the Military Academy was the biggest break he ever got. He graduated into the artillery, served in the last months of the Mexican War and then, five years after his commission, became Professor of Philosophy and Artillery at VMI, a strange combination for anyone but Jackson.

A strong Presbyterian in the days when that was the gloomiest and sternest of religions, he was a strong soldier of the school that stands firm and holds its bayonets strongly. He could take his men out across a field at a dead walk under the strongest counterfire and make them feel it was necessary; his troops never had the feeling that their general was being frivolous or thoughtless or experimental, adjectives that the rank and file frequently felt were applicable to many of the other military leaders.

How he reconciled his deep religious feelings with the trade of manslaughter was between him and his God; he prayed frequently and long, and on occasion he was still praying when he should have been moving his troops. This seems to have been one of those times.

Stuart and his troopers were in the saddle and moving out at dawn; Jackson did not get under way till after ten. At that latitude, and that time of year, this would have been a difference of five hours.

The cavalry did their job well; they covered the front and left flank of the area through which Jackson was to move, leaving the right to Branch's brigade, which would come in and join Jackson, bringing its own screening cavalry as it moved. Really, it didn't matter if McClellan's scouts found out about that brigade; if the Union leaders thought that that was all the troops moving toward Porter, they would not re-enforce him.

Stuart did his work thoroughly. This was not dashing service, though it would not be unpleasant till the heat of the day mounted. Pickets took the advance down the two main roads Jackson would use, and scouted thoroughly, carbines at the alert for Union outriders. Behind the pickets a line of troopers trotted ready to re-enforce any sort of fight; behind them moved the power of the advance guard under Fitz Lee, who sent detachments up every side road to see that he wasn't leading past an ambush.

Rooney Lee and his regiment followed; then the rest of the column came along, safeguarding the horse artillery.

In the first hour, the sun still slanting over the horizon, they flushed some blue-coated videttes, who got out of their way; shortly thereafter they ran into force, dismounted troopers of the Regular Cavalry, horse-holders to the rear, camping well sighted in, with the distance to trees and other landmarks measured to give the range.

This pretty well halted the advance until Fitz Lee's main body came up; then the Northern troopers ran back to their horses, and fought a delaying action, riding back a ways and firing, and then repeating the tactic; their carbines had better range than the Virginians'.

It went on that way till the Union troopers had backed up to where more of their outfit – they were under the command of General George Stoneman – with a good deal of infantry were guarding Northern engineers. Fitz Lee and his men sniped, dismounted, at the engineers; Rooney Lee gave his cousin a squadron of his men to add to the fire, while he took the rest of his regiment upstream. If he could ford they would have the Blue surrounded.

Before this could happen, the Union men set fire to the bridge and the engineers retired, guarded by the Blue Infantry. Engineers were valuable and scarce. Stoneman's troopers stayed put, using their carbines to try and keep the Stuart men from putting out the fire.

But Stuart brought up his artillery, and the Northern cavalry had to get out of there, moving to the east. Stuart dropped off his staff engineer, some freighters and a few axemen to cut timbers to repair the bridge, and fanned out, a small part of his force giving Stoneman enough pursuit to keep him moving, the rest continuing the screening work to the south, where Jackson was to go.

They were now only a few miles – perhaps three – from Fitz-John Porter's line, which was fine; but Jackson's vanguard, Hood's Texans, didn't get there till after two, which was about nine hours after Lee had expected them.

General Ambrose Powell Hill, CSA, had heard Stuart's fire and thought it was Jackson arriving. A vigorous and fierce leader, he at once attacked. If Jackson had been attacking Porter's rear, everything would have gone well for the South. But Jackson was two or three miles from where he should have been. Porter's entrenched, unbothered force burnt A.P. Hill's infantry to a crisp; Hill's men didn't retreat, they just melted away, according to a Union observer.

At four-thirty, Jackson had still not engaged Porter's weak flank; instead he threw his men into camp; he ordered Stuart to do likewise. Lee had told Stuart to take orders from Jackson; he did, though his amazement was plain to his staff.

Jackson sat at his headquarters bivouac, chin on hand, thinking God only knows what dark and gloomy thoughts.

Darkness ended Hill's battle; his survivors hunted their dead in the dark. Stuart and his column camped where Jackson had told them to, on his left, and the devil only knows what Stuart's thoughts were that night.

But at dawn he was out again, with his men, doing the two things – besides obeying Jackson – that General Lee had told him to do: screening and scouting. They cast over a wide fan of country.

Porter was gone. The events of the afternoon and night that had passed had been too heavy to hide; he knew Jackson was behind him and retired – he had lost less than four hundred men in all this – to previously prepared positions, strongly entrenched.

Surprise was no longer on the South's side. Another Hill, General Daniel Harvey Hill, made the next attack, this time on the Union's right. But Jackson, coming up with A.P. Hill on the other side of him, ordered D.H. to cease firing. General D.H. Hill was already displeased with his superior general; in the day's disordered timetable, Hill's vanguard and that of Jackson had blundered into each other and exchanged some fire, each thinking the other to be from the North. But Hill obeyed.

Jackson seems to have been thoroughly confused. He ordered A.P. Hill and Longstreet to throw their brigades against Porter, and Porter, from his strength, brushed them back negligently.

While D.H. Hill attacked on the right and then was halted, Stuart and his column had gotten into an artillery fight on the left. There were only two guns in the cavalry outfit; when the battery they were firing at was re-enforced by four more – a battery is usually four guns in the Field Artillery – they lost one of theirs, a Napoleon.

Jackson took action at that; after all he was a Professor of Artillery as well as a philosopher. He sent a heavy force, more than forty guns, to back up Stuart's one remaining piece, and a long, long artillery duel ensued. Unhappily, it did not have any effect on anything else that happened that afternoon.

Lee came out from headquarters and talked to Jackson, and the long indecisiveness was over. Jackson sent his men charging at Porter's lines, and this was the Stonewall Jackson that Stuart and the rest of the Army had been missing all day. In no time at all an entire New Jersey regiment had been captured and Porter was in some distress.

St. George Cooke had been kicked out of the line, and was now in charge of Army Reserve, not really a fighting position. But he came out with his troops, which included a good deal of artillery and some cavalry. He was about to prove that the Union had been right when it removed him from the field.

It was going for the South now; Porter's men were tired and Jackson's men were angry from their long restraint. Cooke ordered the artillery to limber up and start retreating, and he ordered his Reserve – they were 5th Cavalry – to charge. Apparently, Cooke couldn't believe the strength of the new fire power.

By now the Reserve had been robbed and robbed again; he had less than two hundred and fifty men. But when the Regulars were told to go, they went: right into Hood's Texans.

Their sabers flashed, but they were nowhere near saber targets. Hood's men fired and literally blew the heads off the men of the 5th; every officer but one was wounded almost at once, the troopers broke, and their stampeding mounts carried the gun-horses along with them.

Porter began a stumbling, unorganized retreat. The sun had gone down; McClellan got two brigades up to help Porter, whose men were almost lost in dense woods.

And Jackson? Having been, for a short time, the great general he had been before and would until his death so often be again, he relapsed into the gloomy professor of philosophy, the brooder on metaphysical affairs. He ordered his troops not to pursue Porter's routed army, but to stay on the plain where the main battle had taken place.

Porter got away across the Chickahominy. He left his wounded and his dead where they had fallen, and he left almost three thousand prisoners, more than three times that many shoulder guns, and a good deal of artillery.

The South had lost almost nine thousand dead and wounded. Nobody had won anything he had wanted to win. McClellan had been much too late with the re-enforcements for Porter; on the other side, Jackson had just been late, too often.

But both sides learned from that battle, the first of the Seven Days'. No one on either side of any importance thought this was going to be a short war; each side had learned respect for the other.

151

Too much, really. Between McClellan's heavy army and Richmond there was only one Southern Division, Magruder's. If McClellan had gone straight ahead, he could undoubtedly have taken the Confederate capital.

But he didn't. Gaines Mills, as the Porter-Jackson battle was called, had made him cautious. No doubt the ease with which the Stuart column had ridden around him helped. He shifted his base and his line away from the York River and Magruder. Magruder didn't find this out till two days later; he was being cautious, too, knowing how outnumbered he was.

Lee had been impressed by the stand the Union had made. He simply didn't believe they had gone away, and sent Stuart all along the York, looking for them, with negative results.

Lee did not find McClellan until an engineer colonel heard the rumble of the supply wagons through a fault in the earth; they had carried a terrific distance, silent in the air, but rumbling in the ground.

This Colonel Douglas sent for General A.P. Hill, who sent for General Lee. The Union Army had pulled out and was heading south for the James River; but Lee had sent Stuart scouting north, toward the York, for McClellan.

Lee spread his troops out, from above the Chickahominy in a vaguely west-to-east line, and below the Chickahominy in a north-south line to contain McClellan and to guard Richmond. East of the main line Stuart circled, to guard the right flank of the Federals and keep them below the creek.

Again, the main Southern dependence was put on Jackson, and again he did not strike, though his cavalry leaders, Imboden and Wade Hampton, had found fords over the Chickahominy for him, and his corps was ready and able to go.

The rest of Lee's forces hammered at McClellan, and when he retreated south on June 30, Lee thought the hammering had worked and that McClelkn was through; but he was only withdrawing to a previously prepared position at Harrison's Landing.

Meanwhile, out patrolling, Stuart had had running fights with George Stoneman and William Emory, late of the 1st Cavalry. He had cut the tracks of the York River Railroad, to prevent McClellan's using that line as an escape route. Then Lee had sent him word that McClellan wasn't going toward the York at all, but never mind; Yankee cavalry had been guarding the line, and when they fled, Stuart's Georgia Legion armed themselves with fine new carbines, so the action wasn't a loss.

When the railroad line was sufficiently savaged, Stuart took off after his old superior officers again. He found them near Rooney Lee's plantation of White House, and they were arraigned in force, apparently with artillery backing them up.

Stuart was more like Light-Horse Harry Lee than he was like his own more conventional cavalry background. He at once dismounted one of his regiments – Rooney Lee's – and prepared to make a real dragoon fight out of it, horse, foot, and guns.

But his own artillery scattered the Blue riders almost at once; their artillery had been mock – what were called Quaker guns, usually made out of tree trunks – and their force deceptive, much smaller than it looked.

This was a delaying action, no more. But the North had burnt the bridges, and Stuart's mounts could use a rest anyway. They lay over that night, while their engineers made a crossing. They were all pretty excited; there were supposed to be five thousand of the Blue to be scrapped with the next day.

It was another rumor. The next day they found nothing but stragglers and burnt depots that McClellan had known would fall to the cavalier. That is, at first. Then something caught Jeb Stuart's eye.

There was a Yankee gunboat in the river, off White House Landing. White House belonged to Colonel Rooney Lee; Yanks had no right to use his landing. Stuart declared war on the U.S. Navy.

Cavalry has no right attacking field artillery; much more so, it has no right charging a gunboat armed with 11-inch guns, naval rifles; they are as powerful as a coastal fort.

Stuart threw out a skirmish line of seventy-five men, dismounted and carrying his best carbines, rifled ones. The sailors on the gunboat loaded with shrapnel and splintered the woods behind the Landing; Stuart sent for Captain Pelham and one of his piddling little howitzers; he'd have an artillery duel.

There were three companies of New York Volunteers aboard the gunboat USS *Marblehead*. The Navy's boatswain's mates piped a couple of boats full of them over the side, and the Navy's sailors pulled for the line of skirmishers, who fired, but only wounded one New Yorker.

Then one of Pelham's little cannon balls landed on the gunboat's deck, and the naval commander changed his mind and called his infantry back to the mother ship.

The *Marblehead* pulled anchor and went downstream so fast she capsized and ruined one of the cutters; Pelham and his tiny howitzer chased alongside firing when they could; Stuart is reported to have laughed so hard he was unable to ride. Then he took his column up to Rooney Lee's house for lemonade; Stuart was always a teetotaler and his headquarters was run dry.

The Union had burned what it could, but Stuart salvaged ten thousand rifles, besides those picked up by the Georgians, and plenty of food for his men and corn and forage for his horses.

Stuart sent his report to Lee; there seemed to be no attempt on McClellan's part to move toward the York at all. But the cavalier couldn't believe that the scattered stores around – tinned goods, corn, rifles – had been abandoned by the North; he was sure they would come back.

So, he was still up around White House on June 30, the day that Lee's army beat on McClellan down around Charles City and Harrison's Landing, and the day that Jackson failed to move.

The next day, July 1, Lee ordered Stuart to move south, covering the left flank of the Army as it went after McClellan.

Jackson was moving now; his infantry filled the bridge Stuart had planned to use. Stuart picked up Munford and Jackson's divisional cavalry and as an augmented body they rode around the foot troops, used a bridge of their own, and struck across country to find the head of Jackson's column, and began screening. While they weren't exactly sure where Jackson was, they knew enough to keep the Union from finding out more. They didn't find Jackson that night; but at dark they camped, having ridden forty-two miles that day.

The next day it was apparent that screening wasn't necessary. Stuart took his column out on the forage, trying to find some Yankees to beat, some loot to bring in, anything; McClellan had obviously escaped, and Lee's orders were getting to the cavalry a day or more late.

They saw the USS *Monitor* on the James, but Stuart didn't attack. The rest of the day he encountered some small infantry outfits, which he captured, and an occasional tiny Blue patrol, which clashed and got away. Then it began raining and the foot soldiers bogged down. Stuart screened again, all around the east and north of the Confederate troops; when infantry was tied down by mud was just when Stoneman would strike.

The next day Stuart's scouts found the whole McClellan army stretched below them. They were on a rise called Evelington Heights. Stuart sent word to Lee and dismounted a battalion of troopers to hold the Union Army till the infantry could get there.

Lee dispatched Longstreet and Jackson to cover the five miles to Evelington Heights and relieve the cavalry. Meanwhile Stuart's Captain Pelham was throwing 12-lb. shells at the Army of the Potomac, which was just about like attacking the United States Marine Corps with a water pistol.

Stuart fired every cartridge and every shell he had by two o'clock in the afternoon; he had been waiting for Longstreet and Jackson to come the five miles to his aid since nine in the morning.

This time it wasn't Jackson's fault; Longstreet had the lead and got lost, and Jackson's men followed that lead.

During the next week the Seven Days' Battle – this was the second week of it – petered quietly out. Lee knew the country better than McClellan did;

if the Union Army stayed where it was, it was going to face an epidemic of malaria and maybe even typhoid; this was early July, and the weather in the swampy bivouac could be counted on to be highly favorable to mosquitoes, wearing on the local people, and deadly for Northerners.

McClellan, on the other hand, was busy explaining what he had done, and why it had been so ineffective. Sometimes he wrote that he had saved his army; the next dispatch would say that it was Washington's fault he hadn't saved his army; the third would claim a great victory, and then he would blame one of his subordinates. There wasn't a congressman who didn't get a letter from some one of the brass in the Army of the Potomac that week.

Stuart got more ambition and spent the week clashing with Stoneman's pickets and occasionally pausing on a riverbank to let Pelham shell another gunboat, something that gave Stuart, the horseman, rare pleasure.

The Seven Days' Battle, like most affairs seen long afterward, sounds like a stand-off. But it had a horrible effect on the morale of the North, which had considered the war almost over, and McClellan invincible. Union generals began to dream about Robert E. Lee, and they did not smile in their sleep.

And if Jackson had failed to show that he was Jackson, there would be another day.

But Stuart! The Cavalier composed a poem about himself, called *The Ride Around McClellan*, and allowed the pretty young ladies of Richmond to torture him – with flowers – into reciting it in order to gain his freedom from encircling groups of young Southern belles. After all, he was a married man.

Chapter 14

The North Almost Rallies

L incoln reorganized. He still had the Army of the Potomac, still under the command of General George B. McClellan. It had not been crippled by the Seven Days, and if it had lost a great deal of supplies, the North was rich in that sort of thing.

He called in Generals Henry W. Halleck and John Pope from the war along the Mississippi. Halleck he made his Commander-in-Chief – partly General-in-Chief, partly a presidential adviser; and to Pope he gave a new Federal Army of Virginia, composed of the small armies of Frémont, Banks, and McDowell, which had been up in the Shenandoah not doing much of anything.

Frémont repeated his California performance; he would not serve under Pope. He was relieved and a German volunteer general, Franz Sigel, given his command. This was the end of the military Frémont; he later tried politics and then private industry, always failing. Eventually the government made him Territorial Governor of Arizona, in which capacity he clashed with everyone.

Pope had more respect for the cavalry than had McClellan or McDowell or old Winfield Scott. His job was to strike at Lee from the northwest and release McClellan from his malarial bivouac.

He showed energy. He organized two cavalry brigades, and threw them ahead of his hard moving army; way ahead, as much as twenty miles. They reconnoitered off to the flanks, too, showing their flags in valleys of Virginia that had hardly known there was a war on. He was no believer in the mockery of "civilized war." A Southerner was a Confederate to Pope; if the Reb wasn't wearing a uniform, he would be next week, so strike him now. His men were under orders to live off the country; this was a hostile nation, not a sister state.

One of his brigades was under Brigadier General George Bayard, who had gotten out of West Point in 1856; the other was under John Buford, Captain, 2nd Cavalry U.S.A. and Brigadier General, U.S. Volunteers.

156

Buford had served in the West – against Indians and Mormons – under Cooke, who had twice cited him for excellence. But his ideas about cavalry were quite different from his old colonel's. He saw the rapid improvement in firearms; before the Civil War had started he had felt that the day of the saber was almost over, and the day of the true dragoon – who rode to the fight, dismounted to shoot, and then rode away again – was about to begin. Nobody much listened to him, a young captain on the frontier. But Pope gave him a brigade, and saw that it wasn't snatched away, as Cooke's brigades had been, and Buford showed that he knew how to fight a large body of cavalry.

The Blue riders came slashing down the valley, the Blue regiments foot-slogged after them. Lee sent Stuart up there; civilian Virginians were coming down with frightened reports of the ferocity of this new army.

Lee did something more: he made Jeb Stuart a major general and gave him command of all cavalry in the Army of Northern Virginia. It was a real command, not a paper one like that held by George Stoneman in the Army of the Potomac. There was ample cavalry in the Southern army, and Stuart was authorized to use it as a force to strike in strength, not just as a scouting service.

Stuart had fourteen regiments and two batteries of horse artillery in his new division. John Pelham, now a major, commanded the guns, of course. Wade Hampton, grandson of the War of 1812 man, was brought back from the Infantry to be Senior Brigadier. Fitz Lee got a star, too.

Of course, Pope's two cavalry brigades were nothing against Stuart's division. McClellan's horse troops were still under Stoneman, who had a frontiersman's tendency to split his command into units of less than three hundred men, and to fight them as though they were attacking Apache or Sioux bands, rather than as an organized army that counted its troops in the tens of thousands.

But the two brigades under Bayard and Buford were efficient. One result, and an important one, was that Pope had better intelligence than McClellan had ever had. Washington had turned intelligence work over to the Pinkerton Detective Agency, whose reports read as though pay was by the word. For instance, when Lee had about eighty thousand men in the field, the Pinkertons reported that he had two hundred thousand; as a result, Lee could move sixty thousand men out to strike at Porter, and the North still believed they were outnumbered by the troops he had left guarding Richmond.

Southern intelligence was good because Stuart had sufficient force to penetrate deep into the Northern lines and learn the size of the enemy, something a company or even squadron patrol couldn't do. Pope's two brigades could and did. They cut deep down the valley, deep as Beaverdam, only thirty airmiles from Richmond, and captured John Mosby, still only a captain; burned the houses, ravaged the crops, ran off the stock.

Lee began to have civilian trouble. Virginians complained to Jefferson Davis that they were being left unprotected against the blue-garbed savages from the North. There was clamor to have the railroads and farms covered with small horse guards; Stuart insisted that his men had to be kept together in a strong striking force, and Lee backed him up.

To show what he meant, Stuart struck north, with Fitz Lee's brigade and the divisional artillery under Pelham, into traditional Lee-Washington country; he captured a small Union detachment at Port Royal and then went around and descended on a Yankee wagon train that was moving under infantry escort on the Telegraph Road outside of Fredericksburg.

It was a line charge of cavalry against infantry, but the infantry were spread out thin and dawdling along the hot road – many of the men had put their shoulder weapons in the wagons to ease the duty – and the foot soldiers fled.

The captured wagoners said they were the transport of two brigades, Hatch's and Gibbons', who were south of them, heading toward the Peninsula. Stuart sent two of Fitz Lee's regiments after the Union troops and followed up with his fieldpieces.

The horse regiments engaged the rearguard of the Union movement, and the whole movement stopped and ponderously came around to face north again. Stuart beat an orderly retreat, using the artillery every time it got on a ridge in that rolling country, then moving it fast under a cavalry screen through the next dip. Then he broke away to bivouac, and count his dead, which numbered two.

The Union made no further attempts to send troops down from the Fredericksburg area; they were needed there so long as Stuart could dash in at his leisure and cut the Northern supply line.

But Pope continued to ravage the northern stretches of the Rappahannock and the Rapidan, keeping the Southern forces busy enough so that Lincoln felt it was safe for McClellan to give up the hopeless threat to Richmond and come home to the valley of the Potomac.

Protesting daily, McClellan finally did this, in the middle of August. Pope diverted the South by taunting Stonewall Jackson with Sigel and Banks's corps. Lee sent Jackson re-enforcements, including Robertson's – always the weakest – brigade of Stuart's new division.

Buford and Bayard put up the kind of cavalry fight the South had never seen from Stoneman or Cooke. Robertson was in trouble all the way; the infantry behind him were delayed, waiting for the kind of road clearing they had come to expect of Stuart and the Lee cousins.

But then the cavalry fight moved off to one side, and the infantry corps collided. Jackson was in over-all command, instead of leading his Own Division, as it proudly called itself; Winder, the divisional chief, was killed, and the Union almost had the day.

But Jackson was neither brooding nor praying now. He rode in, saber over his head rallied his men, and Banks, commanding for the North, retreated. Bayard covered the retreat with such diligence that one of his outfits, a detachment of the 1st Pennsylvania Cavalry, lost a hundred and three out of one hundred and sixty-four of its personnel.

Jackson ordered Robertson out in the night. His troopers hit a solid line of infantry and retreated, but not before they had captured some foot soldiers. Jackson learned for the first time that Sigel was backing up Banks and held his position instead of attacking.

The next day Jeb Stuart, out on an inspection tour as head of all Northern Virginia Cavalry, came into Jackson's camp, took Robertson's brigade out, and made a thorough, slashing reconnoiter, overriding the Northern videttes and pickets and flank troops, and penetrating the Union lines deep enough to learn that Jackson was hopelessly outnumbered, that he was facing not one or two corps, but all of Pope's efficient and vicious army.

Jackson withdrew; Pope sent his cavalry scouting and learned that the retreat was genuine and lengthy. He would have followed, but Halleck, in Washington, forbade it; Jackson's retreats were almost always ambushes. Instead, Halleck ordered Pope to hold up, and started sending him McClellan's men as they got away from the Peninsula.

Lee had the railroad within his lines; he sent thirty thousand men by it from Richmond to Gordonsville, where Jackson had gone.

Stuart scouted Pope and got his exact location, and the fact that McClellan was not re-enforcing him as fast as Lee was re-enforcing Jackson.

The South now outnumbered the North in the Pope-Jackson area. Lee came up and took charge at Orange Courthouse, north of Gordonsville, and decided to strike across the Rapidan before the odds changed. Fitz Lee would lead Longstreet and Robertson would lead Jackson into battle. Stuart would swing around to the rear of Pope and cut the railroad, and then Fitz Lee would join him – followed by Longstreet's strong infantry – in harassing Pope's rear and they would have the Yankee savages pincered.

It was a fine plan, but several things went wrong. Stuart did not make his orders to Fitz Lee clear enough; Fitz, answering them, did not get his answer off soon enough to reach Stuart; and the whole Confederate command seems to have suffered from overconfidence.

They were not fighting McClellan now. They were up against Pope, and Pope was not depending on any detective agency. He had his cavalry out

159

in constant patrol; one of his outfits captured Major Fitzhugh, a Stuart aide who had been sent out to bring Fitzhugh Lee to his major general.

In the major's possession, Colonel Brodhead, 1st Michigan Volunteer Cavalry, found a letter signed by Lee giving the full battle plan. Brodhead got out of there. He was commanding one undermanned regiment; he did not want to run into Fitz Lee's brigade or Stuart's division. They rode toward a small town named Verdiersville.

Stuart, with his general's party, had slept there, was still sleeping there. The Cavalier had good ears, asleep or awake. He heard the cavalry approaching, a large party of it, and in his war – up till then – a large party of cavalry was his. He sent Captain Mosby – who had been exchanged – and a Lieutenant Gibson down the road to greet Fitz Lee.

It was just dawn. Mosby and Gibson rode out, went around a bend. Stuart heard gunfire, and then his two officers came around the bend again, riding low as jockeys and yelling "Yankee cavalry" into their horses' manes.

Brodhead of Michigan still didn't want to tackle a large party of Southern cavalry, especially one that had been resting while his horses reached almost the limit of their strength. His men pursued the Confederates awhile and then, outrun, turned back and contented themselves with looting the erstwhile headquarters, capturing Stuart's plumed hat and red-lined cloak, among other things.

The attack on Pope had failed before it began. There had been trouble in the Southern infantry command, too. Longstreet and his subordinate General Robert Toombs had squabbled over the line of command; Toombs was not a West Pointer, Longstreet was, and the brass sided with their own kind.

Fitz Lee got in, exhausted, long after the battle would have been fought. It was a straight case of mixed-up communications, but Stuart reprimanded Fitz Lee harshly. Fitz Lee did not answer. He had always been there before when he was wanted, and he would be again, but a Lee of Virginia did not make excuses.

With Lee's battle plan in his hands, Pope knew what to do. He moved toward the northeast, where he could have better control of the rail lines that were the base of all his logistic plans.

Lee made new plans. Again, Longstreet and Jackson would lead, the former screened and outridden by Fitz Lee and the latter by Robertson. Jeb Stuart would ride with Robertson, which showed that he still had faith in Fitzhugh Lee.

General Lee, that excellent strategist, seemed unable to grasp the fact that Pope was not McClellan and that Buford and Bayard confronted Stuart and Robertson with five regiments of deployed Volunteer Cavalry.

Fitz Lee could not have been in a good humor; he scrapped fiercely with Buford and kept Longstreet's advance moving, though not with the speed it had expected. Fighting on that front was mostly confined to small cavalry skirmishes, very hot and pretty much even.

Stuart, when he saw Bayard's regiments, all in echelon, charged at once. The 2nd New York was in the fore; the heavy Southern charge scattered them, and the 1st New Jersey, behind them, scattered and ran for the river.

But Bayard had three more regiments, and they were willing to fight; Stuart had only the 7th Virginia, having sent the rest of Robertson's Brigade out on reconnaissance.

Robertson went astray, Stuart's staff put him back on the attack, and other regiments began to come in from patrol and were flung against Bayard. Bayard neatly crossed the river, dismounted many of his men as carbineers, and poured fire into the Confederate sabreurs.

Stuart sent for Fitz Lee and Pelham with his artillery. Bayard pulled back and went away; he was heavily outnumbered. But he had done what his cavalry was supposed to do, fight a strong outpost action, and he had fought it in the new, Buford style, with his men partly mounted and partly dismounted; Stuart had never ordered his men out of the saddle.

A new era had started; it is doubtful if Stuart or even Lee realized it. The North certainly didn't; it would be two years more before the full use of heavy-fire cavalry was resorted to by the Federals. The saber was on its way to the parade ground, the military ball, and the wedding arch; the cavalry, from which the title of Dragoon had just been removed, was about to become a true Dragoon force.

It has been said that the Civil War was fought with the bayonet and won with the carbine. This is a little too simple. The rifled artillery piece was a tremendous factor and so was General William T. Sherman's decision to do away with logistics and head an attack that lived off the country. The repeating rifle, carbine or infantry, was a big factor, of course; muzzle-loading carbines, which started the war, were much too slow for the action that ended it.

The battle went on. Lee, as always, kept his cavalry in the front, testing fords, feeling for ambushes, scouting for intelligence. Bayard and Buford fought these forays of Stuart's vigorously, but two brigades were not enough to halt the Gray riders; gradually the Federal cavalry suffered just what its commanders had fought against – being broken up into tiny detachments.

For three days Lee kept his infantry out of action, while Pope lined his army up in good form, preparing to defend the river. Stuart's patrols reported that the Northerners were uneasy and kept shifting their strength from one flank to the other as his numerous horse attacked here and there.

On August 22 Stuart got permission from Lee to try and ride around Pope's upper flank and cut his rail lines. Permission was granted, and the Cavalier took off, with most of Robertson's and Fitz Lee's brigades.

He wrote: *"I intend to make the Yankees pay dearly for that hat,"* a typical Jeb Stuart remark.

It was pleasant riding, through friendly country; there was much nonsense and many admiring girls at Warrenton, the first resting point. Then it began to rain, and when Stuart got to the railroad, at a place called Catlett's Station, it was full dark and pouring. The column was halted, presumably for the night.

But at Catlett's Gray troopers held some prisoners, including Negro teamsters who had been hauling for the Union Army. One of them was from near Stuart's home, and they recognized each other. The teamster had been in Pope's headquarters camp that day and told Stuart all about it; Stuart knew the man and believed him.

Three regiments, headed by Rooney Lee – he was in his cousin's brigade – were told off to make the raid; they took engineers and a detachment of troopers assigned as engineer labor with them.

It was a lovely raid; only two things marred its complete glory: Pope was not in camp, and the rain not only made it impossible to burn the railroad bridge but made the Gray troops give up before they had had enough; Robertson sent them word that the river would soon be too high to recross.

But they captured most of Pope's staff, his records including his battle plans, and they ruined a lot of supplies and captured as many more as they could escort. Moreover, they achieved a coup that delighted Stuart's hatless heart: Pope's dress uniform coat, with the gilt buttons "spaced in threes." Stuart wrote his wife: *"I have had my revenge out of Pope."*

Whether Lee shared his young cavalry commander's delight in the dress coat does not matter much; he was as overjoyed with the capture of Pope's plans as Pope had been to get Lee's from Major Fitzhugh. From them he learned that Pope's strength had grown from fifty-five thousand men to eighty thousand while Buford and Bayard had held Lee back. Soon, according to dispatches, another seventy thousand troops would join Pope; Lee had to strike at once or not at all. But the river was now too high for infantry to cross. Pope would have to be drawn away from the river and forced to fight where Lee could get at him.

The day aftep the raid, and the day after that Stuart's troopers fought skirmishes at every ford along the front; at one bridge they almost passed from skirmishing to battling.

Meanwhile Longstreet demonstrated on the river front. This was screening: behind them Jackson was pulling out and taking up a new front, northwest of the town of Jefferson. By going upstream, they got to fords that were not impassable. They crossed – the men grateful for the wetting, now that the rain had ended and the August heat come back – and marched till midnight. Then they collapsed, at the foot of Bull Run Mountain, and slept till shortly before dawn.

Pope had seen them march, but he had no way of estimating their strength; he had no cavalry to spare from the action along the river. He made a guess, and it was too low: just a flank column.

Jackson's next day's march was again unopposed; one of Stuart's regiments, riding advance guard, just sat their saddles and pitied the poor infantry eating their dust in the rear.

Lee now pulled Stuart away from the river and sent him after Jackson. The Cavalier reported that he had no sleep that night at all. He moved his horsemen out two hours after midnight – it was now August 26 – and rode easily to Jackson's rear, where he dropped off his supply wagons to be guarded by Jackson's men. Then he took a shortcut to the south, and caught up with Jackson's headquarters, Pelham's Horse Artillery always keeping up with the troopers.

Now they were only a little west of the battlefield of the First Bull Run, or First Manassas. Jackson ordered Stuart to provide an advance guard and flanking force, and they moved on toward Bristow, as far from the town of Manassas on the west as the Bull Run is on the east. Pope's lines of communication and supply ran squarely through Bristow; they were now about forty miles from Washington and the broad Potomac, which meant that McClellan's big army was not too far away; about half the distance to the national capital.

Stuart started tearing up the railroad tracks that connected Pope with McClellan. Before he could finish, an engine got through hauling an empty train to the east; then two more trains were taken and derailed. A fourth train scented trouble and retreated to the west, which alerted the Federals; but Stuart's cavalry raids had been so frequent that it was decided this was just another one.

Jackson waited till dark before bringing his infantry into Bristow. Then Stuart made a wide loop and came up on the rear and flanks of Manassas Junction, an important Union ammunition dump and supply depot, while infantry took it from the front. By dawn the Junction was taken, and Jackson could come along with the main body of his army.

They were, by all reports, one of the happiest armies of all time. They were ragged and practically shoeless, hungry and – at the moment – worn out from marching, but here was all that man could desire, and a license to loot the Federal stores. Jackson put a guard over the liquor, took the ammunition under official seizure, and turned them loose.

The troopers were even happier than the foot soldiers; a horse could carry more. Sacks of coffee dangled over cantles and pommels, and hams thumped against the thin flanks of the troop horses. John Pelham had one of the finest times. He not only got new, plump gun horses; he found several batteries of guns.

Stuart did not relax; all day his cavalry sent out detachments to scout out any movement of reprisal. All they encountered were tiny parties of Bayard's and Buford's cavalry, and perhaps some of Stoneman's, all of them in such small numbers that they had to flee. The gray-backed riders – who were probably somewhat blue-clad after looting the Union supply depot – pursued as best they could, but the Union horses were fresher and better fed.

The first reprisal came the next day, in the form of a New Jersey brigade of infantry that came down the tracks from the east. They had brought no field guns; a brigade of infantry was enough to flush out any cavalry raid. Of course, this was the worst sort of intelligence; they should have known that the Junction was full of artillery pieces and ammunition, even if they hadn't learned that Stuart's cavalry carried its own artillery.

Jackson sent out infantry to meet infantry and covered his men with heavy artillery fire. The New Jersey general, Taylor, was killed and his command retreated in disorder, only to run into Fitz Lee; Light-Horse Harry's grandson knew what to do when his troopers sighted routed infantry, and he did it.

But then Hooker came out from Pope's army and was engaged by Ewell. That might have developed into a fight in depth, but Jackson pulled Ewell off: Stonewall had his own ideas of where the battle was to be, and Hooker had not yet reached that site.

Hooker reported to Pope that he had driven the enemy back a full five miles, but he had his own doubts about what kind of a victory it had been, and he advanced with caution.

Stuart, scouting constantly, thought all of Pope's force was converging on them; but Lee and Longstreet were coming up from Salem with re-enforcements. Jackson set fire to the Depot, and marched his army out, toward Washington, which was not exactly retreating.

Pope was working blind. His intelligence had failed completely, and he had learned better than to count on that from the Pinkertons. Longstreet brought his massive column across the Rappahannock only three miles upstream from Pope, and the latter apparently never knew it.

If Pope had had more cavalry scouts … The first years of the war, for the North, was a series of Ifs. If Pope had guarded the warehouses at the Junction …

The next day, August 28, the Yankees, Hooker's outfit leading, marched into Manassas Junction, and found that they were without the rations which they had expected. Stuart's troopers had ruined the railroad; it was the North's turn to march on empty bellies.

Meanwhile, Jackson feinted around the countryside and thus got to his favored scene of battle, the woods and ridges around Sudley. Stuart struck out to bring Longstreet and General Lee in, leaving Fitz Lee to scout the railroad.

Stuart rode into Bayard, backed up with some of McDowell's foot troops. He sent a courier on to Lee and settled down to fight; there wasn't much Union cavalry, but what there was could scrap. The troopers stood each other off all afternoon, and Stuart's men captured a Union courier with messages from Pope: The Northern armies would rendezvous at Centreville. Stuart got a galloper loose from the line of skirmish and sent word to Jackson.

When Jackson was in form, there was no faster man. He could see that if he did not act at once, Pope's army would come together and face Lee in such force that there could be no junction with Jackson; so, Stonewall struck at the only Federals still west of him, King's column, a full division. Jackson hit him with two divisions, those of Ewell and Taliaferro. Almost at once both the Southern divisional generals were wounded, and their troops fought half-heartedly. General King took full advantage and pressed hard.

John Pelham took the Horse Artillery out to back up the Gray; he shelled King with fury and the Union guns zeroed in on him and wiped out his horses and a great many of his men. Jackson's staff sent him orders to withdraw, to which Major Pelham made a simple answer: How do you withdraw without horses? So, he stayed there, and the Confederates rallied, and the fight was a stand off. After nightfall King pulled off.

But now Pope knew where Jackson was, and while that was what Pope wanted, it was what Jackson wanted, too. An attack on the Stonewall army would relieve Lee and Longstreet; and the sombre Jackson had full faith in his fighting power.

The night was spent in Stuart's carefully flanking Jackson by putting Robertson's brigade on the right and Fitz Lee's on the left of the massed infantry. Jackson massed his artillery, too, where it would do the most good, and left to Stuart the job of getting through to Lee and telling him how matters stood.

How they stood was simple; Jackson, with twenty thousand men was prepared to stand up to all of Pope's army, which was about four times as big as his. But the choice of sites had been Jackson's and that counted for a lot.

This, of course, was Second Bull Run, Second Manassas; it was really not so much a battle as a campaign that had been going on for three weeks, more or less intensely; it had been declared when Nathaniel Pope took over the three small armies of Frémont (Sigel), Banks, and McDowell. It almost ended when Fitz Lee and Stuart failed to communicate, and thus allowed Pope to escape across the Rapidan.

Lee on one side and Jackson on the other – with Stuart's strong division scouting and flanking and keeping communications open – had been maneuvering Pope into position, but he did not know it. He had the force, and now he could sledge-hammer the Stonewall and bring the Confederacy down into powdery rubble. All through August 29 Pope proceeded to work at this. Stuart was out and had met Longstreet and they were coming along the pike steadily.

Pope now dispatched Fitz-John Porter, arriving with fresh troops, to hit Jackson on the southern flank; this was Pope's left and Jackson's right, where Robertson's brigade had been posted as flank guards.

What happened next is a matter of dispute; Porter was court-martialed for it, and cashiered from the service, but when Grant came to the presidency he had the case reviewed and General Porter restored to rank.

Whether Porter delayed or Pope did not understand the situation, it was all wrong; by now Longstreet had brought his troops in through Thoroughfare Gap, and his whole relieving army was between Porter and the flank he was to attack. Porter did not attack.

Phil Kearny was on the other flank, facing Ambrose Hill, General A.P. The one-armed Dragoon had left the Army when he married after the Mexican War; he had come back, leading a division with his reins in his teeth and his revolver in his right hand. Nothing ever frightened Phil Kearny. But after A.P. Hill had thrown his division back, it is reported that he wept at how few survivors he commanded.

The next day the South had it all its own way. Longstreet and Jackson, working under Lee's command, could readily pass troops to each other; Pope was pincered and battered at will. The Stonewall had fallen, but it had fallen on him. He retreated toward Washington.

Kearny's division fought rearguard. Jackson and A.P. Hill came on strongly just behind him; ahead of him the column of Pope's army was in a nightmare rout. A lightning storm did not help. The advance guard of the Confederates had Fitz Lee and Robertson's brigades to snap at Kearny and ample, though tired, infantry to back the cavalry up.

The rest of Stuart's division were out, keeping Bayard and Buford – whose brigades were just about demolished – from fanning out and telling Pope if he was about to be attacked on the flanks.

During the night Stuart rode into a plantation owned by some of his friends, near Chantilly, and they put on an impromptu breakfast ball until the Major General of Cavalry had to ride on again.

All through August 30 and September 1 the retreat continued. By the night of the first of September, also near Chantilly Kearny's rearguard was being pushed too hard. They stopped to fight and Major John Pelham brought his Horse Artillery to bear.

It was raining. Phil Kearny galloped at the Confederate lines. It was not one of Pelham's shells that killed him, but a single bullet that hit near the saddle line. The one-armed man – Dragoon, millionaire, general – fell off his horse and into the mud.

The Battle of Manassas – or Second Manassas, or Second Bull Run – was over.

Major General J.E.B. Stuart, CSA, wrote the footnote to it (to his wife):

My Darling One-
Long before this reaches you, I will be in Md. I have not been able to keep the list of battles, much less to give you an account of them. Our present position on the banks of the Potomac will tell you volumes … Parson Landstreet was captured and saw all their generals. Pope told him to tell me he would send my hat if I would send him his coat. I must have my hat first …

Landstreet says all the officers on the other side speak kindly of me. May God bless you.

In haste, ever yours,
J.E.B. Stuart

P.S. I send $200 in draft and $50 in notes. Can you pay my tailor bill?

Chapter 15

The Cavalier Probes North

Manassas had cost the South ten thousand men. It had cost the North about three thousand more casualties than that, and in addition, the rich warehouse at the Junction, seven thousand in prisoners or missing, twenty thousand rifles, numerous artillery pieces. It had reshattered Northern morale. It also ended, for the time being, any forceful use of cavalry. Pope had had two brigades, and still he had failed.

When the army was re-formed, Stoneman had command of the horse troops, and George Stoneman was Cooke-trained, frontier-trained. He would break up his cavalry whenever he could, into units as small as a platoon, and thus be unable to penetrate the enemy lines deep enough to gain any useful information as to numbers, types, intent of the troops.

This seems to be what happened to Pope. For a while Buford and Bayard had used their brigades as brigades – the Jeb Stuart method – and Pope had known where Jackson was and what he was doing. Then the brigades had been broken up, or held as the old classic reserves, and Lee had brought Longstreet in through Thoroughfare Gap with a whole army, and Pope hadn't known it. So, cavalry was pretty useless.

Halleck and Lincoln, cocky little McClellan who couldn't decide whether his troops were expendable soldiers or precious future voters, none of them seemed to be able to learn from J.E.B. Stuart or the Lee family.

Second Manassas is a favorite debating ground for Civil War buffs, of whom there are as many as there were combatants in that hundred-years-ago war. Porter was cashiered for it, Pope was sent West, the Army was sent back to Washington for McClellan to retrain.

Pope said that McClellan had been too timid, and that Porter was a coward. Halleck decided Pope had been at fault. But it seems that the real villain was the Union form of intelligence, the dependence on spy reports garnered by the Pinkertons. Lee was working from hard facts, gathered by the hard-riding, cold-eyed men of Stuart's division. And Lee would continue to win so long as Jeb Stuart was in the saddle.

Stuart missed out at Gettysburg, and no less an authority than Robert E. Lee said of that battle: "Its loss … commenced in the absence of correct intelligence." But that comes later. This was still the fall of 1862.

Henry W. Halleck, like all West Point officers, had a nickname. He was called Old Brains. There is no doubt that he was smart; he had graduated high enough in his class at the Academy in 1839 to be given an engineer's commission; he had written a textbook on military affairs and management; in 1854 he had dropped out of the Army and opened a successful law practice.

What more could you ask of a General-in-Chief than that he be an engineer, author, and lawyer? You could question his military ability.

Halleck was an old-timer, though he had been out of the Army for six years. He knew that McClellan and Pope disliked each other. He should have taken the field at Second Bull Run to coordinate them. Perhaps force alone wouldn't have won against the beautiful manuevering of Jackson and Lee, but it should have been tried; McClellan's troops should have been available to relieve and re-enforce Pope's.

As to cavalry, the General-in-Chief had written that they were useful. He had deplored, in print, the Congressional "wiseacres" who had mounted, dismounted, and then remounted the Rifles in a short period of time; he had seen how expensive that sort of indecision had been.

But now, in the fall of 1862, he sent Pope back to the West, to Minnesota, of all places. Not that there was no fighting in the West; the Sioux were out, there was constant Indian trouble. But Pope was too good a man to waste that way. And if he wasn't, his defeat at Second Manassas was no more disgraceful than McClellan's mess on the Peninsula, or McDowell's at Bull Run. There is the excuse that McClellan was popular with his men and Pope was not. But a war is not won with charm.

So, Pope went to the West and McClellan was given command of all troops in and around Washington. Little Mac was always a good training officer; Halleck ordered him to reorganize his troops and whip them back into fighting shape.

Robert E. Lee had other ideas. He gave his Army of Northern Virginia a short rest, two days, in the hilly country up around Leesburg, where St. George Cooke had been born, and which was the very northern tip of the Confederacy, less than five miles from the Maryland line. Lee's army was triumphant, but impoverished. McClellan's army, resting down the Potomac thirty-five miles away, was defeated, but rich in the commissary and quartermaster departments.

Robert E. Lee figured the time had come for peace. He had whipped the three best generals Lincoln had been able to find: McDowell, McClellan, and Pope; Washington had had to fall back on McClellan again. But he had to prepare to deal from a position of strength.

So far, all the fighting had been inside the Confederacy. (Except for the war in the Mississippi Valley, and this neither he nor Congress would consider as important as the constant threat to Washington. Lincoln, an Illinois man, might think differently, but Lincoln had to get along with Congress.) Now Lee would invade the North, terrorize Maryland and Pennsylvania, and perhaps the rest of the Middle Atlantic, too. McClellan would be behind him, and nothing but Home Guards would bar bis path.

If Lee couldn't capture Philadelphia or New York – and nothing in his writing indicates that he ever thought he could – he could cut the railroads that ran across Pennsylvania, and separate the North's east from its west

The plan sounded well. Maryland had almost gone into the Confederacy; there must be thousands of young Marylanders who would flock to the Army of Northern Virginia. And there was food in Maryland. The troops were starving, and war had stripped the countryside in every direction but north. Lee would go north, and then he would be in the right spot to negotiate a peace.

If he had stayed in bivouac near Leesburg and sent Stuart's cavalry division up into Maryland, he might have changed his mind. Maryland had been violently pro-South at the beginning of the war. Now it was just conservative. It had seen what happened to Virginia; and it did not want to pay the price of secession.

On September 4 – two days after it went into camp – the army moved out again, Stonewall Jackson leading, crossed the Potomac and was in the United States of America.

Stuart crossed the next day. Brigadier Beverly Robertson was detached and sent south to recruit; Colonel Munford took over Robertson's cavalry brigade, minus Colonel Flournoy's regiment, which was left behind to gather what supplies could be found in the wake of the departing armies, North and South. Under Flournoy were all the walking sick and wounded, and all the troopers who were without horses.

Catching up with the foot column, Stuart threw his division along the right flank. Everything went well. There was some Federal cavalry out – mostly Stoneman's – but no detachments big enough to do anything but scuttle from the heavy Confederate division.

Stuart took up his headquarters in Urbana, Maryland, and was courteously waited on by the city councilmen. He was invited to dinner at a prosperous house and had one of his customary flirtations, this time with a girl from New York, who said she loved the Confederacy – forerunner of the New Yorkers, many of them born in Europe, who invariably cried and cheered through the first two decades of the twentieth century every time *Dixie* was played.

Lee was at Frederick. Stuart ordered his Prussian major, Von Borcke, to organize a ball, and sent a galloper to Frederick to invite officers from there to join in. The girl he called the New York Rebel was to be queen of the gala.

She was – until an hour before midnight, when there was an alarm. Yankee cavalry were riding on Urbana; they had already ridden over the pickets, and the 1st North Carolina, which had the duty, were having trouble holding them.

What had happened, of course, was that the small cavalry outfits that Stuart's men had run off had gone home and reported. Brigadier General Alfred Pleasonton had gotten together what horse troops he could and sent them up to do something about the Confederate Army.

It wasn't a big force; by one o'clock in the morning Stuart and his officers were back at the dance. At dawn ambulances arrived at the ball with the wounded; the ladies stopped dancing and started nursing. It was a scene from the almost mythical Civil War of the 1890 novels and the 1930 movies.

There were other scenes. Stonewall Jackson went to church and bowed his head while the preacher prayed for the health of President Lincoln.

But very few Marylanders enlisted in Lee's army, and the merchants grumbled at having to take Confederate money for supplies they had paid for in United States currency. The Army remained shabby and broken-toed, and often hungry. Lee had expressly forbidden violence against shopkeepers who locked their goods in back rooms and denied they had anything to sell; this was friendly country and might yet secede.

There were eleven thousand Yankee soldiers at Harpers Ferry, where Colonel Robert E. Lee, 2nd Cavalry, U.S.A., had led Marines – no soldiers being available – against the forted-up John Brown. This is on the Potomac, where West Virginia now meets Virginia and Maryland. Lee sent Jackson back across the river to march on the garrison; Longstreet put observers on the north shore of the Potomac to watch and give the alarm if Stonewall needed help.

Lee himself, with the greater part of his army, headed northwest out of Frederick for Hagerstown, which is still in Maryland, but always heavily Pennsylvania Dutch. Stuart and his men rode right flank. Pleasonton's cavalry had fought enough of an action at Urbana to test the enemy and find out that it was all of Lee's Army of Northern Virginia.

McClellan moved with better speed than he usually showed. Just a week after Lee had made his headquarters at Frederick, the Army of the Potomac marched into that town and took over; Lee, of course, was gone, but not very far.

McClellan had ninety thousand men; Lee had about fifty-five thousand. But the valuable Jackson was back at Harpers Ferry and engaged; he did not take that garrison until the fifteenth of September, and McClellan was in Frederick on the twelfth.

Another one of the communications fumbles ensued. Lee sent orders of march, rendezvous, and timing to his generals; then sent a second copy to General Daniel Harvey Hill, because the aides couldn't remember whether the first copy had gone to the right place. A Union soldier found this second copy in an abandoned camp; it was wrapped around some cigars. Now McClellan had Lee's plans to read. What happened to the cigars is not certain.

Lee had troops scattered all over the small map of Frederick and Washington counties of Maryland, and McClellan knew it. But Little Mac hated to hurry. By the time he got his troops on the road to widen the gaps between Lee's forces, Lee had learned about the lost orders and closed the holes. Then he chose his own battleground, at Antietam.

Stuart had been skirmishing ever since September 7, the night of the ball. Pleasonton had come up with two regiments, pushing hard, fighting for information and position. Stuart, on the other hand, was fighting to keep tight the cordon he had established, which had kept Washington pretty much in the dark. Pleasonton, stalling until McClellan arrived, did manage to get Franklin's corps of infantry to help, and Stuart fell back on Frederick, the day before McClellan got there.

Now there was not much use in covering the long roads that Stuart had kept closed to dispatch riders. He held the line in front of Frederick as long as cavalry could, using Wade Hampton, Fitz Lee, and Munford as brigadiers. Hampton's South Carolina Brigade fought the horde of bluecoats right into Frederick, and Stuart was reported to be the last Confederate out of town.

Fitz Lee was sent out to determine how many troops had come up the Potomac. He found out – too many. All he could do was harass McClellan's north flank and hang on. Then the cavalry division, on the 13th, re-formed behind the first ridge of hills west of Frederick. Stuart was still not sure how large a force was ahead of him, as he screened Lee's movements to his rear, but he took no chances, and advised that D.H. Hill close the passes through the ridges; Hill sent two brigades of infantry to that job, denying McClellan any intelligence about Lee, who was scouting around Sharpsburg on Antietam Creek, picking a battleground at his leisure.

That was the night the soldier found the orders. There was no longer any reason to put off the battle. But it took McClellan two more days to make up his mind to do the thing he had been sent up the river to do – attack Lee.

The battle of Antietam – Sharpsburg in the Confederate annals – was joined on August 14. It was a bloody stand-up-and-be-killed, heavy infantry battle of the kind that characterized the Civil War. The fighting ran on into the fifteenth, by which time Stuart had left the battlefield for Harpers Ferry to see the surrender.

Not all of the garrison at the Ferry gave up their arms to the Southerners. Grimes Davis got permission from the commandant to take the cavalry out through a sally port; leading their horses, sometimes almost holding them up, they crept away through footpaths in the ridges, and escaped.

There were twelve hundred of the Blue riders. Once in the open and in the saddle, they crossed the Potomac and ran into Longstreet's baggage, coming south from Boonsboro; they completely destroyed the wagons and their cargo.

Colonel David Strother was with McClellan at Antietam. He writes that he begged the general to throw all his strength against Lee; but McClellan ordered him to have Pleasonton send "a couple of squadrons" to see if there wasn't weakness in the center of Lee's line.

Strother rode to General Pleasonton with the order; and Pleasonton ordered out two horse batteries, "which took position … on either side of the turnpike." Which would give Pleasonton – and McClellan – no information at all.

Harpers Ferry fell – eleven thousand prisoners to the South, ample supplies of badly needed commissary, ordnance, quartermaster stores. The besiegers, under Jackson and Stuart, were free to join in at Sharpsburg.

They were hardly needed. Hooker and Burnside had been so battered that McClellan was withdrawing their corps, and sending in that of General Edwin V. Sumner, the same "Bull" Sumner who had ridden down the Mississippi with Cooke in 1846, hurrying their Dragoons lest the two captains miss their only chance at a real war.

He had had to fight his way into this battle; Fitz Lee's brigade and other regiments of Stuart's division had tried to bar him near Boonsboro. He dismounted his advance guard of cavalry the Lees did the same – Rooney Lee was a colonel there – and they cleared the town in house to house fighting; Sumner's men went on to the Antietam. Sumner attacked with vigor, and almost broke through the left center of the Southern line; as always, McClellan was content with half a victory, and leashed the old Dragoon.

Then McClellan went back to stalling. It became September 17, and Jackson got up from Harpers Ferry. The Gray line thickened – it had been perilously thin – and McClellan was brought to a standstill. The next day he let Lee's army march away, and then turned his own troops back toward Washington and further training.

Call it a stand off. It ended, for the time being, any Southern ideas of invading Pennsylvania; it disillusioned the South about Maryland's attitude toward the war. Southern casualties were eight thousand and Northern thirteen thousand; but there had been seven Blues for every three Grays in the battle; and Jackson had won the Harpers Ferry side issue.

The Army of the Potomac stayed up in the north; McClellan went back to Washington still commander of the Army of the Potomac. But Lincoln was through with him; before another campaign took the field, he was relieved by Ambrose Burnside, who is reported to have been reluctant to take the honor. This is the Burnside of the whiskers, now called, curiously, sideburns.

Burnside reorganized his army. He created Grand Divisions, larger than Corps, and turned them over to Sumner, Hooker, and William B. Franklin. Each Grand Division was composed of two corps, and some cavalry. The idea was still to get Richmond, but Burnside proposed to do it through Fredericksburg, north of the Confederate capital, rather than the Peninsula, to the southeast More would be gained than the prestige of capturing Jeff Davis' city; Lee would be cut off from his base by the Army of the Potomac, now swelled to about a hundred thousand. Lee had about half that many effectives; Southern records are not always clear as to who was in the field and who had gone home to convalesce from fever, wounds, starvation.

Lee lay along the Potomac, partly in Maryland, partly in Virginia. Stuart kept his brigades moving, patrolling the line from Longstreet at Winchester to Jackson near Martinsburg. They surely expected the Army of the Potomac to come up at them. September ended, and Lee's strength rose a little, as wounded came back to their outfit. John W. Thomason, writing a biography of Stuart, calls that early October the happiest days that Stuart's headquarters would have in the whole wartime.

There was another of those gallantries that really happened in the war. Phil Kearny's widow wrote, through channels – McClellan to the U.S. War Department, U.S. to C.S. War Department, to General Lee – asking if she could have her husband's horse, saddle, and sword. Lee convened a board of survey, with Stuart at its head to determine what this gear and mount was worth to the Confederate Quartermaster and Ordnance Departments, who held them. A value was determined, and Lee paid it to save the widow time, and sent all off under a flag of truce – with a letter regretting the poor condition of the horse, who had been to the wars and was thin.

There was a raid by Pleasonton early in the month, and Rooney Lee, commanding the brigade because his cousin had been kicked by a mule, did not turn the Yankees back fast enough. They rode into Wade Hampton's lines, and he was not as snappy as he should have been.

Stuart rode up in a temper; he had been sniped at by Pleasonton's troopers. Rooney Lee threw his whole brigade, in columns of four, at the bluecoats, and Pleasonton, who was riding for Intelligence rather than glory, got out of there. He lost some stragglers; Stuart celebrated that night.

It was too bad that Fitz Lee was not feeling well; there were dances every night and charades and recitation by Stuart of original anagrams. At Antietam, it had been Rooney who suffered; he had been knocked off his horse and lay unconscious while Union troops marched by, not noting his breathing or his rank.

Now that Pleasonton knew where Lee's army was, there was less need for horse patrol of the lines. Infantry could fight off any raids.

A week after Pleasonton had been sent home with the intelligence he needed, Lee issued an order to Stuart. The major general of cavalry had not been idle. He had designed, ordered, and presented a new coat to General Jackson, whose old one – that of a professor of VMI – was a joyous disgrace. Jackson, much moved, accepted the gorgeous garment, and would have put it in storage as being too good for everyday warfare, but Stuart made him wear it self-consciously through a dinner at general mess, while enlisted men invented errands there to share in the sight.

Lee's order was simple and to the point, as well as to Stuart's heart. He was to take twelve to fifteen hundred men and ride north from Williamsport, go west of Hagerstown and into Pennsylvania; there he was to cut the railroad at Chambersburg, do as much damage to the right-of-way as possible, grab some hostages to exchange for prominent Virginia prisoners, and get back as best he could. Of course, the primary purpose of the raid was to gather intelligence. The Army of the Potomac was still up that way, while Washington planned the changeover in its commanders.

The orders were explicit as to looting: none. But brigadiers would organize horse-commandeering parties, seeing that a receipt was given to the lawful owner in each case; let the owners present them to the United States for payment. Public property, of course, could be brought back and should be.

Stuart took Wade Hampton, Rooney Lee, and Colonel William Jones, known as Old Grumble, for brigadiers. He picked eighteen hundred men to go along, three hundred more than Lee had allowed.

On the night of October 9, Stuart stopped the dancing at eleven o'clock, and the officers kissed their girls good-bye and went to where the orderlies held the chargers at the head of the outfits. They rode out to banjo music, of course. John Pelham had four guns for artillery pieces; this was like the ride around McClellan all over again. Under cover of fog they almost sneaked through the Union pickets, but a horse clattered and there was some pistol fire. The raiders captured one man, several horses, and went on. The sun began to burn the mist away, and they took in ten infantry stragglers, bluecoats who told them that they just missed Cox's infantry division.

The Yankees knew they were coming, though the 12th Illinois Cavalry, whose pickets they had clashed with, overestimated Stuart's force, putting it at twenty-five hundred, too strong to attack; the word was passed to Hagerstown, almost on the Pennsylvania line.

Stuart was leading his men on a line two or three miles east of what was still McClellan's army – Pleasonton had his horse troops guarding the flank. Lee had sent Colonel John D. Imboden, of Stuart's division, out on a diversionary movement into Virginia just before Stuart started, and a brigade of cavalry and some infantry, quite a large force, had shifted that way, which relieved some pressure on Stuart. But still, his eighteen hundred men were riding around almost a hundred thousand.

And the Union was no longer completely a foot army. Stoneman had what was called a division, some of it dismounted, and so did Pleasonton. Averell's cavalry brigade was the one sent after Imboden. Bayard and Buford both were re-forming their brigades after the last disastrous campaign.

The North, then, had more sabers – the military way of counting cavalry – in the field than Stuart commanded. And some of their horse generals – Buford, perhaps Pleasonton – were good men. But the commanding general, in this case McClellan under Halleck, could not get it through his head that this was like no war the United States had ever fought; that massive power, horse or foot, was the only thing that counted; small detachments were no good for combat, intelligence, or screening.

So, the first definite word that McClellan got was from Washington, from Halleck at the War Department instead of from cavalry in the field. It came to him late in the evening, telling him that Stuart had taken Chambersburg. His answer was typical: he had cut off Stuart's retreat.

He did more than that, as a matter of fact, and what he did was sensible enough. He sent three brigades chasing Stuart and blocked the backtrack with ample infantry, and he brought Averell back from chasing Imboden, and threw his brigade across the backtrack, just above McCoy's Ford on the Potomac, where Stuart had crossed. The foretrack would take Stuart right into Pleasonton's division.

Infantry moved all along the Potomac. Stuart had raided Pennsylvania – the governor of that commonwealth, Andrew Gregg Curtin, was writing Lincoln, Halleck, McClellan, and probably all his relatives – but the Union was seeing to it that the Cavalier and his column could not get back across the Potomac again.

Meanwhile, the force had grown as it trotted through enemy territory. There were now anywhere from three to six thousand riders behind Stuart. Against him McClellan moved twelve thousand foot troops and the three cavalry brigades, probably three thousand horse soldiers. It is hard to say how strong some of the brigades were; McClellan and his generals were re-forming the Army of the Potomac, and it is probable that men assigned to the cavalry and counted on its rolls had not yet learned how to mount a horse.

The Gray riders had taken Mercersburg first. The storekeepers there were disgruntled to see their shoes and boots melt and their tills swell with Confederate bills. Reshod, the column had moved east, through small and unimportant towns, on to Chambersburg, garnering horses all the time, though it is recorded that Stuart would not let his men take any animals being ridden by ladies. Civilians were swept along to keep them from breaking the silence that Stuart was riding in. It began to rain as they hit Chambersburg. The town surrendered at once, and Wade Hampton was named Military Governor. There were Federal stores at Chambersburg, and it was on the railroad. But the railroad bridge was iron, and the troopers could not destroy it.

Colonel McClure of the Pennsylvania militia was in Chambersburg, in civilian clothes, and he was a thoughtful and observant man. Thomason has studied his diary; the colonel reported that the Confederates seemed intelligent and more than gentlemanly; over a hundred of them took tea in his kitchen without saying a harsh or obscene word even to his servants.

Stuart spent the night in Chambersburg, laying over a full twelve hours. It was raining, and his men could use the rest. The horses, for once, were not a worry; the column had ample captured remounts.

At nine in the morning they moved out, and the last men out of town blew up the Federal warehouse. But little private property had been damaged, and what had been was paid for (in Confederate money) and the damagers punished.

The rain worried Stuart. If the Potomac rose ... He called in his engineering officer and showed his plans for recrossing. He asked the officer, Captain Blackford, to vindicate Stuart's plans if the general was killed or captured. The Cavalier could worry about his troops and his cause, but his name and his appearance was never far from his conscious mind.

Now he headed for Gettysburg; while stopping the night, Stuart had let plenty of civilians hear that that was his next destination, certain that they would get word to McClellan.

They did, but Stuart had cut his loop eight miles short of Gettysburg, then an unimportant but pleasant seat of a college and a theological seminary that boasted a library of seven thousand books. There were about half that many people in the town.

In the late afternoon he was back in Maryland, at Emmitsburg; thirty-two miles had been covered since Chambersburg.

Lee was still wooing Maryland; the order came down the line, no more horse commandeering. In Emmitsburg the people brought food but there

177

wasn't time to eat very much; the column had already cut the tracks of their old friends, the Pennsylvania Lancers. As they rode out of town, they captured a galloper from that outfit, with dispatches from Colonel Rush of Pennsylvania to General Pleasonton of the Federals, who was apparently only about four miles away, with a cavalry force half the size of Stuart's.

Changing horses as they needed to, the Gray column rode the night through, another thirty-five miles to Hyattstown. They were still far from the river, and men were sleeping in their saddles.

Left alone, Pleasonton might have caught up with Stuart. But the Pennsylvania politicians, led by Governor Curtin, were still wiring Washington. Convinced that Stuart was in Gettysburg, they forced McClellan to send Pleasonton that way, wasting his time and the stamina of his men. It was after midnight on the third day of Stuart's ride that Pleasonton cut his track and learned from the locals that Stuart had gone through an hour before, at a trot. Pleasonton, without remounts, was slowing down. He headed for the junction of the Monocacy with the Potomac, which seemed a logical place for Stuart to cross. With the water rising, the spot just above the junction would give horsemen their best chance.

But Stuart had taken his chances with the Monocacy water and gone farther east. Getting to the fork, Pleasonton saw the Blue infantry in force upstream from him, guarding the river; not being needed there, he headed downriver. Stoneman and his division were the force at the juncture.

Stoneman had four to five thousand men, half of them mounted. He spread them all along the Potomac, and there was no chance of Stuart getting west again.

Pleasonton rode for the east as hard as he could. Almost half his column had dropped out, and what was left was unbearably weary; only sharp spurs kept the horses going, and the troopers kept falling asleep and forgetting to spur.

A mile and a half from the Monocacy mouth, Pleasonton – perhaps the only man still alert in his command – saw south-moving Blue cavalry. He assumed they were some of Stoneman's numerous troops and rode up to them with some sort of gesture of friendliness.

He forgot – and his fatigue is plenty excuse for forgetting – that Stuart had been out raiding. The uniforms were Union, but they had been seized at Chambersburg, and the men inside of them were Rooney Lee's 9th Virginians. Stuart was with them.

Pleasonton realized his mistake too late. The Southerners saber-charged and knocked his muddled troopers off the road. The Federals tried to retaliate with their carbines, but Pelham's fieldpieces came up fast – they had had fresh gun horses every half hour or more all night – and the column got through, all of it, part of its artillery fighting in the rearguard.

Pleasonton had sent off for infantrymen for artillery transport. His own gun horses could no longer pull.

Rooney Lee was leading the charge for the Potomac, now in sight. But the welcome view was marred by the 99th Pennsylvania Infantry, thrown out in full battle order.

The 9th Virginia went into line, too, facing the Pennsylvanians. Rooney Lee sent word to Stuart, but the general told him to handle his own troubles; Stuart was busy getting his column and his guns up to the front. Rooney Lee tried something that shouldn't have worked. He sent a flag of truce to the Union colonel, telling him the whole Stuart division was about to charge, and asking him to surrender.

All that Rooney wanted was time. What he got was not surrender, but retreat, which was really better; Union troops had heard the skirmish fire and were coming in from all over, and a formal surrender would have been too slow.

Colonel Lee sent the fieldpieces across the river, where they un-limbered and prepared to cover the cavalry as they crossed. But there were still two guns with the rearguard. They came down at a gallop, just as the Union artillery came up and started to go into battery.

Pelham was feeling for the range of the Union guns. He kept them busy while the last of Stuart's men got over, with their prisoners and their commandeered horses and their whole skins.

Nobody had enough energy left to chase the Cavalier. He led his expedition back to Leesburg. Then he wrote his report and took it to Lee two days later.

The statistics are impressive. In one twenty-four hour period, he had ridden eighty miles and won a fight at the end. Sixty horses broken down and abandoned, twelve hundred horses commandeered and brought to the Confederacy. One man wounded, two missing, none dead. Intelligence – Stuart knew all there was to know about McClellan's army. McClellan had learned nothing except that his cavalry arm was incapable. Mr. Lincoln personally wrote indignant notes to Stoneman, and to McClellan, ordering the latter to send his horse troops across the Potomac and down into Virginia to find out if Lee was still there.

McClellan couldn't do it. His cavalry was worn out, though Quartermaster General Montgomery Meigs had been supplying two thousand remounts a week. General McClellan made the reconnaissance by infantry, and reported, yes, Lee was there all right.

Ten days later Burnside and his corps invaded Virginia. It is notable that the cavalry that went with them was Pleasonton's command; of all the Union horse generals, he had the most right to be tired, but he had recovered first.

179

Lee split his army to handle the new drive south; Longstreet took half of it over to the Manassas country and Jackson the other half up the Shenandoah to Winchester. Stuart put his division into the forty miles that separated the two corps, to maintain contact.

October was ending. Soon winter would slow the war down; but in the meantime, there was a chance for Lee to go on the offensive if Burnside – and the waiting McClellan, up on the Potomac – slipped. It was up to Stuart and his riders to look for that slip.

Winter was early that year. Before October was out the horses were breaking skim ice when they were taken down for their morning water. Stuart escorted Lee's headquarters into winter quarters and then took Fitz Lee's brigade out on patrol to the east. The brigade was not at its best. It was down to a thousand men. About half of the eight thousand horses that mounted the division were sick; both Fitz and Rooney Lee were down with something of other.

Riding through a pass called Snicker's Gap Stuart and Colonel Wickham, commanding the brigade, saw the country below them blue with the Army of the Potomac, moving ponderously south. A thousand men couldn't throw themselves on the Union Army. Stuart scouted, and learned that Bayard was riding flank on the eastern edge of the big blue horde. He headed that way, ran into a Rhode Island regiment, drove them back, then dropped his own brigade back to his divisional headquarters and got set for Pleasonton, who would surely be coming down with the center of the Northern invasion.

Stuart's division was in home country; this was the center of the Virginia horse-breeding land, and many of his troopers could count on seeing kinfolk any place they rode.

Stuart had first spotted the Northern Army on October 30; on November 1, Pleasonton led two thousand troopers toward Snicker's Gap, and Stuart tried to block him with Fitz's brigade and, of course, John Pelham's guns. Blocked, Pleasonton headed south along the foothills of the Blue Ridge; if he had gotten through, he could have slashed at Jackson's corps, guarding Winchester. Fighting was constant, skirmishing that swelled into heavy cavalry fights and then subsided again.

Wickham was wounded, Rosser took over the brigade; that was on the second; the next day Pleasonton massed and almost shoved Stuart back through Snicker's Gap; D.H. Hill brought his infantry up to back up the horse troops, and Pleasonton pulled off again. Stuart rode to Jackson's headquarters that night and told Stonewall that he thought Pleasonton wasn't trying for the Blue Ridge at all but was feinting to cover a Federal movement against the Rappahannock.

Jackson sent out infantry to relieve the horse guard on the Blue Ridge passes, and Stuart rode east. He left Wade Hampton behind to patrol the ridges that Jackson's infantry couldn't handle, and almost at once Hampton was clashing with Averell of the Northern horse. Fighting, they came toward the Rappahannock, and ran into a battle between Pleasonton and Stuart.

Rosser dismounted the Fitz Lee brigade and fought them as infantry, which had the unexpected effect of messing up Pleasonton's intelligence. He penetrated the horse lines deep enough to give a pretty good report on Jackson's strength and position, to the left of where Stuart was fighting, but then reported more infantry in strength on Stuart's right; it was only Stuart's dismounted troopers.

Stuart stretched his brigades thin, and they held. All that Pleasonton found out was that Jackson was strong and had good artillery, and the Northern horse general didn't open any access that McClellan's infantry could use.

Stuart, on the other hand, had learned definitely that the Northern Army was heading for Warrenton. Also, he had slowed that invasion down – fifteen miles in six days.

McClellan rested, pondering. There were the reports from the detective agency to consider; there were two deserters from Longstreet's whose information was about what you would expect from second-class privates; there were a good many lies told to his officers by the Virginia farmers. If the Union Army pushed ahead to where they thought Longstreet was, it would leave Jackson free to invade the North again. If McClellan struck at Jackson, the rest of the Confederate Army would be able to pincer him in from the South. McClellan repeatedly reported to Washington that Lee had about three times as many men as Lee ever did have. Pleasonton had gotten some intelligence about the size of Jackson's force but none at all about Longstreet's.

Little Mac waited. On November 7 his waiting ended; he was relieved of his command and Burnside took over, at last.

Stories about Lincoln are dangerous ground for the accurate; everyone who went to call on the President felt he had to come back with an anecdote. One of that week was about a new regiment of Michigan cavalry whose political colonel was taken to meet President Lincoln before the volunteers went into the field. The colonel blustered that he and his rookies were about to get Jeb Stuart and pull him down.

Mr. Lincoln reputedly answered: "I'd rather see Jeb Stuart a captive in this room than see you here," which may have speeded the new troops to the front and out of the zone of politics.

It was in that time of heavy fighting that Stuart's little daughter, Flora, died. Things were too bad for the general to take leave; only his intimate staff knew how miserable he was; it was his duty to keep the half sick, half frozen, half dismounted troopers' spirits up.

It snowed early in November. If Pleasonton had struck, he would have found an almost incapacitated cavalry division holding the line; but Pleasonton didn't strike. There was a battle on November 11, and Fitz Lee's brigade was thrown back against the horseless men of the division, lying as reserves. In rallying his riders against the heavier force of Pleasonton, Stuart had half his mustache shot away. Pleasonton, again, could have pushed his advantage that day, but didn't. Burnside didn't seem to be driving his Army of the Potomac any harder than McClellan had. Stuart promoted Rooney Lee to brigadier and Fitz Lee got well and took over his command again; Grumble Jones was promoted, too, vice Robertson.

It got quiet enough, in that chilly November, for Flora Cooke Stuart to visit her husband at his headquarters. She brought their only remaining child with her: J.E.B. Stuart, Jr., three-year-old Jemmie. Family tradition says that he was first christened St. George Cooke Stuart, and renamed when his grandfather stayed with the Union.

It got too quiet; Stuart took Hampton's and Fitz Lee's brigades and forced his way through the enemy picket lines to discover that Burnside was turning his army to strike toward Fredericksburg.

This was an easterly movement; it could be headed for Richmond. Lee started a parallel march, using Jackson, on the south bank of the Rappahannock.

Burnside waited too long to cross the river, which he would have to do to cover the Richmond country in any kind of depth. Rooney Lee scouted the movement and Jackson was ready for Burnside. Burnside pulled back and made another strike toward Falmouth.

Lee had a big army, for the South: almost eighty thousand men. Burnside had over two hundred thousand, and they were better clothed than the shivering Southerners, better fed, their cavalry much better mounted. But the Union generals who understood cavalry were still all in the West. Burnside was no better at using horse troops than McClellan and McDowell had been, and he was worse than Pope.

Lee, with strong intelligence about the enemy's movements and strength, seems to have set the scene for the battle: Fredericksburg, Virginia. The fault may not be Burnside's. Mr. Lincoln and General Halleck had specifically said that they wanted a big battle before winter made one impossible, and a third of December was gone.

The actual fighting, in depth, took place on December 13, a Saturday. Once the battle was joined, it was all artillery and infantry; Stuart protected Jackson's right flank, but his horsemen were never needed. Jackson wore the fancy uniform coat Stuart had given him, and it is reported that he was much admired.

By nightfall the South had lost five thousand men, the North almost thirteen thousand. Jackson, that sober man, always went crazy in a fight; he wanted to swim his division across the river and fight all night. Lee and Longstreet restrained the one-time professor of philosophy and artillery.

Bayard, of the Northern horse, was killed. John Cooke, St. George's son and Flora Stuart's brother, was wounded; he had risen to brigadier in the Confederacy.

The next day Burnside was expected to continue the attack, but he failed to. The Army of the Potomac went back to the Potomac, and the fighting was over for 1862.

Chapter 16

The Crucial Year

Sherman called 1863 the first "professional" year of the Civil War. The point of view is Northern; Jackson and Lee and Stuart and Longstreet were already professional in all respects.

For the cavalry, 1863 meant that every horse soldier on either side was armed with a breech-loading carbine; the Union had issued them, and the Confederacy had captured its share. The carbine could fire faster than the infantry rifle, but it had a much shorter range of accuracy.

Burnside didn't last the first month of the year. Lincoln replaced him with Joseph Hooker. Almost the first act of Hooker's command was to pull his cavalry together into a corps of three divisions. He made George Stoneman – who was still only a brigadier – corps commander. From now on, according to Hooker, cavalry would stop riding errands for the infantry and become a striking force in its own right.

The new Cavalry Corps would face a distressed Stuart division. The horses had not wintered well. There was little hay or even straw to fill their long guts; corn was in better supply, but the poor animals often had to make do with bark gnawed off living trees.

And, as always, shoes for the humans in the Army of Northern Virginia gave out. Overcoats were rarities; men who could get a spare blanket made a poncho out of it, and those who couldn't walked around with their sleeping cover draped over their shoulders.

Just before the year started, Stuart had led eighteen hundred of his men on another of his raids. The purpose was intelligence but some of the Stuart humor got into it; capturing a live telegraph station fifteen miles from Washington, Stuart put his own operator on the key and complained to Quartermaster General Meigs, U.S.A., about the poor quality of the mules he was sending out for the Stuart troopers to capture. This was to go down in Southern history as the Christmas Eve Raid. It kept Stuart from a party at his headquarters; Flora had come out to attend the party and spend Christmas with her husband.

There were two more cavalry actions before spring released the massive infantry of Joe Hooker and Stonewall Jackson. Fitz Lee led one; he took over Culpeper Courthouse, on the Union side of the Rappahannock, and held the upper river for most of the winter. In March General William Woods Averell led the second raid, for the North; it was supposed to drive Fitz Lee back to the main Jackson army. (Longstreet had gone south, in order to find better commissary for his men.) Fitz Lee had only about eight hundred men in the saddle. Averell was followed by three thousand sabers, but he was cautious; intelligence credited the South, and particularly Fitz Lee, with several times as many effectives as they had troops altogether. Above Warrenton, John Mosby, now a major in Stuart's command, and the leader of what were called Partisan Rangers, started harassing Averell so badly that the Union general detached nine hundred men to ride rear and flank guard on his cavalry column.

Mosby had brought twenty-nine of his mounted rangers along, and annoying Averell into splitting his command was not his original intent. He had already sneaked into a Union headquarters and kidnaped a brigadier general, one Stoughton, and had caused a brigade of Union cavalry to break down completely trying to catch him.

But Averell, for all his split command, came up to Fitz Lee's lines in good strength. By chance, Stuart and John Pelham were nearby; the general to sit on a court and the artillery major to woo a young lady.

The Union men rode down the first pickets they encountered; the officer of the guard dismounted his reserve and sent them up; but only sixty troopers in all were available, and Averell had it all his own way. Word was sent back to headquarters, and Stuart, Fitz Lee, and Pelham went forward with the brigade, all trotting.

Averell had taken his time; he had watered and fed his horses after running off the pickets. Fitz Lee hurled two regiments of his brigade – pitifully small regiments in that bad winter – at Averell's advance guard and broke it up. Then the main body of the Union expedition came through the scattered advance guard, and it was time to retreat; the Gray was hopelessly outnumbered.

Fitz Lee pulled back for three quarters of a mile, till he reached his guns. Sometime in that stretch John Pelham received a shell splinter in the head at Keely's Ford, Virginia; he was taken back to the home of the girl he had been courting and died there the same day.

Covered by his fieldpieces, Fitz Lee made his stand. Averell had a heavy reserve that never got into the hand-to-hand, muzzle-to-muzzle fighting; such men as he did commit stood well, but after a while the Northerner pulled back across the Rappahannock, and the fight was over.

By Northern standards, Averell had not done much; he had penetrated less than two miles into Fitz Lee's territory. But the men of Stuart's staff mourned John Pelham and they mourned a hundred casualties and a third that many prisoners. A hundred and fifty of Fitz Lee's horses were killed or wounded, and this was a hard blow to an outfit that was already nearly dismounted.

Also, Stuart, always the intelligence officer, had noted an alarming thing. This outfit of Union cavalry had stood and fought; and they had managed their horses well, too. Stuart did not use the word Sherman did, professional, but he implied it in his reports.

The winter ended. Stuart, at his headquarters – now called Camp Pelham, in sorrowful memory – had only the two Lee brigades under his hand; Hampton was in the south, Grumble Jones over in the Valley, past the Blue Ridge. Altogether, the troopers of Fitz and Rooney Lee numbered almost three thousand, but half of them were dismounted. The Jeff Davis government had sent out a call for horses from Texas and the South and had ordered some militia cavalry from the southern tier of states to report to Stuart, but nothing happened until after Joe Hooker had struck.

The new general was moving south; he had a hundred and thirty thousand men moving with him. Twelve thousand of these were Stoneman's Blue troopers, under Averell, Gregg, John Buford, and Pleasonton. Stoneman maneuvered first. He left Pleasonton to screen and flank Joe Hooker's army, and he took the other three divisions down into Stuart country, near Warrenton.

Stuart got the reports at once; the Lee headquarters was never in much doubt as to what was intended. Stoneman was on the raid; he would cut between Lee and Richmond, and Stuart would have no choice but to go after him. Then Hooker and his huge foot army would swing at Lee from the west, and Lee would be pincered.

Lee had only Jackson's corps and two divisions of Longstreet's; the main body of Longstreet's troops had gotten tied up in the south. Shorthanded as he was, Stuart couldn't use all his cavalry; some had to be left to get information for Lee, to keep information about Lee from Hooker, to provide flank guards for Lee's army. Of the three functions, the second was perhaps most important; the North didn't know how small the defending army was and would move cautiously till it found out.

Buford attacked first, leading what Regulars the cavalry still had. His move was a feint; when he ran into dismounted sharpshooters of Stuart's division, he engaged them awhile and then pulled off. That was under orders; all the Regulars were supposed to do was divert attention while

Gregg led his division into the main attack of the raid, upstream from them. But Gregg was another of the reluctant Union commanders so common up till then. Rooney Lee beat him back without ever calling on his reserves. The next day Buford and Gregg both went upstream. Buford got all his men across and Gregg got some of his, and if Stoneman had moved, his main body could have crossed, and the raid would have been able to slash ahead with all its heavy force. But Stoneman was slow, and the gods still loved the South; when Stoneman didn't come up, Buford and Gregg had to pull their advance guards back, and as soon as they had done so, the Rappahannock rose, and cavalry could no longer ford. Joe Hooker pressed up behind Stoneman and the whole Union advance stalled.

That was on April 15. By the time Stoneman forded, on the twenty-eighth, Stuart had reformed his thin lines and was absolutely certain of the Union intention. Rooney Lee, with his weak brigade, was told off to harass Stoneman and keep him out of any important railroad or ammunition depots; commissary and quartermaster stores were hardly a problem for the starving Gray army.

That day, April 28, Stoneman got across, with nearly seven thousand men. Rooney Lee could do very little more than snap at the Blue heels, slow Stoneman down, harass him. Now Hooker's main Army of the Potomac moved. Stuart watched them, tried to hold them, was brushed aside. Three whole corps were now in Southern territory; that night Stuart raided their lines and took enough prisoners to identify the names and size of the invaders: The V, XI, and XII Corps, U.S.A.

There was nothing to do but to leave Stoneman to Rooney Lee. Stuart took Fitz Lee's brigade and spread its thin line all along Hooker's front and flank.

Pleasonton brought his Union cavalry up but was never able to pierce Stuart's lines; Hooker never again knew what was happening outside his own lines, had no idea where Stoneman was, and couldn't get orders to the big raiding party. He had a force on either side of Lee now, and he far outnumbered Lee's army. Only he didn't know it. He put up three observation balloons to take the place of the missing cavalry reports; the Confederates took to making their troop movements in the night, or when mists blinded the balloonists.

Lee could be expected to retreat, fall back on Richmond. That was what an outnumbered and flanked army should do, but Lee was writing a new book of strategy. Stonewall had his officers carefully coach some men to desert and be captured by Hooker's pickets, whom they told they were Longstreet men who had re-enforced Jackson. Some of them said that Wade Hampton and the rest of the Gray that had wintered south had come back with them.

187

A New York cavalry regiment ran into Fitz Lee's 5th Virginia in the night, got itself surrounded and confused in the strange country, was soundly beaten and went back – the troopers carrying the dead body of their colonel – to confuse Hooker further by telling him they had run into strong cavalry resistance just where it shouldn't be. Hooker had assumed that Stuart would commit all his men to chasing George Stoneman. Instead cavalry was to the west of Hooker; it must be screening heavy infantry.

The next morning all of Hooker's flanks on the south and east reported heavy fighting. Lee, in some way unknown and sounding impossible to Hooker, had closed in on three sides of the Union Army.

Hooker must have known, by that morning of April 30, that Lee had decided to strike north rather than retreat south. Hooker went on the defensive, had his men start forting themselves up behind felled trees and in trenches. But there were no natural features on his west to protect his flank – no ridges or rivers or forests. Stuart, always scouting, found this out the next day and sent gallopers to Lee.

Lee called in Jackson, and they made a bold and original battle plan. Hooker, from his behavior and from his intelligence reports, must have thought himself flanked on three sides when he was actually only in contact with scouting parties. All right. They would pincer him.

Of course, Hooker had about twice as many effectives as they did, but no matter. At daybreak Jackson would take twenty-five thousand men and move out as fast as he could for the weak flank that Stuart had discovered. While he was doing that, Lee would throw the remaining twenty thousand Gray infantry against Hooker's left, which would make the Union general move his mass over there and ease Jackson's troubles.

It took Jackson all day to make that fifteen-mile flanking movement. Hooker knew there was a movement, but Pleasonton couldn't pierce Jackson's screen to find out just what.

It was five o'clock in the afternoon before Jackson was in a position to strike, which he did along a wide line. At once he knocked the XI Corps, U.S.A., out of position; his men moved in with the bayonets and point-blank fire. The Union rushed up re-enforcements; the sun set about quarter to seven, and the fighting dwindled down.

Stonewall Jackson took his staff out on reconnaissance. Returning to his own lines, he was shot by his pickets. The wound was severe and immediately crippling, and in eight days it was to cause the death of as good a man as Lee ever had.

A.P. Hill took over; almost at once he was wounded, too, and Stuart took command of Jackson's army corps. There were about twenty thousand men left in it; fighting had been heavy.

Stuart had never commanded infantry. He sent a courier to Jackson's bed, but the general simply sent back word to do what he could; Jackson was in too much pain to think clearly. The old professor had always treated his subordinates like students; instead of sending them written orders, he had made them think for themselves. This was both good and bad: good, in that such commanders in the corps who were still on their feet were good, independent thinkers; bad, in that Stuart could only guess what Jackson had come there to do.

The Cavalier did what seemed sensible; laid out his artillery, with which he was familiar, closed up his infantry ranks and rode hard all up and down the line, using his colorful personality to rally the men. Also, he sent strong messages to the rear to get some food up; there would be fighting at dawn, and his troops, not fed for a full twenty-four hours, were starved. An hour and a half after midnight the moon set, the firing broke off, the Union men could be heard digging in. The commissary wagons came up and officers were told to feed their men.

Lee was heard from at three o'clock; a second rider brought the same message three quarters of an hour later. Both halves of the army would attack as soon as they could see; Lee was in front of Chancellorsville, and would press his attack toward Stuart, Stuart was to do the reverse, and the two armies would rejoin somewhere around a little place called Hazel Grove.

Stuart glanced at the sky. The sun would not be up for an hour and a quarter, but you can see quite well for a half an hour before sunrise. He ordered all outfits to stop drawing rations and start getting into line.

Then he renewed the galloping along the lines; Southern armies were famous for starting battles when each man was ready, but this general was J.E.B. Stuart, and when he said "Go!" he meant "Go, damn it!" Stuart, that most Southern of Lee's generals, had a strong feeling of time that was distinctly un-Southern. His men stepped out in unison, moving through the woods and up against the log bastions and earthworks that Hooker's infantry had thrown up during the night.

Hooker retreated. It is hard to see why; he had the force and he had a solid position. But he obviously had been kept from knowing this by the screening of Fitz Lee.

Lee and Stuart's line hooked together just about where Lee had said they would, at tiny Hazel Grove. Meanwhile Sedgwick, who commanded the detached part of Hooker's army, was on the prod, trying to force his way through to Chancellorsville and connect with the main battle.

He got a good start, but too late; the main fighting was over, Hooker was going north, and Lee could send troops to push against Sedgwick's front and turn him north, too.

Official Army publications cite Chancellorsville as one of Lee's most brilliant pieces of strategy, and it was; he had outflanked and outwitted an army twice the size of his. But if Stoneman's raid hadn't been completely stymied by the tired, tiny force of Stuart and Fitz Lee and Rooney Lee, Hooker would have had the intelligence to guide him; and Lee would have been the one fighting in ignorance. The Union now knew it had to have cavalry and it had to have a better cavalry general than George Stoneman. Hooker tried Alfred Pleasonton. Lincoln was thinking of trying someone else besides Hooker for over-all commander.

It is speculation and almost worthless speculation to wonder what would have happened if Lincoln and Halleck had taken St. George Cooke away from his endless round of recruiting and sitting on boards and turned the horse soldiers over to him. He had failed twice, of course, but he had had five hundred troopers or less each time; and in the first failure, when he did not catch Jeb Stuart on the Peninsula, there seemed ample evidence that Fitz-John Porter had not released the cavalry in time. Now Porter was out of the Army in disgrace. If Cooke had been too slow the first time, he had been too precipitate the second, when he had thrown two hundred and fifty cavalrymen against overwhelming fire power.

Still, he had always been a man who could learn; soldiers like Old Brains Halleck knew St. George Cooke as one of the finest minds in the service. Of course, he was old by the standards of that war: fifty-four. But the overwhelming factor seemed to be his Virginia birth, coupled with the desertion from the Union of Stuart and John Cooke and Dr. Brewer. So, Stuart not only fought the Union in the field; by having married Flora Cooke he also prevented the Army of the Potomac from having a good cavalry general in those first years of the war.

Stuart himself was not kept on as corps commander of Jackson's 2nd. Richard S. Ewell got the corps, and the promotion to lieutenant general. Stuart continued to head the cavalry division. It was what he did best.

Chapter 17

The Cavalier Versus the Fop

Beverly Robertson, whose brigade had been turned over to Rooney Lee, came up from the south with a new brigade of North Carolinians. Both sides were now using the draft. Grumble Jones came over from the Valley.

The dismounted troopers went home and came back mounted. The South never had a Remount Corps; each man brought his own horse, and if it was lost in battle – but not disabled by illness or stolen – was given money to get another one. It was not a very satisfactory way to mount a cavalry division; horses were scarce around the theater of operation, and a man sometimes had to cross three states to his home before he could find someone willing to part with a remount.

A short time after Chancellorsville Jeb Stuart could report that he had over nine thousand sabers in his division, all mounted. He also had twenty fieldpieces. Lee had a big army, too: over seventy thousand men, in excellent shape. Summer was starting, and the Valley Forge-type winter had been forgotten.

It was time to hit the north again. Lee's thoughts, written to Davis, were all on shifting the war out of Virginia and relieving that unhappy country. His plan was to hit Pennsylvania, force Hooker to bring the Army of the Potomac there, and then destroy that army. To this end he urged Davis to have General P.G.T. Beauregard move up from the Deep South and back Lee up, so that Hooker couldn't swing back on Virginia.

Jeff Davis would not issue the orders; the Army of Northern Virginia could go north of Virginia, but the Beauregard and other forces in the Deep South would have to stay there. Davis must have been a heavy burden on Custis Lee, his military adviser and assistant. Robert E.'s son and Harry's grandson had stood number one in his class at West Point for all his four years. His father had done the same before him.

There was a mild and rather amusing mixup for the cavalry division before it struck off on the road that would end at Gettysburg. Stuart ordered a full-scale dress review and invited General Lee to come look over the horse soldiers.

Lee was very busy and declined. So, on June 5, Stuart reviewed his own brigades, horses walking past once, then going by again at the gallop; guns firing the thirteen guns for a major general.

Two days later Lee sent over a message; his burden had eased, and he would be pleased to come for the horse troops show. He'd be over the next day. The cursing troopers groomed themselves, their uniforms, and their horses all over again. Lee must have sensed something, or perhaps his son or his nephew told; the general told Stuart just to walk, not gallop his horses, and to omit the seventeen-gun salute he was entitled to. Lee probably had not come over to Culpeper for the review at all; while he was there he gave Stuart orders to march the next day. Ewell and Longstreet would move north with the cavalry on their right flank and the Blue Ridge on their left.

Hooker was still in command of the Army of the Potomac. As always, his information was poor, and he believed that Stuart had more than twice as many troopers as he really did have; the movements northward were reported to the Union general, but he read them as another Stuart raid, and turned out Pleasonton and the cavalry, in two units under Gregg and Buford. Each unit had an infantry brigade and about two thousand horse soldiers: in all, Pleasonton's column had about ten thousand effectives.

This Alfred Pleasonton had been at the Point in the class of 1844; Stuart of the plumed hat and red-lined coat considered him a fop, which is startling. Pleasonton was on the move the night of the Lee review, moving skillfully – for once Stuart's pickets didn't scout the Union. In view of the move the next morning, as many men as possible had been brought in off the vidette lines to pack their gear and get ready for the long expedition; and it is possible that they had been brought in earlier to swell the parade before General Lee.

Culpeper lies below the Rappahannock, which runs more or less east and west there. Buford crossed upstream and Gregg downstream, with orders to converge on Brandy Station, inside Stuart's lines. (Actually Stuart's camp ran from Brandy Station to Culpeper, not quite touching either small town.)

At dawn Buford threw his first brigade across the river. A company of Grumble Jones's troopers guarded the ford there; they resisted long enough for word to get back to Stuart, who sent the 6th Virginia out at a gallop to re-enforce the small party on the river.

The Union brigade was already across; there was bitter fighting in the cutbank of the road where the two forces met, head-on. The North prevailed, killing thirty Gray troopers and their horses, and stormed in among Stuart's artillery park. They almost got his guns and they did get his artillery commander's field desk, with its plans.

Then the guns got away and pulled back to unlimber and find the range. But the fighting was too mixed for artillery support; General Jones had brought another Virginia regiment into it and shortly Rooney Lee was there, too.

The battle mounted. Buford brought his whole force over and to bear, including his infantry and artillery; Jones and Rooney Lee, lacking infantry, dismounted their sharpshooters and used them as foot troops.

Stuart came up, and Wade Hampton was galloping four regiments toward the sound of the fight. Robertson and his new brigade were still uncommitted, and Stuart had sent two of Wade Hampton's regiments away from the rest of their brigade; they would have ridden rearguard in the projected march northward that day.

Gregg crossed the river without resistance and split his force to come in from the north and west on Stuart's camp. But the western force ran into the detachment from Hampton's brigade, and was checked by stubborn fighting.

Stuart had left headquarters on Fleetwood Heights; his adjutant, Major McClellan – not Little Mac – commanded there. He had a six-pound fieldpiece with him, and when he looked down and saw Gregg's thousands of Blue riders, he ordered that they be shelled with the tiny gun.

Gregg halted, unlimbered, and returned the fire with all his heavy force, certain that he was being shelled from a position of strength, probably the main force of Stuart's division. He prepared to charge Fleetwood Heights. Major McClellan no doubt prepared to burn the headquarters papers; he was outnumbered astronomically – one gun section and himself against about three thousand Yankees. He was even out of gallopers; he had sent them to Stuart with his information.

Stuart didn't believe it till he heard the cannon fire; Robertson's rookies should have stopped any invasion from that direction. But Robertson had gotten turned around, and thought he was protecting Wade Hampton's flanks and rear. Actually, he and his new brigade were completely out of the fight that day.

At the sound of the artillery, Stuart sent a regiment and a battalion to Fleetwood Heights. Colonel Harmon, who commanded, was met by a frantic Major McClellan, who shouldn't have been alive but was. Harmon charged at once, but the 1st New Jersey was already on the Heights and set, and they drove the Southerners back down the slopes in disorder.

Stuart rode up to take charge as his cavalry broke; he had left orders for Rooney Lee, Hampton, and Grumble Jones to follow with what troops were not needed against Buford.

Wade Hampton broke away first, then Rooney; Grumble Jones was the big hero of the day, moving toward the hot fight on Fleetwood Heights, but coming backward, fighting a fine rearguard action against Buford, keeping that general from charging through to pincer off the cavalry division.

Colonel Harmon re-formed his command, charged and saw his outfit again broken up; he himself was wounded. But some of his men formed up a third time and put a battery of Union artillery out of the war, killing thirty of the thirty-six cannoneers and drivers, and making the guns immobile.

Stuart threw the arriving four regiments of Hampton's against Gregg's flanks; the Southerners did their work with their sabers, and the hardest horse-to-horse fight of the whole war developed. Hampton's men prevailed, with terrible losses, and the New Jersey people were driven away.

Rooney Lee had gone back, when he could, to help Jones. His men and Old Grumble's were suddenly flanked by Buford; Rooney was wounded, one of his colonels killed, and then Munford, of Fitz Lee's brigade, flanked Buford in turn.

The two split-offs of Pleasonton's expedition now closed in and got in touch with Buford and were in the strongest position they had been in all day; but again, Northern intelligence failed. Pleasonton heard that heavy foot re-enforcements were coming up to help Stuart and ordered a retreat.

Ewell's infantry were near the fight toward the end; but Pleasonton didn't know how many they were, whose they were, what their intentions were. He had nothing to report to Hooker except that he had clashed with Stuart and had lost almost a thousand of his ten thousand men. Half of them were prisoners.

Stuart suffered more than five hundred casualties, wounded or dead. In that war, to be wounded was almost as bad as being killed outright; medical and surgical methods were deadly.

Rooney Lee was to recover, but not happily. He was sent to the home of Colonel Wickham, under the guard of his aide, his youngest brother, Robert E., Jr. His wife went there to nurse him, but while the Lee Army was busy on the Gettysburg expedition, a Blue raid captured him and took him on a mattress to Fortress Monroe.

There was a big legal fuss going on, based on whether Confederate privateers were pirates or not. The North had captured some and threatened to hang them. Jeff Davis said if they did he would hang an equal number of officer prisoners-of-war. Washington said if he did, they would hang Rooney Lee.

They didn't – nobody hanged anybody in that dispute – but Rooney's wife died while he was a prisoner, though Custis Lee, also a brigadier, and special aide to President Davis, offered to be a hostage while Rooney went to his wife's deathbed. Rooney Lee recovered, but it was late in the war before he took to the field again.

The march to the north went ahead, only slightly delayed by the fighting at Brandy Station and Fleetwood Heights. The ride was marked, though, by constant hard skirmishing with Pleasonton's troopers. Stuart spread his regiments out to cover the gaps, the passes, the peaks; so long as the Blue riders could not get over the mountains, Hooker would be uncertain of Lee's troop movements: this might be only another raid of Stuart's division. Except for a garrison at Harpers Ferry, the Valley was all Confederate, and up it moved the heavy column of Robert E. Lee.

Stuart himself was involved in the fire fights. He wrote his wife that in one skirmish all the 1st Dragoons seemed to be aiming their pistols directly at him. Of course, that regiment was now the 1st Cavalry, but that – now the 4th Cavalry – had been the name of Stuart's own regiment.

Lee moved his divisions up in open order; commissary was low, and like grazing horses, the troops could not follow each other without starving. In Maryland, Stuart wrote Lee, the storekeepers wouldn't take Confederate money and Stuart asked if his troopers couldn't seize tobacco. Lee wrote back that the commissary and quartermaster officers could take tobacco, and force Confederate payment.

This dispatch, General Lee to Major General Stuart, concerned other matters than tobacco-starved troopers. Stuart had asked for permission to ride around Hooker's army, as he had twice ridden around McClellan's, to that army's thorough demoralization. Lee's answer was not clear, and he apparently approved the mission, saying that Stuart would be able to judge whether he could make the circuit "without hindrance" and "cross the river east of the mountains."

The confusion arises from the phrase "east of the mountains." Lee apparently meant immediately east. When Stuart got out in the field, he found Union troops thick below the foothills, and swung way out. As a result, he was not at Gettysburg until long after Lee needed his intelligence report; he got in at noon of the second day of July, and the battle was joined on June 30.

This is the sort of thing that fills the lives of the rehashers of the Civil War: Was Lee wrong or Stuart? Neither gentleman was the type to blame the other; whatever happened happened, and let it rest there.

At any rate, once north of the Potomac, Stuart's superb screening would be wasted. A brigade or two could do the work; the other three brigades of Stuart's division could best be used at the head of the Army of the Potomac.

To get there, Stuart would have to ride around either Lee's army, or Hooker's. The Cavalier naturally preferred the latter; it was his trademark, it would provide excellent intelligence, and it had always had the effect of lowering Union morale. On June 24 he moved out, leaving Jones and Beverly Robertson to guard the passes and screen the army; Ewell was already in Pennsylvania and Stuart intended to come up with his vanguard before the fighting started. Ewell already had cavalry, Jenkins' Independent Brigade, not under Stuart's command.

Jenkins had eighteen hundred troopers in the field; Stuart thought Jenkins had three thousand. This is according to Thomason, writing Stuart's biography, and the error is an interesting one. As late as World War II, an Army officer, asked how many men he had, would give the total number under his command, including those on sick or other leave, those left behind to housekeep, those on detached duty. Marine officers, however, told the number actually under the hand at the time. Thomason, besides being a writer and artist, was a professional – he preferred the adjective "mercenary" – Marine.

By sunup on June 24, Stuart was already ten miles on his road, from Salem toward Bull Run Mountain. Five miles later his pickets spotted a Union corps, General Winfield S. Hancock's. Stuart put his cavalry into defilade, shelled Hancock and got away without disclosing his strength; Hancock could report that he had encountered the whole Army of the Potomac or a wandering artillery battery, and Hooker could make what he wanted out of the report; it was sure to confuse.

Stuart sent a message back to Lee about the Federal contact; it never got through. Meanwhile, the cavalry commander made his decision; it was much faster to strike directly for York, the rendezvous point with Ewell, than to back up and go over South Mountain, behind Longstreet's lines. Faster, but not so safe. Stuart turned his horse's bay head for York, Wade Hampton's men riding vanguard.

There was no more trouble till June 27. Stuart could see the dust and hear the racket of Hooker's Army of North Virginia, and he skirted it. When he was about on a level with Washington, Hampton had to wipe out a Blue cavalry patrol. This was at Fairfax; by dark the horses were drinking Potomac water, at Rowser's Ford, and Hampton crossed. Fitz Lee and his men helped Chambliss, who had taken Pelham's place with the guns; the water was deep, the night moonless, and there was some trouble; all the command wasn't across until three in the morning. They had passed within twenty miles of Washington that evening, all three brigades and the guns, but they did not alarm the Union pickets who should have been around.

The next day, at noon in Maryland, they were less than ten miles from the District line when the 2nd South Carolina spotted a loaded supply train and chased it into the District and captured it at Tenallytown, under the guns that were supposed to defend the Union capital.

This was on June 28; that morning – by coincidence, not because of the sight of Stuart's riders – Hooker had been replaced as commander of the Army of the Potomac by George G. Meade.

The captured wagon train was a hundred and twenty-five wagons long. It was an almost intolerable burden to a fast striking cavalry expedition, but the Gray was always hungry; Stuart brought the wagons along instead of burning them.

The raid went on northward, but at a much slower clip: twenty-five miles a day instead of the forty they had made up till then. Fitz Lee darted ahead and cut railroad and telegraph lines; Hampton's brigade surrounded the wagons and urged the mules along. A great many Union soldiers were picked up and paroled; the column was slow enough already, it couldn't take prisoners along.

On the evening of June 29, Stuart's advance guard was ten miles, airline, below the Pennsylvania border, at Westminster. There a detachment – less than a hundred men – of the 1st Delaware Cavalry made a stand, and two thirds of them were at once casualties. Stuart took the column five miles farther and called it a day. Scouts that night told Stuart of Union cavalry near Hanover, up across the state line. In the morning Stuart headed for them.

Meade had gone out to take command of his army; the word followed him in a few hours that Stuart had raided right up to Washington's streets. Holding Buford to scout, Meade sent out Generals David M. Gregg and Hugh J. Kilpatrick to bracket the Southern column, Kilpatrick's division to cut off Stuart's advance, Gregg's to pincer up from the south.

Stuart got a late start that morning of June 30, when Buford's men, up at Gettysburg, were firing the first shots of the big battle. The delay was because of the wagons, of course; get enough mules together and there is sure to be morning trouble. At ten o'clock – four and a half hours after sunrise – the 2nd North Carolina, riding advance guard, was just entering Hanover, ten or twelve miles along their road.

So was Kilpatrick's division. The North Carolina outfit had a few seconds of success, then the twenty-seven-year-old Kilpatrick brought up his main strength. Stuart couldn't – he had no re-enforcements available. Fitz Lee was out on a flank, and Hampton's troopers were tied up with the wagon train.

Stuart and his command party drew their pistols and gave what aid they could. Stuart was nearly captured, but he was on a bay hunter named Virginia, and he jumped a deep and wide ditch that the more plebeian troop horses from the north couldn't manage.

Things came to a standstill. Hampton got his main strength free from the mule guarding and faced Kilpatrick in all his strength. Toward evening Fitz Lee convoyed the wagons off to the east and around Kilpatrick and then headed north for York again. Then Hampton pulled back and went around the other Blue flank, and the whole expedition was free and bound for the rendezvous point, York.

197

A few miles west of York, at Gettysburg, John Buford and his 1st Cavalry Division, U.S.A., had engaged a Division of A.P. Hill's Army Corps. Cavalry, of course, should not charge infantry; John Buford had always felt, since he had been a captain in Cooke's 2nd Dragoons, that a combat man was a combat man whether he got to the battle on foot or on a horse. He brought his two brigades into line in fours; every fourth man led the other three horses to defilade in the rear, and Buford had an infantry line armed with the fast, short-range carbines. He put his line under cover – this was fenced, heavily planted country – and sent his fieldpieces into line to shell the oncoming Gray.

A tower-topped theological seminary nearby provided a good observation point. Buford climbed into the belfry, looked, and climbed down hastily to send gallopers for infantry support; the South was coming up in great strength, and his thin brigades – he could not stop all scouting, and every fourth man was out of the fight holding horses – could not be expected to fight an army corps, especially one with all the artillery he could see going into line.

Help was already on the way; General John F. Reynolds had heard the firing and was hurrying his foot I Corps up toward where Buford's riders were fighting. New York troops got into the line first, along with a mixed brigade of Pennsylvanians and Midwesterners, the famous Iron Brigade from Illinois, Wisconsin, and Michigan.

Buford had been relieved; his troopers came filtering back through the lines to take their horses over from the holders. They had done their dismounted duty well; the battle would be at Gettysburg because they had refused to run against overwhelming infantry force. They went back on patrol.

Stuart was still heading for York, from Hanover. He was closer to Gettysburg, but that had never been his destination, and his pickets did not fan out far enough – eleven miles – to observe the fighting.

The column that had ridden north so fast and so cheerfully was now in serious trouble. Despite their paroling, they had about four hundred prisoners to drag along, and the wagon drivers – Union civilians – were not inclined to cooperate any more than they had to. Mules are individuals, and each one has to be handled differently, preferably by a student of that particular mule. Forage was making difficulties, too.

But Stuart drove them on, and at dawn was at Dover, six miles out of York, only to learn that the Confederate column – undoubtedly Swell's – had been at York but had moved west.

This was not Virginia; local information was not cheerfully given and was inclined to be maliciously inaccurate. It said that the Southerners were converging on Shippensburg, due west, which would have taken Stuart above Gettysburg, but not as far above it as where he went.

He headed for Carlisle, which loomed large in all Regular Cavalry eyes. It was the site of Carlisle Barracks, in modern parlance the cavalry boot camp. Stuart, arriving after a long day's ride – on top of the horrible night ride – found a strong Union division in town.

He prepared to charge, but two of his officers had found Lee, and they now came in to him with news: the battle was at Gettysburg, get there as fast as possible.

Stuart took time to shell the Barracks and to burn the stores of the Union division, then started on the thirty miles to Gettysburg. Most of his troopers were leading, their horses were done for.

There had been heavy fighting all the day of July 1, at Gettysburg. Ewell had routed some enemy, but there had been no cavalry to complete the rout. The next day, when Stuart's battered column came into Lee, they were practically worthless; there was nothing to do but let them rest.

Kilpatrick and Gregg, who had been trying to stop Stuart from ever joining the Army of Northern Virginia, came in and covered Meade's flanks. They were in better shape than Stuart, but the cavalry did not get into the battle till the next day, July 3, when Stuart led his troops out along the York pike, away from the fight.

General George E. Pickett was about to make his infantry charge of fifteen thousand men against the Union center; Stuart's orders seem to have been – they were not written – to harass the Union reserves from the rear.

Harry Lee or William Washington would have held his cavalry behind his own reserve, ready to follow up Pickett's charge; Robert E. Lee didn't see it that way, apparently, and could have been right; the foot soldiers had better guns than in the Revolution, and in any given outfit of soldiers, North or South, there was probably a strong cadre of men who had been at war so long that they had become professional, and could not be routed for long or for far, as had the militia of the War of Independence. Any footsloggers who stood and fired could stand off a cavalry charge.

Around the middle of the day Stuart led the cavalry out on the York Pike. He had Jenkins' Independent Brigade added to his command, four brigades in all, enough to divert a good deal of strength from the Union line and allow Pickett to break through the thick Blue lines.

Stuart had his fieldpieces with him; behind him the heavy artillery was dueling loudly. He went along for less than an hour, then left the road, and started through the woods, with Jenkins' men dismounted and ahead of the riders. These were mounted riflemen, with infantry Enfields, but very little ammunition.

The Union troops they felt out were those of a twenty-three-year-old officer by the name of Custer – George Armstrong Custer, class of '61, U.S.M.A., substantively a captain or lieutenant in the 2nd Cavalry, but on this summer day a Brigadier General of Volunteers, commanding cavalry troops. Hampton was out there with another of Stuart's brigades; he engaged about the same time Stuart did, approximately 2:30 P.M.

Custer had gotten his fast wartime promotions and all his brevets mostly by staff work but he was always a man who liked to fight, and he was determined to do so today. Gregg and Kilpatrick and their Union troopers were out in the same area, and there were all the makings of a heavy scale cavalry battle.

Custer's men came out dismounted, ran into Jenkins' skirmishers, and opened the side-line battle. At first it was all dismounted fighting; Buford came up, and his men and those of Gregg charged on foot; Custer threw in his reserves, mounted, and the horseholders came out of defilade, and there was a terrible charge of Blue horsemen against Jenkins' dismounted riflemen; they were cut up and ruined. Wade Hampton and Fitz Lee countercharged.

Then it was all confusion, the line swaying back and forth; Wade Hampton took a frightful saber cut in the head, his brigade faltered, then re-entered the fight, perhaps more fiercely.

Stuart was waiting anxiously for word that Pickett had broken through, that infantry in Gray would appear through the Blue line and join the horse troops. But it never happened and late in the afternoon the cavalry fight flickered out, indecisively. Pickett's fifteen thousand men made their objective under terrible artillery fire, and then were forced back to Seminary Ridge, where Bufords troopers had started the battle two days before. Pickett had not gotten the support he should have; the battle was lost.

About four hundred casualties were counted in the cavalry battle between Stuart and Pleasonton's troopers under Buford, Custer, and the rest. The whole battle cost fifty thousand men, dead, wounded, prisoner, or missing. Both casualty lists, foot and horse, were about evenly divided between North and South.

The battle was over. The South had lost. Pleasonton threw his horse after the losers, hitting Longstreet's right flank; but Longstreet's infantrymen threw them back with a fury that made the charge seem suicidal, and that was the end of any feeling at Meade's headquarters that the South was routed. Lee was beaten, but still too strong for the exhausted Army of the Potomac to destroy; they would have to let him retreat in some order.

Why Lee lost is a matter of endless discussion. Jackson was dead, and that counted heavily. Longstreet was late, but Longstreet seems always to have been late. The Department of the Army gives a textbook reason: Lee was using the method of progressive attack, which ignores the principle of mass.

But from the cavalry point of view, Stuart's late arrival, his being at Carlisle when the battle was at Gettysburg, seems a major cause. For the first time Lee went into a battle as blind as the North did. Meade had no more intelligence than McDowell or Hooker or McClellan had had, but the Union generals had gotten used to fighting blind; Lee hadn't. It is to be supposed that a trained machine-gunner would lose a fight with a skilled Paleo-hunter if the only weapons allowed were the Folsom pointed spears of twenty thousand years ago; the Indian would know more about using his weapon than the modern man. And at least one infantry officer – a Major Rosengarten of Reynolds' outfit – reported that Buford's cavalrymen scouted the place for the battle and picked it with an eye to Union advantage. This is more or less confirmed by the fact that the action stopped where it had started. Lee was used to having his cavalry, not the enemy's, pick battle sites.

Thomason, who tries not to be an apologist for Stuart, and admittedly fails to achieve a complete lack of prejudice, draws a curious conclusion for a hard-bitten mercenary soldier: God didn't mean for the South to win the war.

The battle was over on July 3. The Glorious Fourth was not so glorious; there was a cloudburst, which worried Lee, who had the Potomac to cross to get his men home; and it worried the North, who had their wounded to carry away. Stuart had cut the rail line, and now the country roads were becoming impossible for wagons and ambulances.

Stuart threw his division out to cover the left flank of the defeated army, reorganizing on the ridges west of Gettysburg. The Gray started reloading their wagons for the long trek home.

In the rain Buford and Kilpatrick took their Blue horse south to lay traps for those wagons.

Robertson and Grumble Jones were down there, around the Potomac; they had been protecting the rear of Lee's army, and had fought a small battle, at Fairfield.

Hugh Kilpatrick, however, got through them, and took a thousand of Ewell's men prisoner. Stuart – it was now July 5 – came through the mountains, fighting off the Blue pass guards, and closed in on Kilpatrick's rear as Grumble Jones hit the Northern cavalry's front. Kilpatrick slipped out of that one and moved out from Hagerstown south to Boonsville, where Buford joined him.

Then, on July 6, they split again. Imboden, of the Stuart division, was riding rearguard on the Army of Northern Virginia; he was heavily burdened with ambulances and stragglers and supply wagons. Buford went after him, while Kilpatrick's troopers engaged Stuart and kept him tied up – or worse.

But Stuart was thinking along the same lines. He left four brigades – including the Independent Brigade, back under his command – at Hagerstown, and led the Fitz Lee and Hampton brigades – John Gordon commanding Hampton's men – to the rear to support Imboden.

Kilpatrick hit Hagerstown a little late. He forced the cavalry guard back into town, only to break through himself just as Longstreet's infantry divisions came in from the north.

Buford was a little better in his timing. He had attacked and completely engaged General John D. Imboden before Stuart got there. Imboden put up a strong defense; he threw his wagons into stockade, in the Western manner, and armed the teamsters and even some of the wounded and fought back valorously.

Stuart came out of the rain at the charge leading his two brigades. Buford fought back, and then rode off; heading south, he joined up with Kilpatrick again, and they counted their casualties: four hundred.

Stuart's losses were two hundred and fifty. In the next three days skirmishes made the score more even; the South lost sixty more troopers and officers than did Pleasonton's generals.

By July 12 the Lee army was on the Potomac, drawn up in a battle line six miles long.

Meade, coming up with his mud-weary, battle-worn Army of the Potomac, did not attack. The Army of Northern Virginia waited for the waters to go down, while Pleasonton and Stuart troopers skirmished on both flanks. On the night of July 13, the army of Robert E. Lee crossed back to Virginia.

Lee did not rest. He sent Stuart out to scout Meade's army, which was reported across the Shenandoah. But that river was too swollen for infantry or guns to get across.

The better-supplied Meade got his army across the Potomac on pontoons and took most of the passes that controlled that familiar theater of war. Stuart, riding hard, and Longstreet's infantry, for once moving with speed, held Chester Gap and Manassas Gap, and both armies were able to get back to the Rappahannock, the North on the north bank, the South on the south bank. Each army was smaller by thirty thousand men, but they were back where they had been a month before.

The troopers grazed their horses on the rich grass of Virginia and pondered an order of Stuart's that told them they were slipping and hurting the good name that the cavalry division had earned for itself. In the last paragraph there is a sample of his style: "Let the artful dodger on the battlefield receive the retributive bullet of his gallant comrade."

The next day Lee wrote a report in which he blamed the loss of Gettysburg on the absence of the cavalry. A year later the First Gentleman of the South wrote a fuller report, fairer to Stuart. Jeff Davis' government published the first, but not the second.

August was quiet, and the cavalry were reorganized into a corps of two divisions. Rooney Lee and the convalescing Wade Hampton were made the major generals commanding them. Stuart was still in command, but as a senior major general instead of as a lieutenant general; the published reports on Gettysburg had made him unpopular.

He got rid of W.E. "Grumble" Jones and had him sent to southern Virginia and out of his theater. He gave Fitz Lee all his old brigade and that of Rooney Lee's; Hampton got his old brigade, Butler's, and a regiment of Robertson's. Beverly Robertson was transferred to North Carolina at his own request.

The war began again, in northern Virginia, on September 13, when Kilpatrick came south and struck at Culpeper. Stuart fought him – at Brandy Station again – and Kilpatrick went back north. He was probably just riding for intelligence, but he destroyed three of Stuart's fieldpieces, and replacements were getting scarcer and scarcer for the South.

On September 22 both Buford and Kilpatrick came down, Buford swinging wide to the west and Kilpatrick bearing straight down. Stuart went across the Rapidan and tried to stop Buford.

Buford was always a hard fighter, and he was gaining the day when Kilpatrick rode in and, charging hard, turned Stuart's flank and almost captured the rest of his fieldpieces. When that happened the Gray troopers suddenly went into a fury.

Fighting rear and advance guard at one time, Stuart broke through Kilpatrick and got clean away, men and horse and guns.

Meade had sent out his reconnaissance, and the intelligence they brought back seemed to discourage him; he made no overtures. Lee decided to try and flank the stronger Army of the Potomac; he would go around the right this time, instead of the left, as he had when Pope held the same ground.

Stuart moved his men out in a screen on October 9 in that third autumn of the war, driving in Kilpatrick's videttes and then skirmishing with Kilpatrick and his main force. Meanwhile Fitz Lee and his division were pushing back Buford, with such success that Meade had no idea the Gray infantry was again on the move. Stuart fought Kilpatrick first at Brandy Station and then Fitz Lee pushed Buford up there and re-formed his line with Stuart's; the spent bullets at that tiny place must have covered the soil with a lead blanket

Meade drew the wrong conclusions from the cavalry clashes; he decided that Stuart was riding vanguard rather than flank on Lee's army. He sent three whole corps down into the Culpeper-Brandy Station area, where Stuart had left only a small force while the main cavalry screened Ewell's corps, moving north but doing it a valley or so west of Culpeper.

Gregg and his cavalry were there, and got away from Stuart to report to Meade, who turned his forces around and got into the country Lee had hoped to use.

Stuart scouted out Meade's movements, got a look at the Army of the Potomac and then tried to get word to Lee. But he was surrounded, all at once, by the heavy Blue movement; nightfall saved him before his two brigades could be wiped out, and they went into cold camp, silently.

There were no fires in the Stuart camp, but it wasn't dark; the Yankees were so close that their cooking fires lit up the Gray lines. Stuart got messengers out to try and sneak through the lines and ask Lee for a diverting attack. Through the night his pickets captured several Union officers, strolling among what they thought were their own camps.

Ewell had gotten the word of the encirclement, and attacked shortly after dawn, but he wasn't at all sure where Stuart was, and his fire was mild and uncertain. Still, it was enough. The Horse Artillery dropped a few shots into the adjacent Union camps; then they limbered up and everybody got out of there, in a mad scramble of yells and shots and confusion. They broke out, losing Colonel Ruffin, but getting away with all their guns and their supply wagons and the intelligence that Meade seemed more eager to retreat than to fight. A.P. Hill attacked, too recklessly, and both armies pulled away from each other for a while and watched.

The next action, five days later, was cavalry again; Stuart against a defending picketing Kilpatrick. It would have been just a frontal skirmish, fire and pull away, except that Fitz Lee, patrolling nearby, heard the guns, came up, and saw a fine chance to trap Kilpatrick.

So, Fitz Lee went into cover alongside a road, and Stuart retreated along that road; they were certain Kilpatrick would pursue and be flanked.

It would have worked, except that Custer was one of Kilpatrick's two brigadiers. Custer, the prima donna, decided to water and feed before helping his major general pursue the routed Stuart men; because of that, Custer's Michigan Volunteers were far enough back to see Fitz Lee's dismounted troopers coming out of the woods to pounce on Kilpatrick's headquarters outfit and Davis' troopers, who made up the other brigade of the division.

The Michiganders attacked Fitz Lee's flank just as Fitz attacked Kilpatrick's; Stuart, on hearing the guns, stopped retreating and hit hard at Kilpatrick's front; it was a perfect merry-go-round, but not very merry for Custer, who lost his personal baggage, or for Kilpatrick, who lost all his headquarters wagons.

The year 1863 petered out, after that. There were skirmishes between cavalry videttes, and once Meade felt his way down, and then went back, deciding an attack would be too costly.

Chapter 18

A Place Called Yellow Tavern

The year 1864 opened with all the personnel for the last act of Stuart's life on the stage except one: Phi Sheridan, still in the West.

In February, Meade sent Hugh Kilpatrick out with five thousand riders to foray against Richmond. That capital had never really been a prime military target, but until Ulysses S. Grant took over the Army of the Potomac, the Union kept trying to strike at it. Besides the usual morale factor and the presence in Richmond of the only real ordnance factory in the South, there were a number of Union prisoners there in early 1864. Also, the riders carried saddlebags full of proclamations by Abraham Lincoln offering amnesty to any Confederates who returned to the Union. It was too late for this, but Lincoln still thought of himself as President of all the states.

Kilpatrick led the raid because Meade kept Pleasonton busy on his staff; it seems as though the larger staff George Meade could get together, the less chance there was of making a firm decision about anything.

The Confederate artillery horses had gone to Charlottesville for the winter; that was an easy place to get feed into. The year before, the Army of Northern Virginia had been in pitiful shape during the cold months; but now the veterans didn't seem to mind being half-naked in the snow; Stuart had a good and active force under his hand.

The first thing Kilpatrick did was split his force into two columns. He commanded the larger one himself, planning to take it around the Confederate right flank and then straight at Richmond. The smaller body, under Custer, was to feint for the left, where Meade would also stage an infantry attack, two corps against Lee's flank. Kilpatrick – or Meade, or Pleasonton, or Lincoln and Secretary of War Edwin M. Stanton, who had sanctioned the raid – figured that Stuart would dash to cover Lee's left and leave the main body of raiders unresisted. The plan was completely based on the Southern forces being in as bad shape as they had been a year before.

They weren't. Fitz Lee was on the left of the Army of Northern Virginia and resisted the infantry attack vigorously; Stuart rode out to take charge, and there was skirmishing all through February 28.

That night Custer struck out, riding hard, and hit at the winter artillery camp at Charlottesville. There were not only horses there, but guns; Moorman, in charge, got one battery around to shell Custer's attack and issued rifles to the revolver-armed cannoneers and drivers. Custer did a good deal of damage and pulled back; he had created the diversion he'd been ordered to make, Stuart got the news, and rode to cut him off.

There was an awful lot of splitting of Federal forces in that raid. Custer's advance guard got several hours ahead of his main body; Stuart rode into the gap and put his shivering men into ambush. But by the time Custer came, the Confederates were too frozen to make much of the trap; Custer rode through and away before their hands could get warm enough to handle their carbines.

Kilpatrick did well at first, managing to skirt Wade Hampton's division, to overpower and capture a Southern vidette party, and to sweep through west of Chancellorsville. There he split his column, sending Colonel Ulric Dahlgren ahead with five hundred troopers to sweep around Richmond and come up from the south, to make an anvil against which Kilpatrick's three-thousand-man force could hammer Richmond flat.

Dahlgren, commanding the new split-off of Kilpatrick's cavalry, was only twenty-one, probably the youngest colonel in the Union Army. He had joined up two years before and had been made a captain: his father was Admiral John A. Dahlgren, one of the most important in the U.S. Navy.

The captain had lost a leg at Gettysburg, rested for a while, and then spent the rest of his recuperative leave at sea with his father. But as soon as he could be fitted with an artificial leg, he had climbed on a horse, found he could ride, and rejoined the cavalry. He led his men, now, sixty miles in thirty hours. This, of course, can be done at a walk – a good troop horse walks five miles an hour easily – but under Kilpatrick, walking was unfashionable; the horses cantered, trotted, did anything but walk, and then, of course, staggered to a halt and were rested, too tired to digest their feed properly.

That sixty miles was not unresisted. Small Gray patrols had to be fought off or ridden over; occasionally parties of winter leave men would get together in haste and do what harassment they could. Dahlgren went where he was supposed to go, south of Richmond and prepared to be the lower jaw of a crusher; but the upper jaw wasn't where it should have been.

Hugh Kilpatrick's troopers called him Kilcavalry; he always drove them too hard. This was one of the worst times. They arrived at the northern defenses of Richmond so worn out that Wade Hampton, pursuing them, could strike at will; Richmond was defended by well entrenched infantry, and Kilpatrick was crushed instead of crushing.

He slipped away to the east, abandoning Dahlgren, who was just then firing at the southwestern quarter of the city. Hampton followed hard, other Stuart corps outfits coming in to strengthen him as he went along, and they made a rich haul of straggling men and horses, until Kilpatrick got back under the shelter of Meade's army.

Ulric Dahlgren fared worse. His five hundred men shrank to a hundred and thirty-five, and then surrendered. The young colonel himself was killed, his artificial leg stolen, and his body shipped to Richmond to be put on show in the railroad depot.

That was the action for the winter; spring had set in before the Blue came out again, and the Gray was more than willing to have it so. Fitz Lee organized a minstrel troupe – this is Major General Fitzhugh Lee – and took it around the camps, entertaining. Flora Stuart's first cousin, John Esten Cooke, was a novelist who was serving as Stuart's ordnance officer; Stuart wrote his wife he was thinking of having Cooke write his reports. But he wrote them himself, including the one on Gettysburg, which was completely free of apology or alibi.

The South was running out of horses. The hotbloods of Virginia had carried Stuart's men through three years of war and were decimated as a result; the reservoir of Southern horseflesh, Texas, had been cut off by the Union when it captured Vicksburg and the whole Mississippi River.

But spring found Stuart with eight thousand mounted men under him, mounted on just about the last able horses available. It was practically the largest force he had ever had. Lee had less infantry than the year before, and no hopes of replacements if these fell. As a matter of fact, there were fourteen-year-olds in the Cavalry Corps; horses were not the only thing the Confederacy was lacking.

Lincoln had finally brought Grant east, in February. He left Meade in charge of the Army of the Potomac, demoted Halleck to Chief of Staff, and made the Western hero – he had taken Vicksburg, cleared the Mississippi and whipped Braxton Bragg at Chattanooga – General-in-Chief, with the rank of lieutenant general. But this General-in-Chief took the field, where he could keep Meade moving. He turned over his old Western army to Sherman and laid out a national plan – the nation being the Confederacy – instead of the old one of taking Richmond first and then going on from there. As Grant saw it, if he could cut up Lee's Army of the Potomac while Sherman cut south from Chattanooga and all the other Union armies moved in on the two main movements, he would cut the South into segments each incapable of defending itself.

There were twelve thousand cavalrymen in the Army of the Potomac then. Their commander was a major general, Philip H. Sheridan, who had proved himself in the West. He had a good force under him, well-horsed, well-armed with repeating carbines, and he knew how to use cavalry.

Meade had fallen into the old error of making Pleasonton lend small detachments of horse soldiers to any headquarters that wanted couriers or guards or parade troops. Grant fought until he had the cavalry back together again, and finally, May was there, the grass was up for the horses, and it was time to strike.

In the first three days of May, Stuart reported a good deal of Union activity to Lee; on May 4, his men uncovered movement in force and depth, crossing the Rapidan and moving south.

Stuart moved out to screen the Lee army. At once he must have known that he was not dealing with Pleasonton or George Stoneman; Sheridan's Blue troopers slashed hard at the screen and kept the offensive at all times. Stuart could not get set to cut through them and raid the heavy and lengthy Grant wagon trains, fording the Rapidan in spring water.

Jeb Stuart went back, leaving his men to harass as they could, and brought up A.P. Hill's corps, Stuart himself riding as guide for the infantrymen. Then he ordered his troopers to pull off to the side and let Sheridan ram headon into the heavy infantry body.

But Sheridan had kept Grant informed, as no previous cavalry commander had informed the general of the Army of the Potomac, and Grant was ready; he threw in all his mass, three corps totaling about seventy-two thousand men, and engaged not only Hill, but the only other corps Lee had, that of Ewell, which had been flanking Grant's movement.

Together the two corps numbered only forty thousand men; Grant could afford terrible losses and still have an army left; and Grant was not timid.

Longstreet was away; Lee sent for him to bring his corps up fast. In trying to do it, Longstreet was wounded by his own pickets. Unlike Jackson, he was not killed, but he was so badly wounded in the neck that he was off the field till fall.

The infantry battle raged through the Wilderness, a heavily wooded area, for two days; the woods caught fire, and it was terrible work; artillery could not be brought to bear, and the infantrymen did all the work. Longstreet's corps came into the fight, and Grant was checked on May 7, but not checkmated. He had ordered Sheridan to mass his cavalry and sweep around Lee's right flank. Sheridan took off, but not with his whole force.

Stuart blocked him, the Blue and Gray troopers fighting dismounted against each other in woods too thick for the horses to work. Then cavalry forays disclosed the whole supply train from the North trying for that right flank, heading for Spottsylvania.

Lee ordered Stuart to race for that town and block it. He barely reached it before Sheridan swept in, but the small margin of time was enough for the

Southerners to get set; they held on until Longstreet's infantry, now under Brigadier General Richard H. Anderson, came up to strengthen them.

Sheridan went back to Meade's headquarters. Meade had been up to his old tricks according to Phil Sheridan, robbing the cavalry of platoons and companies and whole squadrons. Sheridan wanted his twenty-odd thousand men intact, or Meade could have his shoulder straps.

Meade tried to quiet him down. Sheridan was Irish and didn't know how to quiet down once he got mad. He was convinced that with force he could whip Stuart, and that with Stuart out, Lee could be whipped.

Grant, General-in-Chief, overheard the argument between his Army commander and his Cavalry commander, and intervened. The report is that he simply said "Go ahead," to Phil Sheridan. Then he told Meade to move out, too, and strike at Lee.

Sheridan started down the Peninsula; General Benjamin Butler had another Union Army down there, and Sheridan planned to ride through to him, cutting Stuart's screen, reprovision, and ride back to Grant, the sort of slashing separation that had ruined John Pemberton on the Mississippi and Braxton Bragg in Tennessee. Sheridan's troopers were impressed when he took them out at a walk; this was a long expedition, and he was not Kilpatrick, who started everything with a rush and ended up with limping, shaking horses.

Stuart was busy harassing Meade – Grant, really – while Lee's infantry and engineers built breastworks and trenches to stop the Union progress. His patrol brought him word of Sheridan's ride-out. At once he sent Wickham's brigade after the Blue troopers; he called in the rest of his corps and prepared to follow with his full force, which was less than half that of Sheridan's.

Wickham's orders were to strike at Sheridan's rearguard and slow him down till the rest of the corps could catch up; but there was no necessity to slow Phil Sheridan down. His troopers kept up the walk, his rearguard merely fending Wickham off. Sheridan was going to cut northern Virginia through, so that Lee could never again have contact with Richmond, and he wasn't interested in wiping out a brigade; he was going to destroy the Army of Northern Virginia by attrition.

Stuart came up with his main body, saw what was happening, and cut off to take a parallel road and flank past Sheridan, who moved steadily along toward Richmond, doing damage and freeing Union prisoners as he went.

Stuart had time to ride over to the Beaver Dam country and see his wife and Jemmie and their new baby; then he was in the saddle again. At night, Fitz Lee reported that the men and their horses were both played out; Stuart let them stop and rest two or three hours. They moved out again, an hour after midnight, with Stuart decided about where he would make his stand against Sheridan: the little hills behind Yellow Tavern, an abandoned – and no longer yellow – building northeast of Mechanicsville.

At dawn a detachment of the 2nd Virginia clashed with a flank party of Sheridan's column, and Stuart learned that he had headed the Union column, as he had hoped to. Three years of fighting over this terrain – home country for many of his men – gave him a big advantage over Sheridan, freshly arrived from the West. Part of Stuart's force was still harassing Sheridan's rearguard; to head the Blue column there were only about three thousand men.

It was now the morning of May 11. Stuart picked his ground, the ridge above the Tavern, and sent in to Richmond to ask for infantry support. Then he dismounted his men and waited for Sheridan to come.

Phil Sheridan came in midmorning, moving slowly, moving steadily, moving with all the mass of his big column, almost four to one, not counting John Gordon's men on Sheridan's tail.

There was charge and countercharge, Sheridan's men fighting as dismounted Dragoons, and Sheridan feeling out Stuart's thin line, looking for weak spots. But Stuart had always done well with horse artillery, and his fieldpieces were in line that day. There was a stalemate – bloody, not decisive – until four in the afternoon.

Then Custer burst out of the Union line, mounted and leading his Michigan Volunteers on their fresh horses. They charged the guns on Stuart's left, silenced them and drove the whole left flank back; Stuart galloped that way, rallying men, bringing up some mounted 1st Virginians to turn the tide back.

And it was there, as Stuart was in among his men, firing his revolver at anything blue, that something blue fired at him: a Michigan trooper, Private John A. Huff, aged forty-eight, put a pistol bullet through Jeb Stuart's liver.

They got him to an ambulance, and took him in to Richmond, to the house of his sister-in-law, Maria Cooke, who had married Dr. Brewer, now Surgeon General, CSA. They got word to Flora Cooke Stuart, and she started the twenty-five-mile trip into the capital. But Sheridan had cut all the roads, and she got there after her husband was dead.

Fitz Lee fought the corps against Sheridan, but that tough man went on with his raid – sixteen days in all – and the day of Southern cavalry was over. There were no horses left to mount another corps or division. While there was Southern horse action for the next eleven months of the war, it was a series of small raids. The power of cavalry as a striking arm had shifted from South to North, from J.E.B. Stuart to Phil Sheridan.

Chapter 19

An Ugly Little Irishman

When James Ewell Brown Stuart was shot he was wearing – besides his plumed hat and his red-lined cloak – a red rose. Philip Henry Sheridan was not the nosegay type. He wasn't rich, he wasn't handsome, he wasn't big; Stuart was almost six feet tall and broad-shouldered, handsome (after he grew a beard to cover his receding chin) and romantic. Sheridan was a small Irishman with a bump on the back of his head so pronounced he couldn't wear a forage cap and with eyes so slanted they looked Oriental.

Sheridan had graduated from West Point in 1853, a year before Stuart; he would have gotten out before that, except that he lost his temper, lunged at a cadet sergeant with his bayonet, and was suspended for a full year. It is to be noted that the cadet sergeant was a Virginian and an aristocrat; when Phil Sheridan was a boy the Irish were a scorned minority in the United States, and the little mick from Ohio may have felt he was being snubbed.

Sheridan didn't start his Army career in the cavalry. Appointments to the branches were then, as now, allotted to the cadets according to their class standing; Engineers to the highest, Artillery to the next group, and Infantry for the bottom of the class. Sheridan was assigned to the Infantry. He wouldn't have survived at all if Henry Warner Slocum, his roommate, hadn't hung a blanket over the window every night and coached Sheridan on his next day's studies.

He was the first, perhaps the only, of the great generals – the ones who used cavalry in the mass – who had no desire to lead a saber charge. When he had to take his horse soldiers forward at a gallop, he gestured the command with his hat instead of his sword; and he always felt that the best place and way to kill the enemy was from the steady ground and with a gun, rather than from a moving saddle and with a blade.

After leaving West Point – where he had a miserable time – the little Irish-Catholic from Ohio went out as a shavetail to the 1st Infantry at Fort

211

Duncan, Texas, which was where the town of Eagle Pass now stands on the Rio Grande. The "fort" was a tent camp in about as miserable a climate as Texas knows; when it isn't scorching or freezing there, it is flooding. At once almost all the other officers in garrison hated the new little second lieutenant. His appearance, manner of speech and behavior at mess were all unaristocratic, they felt. Furthermore, he promptly built himself a winter quarters of wood and tarp, and smugly announced that he was better off than most of his neighbors, who were wintering in GI tents.

He even managed to make an enemy of the post supplier by shooting so much game that the officers' mess stopped buying beef in any large quantity. Before the winter was over he was transferred to the 4th Infantry, with orders to report to New York. There he was handed three hundred recruits for the West Coast. They went out by boat to Panama, overland across the Isthmus, and then again by boat to San Francisco.

They didn't keep him there more than a few days. It was a very congenial post, that Benicia Barracks; it was there that Grant became alcholic and resigned from the service, and a major died of acute alcoholism, and was buried with ceremonies that, according to George Crook, might soon send some of the other officers the same route.

There was a topographical expedition in the field; Sheridan was ordered out to replace John Hood, commanding forty Dragoons in the escort. Hood had been transferred to the 2nd Cavalry.

So young Sheridan cut out to Fort Reading to find that the exploring party – trying to find a way between the Central Valley and Oregon – had gone on. It was hostile country, but Sheridan was anxious to take over his first command. He picked up an escort of a corporal and two privates and shoved on into the lava beds of the malpais, tracking the engineers. He was not alone in that endeavor; Pit Indians were also on the trail. Sheridan managed to skirt the hostiles and got into camp safely; the combined parties finished their survey and Portland was reached without hostilities.

There they learned that the Yakima Indians were out on the warpath; they had murdered their agent and whipped an Army column sent out to punish them. The infantry lieutenant and his Dragoon command were attached to a mixed force of Regulars and Oregon Mounted Volunteers and sent out to settle the matter. It wasn't a happy column. Like every Regular officer before them, Sheridan and the others found out that they couldn't get along with the Volunteers; it was not till the Civil War lasted long enough to make Regular-acting soldiers out of Militia that the United States and state troops learned to work together.

The commander of the Volunteers was a colonel, Oregon commission; the commander of the 4th Infantry forces (and their Dragoons) was only a major. Bickering over who was in charge, they took off.

Sheridan and his Dragoons distinguished themselves on the second day of the march by scattering a bunch of Yakimas into running fast enough to leave their winter food supply behind. It might have taught Phil Sheridan a lesson, or he might have already figured it out for himself. Many years later, when he was one of the most hated names in the South for his depredations, Sheridan told a friend that he would much sooner burn a man's barn and all his supplies than kill that same man's son; it did more to win a war and was less brutal.

A few days after his first skirmish Sheridan had another. Working on information that the Yakimas were holed up in a certain place, he was leading his troopers on it when a huge cloud of dust rose up behind his command. He turned and charged into it, convinced that tracking Indians had cut off his rear, and he succeeded – this was a saber charge – in herding a squadron of Mounted Volunteers into the Regular major's camp. Good will between the two groups was not increased.

The foray against the Yakimas accomplished nothing; the column returned to base before winter snows blocked the passes. While the major commanding and one of the artillery captains filed charges against each other, Sheridan and his Dragoons were ordered into winter quarters at Fort Vancouver.

By spring, 1856, Sheridan had passed his twenty-fifth birthday and achieved his first independent command. He was sent out from the Middle Cascades with his Dragoons – who seemed to have no horse officers attached to them – to liberate a blockhouse besieged by Shahaptian Indians, several tribes of which were in revolt.

Supporting columns were on the march to back up Sheridan; he didn't wait for them. His men were dismounted; they had come up the river by steamboat. He had a bateau at hand, and tried to ferry his men across the river, since the Indians were on his side and too numerous to be attacked directly. He made the crossing, all right, by commandeering a camp full of squaws to haul on the cordelling ropes.

The relieving columns came up, Sheridan skirmished, captured a number of hostile Indians, and received his first commendation: special mention for gallantry.

It wasn't a very big campaign, not a very significant victory; but it put Sheridan of the Infantry in command of cavalrymen; it showed him how to live off the country and how to keep the enemy from doing the same thing; and it reassured him that the most unpopular of soldiers could be honored if he moved briskly, bravely, and with ingenuity.

He was still up in the Northwest, still a lieutenant, when the Civil War broke out. Sheridan and other Northern officers seized their posts out there and held them against the Southern officers, who were in the majority, but who were more anxious to get back to their fighting states than to worry about Oregon.

After Bull Run had been fought in the East, Sheridan was promoted to captain and ordered to St. Louis, headquarters of the Department of the West. His new commission assigned him to the 13th Infantry, a new regiment. But the 13th was nowhere around Halleck's headquarters in Missouri; Halleck grabbed the Regular and put him at the head of a board that was trying to sort out the accounts of Frémont, recently a general in that area.

It took weeks. Frémont had used Army credit to reward his friends, flatterers, and anyone else who might have a vote in the popularity contest in which the flamboyant Frémont ran all his life. But Sheridan had spent the year of his suspension from West Point working as a bookkeeper, and he rather enjoyed the untangling of the financial maze. When he and his board made its report, Halleck was pleased, and made Sheridan Chief Commissary and Chief Quartermaster of the Army of the Southwest, southwest in this case meaning southern Missouri. Headquarters was at Rolla.

The new job was again mostly paperwork, and not our concern here. Sheridan applied himself to his duties, carried them off well, and found he was not so unpopular in the officers' messes of the wartime army as he had been with the Regulars. His next assignment was a horse-buying trip through Wisconsin. Battles were being fought, his old classmates were temporary colonels and brigadiers and he was still a noncombatant captain. Out in the Mississippi Valley theater, Grant had captured Forts Henry and Donelson, and the Battle of Shiloh was fought while Sheridan was returning to Halleck from his horse buying.

Halleck wasn't there; he had gone to relieve Grant in the Tennessee Valley, believing that Grant was too slow. But General William T. Sherman was. He tried to get Sheridan a colonelcy in the Ohio Volunteers; Regulars offered such posts by state governors were given leave by the Army to accept them without loss of seniority or Regular commission. The governor turned Sherman down, and Gordon Granger, another West Pointer, who had just been appointed a brigadier in Michigan troops, backed Sheridan to succeed him as colonel of the 2nd Michigan Cavalry. The West Point Protective Association must have felt particularly clannish in those days, after so many of its members had defected to the South.

At the end of May 1862, Phil Sheridan had eagles stitched to his shoulder straps and joined the cavalry. He took command of an outfit already saddling up for action. The night of his commission he led out against Booneville, Mississippi, a junction on the Mobile & Ohio Railroad.

Two days later the Booneville yards were a mess of burnt freight cars, twisted rails, and wood ashes that had been railroad ties. Sheridan's

General Francis Marion in a swamp encampment inviting a British officer to dinner, the latter consisting of sweet potatoes and water. (Courtesy of the Library of Congress)

Henry "Light-Horse Harry" Lee. (Courtesy of the National Archives)

Above left: Major General Stephen Watts Kearny during the period of the Mexican War. (Courtesy of the Library of Congress)

Above right: Major General Philip Kearny. (Courtesy of the Library of Congress;

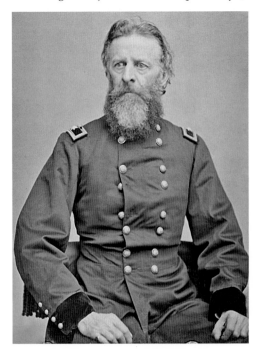

Brigadier General Philip
St. George Cooke during the
Civil War Period. (US Signal
Corps Photograph in the
National Archives)

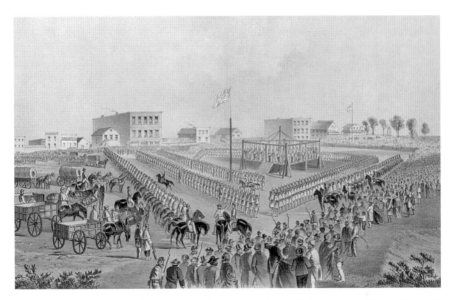

Execution of thirty-eight Sioux Indians, Mankuto, Minnesota, December 26, 1862. (Courtesy of the Library of Congress)

Above left: Major General J.E.B. Stuart. (Courtesy of the National Archives)

Above right: Major General Philip H. Sheridan, Union commander at the Battle of Five Forks. (Courtesy of the National Archives)

Above left: Major General Edwin V. Sumner. (Mathew Brady Collection, US Signal Corps reproduction in the National Archives)

Above right: "Billy Yank", a volunteer soldier of the Union. Note that the only bit used is the snaffle or "watering bridle". (Courtesy of the Library of Congress)

Major General George Crook in the field with his favorite riding mule, "Apache", and two Apache scouts, "Dutchy" at left, and "Alchiso". (US Signal Corps Photograph in the National Archives)

A group of Mescalero Apache scouts with Sergeant F.W. Klopfer of Troop H, 4th Cavalry, at Fort Stanton, New Mexico, 1885. (US Signal Corps Photograph in the National Archives)

A young trooper at Camp Cheyenne, South Dakota, about 1890. Note the curb bit, and that the carbine is in a sling, rather than a boot, which was a cheaper contrivance but not so desirable, as it sometimes jammed. (Courtesy of the Library of Congress)

A large camp at Brûlé Sioux near Pine Ridge Agency, South Dakota, probably in 1891. (Courtesy of the Library of Congress)

Above: The military camp at Rosebud Agency, South Dakota, included two troops of the 9th Cavalry, four companies of the 8th and six companies of the 21st infantry battalions. (US Signal Corps Photograph in the National Archives)

Below: Camp of the US 7th Cavalry at Pine Ridge Agency, 1891. (Courtesy of the Library of Congress)

Above: Members of Company I, 6th Pennsylvania Cavalry, at Falmouth, Virginia, June 1863. (US Library of Congress)

Below: A depiction of the charge of the 6th New York Cavalry at Brandy Station, Virginia, 11 October 1863. (US Library of Congress)

Major General George A. Custer. (US Signal Corps Photograph in the National Archives)

Comanche, the only survivor of the Custer Massacre, 1876. (US Library of Congress)

troopers and those of the 2nd Iowa had completely ruined Beauregard's supply line.

Confederate cavalry attacked the ravagers but were beaten off. When the pileup of trains at Booneville got big enough, the Union troopers pulled out and rode hard for Corinth: altogether, ninety miles in four days, with time out for sabotaging a railroad.

But Corinth was deserted of Confederate troops; Beauregard had left when his rail line was cut. It had been an orderly withdrawal, and it was ten days before Pope's headquarters knew which direction the Southern headquarters had gone; then they sent Sheridan out reconnoitering toward Tupelo.

He ravaged as he went, burning fields, graineries, killing or driving cattle off for the Union commissary. On his return he reported to Pope that his outfit had ridden by "many fine houses … where the women and children were crying for food."

Pope gave him command of the brigade, still with the rank of colonel, but sure of promotion. The pattern was set. Sheridan had come to his command through a very different route than had Stuart – or Harry Lee and his grandsons, or any of the Southerners or other West Point Northerners. He had worked as a bookkeeper in civil life, and actually enjoyed bookkeeping, and his first two wartime jobs had been connected with finance and commissary, the third with purchasing. This was not the sort of general officer who wished he could get a professional writer to handle his daily report.

Sheridan wrote in his memoirs that his first thought was always of his men's mess; Stuart could conceive of nothing more important than being ready to die for his country. Romance and dash had won the war right up to Gettysburg; commissary and quartermaster work would win it from now on. Sheridan had dash, and plenty of it; but instead of entertaining his men with banjo playing and minstrel shows, he fed and clothed them and counted on their having enough brains to be grateful and to see that he appreciated them. Then, when he got on his horse and waved his hat they would follow him. If they didn't they might be transferred to some outfit where the living was harder; it was as simple as that.

During June 1862, Sheridan and his brigade garrisoned Booneville. The acting brigadier sent out constant patrols – in strength, like the Southerners, not in small detachments as the Army of the Potomac was then doing – to feel out the enemy and to improve the maps used by the brigade and regiment headquarters.

The Confederates attacked Booneville on July 1. Sheridan had less than a thousand men under his hand; General James R. Chalmers attacked with more than five thousand Gray sabers.

Sheridan dismounted his men and put them behind trees. They fought as an outfit of sharpshooters, each man armed with a revolving rifle *and* a revolving pistol, twelve shots before he had to reload. That early in the war, the Confederates could be counted on to be using muzzle loaders, or at best single-shot breech loaders; the odds switched from five-to-one for the South to about two-to-one for the North.

Other factors strengthened Sheridan's position. He had occupied the ground for a month, and his men, besides being covered by trees, were flanked by swamps and vanguarded by breastworks. And they were disciplined; the Michigan regiment held its fire till the enemy were within twenty-five yards of them, and then mowed down the attackers. Still, enough got through, Sheridan later reported, so that the bayonet had to be resorted to: possibly the light cavalry saber that could do double duty.

The heavy force of Confederates were as so many of the Southern outfits so often were, suicidally brave. By the middle of the day Sheridan had to switch back to being a cavalry leader or be overwhelmed by sheer numbers. He dispatched a squadron – really only ninety men – to ride around to the rear of the Southern line and charge in column, straight through, making as much racket about it as possible.

While the foray was making its gallop, his skirmish line continued to repulse wave after wave of the Gray assault; then he got a break. A train full of forage came up from Corinth; Sheridan sent orders to the engineer to blow his whistle full blast, which made the troopers on both sides think that Union re-enforcements were arriving. When the diversionary force finally attacked, the noise – shooting, Rebel yells, engine whistle – was so loud that it drowned out the clashing of sabers on the enemy rear.

Sheridan ordered the dismounted attack at the time when Captain Russell A. Alger should be diverting behind the Southern lines. It worked. Alger took Confederate headquarters; the main body of Blue troopers charged with enough density and vigor to convince the Gray that they were surrounded; Chalmers and his large force abandoned their dead and wounded and galloped away. At three o'clock, Sheridan had wired for help; at five o'clock he canceled the order.

As a result of Booneville, Sheridan was mentioned in dispatches, praised – and ordered back to guard General Gordon Granger's divisional headquarters.

It was a dangerous spot; a brigade commanded by a colonel was liable to find itself chewed into message-bearing platoons by a major general of division. Sheridan managed to get permission to take a strong column south on reconnaissance; when he returned he made his report to U.S. Grant, only recently restored to the command of the Army of the Tennessee.

Grant liked everything about the report and the colonel – acting brigadier – who made it.

But the war wasn't going well; McClellan, Pope, and then McClellan again were failing to fight the Army of the Potomac as that massive weapon should have been fought. In the West Halleck was rewarded for fumbling around Tupelo by being taken to Washington as – eventually – General-in-Chief, and his successors continued to move too slowly and without trying to coordinate the three armies in the Mississippi Valley.

Grant's Army of the Tennessee suffered the sort of treatment given the cavalry in the East; it was nibbled away by orders to assign small railroad guard details and tiny garrisons of unimportant places.

Braxton Bragg, fighting for the Confederacy in the West, struck, and along the Ohio the cities panicked. The mayors and governors wired Washington frantically and troops were moved toward Kentucky, Ohio, and Indiana hastily and without much more plan than the Union had ever shown up till now.

Sheridan, still a colonel, was told off to take his 2nd Michigan and four regiments of Illinois and Missouri infantry to Louisville. He was eager to go; there was much more chance of a fight along the Ohio than there was in northern Mississippi, and five regiments were close to being a division; if he used them well, he might get a major general's command.

Grant, encountering the little Irish colonel on the railroad platform, took exception to Sheridan's eagerness to be off; Grant was being left behind with a much depleted army. In their memoirs, both generals said the incident marred their relationship for years.

The Louisville theater was a fouled hive of politics and counter-politics on both sides. Many of the troops were Middle-Western Volunteers, and therefore close to their governors; colonels wired their state legislatures to put pressure on General Don Carlos Buell, commanding, to make them brigadiers; one Regular infantry captain was made a major general of Volunteers by General Wright one week and a brigadier the next by General Nelson.

Across the lines, at Frankfort, Generals Kirby Smith and Braxton Bragg, CSA, were wasting opportunity by deciding on a Confederate governor for Kentucky, and then going through the ceremony of inaugurating him.

The Union won out in idiocy, however, when a general with the unfortunate name of Jefferson C. Davis quarreled with and virtually murdered General William Nelson and went unpunished.

Sheridan got his brigadier's star, and command of an infantry division. Almost a month after he had hurried into Louisville, he got a chance to fight with that division, at Perryville. The South won the battle, but Sheridan and his division were given credit for saving the Union Army by standing firm and holding their position.

After the battle, most of the Union generals laid charges and made complaints against each other; they left Phil Sheridan alone, and he stayed out of the squabbles, and the public press took more and more notice of him; so did Halleck, in Washington.

General Buell was relieved; General William S. Rosecrans – who had praised Sheridan very highly down in Mississippi – took the command; Sheridan's outfit was renamed 3rd Division and reorganized. The army marched over toward Tennessee and ran into the Southern army on Stone's River near Murfreesboro. There they fought a three-days' battle that cost each side about ten thousand men, proved nothing, but added to Sheridan's reputation as a general who could handle a full division. The year of 1862 ended as badly for the Army of the Cumberland as it had for the Army of the Potomac.

For the first half of 1863 the Army of the Cumberland camped near Murfreesboro. There were occasional clashes between cavalry pickets; these were no concern of Brigadier General Philip H. Sheridan; he was commanding infantry. If he had any opinions about the increasingly annoying raids that Morgan and Forrest were making into what was technically Union territory, Phil Sheridan kept those opinions to himself. President Lincoln had suggested that a counterraiding force be formed, but his generals in the field were against it, and as a very junior brigadier, that winter and spring seemed a good time to get along with his superiors.

The 3rd Division benefitted from the fact that its general had led cavalry for a while; he drilled them constantly in how to resist heavy cavalry probes; he took out whole brigades on foraging expeditions, unusual use for infantry.

Perhaps because of this training, the division saw some action. It was sent out, backed up by a cavalry brigade, against General Earl Van Dorn, who was moving about twenty-five miles west of the winter quarters, near Franklin. Sheridan manuevered his column until Van Dorn took the initiative and attacked; the Union division and its cavalry brigade then threw its full force into the field, and captured the Confederate wagon train, loaded with fodder, a cruel blow to any Southern outfit anytime in the war. Van Dorn withdrew, and refused further contact; Sheridan marched his men back to winter quarters in triumph. He came out of the winter with two stars on each shoulder.

Old Brains Halleck was still General-in-Chief. He continued his series of schoolteacherish antics by inviting Major General Grant and Major General Rosecrans to participate in a race for Chattanooga and Vicksburg; the man whose army first captured one of those cities would be made a lieutenant-general.

Grant declined in silence, Rosecrans with an indignant letter, and Lincoln had to smother Rosecrans with a letter full of praise for past glories. The

Army of the Cumberland came out of winter quarters uneasy at all this politicking.

Braxton Bragg had dropped south into the Chattanooga area, where Georgia and Alabama meet, halfway across the southern edge of Tennessee. This is the roughest sort of country: hills and ridges and swamps and forest. Rosecrans moved down on him in a constant series of flanking movements and forceful harassments; Bragg pulled back into Chattanooga itself.

Gettysburg was won in the East. Grant moved south and prepared to take Vicksburg. Again, he gave history a foretaste of Sherman's march to the sea. He sent out his cavalry, under Colonel Grierson, on a wide and fast – and strong – raid from La Grange, Tennessee, down into Mississippi, between two railroads. The column struck both railroads, destroyed public property – about six million dollars' worth – caused a hundred Confederate casualties at outposts and picket guards, and paroled another five hundred Southerners. Then it swept back to Grant with the intelligence that all the Confederate strength in Mississippi was in and around Vicksburg. Grant laid siege and took the town.

Meanwhile, the Army of the Cumberland was preparing to lay siege to Chattanooga, so Bragg pulled out of the city and left the Federals with half-completed breastworks. Bragg pulled up twenty-two miles south, at Lafayette, Georgia, and prepared to do battle.

He had three times as many troops as any one of the three separate Union armies coming at him, but he didn't have Jeb Stuart or any substitute for that cavalry leader; his intelligence failed to tell him that Rosecrans had three columns, instead of two; he planned to hit what he thought was the Union right but was really Rosecrans' center. But he held off; Longstreet was on the way from Virginia with re-enforcements.

Rosecrans began to pull his forces together, aiming for strength and mass, rather than mobility. Bragg attacked when the first three of Longstreet's brigades reached him, but the Union line was too strong for him. That night Longstreet in person brought two more brigades; the next day the attack was renewed. Rosecrans became thoroughly confused and left a huge hole in his line; Longstreet went through it. Rosecrans retreated to Chattanooga and prepared to be besieged himself.

General George H. Thomas made a stand for the Union, and checked Longstreet with mounted infantry, armed with repeating rifles: dismounted fighting by horse troops, again. The single brigade of mounted riflemen – not so-called – checked the Confederates, and Thomas took the rest of Rosecrans' army to him in Chattanooga in order.

Sheridan hadn't seen much fighting in this campaign; his division stood rearguard until the last day, when Rosecrans' confusion broke it up into brigades, mostly ordered to the wrong places. One of his brigades got into position to fire into the enemy; General Jefferson C. Davis promptly marched his own brigade through the field of fire, and Sheridan's men had to hold off.

But in all the marching, countermarching and confusion there were bullets; Phil Sheridan saw hundreds of his men dropped without profit to the Union cause. He rallied what he could of his division – about fifteen hundred men – and cut through till he got to General Thomas, clearly the hero of the day. Thomas shared a flask of brandy with Sheridan, the two of them sitting on a rail fence in the early evening and looking gloomily over the mob of an army that Rosecrans had left in the field. Then they sadly led their men into Chattanooga.

This was the Battle of Chickamauga that had just ended. Sheridan got a good deal of official praise for his efforts there, but it was clear that Chickamauga was another fiasco for the Army of the Cumberland; things were not going at all well.

For two months the Army of the Cumberland was besieged in Chattanooga; and Sheridan's division held the sector under Lookout Mountain. Replacements brought his outfit up to strength again, after the awful casualties of Chickamauga, and in some way, Sheridan had a detachment of the 2nd Kentucky Cavalry attached to him.

He used them in the old Light-Horse Harry method. Joe Wheeler's Confederate horse had the countryside under constant patrol; but Sheridan put his small company of Union Kentuckians into the Sequatchie Valley to forage, with strict orders to stay in hiding, pay for everything they took, and to send him all the food and forage they could buy. As a result, the 2nd Division ate so well it could share with its neighbors; and when the time came to move out, it drove along a herd of cattle, surplus stored up for future commissaries.

Washington had not forgotten the Army of the Cumberland. Hooker was coming down with two corps from the Army of the Potomac – one of them commanded by Slocum, Phil Sheridan's West Point roommate – and Grant was bringing his Army of the Tennessee up by water.

Also, Secretary of War Stanton came out and appointed Grant Commander-in-Chief of the whole Western war. Grant had hardly accepted before Rosecrans' subordinates were wiring the new commander that Rosecrans was planning to retreat. Grant wired Thomas to take over and hold the city at all costs. Rosecrans was relieved.

Longstreet and Bragg were giving the Army of the Cumberland time by quarreling. President Jeff Davis came west and sent Longstreet off to harass Burnside and his outfit of mounted infantry, horse artillery, and cavalry; Grant said later that Davis frequently helped the Union by his wrong decisions.

Sheridan and his division were shifted to Missionary Ridge, so called because it had been the home of preachers trying to convert the Cherokees to Christianity.

Sherman came into the field. Now all the generals who were to win for the Union were there: Grant, Sherman, Thomas, Joe Hooker, and the very junior Sheridan.

The battle, when it came, was an affair of heavy infantry charges; its significance to the cavalry lies in the fact that Sheridan got a chance to fight his infantry division under the eyes of the generals who were to determine the future organization of the Union Army. Sheridan's division was in the IV Corps, supporting Sherman.

Grant had planned the attack for November 24. But two nights before, Sheridan questioned a prisoner his men had taken, and reported to the Commander-in-Chief that Bragg was pulling out. Grant moved the attack up a day and struck the next morning at eleven o'clock.

Sheridan spent the first day of the battle putting his men into rifle pits – Thomas' idea. The next day he offered his division to Hooker, who declined the assistance, saying that he was encountering more noise than fire power.

On the afternoon of November 25, Sheridan's division was ordered to charge up *toward* Missionary Ridge, to capture the first enemy line and cause a diversion from the main battlefront.

Things went wrong, or things went too well, according to the point of view. Sheridan's men hardly stopped at the first Confederate line, but went on charging up the slope, into the face of heavy artillery and entrenched sharpshooters.

Orders came up for Sheridan to stop them; only one of his brigades could be reached; his men had outrun him. He got on his horse and took the lone brigade up to fill the hole its recall had made between his other troops.

It was a military impossibility, but they took the ridge. O'Connor's biography of Sheridan reports that the little general was seen straddling a captured gun and gleefully shouting to his men that they would all be court-martialed for exceeding their orders.

Braxton Bragg and his big army fled. Sheridan and his three brigades – they had almost a twenty-five percent casualty list – pursued. No one else seemed to want to; Granger told Sheridan to go ahead and that support would be sent if the enemy rear was contacted.

Infantry alone could not do a good routing job; Bragg's army was sure to have cavalry fighting rearguard. But Sheridan kept on shoving. Most of the rest of Grant's army were asleep. Bragg got away.

Most Union battles were followed by an epitaph of bickering amongst the generals involved; this time Phil Sheridan chimed in. He claimed that while he was trying to chase Bragg, Wood's division had stolen eleven cannon that Sheridan's men had captured. Wood's man General William B. Hazen answered in fifty-seven pages but kept the guns.

The next day, a heavy pursuit of Bragg was organized. Southern cavalry, under General Patrick R. Cleburne, turned back the pursuers, and the battle of Chattanooga was over.

Almost at once Sherman's corps was ordered to go and help Burnside at Knoxville; Longstreet was attacking him. There doesn't seem to have been any great threat to Burnside, but Knoxville was the heart of the loyal, eastern Tennessee; the battle-worn troops had to make the march for the old purpose of showing the flag. Sheridan and his division went along, under orders. It is probable that Sherman, who didn't want to make the expedition, and Sheridan grew closer together on the march; a good complaint against the authorities in Washington has always been common ground among United States Regulars. Finding that Burnside didn't need them, they marched back to chilly winter quarters at Chattanooga.

In March Congress created the rank of lieutenant general, previously only held by George Washington and Winfield Scott. Grant got the rank and became General-in-Chief.

Grant went East and conferred with Lincoln. The Army was overhauled. Sherman took over the three Western armies that Grant had commanded; Grant left Meade in charge of the Army of the Potomac but decided to make his own headquarters with that army, instead of in Washington.

He brought Phil Sheridan east to command the cavalry corps of the Army of the Potomac. There were twelve thousand men in the corps, which made it half the size of each of the three infantry corps that made up the rest of the Army. Burnside's Army – now brought East and attached to Meade – was only about twenty thousand in strength, smaller than a corps in the parent army.

The long fight in the Wilderness was Grant's first encounter with Lee and Sheridan's first encounter with Stuart. It was Sheridan's encounter with Meade, though, that determined the future of the Cavalry Corps. Meade had again started dispersing the cavalry, drawing off two whole divisions to cover an infantry movement that didn't need covering. Grant decided in favor of Sheridan, the divisions were returned, and, early in May, Stuart was killed at Yellow Tavern.

Stuart was dead, and the Federal cavalry was growing stronger than the Confederate day by day. Most of Lee's rail supply lines were cut as a result, but the Union Army of the Potomac was still not doing well. At Spotsylvania, Meade lost thousands of men unnecessarily; if Sheridan had been allowed to storm the ground before the battle, the infantry would have had an easier time of it.

Returning from his completely successful movement against Stuart, Sheridan was greeted with heavy military humor by Grant, a sure sign of the favor of the commanding general, and told that the whole of Meade's army, re-enforced by the IX Corps – Burnside – and the XVIII – W.F. Smith – was going to drive Lee back into Richmond. Sheridan and his troopers would screen front and flanks.

They moved out on May 27, in wonderful shape. Kilcavalry Kilpatrick was gone, and Phil Sheridan – though not without a sense of personal drama – was a firm believer in the walking of horses.

He was also a great man for seeing that the troopers gave their mounts the full hour's grooming, morning and evening, that regulations demanded. That winter a book on military tactics had suggested that all that currying wasn't good for horses, especially in the evening. It "opened up the pores" and left the animal exposed to the night air.

This may be true. Single-mounted cowboys – as against remuda-mounted trail drivers and roundup workers – wash under the saddle and turn the horse out to roll in the evening, and clean in the morning, through not for a full hour. But the Army never tried cutting down on the grooming, so it will never be known if it was good or bad, necessary or unnecessary.

In any event, the Cavalry Corps of the Army of the Potomac had benefitted by walking to its battles and galloping only when a charge was needed.

The first enemy that they saw was Stuart's corps, now commanded by Fitz Lee; they were dismounted and dug in behind breastworks. Sheridan felt confident he could break through them, though they were firing so hard that he reported back to Meade that he had encountered infantry.

Gregg's division went up against the Southerners first. A mounted charge was quickly repelled. Gregg ordered Custer to attack dismounted. That brave but theatrical general protested; Gregg made it a direct order, and three out of four of Custer's troopers had to climb down and hand their lines to their horseholders.

At nightfall, the Northern division broke through the Southern lines, and came up against Lee's infantry, Hoke's brigade, and Fitz Lee's troopers, who gave up retreating and formed a defense just outside of Cold Harbor.

On May 31 Sheridan cautiously took that town. He was so close to Richmond now that all of Lee's big Army of Northern Virginia was squeezed between him and the Southern capital.

Sheridan was not happy in Cold Harbor. He sent messages to Meade and Grant that he did not think he could hold the town; he wanted to pull back until mass could be put behind his troopers. He was told to hold on; two army corps were being hurried to back him up.

In the morning he captured prisoners from three different Southern brigades. But two divisions of Union foot soldiers were now digging in at Cold Harbor, and the cavalry had some force with them.

Cavalry should not be used to hold positions when massive infantry is maneuvering. Grant knew that, but he didn't act on it. Instead of sending Sheridan's divisions out to explore the enemy's flanks and screen the infantry while it pincered Lee's army, Grant decided to hit Lee's center and batter through.

This, obviously, had an element of surprise to it; Lee could not possibly expect a frontal assault. But the only time a heavy army is weak in the center is when its flanks are being assaulted and strength is being moved from one side to the other. At all other times as good a general as Lee holds his mass in the center, ready to be used on either flank.

Eight minutes after Grant threw his foot strength at Lee's line the battle was over. Eight thousand Northerners were dead, wounded, or captured; there wasn't a change in the Southern line, and Lee lost only fifteen hundred men altogether.

A week later Grant decided to flank. Sheridan was sent out to screen, to harass, and to destroy railroad lines, after which he was to meet re-enforcements from the Shenandoah Valley at Charlottesville and bring them in to Grant, who needed them. Since he had crossed the Rapidan the month before, he had lost fifty-four thousand men and the newspapers – North and South – were beginning to call him Butcher Grant. Generals William W. Averell and George Crook would each have a division of cavalry with the valley troops, and these would now come under Sheridan's command.

Three days after Sheridan moved out, he ran into the Southern Cavalry Corps again. He dismounted two of General Alfred Torbert's brigades and deployed them out as foot skirmishers while he sent George Custer riding around the lines to attack from the rear and cause a diversion. Custer may have thought he had gotten behind all the Confederate cavalry, but he hadn't; he had ridden in between Wade Hampton and Fitz Lee, and while he was happily gobbling up Hampton's rear echelon – ambulances, supply wagons, ammunition, and some guards – Fitz Lee hit him and Hampton turned and pincered.

Torbert and Gregg had to quit the assault on the Confederate barricades and try and cut through to rescue Custer. This took all day; Torbert broke through just about at nightfall. The Union headquarters were not jubilant that night at Trevilian Station.

Sheridan, like Stuart, put great importance on intelligence; unlike the Cavalier, he was a common man, very good at questioning prisoners. That night he stayed up late at that occupation, and learned that General David Hunter, in command of the Union Valley forces, was not going to be at

Charlottesville at all; he had instead marched on Lynchburg. Jubal Early was out that way. A week later he stopped Hunter cold, sent him back to the Valley and out of the war for a while.

In the morning the fight resumed. Tracks were torn up by the Union, to do what damage a stalled expedition could do; while this was going on, first Torbert and then Torbert plus Gregg tried to break through to the west, but Wade Hampton and Fitz Lee were older at dismounted warfare than the Union cavalry, and they could not be moved.

Sheridan turned for home; he was out of supplies, and even his ammunition was running low, and there wasn't much point in going on anyway; he would just run into Southern infantry from the Valley instead of Northern, since Hunter had turned aside. It took them four days to get back as far as White House Landing, where there were orders from Meade to destroy the depot there and bring the supplies – in nine hundred wagons – back to the main army.

Sheridan had fought bitterly against having his cavalry used as wagon guards; foot soldiers could do that work perfectly well. But Sheridan was not in any position to go over Meade's head to Grant this time; last time he had gotten his own way by saying he would destroy Stuart if allowed to stop convoying supplies and allowed to use his troops as a striking force; true, he had killed Stuart, but he had just been thrown back by Stuart's men.

The convoy home was attacked steadily by the Confederates; the weakened, tired troopers barely got their wagons through. Back at headquarters, Sheridan's resentment at Meade grew; the 3rd Cavalry Division had not gone up to Trevilian, and in Sheridan's absence, Meade had ordered it out around Petersburg to break up the rail lines there.

Like its parent column it had run into Gray cavalry and was reputed to be having a bad time. Meade allowed Sheridan to take his weary command out after the 3rd on a rescue strike, but that division managed to get home under its own steam; then the whole Cavalry Corps went into rest camp. Fifteen hundred remounts were received and put into training.

Grant was battering at Petersburg in an entrenched siege action that had little use for cavalry assistance. It wasn't going well, either. Lee had been allowed to re-enforce the city after the action started. Grant had had his engineers tunnel under the Confederate lines and blow them up, but his infantry had then failed to charge through the gap in any sort of mass. He lost four thousand more men in the attempt, too. And Grant's preoccupation with Petersburg had enabled Lee to send out Jubal Early to stop Hunter from coming in out of the Shenandoah.

With Hunter turned back, Early was free; he raided on Washington, skirmishing around the outskirts of the city, close enough in so that Lincoln

225

himself could come out and watch the fighting without a spyglass. Early didn't have the force with him to take Washington; when Grant sent in part of the Army of the Potomac, the Gray troops got away. But they got away safely, and the Commander-in-Chief himself had seen them. It was time to do something drastic, or Grant would not be General-in-Chief much longer.

Now Sheridan was relieved of command of the Cavalry Corps and told to take out a combined force – foot, horse, and guns – and clean up the Shenandoah Valley. Hunter was no longer there; he had retreated into the new state of West Virginia. Jubal Early was using the big Shenandoah Valley as though it were a rest camp, a park, and a fort, all at one time. He could come out of the passes at will and aid Lee; or he could go back into the Valley and feed his army up to full strength. One of his favorite occupations was riding up into Maryland and demanding blackmail money from the towns there in exchange for not destroying them. The Confederacy badly needed gold to buy supplies abroad; Europe would not accept Confederate money.

Grant had not wanted Sheridan for the new, unified command of the departments of Washington, West Virginia, and the Susquehanna. His first choice had been William B. Franklin; Lincoln vetoed that. Then he suggested George G. Meade, probably to get that bungler out of his own headquarters. Lincoln, instead, told Henry W. Halleck to go back into the field, and take the new command.

Grant got drunk. He had resigned from the peacetime Army because of that failing; his officers in their memoirs, however, say he had been sober from the time of Vicksburg until the appointment of old Brains Halleck as the broom for the Shenandoah Valley.

Jubal Early showed his contempt for the appointment by riding safely and contemptuously into Pennsylvania and telling the city government of Chambersburg that he wanted either a hundred thousand dollars in gold or five times that much in greenbacks, or he would burn their town. They didn't, or couldn't, pay that much, so he gave them time to evacuate, and then set the torch to two thirds of the houses and to the ironworks owned by U.S. Congressman Thaddeus Stevens, ten miles out of town. That was when Grant sent for Phil Sheridan.

The General-in-Chief had worked out the problem. Sheridan, at thirty-two, was too young to be given Halleck's command; it would go to David Hunter, who was in West Virginia anyway. But Sheridan would command in the field, leaving the desk work to Hunter.

Sheridan didn't want the command, though it was a big step up. He did not want to leave the Cavalry Corps that he had been shaping up for five months; and the new job had too much politics connected with it. Everyone who had gone out to the Valley had been thwarted by Secretary Stanton and Chief-of-Staff Halleck, not to mention being whipped by Jubal Early.

A few cheering things happened. Hunter turned in his resignation, saying that he felt he had lost the confidence of the War Department and the President. Sherman, fighting Joe Johnston and then Hood in the South, wired that he heartily approved of Sheridan for the new and important job. Sherman wasn't doing well in his drive on Atlanta – his cavalry, under George Stoneman, was particularly ineffective – but his word carried weight. Lincoln had told Grant – who undoubtedly told Sheridan – that he was personally to supervise Sheridan, and that Stanton and Halleck were to be bypassed, a reversal of Lincoln's decision to send Halleck into the field.

Sheridan took the command. It was a big one. The old Army of West Virginia was now only a corps, and not a very large one, called the VIII; to it was added the VI Corps, a division of the XIX and later another division of the same outfit; all of these were infantry.

For cavalry, Sheridan got, at first, only one division of his old corps, Torbert's; but Wilson's division was soon added, and Averell's was already in West Virginia. Torbert was made chief of cavalry, though he had never been a favorite of Phil Sheridan's.

Sheridan moved out to Harpers Ferry, near where the Shenandoah pours into the Potomac, and told an engineering lieutenant to teach him the geography of his new theater of war. The Valley proper slopes from there uphill to Staunton, or thereabouts; water south of Staunton flows into the James rather than toward the Potomac and is not in the true Valley.

It is easy to get out of the Valley to the south; the high ground that separates the Valley of the Shenandoah from the James basin is only comparatively higher than the Valley floor. It was easier to get out to the north, where the Potomac is joined by the Shenandoah. To the east there are all the gaps that Stuart's men had guarded all through the first three years of the war. They are in the Blue Ridge Mountains, and the Southern soldiers knew them as well as they knew their mothers' back yards. The Gray troops were also at home in the gaps and ridges to the west, where the Alleghenies guarded the West Virginia defectors (or, to Sheridan, loyalists).

The Valley, from below Staunton to Harpers Ferry, is about a hundred miles long; the width varies from twenty to thirty miles. The central part of the Valley, from just below Strasburg to above Cross Keys, is split into two floors by a ridge. The north and south roads on the Valley floors were macadam even during the Civil War. However, an embattled Virginia hardly had time or money or manpower to repave the highways after the passage of a five-thousand-horse cavalry march.

At the beginning of the war, Stonewall Jackson had held the rich Valley; then he had withdrawn, and Nathaniel Banks had taken it for the Union. But Banks was needed elsewhere, and was recalled; as he left,

Jackson conscientiously attacked the larger Union force, suffered a lot of casualties, but took over the Valley again.

John C. Frémont went into the Valley famous and came out without much military reputation left; to greater or less degree, the same thing had happened to Banks, Shields, Sigel, and now Hunter. Jubal Early had succeeded Stonewall Jackson, and Early would always be on home ground; he had even been born in Franklin County, just south of the true Valley and, Virginia-style, was sure to have relatives any place he rode in western Virginia. There is an Earlysville behind Brown's Gap, as there is a Mount Jackson on the west side of the ridge.

Besides Early and his army, there was another counter-Union force for Sheridan to contend with in the Valley. Mosby's Rangers were riding there. These irregulars under the command of John Singleton Mosby were direct military descendants of Francis Marion; they scorned uniforms and sabers and were innocent farmers until the word was passed; then they kissed their families good-bye and rode hard and fiercely against Union pickets, stragglers, and small patrols. They had been enrolled in one of the Virginia cavalry outfits to keep the Union from hanging them as bandits, but they were not men to drill or salute or count their rank in brass buttons. Almost the first thing Sheridan did was to tell a Major Young of Rhode Island to organize a ranger force to go after Mosby.

The next thing he did was to declare war on the bountiful crops of the Valley. He got there in August, as the harvests were ripening; by the twentieth he reported that he had destroyed everything "eatable" south of Winchester; the Confederacy would now have to haul supplies up from below Staunton. Of course, he had not destroyed everything; he had first filled his own commissaries. Of all the Civil War commanders, Sheridan, as noted before, was most interested in seeing that his men ate well; in the Shenandoah campaign they didn't eat, they dined three times a day.

There was no major fighting for the first month that Sheridan was in the Valley. He was waiting for his whole command to muster. He threw a defensive line across the floor, where there was least danger of being flanked, and maneuvered gently, feeling out Early's strength while Early felt out his. If he had been Frémont or Sigel, Early would surely have attacked; but Phil Sheridan's reputation had gone into the Valley before he had.

On September 19, Sheridan's cavalry moved out against Early in force. The little Irish general was using a method of fighting – both tactical and strategic – that was new to American warfare, though it resembled Napoleon's methods to some extent. Sheridan regarded horse, foot, and gun as three limbs of one striking force; he did not use his artillery to cover his infantry advance and his cavalry to protect the fieldpieces.

A month before, Fitz Lee's division, backed up by an infantry brigade, had struck at a Union cavalry division under General Wesley Merritt, and been sharply thrown back by dismounted troopers firing repeating carbines. This had, perhaps, given the South the idea that Sheridan's men were more mounted infantry than real troopers; but in the battle of September 19, east of Winchester, the troopers went in mounted, firing pistols or swinging sabers. They completely overrode a battery of artillery and took twelve hundred prisoners, and Early retreated toward Winchester.

Three divisions of infantry were thrown in after Union General Wilson's cavalry division, which then pulled out and started around the retreating Confederates' left flank, instead of leading the routing, in the conventional manner. Early rallied and threw his own cavalry to his left to check the flanking. The Southern general was backpedaling steadily.

That wouldn't have done him any good if Wright, commanding the first infantry division to go into the line, hadn't brought so much impedimenta along that the next division couldn't be brought to bear. Sheridan personally ordered the wagons thrown into the ditch, and pushed on, but Early had had time to get set; he countercharged with foot troops and dented Sheridan's line.

Sheridan threw in another brigade and straightened his line. Then – it was now midafternoon – he got his heavier artillery up on a ridge and got the range, and simultaneously hit both of Early's flanks and his rear with a cavalry charge, Wilson's, Averell's, and Merritt's mounted divisions all closing in at the same time. The rout was now complete; Early and his entire army went tumbling south to rally at Strasburg.

Sheridan and Crook, one of the few West Point classmates who had been friendly with the little Irishman, strolled arm-in-arm in Winchester that last evening of summer. In his *Personal Memoirs*, Sheridan remembered that three very attractive young ladies joined them and "danced around them." Apparently, the girls of this Confederate town were so used to flirting with famous generals that Blue looked Gray to them. It was Crook who suggested that calling attention to themselves was not too wise in the dark of an enemy town; the two generals got off the street by calling on a Quaker schoolteacher who had been doing some un-Quakerish spying for the Union.

Cavalry had followed Early and reported his stand near Strasburg. The foot army marched down that way, while the horse kept Early under observation, telling Sheridan that the enemy was confined to a three-mile front between the Shenandoah and Little North Mountain; specifically, at a rise in the Massanuttens called Fisher's Hill.

Jubal Early was no less a general than he had ever been; but Sheridan was a different attacker than any that Early had been up against. Sheridan's detailed study of the Valley made him think that Early could be flanked on the left, between Little North Mountain and his entrenchments. He sent Averell out with his cavalry to see if this was really so. When he found out it was, he prepared to flank in mass, with Crook's infantry corps up by Averell and his troopers.

Most of the rest of the cavalry were put on the march, away from the battle and around down the side of the Massanuttens to New Market, ready to cut off Early's retreat and pincer him.

Crook and others always claimed that the idea for the flanking movement was Crook's. It might have been. The execution was lovely; the big body of men – a small corps, but still a corps – moved silently, guns blacked or wrapped against haliations, infiltrating their flank position through ravines and little gullies and mountain streams.

By the end of the day of September 22, suppertime for the Southern camp, Crook was in position and struck; Averell and the cavalry were now behind him, due to the roughness of the terrain and the heavy timber.

At the same time a division was thrown against the front of Early's left flank, Sheridan leading it in person, and the rest of its corps, the VI, piling in after it.

Assaulted from two directions by whole corps, the Confederate left went to pieces, and was routed, Sheridan waving his hat and yelling: "Forward everything!"

The rest of Sheridan's army hit the front of Early's. The beauty of the Southern position had been that it seemed unflankable; now that it was flanked, it became a box trap, and the whole Southern force went back as fast as it could before that trap could be worked.

But the cavalry sent around to stop Early at New Market failed to get there; they ran into two brigades of Fitz Lee's riders – Lee himself was out with wounds for the time being – and were licked. The usual explanation is that the Southern troopers were carrying Enfields and those rifles could outrange the Union carbines.

Sheridan did not accept the inferior shoulder arm alibi; Torbert, in command of the cavalry column, had had superior artillery fire, which he had barely used. The Irishman's temper was also up at Averell, who was letting his cavalry slide back into the old ways of overriding and then overresting. It was becoming clear that Sheridan's great cavalry corps decreased in greatness as its distance from Sheridan increased; as overall commander of that corps and four infantry corps, he was too far up the ladder of command.

He relieved Averell of his command and turned over his division to Colonel William Powell. Torbert kept his command, though his troopers were greeted, when they finally rejoined the infantry in camp near

Harrisonburg, with the derisive: "Who ever saw a dead cavalryman?" that had been popular with the foot soldiers in the days of Stoneman and Kilpatrick.

Early forted up near Port Republic and awaited re-enforcements and stores. He got some new field guns, but loaders in Richmond had chalked on them: *For General Sheridan, care of General Early.* Stuart had counted on the Union to be his ordnance corps; now Sheridan had exactly reversed the situation.

Sheridan let him wait. There was more foraging and burning to do in this part of the Valley. This was on direct orders from the White House. Sherman had taken Atlanta at the beginning of the month with the same orders, and with very little help from George Stoneman, his cavalry commander, who had again broken up his troopers into too small parties and had himself been captured. The idea was to starve the South and *then* beat its armies.

Torbert raided Staunton, blew up bridges, exploded arsenals, burned the fields, and drove off the cattle. Custer, now a division commander, was so eager at burning houses that Sheridan had to tell him to stop that work and confine himself to arresting possible Southern soldiers.

Port Republic was up on the high ground. Sheridan was afraid that Early would slip through the familiar gaps in the Blue Ridge and come out in Piedmont Virginia and that the Army of the Shenandoah would be ordered through the gaps and passes after him. The high places in the Blue Ridge had always been fatal to Northern generals. Sheridan felt – in case Early got away that way – that he ought to be let go; the Army of the Shenandoah could then finish its earth-scorching at ease and take the train for Washington and be thrown into the Tidewater where needed, probably at Petersburg against Lee. Early could not stand the knowledge that while he was in the hills, Sheridan was pillaging the beloved Valley. The Southern commander started foraying against the foragers.

When General Thomas L. Rosser's cavalry re-enforced Early, the forays became more serious. Finally, they annoyed Sheridan to the point where he gave direct orders to Torbert to "whip the enemy or be whipped yourself," the enemy being Rosser, and the order was one that was to go down in military history and be repeated almost as often as General Nathan B. Forrest's "get there fustest with the mostest men," which Forrest probably never said; he was semi-literate, but not that bad.

Torbert had seen what had happened to Averell; he was still under a cloud because of his failure to cut Early off at New Market. His troopers were tired of being asked about dead cavalrymen. Also, the Union cavalry outnumbered the Southern. Rosser had Lunsford Lomax along, but Torbert had Custer and Merritt under him.

The fight took place near Tom's Brook, while Sheridan watched from Round Top Mountain. For once cavalrymen could be beaux sabreurs; there was no infantry in the fight at all. Men shot their carbines empty, then their revolvers, and finally drew blade and slashed at each other.

The Gray broke first, and took off from the field of battle, leaving eleven out of twelve of their fieldpieces behind. Gone were the days of Stuart, whose artillery commander, John Pelham, would not take a broken axle as an excuse for abandoning a gun. Sheridan, with the ponderous playfulness that marked both him and Grant when things went well, offered fifty dollars to the trooper who went after that twelfth gun and captured it, but it got away in the general galloping rout and pursuit.

The victory helped Sheridan in Washington. Sheridan was told to prepare to follow his plan of going to Petersburg by rail, and one corps, Wright's, actually moved toward the railroad. Then Early came back into the field in force, and Sheridan recalled Wright and prepared to dig in for a winter campaign. First, however, he was ordered to Washington, to confer with the top staff on future plans.

It is recorded that he hated to leave his army just then. He was right.

Chapter 20

Sheridan Makes His Ride

Escorted by a strong guard of cavalry, Sheridan rode into Front Royal on the night of October 16 to take what were called "the cars" for Washington. To anyone accustomed to the campaigns and distances of the West, the separation between capital and battlefront in the Civil War was often ludicrously – or alarmingly – small. In direct distance, Front Royal is sixty-five miles from the White House; it probably took about two hours on the railroads of the day.

But Sheridan was unhappy about getting that far from his army. His signalmen had interpreted a heliograph message to Early from Longstreet; the two Confederate armies were to get together and "crush Sheridan."

But when Washington calls, a general goes. And, anyway, the Southern message was probably a fake; his code officers had not been able to read Confederate messages for quite a while, and this was sent in a code broken some time before.

Still, the next morning in Washington he told Secretary of War Stanton that he would like to leave town at noon and asked that a special train be made up and ready at that time. The situation was so urgent that Sheridan and his staff had brought their horses up to the capital with them. Sheridan's horse was his big black charger, Rienzi, already famous in contemporary newspapers; the small general had the tallest horse he could find, which was not entirely vanity; it was the sort of war in which a trusted general had to be seen by his men as a rallying point, a necessity which was about to be proved.

The meeting with Secretary Stanton and Old Brains Halleck was completely successful. Two engineers, colonels, were assigned to Sheridan to return to the Valley with him and lay out the plans for entraining his men for the trip to Petersburg, instead of having them follow Grant's plan of breaking through the water gaps and passes of the Blue Ridge when they finished mopping up the Valley.

Sheridan detrained at Martinsburg that night, up above Harpers Ferry; Winchester was on a railroad spur below the Ferry, but there must have been railroad reasons why the special train did not go down that spur. Much hampered by the engineering officers – one of whom was much overweight – Sheridan made the ride from Martinsburg to Winchester the next day, and then got news that he was back in time; all was quiet in the camp out at Cedar Creek. Too quiet, as they say in bad Western movies; Merritt, of Sheridan's cavalry didn't like it.

What was happening was that General John B. Gordon, of Early's command, was being sent out to do exactly what Sheridan had had Crook do to Early on the evening of September 22, almost a month before: infiltrate the heavily brushed ravines all around Crook's left and rear, as Crook's corps lay camped on the Union's left. The Blue pickets were close in, as pickets had to be in broken, brushy country; the danger of capture was too great for them to be thrown far out. It wasn't country for cavalry to patrol the perimeter, and anyway Sheridan believed that infantry should protect itself; the early war had shown how ineffective cavalry became when it had all the duties of night patrolling, wagon escorting, and message running to do for the foot troops.

Crook had struck at Southern suppertime; John Gordon moved out at half-past three in the morning. During the dark of the morning Crook's headquarters heard noises and one of his officers went out to investigate; he was captured before he could give the alarm. Crook was pretty much at ease; though his corps was the smallest of Sheridan's army, its position was strong with natural defenses, and it was believed that if Early came on, it would be to assault Wright, out on the other flank. Whether this would have been believed if Sheridan had been there is conjectural.

The first firing was on Crook's extreme left, and it was no louder or more frequent than if pickets were clashing with each other. Nevertheless, Crook's men were veterans; reveille hadn't sounded, but they all got up and started cooking; if they were to be moved for any purpose, they wanted full stomachs to march on.

Sheridan, in Winchester, heard firing early in the morning, but it was not continuous – the sort of thing that a Union outfit out on reconnaissance would make at Confederate pickets. Still, there was no use taking chances. He got up, ate, and rode out, his staff no doubt grumbling at the early morning start.

A few miles out of town, and fifteen miles from his camp at Cedar Creek, Phil Sheridan met up with the 17th Pennsylvania Cavalry, who had been told to wait there for him, and ride behind him to join his army. The regiment fell in behind the general's staff, and they all went along at the horse-saving walk that was Sheridan's trademark. The sound of firing was louder and steadier.

Crook's VIII Corps had been completely dispersed – crumpled up is the military term – taken by absolute surprise. The Confederates had captured the corps artillery and turned it on the rest of the Union infantry camp. The XIX Corps, Emory's men holding the center of the camp, came directly under the guns and also in the path of Crook's fleeing soldiers.

They held while Wright could bring the right flank around and put it on Emory's rear, now *his* left flank. Then they broke. General George W. Getty, of Wright's corps, was about to throw his men into a countercharge, but when he saw everyone else fleeing, he ordered a retreat; he could not risk being left out on an isolated point while Gray troops flanked and encircled him.

Sheridan, meanwhile, had gone about a mile from where he had picked up the Pennsylvania regiment. The battle noise was now so loud that the general swung down from his high saddle and put his ear to the ground. He remounted with his dark face puzzled. There was certainly a battle someplace, but where? He kept his column down to the walk until he found out, which was almost at once. As he topped a crest, he saw fleeing baggage wagons and artillery limbers – without their guns – and all the camp followers of his army – sutlers, peddlers, self-freed Negroes from the Valley farms – fleeing toward him.

He later said that his first thought was to stay right where he was, halt the fighting part of his army when it got to him, and reorganize it there. But then his chief commissary came along, swept on the fleeing tide, and told him his headquarters had been taken, and that his men were fleeing in all directions.

This was advice from a noncombatant, never very reliable, but Phil Sheridan turned and snapped an order at the commander of the 17th. The general would take an escort of picked men – twenty, or fifty, the number is still in dispute – and ride forward at the gallop. The rest of the column would work as mounted police, turning fighting men back to the battle, untangling impedimenta. Presumably there was still the fat engineer colonel to escort to safety, too.

Sheridan was fourteen – not twenty – miles from the battle. Rienzi and the Pennsylvania horses had had a good morning walkout, just what was needed to put well cared-for mounts into prime condition. Sheridan put Rienzi to the canter. The poem has him covering twenty miles at "eagle flight," but Rienzi or any other horse would have foundered after even fourteen miles at an all-out gallop. Rienzi didn't founder, and the Pennsylvania troop horses kept up.

Sheridan's black hat was seldom on his head during that ride. He would come up to foot soldiers trudging away from complete defeat, wave his hat at them, and they would turn and go back toward the fight. He would ride into a field – often the highway was too tangled with rolling stock for the horses to get through – and find veterans calmly boiling coffee until they found out where the next stand would be made; they would kick over their coffee cans, pick up their guns and follow the little general back to the wars.

What Sheridan said to his men would vary, surely, from group to group. His own version, written later, is certainly edited: "If I had been with you this morning, this disaster would not have happened. We must face the other way; we will go back and recover our camp."

At Newtown, Sheridan met a major of Crook's men, and sent him through the thronged streets spreading the word that Phil Sheridan was back and waving his hat for a countercharge. The mass of straggling foot soldiers behind Rienzi began to form into an army.

Between Newtown and Middletown he came on organized troops: Getty's division of Wright's corps, and the cavalry, under Torbert. These were the only troops still resisting the enemy. Torbert said: "My God, I am glad you have come," which is probably an accurate quotation.

Sheridan jumped his horse over the fence-pole barricade which Getty's foot troops were lying behind while they sniped at the enemy. He took off his hat again – his own account – and the men came over the barricade, cheering.

Sheridan ordered a heavier barricade built, along the line that Getty was still holding. More troops kept coming up; Crook's color bearers had never run, and now two more divisions of Wright's and one of Emory's were found more or less intact and they were thrown into the line.

The rest of the army came back in the form of stragglers. Sheridan told them that no one was braver than they, and to get in there and fight. Twenty-four artillery pieces had been taken by the Confederates; he wanted them back.

A field officer told his men they might as well do it then: "Sheridan will get it out of us some time."

It was the hardest sort of work, reorganizing a routed army; Sheridan was not ready to counterattack for five and a half hours after he arrived on the battlefield. He spent part of that time patiently and personally questioning prisoners, one of his specialities. There were rumors all over the field that Longstreet was about to join Early, as promised in the intercepted message; the intelligence Sheridan got from his captives denied this, and then Powell, cavalry commander watching the gap through which Longstreet would have to come, reconnoitered and sent word to Sheridan that the relieving Gray army was not present.

Sheridan charged, horse, foot, and what guns had not been stolen. Custer took his division in mounted, screaming their heads off. Crook's men fought harder than anyone; at one point they outran the Cavalry. Infantrymen, stopping for breath, were told by Sheridan that if they couldn't run they could at least holler: "We've got the god-damndest twist on them you ever saw," probably also an unedited quotation.

The charge had gone forward at four in the afternoon. Nightfall in Virginia that time of year is about five-twenty. By full dark the Confederates were fleeing, their wagon trains and artillery cut up by Custer's, and Merritt's troopers under Torbert, their guns abandoned. The cavalrymen kept after them in the dark; the foot soldiers rested, and the sack of the rest of the Valley was certain; the food cupboard of the Northern Confederacy was doomed.

Grant was still besieging Petersburg; Sherman was in Atlanta, preparing to do to the southern Confederacy what Sheridan had done to the northern, but on a larger scale. The swathe he cut from Atlanta to Savannah was twice as wide and more than twice as long as the Valley.

The war was ending. Whether the South knew it or not is another matter; Lee probably did; John B. Hood, leading thirty thousand men in the Tennessee country, probably didn't; he was a last-ditch kind of general.

Sheridan was rewarded for his work in the Valley. He was made a major general in the Regulars. This was the greatest reward any soldier could get; brevets were empty honors, and generals of volunteers had only dubious futures; Custer, for instance, was still a major of Regulars. But Phil Sheridan was now assured of high pay the rest of his life. His army went into winter quarters. The officers' wives were allowed to come out to the bivouacs, and things got social; rumors spread back to Washington that Sheridan himself was engaged to somebody's niece or sister. Nothing came of it.

All was not eating, dancing, and foraging. Mosby was still out with his partisans. Custer, never cautious, captured six of the irregulars and hanged them; the North was not certain that John Mosby was much better than a common highwayman. Mosby hanged seven Union soldiers and wrote Sheridan a note that implied the tiny force of partisans was as important as the Army of the Shenandoah.

Sheridan had been working against Mosby with what would now be called psychological warfare; he had had his men telling the inhabitants of the Valley that their barns would not have been sacked if it had not been for the fact that they had helped the partisans. He decided that local anger against Mosby was not high enough; he sent Wesley Merritt and his cavalry division out to garner in every speck of food, every food animal, every bit of grain and hay; all the barns were to be burned. There was a heavy Quaker population, and these were spared; the Friends had never gone with the slave-holding South.

Merritt's division did all the work; Custer could not have been trusted to spare the Quakers, or the homes themselves, which were not to be burned, by orders of Grant and Sheridan. Sheridan, formerly commissary, quartermaster, and civilian bookkeeper, kept careful record of what was burned and what was commandeered.

Sheridan succeeded in turning public opinion further against Mosby, and in making Mosby's provisioning difficult; but he did not capture the Rebel chieftain. He did take – by ruse and surprise – another raider named Gilmore, whose men reciprocated by capturing Crook and a lesser general. The generals were soon exchanged and returned to their commands, but not before George Crook had become engaged to the sister of one of Gilmore's riders; when peace came they were married.

Chasing guerrillas was not work that called for a major general in the United States Army. Sheridan turned over his Shenandoah command to Winfield S. Hancock and was again a cavalryman.

Early in February he took Merritt's and Custer's cavalry divisions and set out up the Valley; the two divisions were to become part of the Army of the Potomac, of which Phil Sheridan would again be cavalry commander if he could not get through the upper Valley to join Sherman in the south.

At Waynesboro he ran into Jubal Early, and defeated him decisively; then he destroyed a number of railroads, turned around, and rode out of the Valley to show up at White House Landing, where he reported to Grant that he'd be at the Petersburg siege as soon as his troops rested after more than two weeks of riding and fighting in the mud. Grant had thought he had sent Sheridan to Sherman; he was surprised. But he was in need of help at Petersburg, and the little Irish general got his way.

Chapter 21

The Mop-Up

The Army of the Potomac cheered when they saw Phil Sheridan; he waved at the ranks with his black hat. It was a new one, a sort of pork pie, more rakish than his old plug, but still calculated not to be pushed off by the ugly bump on the back of his skull.

Grant did not cheer. He had wanted Sheridan to go down, help Sherman lick Joe Johnston, and then lead the armies of Sherman north to hit Lee's rearguard. He still wanted that; Lee was still the primary target of the North, correctly. There were several theaters of war, but they were all – Shenandoah, Georgia and the Carolinas, the Mississippi Valley – peripheral to the battle for Virginia. When it was won, the South would surrender.

Petersburg was a siege operation, and a siege has little use for a crack cavalry commander. But when Grant heard his men cheer Sheridan, he knew he needed the man, if not the cavalry leader. His men were dispirited, as soldiers always are when a siege drags on and on. Sheridan, who personified movement and dash and complete destruction of the enemy, gave them hope.

The little man from the Valley did not want to go to the Carolinas and he did not want to ride among the trenches bringing cheer to the troops as a sort of mounted Gray Lady.

He didn't need Sherman, he said. In fact, to bring up Sherman would imply that Grant's Army of the Potomac couldn't do the job. Sheridan's cavalry was part of that Army; he proposed to ride around Petersburg, cut the rail lines and pikes supplying the besieged Lee, and starve the Confederates out. Grant didn't think so. He had a healthy and sensible repect for Lee, and another for Sherman, always his closest military adviser and strongest striking arm.

At this point Lincoln came south and said he wanted a conference. Grant took Sheridan out to Lincoln's boat with him. The President was dejected about the siege. The cavalry general's lively spirits seemed to reassure the gaunt Lincoln, and Sheridan's plan for handling Lee's supply lines were approved. Grant gave Sheridan a new title of Commander-in-Chief of the Army of the Shenandoah, serving with the Army of the Potomac, an honor that seems to have been designed to keep Meade from slowing down the Irishman's plans; both men were now Army commanders.

Sheridan went out to the cavalry lines to get his troops in order; for such a volatile man, he was always endlessly patient with the details of grooming and stabling – and the feeding of his troopers. This was long before the Army took any real notice of how soldiers ate; twenty years later on the prairie, scurvy was more common even than beans for boiling; troopers got bread and bacon and sowbelly.

Then Sheridan was called back to Grant's headquarters at City Point to meet and talk with Sherman, up from the South. Grant and Sherman and Sheridan had come a long way since Colonel Sheridan had commanded a brigade at Booneville and hoped that Generals Grant and Sherman would notice him. Sheridan was peppery. "My uneasiness made me somewhat too earnest, I fear," was his description of the scene.

Sherman was redheaded. Grant smoothed the two generals down, but after Sheridan had gone to bed, Sherman came and woke him and renewed the argument, sitting on the edge of the cot. Sheridan had the advantage; he was lying down and resting. He simply out-waited the older and senior general, and Sherman gave up.

Sheridan got his riding orders the next day. After his troopers had ruined the railroads into Petersburg and Richmond, they were to be led either back to the Army of the Potomac or south to join Sherman, an either-or that seemed to make everybody happy.

As Sheridan rode out from Hancock Station, he had about twelve thousand troopers behind him, and two Army Corps backing them up on foot. The cavalry were divided into three divisions, under George Crook, George Custer, and Thomas Devin; Wesley Merritt was Cavalry Commander of Corps, vice Albert Torbert, who had gone on leave. However, Crook's division was directly under Sheridan, an unusual arrangement.

Lee's intelligence was good; as the Union horse moved out, so did Fitz Lee, in an attempt to cut the Blue riders off from their infantry support.

That first day – March 29 – the worst enemy encountered was the weather. It rained with the fury that all soldiers in all battles in all wars have always been rained on. Sheridan took his first point, Dinwiddie Court House, midway between the Southside and the Weldon rail lines into Petersburg. The mess wagons were floundering out in the mud somewhere, but there was coffee for Sheridan and his staff at the tavern, and also some flirtatious Southern ladies who still seemed to think that the war was a giant jousting of knights and that Union generals could be turned from their course of destruction by the fluttering of eyelashes.

The evening was improved for Sheridan by a dispatch from Grant, who had moved his headquarters out toward the cavalry point. Grant told him to forget about joining Sherman; just flank Lee and forget everything else. The General-in-Chief had apparently given up trying to change Sheridan's mind, just as Sherman had done.

But later that night, Phil Sheridan got another dispatch; maybe the cavalry maneuver and everything else ought to wait on better weather; horses were going down to their bellies in the mud at Gravelly Point. Sheridan gave orders for Custer's divisions to spend the morning laying logs on the roads for a corduroy and rode over to Grant's headquarters. He harangued Grant's staff, but not the General-in-Chief himself. Sheridan may have begun to think that Grant was getting tired of being bawled out by his junior general. One of the staff officers, however, went and woke up Lieutenant General Grant, and Grant came out of his tent and told Sheridan to go ahead. He did, but not the next day. That was a mess of day labor and small skirmishes and desperate attempts to get the fieldpieces up with the cavalry, not to mention the supply wagons to feed the troopers.

But Merritt justified Sheridan's faith in him by leading a Stuart-type reconnaissance in force, all of Devin's division and a brigade of Crook's. They penetrated far enough into the Southern lines, fighting all the way, to find out that the Confederates were massing for an attack the next day.

The information proved correct. On March 31, A.P. Hill attacked Warren's infantry – half of Sheridan's support – and drove them out of column. Then he was counterattacked by both Warren and the commander of Sheridan's other foot corps, Humphreys, and stopped dead, immobilized out of the battle.

Pickett was given the job of attacking Sheridan himself. Sheridan feinted backward, drawing Pickett toward him until the horse artillery could come up and get into the Union line. Pickett had two infantry divisions and three of cavalry, under the two Lees and Rosser; but the Union had repeating carbines and these, with the field guns, retreated to the woods after inflicting terrible casualties.

All this maneuvering had split the Confederate forces wide open. Sheridan wired Grant and Meade, and then, with their concurrence, ordered General Gouverneur Warren and his infantry corps in to smash Pickett before A.P. Hill could re-establish contact.

Warren held back through the night. Perhaps he couldn't do anything else; it had stopped raining, but the ground was still boggy, his men were exhausted, streams were out of their banks and had to be rebridged. Another theory is that the thirty-three-year-old infantry general resented taking orders from Sheridan. In any event, morning found little Phil Sheridan stamping on the mud in front of General Warren and bawling the taller man out in the unmerciful Sheridan way.

New plans had to be made. Sheridan got Warren started north and west, into a position of poised rest at the farm of a man named Boisseau. Meanwhile, Devin and Custer went in direct pursuit of Pickett, with Crook and his division riding in reserve.

The cavalry massed to attack Pickett's right as noisily as possible; they even had their bands playing. While this worried Pickett, Warren would hit his left, and the Union's superior force would roll all of Pickett's force in on itself. But again, Warren held back, and again Sheridan rode to the fool general's headquarters and raged at the aristocratic Warren, who seemed coolly unmoved by the whole thing.

It was four o'clock in the afternoon before Warren got his V Corps going; Sheridan wanted everything washed up by sundown, which would be about twenty minutes after six. Then Warren swung two of his three divisions too far out to protect the third as it went around Pickett's flank. Sheridan tried to get word to Warren, failed, and rode into the attack on Pickett's left flank himself, rallying the men of the unsupported division.

As always, men fought harder when Phil Sheridan was there. He loved battle, he was precisely and absolutely fearless, and the spirit seemed to come out of his small body and enter into those of thousands of privates and lieutenants and anyone else he commanded, making them refuse to believe that they could die, either. On the other flank, Custer had taken his cavalry in against Rooney Lee, and the Union troopers were doing more than they had been ordered to; they were not just creating a diversion, they were rolling up the enemy themselves. A lot of them went in dismounted, using their rapid-fire carbines with devastating force; others made saber charges effective.

Devin's cavalry made the charge on the front and center of Pickett's line, and made it take. Sheridan was all up and down the line by now, Rienzi keeping up the gallop and seeming to be as bulletproof as his rider. At one point the little general found himself a mounted policeman, directing Southern prisoners where to lay their guns down and walk to what he assured them was safety.

The battle ended before sundown, as Sheridan had wanted it to. Pickett's army was routed, and Lee was left stranded in Petersburg, with no striking arm to come help him.

Sheridan relieved Warren of his command and had his orderly build a fire. Then he lay down beside the blaze, his head resting on a saddle, his hat still on; he had once said that the pork pie that replaced his Plug made a "night cap without equal."

Sheridan was tired; he lay there and made disposition of his infantry and cavalry in the pursuit of Pickett. He did this without a map, according to a New York *World* correspondent who stayed near him and got, in the general's spare time, an interview on which he based a story-reprinted as far away as London. Then Sheridan got up and went around the camp, apologizing to officers he had been rude to during the battle.

Lee had to come out of Petersburg, now; Sheridan commanded all the lines leading into the city; it had become a cheeseless rat trap, Petersburg protected Richmond; the day after the Battle of Five Forks, Jeff Davis had his clerks burning the government records.

Lee and Jeff Davis arranged a rendezvous down at Danville, almost on the North Carolina line. There was no place to go but South, where Joe Johnston still survived. Getting south was another matter. Grant was now charging straight at Richmond, with all his mass. Sheridan was out riding, feeling for the line of retreat the Southerners had taken from Five Forks. It was mostly a cavalry retreat; the men of Stuart's old corps had re-formed and retreated in order, but the infantry had drifted off in little knots of men, mostly disarmed, to the north and west, and were lost to the Confederate Army. They would study war no more; Phil Sheridan had been too stern a schoolmaster. The best thing to do was to go west, first, into the Virginia highlands. Lee split his command into two wings, giving one to Richard Ewell and the other to James Longstreet.

Sheridan, always probing, found this out at once; Grant and Meade had already guessed that west was where the Army of Northern Virginia would have to go. The trick was to guess where it would reunite, the two wings joining for a swing to the south. Grant and Sheridan both thought that the meeting point would be Amelia Court House; this was confirmed when they intercepted a message at Jetersville, southwest of Amelia, asking for three hundred thousand Confederate rations to be delivered there. Since Jetersville was so small that the *Gazeteer* didn't give a population for it (the same book described Amelia as having "very few dwellings"), large movements of troops could be expected there.

Sheridan moved all his horse and foot up that way, fifty-odd miles out from Richmond, and cut the line of retreat to the south and part of that to the west; the Army of the James sent up infantry divisions to extend the Western barrier.

Lee tried to go south from Amelia Court House; Sheridan sent Crook riding hard after him, harassing the Southern rearguard, capturing the essential wagon trains. Meade was moving infantry in the same effort, but he was moving them too slowly. Sheridan moved Custer and Devin in behind Crook; if his cavalry couldn't have infantry support, it would support itself.

Sheridan managed to cut into Ewell's column, pinching Anderson's corps off from the main body. Ewell should have, and probably would have, let Anderson go; but Sheridan wanted the whole wing, half of Lee's command.

Crook's division had cut off Anderson; Sheridan ordered him to attack the dug-in division, while Devin and Custer rode around to attack on what was really Anderson's front. Then Sheridan used the VI Corps, infantry still attached to his command, to engage the rest of Dick Ewell's wing.

By nightfall he had captured nine thousand Confederate rank and file, including several generals. One of the latter was Custis Lee, who had been Jefferson Davis' military aide – George Washington Custis Lee, Robert E. Lee's son, who had graduated first in the class of 1854 at West Point which also included J.E.B. Stuart, a year after Phil Sheridan got out, near the bottom of his own class.

Grant sent Lee a tender, but the Southern general still had Longstreet's wing of his army. Grant told Sheridan to keep pressing. The cavalry moved out against the retreating Lee; they hit him on either flank, in the rear, any place they wanted to. Crook attacked the main column, and his brigadier, Gregg – not the same one who had held higher rank in Sheridan's force – was captured.

On April 8, Sheridan got to Appomattox Depot, five miles south of the Courthouse. He tore up the tracks, seized the supplies for Lee's army that were waiting on a siding – four trains of them – overcame a Southern battery trying to defend the Depot, and captured twenty-five guns. There was no doubt that he had guessed right, that he had now headed Lee, and more than that, stripped him of all the materials needed to sustain life in the Army of Northern Virginia. He wired the commanders of all the infantry corps round about to close in for the kill.

Nobody in the Cavalry Corps, USA, slept that night. When Lee came out in the morning, his stand at Appomattox Courthouse was completely surrounded by Sheridan and his men, dismounted, repeating carbines at the ready.

The South died hard. Lee threw John Gordon's corps – down to strength of a large division – at the enemy. Sheridan gave ground; carbineers couldn't stand up against heavy infantry attacks. Then the troopers parted their ranks, simply moved to the flanks, and General Edward Ord's Army of the James came through the gap; they had marched all night in answer to Phil Sheridan's message.

That was it. The war was over. Lee and Grant signed the peace that afternoon. There were incidents. Custer, dressed in a manner that Kilpatrick, whom Jeb Stuart had thought a fop, would have called overelaborate, walked up to old Longstreet, and demanded his surrender. Longstreet, who had been a major when Custer was a cadet, snubbed him, and the twenty-five-year-old major general of Volunteers went quietly away, white sombrero, flowing scarf, gold sleeve galloons, long hair and all.

Sheridan was less cordial, less sentimental than the other West Point Union generals. The Southerners had snubbed him for a mick when he was a cadet; he hadn't forgotten. After the signing, the officers present were allowed to buy the furniture in the historic room of the signature. Sheridan bought the little pine desk on which the peace agreement had rested, and sent it to Custer's young wife Elizabeth, whom he admired.

There was some war left. Grant sent Sheridan south before the big peace parade in Washington; Joe Johnston and Kirby Smith still had armies in the field. But they both surrendered before he got there. He had missed the glory of leading his troops along Pennsylvania Avenue for nothing.

Still, those same troopers – all of them – had gone far out of their way to pass his hotel while he was packing to go south. It was raining and uncomfortable for them, and Sheridan appreciated the honor; it is reported that he cried. That was the end of Phil Sheridan's career in the Cavalry. He remained, however, in the Army, and when Sherman retired in 1884 became its General-in-Chief, by then called General of the Army, though Sherman and Sheridan never wore more than four stars.

But his work after Appomattox was all administrative. He commanded the occupying force in Louisiana and Texas, he schemed with Juárez to get the French out of Mexico, he headed the Department and then the larger Division of the Missouri.

The short, ugly, swarthy but lithe and graceful cavalryman became a short, fat desk officer. He made himself hated in the South; he got the reputation of being a slaughterer of Indian women and children, somewhat undeservedly. He was sometimes talked of as a presidential candidate, though nothing could come of that for a Catholic Irishman in those days. But he never again led a cavalry charge, waving his hat and somehow making small men into big ones.

Jeb Stuart was gallant, Jeb Stuart was handsome; all of Light-Horse Harry Lee's grandsons did him and his son credit. Sheridan was ugly, ill-bred and frequently nasty and profane; his later development shows a gross streak in him. But he had won a war as Grant's most efficient striking arm. The poor boy from Perry County, Ohio, had paid back his country for his free education at West Point.

Chapter 22

Three Highly Independent Operations

There were theaters of war in which neither Stuart nor Sheridan figured, of course. But none of the Cavalry work in those places was distinctive enough to be recounted here; the stories of Phil Sheridan and the Cavalier tell it all except for the exploits of the Southern raiders.

John Mosby harassed Sheridan in the Valley, and so came into that picture. John H. Morgan's raid through Kentucky, Indiana, and Ohio was the deepest penetration of the North that any Confederate ever made. Bedford Forrest was both a general of the line and the wildest raider of all.

Out on the Missouri-Kansas border, where St. George Cooke and his Dragoons had kept the peace in the late '50s, William Clarke Quantrill for the South and James H. Lane for the North led their wild Raiders and Jayhawkers in forays that were called patriotic or pure banditry, depending on which side the observer was. But men on horses are not necessarily cavalry. So, the accounts of Mosby, Morgan, and Forrest complete the cavalry story of the War Between the States.

Mosby first. Like so many of the horse officers, he was a writer; his *War Reminiscenses* and his *Stuart's Cavalry Campaigns* came out in 1887 and still make good reading. Before the war he had been a lawyer. Afterwards he was a Republican, and seven years after the peace, could be found canvassing Virginia for Grant's candidacy, of all things; this alone must make him unique among Southern leaders.

Mosby was as full of contradictions as any fiction writer could ask for. The lawless streak in him is widely remembered; but he had been a lawyer, was to be one again, and in the tri-country area he set up for his own kingdom, he made himself the law when the war suspended regular courts and peace-justice proceedings. Munson, one of his men quoted by Henry

Steele Commager in *The Blue and the Gray*, boasts that "no country, before, during or since the war was ever better governed."

John Singleton Mosby at the age of twenty-eight started his way in 1861 as a private in one of the numerous fancy-dan outfits raised in Virginia. This one was called the Washington Mounted Rifles, and the company commander was no less a cavalryman than William E. Jones, late of the Mounted Rifles in the Regular Army – hence the name – and later to be the Grumble Jones who was a general under Stuart.

Grumble, who liked practically nothing in the world, seemed to take a fancy to the slim ex-lawyer. When the outfit was taken into a regiment with Grumble as colonel, he had Mosby commissioned a lieutenant and adjutant of the regiment.

But, in the peculiar course of democratic war in the mid-nineteenth century, the Confederate government passed a law allowing soldiers to elect their own officers. The men made Fitz Lee colonel and Grumble Jones lieutenant colonel. Whereupon Mosby resigned his commission, which also seemed permissible in wartime under the early Confederate laws.

He had no official standing at all when he joined Stuart and acted as his guide in the first ride around McClellan's army. Stuart took to him and eventually gave him a commission in the Virginia forces, which happened to be non-existent legally by that time; the Confederate Congress had abolished state guards and made the Army into a whole, officers commissioned from Richmond or not at all. But life in that outfit of gallants, hard riders, and daredevils was too tame for the Virginia lawyer. In the first month of '63 he asked Stuart's permission to go raise his own force and use it to operate in the parts of Virginia that were in Union lines.

He got the permission, more or less informally; later the Confederate Congress passed a special law concerning "partisan rangers" that was supposed to cover Mosby's men if they were captured; the Union regarded them as illegal highway robbers, to be hanged rather than imprisoned.

Mosby himself was eventually given a commission in the Confederate Army, rising to full colonel, but after Appomattox, many of the Union generals wanted to hang him. Grant got him paroled, which may have had something to do with Mosby joining the Republican party when the other Republicans in the south were all carpetbaggers or Negroes.

He operated in Fairfax, Fauquier, and Loudoun Counties, northeastern Virginia, where the Old Dominion pushes into Maryland. His men resembled those of Francis Marion, of course, but they were even more irregular; one of them wrote later that making coffee, frying bacon, or chewing hardtack was unknown amongst them; each man knew a farmhouse he could call home, and they always ate at tables bountifully set by Southern sympathizers.

247

After raids on Northern supply trains and depots they would repay their hosts with livestock, grain, and the notions that were so hard for farm wives to get in war-ridden territory. The area was not completely Southern. It included the home district of St. George Cooke, around Leesburg, which declared for the Union just before the colonel of Regulars did the same thing.

Mosby's lighthearted Rangers – "blithe in the face of danger, full of song and story, indifferent to the events of tomorrow" according to one of them – did a lot to encourage loyalty to Virginia rather than to the United States in the divided area.

John Mosby, after he left Stuart, raised about thirty followers. Each was to uniform himself, with the only proviso being that every man had to wear something gray. Each man brought his own horse, but this was the rule all through the Southern cavalry. Arms consisted of Colt's army revolvers, muzzle-loading, but with removable cylinders, so that a ranger with two of them on his belt could fire four cylinders in fairly fast order. Some of the men wore two pistols on their belts and two more in their boot tops, but the sort of fast skirmishing that Mosby led them on didn't call for heavy fire power; shoot, ride through, and outgallop the enemy was the usual order.

These, in other words, were not Dragoons, who could make a stand dismounted or charge through enemy horse with sabers slashing; they didn't carry either carbines or swords.

Nor were they foragers, in the old tradition of Harry Lee, Mad Anthony Wayne the Drover, or Sheridan's men in the Valley. Mosby would not tolerate the robbing of the local farms, even if their owners were Northern sympathizers; he caught one of his Rangers kicking over a Quaker farmer's milk bucket – and the Quakers were always Loyalist – and dismissed him from the force, sent him to Early in the Regular Anny with a message that the man was "unfit to be a Guerilla."

But within his command, the Ranger chief didn't care for the military legalities. The only officer ever addressed by the title was Mosby himself; the others went by their first names, never called a drill, and seldom even had a roll call.

If Stuart was Lee's Intelligence Corps, Mosby was Stuart's; in plain clothes or under cover of darkness, he and his men steadily found where Stuart could best apply his penetration-in-force system of news gathering. He was also Stuart's Remount Corps. Stealing horses and mules from the Union forces became a major part of his service; the most valuable kind of service he could have rendered a cavalry commander in an army where each man brought his own mount and might have to go home to find a replacement in case of loss.

Until March 1863, Mosby was only a gadfly to the Union. Then he and his men – quite a large force for him, thirty in all – descended on the headquarters of Brigadier General Edwin H. Stoughton at Fairfax Courthouse and took that Union dignitary out of his bed, first waking him with a slap on his bare rump.

They returned to Stuart with the general, two captains, thirty private prisoners and fifty-eight horses. Fitz Lee accepted the booty for his commander, further annoying Mosby by inviting Stoughton, but not Stoughton's captor, into his quarters. Stoughton and Lee had been classmates at West Point. But Mosby was rewarded when Stuart got back to Culpeper a few hours later. The Cavalier stood on the railroad platform, listened to Mosby's account of his night, and roared with his famous laughter. He mentioned him in General Orders, bringing a response from General Robert E. Lee that "Mosby has covered himself with honors."

E.H. Stoughton, '56, U.S.M.A., was perhaps no great loss to the North. In fact, official records deny that a general was taken out of his bed, by listing his appointment as expired a few days before his capture. He never reappears in the official reports. The fact that a Southern force of irregulars, however – generally reported as ten times its true size, but still a tiny force – could take a general from his bed in his headquarters shocked the Northern papers. Mosby became famous, at first under such newspaper names as Moseby and Mosely.

Investigation led to the arrest of a young lady of Fairfax, Miss Antonia Ford. She was accused of having acted as a spy for Mosby, of being "very intimate" with him, and of having worked with him in the actual raid itself. She was arrested and interned in the Old Capitol Prison in Washington for a while.

The scandal was probably skewed. If Antonia was "very intimate" with anyone, it was probably Jeb Stuart, whose "flirtations" were notorious. In fact, Mosby had first come to the Cavalier's notice when the young lawyer drove a couple of Stuart's lady acquaintances from Fairfax to Centerville, while the Cavalier rode outrider. In Antonia's possession when she was arrested was a commission as honorary aide-de-camp issued her by Stuart in 1861.

Having become a newspaper personality, Mosby's small raids and horse stealings made headlines from then on. This was before Sheridan came East, and the Union forces in Virginia were all operating in the murky light shed by the Pinkerton intelligence agents. The presence of a Confederate force that seemed to penetrate their lines at will contributed heavily to the nervousness of the Army of the Potomac, and Jefferson Davis issued Mosby a bona-fide commission as a captain, CSA.

His command grew and shrank. It became the custom for dismounted troopers and officers of the Regular cavalry regiments of the Confederacy to go with Mosby on borrowed horses till they could steal permanent mounts from the Union lines. It also became the custom for discontented soldiers to desert the hard-marching, hard-drilling Regular lines of the Confederacy to join up with Mosby's Partisan Rangers, who were reputed to be getting rich on loot, and who were certainly eating better and drilling less than any other Confederate military in the spring and summer of 1863.

Mosby was warned about accepting deserters in his band, and there is evidence that he tried hard to screen his volunteers. Men who did not fight as hard or ride as hard as he wanted were sent to the Regular lines with the request that they be put into less dashing companies. That Mosby was more of an aid than a nuisance to General Lee is evidenced by the fact that when the Confederate Congress repealed the Partisan Ranger Act and outlawed the independent raiders who had been working around the South, Lee had the congressmen make an exception of Mosby's command, which was taken into the Army as the 43rd Battalion. However, the 43rd never drilled, mustered – Mosby himself said he never saw all his command together at any one time – and continued to divide loot among the members of a raiding party.

On October 14, 1864, Mosby's Rangers hit the Baltimore & Ohio Railroad, derailed a train, cut the line and captured a Union payroll of $173,000. There were eighty-four men on the raid – each one received twenty-one hundred dollars for his work. When Mosby refused a share, his men pooled together and bought him a thoroughbred horse named Croquette. Cash sublimated into horseflesh did not offend the Rebel raider.

Grant and Sheridan were running the Virginia theater of war by then, and Sheridan, particularly, was determined to capture Mosby, who had looted and burned the little Irishman's wagon train back in August; the loot consisted of five hundred or more horses and mules, two hundred beef head, and the contents of seventy-five wagons. Mosby took two hundred prisoners, but missed a chest containing over a hundred thousand dollars in greenbacks.

After that, Grant had ordered Sheridan to hang any of Mosby's men he caught and hang them without trial. Now, two months later, Mosby was operating more successfully than ever.

A few days after the Greenback Raid, as the strike on the B. & O. came to be called in derisive headlines North and South, the Mosby people repeated the exploit that had first brought them to fame – they captured another brigadier, General A.N. Duffie, a Frenchman who had bested Stuart at Middleburg, when the Cavalier should have been at Gettysburg.

Grant's order to hang Mosby men without trial had been obeyed; it is not surprising that the general who shot four partisans and hanged two was George Armstrong Custer, always a little more bloodthirsty than anyone else.

Later that same October Mosby forced twenty-seven prisoners from Custer's command to draw lots; the seven losers were to be hanged. The increased number was in retaliation for a partisan hanged by Brigadier General William H. Powell of the Union. One of the seven escaped, two were hanged, and Mosby's men impatiently shot the other four.

When Sheridan scorched the earth of Mosby's kingdom, the raider's activities declined. Also, the raider chief came down with a serious cold; he had never weighed more than a hundred and twenty-five pounds, and he had been wounded repeatedly, once so badly that Union officers looking at him went away, sure he could not last the night. They did not, however, know who it was they were looking at, or they would have taken him with them, dead or alive. Even with his belly ripped open by a bullet, he had still managed to convince them he was a lieutenant named Johnson.

The Valley was no longer of much use to the Confederacy, but Sheridan could not abandon it till he captured Mosby. He never did. At the height of the search, the partisan chief dressed in full uniform and took the train to Richmond to confer with Lee.

It was proposed that Mosby move his men to the Peninsula, where troops were needed and where forage was still available. But it was feared that if Mosby himself went into that easily blockaded country, the entire Union cavalry would be sent there to take him. So, he split his command, sent four companies down to Tidewater, and continued to stay in the desolated valley with his three remaining troops.

Mosby had not only hanged Union men, stolen a Union payroll, captured Union generals; he had also mortally wounded the vanity of the Union Army. So, when Generals Grant and Lee announced the terms of peace, Mosby was specifically exempt from parole.

He spent years after the war in and out of trouble, in and out of jail. He would correspond with a parole officer of the Army of Reconstruction, arrange to surrender, and then be met by a different officer who would deny knowing anything about the correspondence and would attempt to arrest Mosby. He always wore two six-shooters to any parole conference. Few men dared stand up against them and his reputation.

Early in 1866 Mrs. Mosby went to see General of the Army Grant, who received her courteously and gave her a letter of parole for her husband. The letter was dated February 2 and should have ended Mosby's troubles; but in April, for reasons known only to himself, Mosby appeared on the streets of Leesburg in complete Confederate uniform, buttons, sidearms, and all. This was in direct violation of his parole; a guard was turned out, and how the Rebel colonel escaped has never been made clear.

Mosby settled down in Warrenton, as much as he could settle down, built up a good law practice, made money in real estate, challenged various people to duels, campaigned in Virginia for President Grant's re-election in 1872, and, according to the old Union general, carried the state for him against Horace Greeley. But feeling against Mosby never died down. After Grant was out of office, Mosby appealed to him; the old partisan's life was being threatened – he had been shot at in the night on the streets of his home town.

Grant went to see President Rutherford B. Hayes, who, in 1878, appointed Mosby consul to Hong Kong where, presumably, few people would care which side he had fought on in the Civil War. Mosby served in that port for seven years, hating it all the time except for a short visit from Grant and his family.

John Singleton Mosby lived a long, long time – he died in Washington in his eighty-third year, on May 30, 1916. He served as attorney for the Southern Pacific Railroad, and for the government in the General Land Office, and in the Justice Department.

As late as 1915 he was still fighting, this time with letters to newspapers in defense of Belgian civilians executed for sniping at the German troops occupying their homeland. This was the way he had operated in his war, he wrote, and he had had a German soldier or two in his command, at that.

John H. Morgan of Kentucky was different from Mosby in many ways. One of the few things they had in common was an early reputation for being ready fighters. But while Mosby had been thrown out of college for shooting a fellow student in the face – the student recovered, and Mosby was only in jail six months – Morgan never went to college. His father had a store, and the young Morgan went to work there. By the time the war broke out he was, at thirty-five, a wealthy man, with two "manufactories" of his own.

Since he had been a first lieutenant of Militia in the Mexican War, he was elected captain of his militia company, the Lexington Rifles, in 1857. When war came, he promptly enrolled this outfit in Albert Sidney Johnston's Confederate Army of the Western Department.

There seem to have been only one or two resignations. Unlike Virginia, Kentucky was Union or Confederate mostly by towns instead of by houses; there might be two or three Northern sympathizers in a Southern town, or the other way around, but they were well-known, and would not have joined a militia company – basically a social group – in which the majority held counter political opinions.

The towns of Kentucky – like those of Missouri – did not go Northern or Southern by geography; sometimes there would be a solid county, but more often a few miles would separate Union from Confederate sympathizers.

This made the big difference between Morgan's command and that of the Virginia partisans. Morgan could lead a fair-sized division, confident that he could feed and forage his command; Mosby never could take out, at any one time, more than a large-sized company.

Morgan's Men, as they liked to call themselves, were not all Kentuckians. At times he had a Texas regiment with him, later he had a Tennessee regiment in his division and other troops joined him from time to time; so did individual soldiers, many of them militiamen whose time was up, and who had drifted back from the Eastern theater of war. No doubt, too, Morgan's easy discipline and gainful looting attracted deserters from more rigid Confederate forces. The government at Richmond complained all during the war about the loss of men to partisans.

The Morgan company, then regiment, then brigade, and finally division, served in several battles; the earliest was the disastrous evacuation of Nashville. His men were counted as a squadron, by then, and were detailed with the 1st Missouri to act as military police in the terror-stricken city.

Except for Forrest's regiment, which had escaped from Grant at Fort Donelson intact, there were no organized troops in Nashville except the Kentucky-Missouri provost guard. The South had not expected any setback like Fort Donelson, where over eleven thousand Confederates surrendered. The troops pouring into Nashville from the defeat came in little knots, not even formal squads. It seemed probable that all of Kentucky was going to have to be abandoned to the North, and discipline vanished in the mood of despair.

Forrest's regiment recuperated a little from its retreat and were thrown into the military police; they were needed; looting and rioting filled Nashville. One of Morgan's troopers noted that the Forrest troopers used the flat of their sabers to drive looters away from warehouses of stores wanted by the troops; this is interesting, in that Morgan's Men never carried swords of any kind except as trophies taken from Yankee troopers or officers. Morgan rode rearguard out of the city, his men driving infantry deserters and stragglers ahead of them.

They were heading for the Battle of Shiloh, but they didn't know it. The main body of A.S. Johnston's army had re-formed at Corinth, Mississippi, and was ready to strike north again. It was Johnston's idea to strike Grant at Pittsburg Landing, where Shiloh Church was; all the troops left in Tennessee were coming to support the Southern force. Shiloh was indecisive. The South lost eleven thousand men, the North thirteen thousand; Albert Sidney Johnston received a fatal wound; the Confederate troops went back to Corinth.

Morgan's Men had done well at Shiloh, however; together with the 8th Texas – Terry's Rangers – they had made a cavalry charge against skirmishers who were trying to prevent a Southern battery from firing and had gone through the skirmishers to run into a whole regiment of infantry, fortunately already milling.

Basil Duke, Morgan's brother-in-law and second-in-command, who was to write the history of the Morgan raiders and command them after Morgan's death, noted in the subsequent rout that those men who had sabers found them useless compared to guns and pistols.

After the battle, the Confederate Army, now under P.G.T. Beauregard, entrenched itself at Corinth. Morgan got permission to ride into Tennessee to forage and loot before Halleck's approaching army. He led three hundred and twenty-five men, according to Basil Duke.

The foray was successful; Morgan took prisoners, burned Federal supplies, looted stores with Union flags over them, destroyed an engine and forty cars, stopped another train and took eight thousand dollars in Federal greenbacks, and in general had a fine time. Also, he restored the spirits of Southern sympathizers in western Tennessee, always a dubious part of the Confederacy. In one town Morgan had to hide his prize mare, Black Bess, from feminine sympathizers who wanted locks of her mane and tail; he said that otherwise she would have been completely shorn.

At Chattanooga, Morgan was joined by some of his own men, wounded at Shiloh and now convalesced, by Captain Gano's troop of Terry's Texas Rangers, and by three hundred men from the 1st Kentucky Infantry, an outfit just disbanded as having completed its militia term of enlistment. He mounted them and was in command of a full regiment; Johnston had made him a colonel, and now the title meant something.

Morgan drilled his men in Tennessee, preparatory to taking the war back into Kentucky. Mosby, like most partisan rangers, never bothered with drill; Morgan, according to Basil Duke again, didn't bother with guard mounts and parades until recruits poured in so fast they had to be disciplined quickly, but he was devoted to what was called "Maury's skirmish tactic for cavalry," a method developed for fighting Indians with small bodies of horse troops, and adapted by Morgan for the use of any size force against infantry. It was a maneuver for dismounted troopers, really, mounted riflemen. Morgan favored the "medium" Enfield rifle; the carbine, Enfield or otherwise, was too inaccurate and short-ranged, and the infantry, or long Enfield, was too unwieldy on horseback. Each man carried two revolvers, preferably Army Colt's. Duke had no use for breech-loading rifles; the Enfield and Springfield at that time were still muzzle loaders. We presume his views were those of John Morgan's. The time taken to load through the muzzle, and to ram home the load with a rod kept a soldier cool, Duke said. Having gone to all that trouble, he was not going to shoot wildly, but to take his time, aim, and make every bullet count. But if a soldier just had to slip in a cartridge, or "turn a lever," he would get careless and let fly at the blue sky. "Dead shots with an Enfield shoot as if they were aiming at the sun with a Spencer," he wrote, though he regarded the Sharp and Spencer as the best of the breech loaders. The rule with Morgan's Men was: use the revolver if you have to fight on horseback; dismount whenever possible, and fight as mounted riflemen with your muzzle-loaders.

Every fourth man in mounted column was a horse holder. As the outfit went front into line, he grabbed the reins of the other three and rode to the rear, to hold himself and the four horses in readiness for a charge if the enemy was routed, or a retreat if the battle went against Morgan's Men.

On the flanks a few men remained in the saddle as skirmishers. If the detachment was big enough, some of these rode behind the dismounted line as the battle was joined, prepared to act as cavalry routers in the classic manner. If numbers meant anything, the skirmishers soon dismounted and sent their horses to the rear, too. The line then advanced in single depth, at the double or dogtrot; the two flanks went ahead of the center; in this way, if any part of the line was attacked, it dropped back and the charging enemy found himself surrounded by the Morgans.

Artillery backed up the Morgan raiders; preferably two to four mountain howitzers, short range, high ballistic guns that could be pulled at a gallop by horses or manhandled into line by a very few troopers, or even dismantled and carried on pack saddles.

Later, just before Morgan's great raid into Ohio, Braxton Bragg's staff ordered Morgan to turn his two howitzers into the general ordnance, and Morgan's Men nearly mutinied. Duke wrote that he would have gladly seen the ordnance officer who seized the guns "tied to one of their muzzles and shot off."

For the next year Morgan and his men stormed in and out of Kentucky, serving also in Tennessee and fighting at Cairo, Illinois, once; Cairo is where Kentucky, Illinois, and Missouri come close to Tennessee and Arkansas, so this was still pretty much Southern country.

Morgan was not always an independent commander; he worked with the Western Army under Bragg when needed. He also worked with General Kirby Smith, whom he thought a much better commander than Braxton Bragg.

By the end of that year of foraging he had a huge command, about nine strong regiments, broken into two brigades, so that he should have been a major general. But he did not even make brigadier until he had been in the field five months; his men called him general long before Jefferson Davis conferred the title on him.

Six months later Morgan got the great notion for which he is remembered; he would take his division across the Ohio River and raid into Indiana,

Ohio, and maybe even into Pennsylvania, taking the war farther north than it had ever been.

Actually, he did succeed in taking it slightly farther north than Stuart went on the raid that burned Carlisle and raided Middleburg when the Cavalier should have been farther south helping Lee at Gettysburg. Morgan got to Beaver Creek, Ohio, northwest of Pittsburgh, about three weeks after Stuart got to Gettysburg.

There is no correspondence to show that Morgan was aware of Lee's plans to strike north into Pennsylvania; but it is not strange that the Midwest expedition coincided with the Eastern one. The military maxims – or cliches – of "when in doubt, strike," and "the best defensive is a good offensive," were beginning to apply. But they applied for opposite reasons.

In the East – to use another cliché – the iron was hot. Chancellorsville has been called Lee's most brilliant battle, and it was up to him to follow it up with an invasion. This was his chance to move the war out of famished Virginia and into the rich enemy country.

In the Mississippi Valley, Vicksburg had given control of the river to the North, and Braxton Bragg had retreated out of Kentucky again, and gone far south, to southern Tennessee, with the army that had been meant to keep Rosecrans from cutting the Western Confederacy in half. Bragg would rally and come north again to Chattanooga; Generals Ambrose Burnside and Henry M. Judah were moving to re-enforce Rosecrans. A move against the northern Midwest would divert the troops – there were about a hundred thousand of them in the territory of the proposed strike – that would make the difference between heavy odds and an even chance for Bragg. He gave Morgan permission to ride out.

Bragg was reluctant to let Morgan loose; he kept changing his mind, giving permission one day, withholding it the next. Bragg did not share the prejudice of some commanders against cavalry; he used them in force for screening, he appreciated their intelligence work, and he had good cavalry in his own command, including a brigade under Brigadier General Abraham Buford, no relation to General John Buford of the Union. However, Bragg regarded Morgan as "dangerous," because of the raider's independence, his almost point-blank refusal to stay long under anyone's command. Braxton Bragg was the Confederacy's Commander-in-Chief in the West; quite naturally he felt uneasy about there being a second Confederate Army in that area, and this was virtually the way Morgan thought of his command.

But finally, General Bragg gave Morgan permission to raid into Kentucky. This should keep Union cavalry General Judah up there and away from Bragg and Rosecrans; it might even divert Burnside. First, however, the Morgan Division went out to stop Brigadier General William Sanders, USA, who was threatening Knoxville, over in East Tennessee.

Morgan took two of his three brigades – any time there was a delay, Morgan's command grew – and left the third one to guard Bragg's front. The dash against Sanders was successful, and the Union troops left Tennessee when Morgan approached. Weeks had been lost. During most of that time it rained, and the Cumberland River flooded, barring Morgan from the Kentucky-Tennessee border.

The river was still out of its banks on July 2, but Morgan ordered Duke to take the 1st Brigade across, anyway. The horses swam, the fieldpieces teetered precariously on two rickety little flat boats. Colonel Johnson, commanding the 2nd Brigade, didn't even have the use of the two flat boats, but got his thousand men across somehow. Altogether the force was just under twenty-five hundred, not bad for two Confederate brigades in the summer of 1863.

Twelve miles north of the Cumberland, Judah had a couple of his divisions. The Union leader had forces scattered all over the country; he had been in an argument with one of his subordinate generals, and orders and counter orders were floating all over the place.

Judah didn't expect Morgan; the river seemed impassable. But there were scattered Union men along the river, and soon the 2nd Brigade was engaged fairly strongly. Duke's 1st Brigade, which had the artillery with it, had its vanguard well inland before the scouts, riding rearguard, were out of the river. Duke ran into Union Kentucky cavalry; Duke had numbers on his side, and attacked at once, before many of his men had time even to pull on their underwear and boots. The psychological effect helped drive off the Federals, according to the diarists.

Then Duke sent help to Johnson and the 2nd Brigade. The Union horsemen, under Colonel Frank Wolford, were pushed back far enough for Morgan to make a stand at a crossroads beyond Burkesville, the seat of Cumberland County. When the Union got enough men together to attack in force, Morgan had his fieldpieces – heavier ones than Duke liked for fast cavalry work – covering the roads.

On July 3, Wolford and Morgan both headed for the town of Columbia, about sixteen miles north of the river crossing. Morgan got there first and took the town by noon; twelve hours later his rearguard was still passing through the village. Colonel Richard Morgan, the general's brother, guarded the advance, about nine miles above Columbia, with the newly formed 14th Kentucky, an understrength regiment newly formed and attached to Johnson's 2nd Brigade.

The next day was Saturday, the Fourth of July. Astrologers would make something of the fact that the Fourth of July weekend has always been a lucky one for the United States of America; in the Spanish-American War, the Spanish fleet was destroyed on July 3-4.

Independence Day, 1863, was a black one for the states that wanted their independence from the Union. Lee was turned back at Gettysburg, Grant took Vicksburg; and General John Hunt Morgan, with his more than two thousand troopers, tried to knock four hundred Michigan infantrymen out of a well-built fort and was thrown back for a loss of thirty-six dead and almost fifty wounded. The dead were buried under a flag of truce, the wounded were left with a surgeon to tend them.

It was a bad start for the raid, not only because of the casualties, but because the delay to try and take a blockhouse that could have been bypassed gave General Judah time to decide what he ought to do about Morgan. He started in pursuit with his heavy Cavalry corps. So did Colonel Wolford, sore from his defeat at Columbia.

The raiders kept moving. They didn't stop officially at Campbellsville (forty-one miles from the Cumberland) but a Captain Murphy hesitated long enough to question a civilian – and steal his gold watch. Captain Magenis or Maginis (these are Duke's spellings, and he was weak on proper names) of Morgan's staff caught his fellow-Irishman, turned him in to Morgan, and Murphy murdered his fellow officer. There was no time to hang the felon. He was taken along as a prisoner and escaped just before the column crossed into the North.

Looting was always a problem for Morgan, and for all the other raiding chieftains. The kind of men they wanted, troopers who could live off the countryside and get paid when and if the outfit ever met up with a loaded paymaster, were naturally wild. Encouraged to steal food for themselves, to forage for their horses, to find ammunition and clothes and saddles and guns as they needed them, and money if it was Federal, they were hard to restrain from taking valuables from people who were, or might be suspected of being, Union sympathizers.

On his very last raid, Morgan was accused of encouraging his men to rob a bank, and a civil suit was instituted against his estate after the war. But at the time of the robbery Morgan himself admitted that the quality of his following had badly deteriorated, and that he had men in his ranks he wouldn't have tolerated when things looked bright for the Confederacy and the pick of Kentucky's young men all wanted to ride with the glamorous Morgan.

The next stall-up was at Lebanon, fifty-six miles up from the Cumberland. The town was held by Union Kentucky troops, the 20th Kentucky USA, and Morgan knew them well and wanted to avoid a showdown with them. He tried to bluff their Colonel Hanson, failed, tried an artillery assault and had his cannoneers driven back by sharpshooters, and then was told the Michiganders were closing up his rearguard.

When in doubt, charge. Morgan ordered a rearguard action against Wolford and his Michigan troops, and threw everything he had at Lebanon, Duke leading with the 2nd Kentucky, who had had some experience with street fighting when he was their colonel instead of their brigadier.

The town was taken with a loss to Morgan of less than ten men killed and thirty wounded. But one of the dead was Morgan's nineteen-year-old brother, Tom. There were three Morgan brothers, as well as brother-in-law Duke, serving under the general; Colonel Richard commanded the 14th, and Captain Calvin was beside First Lieutenant Tom when the boy was shot. Duke reports that Lebanon gave them a rich supply of ammunition, fine rifles, and an abundant supply of medicines. The column moved on toward Bardstown, close to the Ohio River.

Burnside was reported to be over near Harrodsburg, and Morgan sent Company H of the 2nd there to occupy his attention. Sending a single company out to divert an army seems insulting to Burnside's reputation.

Bardstown was reached at four o'clock in the morning, but apparently not everybody rode steadily. At least one officer, a Lieutenant Colonel Alston, took a nap on someone's porch and woke up a prisoner of the Union.

The column moved out at ten in the morning, going due east to where the river passed Brandenburg and Garnettsville. Morgan learned that he was expected to try for Louisville, heavily held by the Union and now being re-enforced.

This information was gained at nightfall when the raiders captured a train on the line that ran from Nashville to Louisville. One of Morgan's men was named George Ellsworth; he was the greatest wire-tapper in the world, a man who could imitate any other telegrapher's "fist" or style of sending. Union brasspounders always seemed anxious to tell him anything Morgan wanted to know. After the war Ellsworth invented and patented a device that would prevent future tappers from using many of the tricks he used.

When they crossed the Salt River that night they were in Ohio River country; Morgan sent two officers to steal boats for the crossing of the big river. Another officer took two companies ahead of the main column; they were to get into Indiana and keep the Indiana militia busy while the main column crossed. This made the main force five companies smaller than when it left Sparta. One company was "occupying the attentions" of Burnside, and another had been sent off from Columbia to cause diversions around the Crab Orchard country. A third had simply deserted in a body. The new detachment was supposed to rejoin Morgan at Salem, Indiana, but never did; they ran into an overwhelming Union force and were captured.

When the raiders got to Brandenburg, they found that Captains Merriwether and Taylor had proved themselves highly successful boat thieves; they had commandeered two fine steamers. The adjective "fine" is Duke's, and a real tribute; the Kentuckian hated everything about the water – scenery, boats, the very air. He denounced as hypocrites people who professed to go sailing or water traveling for pleasure; it was simply out of the question that there could be, anywhere in the world, any such fools. He flew into a grumbling rage at the very sound of seaman's language.

Snipers on the Indiana side, aided by some sort of cannon, tried to prevent the Kentuckians from boarding their vessels, but Morgan's artillery drove the enemy away from the bank, and the 2nd Kentucky and 9th Tennessee crossed, without their horses.

Then a Union gunboat came down the river and started firing on both parties of Southerners. The horse artillery returned the fire, though the boat was too heavily armored with oak planks for a fieldpiece to hurt her. After an hour, though, she went on downriver – perhaps out of ammunition – and the embarkation went ahead. The first thing across were the horses of the two dismounted regiments. As the first brigade finished crossing, before nightfall, the gunboat came back with another boat, described by the landlocked Duke merely as a "consort."

For some reason, the Parrott fieldpieces were now able to drive away both boats, and by midnight the 2nd Brigade was in Indiana. The raiders burned one of the steamers they had used because it was in government employ; the other was spared, on the promise of its captain that he'd steam for Louisville so the Federals couldn't use his boat.

The raiders were in wonderful spirits that night. Everyone who lived in the country just north of the river seemed to have left when the 1st Brigade landed, just before suppertime. Bread was rising, but not yet baked, and chickens were plucked but not yet fried. The troopers completed the cooking and camped where they had eaten.

The next day militia tried to hold Morgan up in Corydon and did succeed in killing and wounding a few Kentuckians before they were routed. The column moved on, and camped about sixteen miles short of Salem, which would be their first substantial Indiana town; it had a population of about two thousand, three times as big as Corydon. Militia and volunteers tried to stop them at Salem but were easily overpowered. The Morgan Men fed their horses, burned several railroad bridges, and did some pillaging, against Morgan's orders and the efforts of his military police.

Astoundingly, what the troopers most wanted to steal was calico. The puzzled Duke recorded that each man would tie a bolt of it to his saddle and leave it there till he could replace it with a fresh one, behavior that would puzzle a congress of psychologists. Later, in Ohio, one trooper risked shooting by a provost-guard in order to fill his pockets with horn buttons.

In Vienna Ellsworth forced the telegraph operator to send a message, studied his style, and sat down at the instrument to get the news from

Indianapolis and Louisville. Alarm was spreading all through Indiana and Ohio, Morgan learned with satisfaction: no troops would be sent South from those states to help Rosecrans.

The column camped near Lexington, and General Morgan availed himself of his rank by going into town to rest in a bed. During the night a Federal cavalry patrol rode right up to the porch of the house where the bed was located, and then rode away again.

Morgan found little resistance as the second week of July went by. He kept moving; the men were in the saddle twenty-one hours a day, on an average. But they didn't complain; they and their horses were eating magnificently. At Dupont they raided a packinghouse and each trooper rode off with a ham tied to his saddle; and at every place the Kentuckians noted with wonder that the Yankees baked once a week instead of every day, and the houses were all full of bread, a very important item to the hard-tackless Southerners. Duke, at another time, said that a trooper could eat five or six pounds of meat and be hungry in a few hours if there wasn't bread or potatoes to go with it.

As they went, they burned bridges and any railroad equipment they could find, but not the houses, except for one, from which they had been fired on; this even though an Indiana regiment had burned the homes of Company F, 2nd Kentucky, who were Mississippians.

Flour mills called for individual decisions. The miller either paid ransom, or his mill was burned down. Horses, of course, were needed and taken as found. The men were dissatisfied, however, with the inferiority of Indiana horses to Kentucky stock.

Ellsworth tapped another wire and told the North that Nathan Bedford Forrest was heading for the Ohio to follow Morgan. The Governor of Indiana wired Burnside to send home a regiment and a battery recently dispatched south. He also asked for seventeen thousand rifles from the arsenal at St. Louis and for his friend General Lew Wallace, who would a decade later write a novel called *Ben-Hur*, to come and take charge of Indiana's defense.

He got Wallace, who loaded about thirteen hundred soldiers on a train and started rocketing around southeastern Indiana looking for Morgan. But Morgan was hard to find. The only means of rapid communication was the telegraph, and half the messages it supplied were fakes sent out by Ellsworth. Actually, Morgan was heading due east, for the Ohio River again, at Madison. Ellsworth had found out that Indianapolis, New Albany, and other places in central Indiana had all been heavily garrisoned against his cutting back west again. When Morgan led his men out of Salem, the authorities there counted his force as three times as large as reality, and so wired the Federal military.

By the afternoon of July 13, the column was at Harrison, almost on the Ohio line. Morgan pulled up here for three or four hours. It was time to maneuver around enough to fool the authorities at Cincinnati, where there was certain to be a strong force of Federals. He sent detachments off in all directions, the strongest going toward Hamilton, Ohio, due north of Harrison. Then he headed the whole division straight for Cincinnati, the Hamilton expedition joining up on the way.

The troopers rode hard through a long, long day, covering fifty miles. Duke said that the raiders were indescribably tired; nervous strain made this worse than an ordinary two days' march done all in a day, and while they had foraged well in Indiana, before that time they had been on half rations or less in famished Kentucky and battle-ravaged Tennessee. Nevertheless, they rode around Cincinnati that night. Scouts picketted out in front of the column; then came General Morgan, followed by Duke's 2nd Brigade.

The 1st Brigade rode rearguard and got all the trouble. Most of it, according to Duke, was caused by the 2nd Regiment, which was riding just ahead of the 1st Brigade, and constantly straggled, then galloped to catch up, opening a gap between Duke's 1st and the rear of the 2nd.

While these gaps were open, Duke would lead the 1st to a crossroads. These were suburbs they were riding through, and crossroads, five-points, and Ys were constant; Duke and his men would have to halt, climb down, and light bundles of paper to get enough light to read the hoof tracks and see which way Morgan had gone. But suburban traffic is heavy, and they would have to use such difficult and trivial signs as the freshness of slobber dropped from the mouths of the 2nd Brigade's horses. Duke does not mention manure, usually a good sign of how much time has passed since a horse went by; perhaps he was showing Victorian delicacy, or perhaps in July in that moist river country manure was slow in cooling or drying. The bubbles in saliva, of course, burst under any condition.

It was a slow, painstaking way to conduct a brigade down a dark road in the outskirts of a strong enemy city, fifth largest in the nation, with over a hundred and sixty thousand population ten years before and now perhaps a quarter of a million. Every time there was a halt, the troopers would climb down and go to sleep, or simply pass out in their saddles; the officers increased their own exhaustion by hauling men to their feet and making them remount; strong soldiers were hurt by falling off their stalled horses. Quite a few men evaded their officers, went to sleep in the fields, and were waked the next day by the enemy.

Sunrise found the column past Glendale, about five miles north of the present city limits, twice that far from the Ohio riverfront. They were almost out of danger, Duke felt; there was the Little Miami Railroad to cross, and after that they could expect nothing they couldn't handle in the way of enemy troop concentrations. The men revived. They halted near Camp Dennison, and the horses ate while the troopers skirmished with the Dennison pickets and burned a number of Federal wagons. Then they marched on, riding till four in the afternoon and halting at Williamsburg. They had been on the move for thirty-five hours and had covered ninety miles and were deep into Ohio.

Burnside rushed his troops across from Indiana and quartered them in Cincinnati. The residents of that city still didn't believe they had been spared; hoarding and pilfering and some looting and rioting broke out. Judah was down river with three thousand cavalrymen, about half again more than Morgan led. But the river was too swollen for boats to struggle upstream quickly; Judah got a day behind Morgan and never did catch up.

Telegrams streamed into General Jacob D. Cox's District of Ohio headquarters in Cincinnati. Morgan was in a dozen places at one time. While some of these telegrams must have been sent by Ellsworth, others were genuine, even if their senders' observations weren't. Morgan was doing what he had come north to do; panic Ohio and Indiana. Now, at Williamsburg, he let his men have their first full night's sleep since crossing the Cumberland eleven days before.

There were hardly any Kentucky horses left in the column. As a horse played out, his rider would lead him to the next barn, steal an Indiana or Ohio mount, and ride him down. Sometimes a man would use up three or four horses a day, and the Kentuckians complained constantly about the poor quality of mounts they were stealing. Many of the farm horses were not even shod and went lame almost as soon as they felt Confederate weight on their backs.

The raiders had gone southeast from Glendale to get to Williamsburg. Now they rode straight across the second tier of Ohio counties, through such towns as Piketon and Jackson, which still exist, and a dozen others now gone; many of them were so small that Duke had forgotten their names when he wrote his account in 1867.

Small bands of militiamen attacked Morgan's two-thousand-man column daily, occasionally killing a trooper, usually wounding two or three, and being captured in the hundreds. But there wasn't a thing the raiders could do with prisoners but turn them loose again.

On July 18 they encountered their first Regulars. This was near Pomeroy, on the Ohio River which, after it finishes separating Ohio from Kentucky, sweeps northeast to mark off what had become West Virginia just the month before. Morgan had crossed Ohio.

Pomeroy was a complex place with many crossroads leading to such places as Portland, Buffington Island, and Chester. Morgan put Colonel

Grigsby and his 6th Kentucky in the vanguard, to fight off organized militia and the Federals – they weren't sure whose troops these Regulars were – while the rest of the column passed each crossroad.

Grigsby used his men as dismounted riflemen each time; when the column had gotten by, Major Webber fought rearguard, and the Kentucky division moved on.

The division nooned at Chester for an hour and a half. Duke ascribed all their later troubles to this; it brought them to the river after dark, and on the river, they found Regular infantry, dug in behind breastworks and ready for them. He reports the town on the river as Chester; it was probably Cheshire, about eight or nine miles downriver from Pomeroy, but the 1855 *Gazeteer* lists several Chesters in Ohio.

No matter. The encounter with Regulars that day had informed Morgan that the Ohio River was now probably open to traffic and that the troops had gotten ahead of him by boat. If this were true, there would be more Regulars ahead of him at Pomeroy, and he had better get into West Virginia that night. But the breastworks commanded the ford, and the night was pitchdark, and attacking strange fortments blindly was almost suicidal.

So, Duke went into position, during the night, with the 5th and 6th Kentucky Regiments, placing himself – by feel, really – in a position to attack the earthworks at daybreak, while the rest of the division started crossing.

Duke attacked at dawn – and found the Federals had pulled out during the night, rolling their fixed artillery off its positions and leaving the empty breastworks for the Confederates. He sent word to Morgan of the evacuation and started his regiments up the Pomeroy road, looking for the Federals; it wasn't safe to cross the river until a possible and probable attacker had been pinned down.

At one his advance guard ran into a fire-fight. They had brushed the vanguard of Judah's force who had been ferried up the river and were fresh and reputed to be now eight or ten thousand in number. Duke's Colonel Smith dispersed the Federal riders, killed and wounded a few of them, and captured a fieldpiece and Judah's adjutant general. Morgan sent word to Duke to hold the enemy at any cost, and to call for what re-enforcements he wanted.

All of Morgan's divisions were in a tiny valley, not more than a mile long, and eight hundred yards at its widest, the southern, end. A ridge pinned them down on the west, the broad river on the east. Escape to the west was possible on the Chester road, where Morgan's Men had entered, in the middle of the valley.

Duke dismounted his troopers at the abandoned breastworks and formed a line. Judah's men attacked, three regiments of them, two of which Duke reported as being very good. Some Southern officer gave the command to blow to horse, the holders came up, and the Kentuckians were driven off by the dismounted troopers of the North.

Duke rallied them, and brought them back, and General Edward H. Hobson, USA, came marching down the Chester road. Hobson and Judah were not working together but had been independently hunting Morgan; Hobson with about three thousand men, Judah with twice that many, at least.

The Morgan division was pinned down from two sides. Now fire opened from a third – gunboats on the river. Morgan himself took charge of the evacuation of the valley by his main force; he led them – slowly, for the tired men were in great confusion – out the north end, while Duke stood the terrible cross fire behind him. The terrain was so limited that Duke could not bring most of his troops to bear on the enemy, though they were under fire all the time.

Morgan out, Duke ordered his own men to horse, and they retreated after their main body. The 6th Kentucky fought rearguard – *completely without ammunition*. Their bullet pouches empty – each man had only had four or five rounds when they went into the fight – they formed rear into line (from columns of four) three times and repulsed enemy charges with the sheer weight of their bodies and those of their horses. Men who had trophy swords used them, of course. It pays to have a good reputation.

But when the troopers saw how narrow the valley got at the north end, they broke, clogged the two northbound roads, and were charged by the 7th Michigan Cavalry, while the gunboats sent screaming charges of grape over the heads of the fireless Kentuckians. Duke, with fifty officers and men, was forced up a box canyon and captured. So were about six hundred and fifty more Morgan Men.

Morgan got away with about eleven hundred of his riders – less than half the number he had crossed with into Indiana. Some others made their way across the river and got away independently. For another week, and almost two hundred miles, Morgan rode to the northeast. But he was marked now, and the enemy had railroads and the river to use to bring troops to bear. On July 26, on the West Fork of Beaver Creek, he surrendered; he was about ten miles from the Pennsylvania line to the east and the same distance from the panhandle of West Virginia to the south.

Morgan was taken to prison in Columbus, Ohio; Duke ended up there, too, and so did Colonel Richard and Captain Calvin Morgan, the general's brothers, and several other officers of his command. Morgan got there at the end of July; before the end of November he, with six of his younger officers, had escaped, by tunneling down through a cell to an old ventilating shaft, and then tunneling up from the shaft to six other cells.

Duke and Richard Morgan and the other senior officers did not attempt to escape, though they helped their general and his young captains. Richard Morgan sat in his brother's cell and impersonated him, taking advantage of the dim prison lighting.

Once out, the Confederates split up. Morgan and Captain Hines simply went down to the railroad depot, bought tickets for Cincinnati, and the general spent the trip talking to a Union officer, feeling that being in high company would keep trainmen and provost marshals from examining his spurious papers too closely.

Outside Cincinnati, Hines and his general pulled the emergency stop rope, and then each went to one end of the car and furiously applied the handbrakes. The train stopped, they jumped off, and made their way to the waterfront and paid a boy a couple of dollars – Union – to row them across to Kentucky.

Morgan was loose, and in Kentucky, where he knew how to find friends. His trip across the state was triumphal; but this was the end of 1863. A year, two years before, a feat like his would have rallied great strength in the border states, but nothing could save the Confederacy now.

General Morgan rode east with a small party of troopers, and then went up to Richmond, where he appealed to the Confederate government to do something about the officers still in Union prisons. They did nothing – perhaps there was nothing they could do.

Colonel Adam Johnson had gathered up all of Morgan's Men not captured, wounded, or killed in the disastrous battle on the Ohio – about four or five hundred. For awhile they were attached to Nathan Bedford Forrest's command, duty similar enough to their old life; at other times they were used elsewhere.

Naturally, Morgan wanted his old division back, but Richmond, with the idiocy that attacks legislators now and then, had a new policy, based on a wild theory that men would fight better under strange officers. The idea was to make a machine of the Army; Duke commented that it "would be difficult to conceive of a more utterly worthless machine."

In the spring of 1864, General Morgan was given command of the District of Southwestern Virginia. The troops under him were largely Kentuckians, but only one battalion – Kirkpatrick's – had been in his old division.

Officially or not, Morgan's Men kept coming into his department, and by May, when the salt and lead mines of his area were threatened by Crook and Averell, he could put six hundred old raiders, about a fourth of his Regulars, into two battalions. Another four hundred of his men were dismounted. The South had used up its horseflesh.

The ensuing battle, in Wythe County, Virginia, was inconclusive; Federal losses were heavier than Confederate, but the North could afford them, and it was the South that was forced to retreat.

Morgan decided to go back to raiding. He planned to swoop back into Kentucky, rallying recruits and getting horses for his walking troopers, now organized into his 3rd Brigade, about eight hundred strong. He had to move fast; Crook and Averell were awaiting strong re-enforcements from Kentucky.

The division started out happily enough. Federals were barring Pound Gap in the Allegheny country of far-western Virginia; the 3rd Brigade cleared them out, and captured several horses, a good omen for the raid. Morgan detached scouts to make sure that the displaced Gap guards were not outriders from some strong command, and took his division northwest toward Mount Sterling, where the Union had its biggest supply and ammunition dump in Kentucky. He felt he was in a race. The re-enforcements that had been sent to Virginia and eastern Kentucky would probably turn back, now that he was in the raid; if they got to Mount Sterling before he did, he wouldn't have a chance.

But the Union forces, under General Stephen G. Burbridge, had artillery to slow them down, and Morgan didn't. His mixed force, mounted and dismounted, covered a hundred and fifty miles of rugged, hard Appalachia in seven days. The 1st Brigade alone lost one horse out of five, more than two hundred in all; forage was as scarce as rocks and mountains were plentiful.

When he was sure he was going to win the race against Burbridge, Morgan started sending out detachments to cut rail lines, burn bridges, and take the town of Maysville. This was the old Morgan, giving the illusion of being in several places at once, taking over a large area and keeping it by making sure no re-enforcements could come in by rail.

On June 8 they were out of the mountains and into the blue grass around Mount Sterling. They cut the telegraph lines, hit the depot with all of Morgan's old fury, captured what they needed and destroyed the rest of the big depot.

The next day disaster struck. The scouts sent out in the mountains had reported that Burbridge had given up and headed back for Virginia. He hadn't. He had feinted and then come on fast toward Mount Sterling – faster than Morgan had thought possible.

Morgan's rearguard pickets were under the command of an officer new to Morgan, and they were exhausted men, barefoot and bleeding from the march through the mountains. Burbridge went through them without causing alarm and hit the main camp at three in the morning. Martin's 3rd Brigade lay in their path; a lot of Confederates were killed in their blankets. Then the Southerners rallied, resisted constant Federal assaults for an hour, and fell back through Mount Sterling, which Burbridge had already occupied.

On the other side of town they were joined by the 1st Brigade, which had been on a different road, unable to help up till now. The two brigades thrust back at the enemy, with success until the 2nd Brigade ran out of ammunition. Then the whole Morgan Division withdrew, leaving Burbridge's men too crippled to pursue them.

The next day Morgan hit Lexington, finding only slight resistance. Here were enough Federal horses to put every Morgan survivor in the saddle. The old raider feinted at Frankfort, and hit Cynthiana in force, capturing more stores, a four-hundred-man garrison and the Union General, Hobson.

But on the morning of June 12, Morgan had only half his original command under his hand – about twelve hundred men. Some were off destroying railroad bridges and tracks, some were guarding prisoners, and there had been casualties. Then Burbridge came up with over five thousand men and hit the 1st Brigade at a time when it was almost out of ammunition. The raid of the day before had taken bullets but they didn't fit the captors' guns.

The 2nd Brigade moved to the rescue of the 1st, but even combined they couldn't stand up against Burbridge's heavy force. Morgan ordered a general retreat, fighting rearguard with a mounted charge of his reserve, and headed back for Virginia. He had suffered heavy losses, and he now tried to recruit back to strength. But it was too late. The people of Kentucky and southwestern Virginia had lost faith in the Confederacy, and a soldier was no longer a hero, but a nuisance who took food away from starving families and fodder away from gaunt cows.

Lawlessness was taking over the country; unpaid soldiers simply took their horses and their guns and went into business as bandits, called guerrillas in that theater.

Burbridge, coming back after Morgan, shot any guerrillas he captured, and frequently shot legitimate prisoners of war, hard to distinguish in their tattered clothes. This didn't help Morgan's recruiting officers.

Also, Morgan was in trouble with Richmond. A bank had been robbed at Mount Sterling, and it was charged that he had given orders for the robbery; Duke denies the charges, and the truth is, Morgan had a long-established reputation for keeping his men in hand and honest; no charges of unpunished crimes against civilian property rose out of the long Ohio raid, for instance, and it was through enemy country.

Duke rejoined his general; he had been exchanged at Charleston, South Carolina, along with a number of other Confederate general and field-grade officers. Morgan took his command, now about sixteen hundred men in poorly armed and equipped condition, out into the field in August. He had an idea that he could drive the last Union forces out of his Department.

On September 3, 1864, at Warrensburg, east Tennessee, he ran into a Federal cavalry force under General Alvan C. Gillem, was shot by its vanguard, and died the next day.

Duke took over the division and found only two hundred and fifty-four officers and men under his command. It was renamed a brigade, though it was no larger than a healthy battalion.

Only fifty of his troopers had rifles that would fire; these were of all imaginable makes and calibres, and impossible to keep in ammunition. A Kentucky member of the Confederate Congress, E.M. Bruce, got the brigade rearmed, largely out of his own pocket, and Duke led it through endless fighting all that fall of 1864 and into 1865. Among the generals fighting for the Union in the South, George Stoneman showed up.

But it was over, and Morgan's Men knew it. When Lee surrendered, they hoped he would join Joe Johnston in the South, and they headed east to be in the combined army. They were at Charlotte when Jefferson Davis arrived there. A few days later they heard about the assassination of Lincoln and didn't believe it.

Davis still didn't believe the war was lost. With Duke's and four other brigades he went through the Carolinas to Washington, Georgia, where President Davis left them; there were threats to lynch the chief Confederate, and he planned a secret escape.

Duke took the brigade to Woodstock, Georgia, to surrender. And that was the end of Morgan's Men.

It is practically certain that Nathan Bedford Forrest never said that he "got there fustest with the mostest men." Forrest said "mought" for "might" and "fit" for "fought" but otherwise his spoken English was standard middle-class Southern. It is true, however, that he could not spell, and that he had no more than six months of schooling.

He was the oldest of the three Southern raiders, forty when the war started; Morgan was thirty-five and Mosby twenty-eight. Like the other two, he has been called the Francis Marion of the War between the States, but, like Morgan, he much more resembled Light-Horse Harry Lee, in that he could raid independently or work with an organized army; the men that Morgan, Forrest, and Lee led were disciplined, uniformed troopers; those of Mosby and Marion were not.

In 1861, Nathan Forrest was one of the richest men in the South; the son of a rather unsuccessful blacksmith, he had accumulated a fortune in lumber, slaves, and other industries. He enlisted when the war broke out, and then raised and equipped a battalion of Cavalry at his own expense, raising himself from private to lieutenant colonel in the manner, of the day.

Raising the battalion was not easy. In the first place, Forrest enlisted at Memphis, and western Tennessee was not strongly Confederate; in the second place, military stores – saddles, guns, ammunition, and so on – were not available closer than Kentucky, and that state had been declared neutral while both sides courted her.

Forrest went up into Kentucky and bought what he needed and smuggled it back to Memphis. He also raised his first company there, the Boone Rangers. The name of his battalion had been designated as Mounted Rangers.

From the first, the Confederate powers regarded him as an irregular, a partisan Ranger in the language of the day. For one thing, he wasn't educated; for another he had been a slave dealer and conducting a brokerage in slaves was a very low occupation in the South. It was all right to lose slaves in a poker game or over a horse race but buying and selling them for profit was lower class. In all, the South raised twenty-four men to the rank of lieutenant general. Twenty of them were professional Army officers before the war; three others were men of wealth and social standing, officers before Forrest joined up; he was the twenty-fourth.

It was impossible for such generals as Braxton Bragg and Robert E. Lee to see how a man of Forrest's crude background and semi-literate estate could lead anything but wild woodsmen. But whenever he was given a high command, he fought it better than the Regulars. If the South had recognized his military genius early in the war … The history of the Confederacy hardly has any punctuation but question marks.

Back in Memphis a second company joined the battalion: the Forrest Rangers (horrible pun) under Charles May. This, of course, was not the Charles Augustus May who had garnered so many brevets in the War with Mexico. C.A. May, a Northerner, had resigned from the Union Army when war broke out, because of the many Southern friends he had made in the Corps of Officers. He became head of a New York city street railway system, and a very wealthy man.

A third company, that of Captain D.C. Kelley, a Methodist minister, was already formed as an independent command. The Reverend Captain Kelley brought it into the battalion of the rich Forrest when the captain found that he could not equip his men through regular channels. Forrest already had the equipment.

Eventually the battalion filled its strength with eight companies, six hundred and fifty men. Two of the companies were from Kentucky, four from Alabama, one from Texas, and only one from Tennessee, the original Forrest Rangers. Forrest was lieutenant colonel and commandant; Kelley major and second-in-command. They marched out under orders to report to a Tennessee regiment nicknamed the "Irish," though the colonel had the non-Gaelic name of Adolphus Heiman.

270

Forrest had enlisted in June and started raising his battalion shortly after that. Until the middle of November, the battalion did nothing much but ride around middle Tennessee; on November 14, Forrest asked permission of A.S. Johnston, over-all commander in the West, to move north of the river, where the land was more suitable for cavalry. The battalion had already captured a Union transport on the Ohio; like all good Southern cavalry, Forrest learned early to supply himself from the Northern quartermaster and commissary stores. Then the battalion did some long range riding, without contacting the enemy, and started to go into winter quarters at Hopkinsville in the southwest corner of Kentucky; south, but still north of the Cumberland.

Shortly after Christmas, 1861, they brushed with Union cavalry near Sacramento, Kentucky, one of the many Middle Western and Eastern towns whose names testify to the nostalgia of some veteran of the Mexican War. Forrest ran the Yankee riders off with a combined flanking movement and frontal charge that – though the thing was nothing more than a minor skirmish – awakened the curiosity and admiration of his superiors. The man had probably never even seen a book on tactics, but he seemed to know all about them by instinct.

Six weeks later, Forrest and his men were at and around Fort Donelson as Grant moved to take it, by river transport and over country that was more ice than soil. Though Donelson was on the south bank of the Cumberland, which it was supposed to command, the terrain was not very suitable for cavalry. What wasn't ice, now in February, was thick undergrowth or plain swamp.

Forrest's Rangers first served as sharpshooters to cover engineer troops improving the defense of the little fort, then, on February 14, as the fighting started, charged and captured a battery of six guns, then another – three guns taken this time. Charles May was killed and Forrest had the first two of a legendary number of horses shot out from under.

Then General Gideon Pillow ordered the Confederates to cease attacking, and left Forrest out on the field to gather wounded and abandoned guns and ammunition. Toward midnight Colonel Forrest, his scavaging done, was in Pillow's headquarters where he was told that the field he had just left was reoccupied by Union re-enforcements.

Forrest said bluntly that he didn't believe it and pointed out that he had been the last person present to look the field over. While the genteel generals winced at his crudity, they argued back and forth. Finally, two scouts – both later high officers in Morgan's command – were sent out on reconnaissance.

They reported no strong Union movement on the day's battleground, but the generals continued to argue. General Simon Bolivar Buckner

271

wanted to surrender; Gideon Pillow didn't; General John B. Floyd thought surrender was inevitable but did not intend to let his own person fall into Union hands.

Forrest, apparently there to escort out any generals who felt as Floyd did, said he didn't think surrender was at all necessary, but if retreat – not surrender – was to be made, he offered to shield the retreating column with his cavalry. Nobody paid any attention to him. But when it was agreed that Buckner would head a surrender – he had done favors for Grant in the Union man's time of trouble – Forrest pushed back into the conversation by telling Gideon Pillow that he and his troopers had not come there to surrender. Pillow told him, somewhat brusquely, to cut his own way out if he felt like doing so.

Forrest walked out of the brassbound conference at once, called in his company and field officers, and told them what he planned. They all agreed to follow him; so did several other outfits, numbering about two hundred men from all over, and a Captain Porter, who was anxious to rescue his artillery horses. Forrest took his brother, Lieutenant Jeffrey, and rode advance picket himself.

The column got out of there without having a shot fired at it; the only Union soldiery they saw were wounded men huddled over little campfires. Forrest later said that these fires were probably what caused the brass to think the field had been occupied by Union troops.

The surrender of Fort Donelson gave U.S. Grant the nickname of Unconditional Surrender Grant; his old friendship with Buckner had not counted for much. It also raised a furor in Confederate movement and military circles. Forrest was called on to write – dictate – at least three reports on it in the next few months; Buckner volunteered no less than twelve.

Forrest led his column to Nashville and found it in a panic controlled only by Morgan's Men and the 1st Missouri. The whole eighty miles from Donelson to Nashville had been through terrorized country.

Before entering one little town, Forrest had taken the precaution of having his men discharge their arms and reload with fresh powder, in case the enemy was there. The enemy wasn't, but a Confederate cavalry regiment was; at the sound of the guns they galloped away and abandoned their wagon trains. Forrest's men happily replaced their own supplies, which they had had to leave in Donelson.

Forrest rested his men on the edge of Nashville and went into town on the twentieth to find civilians charging food warehouses and looting wastefully and riotously. He used his cavalry to stop the trouble and sent for wagons to move the food in an orderly fashion. The next day he called out a fire engine to help, and for three days thereafter he loaded and shipped

South supplies the Army needed down there. Kelley had gone ahead with the larger part of the battalion.

On Sunday the work was done, and Forrest rode down to Murfreesboro at the head of his men. There he was informed that his battalion and the Texas Rangers were to be attached to Albert Sidney Johnston's army as "unattached cavalry," not in any brigade or division.

Forrest had been free with wires to Johnston from Nashville about the way such things as railroads, artillery, commissary, and quartermaster affairs were being handled. The generals apparently didn't want Forrest in their brigades or divisions; as for the Texans, they had not come the long way to Tennessee to be disciplined; when not fighting, they were usually out of control.

After three or four days at Murfreesboro, Forrest was told to march to Huntsville, Alabama, where many of his men lived, and to grant two-weeks' furloughs to his troops. Another Forrest brother, Jesse, showed up there with a fresh company of troopers. Then the outfit moved out to Iuka, Mississippi, and picked up a final company, this time from Tennessee.

Now the battalion was a regiment and elected new officers. Forrest became a full colonel, the Reverend Kelley lieutenant colonel, and a private named Blach was chosen as major. The new regiment marched toward Pittsburg Landing and Shiloh, where they would again meet Grant. The Forrest regiment skirmished with Union Cavalry on April 5, and then was assigned to guard fords as small picket parties.

The next day, Sunday, forty thousand Confederates landed on a completely surprised Union Army. Forrest's men were held back, still guarding fords. But when the noise of the battle started up, their colonel couldn't stand it. He hastily assembled his men and told them the noise meant that their friends were falling to Union bullets while they guarded a "damned creek." The regiment roared, Forrest roared, and they went toward the battle at a gallop.

They found General Benjamin Franklin Cheatham's brigade of infantry thrown back after several charges against a strong Union position called the Hornet's Nest; not only thrown back, but thoroughly sick of the whole thing and not of a mind to make another charge. So, Forrest and his troopers charged for them. And, short of their goal, bogged down in a swamp.

But they had gotten Cheatham's foot soldiers going again; the infantry went through the mired horses and completed the charge. The Hornet's Nest fell at five-thirty in the afternoon.

By then Forrest was out of the bog and over on the right flank, helping to capture the Union reserves. Then he skirmished and sent word to Polk that the Union line seemed weak. But Polk did not send enough force to break through, and what he did send was worn out; perhaps his other troops were, too.

Forrest never seemed to get tired, and "Ole Bedford," as his troopers were beginning to call him, kept his men so busy following him they didn't know whether they'd been used up or not.

When the fighting stopped at the end of that first day of Shiloh, he led his men out on a double scout: he was looking for Union re-enforcements, but he was also looking for his fifteen-year-old son, Willie, who served as his orderly or aide-de-camp, and who had disappeared during the battle. He didn't find Willie till a couple of days later, but he found Union General Thomas L. Crittenden bringing in fresh bluecoats from river boats, and having trouble landing because of the stragglers along the shore.

It was about midnight when Forrest woke up Brigadier General James R. Chalmers with the suggestion that they find Generals P.G.T. Beauregard, Braxton Bragg, and William J. Hardee, and hit Crittenden before he could make a beachhead. Chalmers said he didn't know where those officers had set up their headquarters – and, presumably, their sleeping quarters as well – and Forrest cursed him and went charging off. He eventually got to headquarters, where he was told to keep up a strong picket line through the rest of the night. He did, occasionally sending word to Generals John C. Breckinridge and William Hardee; he never found Beauregard.

Having worked the night shift, Forrest's Rangers started the day shift at half-past five in the morning, fighting a slow retreat against a fresh Union Army under Buell for an hour and a half, holding the bluecoats down until the Southern infantry was ready for them. When this was accomplished, the troopers rode through the infantry lines and went to work as police to keep the foot soldiers from straggling.

Then, from eleven to one, they guarded the right flank of the main army, closing with the enemy no less than three times; after which they moved to the center, dismounted, and fought as infantry until the Union infantry could withdraw three-quarters of a mile and bivouac for the night.

Presumably they served on picket duty that night; the conventional generals under whom Forrest was serving always left this duty to Cavalry. In the morning, with Forrest in over-all command, and Morgan, the Texan Rangers and a company of Mississippi horse added to his command, they fought rearguard while Breckinridge continued his orderly retreat.

Brigadier General William Tecumseh Sherman was fighting vanguard for the Union. Seeing there was only a small cavalry command in his way – Forrest led less than four hundred men in all – Sherman threw an infantry regiment at the charge and held a regiment of cavalry in classic reserve.

Forrest's men – some or all – were armed with shotguns. They made their stand just above a small stream, and blasted buckshot at the Blue infantry as the foot soldiers were wading. The whole Blue regiment broke and ran, abandoning their shoulder guns, and the Forrest riders chased them with sabers, pistols and – Texans being present – probably Bowie knives.

The Blue Infantry charged into the Blue Cavalry. The Union troopers fired their single-shot carbines too soon, and then fled back to the strength of Sherman's main line. Here they were safe, against a solid brigade, and the Southern troopers gave up the chase. Not so their commander; Forrest charged, single handed, to within fifty yards of the Union line.

Then he grabbed up a Union soldier, held him behind him on his cantle for a bullet shield, and galloped for home. Again, he had a horse shot out from under him, and took a bullet through his own hip bone.

The Confederate Army now retreated in full mass; Forrest went back to Corinth shifting from horseback to a buggy and back again, trying to ease his wound, which, at Corinth Depot, was declared to be mortal. He was given sixty-days' leave in which to die.

Three weeks later he was back, storming at the commissary because his regiment hadn't been fed well enough in his absence. He still carried the Minie ball that had been called fatal, but a week after he was back in the saddle it left its lodging near his spine, and a field surgeon removed it, without anesthetic. Forrest took two more weeks of leave as a result of that. He never left the field again till after the war was over.

His leave, of course, was not spent just recuperating. He ran a recruiting raid and raised a few more rangers for his regiment. But less than two weeks later he lost the regiment; he was kicked upstairs, given command of several other cavalry regiments, and told to organize them into a brigade, though his commission as a brigadier was not made out for more than a month later. The Reverend Colonel Kelley took over the old Rangers.

This was to happen to Forrest several times in the course of the war; he would get an outfit into shape, fight it, and then have it taken away from him. In this respect he was completely different from Light-Horse Harry Lee, Marion, Morgan, or Shelby, all of whom ended the war with at least the nucleus of their original troops, constantly renewed after casualties. Ole Bedford, apparently, could make slashing, raiding troopers out of any men given him.

Through the summer of '62, Forrest trained and supplied his men; his method of doing these necessary things was to put them in the field against the enemy and tell them to take what they needed from the Union. As they moved through the field, more troops were sent to the brigade for training and equipment, and when he struck the Federal Depot at Murfreesboro – on July 13, he had as many men as Crittenden's garrison there – fourteen hundred.

Crittenden had not been in charge of the rich depot very long and was planning to tighten its defenses when the work week started, the next morning. But Forrest came in at four-thirty Sunday morning. Before noon the town was taken, the depot surrounded, and General Crittenden captured. Some of Forrest's officers thought enough had been done; the railroads into the depot were uncut, and there were heavy troops out along the lines. Forrest answered that he didn't like to see a job left half done, and demanded unconditional surrender of Colonel Duffield, Crittenden's deputy, because of Forrest's "overpowering force" which had been almost exactly even a few hours before. Duffield was wounded; the next in command, Colonel Parkhurst, surrendered; half the Union garrison were casualties.

There was still a force west of town. Its commander came in to ask Duffield – now a prisoner, of course – whether he should surrender. As he rode through the town, Forrest played a trick on him that he was to use again in his career: he put his men into a circular march that threw the same troops past the Union officer several times, giving the illusion of a great body of graycoats.

Forrest pulled out at six in the evening, now completely equipped and supplied. He had three fieldpieces too, the first for the Forrest Brigade, and twelve hundred prisoners. Fifty Union wagons, loaded and drawn by fine teams, went with the column.

The next day, while some of his men worked away from the column destroying bridges, Forrest found he didn't have enough troops left to guard all that column, so he paroled most of the enlisted prisoners.

The capture of twelve hundred men and about a quarter of a million dollars was not going to change the course of the war, certainly; but it caused the Union to move almost all the troops in the area around in a grand checkers game whose objective was the protection of Nashville and Chattanooga. Forrest spurred on these frantic movements by raiding almost into the outskirts of Nashville and then riding into Lebanon, a week after he had ridden into Murfreesboro, to find that the garrison had heard he was coming and pulled out. But it wasn't all wasted; the liberated Lebanese not only furnished the Forrest troopers with a magnificent Sunday dinner, but supplied them with enough delicatessen to let them eat Sunday style for the next three days. The first of those days found him five miles out of Nashville again, cutting the telegraph wires, destroying bridges, and using his new artillery against the defending stockaders.

Brigadier General William Nelson spent a good deal of energy moving his division to and fro as the Buell's headquarters got word of Forrest's location. Nelson was annoyed. He reported to Buell that he would shortly have twelve hundred cavalrymen in his division, and that he would lead the troopers into the field personally, and soon end the career of "Mr. Forrest." For the next five days he continued to wire Buell, asking where his twelve hundred riders were; it was too hot, he said, for infantry to chase Forrest's men, who were mounted on "race horses."

Forrest continued to harass the Union all over middle Tennessee; finally, on August 2, two weeks after he had made his boast, Nelson started after the raider with a combined infantry-cavalry force of about four thousand. Other heavy commands stood by ready to help when Forrest was pinned down. But before Nelson could get very far, Buell called him back, because of a false rumor that Braxton Bragg's whole army was coming north.

Bragg, however, did come up to Chattanooga, where Forrest went for orders. The orders were to pin Nelson down; Morgan was out with his partisan rangers harassing Buell's main column effectively enough. Forrest was also promised some more cavalry for his brigade and was told his promotion to brigadier general was now official.

Forrest rode around skirmishing with Union troops, keeping Buell pretty well confused until the forces trying to encircle him got so heavy that Bragg ordered him out of the country, and into the Sequatchie Valley east of the Cumberlands. If he received the order, he didn't obey it until late August when he was about where Bragg had wanted him to be to wait for the arrival of the main Confederate force.

Here he found himself surrounded by four different Federal columns, all marching directly for him. He tried to get out somewhat southwest of McMinville and was thrown back by a heavy garrison. But the fight caused the Union forces to swing around, and while they were doing it, Forrest and his troopers hit again, at Little Pond.

More than once reports went into Buell's headquarters that Forrest had been routed and his men dispersed which was enough harassment. Forrest went on his way and rendezvoused with Bragg at Sparta. Four companies of his old Ranger Regiment joined his command here, and the brigade moved back to slow Buell down by foray rather than by confusion.

Just south of the Kentucky line, Forrest reported that he had brought the Union Army to a complete halt and left a Northern artillery outfit shelling a patch of completely empty woods.

Forrest was always to do the enemy as much damage by rumor as he was by gunfire. Part of the panic that Indiana and Ohio went into during Morgan's raid was caused by reports that Forrest was coming over the river in Morgan's tracks, though Forrest was actually in Alabama at the time.

Bragg never clashed with Buell in that Kentucky campaign. But Bragg had learned more and more about his ungentlemanly general officer. At the end of September, he sent for Forrest, relieved him of his command, and told him to go back to middle Tennessee and raise four new regiments of infantry and two of cavalry. He was also to take charge of any troops he found in that area, and for escort he could take what was left of his original

Ranger Regiment, four companies. Once his force was raised, he was to pursue partisan Ranger activities, cutting communication and supply lines, capturing supplies, harassing the enemy in all ways.

Bragg would not, perhaps could not, see Forrest for what the Ranger general really was, a master strategist and tactician. Another big "if" forms in Confederate history here. Forrest proved, as the war went on and the opportunity showed up, that he could handle any size body of troops he was given, and that those troops could be parade-ground, manual-of-arms troops or just plain recruits from the cities and farms – all he needed was men and guns, and he preferred that some of the men be on horseback.

Unlike Forrest, Morgan never commanded infantry willingly; his first concern was always to get dismounted men into the saddle, after which horse-raiding became general raiding. Mosby was miserable for the short time he was with Stuart in the regular hierarchy; he was a plain irregular, bringing his men together when there was work to do, sending them home between raids, and strictly limited to an area in which he was at home.

Grant would have used Forrest as he used Phil Sheridan, to command infantry or cavalry, to take charge of a battle or a raid; Lincoln would have done the same thing. But the top brass in the South were all gentlemen, and Forrest was not. He couldn't even spell.

So, Bragg wrote Jefferson Davis that Forrest (and Morgan) were to be kept on "partisan service, for which alone they are ... suited," and Forrest kept on raiding, with a larger and larger command until January 1865, when he was made Commander of the District of Mississippi and East Louisiana. By then, of course, it didn't matter who commanded; the South was done for.

The details of Forrest's raids would be repetitious; he led more men than Morgan, but he operated in the same way; and he never did anything as dramatic as Morgan did when he rode across Indiana and Ohio. However, Forrest – or his men – committed, on April 12, 1864, one of the worst atrocities of the war, murdering Negro soldiers who had surrendered at Fort Pillow.

Forrest fought all over the western South, from Kentucky to Mississippi. He was frequently mentioned in Union reports as being a threat to Northern objectives all out of proportion to the size of his command. He held the North back a long, long time.

If he had been in Washington's army in 1776 he probably would have driven the British out of the South sooner than they were driven; but the war of 1861 was fought with mass, logistics, and industrial production, and nothing that any raiding general could do would ever alter the outcome.

Mosby, Morgan, and Forrest didn't change the course of history; but they embellish history's pages as a three-colored pie-chart brightens the tables of a financial report.

Forrest's own history ends on a grim note. After the war he was credited with founding the Ku Klux Klan. He didn't; apparently it was formed by a few young ex-officers of the Confederate Army as a social group, but there is no doubt that Forrest welded it into the force for terrorism or law-and-order – depending on the point of view – that it became; and there is no doubt he was its first Grand Wizard. In 1871 he was brought before a Congressional Committee and investigated: the record fills thirty volumes. It appears that he had dissolved the Klan no later than 1869. Of course, his Klan had no connection with the later ones of the 1920s and the present time.

Forrest died in Memphis in 1877 at the age of fifty-six, after several attempts to restore his prewar fortune – a million and a half dollars, according to his own testimony – by cotton planting, heading an insurance company, trying to build a railroad. He was not always broke; he contributed five thousand dollars to the founding of Vanderbilt University – and he had many friends, some of them ex-Union officers. Memphis honored him with a statue after his death, and he and his wife are buried under it.

Chapter 23

Meanwhile, Back in The West …

The Civil War had a side-effect on the West. Deserters and draft evaders swarmed out on the prairies to avoid arrest and, perhaps, to make their fortunes. The gold strikes in California in 1849 and in Colorado in 1859 inclined people to think that the West was one big mother lode.

Naturally, these drifters were not the highest type of citizen. The Union did not draft men who owned a certain amount of money; the South exempted holders of more than a few slaves; and anyway, there is an old expression: dukes don't emigrate; patriots were in the service, Blue or Gray. It is probable that most of the emigrants were wanted for breaking a few other laws than the conscription ones.

If there were any conscientious objectors, pacifists with higher motives than evasion of the law, they were few and have gone almost unmentioned in the Plains-Rocky Mountain annals. The North exempted only Quakers from fighting, and those only late in the war.

The incursion of white men into Indian territory produced the inevitable result; the buffalo-hunting Indians took alarm and made reprisals; the Apache-Navajo Athapaskans southwest of the buffalo country slaughtered the intruders for less obvious reasons.

Another factor contributed to the unrest of the Indians in the first half of the 1860s; the Regulars who had ridden amongst them showing the flag had other and heavier commitments in the East. A small detachment of the 2nd Cavalry, the old 2nd Dragoons, stayed in New Mexico during the war, but lieutenants were flying their starred generals' flags back East, and assignment to the frontier meant the death of a West Pointer's career. The Regular cats were away, the Indian mice played.

The Navajos were taken off the warpath for good in 1863 by no Jess a person than Kit Carson, temporarily commissioned a colonel of New Mexico Militia by the Territorial government. Leading a group of citizens serving as temporary militia, he herded what Navajos he could find into Cañon

280

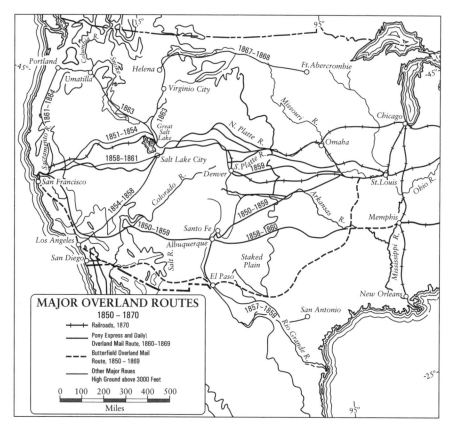

Map 3 Major Overland Routes, 1850-1870

de Chelly and the adjacent Cañon de Muerte, held them in the quicksands between the towering smooth red granite walls till they were thoroughly cowed, and then marched them out of Navajo country all together to Fort Sumner over on the Staked Plains part of the Territory.

Carson thought he had rounded up all the Navajos, or nearly all. He hadn't, but he had captured more than half the tribe, certainly, about seven thousand men, women, and children. Later, more than another thousand Navajos, and about four hundred Apaches were herded to the Bosque Redondo under the guns of Fort Sumner. They were held there until 1868. Profound changes were made in their habits – for instance, the present "traditional" dress of Navajo women today is modeled on the officers' wives' clothing of the 1860s – but all this is no part of the history of the cavalry. This was the second time that Kentucky-born Christopher Carson had been commissioned a horse officer, the first being when he rode messenger for Frémont and then guide for Kearny, but Carson would

281

have been the last person in the world to call himself a cavalryman. At any rate, the Navajos as cavalry opponents were really knocked out of the wars while the cavalry was fighting the South.

The Sioux, as a force of hostiles, came into the field during the same period. In 1862 they were very largely in Minnesota, where the late arrival of annual gifts from a government busier with larger affairs caused an uprising; the Sioux were pushed southwest by a state general named Henry Hastings Sibley, who is not to be confused – though confusion is hard to avoid – with General Henry Hopkins Sibley, West Point '38, who was a Confederate brigadier, and who led the Texas troops into attacking New Mexico just about the time that Minnesota's Brigadier General H.H. Sibley was attacking the Sioux.

The Sioux ended up in the country between Omaha and the Rocky Mountains, roughly comprising Nebraska, eastern Colorado, northern Kansas, and part of Wyoming. They gave no signs of settling down just because they had left Minnesota, and in 1863 Iowa raised a regiment to go quiet them down: the 7th Iowa Cavalry. Their story, also, is really no part of the history of the United States Cavalry; they were a state outfit, though in a time when state outfits were the larger part of the United States Army and when most Regular officers were serving with state troops.

The 7th Iowa Cavalry would be forgotten if it were not for Eugene F. Ware, who served two hitches as an enlisted man in other Iowa troops before joining the 7th in February '63. He was made second lieutenant of Company F; he became captain of the company just before he resigned in 1866 to become a newspaperman.

Because he was not a Regular, Ware brought a fresher viewpoint to Indian fighting on the Plains than did the West Pointers, who took as routine many things he thought were bizarre. And because his enlisted men were emergency rather than mercenary troopers, he was not as far removed from them as were the Regular officers from the Regular barracksmen.

Despite their civilian background, the 7th Iowa seems to have led approximately the same life that the Regulars were to lead on the Plains for the next thirty years. So, Ware's account is worth studying as a sort of introduction to the final chapter of the United States Cavalry as an effective, mounted force, a chapter that ran from the surrender of Lee to the massacre at Wounded Knee.

The 7th Iowa told itself, repeatedly, that it was fighting in the Civil War, that the Sioux would not be on the warpath if Confederate agents had not incited them. There is absolutely no evidence to back up this claim; the South and North had both tried to get the Five Civilized Nations of Oklahoma – not the Sioux – into the war, with some success; that is, there were Cherokee and other Oklahoma Volunteers on both sides of the War between the States, though no one tribe ever declared itself an ally of either the Union or the Confederacy. But the belief was necessary if young, ambitious men were to drop their mercantile careers, leave their farms or halt the study of their professions to go out on the Plains. It is heartbreaking to be a soldier in a little, unknown war when your country is fighting for its life in a big, world-renowned war.

So, the young men of the 7th Iowa saw the Indians as Confederate-inspired and paid, and would have liked to see Robert E. Lee in person leading the Sioux riders against them at Julesburg. As a matter of fact, Ware had actually encountered Indian Confederates when he was in the 4th Iowa Cavalry, fighting in southern Missouri. In the battle of Pea Ridge, in March 1862, a number of Oklahoma Indians were captured, and Ware was with the detachment detailed to take the red-skinned prisoners – eleven of them – and four hundred other captives to the railroad at Rolla, Missouri, where it was planned to put the Indians on the cars and send them touring around the border states to show what barbarous methods the South was resorting to, all Indians supposedly being scalpers, rapists, and torturers. But ten of the Indians were killed, one by one, "trying to escape," the old Mexican excuse for losing prisoners. The last one was admittedly murdered before the column got to Springfield, Missouri, on the way to the railhead.

So, Ware had some reason for believing that the Sioux and Cheyennes might be Confederate agents. He had seen Indians who were, and he had later heard that the death of the eleven Oklahomans had caused a great wave of Indian enlistments in the Southern Army. It seems dubious, though, that Southern soldiers would have served alongside men as dark as most Indians. After the surrender, a Confederate general raised a brigade of troopers to go to Mexico and fight for "Juárez and Freedom" rather than apply for Union amnesty; but when they crossed into Mexico, and saw how dark Juárez's soldiers were, they went on down to Mexico City and offered their services to the white, though oppressive, Maximilian, who declined them.

At any rate, Company F, 7th Iowa Cavalry, found itself in Omaha, in the middle of September '63, bound for the frontier, newly uniformed, but poorly armed. Each man had a Gallagher's carbine, "an exceedingly inefficient weapon," a muzzle-loading Colt's .44 revolver, and a heavy cavalry saber. Before they left the city, they boxed their sabers for storage; the cavalry sword was already outmoded, and these Westerners knew it.

Even this far north, Ware reported a large number of deserters from the Confederate Army, most of them still wearing parts of their uniform, all of them declaiming that they had just picked their bits of gray clothing up someplace.

The second day in town, the company drilled by the bugler. Ware said that this was the only way to prepare for Indian fighting; he laid great stress on it all during his time as an officer or sergeant. Whether the Iowa troops actually used bugles, or whether they had true cavalry trumpets is beside the point; the interesting fact is that the troopers worked in true unison, listening for commands over the noise of battle, instead of simply charging and then fighting ad lib as the hostiles presented themselves.

Ware was junior commissioned officer in the regiment. That night all the other officers turned over the command to him and went to town; he had no one to pass the buck to, and by taps was trying to discipline a drunken regiment with a corporal's guard of duty men. Finally, he found twenty-five men who were sober, and used them to tie the worst of the celebrants to wagon wheels. About three hours later some of the officers started straggling back to camp, and he had help.

On September 26 the outfit started West, some of the troopers rolling drunk in their saddles. Ware and the other officers went along the line of column sniffing canteens and emptying those that contained whiskey.

The second night out Ware ran into two Iowa time-expired soldiers who were batching on a homestead. They told him that almost all their neighbors were Southern deserters who were still strongly anti-North; each Union homesteader had two revolvers and a rifle to protect himself with.

A couple of days later the men discovered a distillery near their camp; a German was making what he called White Wheat Whiskey, and Ware had quite a time keeping his men from ruining their military careers before they were fairly started.

Here orders came to escort a U.S. Paymaster to what Ware wrote as Fort "Kearney"; in fact, the extra "e" was now so firmly planted in history that the *United States Service Magazine* was inserting it in General Phil's name.

On the way they stopped to pay annuities to the friendly Pawnee Indians. Their government agent, a man named Lushbaugh, stayed drunk all the time they were with him, but had an effect on Company F; many of the troopers began growing whiskers the shape of the agent's red sideburns; they called them Lushbaughs, which were different from Bumsides because they did not connect with the mustache.

All the way to the O.K. Store, which Ware, writing later, thought was the site of the town of Grand Island, the twenty-two-year-old lieutenant and his captain, Nicolaus O'Brien, had whiskey trouble; the men were constantly getting drunk, and threatening something more than disobedience and only slightly less than mutiny. However, the two officers – the first lieutenant was on detached duty, and of little use anyway – were the strongest men and the hardest fighters in the country, and, unlike the Regulars, perfectly willing to touch the body, chin, or eye of a trooper. Quoting Ware: "A company of volunteer soldiers will grow clannish and inclined to hang together for good or evil, and to see how far they can disobey the military law and ... scare or baffle their officers ... When on detached service, such as we were, it is sometimes about all an officer's life is worth to maintain his own standing."

All of which sheds further light on the problems of the militia, even when federalized. Since officer and trooper were frequently neighbors and expected to remain so for the rest of their lives, the harsh penalties of a formal court-martial were to be avoided; but knocking out a drunken trooper would probably cause no permanent resentment.

Ware, after going on for quite a while about the disciplinary problems of his volunteer soldiers, adds that there was one thing they wouldn't do. "They wouldn't get scared. And they wouldn't dodge any hardship or danger, and they would march all day and all night." They passed through the Pawnee country and into that of the Omahas and Ponkas. All these tribes, they observed, were made up of effeminate men and calm, sturdy women. They came to Fort Kearny, at the junction of the Omaha and Leavenworth trails and two minor roads from St. Joseph, Missouri, and from Weston, a post just above Fort Leavenworth.

On the west the fort had as a neighbor a settlement called Dobeytown, though the houses were daub-and-wattle rather than true adobe. Ware described it as "containing the toughest inhabitants of the county, male and female ... Large quantities of the meanest whiskey on earth were consumed here, but, strange as it may appear, there were also large quantities of champagne sold." Travel was heavy; old friends meeting there toasted the occasion in the bubbly wine. Captain O'Brien and Lieutenant Ware again had disciplinary trouble.

Here Ware met what must have been one of the best pistol shots the world has seen, a man named Talbot. He would put his horse at a dead gallop alongside a telegraph line and put eleven out of twelve bullets into the poles as he went along. Accurate shooting from a moving horse is more of a movie stunt than an actuality; this man Talbot was a phenomenon. Young Ware practiced imitating him, but never got that good.

They restocked at Fort Kearny, and the commissary told Ware that fatigue parties were allowed to buy whiskey to take out on detail with them; the commissary showed him barrels stored since 1849, and offered him one at twenty-six cents a gallon, with no allowance for evaporation. There was only a tiny garden at Kearny; the stable manure had been shoveled under the sandy soil, and a few vegetables did poorly there. Troopers were told off to tend them. Besides the whiskey, supplies, and building tools picked up at Kearny, O'Brien and Ware were each given a greyhound by the post commander.

Their orders were to build a fort a hundred miles west of Kearny, at Cottonwood Canyon. They moved out, and were overtaken by their regimental assistant surgeon, who was to be medical officer for the fatigue party.

The next day O'Brien tried to light a cigar on horseback in a high wind and started a prairie fire. In a few minutes it was a half mile wide; the Platte River stopped it, but not before it had killed several cattle. Captain O'Brien, not so devoted a drinker as his troopers, gave the owner of the cattle a deep drink out of his canteen full of '49, bought the meat with a government voucher, and everybody parted friends.

The column now had with it a Vote Commissioner from Iowa, sent out to take the men's ballots when it was time to vote; there was a strong Copperhead element in the state, and every Union vote was needed. Election Day was nearly a month off; this was early October, and the Platte was dry, though the riders could always get water eighteen inches down. The Commissioner went along and was useful in hunting and observing buffalo; they were getting into hostile Indian country, and the movements of the buffalo would tell them about those of the Sioux. Until Election Day, the Commissioner observed buffalo.

They got to Cottonwood Canyon, and found a little settlement there, a log store, a blacksmith shop, a liquor store that also sold canned goods, a stage station; this was the only spring "along the Platte for two hundred miles."

The place had prospered from Indian trade, but now was dying and in mortal fear that the former customers would come back in anger. McDonald, the trader, was glad to let the soldiers use part of his building for Post Headquarters.

Fine cedar trees – straight and sometimes two feet in diameter – grew up the canyon. O'Brien organized the men into felling, trimming, and crosscutting squads; trees a foot in diameter were selected and cut into twenty-foot logs. The supply wagon mules snaked them down to the fort site. Every night each man who had worked in the woods was given a jigger of the '49 Vintage, Ware reported, adding: "We were racing against the weather and I never saw men work with more activity."

These were frontier men, as opposed to Regulars, who were more often either foreigners or city pickups. When a job came up – like cornering a log cabin – there was always someone who had done it before. By the end of November, the whole outfit was under cover.

The enlisted barracks was a hundred and twenty feet long, twenty feet wide, and cut into six rooms. In each room one non-com and sixteen privates slept; the north room was reserved for a non-com mess and the privates cooked and ate in their barracks room. Bunks had been made out of whip-sawed lumber and padded with filled haybags.

Company Headquarters was twenty feet square and so were the hospital and the guardhouse; the warehouse was forty by twenty. The stable was built like a palisade, of twelve-foot-long cedar posts standing upright; it was two hundred feet long, and so built that it could be added on to later to form a rectangular stockade. Everything was chinked with mixed cedar chips and clay and plastered over.

By the time the fort was built, Election Day had come and gone. The votes were taken on the lunch hour, after both officers had made speeches urging the men to vote for Lincoln and total victory, rather than for McClellan and peace with the Confederacy. Only eight men voted for McClellan; Ware never did find out who they were, but he wrote: "I think five of the eight became deserters, and ... one was killed by whiskey and the other two had poor military records." Ware did not admire people who didn't share his political views.

With everything safely under cover, the officers arranged for beef and hay from a pair of brothers in the oxen-exchange business; that is, they kept well-trained, rested oxen on hand, and swapped them for foot-weary cattle from the travelers, charging a boot, of course; they had become very wealthy at the trade. They had also been merchants to the Sioux, and they warned O'Brien to expect trouble in the spring when the prairie greened up, which would be about June 1.

Work went on; a well was dug, and a beautiful cedar flagpole was erected. A sergeant and ten men escorted the wagons back to Kearny and returned with two fieldpieces, which were mounted on the parade ground. O'Brien had been in the artillery and drilled every one of his troopers into a gunner. When Indians appeared on an island out in the river around the middle of December, the howitzers were fired short of the island, and the Indians ran away. They were probably Sioux. Two days later two braves of that nation came to the post and were treated to molasses and hardtack. They ate enormously, and then ran away. The soldiers thought they were probably spies, though they said they were from the South, and not connected with the local hostiles.

Before the winter settled in, Company G of the 7th Iowa Cavalry joined F, who sheltered them until they could build quarters. A sutler had come in, too, and hired civilians to build him a post. There were about a hundred and fifty able-bodied men between Gilman's, fifteen miles east, and Jack Morrow's, ten miles west of the fort, which had been named Cantonment McKean; later it was changed to Fort McPherson. Present McPherson County, Nebraska, would be due north of the site; the Platte does not touch the county.

Major George O'Brien – the older brother of Captain Nicolaus O'Brien, commander of F – was sent out to command the two-company post; Ware was made adjutant and later commissary and quartermaster as well.

Some of the statistics he recorded are worth pondering on. The post bought good hay in the fall for fifteen dollars a ton; the ranchers charged winter-starved travelers – "pilgrims" – fifty dollars a ton.

Rations for a man, per day, as ordered by the government, consisted of bacon or salt pork or salt beef; hardtack or bread or flour or cornmeal; dried beans, peas and rice; green or roasted coffee or tea; salt, pepper, a small amount of molasses and sugar; vinegar; and potatoes (if practicable). The men also got candles and soap from the government.

These, though State troops, were federalized, and that was about the standard ration until the very late '80s, when canned tomatoes were issued against scurvy. But the beans and the potatoes were rarely available to field parties; bacon and coffee and hardtack were expected to nourish a trooper.

O'Brien's men got fresh beef and probably game; Regular troopers were to complain that these luxuries were only available to the officers. Shortly after the fort at Cottonwood Canyon was built the last buffalo disappeared from the vicinity, but there was other game: antelope, beaver (the tails were delicious), prairie chickens, and probably waterfowl when the Platte was running. Vegetables were simply not considered. The small garden at Kearny was not official, and no root crops were issued, though onions, carrots, and turnips would have kept well in cellars and would have made a vast difference in the state of the troopers' health and morale. Dried apples were available at the sutler's, and canned vegetables could be bought, but not by eight-dollar-a-month privates.

The next year Ware – now out near Julesburg – speaks of being issued "desiccated vegetables," consisting of "onions, cabbages, beets, turnips, carrots and peppers, steamed, pressed and dried." These the men ate as they were issued or made into soup; but they got scurvy anyway, until their surgeon discovered that the de-prickled flat stalks of the tuna cactus, opuntia, could be boiled up with sugar and made into something that not only tasted like applesauce, but cured and prevented scurvy. Other surgeons, other places, were to recommend plucking the wild onions from the prairie, with good results. But the government never issued onions or lime juice, though the latter had long been used by the British Navy, and British ships were required to issue the antiscorbutic to their merchant seamen from about the time of the Civil War on.

Ware does not say whether his Iowa troops were issued standard cavalry horse furniture, but since they were federalized, it is probable. By 1863 the method of saddling and bridling and equipping a troop horse was set, and never changed again in any important respect.

The saddle was the modified Hungarian one that George McClellan had brought back from Europe and named after himself. It was cut away down the middle, airy under the hornless pommel, light in weight. The tree was made of beechwood and covered with bull-hide by preference; the Civil War probably caused a shortage of that tough leather, and saddles were more often covered with less durable steer or cowhide. Some troopers mentioned rawhide saddles in their diaries; a good McClellan is covered with rawhide, shrunk on the tree; then smooth leather is stitched over the raw, which is inclined to split when dry.

Two bridles were issued, one called *the* bridle, which had a curb bit with chain, and the other the watering bridle, with a snaffle bit, which means a hinged, flexible bit with rings on each cheek to hold the reins.

Official War Department paintings show the troopers using both bridles, with the snaffle reins lying between the pommel and the trooper's lap. The most widely distributed photograph of a trooper shows only the watering bridle. Probably the method of bitting used depended on the individual horse and his rider's preference.

A standard Army blanket was issued for a saddle blanket and folded according to strict regulations. Ware says that he had his men spread a smooth burlap sack under the woolen blanket to keep from scalding the horse's back; other riders have found that wool absorbs the horse sweat better than burlap; it is possible that the issue blanket of 1863 was coarse and abrasive.

Saddle bags were clipped to built-in metal pieces behind the moderately high cantle. The blanket did not extend back all the way under them, and anything carried in the larger pockets, which rested on the horse's flank, would get sweated through if the trooper was not constant with his neat's foot oil. Smaller pockets rested on the large ones and were protected against weather by flaps stamped *U.S.* Experts in military furniture and uniform cite exceptions to the description above, which has been taken from an 1863 War Department's publication.

Skirts were originally riveted to the McClellan, some say; and the smooth leather covering over the rawhide was a later addition. These and other modifications were possible, and even probable; certainly, in a war where soldiers frequently went barefoot, cured leather was in such demand that supply officers must have frequently accepted rawhide as better than nothing, and until troopers were thoroughly hardened, the effect of horse sweat on the inner thigh would have been crippling. The skirts may have been added by order of McClellan, a lesser general, or some other officer.

Also, the carbine was certainly carried in a clip during a good part of the war; again, the shortage of leather would have made this a necessity. The canteen of that day was stopped with a cork; toward the end of the active horse cavalry a screwtop type replaced it; toward the very end black plastic took the place of metal and kept the water tasteless.

A carbine boot went under the left leg; saber slings were also available, but by Ware's time only officers wore sabers in the field, and these were more for signaling to the troopers than for offense. A flashing blade at the head of a column could raise or lower the pace – walk, trot, canter, gallop – without the use of the trumpet to warn Indians that the pony soldiers were near. But after 1866 the Army was so small that columns could easily be commanded with a raised fist, and gradually the officers, too, left their sabers in the fort.

Each man carried a couple of days' grain for his horse, and canned bacon, roasted coffee, and hardtack for himself; he might also carry a candle or two for dressing before dawn or even cooking when a fire would have attracted hostiles. A tin cup and plate served both for cooking and eating. A change of socks was usually all the wardrobe a trooper went out on patrol with; when changing posts, wagons brought his extra uniforms, underwear, and so on.

On detached duty – in other words, when not in a fort or cantonment – hats were optional; men wore their forage caps, black or tan campaign hats, or even some remnant of civilian life. In winter, starting after the war, fur caps, Russian style, were issued.

Blue pants, yellow-striped always for non-coms and officers, often for troopers drawing mounted pay – a couple of dollars a month more than infantrymen or cavalry recruits drew – were held up by broad suspenders. The revolver was carried on a belt that might also help hold up the trousers or be worn loose to slouch over one hip – trooper's option, except when on parade. Ware's men had muzzle-loading, paper-cartridge Colt's. Whether they carried an extra cylinder, already loaded, he doesn't say.

That first winter at what the men called Fort Cottonwood drew a blizzard in December. With bad weather, it became difficult to exercise the horses until the quadrangle of stable was completed sometime in the distant future, it was not possible to let the animals out to roll and frolic and kick up their heels in the snow; hostiles might stampede them. When possible in winter some mounted drill was practiced. Later outfits found this virtually impossible; dismounted drill for parade purposes, fatigue, including new building, and horse-tending filled the day. But Ware's Iowa troops probably did not care about fancy guard mounts and retreats and let the dismounted drill go. Also, they contracted their firewood, paying a civilian who passed through with a large crew of men to go into the canyon and buck up the lopped off cedar branches left from the post construction. Regulars would have been sent to do this and also to cut the hay that Ware, as quartermaster, bought for the post.

In bad weather they had "bugle" practice in the barracks. The officers found that the men quickly forgot the trumpet calls, and it was planned to use no voice commands when they went out against the Sioux in the spring. The command was too large to hear a voice order and planned to spread out too thinly to see hand signals, which were effective – as were passed-along voice calls – only against organized troops, not against Indians on horseback, according to the Iowans. Later George Crook of the Regular Army always ordered his trumpets silent when in hostile country.

While they were snowed in, the Cheyenne agent rode into the post and said there were twenty thousand of his people south of the fort, as many to the north, and they were all out of hand; he wanted the chief and the principal councilmen arrested. The agent then proceeded to go on a three-day drunk.

While he was out of use, one of the civilian ranchers came in, and Major O'Brien consulted with him. It was planned to send Lieutenant Ware and a detachment out as soon as a break in the weather coincided with a stretch of sobriety in the agent. The rancher said that the agent was a pure politico, completely worthless, and that if Ware did go out, he was not to go within five miles of the Cheyenne camp, but to stop and ask the chief to come out for a parley.

The agent sobered up and was told of this plan; he blustered that he was not going near his charges again, that it was up to the Army to execute his orders. Then he took the stage to Kearny, from where orders were wired back not to move against the Cheyenne until the general commanding had thought the matter over. Presumably the Indian agent hadn't impressed Fort Kearny any more than he had Cantonment McKean. That ended the matter, though everyone expected the Cheyenne as well as the Sioux to take the warpath in the spring.

Eugene Ware mentions no further telegrams about the Cheyenne agent, but explains why the wire was not cut by the Indians. A Cheyenne who had been East and considered himself an expert on white matters had once induced a group of Indians to cut and drag a length of wire away; previously they had been a little shy of it from superstition, but the shiny copper was a great temptation. While the braves were trailing their booty across the prairie lightning hit it and knocked all of them off their horses; some of them were badly hurt. Superstition took over again, and the telegraph line became sacred.

In March, Lieutenant Eugene F. Ware took over Company F, Major George O'Brien went back to Fort Kearny, and Captain Nicolaus O'Brien became post commander. Ware was relieved of his adjutant, commissary, and quartermaster duties – each of which should have paid him an extra ten dollars a month, though he doesn't mention extra pay – and started drilling his men and horses, twenty-five at a time. The rest of the company went back to construction fatigue.

The only drills he taught were skirmish, both mounted and dismounted. In mounted skirmish the men rode twenty to fifty yards apart, and "raced over the prairie, wheeling, deploying and rallying on the right, left and center, all by the bugle."

Dismounted drill was the drill by fours, counting off, the fourth man becoming horseholder and the other three skirmishing to the front, ten paces (thirty feet) apart. The three skirmishers would drop to the ground and load their carbines; then number one would rise, fire and dash forward, falling to reload while number two and then number three imitated him. In this way two men with loaded carbines were always covering the third man. This was good practice. Ware said they fired immense amounts of ammunition at it, and the horses got used to the sound of gunfire, the men to the use of guns. But later Regular outfits had no chance at this sort of work; ammunition was not issued for target practice or drill after the Civil War until very, very late in the Indian Wars.

All of Ware's men could write their own names, and most of them could read and write easily; the weatherbound troopers had a great quantity of newspapers and read them constantly. This was another contrast from the Regulars who were to follow them; few of the mercenaries of the next thirty years were literate.

The '49 whiskey didn't last long; Ware went back to Kearny, discussed the matter with the quartermaster, and returned with seven more barrels; he doesn't state the vintage. A man on fatigue was given a gill of whiskey – four ounces – in the morning; if he didn't shirk through the day, he got another gill at quitting time. A half pint of whiskey is enough to make some men unruly, but the men had to drink each gill as issued, under the eyes of a strong dispenser, or pass it up.

Liquor could be bought across from the post, at Boyer's store. When Artemus Ward, the humorist, passed through on a stagecoach, O'Brien and Ware invited him to a drink; but Boyer had nothing left but a case of Hostetter's bitters, a popular and – according to Ware – tasty drink of the day. Ward drank with the officers, and then bought out all of Boyer's stock, except one bottle, to comfort him on his travels.

The grass came up in April, and travel increased; so did the possibility of Indian war. It was planned to hold council with the Sioux around the middle of the month; if they didn't go on the warpath, it was thought that the Cheyennes and Arapahoes would remain peaceful, too. The 1st Colorado Cavalry sent an officer to Fort Cottonwood from Denver to see what the Sioux situation was; he felt that it didn't look good.

General Robert B. Mitchell came to the post for the council; the Indians started drifting in and were kept camping two miles from the fort for safety. However, any one Indian delegation of not more than a hundred men could come in to talk; the troopers went armed at all times, but the general and his officers threw off their weapons when actually parleying, as did the councilors for the Indians. Thus, each party to the parley was unarmed for etiquette, but backed up by heavily armed fighting men.

The Indians sat on the ground, the general sat on a folding chair, the officers on cracker boxes. They – the officers – wore red silk sashes for some reason; this was the color of the artillery, and of generals, rather than that of the cavalry. Possibly there was no yellow silk in Omaha when they were outfitting. All four tribes of the Sioux nation were represented. Again, Ware comments on how feminine-looking they were, with one exception; but he was facing the pick of as rough-fighting Indians as the Plains ever saw.

The Indians smoked, the officers smoked, then the Indians smoked again; the standard procedure for the opening of a council, a scene that was to be repeated frequently in the next thirty years. Finally Spotted Tail, senior warrior present, asked what the white men wanted to talk about.

General Mitchell replied at length, giving the usual preamble about how good the white man had been to the Sioux, how white men's guns had made game killing easier, how the white man wanted, only and always, peace. Then he delivered the snapper: the Sioux were to get out and stay out of the Platte Valley.

Each of the Indians replied in turn, speaking of the poverty of the Indians since the white man had come to drive the game off. After each Indian speech General Mitchell spoke of the benevolence of the white man, who gave the Sioux annual rations of bacon and flour, and who wanted the Sioux to settle down, live in houses, and become farmers.

The interpreters interpreted, the powwow went on, the day wore away. Finally, the Sioux asked again why the white men had sent for them; the general dropped his oratory – he had gotten around to invoking the Great Manitou who had not meant for the Sioux to own all the world – and again said flatly the white man wanted the Sioux to stay out of the Platte Valley.

Spotted Tail, though he had brought more oratorical men with him, answered that one himself. He said that his people didn't want to hunt in the Platte Valley, because the white men had driven all the game out, but they did want to come down there and trade their buffalo skins and beaver pelts; they couldn't live on the government issue rations, and there was no use promising them greater issues, because the government seldom backed up promises made by Army officers. They might give up the Platte if they had a treaty saying that this was to be the only road through Sioux country; otherwise they would soon be asked to stay out of another valley, and then a second and then a third till they had no place to hunt at all. Even as they spoke surveyors were going down the Niobrara Valley.

General Mitchell said that if the Sioux didn't stay out of the Platte, he would station a soldier to stand over every blade of grass in that broad pass. Spotted Tail said that the Sioux didn't scare easily; there were more Sioux than there were white men, and everyone knew it. The Sioux could put twenty-six thousand warriors into the field at once.

It is curious that Spotted Tail used that figure. Twenty-six thousand men – including officers – was to be almost the authorized strength of the United States Army – East, West, North, and South – from 1869 till 1898, five years after the Sioux were broken at Wounded Knee. This parley took place in the spring of 1864; the Civil War was grinding to a halt back East, and in another year the great armies would be going home.

The parley ended peacefully, in a feast of molasses and hardtack and coffee and boiled beef. Nothing had been decided. There was to be another parley in fifty days but it, too, would decide nothing.

The thirty years of the Sioux wars had started, and the death warrant of General George Armstrong Custer – not to mention the death warrants of hundreds of less flamboyant soldiers – had been signed.

That was April 16, 1864. Custer, under Phil Sheridan, was heading for the Battle of the Wilderness. Rumors came in that the southern Cheyenne and the Oglala Sioux were allying themselves with the Confederacy. Ware felt that the reason the northern Cheyenne and the rest of the Sioux were not Confederates was because the 7th Iowa Cavalry would promptly shoot any Southern emissaries who came into the Platte area.

A woman named "Salt Lake Kate" came in and reported to O'Brien that she had been raped by no less than eighteen Cheyenne. Ware took ten men out to avenge this insult to American womanhood; the drovers and ranchers along the trail told him to forget it, that Kate was the toughest woman in the world. He went back to the post, though he half-suspected the woman's story was true.

One of the ranchers started fortifying his home; trouble seemed certain. On May 21 two hunters came in and said the fighting had started, that the Cheyenne and Brûlé Sioux had surrounded a party of Colorado troops about forty miles south of Fort Kearny. The information was wired to Kearny, but no answer ever came. O'Brien sent all the women on the ranches and the road into Kearny for safekeeping. It was just as well; two days later Indians raided a wagon right across the Platte from the cantonment, killed two men and stole the horses. The Iowa troopers saddled up and poured across the river, but they could not catch up with the hostiles.

Sniping, harassing Indian action continued; it was probably complicated by the fact that a "squaw" camp for women, children and professedly friendly braves was maintained two miles from the fort. Seen at a distance, or known only by his work, a hostile could impersonate a friendly Indian with ease.

There were rumors that the Cheyennes and the Comanches were now officially aligned with the Confederacy. There were all kinds of other rumors; General Mitchell came to the conclusion that the summer would not see a formal Sioux or Cheyenne uprising, but that the younger men of the tribe would continue to operate against the whites in small, unofficial groups. This was just about what happened. Spotted Tail himself seemed determined to keep the tribe, as a tribe, off the warpath, but he couldn't control all of his people all of the time.

Ware was ordered to Fort Kearny to sit as junior member of a nine-man court-martial. Proceedings were dull; without shorthand the keeping of the voluminous record held everyone up. Only one case is worth mentioning: the trial of an officer for buying dried apples, sugar and flour at Subsistence (modern Post Exchange) rates and then having his wife and son bake them up into pies, which they sold for fifteen cents apiece. They had made "several hundred" dollars by the time of the trial; the officer was dismissed from the service.

The court was still sitting when news came of heavy Indian depredations to the west; Lieutenant Ware was excused and told to get out to Fort McKean as quickly as possible. Captain O'Brien and General Mitchell would follow by stage.

Ware rode thirty-five miles the first afternoon, much tortured by mosquitoes. At a ranch he paid five dollars for a yellow silk handkerchief to use for a face mask. The next day he covered sixty-five miles by swapping horses at a ranch and pulled into McKean to find a great many pilgrims – travelers – stopped there because of the rumors.

There were a number of women in the parties, so a dance was put on, and young Ware, having ridden sixty-five miles that day, danced till dawn. Then he lined up Company F, inspected and drilled it, and had the company wagons packed with thirty days' supplies.

General Mitchell came up with Captain O'Brien, and Company D of Ware's regiment as a guard. The time had come for the next Sioux council, and the squaw camp was full. Also present were a number of Pawnee Indians, allied with the whites, and at war with the Sioux.

Mitchell now had a yellow silk sash instead of the red one he had worn at the first council; he was a cavalry brigadier. He opened the council with a good deal of ceremony, among which was the flashing of sabers by Company D. This is one of several times that Ware mentions sabers, though he opened his account by saying that they were left behind.

Everything had to be interpreted, not only from English to Sioux, but from Sioux to Pawnee, Pawnee to English, and so on. The Indian speakers accompanied themselves with sign language insulting to the other tribe.

Again, nothing was decided; General Mitchell had said he didn't think anything would be. He called a halt to the council and ordered, rather than advised, the Sioux to cross the river and keep going for at least three days, out of the valley. They went off yelling and whooping, the Pawnees shouting insults after them. A few minutes later the column moved out on its patrol expedition: the general, his staff, Company F, Company D, interpreters and guides, and a "battalion" of eighty Pawnees under command of a Major North. The title before North's name seems to have been the courtesy title usually accorded Indian agents; when the Pawnee Battalion was dissolved, Ware began referring to North as a lieutenant.

This was pretty much a show-the-flag march, such as the Dragoons had used before the war to warn the Indians to keep the peace. Perhaps to build up its impressiveness, the Pawnees had been issued blue uniforms. But almost at once they started shucking out of them, first the shirt, then the hat – out of several of these they poked earholes and put them on their horses' heads – and then the breeches which, if they were not just thrown on the ground, were split down the middle and reconnected with a rawhide thong. The general effect, according to Ware, was unmilitary.

They rode by Julesburg, Colorado, named after a French-Canadian rancher named Jules Beni, now moved on; Ware was to be stationed there later. Here they picked up a number of pilgrim wagons which wanted to follow the column for protection; this was to be a constant thing on cavalry patrols until the railroads took over the east-west travel.

There were three miles of wagons; and the Platte was "quicksandy" here. The word was used loosely, and still is as a matter of fact, for any sort of shaky river or stream bottom. The troopers firmed it up by driving the wagons across it fast; each passage tamped the sand or mud or whatever it was down, and the pilgrims crossed all night by lantern light. One wagon went off the trail and was lost; its mules were saved, but a Major Wood of the 7th strained himself so badly trying to wrest the wagonbody loose that he had to be put in an ambulance and sent back for treatment.

Ware, in talking about the Pawnee Indians who were with the column, contributes a word of Western slang, 1863 style, worth knowing: Abbrigoin for aborigine or Indian. It seems to have been one of General Mitchell's favorite epithets; the yellowlegs did not care for the Pawnees, who behaved, according to Ware, like monkeys, and had "unprintable manners and unspeakable habits." They also, he was interested to note, could swim in the Platte at the end of the day, and come out dirtier than they went in.

The troopers went through the Lodgepole Valley, past Mud Springs, to Court House Rocks. No hostiles were in sight, but there were burned wagons along the road, and forty-seven dead oxen; two or three of them had been killed by arrows, the rest by thirst; water was thirty-two miles apart on one stretch.

As they approached the Platte River bluffs again they saw numerous smoke signals; the Pawnees went mad, riding in all directions and pretending to look for Sioux signs on the brushless prairie. The general decided to send the "blankety-blank" abbri-goins back; they were completely out of control. So Major North led them away, after the general had flattered them on their martial military behavior; they probably sensed the sarcasm in his voice.

At Fort Laramie, Lieutenant Ware was appointed Post Adjutant. The fort was manned by three companies of Ohio Cavalry. The two nearest ranchers were both French, Bordeaux and Beauvais. Bordeaux found Indian signs around his place, and the post commandant sent Ware down with ten men to show the flag. He spent the night talking to M. Bordeaux – Ware could read French, which delighted the rancher – and they finished off by Bordeaux going down in the cellar and coming up with two dusty bottles of champagne. Ware demurred; a quart of champagne was too much for him. So, Bordeaux knocked the head off a single bottle, and they split it, drinking out of tin cups to the honor of La Belle France.

There was a vegetable garden at Fort Laramie, heavily manured for years, and watered by a ditch; but it grew "some vegetation" only. Then grasshoppers came and wiped it out; this was one of the years when the hoppers got so thick that everything except the native grass was eaten. Later this was to be taken by some of the Indian tribes as a sign that whatever God ruled the skies favored them over the white nesters, since the buffalo feed was untouched, but the white man's plowed crops destroyed. In 1863 there were no sodbusters as yet.

Jim Bridger, the famous scout, was at Fort Laramie, as was the less-famous Charles Elston, reputed to have two Sioux and one Cheyenne wives, but reported by Ware as "a sort of high-toned fellow" nonetheless.

Sometime in August a detail returned from making a twenty-five-mile scout around the post; they reported no Indian sign. Their commander told them to strip the tired horses and let them roll on the parade ground; the sweaty mounts at once started frolicking and easing their backs, the best possible treatment for a horse after a day's work. No man can see his horse having such a good time without grinning; there must have been smiles on all those prairie-tanned faces when suddenly a warhoop was heard, and a party of less than thirty Indians rode through the post, waving blankets and yelling. They stampeded all the loose horses and then were gone out the other end of the parade ground.

The post commander had Boots and Saddles blown, and a mixed detachment of Ohio and Iowa troops took off after the horse thieves. But –

note well – the Indians had "plenty of relays of horses ... we did not seem to overtake them."

The mystery of why no one in the Army ever thought of using the remuda system of traveling deepens. Eugene Ware was not a West Pointer, nor were any of the other officers present. They had more open minds than the Regulars, but the thought did not occur to them that a man on a single horse could never run down a man who changed mounts every few miles.

The detail recovered a dozen horses that the Indians had abandoned as worthless, used up; they were't worth taking back to the fort, and some had been arrow-shot by their captors in parting. The troopers nearly ruined their own horses in the hundred-mile pursuit.

Two of the officers "bought" Indian wives at Fort Laramie; the Sioux price was one or more horses. But the father of one of the brides just got on the purchase price and rode away in the night; the other bride – a two-horse girl – accompanied her groom to his quarters, scratched and beat him, ran out the back door and disappeared. General Mitchell mustered both men out without charges, and Ware commented that the Sioux women were among the most virtuous in the world.

Mitchell started sending out detachments to build small forts to protect the westering road. Captain Jake Shuman went out first, to build Camp Shuman; a father and son had Fort (William) Collins and Fort Caspar (Collins) named after them; Company F was sent to Julesburg to build a small fort.

At Camp Shuman – the captain later renamed it Mitchell for his general – Jake Shuman broke out a bottle of St. Croix Rum Punch for O'Brien, Ware, and Shuman's own first lieutenant. But Ware was more interested in getting together with Camp Shuman's first sergeant, with whom he had soldiered down in Arkansas. The fact that one was now commissioned and the other not made no difference to them; they greeted each other by their old 4th Iowa Cavalry nicknames and fraternized without shocking officers or troopers. When the Regulars took over the West again, after the Civil War, this would become impossible.

The road from Fort Laramie to Julesburg was deserted, though the soldiers saw no Indian sign, and concluded that the Cheyennes had gone south and the Sioux north. But at Julesburg there was a mob of pilgrims and freighters, under the protection of Colorado troops. The Rocky Mountain troopers set up a patrol to Julesburg, the Iowa boys patrolled the other way, and the road opened up somewhat. Julesburg was thirty-five miles from any kind of tree, and bull-chips were scarce and unsatisfactory fuel; the troopers had been eating a good deal of uncooked bacon. O'Brien sent Ware out with wagons and a guard detail to Ash Hollow.

They saw plenty of signs of wild horses; deer, antelope, rabbits and wolves were plentiful, but the only Indian sign was a signal fire on a knoll, so cold that they could not tell how long ago it had been used. In camp at the foot of Ash Hollow, Ware threw out strong pickets. "I was only twenty-three ... and felt the responsibility heavily." The troopers were just falling asleep when one of them thought he saw a fire arrow in the sky. They got up, bridled, and loosely saddled their horses. Each man lay down with his reins in his hand, ready to jump up, cinch, and ride at any alarm.

Wolves were all around them, and all howling. Ware was afraid that some of the howls were being made by Indians. But the worst thing that happened to him in the night was that a wolf tried to steal his bacon ration. He frightened the animal off with his saber.

That night was not so bad; the wagonloads of wood made good barricades if it came to a fight. Another soldier saw a "fire arrow" but Ware saw it, too; it was a shooting star. They got back to Julesburg without trouble.

It was too late in the year to build a fort; O'Brien moved the detachment into the ranch of a man named Bancroft, and the company re-enforced the place with sods. The method is worth repeating. Five spans of mules pulled a plow with a thin share, especially hardened by the company blacksmith; a trooper rode the near leader, field artillery style. Axmen followed the furrow and chopped the turned-up sod into three-foot lengths; other troopers puddled mud for mortar, and the walls went up fast, in alternate cross and long courses, broken to baffle rain or melting snow.

Cedar poles were freighted down from their old fort at Cottonwood Canyon, and the men built stables and quarters to augment the ranch buildings. It was arranged with a party of Mormons to bring in more timber on their empty wagons; the Mormons traveled through the country unarmed and unalarmed, having some sort of rapport with the hostile Indians that continually puzzled the military.

Indian scares continued into November. One night a stagecoach came in, the driver wearing an arrow shot through the slack cloth of his coat just below his neck; the head of the limber arrow had whipped around and slapped him in the face.

It was the duty of a post commander out there to act as civil authority, too. When a rancher came in and said a wagon train had stopped at his place and refused to pay for supplies taken, Ware, in temporary command, sent a corporal down with a squad, brought the wagon-master and two of his cronies in, sat as judge, and put the wagon-master in jail till he paid a judgment of $162.50. Presumably this extra duty was because it was wartime; organized territories usually had justices of the peace and higher civil courts available.

Late in November the first sergeant took out another party, for firewood again; it was getting cold. The first week in December was marked with a hurricane that lasted three days, and the last of the pasture on the prairie went. Wagons that carried hay could still go on, but the Indians were pretty well pinned down for the winter.

Ware helped a Mormon train across the frozen Platte by taking his men out and chopping a twelve-foot-wide ford. But then the men were reluctant to get into the water to heave out the ice blocks. Ware jumped in and set them an example, and the ford was cleared by the men working up to their waists in the freezing water. Then he double-timed them to the post to change their clothes; they came back with bull whips and hurried the Mormon mules across before dark could fall and the crossing freeze up again. The man whose ranch the outfit had converted into a fort was so impressed that he brought out two quarts of champagne, one of which Ware drank – completely this time – in the lee of a windmill.

The champagne-drinking West has been obscured by the red-eye drinking West of screen and fiction, but there seems to be no reason why Ware would have invented it.

In December 1864 word came to the cold, high Plains that General John Hood had been whipped in Tennessee and the Confederacy was crumbling. The soldiers celebrated. A number of troopers got roaring drunk, and Ware investigated. He found a bootleg, crooked-poker joint about a mile below Julesburg. This seems a logical and profitable venture; but the existence of many similar ones is rather astounding. Most of the time that the troops were in the West a private got eight dollars a month, sometimes less, sometimes as much as thirteen.

Still, let a hundred-man post open up, and prostitution, bootlegging, and gambling joints open up at once; usually several of them. Where was the profit in all this? Even if four or five people split the whole payroll – and not more than half of it could have been spent on roistering since the men had other obligations – the cost of moving women and keeping them alive, of liquor, and of building the hog ranches and blind tigers seems too big an investment for the possible return.

To get back to Ware's case, that last Christmas week of the Civil War, he heard that his men had been cheated and mistreated, and that they were going to lynch the two gamblers who ran the speakeasy-gambling hall. O'Brien was away buying remounts; so, it was up to the young lieutenant. The non-coms figured out that the hanging party was slated for December 29. Ware posted a heavy guard and ordered its corporal to report to him every thirty minutes; but in the middle of the night the corporal said that two men had slipped by one of the guards, and a barracks check showed a full ten troopers missing.

By the time Ware could saddle up, another twelve rushed the guards and got away. He circled wide so as to give the lynch party no warning, and cut in ahead of the AWOL men, who were, of course, on foot. Dismounting, he raised his carbine, barked them to a halt, and made a speech: they proposed to commit a crime, and he would not be a proper officer if he permitted it; and if they rushed him, he would kill one or two at least; it was impossible to miss with such a mob of men.

One man cocked a pistol at him in the dark, and Ware clicked his carbine and told them to make up their minds; rush him and kill him, or march back to the post. They turned around and started marching. He let his pony go to find its own way back to the stables, and on foot marched after his men, who began to run, presumably to get back before they could be identified.

Lieutenant Ware – the only officer on the post that night – sat up with his two Colt's strapped on; after about an hour one of the sergeants said the men were not sleeping but were planning to go back down to the blind tiger and take up the lynching where they had been interrupted. Ware walked into the barracks and made another speech; he issued a direct order which he backed up by saying that he would see that any man leaving the barracks was court-martialed and shot. The project broke up.

Regulars would have behaved differently. Ware was much closer to his men than the West Pointers could ever be to the foreigners and slum-dwellers and misfits who would fill the ranks when the State troops went home. In all probability a West Point lieutenant would have had to send a sergeant on the sort of job Ware did that night, since anything short of immediate obedience to a commissioned officer's command was a serious, sometimes fatal, offense. Perhaps Regular sergeants wouldn't have told a lieutenant what the men planned. There was a line between sergeants and troopers, but there was a deep ravine between officers and enlisted men.

News came to Ware's post of the Chivington massacre; an attack by Colorado troops on snowbound Arapahoes and Cheyennes. Chivington and his State troopers killed about five hundred Indians, indiscriminately; most of the dead were reported to be women and children. Ware's only regret was that fifteen hundred other Indians got away.

As 1865 opened, Ware was ordered down to Cottonwood Springs again to take over a company of recruits; but before he could train them he was made aide-de-camp to General Mitchell, and then, before he could go to Headquarters at Omaha, a wire came in that Company F at Fort Sedgwick had been hit by Indians. Mitchell wired Ware to take forty men and go back to Julesburg.

He took ten trained troopers, a howitzer fieldpiece, and thirty-two of his recruits. The rookies were not yet mounted; he put them in wagons and covered the fieldpiece to make it look like another wagon. His strategy was to induce the hostiles into attacking what looked like a wagon train with an escort of twelve men and an officer. They didn't.

Julesburg was quite a battle, but Ware missed it; part way there he was ordered to return to Cottonwood Springs again. He sent his company back, but went ahead himself, till further wired orders recalled him sharply. The company lost fourteen men in the battle and found fifty-four Indian bodies after it; the Plains Indians were devoted in their efforts to carry off their dead, so it is probable that more had been killed. O'Brien told Ware that there had been a thousand Indians against his sixty men; this is probably an exaggeration; the enemy always looked more numerous than they were, as can be proved by comparing Union and Confederate accounts of battles.

General Mitchell led a column into the field after the Julesburg fight: about six hundred and forty mounted men and a heavy wagon train. O'Brien was detached from his company and made commander of the six-piece artillery battery; Ware was assistant Adjutant General, acting; the troops were all Iowa or Nebraska State or Territorial Cavalry.

For once a remuda went along: fifty extra horses. But the number indicates that they would be used as replacements for casualties, rather than as change-over mounts in the course of a single march. All the animals were corn-fed; the prairie grass was frosted and unappetizing. The grain-fed, hay-fed Army horse, so ponderous against Sioux ponies in the summer, had a distinct advantage in the winter, when about the best an Indian pony could hope for was cottonwood bark or brown grass from which the seeds had heen frozen.

This was, in one sense, a show-the-flag march. William T. Sherman had reached the sea from Atlanta, John M. Schofield had taken Nashville, Phil Sheridan had scraped the flesh off the Shenandoah Valley. Robert E. Lee was about to fight his last battles.

The Union could release troops for Indian fighting; it would be impressive for the hostiles to see a column as big as Mitchell's. If O'Brien, with sixty men, could fight off a thousand braves, a column like Mitchell's could handle anything the Sioux-Cheyenne alliance could send against them.

But a winter attack on the Plains was a very good idea for other reasons than propaganda. The horseborne Sioux and Cheyenne had to stay near the cottonwoods in winter or lose their horses; if they could be driven away from the streambeds, they would come into the spring dismounted and no particular menace.

For the first week the column kept seeing signs of large Indian camps; the Indians had scattered ahead of them. One scouting party had its camp overrun by braves, but without damage. Then they crossed into Kansas, and back out again; the thermometer fell to zero, but the skies stayed clear. General Mitchell got philosophic and speculated that it cost the Army three million dollars a year just to run his little district; for two thirds of that he could have bought the Indians broadcloth suits, fed them on fried oysters, and given them all the poker, whiskey and tobacco money they wanted, and thus end the Sioux War. It is too bad that the general's plan was never tried; the meeting between the Sioux and the fried oysters would have been full of interest.

They went up the Republican River to the edge of timber, and then back down it again. Heavy winds had nearly ruined both horses and men – every man in the command suffered from frost bite. Fifty men had to be discharged because of illness, and the expedition had not killed an Indian, though it had kept the Indians on the move. The philosophic general thought of resigning from the service and did send in a request for Southern duty.

Back at Cottonwood, he took some action on January 27; the day was clear and bright, with a strong wind out of the northwest. Mitchell wired all his commanders from Fort Kearny to Denver to set the prairie on fire. The men of his command didn't know it, but this would be the last chance to strike at the Indians that way; the end of the war was about to loose a flood of settlers on the Plains, who would be as badly hurt by a grassfire as would the hostiles.

For three hundred miles the frontier blazed. Most of Nebraska, at least half of Kansas, the southern half of Colorado burned; the flames started at the Platte and South Platte and ran to the Arkansas; in some cases, they jumped that river and went on into the Panhandle of Texas.

A gameless, grassless cordon sanitaire had been laid across the Plains, two hundred miles and wider. The Indians would have to go north of rt, where the water was bad, or south, into Apache-Comanche country. Neither choice was very appealing.

But there were plenty of Indians north of the river when the fire started. They renewed their raids on the riverbank ranches; cattle raids became constant. O'Brien and Ware, leading a detachment from Cottonwood Canyon to Julesburg, saw smoke signals constantly, and every so often a solitary Indian would fire at them, but from too great a range to be effective.

They found Fort Sedgwick, at Julesburg, the soddy fort they had built, surrounded by large hordes of Indians; more were crossing on the frozen Platte. A great many Indians had survived in the fire belt; backfiring was well understood before the white man ever appeared. Now they were swarming north.

The Iowans had only a dozen troopers with them, but they were hauling a howitzer; they loaded with canister – an anti-personnel shell filled with iron balls – and prepared to make a dash for the fort. The howitzer was small enough, with a light enough charge, that it could be fired from horseback without recoiling forward and knocking over the horses hauling the fieldpiece.

The Indians were using fire, too; the stage station and stores around the little fort were burning. This helped the troopers, who went forward fast under a dense enough smoke screen to within two miles of the fort. Then they put their horses at the gallop and went forward in open order, at intervals of twenty yards, fanned out on either side of the gun. There were hostiles on both flanks and their rear, now.

Ahead of them, by the burning stage station, the Indians scattered out and let the little column through. When the Sioux made a stand in front of them, O'Brien ordered the howitzer to wheel and fire when the charge was still a mile from the fort; the garrison heard them and brought out its own howitzer to cover them.

But instead of covering them, the gunners aimed directly at the relieving party. O'Brien ordered the sabers (?) drawn, though the Indians, puzzled, were staying well off the front of the charge and firing from a safe distance. The whole column rode into the fort uninjured.

There were supposed to be about fifteen hundred hostile braves around the fort. Toward dark they went back across the frozen river – a wide crossing had been sanded to keep the unshod ponies from slipping – and went into camp. Ware was told that they were a mixture of Arapahoes and Cheyennes, not Sioux at all.

The Indian camp was full of loot from the ranches and wagons they had raided. There was a huge fire going, made of chopped-down telegraph poles, and a drunken war dance started up after nightfall; they had captured great supplies of bitters. O'Brien and Ware climbed up on the fort haystack and saw large numbers of cattle and "American" horses driven into the Indian lines. Then an Indian shot a fire arrow into the hay, but one of the troopers put it out neatly with a cupful of water, thrown with marvelous precision.

The Indian campfire spread to the prairie around it; General Mitchell's feat threatened to be repeated north of the river, too. Smoke obscured things, and when the sun came up, the watching officers could not see a single Indian. They reconnoitered the Indian camp; from the signs they estimated that five thousand cattle had been driven off. The hostiles had gone away, up Lodgepole Creek. Relief was coming toward the fort, a large detachment under a Colonel Livingston. The Indians had learned about it from smoke signals and taken off.

General Mitchell was transferred south, as he had requested. The war ended, and the Iowans went home to make careers for themselves. Ware took up newspaper work, the law, and politics; his military life was over. But he left us one of the best accounts of life on the Sioux frontier that we have.

304

His outfit – the military department headed by General Mitchell, manned by Iowa and Kansas and Colorado troops – didn't make much of a dent in the Sioux world, and more than a dent was needed. Right was on the Indians' side. They had gotten there first, driven out of Minnesota by troops, out of Wisconsin by harder fighting Indians. But history was on the white man's, the European man's, side. There were less than three hundred thousand Indians in the United States according to the 1860 census; of course, only a fraction of these were on the Plains. But in 1865 alone, half that many Europeans migrated to the United States.

Men who could farm and make a living on a quarter section of good prairie were starving to death in the Eastern cities, in Europe; but the Plains Indian needed section upon section of land for each member of the tribes; buffalo hunting is a spacious way of life. It had to go. Shed a tear for the Arapahoe, the Cheyenne, the Sioux, the Kiowa; they were colorful, they loved the life they led, they fought furiously against becoming plodding farmers. But they had to go, to trade schools, to reservations in dusty Oklahoma, to hanging around pool-halls in the Dakotas.

Wyoming is the least populated of the old Plains battlegrounds; yet it contains as many people as the whole Indian population of the country in Ware's time. By 1870 Kansas alone counted more people than the nation counted Indians.

General Mitchell's giant grassfire split the Plains when they most needed splitting, in the transition time when the citizen soldiers went home and the professional troopers and their Regular officers took the duty back.

Chapter 24

The Man who Hired Hostiles

Not all of the old Dragoons got to the Eastern theater of the Civil War. Part of each of the first three regiments stayed in New Mexico. The commander of the Military Department of New Mexico at the beginning of the war was Colonel W.W. Loring of the Mounted Rifles, now the 3rd Cavalry. But Loring was a Southerner, as was his deputy, George Crittenden and Major H.H. Sibley – again, not to be confused with the Sibley who drove the Sioux out of Minnesota. Colonel Edwin Canby took the command.

A month later he knew he was in bad trouble. Navajo and Apache raids had never stopped; and now word came from Texas that Major Sibley had been made a brigadier general, CSA, with orders to lead a column to New Mexico and seize that territory.

Down in Southern New Mexico, the Texans – the New Mexicans always called them that, rather than Confederates – came across from Fort Bliss at El Paso and took Las Cruces-Mesilla and the valley it commands without a struggle on the part of Major Isaac Lynde, the commandant at Fort Fillmore, though his force was about the same size as that of the *tejanos*.

Canby sent out orders to the forts in what is now Arizona, Buchanan and Breckinridge. The stores there were burned, and the troops came back to the middle Rio Grande Valley.

The Apaches now had Arizona to themselves. In effect, this was an anti-Confederate move; even if the Texans took New Mexico it cut them off from California, whose gold would have shored up an international credit that was shaky from the very beginning of the war. The South did send a small detachment – about a battalion – of Sibley's men over to take Tucson, but California had remained loyal – it wasn't expected to – and a California column came out and drove the Texans back to El Paso. Then the Californians, under Colonel Carleton, settled down to fight Apaches.

In the fall of 1861 Sibley and his Texans – called Rangers, of course – started up the Rio Grande; by February 1862 they were at Mesilla. Canby had sent his cavalry south to contain them; besides Kit Carson's mounted New Mexico Volunteers and some rather worthless New Mexico militia, he had eleven companies of Regular infantry and nine companies from the first three cavalry regiments. He was using troopers from the 1st and 3rd Cavalry as artillerymen, but he relieved them of that duty for the Southern Rio Grande expedition, and turned the fieldpieces over to volunteers, who allowed some of the Texas force to get across the river at Panadero Ford, below Fort Craig. Canby turned the guns over to the cavalrymen again, under a Major Roberts; he armed the upper ford, Valverde, and stopped the crossing.

Canby had been directing the battle from the march, by couriers; around noon he arrived in person, and took charge. He shoved his guns forward, and backed them up with his whole force, but the Texans made a mounted charge of over a thousand men – some of them lancers – the Federals were thrown back to the fort, and the Confederates crossed and marched up the river to Albuquerque without opposition.

Then Sibley split his force, using the smaller part to occupy Santa Fe, with its Palace of the Governors and Fort Marcy; the larger part went on up to Fort Union, where the Santa Fe Trail split into its two routes, and took over about three hundred thousand dollars' worth of military stores. A detachment from Santa Fe went out and overpowered the weak garrison at Apache Canyon-Glorieta Pass, names for contiguous cuts in the mountains that protect Santa Fe on the east.

This was the same natural bastion of Santa Fe that St. George Cooke had scouted for Kearny in 1846. Captain Cooke had reported that the pass seemed impregnable, but that he had figured a way through it; then he had gone on in and bribed Governor Armijo not to put up a defense. Cooke was one of the best Western fighters ever known, his Civil War record to the contrary. He was talking about a defense by fat, lazy Armijo; and even so, his tone was dubious; he *thought* he had found a way through Glorieta Pass and Apache Canyon; he wasn't sure.

Sibley's people had time to set up a defense, and their arms were a thousand percent better than the Mexican Army had had in New Mexico sixteen years before. If they had put snipers on the ridges and set up their field batteries better, the Union could never have gotten through.

But Texas wanted to occupy all of eastern New Mexico, not just the capital. When the Union force came on, the Texans did not content themselves with just trying to stop them; they ventured out on the wider spaces past the canyon.

Some of the Colorado Cavalry Volunteers who were later to show up to help the Iowans on the Plains were already with Canby; more were now on their way south to New Mexico, together with a small detachment of

Regular infantry and some field artillery. Among the Colorado officers was Chivington, who later led the Indian massacres that so provoked the northern troubles.

There was a Texas battery in the mouth of the canyon. Chivington was leading the vanguard of the Federals with four hundred men, evenly divided between foot soldiers and troopers; he foot-skirmished the battery while his cavalry hid behind a spur. The battery pulled back, but that brought it too much out in the open, where Apache Canyon widened out.

Chivington dismounted half his troopers to fight flank guard for the infantry and ordered all his footmen forward. As they harassed the enemy, the hundred remaining troopers charged at the gallop, "looking like so many devils," according to a letter a Texan sent his wife after Sibley's men had been defeated.

The Confederates outnumbered the Colorado troops strongly; but Chivington dismounted his men again – he already had over a hundred Regular infantry – and single-filed them over the ridges and cut off the Texans. Sibley abandoned Santa Fe and then Albuquerque, and eventually all of New Mexico, retiring to Fort Bliss. He left more than half of his force behind, wounded, dead, or straggled.

Had the Texans held Santa Fe, history would probably have been changed. The Lone Star State had always considered at least the area of New Mexico east of the Rio Grande as part of Texas; and though the Texans were rebels, the Texas politicians who came up in the Reconstruction days would have backed their claim, and the underpopulated Territory of New Mexico, with no congressional power at all, would have been split in two.

General James H. Carleton became military commander of New Mexico in 1864; he was, in substantive rank, a major of infantry, brevetted major general of volunteers. After he put Colonel Kit Carson and his New Mexico Volunteers out against the Navajo, that tribe ceased to give much trouble, though half the Navajos were still loose, and others kept escaping from the Bosque Redondo concentration camp. Other tribes, Apaches, Utes, Comanches, Kiowas, plagued the territory with sporadic raids. Carson's regiment of volunteers seems to have been the only New Mexico Territorial outfit of any use to Carleton; Canby took a good many of the Regular cavalry troops with him when he went East to get in on enough of the main war to be made a brigadier general of the Regular Army in 1865; after Reconstruction duty he returned to the West and was killed in the Modoc Indian Wars in 1873.

Fighting in the Southwest was by detachments; a full company of troopers was seldom involved. White habitation pretty much shrank to the Rio Grande Valley. Arizona was separated from New Mexico in 1863, given its present name and attached to the military Division of the Pacific for defense. Arizona had already been made a territory by the Confederate government; its boundaries were those of the Gadsden Purchase that had been made to include Cooke's wagon road. This made Arizona lie directly below New Mexico; if the Union had followed this division, Las Cruces would be in Arizona, Flagstaff and Williams in New Mexico.

But Carleton's California Column drove the Confederacy out of Tucson, and the Union flag went up. Unlike the rest of Arizona, Tucson and the Santa Cruz Valley below it were never completely abandoned to the Apaches in the early '60s and there were a few other towns living in a virtual state of siege. By 1870, the first year Arizona was given its own census figures, there were still less than ten thousand people living in the Territory; New Mexico had more than ninety thousand.

When the war ended, four problems faced the Army. First, and considered the most dangerous, was the occupation of the Confederacy; there were only two great classes of people there, freed slaves and former rebels. Without military law, the former would wander, loot, do anything; the South was not set up to employ them. And the latter might very well take law into their own hands, which, of course, they did to some extent; witness Nathan Bedford Forrest and the Ku Klux Klan.

The second Army assignment, in the Eastern-oriented eyes of Washington, was the presence in Mexico of an army of Napoleon III's, keeping the weak and nervous Maximilian on the throne, contrary to the Monroe Doctrine and the safety and peace of the United States.

Then there were the two minor menaces, the Plains Indians and the Southwestern Apache-Ute-Comanche uprisings, not to mention some rather dissatisfied Modocs, Nez Percé, and Salish tribes in the Pacific department.

A strong army was needed. There were a million men under arms in May 1865. By November eight hundred thousand of them had been discharged; this was a volunteer army, of course, enlisted for the duration of the war, and every man in it was anxious to go home and vote for the politicians – Congressmen, Senators, governors in their capacity as commanders of State troops – who had sent him home faster than the next bluecoat.

Ulysses S. Grant was made General-in-Chief. He asked for an army of eighty thousand men. Edwin M. Stanton, still Secretary of War, thought that fifty thousand was enough, and asked Congress for that many. By September '66 there were a few more than thirty-eight thousand men under arms, to carry out all the missions the Army had to fulfill. A year later, as the veterans found peace not all it should be, there were fifty-four thousand men in the rank and file; this was to be the high for the postwar years. In 1874 the size of the Army was set by Congress at twenty-five thousand, and what with desertions, disability, and the usual troubles that dog all military operations, there were probably never as many as twenty thousand officers and men available for field duty until the Spanish-American War. There were ten regiments of cavalry in the peacetime Army, and there were not to be any more than that until after World War I, when cavalry had been proved obsolescent.

The first three regiments were the descendants of the two Dragoon outfits and the Mounted Rifles; the 4th and 5th were the 1855 regiments created by Secretary of War Jefferson Davis. The 6th had been formed just as the Civil War started and was retained on the Regular list. The 7th and 8th were new; so were the 9th and 10th, but these were different from all the rest, in that they were Negro outfits, officered by white men, and were to remain so until after World War II, when the Army was desegregated.

The United States Volunteer Cavalry – as against State or Territorial Volunteers – was dissolved. These were the so-called Galvanized Yankees, Southern prisoners who had gotten out of prison camps by agreeing to wear blue and fight Indians. Though the concept is glamorous and has occasioned great imaginings on the part of fiction writers, the Galvanized Yankees did not amount to much, and while used in the West, didn't really cause as much bother to the Indians as they did to their own officers.

In May '65, before the great mustering-out was well under way, Sherman had taken fifty thousand troops to the Mexican border. He never had to invade Mexico, but his presence on its northern frontier caused Napoleon to pull the French troops home; then Juarez and his revolutionaries defeated Maximilian's Mexican troops with ease, and the Monroe Doctrine was in force again.

If Sherman had taken his army north through New Mexico and Arizona and into the Plains, the Indian troubles would probably have ended before 1870. But some of his men were entitled to discharge and some were needed in the South, which was under military law until 1870; for the seven years after that civil law was in force on paper, but it was carpetbag civil law, and the troops had to stay there to enforce it. Thus, as late as 1876, when Custer assembled all twelve companies – only eight hundred men, at that – of the 7th Cavalry at Fort Abraham Lincoln, he had to bring two companies in from coastal duty on Staten Island in New York, and three from duty in Louisiana.

Backing up the ten horse regiments were forty-five infantry regiments, and then, after 1869, only twenty-five. These were useful, in the West, to guard railroad construction crews, and even more useful for the building of the many forts that were constructed to guard the many trails used by the emigrants rushing out of the depressed East.

There weren't enough infantrymen; the troopers had to pass up mounted drill in favor of construction work. As for target practice, unless an officer had private means and bought cartridges for his men, it was out of the question; ammunition was not to be wasted by learning to use the carbine.

George Crook, Brevet Brigadier General, U.S.A., Major General U.S.V. during the war, fought right through all the Indian Wars; he was, probably, the only general officer to take the field in the Pacific, Arizona, and Plains theaters. Sherman called him the "greatest fighter and manager of Indians" he was ever to know; and Crook's career in the West is delightful to follow because of Captain John Gregory Bourke, 3rd Cavalry, who served as aide to Crook and was his greatest admirer.

Bourke was one of the finest writers the horse soldiers ever turned out, and the cavalry was rich with good authors. Light-Horse Harry himself started the tradition when he wrote his *Memoirs of the War in the Southern Department*, still good reading if one allows for eighteenth-century elaboration. Charles King, another of Crook's men, turned pro when he was retired for wounds thirteen years after he got out of West Point; he became a fiction writer, however, rather than a historian; it is hard to find a high-class magazine of the '80s or '90s without one of his stories in it. Philip St. George Cooke held the title of the cavalry's greatest wordsmith until young John Bourke came along to dispute it. George Armstrong Custer wrote prodigiously, and when he was killed his wife Elizabeth took up the pen, mostly in defense of his memory. Everyone who rode with Stuart wrote a book about it, it seems. Sheridan's two-volume *Personal Memoirs* is as truculent and bluff as its author. Crook started his autobiography, too, a rather dull account of his numerous wars which he never finished. But Bourke or Cooke, one or the other, remains the champion.

George Crook was a classmate of Phil Sheridan's at the Academy, though he did not hit any cadet officers, and so graduated a year earlier than Sheridan. Both men were from Ohio, and close friends in so far as Sheridan ever had any close friends at West Point. Crook, of course, commanded brigades and divisions under Sheridan during the Civil War, and they were together in conquered Winchester the night the Southern girls let habit overcome patriotism and danced around the strolling generals.

But after Chickamauga, Crook cooled toward his chief. Sheridan wrote up the report of the battle in such a way as to make it appear that Crook had commanded a corps, when Crook had only led a division, but had fought it so hard that he had accomplished as much as a corps could have; Crook felt that the report belittled his achievements. Actually, looking back, Sheridan may have meant more than well. Field promotion in the Army usually comes after the fact; until a man has commanded a regiment, he is not likely to be made a colonel. The coolness seems to have been one-sided. In the dreary days of the small post-war Army, Sheridan appears to have been Crook's chief sponsor.

Crook, like Sheridan, started wearing shoulder straps as an infantry officer. This was because they had graduated very low in their classes – Crook even lower than Sheridan – and the infantry appointments were filled from the bottom of the class.

But during the war Sheridan gave Crook a cavalry brigade and then a division to command, and after the war Crook, assigned to the 23rd Infantry as lieutenant colonel, quickly started snatching up any cavalry companies that were around and attaching them to his command.

He went to Oregon after the war, with part of the 23rd. He had been there in the '50s, theoretically an infantry lieutenant, but he had managed to serve as a cavalry subaltern under the same A.J. Smith, then a captain, 1st Dragoons, who had messed up the Mormon Battalion and who was later to be a run-of-the-mill major general of Volunteers in the Civil War.

The Oregon-Idaho frontier was stormy in 1866. The migration into that country had not stopped during the war, and now it came on stronger and stronger, and the Indians looked on with horror and outrage as valley after valley was taken over by farmers who drove the game out and shut off access to fishing waters.

Early in the year, Company M of the 1st Cavalry skirmished with Indians; then Company A had trouble, as did H and I and finally F. The three old regiments were scattered all over the West, from Arizona to the Dakotas. The Plains was rather quiet that year of transition possibly because of General Mitchell's fire; the 4th, 5th, and 6th Cavalry, and the next four as formed, were not yet used on Western duty.

Up in the Northwest Crook developed the method of Indian fighting he was to use until the West was subdued. He differed from any other of the great Army Indian fighters – Kit Carson was not really Army – in that he loved the men he fought against with a deep and genuine love. In this he resembled many of the Indians he fought, who held dances honoring animals before they went out on the hunt; a deer dance before going into the mountains, a buffalo dance before riding out on the Plains. The Indian – some Indians, because no generality about Indians ever holds for the whole United States area – kills animals to eat or even for ceremonial reasons, but he does not hate the animals he kills.

And Crook did not hate the Rogues, the Pit Rivers, the Apaches, the Sioux and Cheyenne that he fought. Nor did he hold them in contempt, as had Ware and Chivington and their fellow State officers. The pre-war Army had maintained that the only good Indian was a dead Indian; the Iowans had sent their Pawnee scouts home as useless.

Crook's first principle was always to have as many Indian scouts as possible, and always to recruit them, when possible, from the hostiles; he liked them wild, right off the warpath, so that they would know as much as possible about the strength, plans and movements of the hostiles. White men recruited this way in an intra-white war would carry a strong strain of spy in them; Crook was convinced that Indians wouldn't, and his faith seems justified by the record. The difference arises out of the philosophy of the two races; fighting is an honorable way of life for most Indians, more important than racial or tribal loyalty. Crook was firmly convinced, in war and peace, that the way to an Indian's heart lay in the profit motive. He paid his scouts, of course, and he tried to solve the Apache troubles by showing the desert warriors how to farm, and *then buying their produce to feed indigent Indians and his soldiers.*

This was heresy. It worked, but it took the profit out of the Indian trader's pocket; and Crook was fought by the Indian agents, then, as now, part of the Department of Interior. (For an interval they were under the War Department.)

It worked, as did his wild scouts, but it seems dubious if it would have worked for – say – Custer or Miles or St. George Cooke, or most of the generals who commanded in the Indian Wars. Crook's personality appealed to the Indians. He was profoundly interested in their way of life, he went to them as a student rather than as a Great White God, and that attitude showed through. Whenever he could, he rode with the Indian scout part of any column he commanded, and he was not above tasting anything the Indians ate.

His second principle, then, was to know as much as possible about the country; not just the terrain with an eye to cover and enfilade, but all about the vegetation, insect rife, mineralogy, geology, and zoology.

Crook was a tireless hunter. At the end of a day's march and maneuvering, when younger men would rest gratefully in camp, he would take his sporting gun and go after game, usually successfully, and preferably alone, though in very hostile country his subordinates often persuaded him to take a covering escort.

All this knowledge paid off. He never made camp on sacaton grass when a little extra travel would put his horse on rich black grama; he never herded Indians into rich berry country when a flanking movement would turn them into areas where there was no natural food for them. He dismounted his troopers when the conformation of the rocks indicated that the horses would soon start slipping and spending strength they could husband by being held back on the flats.

Crook's third principle was to get on the tail of hostiles and keep there until they were run down. This was in complete contrast to the Civil War method of trying to encircle the enemy; the day the complexion of the enemy changed from Southern white to Western red, he changed his methods.

Crook was successful in Oregon, and in 1871 was ordered to take charge of the Department of Arizona, a part of the Division of the Pacific, with headquarters at the presidio in San Francisco. The Territory of Arizona was a part of the Division of the Pacific, with headquarters at the presidio in San Francisco. The Arizona headquarters, ridiculously, was in Los Angeles; Crook changed it to Tucson. In his command – a brigade – were the 23rd Infantry, and the 1st, 3rd, and 5th Cavalry.

Conditions were very different from those the Iowans had found on the Plains. There was no telegraph through Arizona, and there were few Anglo ranchers; the town of Tucson was really a Mexican town. Prescott, the Anglo town, had been founded and then shrunk almost to extinction, but now a gold boom was building it up again. The daily Butterfield Stage Coach Line that ran across the old Cooke-Mormon Wagon Road in the south of Arizona had been discontinued a couple of years before Crook arrived, because of Apache trouble. In the north, the road from Santa Fe to Los Angeles had not been fully opened since the beginning of the Civil War.

Crook arrived in Tucson on one of the occasional stagecoaches, un-escorted, unannounced, unmet. His baggage, according to Captain Bourke, would have fitted into the cover of a Remington typewriter. He spent the morning talking to Governor Safford, and the afternoon issuing orders to all the officers in his department to report to him, right then.

Rumors were floating around Tucson that the government had issued orders to the new commander not to attack the Apaches, but to wait till Washington decided on a reservation for them. The chiefs of the Warm Springs Apaches had been camped for two years in front of Fort Craig, over in Mesilla, waiting for this decision.

Crook grunted, mounted five companies of cavalry and a bunch of Apache and white scouts, and took to the field. He was not a show-the-flag man. By now, the shameful truth was that there was no flag to show. Hardly a tribe in the West had not been promised something by some Army officer and then had the promise broken by another officer or, more often, an Indian agent.

Five companies of cavalry – perhaps three hundred men – might impress Apaches. But the Indians knew that some whim of Washington's might pull those five companies out of Arizona completely by tomorrow; and the Apaches were desperate. What more could a people do than sit two years before a fort, waiting for an answer to a sincere peace offer?

Only two months before Crook took the campaign trail, there had been a mixed-up matter at Camp Grant, north of present-day Douglas. The Chiricahuas had come in to dicker; time and more time had gone by, as reports were returned from headquarters to the officers at Camp Grant for redrawing, clarification, briefing. Then a party of Mexicans and Papago Indians had suddenly struck the Apaches in the treaty camp, the Apaches had struck back, and a number of people, including an officer of the

314

3rd Cavalry, had been killed. The Apaches had decided you couldn't talk to the white man.

The day, July 11, that Crook led his little column out toward Bowie, the temperature reached a hundred and ten degrees before ten o'clock in the morning. This might well have been called a "try-the-men" march.

Crook marched his men almost to the border of his command, Fort Apache, way to the east, near the New Mexico border, and midway between Mexico and Utah. He asked questions constantly, on the march, in the camp, on evening hunting forays. He sized up the scouts, he appraised his officers. He learned more about the country than officers who had been there three years and more.

The only encounters with Apaches were trivial; flanking parties and videttes twice scared off raiders, once recapturing some cattle after they had been slaughtered but not cut up and once causing the raiders to abandon a few stolen burros.

There were a few bands of Apaches around Fort – then called Camp – Apache who were still hopeful of peace. Crook took his time and let their chiefs talk to him Indian fashion – that is, endlessly – until every man had said everything he wanted to say in as many fashions as he could think of.

When he left Camp Apache he had made a good impression on the local chiefs; and some of his officers had made good impressions on him, because he dispatched three companies out on independent scout duty back toward the west.

His own party, two companies, cut into the Mogollon – always pronounced Muggy Owen by local whites – country and the Tonto Basin. This was cool, upland country, and rich in game and natural fruits and nuts. Here lived the Tonto Apaches, strongholded and well-supplied, and with a reputation for being the wildest in Arizona. Crook got what he wanted in the Tonto Basin – a fight with the Tontos.

It was only a small band that attacked him, and it was an arrow attack rather than a rifle fight, in such dense forest that the Indians couldn't take decent aim. Crook cut off two of the Apaches, which was what he wanted; he planned on making scouts of them, showing them he was a straight-talking man, and sending them back to dicker with the chiefs of the Tontos for him. But they escaped, down a slope so steep and rough no one but an Apache could have made it, Crook fired after them himself, and wounded one of the fugitives in the arm, but the brave kept on going.

So, Crook finished his long patrol at Prescott without really fighting Apaches. But he had showed willingness to fight, willingness to talk, willingness to learn; he had found out which officers, mule-packers, and guides were good – though a dispatch received at Camp Apache had made him pay off his scouts – and he had learned an awful lot about how to survive in both desert and mountain Arizona.

Now the government had sent a Quaker named Vincent Colyer out to make peace with the Apaches; Crook was ordered to stay out of the way. Gloomily – he had learned enough on his long expedition to know that the Apaches did not trust civilians – he did so. But there were other hostiles in Arizona. There were the Hualpais – sometimes called Wallapies – and tribes of the Mohave and Yuma stock, called Apache-Mohave and Apache-Yuma, though they were not in any sense Apaches. The confusion came about because Apache is the word for enemy in the Pima language, and since Kearny's and Cooke's time the Pimas had been the principal Indian contact the Army had in Arizona.

About a thousand mixed members of these three tribes – mostly Apache-Yumas – were around a miserable Camp Date post, near Wickenburg. They were not warriors, but petty larceny raiders, quite possibly outcasts from the main bodies of their tribes. Some of them were on the prod over toward Wickenburg when they trapped a stagecoach and murdered most of the passengers and the driver, before looting the coach and baggage. One of the passengers was a fairly well-known young scientist, named Loring. He had connections; there was a clamor for revenge.

It was a crucial moment in the history of Arizona. If General George Crook had followed the usual Army procedure, he would have taken his troopers and wiped out the Camp Date Indians. If he had been a little more merciful, he would have demanded the guilty men from the camp and been handed anyone the camp leaders wanted to get rid of.

Instead he used the incident to demonstrate what he had been telling every Indian he talked to: he was going to treat Indians, Anglos, and Mexicans all alike. If a man committed a crime, that man was going to be punished and no other.

It took weeks and months to ferret out the proper Indians to punish. Two passengers had survived the raid, a man and a woman, but they were not better than the average Anglo at telling one Indian from another.

Crook got hotter and hotter on the trail; one of the culprits left and went to California and passed for a Mexican to avoid arrest. The others decided to parley with Crook next time he came to Camp Date and murder him during the talk; each would have a carbine under his blanket, and the signal would be the rolling of a cigarette, a very un-Indian way of smoking. But the Hualpais heard about the scheme and told the general; they had become convinced that he was the man their country needed.

Crook came to the council fire, strolling casually, unarmed. His only military escort was one of his aides-de-camp – not Bourke – but a dozen of the civilian packers drifted up, armed with the revolvers and knives that were part of their everyday clothes.

The talk droned on, the signal man asked for tobacco, and then started to roll it, rather than put it into a pipe. At once the carbine appeared in the hands of the man next to Crook; the trigger was pulled, but the general's aide had knocked its muzzle up harmlessly. The packers fell on the Indians, the Indians grappled with the packers. Some of the Indians were killed, some wounded; a few escaped. They found their own people against them, however. Word was sent out from the tribal leaders that they would have to surrender.

There was no answer, so Crook sent out troopers of the 5th Cavalry, guided by Camp Date Indians; they surrounded the outlaw camp at the head of the Santa Maria River and captured or slaughtered the forty runagates. The Apache-Yumas made peace; the Hualpais already had; the Apache-Tontos followed suit.

Crook had everything in hand in Arizona except the Apache situation; Vincent Colyer was still talking, and the Army was still leashed. Down in southern Arizona, the Chiricahua Apaches in the Dragoon Mountains – named when Kearny and Cooke passed that way – amused themselves by sniping at the 3rd Cavalry garrison of Fort Bowie, killing a guide. Twenty-five miles from Tucson other Apaches killed a lieutenant of the 5th. Colyer went on talking.

Two months after the incident at Camp Date, Crook got the word to go pacify the Apaches. He moved out on November 15, 1872; this was late to campaign in the Arizona mountains; the line of march went across the Colorado Plateau, and most of the streams were frozen. Crook got his men up at two every morning and put them on the march by four; they moved until late afternoon, the troopers getting down to walk when the cold stopped the circulation in their feet.

At Camp Apache Crook enlisted scouts and then headed for Camp Grant. He was pushing hard; when the column got lost behind a peak, he kept it moving from six o'clock one morning till eight the next. Then he watched till the men put their animals out on graze, and while his scouts and troopers slept, he walked a mile or so up the river to shoot reed birds for the staff mess.

After picking up the 5th Cavalry garrison at Fort Grant, he proposed to make a clean sweep of the Tonto Basin. He used the converging column method here, a rare thing in the annals of Crook in the West. But the columns were not to depend on each other; each was completely supplied, completely independent, and completely able to handle any hostiles they flushed. Crook was not depending on a rendezvous between columns before fighting; he was, in effect, putting six separate armies into the field, each, of course, peacetime small.

Orders were to stick with any Tontos flushed and follow them till the horses gave out; then follow them on foot till the feet gave out; and then crawl after them.

If the center of the Basin – a vague point – was reached without contacting hostiles, the column was to turn back to its base and hunt in that direction. Any Indians who wanted to surrender instead of fight were to be taken at their word; Crook was violently eloquent on that point.

John Gregory Bourke is graphic, almost poetic, in describing the country; they would be in rich valleyland in the morning, on a snowy peak for the night, then down again. They flushed the *ranchería* of Chuntz, a Tonto leader whom Crook wanted for the murder of a Mexican boy, but Chuntz and his people escaped; the column burnt his winter supplies and shoved on.

On Christmas Day they joined up with another column of the 5th, which had had a little better hunting; they had burned a *ranchería*, killing six Tontos and capturing an Indian woman and a six year old boy, whom they had named Mike Burns, after their captain commanding. The outfit had adopted the boy, of course, and were delighted with his able use of the bow and arrow; even more useful was his ability to knock down quail with stones, since no game shooting was allowed.

Later Mike was sent East to Carlisle Indian School, where he received what Bourke called "the rudiments of an education"; Bourke and his general were opposed to sending Western Indians East, but thought they ought to be educated in their own country without losing contact with their own tribe and tribal ways. Sixty-odd years later the Indian Bureau finally came to the same conclusion.

Major Brown, in charge of the column, had a conference with Natanje, one of the Apache scouts, on December 27. Natanje said he was now convinced the Indians didn't have a chance against this calibre of troops, and he offered to lead Brown and his column to a Salt River cave where a large band of hostiles were holed up. But the trip had to be made by night; in daylight the cave was impregnable, and the column would be wiped out.

The less able of the command were left behind with the horses, mules, and supplies arranged in a combined breastwork and corral. The rest of the men inspected their guns and moved out, cartridge belts filled and twenty extra rounds wrapped in a blanket and slung over each man's shoulder. It was bitter cold. A mule had died in the night, and the Apache scouts cooked and ate it before leaving. The white soldiers each carried a little hardtack, bacon, and coffee.

Lights were seen ahead; the scouts fanned out to investigate, while the freezing troopers lay with their heads wrapped in their blankets, in fear of coughing up an alarm. The lights turned out to be from a four tepee

318

camp, abandoned by raiders returning from the Gila Valley; fifteen foot-sore horses and mules were recovered there.

Natanje led out with a vanguard of a lieutenant and about a dozen troopers, picked for being sharpshooters. The trail led down over slippery rock, with the Salt River rolling to one side, hundreds of feet below.

A terrible uproar, unidentifiable, was heard from the vanguard; the major ordered Bourke forward with the first forty men he could grab, scout or trooper. The frightful noise the column had heard had been a volley poured into the raiders as they danced a celebration of a successful foray. Six of the Tontos had been killed; and the rest had run for the cave where the main party was forted up. If they had stood and returned the fire of the vanguard they could have caused terrible damage; men poised on steep and slippery rocks are in no position to win a fire fight; but the cave had always meant safety, and they dove for it.

Their thinking was sound enough. The cave wasn't deep or large but naturally deposited high boulders in front of it made it almost impregnable; in fact, no force the Apache had ever seen this deep in the mountains could have done anything about it before the attackers' ammunition ran out.

But with the men that Bourke brought down, the advance party was now over fifty in number, each man with full cartridge belt and twenty extra rounds. They settled down to keeping the Apaches in their fort, as Major Brown had ordered them. One brave tried to make a run out, presumably to get help from other *rancherías* in the canyon; the troopers shot him dead at once. A Pima scout in Major Brown's party was killed almost on arrival, having exposed himself carelessly. All the other people in the column, troopers, Pimas, Apaches, took adequate cover behind rocks, and the siege was on. It was not the sort of situation in which the besiegers had it all their own way and could starve out the besieged. It was too cold, and the Army column had only scant supplies; but the Tontos had their whole winter's supply in the cave with them, including ample firewood. In other words, it was a siege in reverse; the insiders could starve out the outsiders.

The sheer numbers of the attackers brought victory. Brown placed all his men in careful cover and told them to fire at random at the ceiling of the cave; ricochets were sure to hit down among the Tontos.

First, of course, he tried having his interpreters ask the hostiles to surrender. All he got for that were cries of defiance; the cave had always been safe. The troopers and their Indian allies opened fire. The Tontos at first tried to draw the fire down from the roof by the old trick of putting hats or headdresses on the end of bows and shoving them above the rock barricade; when the attackers paid no attention to these classic lures, the cave defenders started firing arrows in mortar fashion, pointing them almost straight up in the air, so that at the end of a short, high flight they would come down on the Army's rearguard, where men could be presumed to be more careless of cover than up on the firing line. Only half of the troopers were firing; the others were held in reserve, in case of a charge out of the cave.

Brown had hoped that the ricocheting bullets would land among the braves, who could be presumed to be in the front of the cave, firing out or getting ready to fire if anybody tried to scale the rocks. But when the wails of a squaw and baby were heard, he called a cease-fire, and again asked the Tontos to surrender.

For a minute or so it seemed that they might; there was silence in the cave. Then one of the Apache scouts, excitedly yelled to the troopers to look out; the Tontos had started singing their death chant and were certainly going to charge.

About twenty of them did, splitting into two parties, half the braves trying to pin down the attackers while the other half flanked the holed-up Army people. The troopers charged out of their shelters, and about six Tontos were killed before the charge was abandoned and the survivors retreated back into the cliff dwelling.

But one of the Apaches had gotten away unnoticed. He slipped between the rocks and suddenly appeared just behind the troopers' firing line, where he jumped up and started whooping, evidently asking for cover from the cave while he attacked the firing line from the rear. He was right between the skirmish line and the men held in reserve; the rearguard men wiped him out.

Brown brought up his reserve and the fire against the roof of the cave doubled; so did the whooping and war chanting from inside the shelter. A little Apache boy came out, sucking his thumb, to stare at the intruders; a spent ricochet creased his skull and knocked him down and Natanje, the scout, ran out and scooped the child up and carried him to safety in the Army line. The men cheered and went back to shooting.

When relief came, it was not for the Tontos. Burns's company of troopers, together with some Pimas, had been backtracking the ponies found earlier in the morning. Hearing the firing, their captain had brought them back up the mountain. They came out above the cave, looked over the crest, and saw what was going on.

Burns had four of his men take off their broad suspenders and make harnesses for two others, who leaned far enough out – held by three sets of suspenders each – to fire down at the cave. But the men he had selected were Irish, as was so much of the enlisted force, and when their revolvers clicked empty, they lost their tempers and threw the guns down on the cave people. So, Burns had them pulled back in, and set his company to throwing down rocks instead of GI guns.

The falling boulders landed in the only part of the cave safe from the ricochets, the very front, where men could huddle behind the rock barricade.

After awhile Brown signaled to Burns to hold his rocks and ordered another cease-fire from the original attackers. There was absolute silence from the cave.

The troopers went forward, helping each other up the natural barricade; Bourke wrote that they had the feeling they were entering a cemetery. To their absolute amazement, however, there were over thirty survivors. Some of the squaws had made shelters out of stone metates that the Apache use for rolling out bread or for grinding seeds and grain and acorns; others had made bulletproof shelters for themselves and their children out of the dead bodies of their men. Only one man was still conscious; all the other braves were dead or knocked out. Half of the so-called survivors had mortal wounds and died shortly after the firing stopped.

The cave was found supplied with jerked meat – probably mule, perhaps horse – roasted mescal, seeds for grinding, and an abundance of ammunition and guns and bows and arrows. The Indian scouts were told to take what they wanted, and the rest was burned.

The only man buried was the Pima scout; the Tontos were left where they had died. The eighteen women and children who lived were put on the recaptured ponies and sent out to Camp Grant. Bourke says they could have saved more of the wounded if they had had any sort of medical supplies with them; but Arizona was then considered so far from civilization and such an unhealthy place to live that the Army could not get medical officers for the troops there.

The Battle of the Cave was a big one; other encounters with the Apaches went on through the winter. In April Crook was satisfied that he had thrashed all the hostiles around except Cochise's band, then in the Dragoons. Despite Hollywood's rewriting of history, Crook considered Cochise's people as bad a band of hostiles as Arizona has known. Crook brought all his forces together and prepared to start after Cochise.

But General Oliver Otis Howard had been sent out to Arizona, with stronger powers than Vincent Colyer had had, and before Crook could take the warpath, Howard made a deal with the Indian leader, giving him all the Dragoon and Huachuca Mountains for a reservation. Crook wrote in his autobiography that the tactic arrangement was that Cochise would confine his raiding to Mexico and use the reservation for a sanctuary; Crook considered Howard a weakling and a fool, but not even the man who had just made an unholy mess as head of the Freedmen's Bureau in the South could have been silly enough to make that kind of a deal with a hostile Indian chief.

John Gregory Bourke had a different version of the Cochise affair, but it must be remembered that Bourke was still in his twenties and only a second lieutenant at the time. He was not in on the highest councils. He felt that Cochise really meant to go off the warpath, but that when the Army was ordered to leave him alone because of his treaty with Howard, white bootleggers moved in and corrupted Cochise's braves.

At any rate, the double jurisdiction – Howard over Cochise and the Chiricahuas who followed him; Crook over all the other Indians – didn't work out. Crook put his thoroughly whipped Indians to work, at San Carlos and Camp Verde. He gave them condemned – almost wornout, in Army language – tools and had them dig an irrigation ditch at Camp Verde.

The ditch was five miles long and four feet wide; all the Indians camped along it, by bands, and each man dug with what he was given – an old file, a hammer with one prong broken off, a shovel with a hole in it, a camp kettle that leaked, or just a fire-sharpened stick. When it was dug, the Apaches were irrigating Indians, and Crook took their chiefs up to Fort Whipple to meet the heads of tribes that had always irrigated – Maricopa, Pima, Papago, Yuma, and so on. The Apaches shortly had fifty-seven acres under ditch and planted to melons and other delicacies familiar to their own diet; corn and barley would go in next.

The cavalry officers were particularly proud of the large water wheel they built at a total cost of thirty-six dollars; the wood came out of old packing boxes.

Crook's idea was that the Apache would become a farmer if he was paid cash for his crops; the government was buying supplies to feed the treaty Indians; why not buy them from the Indians themselves? It was cheaper than freighting food to the reservations and much cheaper than mounting constant Indian wars. But the contractors who had been selling supplies to the Indian Bureau saw nothing except profits lost; and the Indian Bureau officials frequently owned part or all of the contracting and trading companies.

Pressure was put on President Grant, his Secretaries of War and Interior, on the Commissioner of Indian Affairs. It is possible that pressure did not have to be applied to all of them; Secretary of War William W. Belknap resigned in 1876 under charges of corruption.

Crook was ordered to move the Apaches to the mouth of the San Carlos River, which Bourke describes as a "sickly" place. It is now under the backup of Coolidge Dam. Crook said there was malaria there, and that his mountain Indians couldn't stand the dust at San Carlos. Besides they were doing so well – in addition to the work at Verde, Apaches at Camp Apache had raised two hundred and fifty tons of corn and fifteen tons of beans, farming with burnt sticks and condemned hoes.

But the Indians were not under Army jurisdiction until they went to war; the Apaches were removed to San Carlos, except for Diablo's band which threatened to die sooner than move. These were left at Camp Apache.

Crook bought horses from Arizona and paid off his scouts in them, so that they would have something to show for their work and their fighting. He mentions in this connection that the Apache was *not* a horse Indian; he was too often in the mountains to use horses. The Apaches' own name for themselves is "men of the woods"; it is the Reservation system that has made them into desert Indians.

The Chiricahuas, due to the Howard-Colyer treaty, were not under the Army; they were to be treated separately, and not by Crook under any circumstance. This caused all kinds of trouble; when he got the other Apaches working and making money, wild Chiricahuas would come down and taunt them for living like women. On the other hand, sensible Chiricahuas would see which way destiny was taking Arizona and would infiltrate his working bands and pretend to be members of tame bands. Crook would pretend not to notice; of course, he knew, but he couldn't say so.

For this was Crook's greatest strength. Other Army officers, other government men, saw Indians as a mass; a friendly Pawnee was little different from a hostile Sioux, and a Cheyenne who was trying to make up his mind about his attitude toward the whites was very likely to be suddenly seized and punished for something a Kiowa had done.

Crook not only knew the difference between an Apache and a Pirna, but he knew the difference between a White Water Apache and a Chiricahua; and then he went on to know as much as was possible about each individual Chiricahua. As a result, he could fight an almost Mosby-type battle; he had men friendly to him inside every hostile camp, most of the time. When he didn't he had men who were neutral toward him and respected him. When the hostiles were being driven hard they would counsel the wilder men to give in to Crook, knowing he would be as lenient as possible, and that he would never punish one man for something another had done. Bourke's books, and even Crook's badly written fragment of an autobiography, are full of the names of individual Indians.

However, individual enlisted men did not impress Bourke, unless they were non-commissioned and killed. He regarded them as a bunch of comic micks, apparently; his Irish-Catholic parents from Galway had been in the United States eight years when he was born in 1846, and he seems to have had the scorn for an immigrant that only a second-generation American of the same origin can have.

Once on reservations, the Indians flourished amazingly; they not only raised their own supplies, but accumulated surpluses they could sell in such Arizona towns as Globe, where the decent people of the town saw that the Indians were paid decent prices and given decent weights in the stores.

There were breakouts, of course. Delt-chay (or Del-tche), the Red Ant, nicknamed the Liar, broke out of Verde while Crook was at Prescott; the general wired – with peace he had been able to build and maintain a military telegraph line – Lieutenant Schuyler at Verde to smoke signal the Red Ant to come back to camp. He came back.

But later Delt-chay broke out again and led a band into the mountains; and the Apaches at the miserable San Carlos Agency went on the warpath into the San Pedro Valley and started murdering and robbing the ranches there.

Crook sent troops after the San Carlos Indians and told the Apaches themselves to bring him the head of Delt-chay and his co-leaders. The troopers caught up with the San Carlos people, killed some, and accepted the surrender of the others.

The Apaches brought in the required heads, and one over; Crook wrote drily that Delt-chay had two heads, one at Verde and one at San Carlos. Unable to decide which was authentic, he paid for both grisly trophies.

Crook parleyed with the renegade San Carlos band. He told them that since they had surrendered, he could not kill them out of hand; but he proposed to give them a headstart, drive them into the mountains, and there slaughter them in a fair fight.

They begged to be allowed to stay on the Reservation; finally, he graciously forgave them. That, Crook said, "about quieted them."

There were small forays; Crook took each one seriously, knowing that the peace of the whole Arizona Apache nation depended on his punishing the smallest infraction. He had to send out two parties, mostly scouts, to track down and massacre a band of Indians – men, women, children – for murdering a single man near Wickenburg. The other Apaches did not resent this.

He found out that the hostiles, few as they were, were being sold ammunition by the Hopis; he took Bourke and went up into the Hopi country and "the fright we gave them put an end to it."

The Apaches – except for Cochise and the Chiricahuas – were at peace; the Tucson Ring and the Indian Bureau were not. The Hualpais complained that they were starving. Crook sent Captain Beale up and the captain found out that a family supposed to draw ninety-five pounds of beef was actually getting fifteen. Beale took over the weighing of the rations himself; the Indian Superintendent screamed at this interference in Interior matters by a soldier. A court of inquiry was held, and it was learned that the Indians' supplies had been sold to mining camps for the credit of the superintendent.

Crook was home safe on that one. But he could do nothing when the Interior ordered all the prosperous Verde Indians to move to San Carlos; he moved them.

In the spring of 1875 Crook, who had made permanent brigadier general a year and a half before, was relieved of his duties as commander of the

Department of Arizona and ordered to take over the Department of the Platte. The Sioux and Cheyenne were giving trouble.

The Platte department was part of the Division of the Missouri, Lieutenant General Phil Sheridan commanding. On the way there, Crook attended Sheridan's wedding in June 1875 to Irene Rucker, the daughter of General D.H. Rucker, later to be Quartermaster General of the U.S. Army.

Bourke seems to feel there was still coolness against Sheridan on the part of Crook, that Crook continued to feel that Sheridan had kept him from making full colonel after the war, though two of Crook's subordinates, Gregg and A.J. Smith, had gotten the grade. Looking back, it is probable that these were seniority grades; both John Gregg and Andrew Jackson Smith had been in the Mexican War, six years before Crook got out of West Point. Now Sheridan had sent for his old division commander when the Plains started to boil. There had been a gold strike in the Black Hills, and prospectors were pouring into the Sioux reservation; the treaty signed with the Sioux was being broken daily.

Crook's orders were to get the miners off the reservation and to destroy their guns, wagons and supplies. It was an assignment calling for tact; Sheridan had had experience with the coolness of Crook's head, a quality that Little Phil did not share.

The Northern Plains had never been really quiet since the Iowa-Colorado-Kansas State troops had left. General Grenville M. Dodge was building a railroad – an occupation he had given up for a few years to become a war hero, and commander, toward the end of the war, of the Department of the Missouri. The road is now the Union Pacific, and it was built under attack by hostiles, Dodge himself getting blasted at least once.

There was the gold strike, already mentioned, and there were hunters mowing down buffalo with swivel guns in order to strip them of their hides and leave the good Indian meat on the prairie to rot. It has been estimated, and unchallenged, that the kill was about two million in each of the years from '71 to '73.

Besides the Sioux and Cheyenne, always hostile those days, the Pawnees, Arapahoes, Utes, Bannocks, and Shoshone hovered on the knife edge between friendship and war with the whites. The last three tribes were mountain people, but Indians as far from the Plains as the Rio Grande Pueblos made annual expeditions to stock up on buffalo meat, to be smoked or jerked or sun-dried for the winter.

It was a good time for Phil Sheridan to bring his classmate in. The Regulars who had taken over from the State and Territorial troops were no better than the amateurs at telling one Indian from another; Crook's peculiar – in the sense of personal – talent for impressing and analyzing individual Indians was about the only weapon that could be used – especially when it was coupled with his driving method of using a cavalry on a continuous pursuit, rather than in intermittent forays.

A Sioux chief named Crazy Horse had killed an incompetent and inexperienced officer by the name of William Judd Fetterman in 1866, along with Fetterman's party of eighty men. This was on the Bozeman Trail, laid out by Colonel Andrew Carrington, of the infantry, that year. The next year a woodcutting guard of thirty-two infantrymen stood off an estimated fifteen hundred hostiles by forting up behind the wagons and holding their fire till the Indians were almost upon them; this seems to have influenced the Army into thinking that a good defense constituted an offense, and the Plains Indians got more and more out of hand.

In July Crook took a small party into the Black Hills, and "circulated around," in his own words, among the trespassing miners, explaining to them that he felt bad about it; but they had to get off the Sioux land. Some of the miners left; others stayed, constantly harassed by military patrols.

Then Colonel R.I. Dodge, an infantry officer but commanding six full companies of the 2nd and 3rd Cavalry as well as some infantry and artillery, went into the country ostensibly as guard and guide for a party of Interior geologists and engineers. This was a strong force; hardly any miners stayed on the reservation.

But, on Crook's advice, the departing miners had left their claims clearly staked, in case the government decided that they could come back. The Sioux and their allies the Cheyenne saw these stakes and felt that they meant that it was only a matter of time before the valleys of the Belle Fourche, their traditional cornfields, were taken from them.

The inconsistency of the Indian policy in Washington was never more clearly shown up as idiotic and inconsistent. Down in Arizona, Crook had turned nomad warlike Apaches into peaceful farmers. Here in the Plains the Sioux themselves wanted to farm, but the government, whose Indian agents were constantly trying to make farmers out of belligerently anti-farm people like the Utes, kept interfering with the Apaches and Sioux and moving them where subsistence farming was virtually impossible.

In the fall of 1875 Washington sent out a commission; the chairman was a civilian, but Brigadier General Alfred H. Terry, commander of the Department of the Dakotas, was a member.

The Indians came to the conference in a belligerent mood. One chief, Little Big Man, was for murdering the commissioners on the spot. The single company of cavalry guarding the parley was suddenly thrown into line with carbines at the ready; Little Big Man quieted down and turned the talk over to Spotted Tail.

Crook had apparently made friends with this respected Sioux Chief, whom he called Old Spot in his autobiography. Spotted Tail announced calmly that any Indians who wanted a fight could fight him and his band. The conference broke up in idle boasting and chatter, and Crook noted that the commissioners were glad to get away, and "didn't recover their courage till they got the Missouri River between them."

Early in 1876, before the winter had really broken, Crook took to the field with six companies of cavalry. They worked up into the Powder River country, were snowed into their blankets for twenty-four hours by a buzzard and then, as they worked from the Tongue toward the Powder River itself, spotted two sets of Indian tracks.

Crook ordered Joseph Jones Reynolds, colonel of the 3rd Cavalry, to take half the column and backtrack the bucks, who were either out hunting or were scouting Crook's march.

Reynolds was a friend of Crook's, and Reynolds was in some sort of trouble with the brass; he had general's brevets, and had recently commanded the Department of Texas, but had then been ordered back to his regiment; it was not customary for full colonels actually to command regiments – though they were carried on the rolls as regimental commanders – in the depleted Army of the postwar '60s and the early '70s.

This was General Reynolds' chance to do something outstanding. Crook stayed behind to guard the packtrains; the mules' shoes had worn so slick that he was afraid to take the animals into hostile and probably rough country. Bourke says that the country, if it had been in Arizona, would have been called rolling mesa.

There were ample half-breed scouts along with Reynolds, as well as Frank Gruard (or Grouard), a Hawaiian plainsman, who was very good at guiding and scouting and believed by the Plains Indians to be some sort of an Indian himself.

Bourke went along, apparently as an observer; he rode with a newspaper correspondent named Strahorn and with Hospital Steward Bryan. He reported that the going was rough, with lots of natural ditches to be slid down into and arduously climbed out of again; water was frozen over two or three feet deep, so that the horses could not be watered; but the horses were eager, and they made good time.

A smoke was sighted, and Frank Gruard scouted out; but it was a burning coal deposit, not an uncommon thing in that country. Gruard scouted out again and came back reporting a big Indian village at the base of a cliff; it was flanked and protected by bluffs.

Reynolds ordered one company – Bourke calls them battalions, but Crook says companies – to make a revolver charge into the village and then split, one half to keep the braves pinned in their tepees, the other half to run off the pony herd. A second company was to move in as an occupation force, fanning out and destroying all the Indian tents and their contents. The third outfit was to occupy the bluffs and prevent the Indians from fleeing to them and turning to harass the troops in the village.

An officer named Teddy Egan led the charge; Bourke and his little group of non-combatants rode with him. They came upon the village in a column of twos, wheeled left front into line and charged at a trot until they reached the first tepee; then they picked up into a gallop.

An Indian boy, taking horses to water in the early dawn, saw them and gave the war whoop; a squaw come out of her tepee and stared, and stray ponies started trotting away from the charging soldiers.

Then the bullets started coming at them, and the troopers fired back. The hostiles ran for the bluffs, turning every few paces to fire back with their Winchesters; they aimed at the cavalry horses, rather than the raiders. Several horses went down, one pinning a blacksmith under it, and Bourke's bridle line was cut clean by a bullet.

But the Indians – there were both Sioux and Cheyennes in the village – were horseback fighters, and they had been cut off from their herd. Less than forty men had been in the charge; six horses and three men were wounded almost at once, but the wounded men were not on the wounded horses. Then a private was killed, and Egan dismounted his men and took cover in the wild plum trees that edged the frozen Powder River.

The rearguard, or occupying, force moved out toward the bluffs to give a crossfire; the company sent there had never shown up, and the Indians were forting up behind the rocks on the bluffs. The troopers could not hold out long; they had dropped their heavy robes and greatcoats at the edge of the village to free their arms for the pistol charge, and frostbite was hitting hard; the Hospital Steward went around and dabbed iodine on the frozen flesh.

The soldiers had set fire to the tepees, and now these began to explode; powder was stored in every one. The eighteen-foot lodge-poles would fly in the air and then come crashing down; but none of the invaders were hit by them.

This was the village of Crazy Horse, the Oglala Sioux who was to help Sitting Bull kill Custer before the year was out. The camp was as richly supplied as any on the Plains: ample ammunition, dried and fresh meat, hardware, saddles and a profusion of richly ornamented clothing and blankets.

Everything was going the Army's way, when Reynolds ordered a retreat. Bourke could never figure out why. Reynolds could have fortified the town and sent for Crook and the rest of the column. A lot of the ponies got back into Indian hands, but the braves driving some of them ran into Crook and lost them again.

The two Army parties came together where Lodge Pole Creek flows into the Powder. Crook preferred charges of misbehavior in the presence of the enemy against Reynolds, and two of the captains commanding companies (or battalions). The confusion as to just what an outfit was came about from the small size of the Army; on a single page Crook calls Reynolds a general, a captain, and a colonel.

Before Crook got to them, Reynolds' exhausted men lost more ponies to the Indians; the cold, the fight, the hard march had made it impossible to keep an adequate herd guard going; more then seven hundred ponies had been taken.

Crook ordered a turnback to old Fort Reno, about ninety miles away. The Indians harassed their march, still trying to recover the ponies; Crook ordered the Indian horses killed; this not only removed the temptation from the marauders but provided food for the starving troopers.

Reynolds' indecision and retreat, his captain's failure to occupy the high ground around the village, seemed to cause the Army to lose face on the Plains; more and more bands of Sioux and Cheyennes went off on the warpath to join the hostiles.

Sheridan ordered both the Department of the Platte and that of the Dakotas to put all their troops in the field and run down the renegades. Terry commanded the Dakotas; Custer was in command of the 7th Cavalry at Fort Abraham Lincoln, Dakota Territory. Custer had commanded a division under Sheridan when Crook had a similar job. Crook had very little use for the gaudy boy-general; at Sailor's Creek, back in Virginia during the war, he commented that Custer ordered his division to charge: "His bands struck up, ... but not to exceed 300 men broke cover ... Nothing was accomplished ... As soon as the enemy hoisted the white flag, General Custer's division rushed up the hill, and turned in more prisoners and battle flags than any of the cavalry, and probably had less to do with their surrender than any of the rest of us."

George Armstrong Custer was not at his post of Fort Lincoln when Crook sent Reynolds out to regain his prestige. The yellow-haired general – no longer a boy in 1876 at the age of thirty-six – was back East, reminding the public that they loved him, bragging that his 7th Cavalry could lick all the Indians in the world, infuriating President Grant with charges of corruption against Grant's relatives, and generally behaving like anything but a lieutenant colonel of frontier troops.

But on May 10 Custer got back to Fort Lincoln, court-martial and cashiering hanging over him for insubordination. His whole 7th were in camp around the fort, a very rare thing; the Army was so small that every regiment ordinarily had a few companies out on detached duty; many garrisons were only one company strong.

Custer had been conditionally released from a hearing in Washington to take the field under General Terry. His orders specifically stated that he was not to take any correspondents out on his expedition; but of course, he had a couple of newspapermen in his entourage; without publicity, he would not be Custer.

Before the big, combined campaign could get under way – and an old staff slogan was: Combinations seldom work – Crook moved out with his own troopers. The situation had gotten almost unbearable. The Union Pacific, completed a few years before, was under almost daily attack; Red Cloud lost his son-in-law in one raid, ample proof that senior and widely followed Indians were involved, and that these weren't sporadic attacks by young bucks with spring fever. Late in May Crook went on the march with fifteen companies of cavalry and five of infantry.

Before he went, he had gone to Red Cloud Agency and talked to some of the Indian chiefs, in line with his lifelong policy of going to any pains to distinguish one Indian from another. Such important men as Rocky Bear, Three Bears and an old sachem called Sitting Bull of the South attended. Crook told them that the Sioux and Cheyenne were a rich people, heavy with ponies and other valuable goods; if they went to war they would lose these, even if they won a few early battles.

The chiefs agreed with him. Sitting Bull (whom Bourke says was as good as the other Sitting Bull was bad) said that while he couldn't take the field himself, because of age, there were thirty-five or forty of his young braves available to help Crook against any hostiles who fought the government.

But the Indian Bureau functionaries were still around. The Sioux Agent, Hastings, tried to forbid the chiefs from helping the Army; it was not until Custer was dead and Crook was campaigning in the fall that the three men he had talked to at Red Cloud could get scouts to him to help him. Then they were the greatest help a general could ask for.

There were five national war correspondents with Crook as he crossed the Platte with his twenty companies of men, his more than a hundred wagons, his hundreds of pack mules; the expedition was as well-covered as any military move since the Civil War. The drowning of a teamster named Dill was immortalized by hundreds of expensive words. John Finerty of Chicago later published his Crook annals as a book.

Every morning the infantry moved out at four o'clock; the cavalry grazed their horses on the spring grass before the frost was off it, then caught up. Precautions against a stampede of the horse herd were thorough; mounted guards rode round and round the grazing animals, while whole companies did point duty out a ways, ready to turn any kind of a run started by Indian charges.

Frank Gruard, the Hawaiian frontiersman, had gone off to find the Crows who were supposed to scout for Crook. He got to the Crow encampment, where he was nearly shot as a Sioux, and recruited a hundred and twenty-five men, who came reluctantly; they said that their women and children would be massacred if the Sioux found out that the Crows were helping Crook. Gruard pointed out that if the white man was driven off the prairie the Sioux would massacre their hereditary enemies anyway; so, the young men went with him, under the leadership of an old chief. But on the way to rejoin Crook, Gruard came upon one of the expedition's abandoned camps; the Crows saw it as a field from which Crook had been routed, and hurried back to protect their families. Gruard came into Crook's camp with just the old chief. The Army column had been strengthened by a party of sixty-five Montana miners, extremely prairie-wise men, who joined on as volunteers.

On June 9 Crook got to the Tongue River and camped; then his lines were attacked by a party of Sioux and Cheyenne. Crook had expected this; Crazy Horse had warned him not to go as far as the Tongue. The attack was energetic, but not too serious; only a bluff to show that Crazy Horse would keep his word, according to Bourke. The hostiles forted up in the rocks from which they had driven in Crook's pickets, and poured rifle fire into the camp, aiming at the white tents. But the troopers weren't in their tents just then; the damage was mostly to stoves, canvas, ridge poles, and wagon tailboards. Three rifle companies of the infantry and four companies of the 2nd and 3rd Cavalry routed the hostiles. Two troopers received glancing bullets, not serious, and three horses and two mules were shot; most of the five later died.

Crook moved on to the forks of Goose Creek, where the grass was better. The expedition crossed the camp of the Crows. Gruard's friend, the old chief, was sent to parley for Crook; a Major Burt was made commander of a good-sized detachment of Crow warriors, with "grotesque head-dresses, variegated garments, wild little ponies, and war-like accoutrements," according to Bourke.

On June 14 eighty-six of the hundred and twenty-five Shoshone scouts Crook had been promised arrived. Gruard had found fresh hostile sign, and Crook marched toward the Rosebud, where the hostiles were understood to be camped in force. The wagon train was left behind.

Crook would have been happier to have Sioux or Cheyenne scouts, as well as Shoshones and Crows, who could not possibly know the plans of the hostiles, but only their past behavior. But the Indian Bureau had blocked the Sioux who wanted to help the Army.

A hundred and seventy-five of the infantrymen had decided to join the cavalry. That many mules were taken from the pack-train and for an hour on the next day (June 15) the camp was amused by the meeting between inexperienced riders and equally inexperienced saddle animals.

The Shoshone and Crow reported that they had located a big herd of buffalo dead ahead, and that the buffalo were acting as though they were moving away from a large Sioux hunting party. Crook took them at their word, at once; he had never found an Indian wrong in such matters, and he was accustomed to Indians telling the truth. He told his copper-skinned allies to deploy at will; this was a business they'd been born to, but he had had to learn. The camp ate fresh buffalo that night of June 16.

The next day Bourke was out on scout with some of the Crows; the general's aide was as fond of Indians as the general. Suddenly shots were heard; two of the Crows, one badly wounded, rode back in from the vanguard, crying: "Sioux, Sioux," as loud as they could.

The scouts rode in to Crook; the Shoshones, two companies of infantry, and some dismounted cavalry moved out to the left of the column, where there was high ground to be taken.

Crazy Horse, in command of the Sioux, later surrendered to Crook, and told him what the Indian plan had been that day on the Rosebud. Crazy Horse had led sixty-five hundred warriors; but he had only thrown fifteen hundred at Crook, a force no larger than Crook's.

This initial contact would – if Crook behaved as other Army men had – break the Army forces up into small detachments, each chasing a fragment of the fifteen hundred braves; after a while, each fragment would turn, engage the troopers, and get enough re-enforcement to wipe out the pursuers.

If, on the other hand, Crook used the principle of mass and power which the Sioux leaders well understood, he would throw his whole twenty companies, his Shoshones and his Crows after the equal force of fifteen hundred Sioux-Cheyenne, who would slowly withdraw into the canyon of the Rosebud, walled by sheer cliffs and blocked by a debris dam piled up by the spring freshets. Then the five thousand unengaged hostiles would box the column in from the rear and wipe it out.

But this was Crook they were fighting, not Custer or Nelson Miles. Crook put a big clump of horseholders in the bottom of a ravine, where they could be seen by the pony-hungry Indians; the hostiles charged down the ravine whooping, and the dismounted cavalry and infantry and Shoshones rose from their cover on the high ground and volleyed down on them; the long rifles of the infantry were particularly effective.

The Sioux whipped their ponies out of there as fast as they could gallop, turned and re-formed behind a ridge about three hundred yards away, and sniped back at the snipers. Then the hostiles thought they saw a weak spot in the Army to be met by a countercharge of the Shoshones, who galloped in close and then mostly dismounted to fire.

But the Sioux were dressed so much like the Crows – who were attacking the hostiles on the other flank, a thing the Shoshone couldn't know – that the ally-Indians couldn't accomplish the slaughter they might have; Crows and Shoshone were allies, and a mistake could lead to a disastrous feud.

Crook continued to thicken his line, the Indian allies and the infantry fighting in from the flanks, as he advanced. The whole Sioux-Cheyenne body turned into a rearguard, fighting backwards for seven miles before they pulled off for the day.

A dozen of Crook's men were dead; the Shoshones and Crows had taken that many scalps, and a number of Sioux and Cheyennes had been seen leading wounded or dead men out of the fight; the Plains Indians – most Indians, in fact – never abandoned their dead if they could possibly help it.

Two days later Crook was back at his wagon train camp, which had been heavily breastworked by the officer left in charge, a Major Furey. Wagons were sent back to Fort Fetterman with the wounded, under orders to return with fresh supplies for the column. The Shoshones and Crows went home long enough to show the hostile scalps and have a dance of celebration with their people; Crook said he would wait where he was for them.

No word had been received from Terry and the Department of the Dakotas; Crook could not tell whether the other arm of the great Sioux-killing pincers was moving or not

It was – at last. It had taken longer to get the 7th Cavalry together than had been planned; they were just about moving out of Fort Abraham Lincoln while Crook was fighting on the Rosebud.

The Battle of the Rosebud wasn't a triumph, but it wasn't a rout. Crook, in his report, didn't brag about it, but he did point out that by War Department standards he had won; the Indians had been driven off a battleground of their own choosing. The latter-day charge that it was Rosebud that kept Crook from joining Custer doesn't hold up. The loss o£ twelve or thirteen men wouldn't slow him down. The truth was that he was out of supplies because the treaty with the Sioux in 1867 had caused the abandonment of the outpost forts in the Sioux-Cheyenne country. Also, Crook had received nothing but Sioux rumors concerning Terry's plans.

While he waited for fresh supplies, Crook did get some news; the 5th Cavalry had moved up to the Red Cloud Agency as a reserve, and Rutherford B. Hayes had been nominated for the presidency on the Republican ticket. Hayes had been a brigade commander under Crook; William McKinley had been a Crook staff officer, but Crook was to die six years before McKinley became President.

If Crook had known where Terry or Custer were, he could have gotten to them in time; it is about fifty miles from the battlefield of the Rosebud to that of the Little Big Horn, and the battles were a week apart. Crook had shoved unsupplied troops before and was to do so again. But a week after Custer died on June 25, Crook was still trying to get intelligence; he and his aides and some correspondents including John Finerty were out at the beginning of July hunting and trying to get some information about the Army from the Department of the Dakotas.

Frank Gruard was scouting to the northwest, where smokes had been reported. Bourke always thought that one of the smokes was that of Custer's battle; distance would have made it appear no more than the pall over a large group of Indian cooking fires. Gruard returned to camp – which was moving steadily along the Tongue – about the same time Crook did, and at Crook's request took off toward the Big Horn with a guard of 2nd Cavalry troopers and a lieutenant; he proposed to make a light, quick scout in depth. Finerty went along.

At the head of the Little Big Horn they were hit by a monstrously large party of hostile Sioux and Cheyenne. Several of the Army horses and one mule were shot and crippled when they reared in answer to the hundred-round volleys that the Indians poured in on the column. But Frank Gruard slipped his escort away, after killing White Antelope, a Cheyenne chief, and the expedition got back to Crook alive, though two of the young troopers had gone completely insane from fear and hardship.

Couriers and mountain men and the like kept coming into camp with wild rumors about Terry, Gibbon, and Custer; but all of these came through the Department of the Platte country, second- or third-hand. Bourke reports that Crook was worried about Terry's silence but would not admit it to anyone; we can suppose that the aide knew his general well enough to read his thoughts. In any event, under the excuse of hunting meat for the mess, Crook constantly climbed the peaks along the Tongue, from which he could see for a hundred miles; but he saw nothing.

Terry had come up to the Custer battlefield, relieved Major Marcus A. Reno, Custer's second-in-command, and sent the wounded back down the river by boat; they got to Fort Lincoln on the 3rd of July. The hostiles had pulled off as soon as they saw Terry's heavy column re-enforce Reno's survivors of the 7th Cavalry.

A week later dispatches from Sheridan, at Department headquarters, reached Crook and told him of Custer's defeat. The same day the Sioux-Cheyenne forces began trying to burn Crook out with prairie fires. They kept this up for two weeks; the pickets were sure that some of the hostiles were killed or at least wounded, and one body was found later. The fires put a barren circle, a hundred miles in radius all around Crook; but he had corn for his horses and survived until cloudbursts stopped the harassment.

The Shoshones, under the Chief Washakie, rejoined Crook. Two days after he heard about Custer (from Chicago) three enlisted men of the 7th Infantry slipped into camp across the charred and hostile-thick country, with the first dispatches from Terry that Crook had received. The next day the supply train came in, bringing orders from Sheridan; Crook was to hold up until Merritt, of the 5th, could join him with ten companies of troopers.

Crook started drilling his troops. Washakie had already taught some maneuvers to his Shoshones; they could go from columns of two front or left front into line. The chief wanted to keep up this drill but was afraid that pickets and sentries might mistake his Snakes for Cheyennes or Sioux; so, Bourke rode at the head of the wild column, to identify it as friendly, and enjoyed himself terrifically; the Shoshones were reckless riders.

Crow couriers came in from Terry, repeating what had happened in sign language, and carrying the identical message Terry had sent by his enlisted men; he had feared that only one of the several couriers would get through. Crook sent a miner named Kelly down the river to Terry; he was turned back twice and made it on the third attempt.

Crook also sent out heavy scouting parties, one of them completely Shoshone, to determine how many hostiles there were on the prairie. Washakie confirmed the fact that Crook was heavily outnumbered and should wait for Merritt.

On August 3, Crook moved out across the burned prairie to a rendezvous point on Goose Creek. Merritt was waiting for him with his ten companies of the 5th Cavalry, replacement recruits for the 2nd and 3rd, surplus horses and ample ammunition.

This was Wesley Merritt, Major General of Volunteers in the Civil War, another old Sheridan man, who had commanded a corps in the war, more than Crook had done; he was not colonel of the 5th. Bourke speaks of him as a "very young man," but he was forty, only eight years younger than Crook and five years younger than Sheridan. Bourke himself was thirty.

The column was no longer independent; it had become what it started out to be, the southern arm of the Yellowstone Expedition, commanded by Terry, who was with the northern arm.

The general aim was, as it had been at the beginning before the Custer fiasco broke things up, to pincer the hostile Sioux-Cheyenne between two heavy forces – Crook alone had two thousand men – and end the Plains troubles once and for all. But too much time had slipped by; the hostiles had broken into two columns of their own, one trying for Canada, the other slipping back into the Black Hills, now, more than ever before, thick with prospectors and miners.

Crook knew that the hostiles wouldn't be to the northwest any more; there wouldn't be enough grass there to keep their ponies going. Wiring Sheridan that he feared the Indians had scattered, he started backtracking, down the Tongue and toward the Rosebud country, where he hoped he'd get a fight.

The expedition found the valley of the Rosebud picked clean; it had been a garden when they had marched up it earlier in the year. They also found the evidence of the trap Crazy Horse had set for Crook; and there they hit a trail only ten or twelve days old; Frank Gruard said it had been made by ten or twenty thousand ponies.

Crook pushed on. But on August 11 his vanguard rode into that of Major Reno, now riding spearpoint for Terry. The pincers had come together, but there was nothing in the jaws.

Terry brought very little cavalry to the meeting; a few companies of the 2nd, and the sad remnant of the 7th. He had good infantry, however.

Crook used his own scouts, his trusted Indians mostly, and found three hostile trails; one went up the Tongue, one down, and the third struck across country toward the Powder, to the east.

Further scouting indicated that the eastward trail was the heaviest traveled; the column followed it, now four thousand strong, somewhat deficient in pack animals. Crook's train was fine, but Terry had had to make do with heavy wagon animals, and Bourke said that they lost or destroyed more in a day than was true of Crook's finely trained mules – "as well-trained as any soldiers in the command" – on the whole campaign.

They marched to the Powder and down it to the Yellowstone; the only hostiles they had seen were rattlesnakes, which the Shoshones gleefully lanced from horseback. After a while the Indian scouts left Crook and went home. Terrible rain, hail, thunder, and lightning made the soldiers' lives miserable. Terry and Crook separated; Terry lent Crook some of his Ree scouts to take the place of the departed Shoshone and Crows.

In the last week of August Crook came out of the burned prairie east of O'Fallon's Creek, about fifty miles into Wyoming from North Dakota. The month went out with a night so cold that the men, in soaked summer clothing, nearly froze to death. They were now on Beaver Creek, or thereabouts, which drains into the Little Missouri; on September 4 they hit the river valley proper, and Frank Gruard was sure that the hostiles were dead ahead.

Then they hit a treasure-trove. Where Terry had picketed his horses in the spring, corn had sprung up and the troopers fell on it as forage. Scurvy was bothering the troops; they tried the same beavertail cactus that the Iowans had used, but they roasted it instead of stewing it, and it tasted "slimy and mucilaginous."

The next day the men riding advance guard contacted the hostiles' rear and tried to force a fight; but a heavy fog came up and the Cheyenne-Sioux got away under its cover. Crook's column now had two and a half days' rations left and could have made it into Fort Lincoln on half-rations. But the trail was hot, and by Crook's third principle, a hot trail, if followed relentlessly, would lead to the destruction of the hostiles, as hostiles if not as living men. He sent the Rees into Fort Abraham Lincoln to ask that supplies be sent out, put his men on half-rations, and shoved on.

Familiar with Army quartermaster and subsistence departments, he sent out a train of packers with an escort of a hundred and fifty troopers to try and buy food in the Black Hills towns, probably Deadwood. The column was now living on horse meat and half ripe bullberries (Lepargyrea) and wild plums. The troopers sometimes cornered a jackrabbit, but it took several men to run one rabbit down, and there wasn't much satisfaction in each hunter's portion; and anyway, there usually wasn't anything to use for fuel.

On September 9 the advance guard sent word back that they had attacked a twenty-five tepee village. Crook ordered the cavalry forward at once, and told the infantry commanders to let their exhausted, soaked footsloggers take it more easily. But the infantrymen surged forward almost as fast as the horses. Perhaps they wanted to relieve the monotony of marching hungrily from nowhere to nowhere; perhaps they wanted to lick the Sioux and end the campaign and get back to the fort; and perhaps they were just plain fighting men, happy to do the thing they had enlisted to do.

When the main body of Crook's column came up, the Indians had already run out of their lodges. The village proved larger than thought: forty-one tepees.

Crook was pleased; they had taken two hundred horses, and ample food, not to mention great quantities of furs and buffalo hides. They had also taken a good deal of loot from the7th Cavalry; these were hostiles who had helped kill Custer and half of his regiment.

A small bunch of the Indians were forted up in a gulch fifty or sixty yards outside the village; the rest had scattered across the prairie.

Frank Gruard and a scout called Big Bat – Baptiste Pouriere – crawled cautiously up to the gulch and asked the sniping party to surrender. But the Indians believed Crazy Horse was on his way to relieve them.

Lieutenant Clarke was given the job of dislodging the hostiles; he assembled a party of volunteers and began by returning the sniping fire. The Sioux-Cheyenne fire died away, then, as the braves began digging in for shelter. The Indians would not come out of their fort. Crook ringed them solidly with infantrymen and dismounted troopers, who fired at anything that moved.

Bourke and Captain Munson were standing on the edge of one of the winding ravines when the bank suddenly collapsed, and they landed in a squalling mess of squaws and children.

They were unhurt. More children were heard crying in the lava rock fort. Big Bat and another scout again crawled forward and asked the hostiles for a cease-fire so the women and children could get out. The truce was accepted, and eleven women with six children came out to become prisoners; one of the women, a papoose strapped to her back, grabbed Crook's hand and wouldn't let go; she was shaking all over. Then the firing resumed; for two hours the Army poured lead into the rocks; Crook's fire power was so tremendous that, as at the Apache cave, he could count on wiping out the Indian garrison with ricochets. After the two hours he ordered a cease-fire, and again asked the braves to surrender.

Chief American Horse came out; he had been gut-shot, and was biting on a piece of wood to keep from showing pain. He said he would surrender if amnesty was granted the surviving fighters.

Some of the troopers started yelling: "No quarter!" There were wounded and dead all over the Army camp; Lieutenant von Leuttwitz, a Teutonic mercenary, had a leg wound that called for amputation.

Crook did not take orders from his subordinates. He noticed their demands enough to point out that a handful of Sioux made very little difference; then he said he could use some Sioux captives. He had wanted Sioux scouts all along and had always found that he could talk Indians – of any tribe – into working for him and remaining loyal once they started work. This was in contrast to the experience of most Army officers; the discredited J.J. Reynolds – colonel, brevet general – had told the correspondent Finerty that the first rule in campaigning was never to trust an Indian or a horse.

Neither Finerty nor Bourke say how many of American Horse's men came out of the rocks alive. At least two followed their chief; and Bourke says that twenty-eight Sioux, dead or alive women, children, and fighters, had been in the fort.

Crook burned all the supplies in the village that his column couldn't use. He had trouble keeping the scouts, packers, and even some of the soldiers from killing his prisoners. A Ute, the only friendly Indian with his column, scalped the Sioux dead, and Bourke suspected that some of the soldiers took scalps, too.

Crazy Horse had come up with a large party of Sioux; they occupied the bluffs that surrounded the burned village on three sides, and fired, without effect, at a party burying a dead private. Crook did not have enough men to clean the bluffs; he dismounted his cavalry and put them and the riflemen in a circle around the captured ponies, the troop horses and pack mules, and returned the fire from the high ground, his men moving out in a wider circle by foot charges.

In a pinned-down fight like that, infantry rifles were always more effective than anything short enough to be handled by a horse-Indian – or a trooper. Crazy Horse started pulling out of there.

Colonel Chambers led the infantry against the south bluffs, Colonel Royall led the dismounted 3rd Cavalry against those on the north and northwest; Major Noyes ordered the 2nd Cavalry to mount up, and rode out to flank guard on the east and northeast for Lieutenant Sibley, who was rounding up straggling horses and driving them into the camp.

Crazy Horse wasn't licked but he was completely prevented from doing any kind of damage, and no Plains Indians ever stayed around losing men when that was true. But in an attempt to count some sort of coup, a group of young mounted braves dashed down from the bluffs and charged a group of ten or twelve used-up, discarded horses that Sibley had not bothered to round up; if they had followed the column they would have, eventually, been slaughtered for rations, and if they hadn't, the capture of the Indian jerky had relieved the troops' starvation anyway.

Without a command, the troopers and riflemen stopped firing, and let the young warriors charge right up to the strays. When the Sioux found out how worthless the animals were, they turned and charged madly back towards Crazy Horse's retreating body. It is not certain that any of the Army bullets that followed them struck home.

Crook's loss was three dead and twenty-seven wounded; as always on the Plains, the hostile casualties could only be guessed at. American Horse died during the night; and from the number of war horses captured, Finerty felt that the Sioux skirmished against Crook's column and lost four, wounding three of the Army in the process.

It wasn't a big battle, it wasn't the wipe-out that had been hoped for; but it fell right into Crook's standard pattern of how to force hostiles off the warpath: get on their tail, stay there, destroy their winter supplies and they will surrender.

He made a speech to this effect to the captured Sioux and turned the squaws loose to take their children and the word according to Crook back to their people.

A young captive warrior, Charging Bear, refused to go loose; he enlisted as a scout, later became a corporal, and fought for Crook all through the next winter.

Crazy Horse, in Bourke's Army expression, "felt" their lines again the next morning – after a night of rain – but Captain Sumner, fighting rearguard, turned him off.

As the column rode toward Deadwood, in the Black Hills, Crook sent an escort and a pack column ahead to buy supplies and bring them to him; the captured Indian stores would not last forever. He also sent a dispatch to Phil Sheridan in Chicago, telling the lieutenant general that the squaws had said Crazy Horse planned to raid all through the Black Hills during the winter, contrary to usual Indian custom on the Plains. Apparently, the hostile chief figured on capturing forage in the mining camps and towns; otherwise it was impossible for pony-braves to work when the grass was snowed under and frosted into uselessness.

The rain came up. Charles King, riding with Finerty, told the correspondent that the dampness made the wounds he had gotten in Arizona ache; eventually they put him out of the Army and made a novelist of him. Colonel Royall, riding with Bourke, entertained the lieutenant with stories of the Mexican and Civil Wars; no doubt the colonel ached, too, but didn't mention it.

A couple of days after the Battle of Slim Buttes a beef herd reached the column from the Black Hills. It was welcome; the men had been cheering each other up by pointing out how much tastier captured Indian pony was than worn-out troop horse, but the cheers they gave when they heard the lowing of cattle proved that horse-meat is not habit forming.

Bluecoats were always either wildly popular or completely despised in the old West; it depended on the strength of the hostiles and the rumors of hostility. This time the lamp was lit in the window of the Black Hills; the mayors of Deadwood, Crook and Montana cities all turned out to greet Crook and his column.

Sheridan wired that most of the Sioux and Cheyenne were rumored to be about to come into Red Cloud and Spotted Tail Agencies and pretend to surrender so that they would be fed through the winter and be in prime shape to rejoin Crazy Horse and Sitting Bull in the spring. Therefore, Crook was to abandon the winter campaign he had planned, and take over the two agencies, dismounting and disarming the braves before he fed them. Congress had authorized the Division of the Platte to recruit four hundred Indian scouts; this was Crook's chance. Sheridan himself was coming out to Fort Laramie, and he wanted Crook to join him there, forthwith.

Crook turned over his command to Merritt, and headed for Fort Robinson, on his way to Fort Laramie. His aides, an escort of twenty men under Sibley, the newspapermen, and some infantry officers due for leave went with him.

They passed through such towns as Deadwood, Custer City, Crook City. Deadwood and Custer (the city has been dropped from the title) still exist; Crook City is gone, though there is a Crooks across the state, and it is probable that General Crook has suffered a fate similar to that of P. St. George Cooke and the Kearnys. Deadwood has about three thousand inhabitants, Custer is even smaller.

But Deadwood was booming in that fall of 1876. There were two newspapers and a "Deadwood Theater and Academy of Music." Bourke attended this palace of entertainment and found it rather sad.

Finerty, on the other hand, strolled around town dressed in cavalry breeches and accepted free drinks from Indian-scared miners who thought he was a thirteen dollar a month trooper. It was not at all sad for the Chicago reporter, that night.

Custer City, south of Deadwood, was already collapsing; the gold dust had run out, and the gold that remained was in quartz; only big companies, paying day wages, could afford to extract it.

Sheridan and Crook talked at Fort Laramie, and Crook went back to protect the Black Hills and disarm the hungry Sioux and Cheyennes as they came in to the agencies. For once, the Department of Interior Indian Agents were glad to leave Indian administration to the Army. When the Oglala chiefs Red Cloud and Red Leaf came in to draw supplies they were surrounded and seven hundred ponies and fifty rifles were taken from them. This was in the last week of October; it officially ended the summer campaign called the Yellowstone Expedition and cleared the deck for a winter campaign.

That started a month later, and due to Sheridan's orders, Crook commanded from Deadwood City and the Indian agencies, sending General Ranald Mackenzie out into the field. The campaign was a repetition of that of the winter before, with one huge change. This time there were numerous Cheyenne and Sioux scouts available; in the winter of 1875-76 the Indian agents had prevented any of the hostiles' tribesmen from helping the Army.

Crook was also using the Pawnees as scouts, successfully; they were again led by the "Major" North whom the 7th Iowa had sent away, deeming his scouts as worthless. Nothing more clearly underlines the reason for Crook's consistent success with Indians and Indian trouble; he was, as Sheridan said of him, not only an Indian fighter, but an Indian manager as well.

In October Red Cloud and Red Leaf had surrendered; in the last week of November Mackenzie and his troopers landed on the camp of the Cheyennes under Dull Knife with all the force of the Army, the Pawnees, the Shoshones, and even some Bannocks, who were pretty far east of their usual territory.

It was a big village, with two hundred and five lodges, crammed with winter and war and ceremonial supplies. Bourke figured there were fourteen or fifteen hundred ponies in the remuda; the Army captured half of them, and the frustrated Cheyennes, their supplies in flames, killed some of the rest for food and others for warmth; a horse would be slaughtered and slit open so that the old people of the tribe could put their feet inside the carcass and get through the night without freezing.

It was rough country; the Cheyenne braves hid out in the gullies and rocks and bluffs. Mackenzie sent back to Crook for help in routing them out; Crook brought eleven infantry companies and some artillery batteries serving as infantrymen up in twelve hours – twenty-six miles over frozen, slippery ground.

That was amazingly fast, but not fast enough. While the march was being made Dull Knife and his subordinate chiefs pulled back; their people were dying of cold; eleven babies were lost the first night after the battle.

Crook sent the Hawaiian, Frank Gruard, and another Cheyenne-talking scout out to parley. But Dull Knife would not surrender. He was in a sullen fury because of the Sioux and Cheyenne scouts who were fighting on Crook's side; he said he could beat all the white men in the world, but not his own traitorous people. He had just killed seven soldiers and wounded a couple of dozen more. He invited Crook to kill him and his people then and there.

If the 7th Cavalry had been there, that is what would have happened; the wiped-out camp had been rich in Custer trophies. But this was a broken-backed bunch of warriors. Their winter supplies, their ammunition was gone. Crook let them go free – the Volunteers would not have, Custer would not have, Miles would probably not have – and see how they liked wandering hungry and friendless on the Plains; when they had had enough of that, he'd be willing to shelter and feed them at the Agencies.

Dull Knife did not believe he was friendless. He led his Cheyennes down the Powder River to the camp of Crazy Horse and his Sioux; Crazy Horse turned the Cheyennes down completely; they had been his allies at the Little Big Horn, but now he didn't know them.

Sitting Bull had gone north, toward Canada, and was probably there by then. There was no one left for the Cheyenne to turn to. A month after the battle at their camp the Cheyennes started coming in. They not only wanted to make peace, they wanted arms to go kill Crazy Horse and his Sioux.

How Crook had known that Crazy Horse would not help Dull Knife has never been explained. The general stopped his memoirs before they got that far, and he never confided in anyone; his dispatches to Sheridan are ambiguous on the point.

Now that the Cheyennes were out of the fight, all the tribes of the Plains wanted to go exterminate the Dakotas, the Sioux's own name for themselves. Crows, Shoshones, Utes, Bannocks, Winnebagoes, and Arapahoes all wanted to enlist in the scout corps. Crook sent most of them home to tell their people about the might of the bluecoats.

He sent Spotted Tail – his "Old Spot" of the Black Hills summer peace talk – out to reason with Crazy Horse; Spotted Tail was the hostile chiefs uncle and felt he could make his nephew realize the odds against him.

Crook was fighting against time, but he couldn't let the hostiles know it. Sherman, now General of the Army rather than General-in-Chief, had written Sheridan, who had written Crook, that Congress was about to reduce the size of the Army. At the same time, it was going to increase the size of the cavalry, but Crook might not get any of the new horse troops for a summer campaign; and even if he did, they would be lacking in the long training needed to make a horse soldier out of a recruit or even a seasoned footslogger.

Some of Crazy Horse's young men came in with Spotted Tail; but the main body waited out on the prairie. Crook had told Spotted Tail to make it clear that the Army was not suing for peace; it was just giving the Minneconjou Sioux – Crazy Horse's division of the nation – a chance to surrender and be given some land – not all they wanted, but some – on their own high Plains. In early May Crazy Horse and the rest of his people came in.

Then the Indian Bureau stepped back in. They announced that the Cheyennes would have to go to the Indian Territory – Oklahoma; and the Sioux would have to be moved to the Missouri basin, east of their natural home in the Black Hills. Having stepped in, the Indian Bureau stepped out again. The Army could break the news to the Indians, the Army could do the moving.

Crook went to Sheridan at Chicago, Sherman at Washington, anyone who would listen to him. He couldn't get the order changed.

Crazy Horse was getting restless. Out in the northwest Chief Joseph had led the Nez Percés – Christian Indians, long suffering under Indian Bureau rule – on a highly successful path away from the reservations and the white men; the word of this surely reached the Sioux.

General Crook started out to head off Chief Joseph, but Sheridan recalled him as rumors spread about an imminent revolt in the Dakota agencies. Crook was barely back in his own bailiwick when Crazy Horse broke out and went off the reservation with all his village.

He got only about six miles; eight companies of the 3rd Cavalry and about four hundred Indian scouts swarmed after him and surrounded the village. Their orders were to arrest the chief and send him to Omaha for trial; but Crazy Horse was a fighting man; he was fatally stabbed in the arrest.

There are two or three accounts of this; one is that when they were putting the chief into a cell he suddenly produced a knife, stabbed Little Big Man, who had been a Sioux chief and was now a scout, and that Little Big Man fought him to death. Another is that Little Big Man held Crazy Horse while a soldier killed him with a bayonet. A third account says that Crazy Horse attacked the jail sentry with the knife and was bayonetted in return.

It doesn't matter. His people were glad to see him dead; the trouble on the Plains was over. The Cheyennes had gone to Oklahoma, from which

Dull Knife was later to lead them back to the Plains; Sitting Bull was still in Canada.

Crook had quieted the Apaches in Arizona and the Plains Indians in the Dakota country. Neither territory stayed completely quiet; the Chiricahuas were still on the loose down south, and Dull Knife and his Cheyennes came back to the Department of the Dakotas in the summer of 1878; the survivors were allowed to stay there; Crook enlisted all the able-bodied men as Indian scouts. But mostly, for the remainder of Crook's command of the Dakotas his military service consisted of lending his troopers to adjacent departments for Ute trouble, Bannock trouble, Shoshone trouble.

The Indian Bureau sent a good agent to Red Cloud, for a change, and the Sioux remained quiet. Sitting Bull was still up on the Canadian line, but he didn't cause the Department of the Dakotas any trouble until Crook had gone back to Arizona.

That was in 1882; Crook had been away for nearly ten years, and the Chiricahuas had never been completely quiet in all that time; recently they had tried reservation life, been thoroughly robbed by the Indian agent, and gone out foraying again, sometimes in Sonora, sometimes in Arizona. They killed their agent and fought across New Mexico and then back into Arizona.

By then all the other Apaches were out, too; the Southwest was in an uproar. Phil Sheridan was in command of the Western and Southwestern Divisions of the Army; Sherman was still General of the Army; they sent their old Indian fighter back to take command of the Department of Arizona.

Crook got himself a mule and started around the Territory to see what was really happening. He had had experience with traders who cried about hostiles and Indian outrages because they wanted the Army, and the Army's payrolls to come in. He had also had experience with miners and mining companies who yelled outrage because they wanted to take over the Indians' lands. Ranchers and farmers were not above coveting their (Indian) neighbors' land, either.

He found what he undoubtedly expected to find, that except for the Chiricahuas, the Apaches were not beyond reason. Some of his old friends were dead, but their successors among the chiefs remembered Crook, the man who could tell one Indian from another, and they were happy to talk over old times with him.

Having talked over old times, the bushy-bearded general got around to current events. The Apache chiefs told him their grievances, and he promised to do something about them. They knew that this was one soldier who not only was on their side; he was a man who was not afraid to tell the Department of the Interior and its Indian Bureau what to do. They quieted down.

344

That left the Chiricahuas, who had not only murdered their Indian agent, but reportedly had played football with his head after they had cut it off. Geographically the Chiricahuas had it all their own way. The eastern border of Arizona is a pencil line, drawn in 1863 by someone in Washington. Crook could not cross it into New Mexico; he was commander of the Department of Arizona, Division of the Pacific, and New Mexico was under a different chain of command.

The southern border of Arizona is another straight line, with a slight angle in it; it was drawn by envoys of the United States and Mexico after the Mexican War.

Crook could not cross that line either, except in "hot pursuit," and the Chiricahuas were not coming close enough to let him start chasing them; Crook's reputation for never leaving a trail once he got on it was one of the things Arizona remembered about him.

He ambled down to the border on his mule and sent word into the Sierra Madre mountains of Mexico that he was as far south and as far east as he was allowed to come, and that he would like a peaceful talk with the Apache chiefs.

It didn't work. But he got some intelligence from two Apache squaws who, tired of mountain life, were returning to the reservation at San Carlos from the Sierra Madre stronghold. Their report – and Crook believed them, as he almost always believed Indians – was that Chato and Nachez and the other chiefs had built and stocked a fort far below the border that could barely be reached by soldiers and couldn't be taken if it was reached. This was in October '82. Crook had had experience in the high mountains in winter; he had every reason to believe that anyone well fortified and provisioned would stay holed up till spring. He turned his attention back to his friends, the rest of the Indians of Arizona.

In November he held a big council with them. Previously he had had a small council with the representatives of the Indian Bureau and a compromise had been worked out that should be analyzed by the editors of the *Harvard Law Review*.

The Indians *on* the San Carlos Reservation – most of the Apaches of Arizona and some that were being shipped in from New Mexico – were under the jurisdiction of the War Department, that is, Crook. The Indians *at* the San Carlos Agency, however, were under the jurisdiction of the Department of the Interior, that is, the Indian Agent.

Just to complicate matters, Captain Emmet Crawford, whom Crook appointed his senior representative in Apache matters, would be stationed at San Carlos; his assistant, Lieutenant Charles Gatewood, would be up at Camp Apache. For modern readers, familiar with Arizona, this put Gatewood in charge of the present White River Apache Reservation and

Crawford in charge of the present San Carlos Apache Reservation; the two were then both part of the San Carlos.

With this sort of setup, Crook had things all his own way, which meant all the Apache way. They were told to raise their own police force, set up their own judges, and call on the military only when things got too much for them, either from white infiltration of their lands, or from dissident members of their own nation.

They could cut wood and sell it, raise grain, plant what crops they wanted and reap the harvest for their own use or for sale; the Army would protect them. Each Indian could settle down where he wanted to, *at* the Agency or *on* the Reservation. Few chose the former; and Indian councils settled who was to get which land among their people, according to need and farming ability.

This was the Apaches' promised land. They grumbled suspiciously for a short while, and then remembered that this was old General Crook, who kept his word. Some of the Apaches, of course, did not want to take to farming; that was fine with the general; he needed scouts. The Apaches happily took up the offer. They never caused trouble while Crook commanded in Arizona, though a small band of Warm Springs Apaches did leave Arizona for Sonora and the wild life with the Chiricahuas; however, they claimed they had been forced to do so by the hostiles: join us or die.

Captain Crawford, 3rd Cavalryman turned Indian agent, made a report at the end of 1883 that is statistically astounding. The Apaches at White Mountain (Fort Apache) reservation had raised two and a half million pounds of corn, and a hundred and eighty thousand pounds of beans, not to mention large quantities of potatoes, barley, wheat and the melon-pumpkin-squash crops that are hereditary to Southwestern Indians. All this was in one year, Crook's first back in Arizona.

But war, rather than the prevention of war, is a soldier's first occupation. Crook got ready to go after the Chiricahuas, when and if he got the word to go into Mexico, or when and if the hostiles crossed into Arizona.

Crawford and Gatewood recruited and trained scouts. Tom Moore, a packer who had worked with the general before, in Arizona, on the Yellowstone expedition up in the Sioux country, and elsewhere, formed up a civilian pack unit. White scouts showed up, men such as the famous Al Sieber, who had worked for Crook and then quietly disappeared when Crook was relieved. Crook began pulling in all the troops – undermanned companies – posted around his department; he concentrated them at Willcox, where they could be supplied by train.

The break came in March. The Chiricahuas, under Chato, crossed the international line below Fort Huachuca and killed four charcoal burners.

Then they struck out east, raiding as they went. Below the border more of the band under Geronimo – Cochise was dead – struck through Sonora.

One of Chato's men, Panayotishn (or Pe-nal-tishn) deserted as the hostiles turned east, and went north to San Carlos, where he was arrested at the agency. Crook got him out of jail and brought him to Willcox; here was the ideal scout, by Crook's rules, to guide him to the Chiricahuas.

A couple of days later the leash was slipped. Sherman, as General of the Army, ordered him to destroy the hostile Apaches, to pursue them regardless of "department or national lines."

Crook got on what he undoubtedly called "the cars." He took the railroad to Guaymas and Hermosillo, in Sonora, and talked to both the civil and military leaders of that state; then he did the same thing in Chihuahua. He was promised all the cooperation he wanted; the Mexican Generals Topete and Carbo promised to place their troops where they could back up the United States force.

It wasn't much of a force, but then the Chiricahuas weren't numerous; they were just brave, hostile, and at home. Even with the addition of the Warm Springs, Chato and Geronimo between them could not put more than two hundred braves in the field.

Crook took along that many or more Apache scouts; he also had forty-two troopers of Company I, 6th Cavalry, heavily over-officered: ten commissioned men, including a doctor. There was also a private from the Army's General Service, whom Bourke never explains; quite possibly he was a mapmaker.

The telegraphic orders from Sherman had not cleared international matters. The "hot pursuit" or "close pursuit" law said that the chase must stop when the border-crossing soldiers reached inhabited country; this could mean that Crook could chase the Chiricahuas as far as the first brush hut and no farther.

He and General Topete both wired their governments asking how much freedom was allowed. Sherman wired back that Crook was to abide strictly by the convention, meaning the close pursuit law, presumably. It sounded as if Sherman was giving Crook complete liberty, but if Mexico protested it would be Crook's fault, not Sherman's.

Crook marched his men the hundred miles from Willcox to San Bernardino, Arizona, where St. George Cooke and his Mormon Battalion had fought the Battle of the Bulls. Chato and his people were far to the east by then, but this was the edge of Arizona; despite the General of the Army's orders, he apparently didn't want to step on the toes of the military in New Mexico.

The march took five days; it was the end of April when Crook led his expedition across the international line. Behind him he left a supply camp guarded by the tiny cadres of seven cavalry companies.

347

Each officer and man in the expedition carried a blanket and forty rounds of ammunition. Five pack trains went along, the packers armed but under orders merely to defend their animals in case of a fight. Three white guides – Sieber, Bowman, and McIntosh – would fight and do it well; Crook had about two hundred and fifty effectives, four out of five of them Apaches.

The troopers renamed Pe-nal-tishn (or Panayotishn) Peaches; Crook counted on him to find his way back to the Chiricahua stronghold. Peaches told the interpreters that he wasn't a Chiricahua himself, but a White River Apache; however, he had married two Chiricahua women. Southwestern Indians are more likely to follow the clan of the mother than of the father; among the Diné the mother's brother is usually a boy's sponsor in tribal and religious life; it must have been hard for Peaches to leave the Chiricahuas, since he had several children.

The column followed the San Bernardino River below the border and then went up the tributary Bavispé. The "habitated country" of the close pursuit law didn't apply; the country had been deserted, given over to the hostiles, whose moccasin marks were on every trail. When shod footprints were found, they were those of heavy parties of Mexican soldiers, escorting packtrains.

When they did find people, it was at the squalid villages of Bavispé and Basaraca. The inhabitants, Bourke found, were in a deplorable state of raggedness, except for the men's silver-banded hats and flaming silk-and-wool sashes. He liked the country and thought it potentially prosperous.

The Mexican peons told them that the Chiricahuas raided constantly; no man dared go half a mile from the village without being covered by the guns of the Guardia Nacional, a couple of dozen of whom were stationed in the valley.

Bourke amazed the villagers not only because he spoke Spanish, but because he went and prayed in their churches; they had never heard of an Irish-Catholic.

The man who seemed to be *alcalde* of Basaraca told Crook he had orders to aid the expedition in all ways; there wasn't much he could do except sell four beef animals to feed the Apache scouts, but apparently the Mexican government was not going to split hairs about Crook's very cold pursuit of the hostiles.

All down the valley the conditions were the same, or worse. The column went twenty miles south of Basaraca to the ranch of Tesorababi, where they camped until May 7. Then they headed for the mountains. In the scrub-oak foothills they picked up a heavy cattle trail, and knew they were on the track of raiding Chiricahuas.

One of the white men had caught an owl and was keeping it tied to his pommel; the Apache scouts wouldn't go on till he set it free; owls brought bad luck. The next day the vanguard rode up on freshly slaughtered cattle; from then on, they were never to be out of sight of them. The Apaches had captured so many animals that they could indulge their favorite appetite for tongue and liver only.

The way became dangerously steep; they could look down and see where a stumbling steer had fallen hundreds of feet.

They came to the abandoned camp of a Mexican army party, which had sent out scouts only to have them beaten back by the Chiricahuas. The trail went up and down, from scrub oak up through juniper to fine pine country, then down again into another valley; the ridges were almost knife-sharp.

The medicine men became active. In camp that first night out from Tesorababi they went into trances, trying to see the Chiricahuas. One of them said it would be two to six days before they caught up with the hostiles.

The next day, the troopers and officers dragging worn-out horses behind them over the increasingly steep trail, the column came to the stronghold Peaches had told them about. It was deserted. However, it was, in every respect, as good a fort as the guide had said. And as difficult to get to; five pack mules had already fallen to their death.

Now the Chiricahuas had pulled even farther back into the mountains. The soldiers could expect the country to get worse; it did. While bands of Apache scouts guarded rear, front, and flanks, axmen had to cut trails. They, passed Chiricahua *rancherías* of thirty and forty jacales and some smaller ones; all abandoned.

The trail climbed a thousand feet above the tiny, shining headwaters of the Bavispé; the animals in the vanguard constantly started little rockslides to endanger those behind them; the Apache scouts scrambled up and down the slopes like squirrels and the white men sweated and gasped for breath.

A scout gave the alarm; he had sighted two hostiles; Apaches stripped quickly, grabbed up their weapons, and trotted off. False alarm; the men sighted were their own scouts.

But Chiricahua signs were plentiful. Children had abandoned their dolls, women their pitch-lined water jugs. The Apache scouts held a council, then went to see Crook. They would never catch Geronimo, Chato, and the rest this way, they said. The horse soldiers and the packtrain were holding them back. They proposed that the scouts with their officers, Al Sieber and his two assistants, go ahead alone, while the troopers and packtrain stayed in camp.

If they came on the new Apache strongpoint, they would attack if it seemed safe, engage the hostiles, and send back for the cavalrymen to act as re-enforcements. If it didn't seem safe they would hold off and send for Crook and his forty or fifty soldiers, then storm the Chiricahua redoubt.

Crook told them to go ahead; and this accounts for a good deal of his success. It is an Army habit – a habit of most civilians, too – to use over again a method that worked last time. Against Crazy Horse, Crook had engaged with his cavalry, then clinched the battle with his infantry. Now a bunch of ignorant Apaches were proposing to do just the opposite.

He may have recognized that in these mountains Apache infantry became cavalry, troopers became infantry; the former were faster, the latter more phlegmatic and likely to aim more accurately and to hold their fire more economically than the Indians. If he didn't, he made his decision purely on his deep faith in Indians. He put strictures on them, however. They were not to kill women or children, and any braves who surrendered were to be held for return to the reservation.

This was probably in accordance with their wishes. The Apache scouts invariably took great pleasure in tending any hostiles' offspring they captured; the women were not to blame for anything their husbands had done; and later on the Chiricahuas were easily absorbed into the other bands on the reservations.

Bourke described the scouts' preparations for the move out. They baked four days' supply of bread over little fires; they mended their moccasins; they ground coffee on improvised metates; they cleaned and checked their weapons; and some of them took sweatbaths for religious or health reasons.

Crook sent strong detachments out to the south, where it seemed that the hostiles had ambushed a large Mexican party of soldiers; the move was strategic rather than tactical; the Chiricahuas might do it again or try to.

The medicine men counseled with their spirits and said that the scouts would find plenty of Chiricahuas in two days and kill them on the third.

The advance guard – more than three quarters of the whole column – moved out on Friday morning, May 11. That night Captain Crawford sent back a runner; there was an excellent camping place about fifteen miles farther on.

For three days the base camp moved slowly after the scouting party, through country littered with quantities of Chiricahua loot and supplies.

It was the same up-and-down country they had had all along; wonderful piny peaks, scrubby chaparral-filled gullies, and then up again. Stray ponies abandoned by the hostiles were gathered into the pack-train, or joined of their own accord, out of the constant horse-loneliness.

The work was clean; the Bavispé headwaters were dotted with deep, cool pools, and the men had plenty of chances to bathe.

They pushed supplies ahead to Crawford and got back word from him that he had found a village of almost a hundred jacales – deserted. Then at noon on May 15, he sent word that his men had seen and fired on two bucks with a squaw; the action had started the main body moving again.

Crawford timed his note 12:05 and Crook got it at 1:05; the vanguard and the chase party were closing up. While the note was still being passed around the officers with Crook, they heard firing; Crawford had engaged the enemy!

Crook gave the order to mount up, but the firing died away, and the outfit stood to horse, ready to move out when better intelligence was available.

It didn't come till after dark, when Crawford led his whole command into camp. Crawford reported that he had jumped two villages of hostiles, those of Chato (the flat-nosed) and Bonito (the handsome.) His younger scouts had fired before he could stop them, and the Chiricahuas had scattered over incredibly bad, rough, broken country. But he had killed nine hostiles, and captured two boys, two girls, and Bonito's daughter; also, four good rifles and a new Colt's revolver. He had burned the villages and taken the animals, forty-seven of which were needed to carry the hostiles' loot – coin, watches, all the plunder of raids in New Mexico, Arizona, Sonora, and Chihuahua.

Bonito's daughter was past childhood. She said that her people had panicked when they realized that the force attacking them was mostly Apache, though Army-commanded; they had been particularly shocked to recognize Pe-nal-tishn, the troopers' Peaches.

She thought the war was all over, that the Chiricahuas would give up, knowing they now had their own people to fight. She was sure the White Mountain Apaches, under Loco, would quit at once; so would Chihuahua's band; Geronimo and Chato she wasn't too sure about; a chief named Ju would go on fighting, but all his braves were dead, so he didn't matter.

At her suggestion, Crook turned her loose with two days' supply of food and the older captured boy to help her take the word to her people that they would be honorably treated if they surrendered.

The column waited for results from the girl's embassy; the scouts made a jacal for the three remaining children, whom Bourke watched with the great interest that was later to make that soldier turn ethnologist. The older girl had apparently been taught the Apache equivalent of the saying that the devil finds work for idle hands; she kept basting a skirt for herself and then ripping out the stitches and doing it over again. The younger girl cried, but the little boy stared out stoically through eyes that were "as big as oysters and as black as jet."

Crook threw out heavy pickets to take any hostiles who wanted to surrender, and the column moved forward that way, strongly videtted and progressing very slowly.

It was raining, but the pine forest supplied pitchy wood. A smoke signal was seen, answered by the scouts, and when the party went into camp, they sent up another signal, and two squaws surrendered; they were sisters of one of the scouts and brought not only themselves, but the word that the fight with Crawford's scouts had taken a heavy toll. Apparently, they were

351

part of Chihuahua's band; Bourke isn't entirely clear, but they said that Chihuahua was anxious to come in.

Then six more women surrendered, one of them Chihuahua's sister, who said the same thing. Crook said that that was fine with him, and the chief walked in, with fifteen of his followers, all ages, both sexes. He said that he wanted to surrender, that he was sick of war. But he added that Geronimo and Chato, with most of the braves, were off fighting Mexicans.

Before night forty-five prisoners gave themselves up. Crook allowed Chihuahua to take two of his young men and go out looking for more of his people. The next morning, he wasn't back, but the camp was moved five miles to better grass, and when the prisoners were counted, there were seventy of them; some had joined up unnoticed during the move.

The next morning there were a hundred and twenty-one, Bourke's count: old men, boys, women, and children; no braves yet. But the prisoners assured Crook that Chihuahua was to be trusted about surrendering.

Then there was a "fearful hubbub," as armed Apaches appeared on the heights above the camp, shouted, and then hid themselves behind rocks. The Apaches in camp shouted, the hidden men shouted back, and then two old squaws clambered down from the cliffs, to ask if their men could surrender safely.

Crook sent a scout and a Chiricahua prisoner out to tell them it didn't matter; if they didn't surrender they would be wiped out; but that today, while Chihuahua was out, there was a truce.

The whole thing was complicated by the fact that the Chiricahuas were supposed to have, and said they did have, a captive American boy; naturally Crook wanted him back alive.

The hostiles came down in ones and twos, cautiously; they were Geronimo's men, returned from raiding in Chihuahua; they were also the first braves – thirty-six of them – to surrender.

Geronimo wanted to talk to Crook, but the general scorned the offer; he told the chief there was nothing to talk about; all he had to do was look around the Army camp and see how many Apache hands were against him; but Crook did think that Geronimo ought to know that the Mexican Army was sending heavy troops out to back Crook up.

Geronimo thought this over and surrendered unconditionally; he said that he wanted to go back to San Carlos and work for a living; he couldn't fight Americans, Mexicans, and Apaches all at once. He wanted to go out and round up his people as Chihuahua was doing; then they'd all go back to San Carlos and live on the reservation.

Crook could always tell one Indian from another; he didn't send Geronimo out yet.

The problem of feeding the captives began to be serious; they were pouring into camp, sent by Chihuahua. The prisoners were put to work roasting mescal, and such ponies as could be spared were slaughtered for them; there were some beef cattle, too.

Bourke found it a curious outfit for a military camp; children laughed and played, two old ladies fought over a stretch of tripe, Apaches played their fiddles and flutes.

Geronimo kept trying to dicker with Crook; the general kept on being indifferent to the man who considered himself the greatest of all Apaches. Finally – Chihuahua and other chiefs had rounded up two hundred and fifty hostiles by then – Crook felt that Geronimo was sufficiently impressed with the inevitability of defeat if he betrayed Crook and the Army.

Crook started his unwieldy column home and told Geronimo he could stay behind and round up his people, then bring them to the San Carlos reservation.

The white boy, Charley McComas, was never found. The Indians said, and it seems likely, that he had run away when Crawford had his first fire fight and had died from exposure in the rough mountains.

Geronimo was thoroughly subdued. He sent in word that rounding up his people was harder than he had thought; he asked Crook to stay in camp for a week and wait for him.

Crook did not do this, but he moved slowly, and on May 28 Geronimo and the chiefs who had been helping him led more than a hundred Apaches meekly into camp. There were now nearly four hundred captives, plus six Mexican women recaptured from the hostiles.

As they moved northwest, they came into game country, and lived better; they also hit a forest fire in the valley of Janos, and prisoners, scouts and troopers fought it side by side.

On June 15 they crossed back into Arizona and marched to their base camp in the San Bernadino country. At once there was trouble; the white men around the San Carlos agency had been stirring the farming Indians up, telling them that the reservation would become a concentration camp if the hostiles were allowed to resettle there.

This had caused the territorial and other newspapers to demand that the Chiricahuas all be hanged; when the prisoners learned this, some of them broke back into Mexico, clashed with the Mexican troops, went into hiding.

But eventually they came back across the line and up to San Carlos. Crook broke the Chiricahuas up into little groups and attached them to bands of Indians already farming.

He was then charged – by the press – with having been taken captive in Mexico and forced to grant easy surrender terms to the hostiles. He was summoned to Washington, and eventually the old arrangement was reinstated: the Army had charge of Indians on the San Carlos Reservation; the Indian agent, a Mr. Wilcox, had charge of Indians at the Agency. Crawford and Gatewood went back to teaching Apaches how to make money.

All was quiet for two years, so far as the Apaches went. Geronimo turned out to be one of the best farmers in the tribe. But the Agent, Wilcox, was far from quiet; he was third government man on the reservation, instead of first, and the two top men were yellow-legged Bluepants, whom most civilians in the West despised when there wasn't any trouble. Wilcox resigned and a man named Ford took his place, and promptly got just as unhappy as Wilcox had been. Finally, he confiscated the picks and shovels Crawford had issued for the digging of an irrigation ditch. It was a small thing, in one way, but it dirtied the face of the Army, which was General Crook's face.

Captain Emmet Crawford, who had taken such pride in the agricultural accomplishments of the Apaches, asked for and was given permission to return to duty with the 3rd Cavalry. Crook himself asked several times to be relieved of all responsibility for the behavior of the Apaches. His wording is peculiar. It would be thought that he would advise the War Department to turn the Indians over to the Interior and be done with it; but in each of his requests through channels he uses the singular first person; *he* wanted to be relieved, etc.

He was called to Washington; a conference between the two departments included him, the Commissioner of Indian Affairs, and the two secretaries. It was inconclusive; like all the orders sent to Arizona, it ordered Crook to keep the Apaches peaceful, but not to interfere with the agent's view of how they should farm, unless they were prisoners.

Crook specifically did not want to differentiate between prisoner Apaches – Chiricahuas – and non-prisoner Apaches – ex-scouts and their families. He had separated Geronimo's people up, putting them with the ex-scouts and their relatives, and he felt that was the way to control them.

Major General John Pope commanded the Division of the Pacific, making him Crook's immediate superior. He backed Crook time and again, but it did little good.

Geronimo had been one of the big proponents of the ditch that the Indian agent didn't want built. Geronimo had been a big man on the warpath. With no ditch, he fretted; he wasn't a big man at all any more. And he could tell that Crook was losing face. Anyone who has ever lived on or around an Indian reservation knows that everything that happens in Washington is immediately known to all of the rude aborigines; the Apaches were no exception.

In May 1885, nearly two years after he had come down out of the Sierras and turned to farming, Geronimo, with Nachez and about a quarter of all the Chiricahuas on the reservation – one hundred and twenty-four – went on a protracted drunk.

Crook had forbidden the brewing of tizwin, the cactus-pear (or mescal) wine of the Apaches, but he had never hoped to enforce the ruling completely. In fact, he had advocated, in a letter to the Indian Rights Association, that Indians be allowed to buy liquor like anyone else; he had never seen a group of Indians untended by a bootlegger.

Geronimo, when he had drunk enough, led his party off the reservation. Three-fourths of the Chiricahuas, including such big chiefs as Chato, stayed behind.

The nearest officer, Lieutenant Britton Davis, 3rd Cavalry, wired Crook at once. If Crook had gotten the wire, the party might have been stopped before it went completely hostile, but Crook never got the word. Bourke says simply that the telegraph wasn't working well. Lieutenant Davis himself – who later wrote a book – says that he sent the message through channels, as he should have, and that when it got to a Captain Pierce at San Carlos, Pierce took it to Al Sieber, serving as head of scouts, before passing it on. Sieber – this could all be legend – was suffering from a hangover, and advised Pierce to forget the whole thing, not to bother Crook about "another tizwin drunk."

Geronimo got two days' headstart on his way back to the Sierra Madres and the glory that meant so much to him. The troopers rode out of Camp Apache after him, but Crook ordered them back to prepare carefully for a long campaign, while detachments across southern Arizona rode out and tried to stop the hostiles, without success.

Geronimo and his people killed thirty-four whites in Arizona and thirty-nine in New Mexico, dashing back and forth. Bourke does not list how many peaceful Apaches they murdered, but the numbers were large. The White Mountain Apaches managed to kill one Chiricahua brave and play football with his head in the Apache manner, a sport that has now died out, but would perhaps be popular on television.

General Phil Sheridan, in Chicago, was furious. He asked Crook, by wire, how a handful of Indians could escape when Crook had forty-six companies of infantry and forty of cavalry to hold them back.

Crook held his tongue, and organized parties of scouts to comb the Black Range and the Mogollons, both in New Mexico, but his men never contacted Geronimo and the hostiles crossed back into Mexico and the Bavispé River country from which Crook had chivvied them once.

Captain Emmet Crawford was recalled from the 3rd Cavalry in Texas and put in charge of a detachment of Chiricahua scouts; Crook was using his old methods, his old men. Lieutenant Davis, with more Apaches, joined Crawford, as did a troop of the 6th Cavalry, and they followed Geronimo across the border and into the Sierra Madre. Crawford's thoughts on going back to the Sierra Madre would be worth knowing.

Crook set up his headquarters at Fort Bowie, on the railroad, about seventy-five miles north of Douglas on the border. Lieutenant Gatewood combed the country just into New Mexico with a hundred Apaches; then Major Wirt Davis came in with a company of troopers and a packtrain; Gatewood joined him and they followed Crawford into Mexico.

Crook stopped the border as tight as he could – it would have taken an Army five times the size of that of the United States to do a complete job – by putting a detachment of troopers at every waterhole from Nogales to El Paso. Apparently, nobody any longer cared if Crook went into New Mexico.

While Crook made his massive and careful preparations, Crawford contacted Geronimo, in late June, and drove him out of a camp northeast of Opunto or Oputo, still in the Bavispé valley. But Crawford and his Chiricahuas were not numerous enough to surround the hostiles, who got away. Three weeks later Major Davis and his combined command of cavalry and Apaches crossed the line, and hit Geronimo near "Nacori," probably Nacozaria, which would be northwest of where Crawford found them; this is in the Sierra Madre Occidental, very rough country, closer to the international line than Oputo. A village was destroyed, without casualties, and a few women and children were captured.

The two columns worked together after that and kept pushing the hostiles north. At the end of September Geronimo crossed into the United States once more, passing between two cavalry outfits guarding waterholes only a few miles apart; Apaches could go longer without water than any other people in the history of North America.

The troops on patrol through southern Arizona kept seeing Geronimo or hearing about him, but they couldn't get close enough to make him stand and fight; he got his band into the Dragoon Mountains, in New Mexico.

At the end of November New Mexico was officially made a part of the Military Department of Arizona, under Crook's command.

But Geronimo's hostiles had recrossed the border. Crawford found them there in January and hit them hard; the old Crook tactic of forcing hostiles to go into a winter in the mountains without food or supplies or tents worked again.

Geronimo sued for peace. Crawford prepared to council, but before he could set up the talks, his camp of Chiricahua scouts was hit by a detachment from the Mexican Army, Tarahumari Indians, long-time enemies of the Apaches.

It is probable that it didn't matter to the Mexican Indians whether they killed Apache scouts or Apache hostiles; whom they killed was Emmet Crawford. The captain had spotted the Tarahumaris as Mexican soldiers and stepped out in front of his prone Apaches to show them his uniform, or whatever part of it he wore in the field; certainly, the Mexicans could see that he wasn't an Apache himself. A single shot killed him.

Lieutenant Marion Maus, his second-in-command, reported later that it took some time to bring his scouts under control; in that time, they had killed the Mexican officer and fifteen of his Indians. Geronimo's Indians were reported to be interested spectators to this exchange.

Geronimo had had enough, even so. He agreed to round up his people and bring them to the border in March, two months away; he'd meet Crook at the Cañon de los Embudos, in the country where Sonora is divided from Chihuahua and Arizona from New Mexico.

Maus reported to Crook; Crook took Geronimo at his word and called the troops out of the field. Telegrams poured in on him, asking how he could take the word of a heathen, blood-thirsty hostile; Crook went hunting. The press of the United States attacked him almost unanimously; but it is dubious if General George Crook kept a scrapbook; he was never much of a reader.

In March he had Lieutenant Maus and his scouts camp in the Cañon de los Embudos and he himself followed on, careful to bring civilian witnesses with him: Mayor Strauss of Tucson, a photographer and the photographer's assistant.

Geronimo and Nachez came in when they had promised; the parley opened. Geronimo opened with one of his usual reform-school speeches. He had left San Carlo because he was afraid of Chato, the chief Mickey Free, and Lieutenant Britton Davis. His feelings had been hurt because bad stories had been published about him in the newspapers; in other words, it was all somebody else's fault. And now he would like General Crook to stop frowning and smile at him.

Crook was not bowled over by this eloquence. He answered that it was a wonder that Geronimo and the forty braves who went on the warpath with him were afraid of the three men he had named; but even if they were, did that give them a reason to kill innocent people all over the country? No, Geronimo had once sworn to a lasting peace, and broken his word, and now Crook wanted to know how he was ever going to believe the chief again.

As the sweat broke out on Geronimo's forehead the photographer dodged around taking pictures of the hostile chief and his men; Crook had not bothered to disarm them; he seldom did, thinking it would show a lack of self-confidence. That ended the council; Crook left Geronimo to think it over.

The next morning Bourke and Mayor Strauss took a stroll through the hostile village, and found it heavily fortified, and the Chiricahuas well clothed in Mexican shirts and blankets.

The day after that Geronimo surrendered unconditionally; he only asked that when they traveled up to San Carlos together, Crook talk to him once in a while; apparently, he couldn't stand the general's coldness. The whole thing sounds, in modern light, like a transcript from a juvenile court; it would be interesting to have Geronimo's career analyzed by a psychiatrist specializing in delinquency.

That night there was trouble, but Crook didn't learn of it till morning. The Cañon de los Embudos was near the San Bernadino ranch from which Crook had started his first campaign after Geronimo, and at which the Mormon Battalion battled the wild bulls. A man named Slaughter had taken up the United States part of the ranch, but a man named Tribollet was squatting on the Mexican side, about four hundred yards from the border.

He was a bootlegger of mescal. There couldn't have been an awful lot of business in that remote southeast corner of Arizona; not content with selling to the hostile Chiricahuas he filled them with wild tales of the dreadful punishments they were going to get at San Carlos. It was common for white men in that country to want to stir up Indian trouble; it brought in the troopers, potential customers for anything, particularly bootleg.

Geronimo and some of his people took off, drunk, but riding hard; Crook sent Lieutenant Maus after them. Chihuahua and eighty of the hostiles surrendered and went on up to San Carlos. But Geronimo and Nachez and thirty braves were again on the warpath in Mexico.

It seemed certain to Crook and his officers that Geronimo would come back when he sobered up and considered the difference in source of what Tribollet had told him and what General Crook had told him.

Sheridan, General of the Army, didn't agree. Sheridan knew the Plains and he knew the Valley of the Shenandoah, but he didn't know Arizona; he ordered Crook to protect the settlers there and Crook wired back that troops working that way were effective for about a half-mile radius and no more; if he couldn't handle things his own way, he asked to be relieved. He was.

General Nelson A. Miles, who had commanded in Arizona while Crook was fighting Sioux, and who had done it in such a way that Crook had had to come back to the Southwest, took over again; Crook was given the command of the Department of the Platte, with headquarters at Omaha.

Miles – to finish the story of Geronimo – conducted a campaign that might have been effective against German hussars in the Valley of the Rhine. First, he chased the hostile with cavalry, then he added infantry, and then, in exasperation, he called on Lieutenant Gatewood, who had been Crook's junior Indian agent. Gatewood sent out word that he'd talk; the Chiricahuas came in, and all but six surrendered.

The Plains were quiet and had been since Crook defeated the Sioux and Cheyenne. Crook had been in the field a long time since his graduation from the Point so long ago; he was glad to take it easy. He rode his Department hard, however, especially about target practice, something the Army had long been delinquent in. He went East to be honored in Boston for his justice to the Indians; and he attended veterans' dinners whenever he could.

Then, in the fall of 1887, the Utes broke out in Colorado. There was feeling against these Utes in Colorado; in 1879 they had massacred their agents and their agents' families. But this time they had not gone on the warpath, just on a hunting trip. However, they were hunting off the reservation and out of season, and a game warden tried to arrest them. Guns went off, and three of the Indians were wounded. Then the sheriff joined up with the game warden, each leading a posse, and tried to serve warrants on two Utes suspected of horse stealing. More shots were fired; the posses pulled back.

The governor of Colorado sent the militia and called on Crook for Regulars. Crook pointed out that game laws and civil warrants were not Army matters.

Crook was certain the outrageous reports coming out of Colorado were mostly the usual uproar about Indian outrages that, when investigated, would come to little or nothing. He was right; two white men from Meeker, Colorado, went out and talked soft to the Utes, and the Indians agreed to go back on the reservation; they only wanted fifteen days in which to gather up their stock.

The sheriff, the newspapers, the militia all regarded this as a stall in order to get re-enforcements.

As part of the Utes – about twenty-five braves with their families – were slowly driving their stock home a hundred militiamen and a posse hit them full force. Three white men were killed, and four Indians, three of them children. The Utes broke and abandoned their stock, a few hundred horses and twenty-five hundred sheep and goats.

The militia reported it had killed fifteen braves or had at least wounded that many. This made a dangerous situation, apparently; the Utes still had ten effectives in the field, so the governor appealed to President Grover Cleveland's Secretary of the Interior, Lucius Lamar, for protection. Federal wards, the Indians, had been killed. Secretary Lamar sent his agent, and the War Department lent General Crook to go along. Crook did. He told the governor – firmly – that before he could do anything or would do anything, the white citizens would have to give the Indians back their stock.

The governor protested. Finally, he gave in, the county commissioner promised to see that the animals were returned to the Indian agent, and the Ute war ended with Crook where he had always been: in the position of seeing the Indian as an individual and a human being. The next year he was made a major general, given command of the Division of the Missouri, headquarters in Chicago, and became a desk officer. That he had not changed much, except as to age, is witnessed by the fact that two weeks after taking over his office in the Pullman Building he sent three turkeys and six chickens to a Sioux friend in the Dakotas.

He served on Indian commissions, he commanded his huge Division – it held the Departments of the Platte, Dakota, Missouri and Texas – and he went hunting. But he was never again a cavalryman. He wrote articles protesting the treatment of the Chiricahuas by General Miles, who had sent not only the hostile chiefs, but also most of Crook's scouts to prison in the southeast.

Crook had calmed down, though; he got General Oliver Otis Howard on his side, and between them they sent the Chiricahuas west. Considering his troubles with Howard when Crook first went to Arizona, this was a triumph of diplomacy for the bristle-whiskered sixty-year-old general. He was still commanding his division when, on March 20, 1890, he suffered a fatal heart attack while taking his usual morning exercise with the dumbbells.

The Apaches wept; the Sioux danced the Ghost Dance and said that hope for them had died with Crook. But though John Gregory Bourke – whose big book *On the Border with Crook* was about to be published – said that Crook could have prevented the trouble of 1890 at Wounded Knee, it seems a very good thing that the old Indian manager was dead before he saw the depths to which a United States Cavalry unit could fall. A few minor notes, and we'll take that up.

Chapter 25

Some Small Wars

There had, of course, been Indian wars between 1865 and 1890 that George Crook didn't go to. The Modoc Indians of northern California revolted in the early '70s. These are the Rogues after whom the Rogue River, where Crook first led cavalry, was named.

They had been taken from their home and put on the Klamath Reservation in southern Oregon; the Klamaths and Modocs are close relatives. But there were a good many more Klamaths than there were Modocs, and the stronger tribe made life so miserable for the smaller one that the Modocs left the reservation in 1870 and moved back to northern California.

Nobody did much about this for two years. General Edwin R.S. Canby was commanding general of the Department of the Columbia; like Crook, he felt that Indians had rights. But the Indian Bureau insisted, and Canby ordered Company B, 1st Cavalry, to move the Modocs back to the Klamath Reservation.

Company B's captain, James Jackson, put his men around the Indian village; he had almost as many troopers as there were braves. He ordered a general Modoc disarmament, which netted him a few muzzle loaders. Then Jackson – the orders were the Indian Bureau's, not Canby's – told Captain Jack, the leader of the Modocs, that he was under arrest. Almost at once the Indians produced pistols, and a fire fight started.

It wasn't very decisive; the Modocs seemed to have planned their moves well. They broke away and holed up in the Lava Beds that now feature a National Monument between Tule Lake and Glass Mountain. There they had cached ample supplies, and there they were re-enforced until they had about a hundred and twenty effectives in one of the finest natural forts north of the Sierra Madre country.

Jackson got re-enforcements, too; he tried to take the malapie – as most Westerners call lava beds – with two hundred Regulars and an equal number of outraged citizens, who felt that the couple of hundred Modocs were crowding them.

That was at the end of November '72; the Army was still trying to get Captain Jack and his men out of there in April '73. Canby kept saying that if the Modocs were given a decent piece of land away from the Klamaths they'd come off the warpath happily; the Indian Bureau kept saying that the Klamath Reservation was the only place for the hostiles.

Canby was ordered to go into the malapie with a peace commission. While he was giving Captain Jack the word from the Department of Interior, one of the braves shot and killed the general and a missionary also serving on the commission.

General Jefferson C. Davis, who had fought a duel back along the Ohio, succeeded Canby. He brought in artillery, and in June the Modocs surrendered, and were given a reservation of their own, as they had wanted and as Canby had advised.

This really wasn't a cavalry war, though the 1st started it. It has been called the most expensive of all Indian wars, and was, counted at per capita cost per Indian; half a million dollars to subdue seventy-five braves and their families. It tied up a thousand men of the Regulars when the Army was less than thirty thousand in all, and it killed Canby.

This was the Canby who had graduated from the Point in time to fight with the Dragoons in the damp Seminole War, the Canby who had done well in the Mexican War, gone up to Utah with St. George Cooke in the Utah troubles, driven the Confederates out of New Mexico in the Civil War, and fought at Mobile. He was murdered in 1873. That was the year that St George Cooke turned sixty-four and was mandatorily retired. The last of the men who had once called themselves Dragoons were passing out of the Army; Cooke was to live another twenty-two years, but only as a writer and ex-soldier.

Chief Joseph's War was a little later, in 1877, and this chief had more men than Captain Jack – about four hundred and fifty. This time the Indians were the Nez Percé, which mean pierced nose in French; like almost all Indian tribes, the name was given them by neighbors, telling white explorers who lived over the hill. The Nez Percé did *not* pierce their noses, but the local sign language for neighbor was a pass of one finger under the nostrils, by legend. Some anthropologists say that the Nez Percé had once pierced their noses, long before the white man arrived in the country; some say they never did; at least no Europeans saw them that way, and it really doesn't matter.

They had always been peaceful and were one of the first tribes to be Christianized. But their white Christian neighbors crowded them out of the Wallowa Valley in the heavy emigration days that followed the Civil War and Chief Joseph led them on the warpath.

General O.O. Howard, who a few years before had complicated the Apache situation, took after them; he had about as many soldiers as did

Chief Joseph. He caught up with them in July; this was 1877, when Crook was busy with the Sioux-Cheyenne, and Sheridan wouldn't let him go after Chief Joseph.

Howard hit the Indians hard enough to force them over the Clearwater River and into a force of soldiers and civilians posted to stop them. So, Joseph and his people simply faded into the hills, by deer-paths and creek bottoms. They came out in the Big Hole Basin and rested, thinking they had left Howard far behind, which they had. But Howard had used the telegraph, and Colonel John Gibbon was ready for Chief Joseph with about two hundred foot soldiers.

Chief Joseph was getting the better of Gibbon when Howard caught up; in fact, he had besieged his attackers. But the combined forces of Howard and Gibbon were more than the Indian general cared to face; again, his band melted away and re-formed in the Bear Paw Mountains.

Here they were struck by General Nelson A. Miles, who had been so useful in mishandling the Apaches when Howard wasn't busy at that work. Miles had eleven companies of soldiers, six of them troopers, and two field guns; even so, it took him four days to make Chief Joseph surrender. Three companies of cavalry were from the 7th, the rest from the 2nd. Lieutenant Marion Maus, who was to be with Crawford, commanded scouts.

This was not the most glorious chapter in the history of the Cavalry, unless you call Chief Joseph's people cavalry. They were the only tribe that ever bred horses genetically; the modern Appaloosa is descended from their stock. In eleven weeks the Nez Percé fought thirteen battles and skirmishes against ten different Army outfits and traveled sixteen hundred miles. If Sheridan had let Crook go west to meet these extraordinary horsemen, he would have undoubtedly enlisted them as scouts, despite their naturally peaceful ways; he might even have formed the first Remount Corps out of them.

There were other fights; the Comanches made trouble in the Southwest as they had before the Civil War. But they never produced a great chief, nor did their wars bring forth a great Indian fighting general, as the Apache-Sioux troubles brought forth Crook.

In New Mexico, the Mescalero, Jicarilla, and Warm Springs Apaches gave trouble; the last band was shipped off to Crook in Arizona and behaved well from that time; the former two were moved around the state – the 10th Cavalry was often the mover – by General John Pope, and finally settled down in 1883. Like the Pueblos and the Navajos, any trouble they have given the government since then has been in the law courts.

Cavalry patrolled Indian Territory and had little more to do than show the flag there. Cavalry patrolled the Mexican border, and occasionally skirmished with bandits where the border wasn't clear.

Chapter 26

Disaster on Horseback

Nothing in the history of the United States Cavalry is more amazing than the fact that the best-known horse soldier the United States ever turned out was probably as useless as any man who ever wore stars on his shoulders.

George Armstrong Custer was conceited, impulsive, disobedient and incapable of learning. He was also just about as brave as anyone in the world, physically; morally he cringed from criticism as he did from obscurity.

He suffered, of course, the worst defeat, considering men involved, in our history, but this seems little reason to commemorate him as widely as has been done. There is a story – true or not, it doesn't matter – that the British name one class of men o' war after great British defeats, in order to remind their captains that they are not invincible. By this principle, cavalrymen after 1876 should have been called custermen.

But the generals, including Phil Sheridan, who turned Custer loose on the Plains should have known better. He had never had anything but his extraordinary courage and his flair for the dramatic, and his ambition. Those are good things for a cavalry leader to have, essential things. An officer can't order a charge, he must lead it; soldiers, particularly troopers, like to follow a man they think is doing something important and dramatic; and lack of ambition makes men cautious, which cavalrymen can't be. It was possibly indifference after his son and two daughters went with the Confederacy that changed St. George Cooke from the country's best cavalryman to one of the least useful; he no longer cared, he'd lost his ambition.

Custer graduated from West Point in 1861 at the age of twenty-one and was assigned to the 5th Cavalry, brevet second lieutenant. That was the usual rank for a graduated cadet; the brevet was removed when there was a vacancy in the regiment. In 1861 that didn't take long, as the Regular officers were allowed to join the Volunteer and Militia regiments who were crying for experienced men.

Custer became aide-de-camp to General Phil Kearny shortly thereafter. The one-armed, dashing millionaire general became his ideal. But in the fall McClellan ruled that Regular officers could not serve on the staff of Volunteer generals, and Phil Kearny was leading the New Jersey Brigade as a Volunteer. So, Custer was relieved of his staff job; he promptly applied for sick leave, and from October '61 to February '62 stayed at his half-sister's home in Michigan. What his illness was is now not known; he was only to be sick once again in his life when he got what would now be called influenza, possibly virus X, out in the Dakotas.

The regiment he reported to after his sick leave was now the 5th, rather than the 2nd Cavalry. It followed General George Stoneman on a "raid" that failed to find Johnston's army; however, the riders did pass a Southern picket, against which Custer led Troop G, succeeding in getting one of his troopers killed, the first casualty of the Army of the Potomac. Stoneman then lent the young officer to a Lieutenant Bowen of the engineers, who needed an errand boy.

Like the admiral in Pinafore, Custer polished his doorknob so industriously that he caught McClellan's eye. Little Mac offered the lost West Pointer a job on his staff. Still a substantive second lieutenant, Custer could now be called captain.

McClellan liked Custer, in his own autobiographical phrase he "became much attached to him," and there is no doubt that the yellow-haired kid was reckless and gallant and fearless.

McClellan let Custer take a company of cavalry and two of infantry across the Chickahominy and capture a Southern outpost; such things were necessary in a cavalry officer's dossier, if he was ever to make high grade in the Army. Custer was promoted to first lieutenant in his regiment.

On another tiny foray he and another captain captured double-armfuls of Southern weapons; he was with his own regiment, under Averell, when he managed to shoot a Southern officer and capture his sword, which Custer carried through the rest of the war.

McClellan was removed from command of the Army of the Potomac, and as one of his last acts in office, gave Custer some more leave. From early November till the middle of January, Custer stayed in Michigan, wooing Elizabeth Bacon, the daughter of Judge Daniel S. Bacon, who later became his wife, and trying to convince her father that he amounted to something. He also applied to Austin Blair, Governor of Michigan, for a colonel's commission. Both the judge and the governor turned him down.

McClellan called him back to help write the final report on Little Mac's command of the Army of the Potomac; in April '63 Custer was ordered to rejoin his regiment as a first lieutenant.

But that didn't last long, for, in May, Pleasonton was made a division commander and he invited Custer to join his staff. The yellow-haired boy was an ardent believer in himself; the other members of the staff started calling him general, because he was convinced he'd wear a star before the war was over.

In June he got into action. As in so many of the events of Custeriana, it is impossible to discern now what he was doing where he was. This was an engagement of Kilpatrick – old Kilcavalry – who was in Gregg's division, rather than Pleasonton's. Kilpatrick charged Stuart, rather disastrously; the general and his second-in-command were both dehorsed; Stuart fought the Blue to a standstill and started to pull off. Custer dashed after the Confederates, into their lines and then out again, waving a bloodied saber; he wrote his sister that he thought he owed his escape to his hat, a straw model like those the Southerners were wearing.

All right. Nothing he had done by then was outstanding for a lieutenant, except the amazing amount of leave he had managed to take. But on June 27, 1863, the lieutenant, acting captain, was appointed a brigadier general of Volunteers. Why?

There is no possibility now, a hundred and more years later, of finding out why. He had always stuck close to headquarters, of course, where anything he did could be seen by the generals. He was a McClellan man, of course, and there was a strong McClellan clique among the West Pointers. He was a West Pointer, of course, and the West Point Benevolent and Protective Society was operative then as in later wars. But he had never commanded anything larger than a company, and seldom that. He was out of the Point just two years, after running up a very poor scholastic and disciplinary record there. He had had more than six months' leave in his twenty-four months of service. He had been refused a colonelcy in the Michigan Volunteers by the governor. Now he was being given a brigadier's shoulder straps over the same outfit.

The only explanation is so frivolous that it is impudent to mention it. Stuart the flamboyant had called Pleasonton, his classmate, a fop; maybe the fop saw a super-fop in Custer, who up till then had been one of the most sloppy of officers.

At any rate, General Alfred Pleasonton and his youngest brigadier had their pictures taken together and the inferior quite outshines the major general. Custer's hair in the photograph is long and curly; all possible edges of his jacket are gilt-edged; his boots shine magnificently; and his sleeves, from elbow to cuff, are covered with gold galloons, intricately and mysteriously embroidered into a pattern of glory.

Pleasonton is not in fatigues, of course. His boots rise above his kneecaps, and there is a white handkerchief in his breast pocket, and, of course, he was entitled to wear the eighteen gilt buttons of a major general, while the brigadier was restricted to the sixteen of his rank.

The twenty-three-year-old general joined his brigade with his own entourage – two horses, a dog, and a pair of trumpeter-orderlies.

Less than a week later he led the Michigan Brigade to Gettysburg. There, as half of Kilcavalry's division, they ran into Wade Hampton of Stuart's corps. Followed only by Company A of the 6th Michigan Cavalry, young Yellowhair charged the Confederate veterans. Hampton's troopers blasted the troop off the road. Custer's horse was shot from under him, and he would have been killed if a private named Churchill hadn't shot the man who had a bead on Custer. Churchill thus condemned half the 7th Cavalry to death thirteen years later, but he could hardly have known that at the time.

Artillery fire caused the canny Hampton to pull back. The next day Custer was on the flank. His orders were to stay where he was till Gregg relieved him, then report back to Kilpatrick. But there were Southern troops facing them; Custer stayed up on the line.

Stuart sent up a line of skirmishers from his horse troops, heavily backed by solid infantry. Custer ordered his men to rapid fire in volleys; by the time Fitz Lee's 1st Virginia was ready to charge, the Michigan troops were almost out of ammunition.

Custer saber-charged. Always brave, always dashing, he broke Stuart's charge with his brigade; but he had two hundred and fifty-seven casualties doing it, though some of these were only wounded or missing. At the Little Big Horn there were more than two hundred and sixty killed.

From the fact that it was Stuart he fought, it is apparent that Custer did not influence the decision at Gettysburg much one way or the other; that was the battle that Stuart was late for, and the cavalry action was a side issue.

Two months later Custer led his brigade behind Pleasonton on one of the numerous raids on Culpeper Courthouse. This time young Yellowhair rode his whole brigade into a swamp. Their commander then deserted them and tried singlehanded to capture a train; he lost another horse, was wounded in the thigh, and got twenty days' leave.

Returning to action in October, his brigade was nearly captured by Stuart, and Custer showed the one thing he was really superb at – a dashing charge that cut through Stuart's lines and let the brigade get away, battered but free.

The next day Custer and his men loitered so badly behind the rest of Kilpatrick that they spoiled a trap Stuart and Fitz Lee had set for Kilcavalry.

Stuart sucked Kilpatrick forward, Fitz Lee swung around to take him from the rear, and rode right into the straggling Michiganders. Both Lee and Custer opened fire, and the noise warned Kilpatrick. The whole division fled. This was the affair in which Stuart captured Custer's baggage train and his personal effects and a hundred and fifty troopers of Custer's brigade. The year 1863 closed on that note.

Custer was married on February 9, 1864. He and Libby enjoyed a short honeymoon, and then Custer was called on to help Kilpatrick in a raid that was going to capture Richmond. This time it was Kilpatrick himself who mired the command down in the swamps of Virginia. Custer, deployed to keep Stuart out of the battle, missed the mud. Kilpatrick ruined three thousand horses and accomplished nothing.

Then, as spring was about to renew the war, Sheridan came east, and Pleasonton and Kilpatrick were removed from the Army of the Potomac. There was a general shakeup, as the short, surly Sheridan began making a real Cavalry Corps for the Union.

Custer and his brigade were put under the capable Major General Alfred T.A. Torbert. The days of the saber charge and the wild dash were over. Torbert and Sheridan taught the troopers and their officers to fight dismounted and to aim before firing. They taught them to march at a horse-saving walk instead of at a dashing gallop.

Sheridan put Custer to fighting vanguard for him, and it was one of Custer's men who killed Jeb Stuart at Yellow Tavern. After that, the war shifted, and Custer earned his brigadier's pay. Sheridan saw how to use him; as a dashing feeler ahead of steadier commanders.

The rest of Custer's war is subordinate to the story of Sheridan, already told. Sheridan had to restrain Custer in the Valley, when, goaded by Mosby, Custer started setting fire to farmhouses, without regard for the political views of the occupants. Custer hanged some of Mosby's men, and Mosby promptly captured some of Custer's troopers and hanged them. The order went out to regard Mosby and his Rangers as legitimate soldiers.

Crook, brought in to Sheridan's force, observed Custer and thought little of him, as he reported after Sailor's Creek; Custer's band played, but his men were busier trying to capture flags than they were in fighting Confederates.

But Sheridan liked Custer. He liked Mrs. Custer even more; the gloomy little bachelor general was to buy the peace-signing table at Appomattox as a gift for Libby Custer.

Nothing scandalous is implied or even to be dreamed of. Custer had a pleasant-talking, pleasant-looking young wife; Sheridan had a lonely life and Libby Custer's teasing obviously pleased him. She was constantly after him to get married, constantly picking out brides for him. There wasn't much lightness in Sheridan's life, he never had many friends – Crook was as close a one as he seemed able to achieve, and Crook was himself pretty dour – and Mrs. Custer's husband was to stay in Sheridan's favor until the lieutenant general married, a few months before the Battle of the Little Big Horn.

Custer was made a major general of Volunteers in April '65. He was the youngest man of that rank in the Army. He finished the war as brevet major general, USA, entitled to be called general the rest of his life, though he was only a captain in the 5th Cavalry.

In the victory parade his horse ran away with him – not by accident – so that he passed the reviewing stand alone, and alone was cheered; then he reined up, rode back to his troops and took a second round of cheers, sharing them cheerfully with his men.

The Army didn't dissolve immediately. Custer still held his wartime rank, with command of a division which he was to pick up at Alexandria, Louisiana, and march to Texas and border duty; it might be necessary to invade Mexico to get Maximilian and the French out. He would be under Sheridan in the Southwest, Libby went with him to Louisiana.

The soldiers of Custer's new command were Volunteers, and the war was over; they wanted to go home. They muttered and they grumbled, and the humorless Custer got harder and harder with them; he even had some of the citizen soldiers flogged, though flogging had been officially outlawed early in the war and had been unpopular back in Stephen Kearny's day.

The harder Custer's nose got, the higher rose the spirits of his troopers. Finally, several men of the 3rd Michigan – not an outfit that had been with Custer during the war – showed up at morning formation with their blouses inside out and all their other equipment, man and horse, in as much disorder as they could achieve.

Custer did not laugh. He put the troopers under arrest and ordered a sergeant who was supposed to have been the author of the joke shot. Shot to death.

The regiment signed a unanimous letter asking pardon for the sergeant. When Custer refused, his staff started hearing rumors that the general would be shot if he attended the sergeant's execution. The officers begged Custer to at least wear sidearms. Now Custer laughed.

There was a deserter to be shot – legitimately – at the same formation. Custer, his staff unarmed, he himself on a horse, slowly reviewed the troopers, man by man, the troopers presenting their carbines, which could or could not be loaded.

The sergeant and the deserter, both blindfolded, were lined up before the firing squad. At the last minute, Custer's provost marshal pulled the sergeant aside, and as the deserter fell dead, the sergeant fell, too – he had fainted.

Custer marched his division to Texas without further mutiny; when he got there Sheridan congratulated him on the appearance of his outfit; they were soldiers instead of citizens now. Custer's bravery had paid off; when only bravery was needed, he was always successful. The Mexican threat ended, and Custer was ordered to report to the 5th Cavalry as a captain. He applied for, and got, indefinite leave of absence. He was broke; furthermore, his future pay would be two thousand a year, instead of the eight thousand he had drawn as a major general. His plans were typically Custer. He would go to Mexico and become a general in Juárez's army.

The Mexicans were agreeable to this. If he would bring a thousand experienced troopers with him as a personal command, he would be paid sixteen thousand dollars a year – in gold – and have the rank of adjutant general. Presumably he would be allowed to design his own uniform, too. He applied to General of the Army Grant for a year's leave of absence, with permission to "take service abroad."

Grant seemed to think this was all right. He even gave Custer a letter to the Mexican ambassador, in which he highly praised Sheridan, and said that if Sheridan had favored Custer, Custer must be all right. But before Custer could sign up with Juárez, his wife's father died and left her enough money so that the Custers would be able to live on a captain's pay; and Congress authorized five new regiments of cavalry; the young captain now had some chance of promotion.

Besides, President Andrew Johnson had not seen eye-to-eye with Grant about Custer's proposed adventure. Leave had been denied. The President softened the denial by inviting Custer – and the charming Libby – to accompany him on a speaking tour. Custer was to be his bodyguard.

At the end of the tour Custer could have become a colonel; but the command was that of the 9th Cavalry, one of two Negro regiments being formed, and he declined. The idea of American Negro soldiers was too new, though Negro Volunteer troops had often done well in the war, but the West Pointers distrusted the future of the 9th and 10th Cavalry.

Sheridan came to the rescue. Custer was made lieutenant colonel of the new 7th Cavalry. A.J. Smith – the 1st Dragoon – was to be colonel, but it was understood that full colonels would be used for staff work away from their regiments. Custer would have virtual command.

The Custers packed. He was to take over command at Fort Riley, in Kansas, the future Cavalry School. Packing wasn't exactly the word for it; there were four horses and innumerable dogs to be taken along.

In St. Louis they stopped to see their old friend Lawrence Barrett who was acting on the stage of a local theater. No one writing about Custer can resist quoting Libby on the subject of the friendship between General Custer and actor Barrett: "They joyed in each other as women do, and

370

I tried not to look when they met or parted, while they gazed with tears into each other's eyes and held hands like exuberant girls." No comment.

Custer drilled his regiment through the winter; in the spring he led out eight of his companies behind General Winfield Scott Hancock on a show-the-flag demonstration of unheard-of proportions: a thousand infantry and artillery and a vast wagon train would go along. Hancock was sure that the seething Southern Cheyennes and the Arapahoes would become peaceful at once when they saw all this might.

The exact opposite happened. The Cheyennes were nervous and jumpy and had been ever since Chivington's Colorado troops had massacred some of their people at Sand Creek. Their agent, Colonel E.W. Wynkoop, however, was a good man and they recognized him as such; he was gradually calming them down, perhaps pointing out the difference between Regulars and the Indian-hating State and Territorial militia. Wynkoop told Hancock that a heavy troop movement into the Cheyenne country would surely be taken as a preliminary to another slaughter of Cheyennes and would force those Indians into becoming hostile.

Hancock marched anyway. He told Wynkoop that "no insolence would be tolerated from any Indians." The general commanded from an ambulance instead of from horseback and picked up his troops as he went from Leavenworth to Riley, then to Harker and finally to Fort Larned, where the ponderous column was completed. Wynkoop made a final effort to stop the troops at Harker, but Hancock went on into Cheyenne country.

A few Cheyenne chiefs came into the camp; Hancock insisted on counciling with them at night, which went against Cheyenne superstition or religion or both. Nothing was decided; Hancock announced that he would march on the big Cheyenne village at Pawnee Forks.

The chiefs met him a few miles out from that village and begged him to keep back; the sight of blue uniforms in force would panic the Cheyennes, and the chiefs could not predict what would happen. All afternoon the Indians had been burning the prairie grass to stop the troops; it was obvious that they were desperate.

Hancock didn't commit himself, but he waited till eleven the next morning for the chiefs to come out for further counciling; then he moved toward the village and met the chiefs right on the edge of camp.

He greeted them by having the 7th Cavalry draw their sabers and gallop along a line of deployed infantry; the artillery was wheeled and unlimbered to cover the Indians; it was a queer setting for a peace conference.

Custer wrote later that he was impressed by the *number* of Indians; every diarist who ever encountered the Plains tribes had this first impression. As a matter of fact, more experienced hands said that there were only about three hundred Cheyennes at Pawnee Fork; about a tenth the number Custer was to meet in 1876.

Hancock promised to leave the Cheyenne village alone; but that night he got reports that the Indians were dispersing. This, of course, was just about the purpose of the expedition; but Hancock was not the clearest thinker in the world. He sent Custer out to contain the Cheyennes.

It was too late; the Indians were gone. Custer rode in pursuit, but the fugitives broke into a hundred parties, and got away. When they re-formed they were formally on the warpath.

Custer then marched his troopers to Fort Hays, shoving hard all the way, trying to make veterans out of them all in a rush. He was absolutely tireless himself, and never, in all his short life, understood that other men did not have his endurance and energy. Deserting from the 7th Cavalry was a constant occupation. In 1868, according to Godfrey, then a lieutenant in the 7th, a sergeant equipped and mounted thirty men, issued rations to them, marched them thirty miles from the post, and then told them that he was deserting and they could, too. A couple of them went back to the fort and told the story; the rest scattered.

The summer of 1867 was reasonably quiet for a while; the Sioux-Cheyenne preferred to stay out of sight of the Army. But late in June a Sioux band tried to stampede Custer's horses, and the colonel, in a red nightshirt, turned out and led his men in driving the hostiles off.

Then Custer ordered a Captain Hamilton and his company after the frustrated horse thieves; Hamilton got himself into an ambush, from which his colonel and the rest of the garrison rescued him.

Libby was on her way to her husband at Fort Wallace. Three days after the Sioux attack on the fort, they attacked her train; the escort, under big W.W. Cook, Custer's adjutant, fought them off unil re-enforcements came out from the post and the Sioux fled.

Custer drove his troopers around the Platte all summer, trying to make real soldiers out of them, never really contacting the Indians, but getting harder and harder on the men as the realities of Plains fighting and Plains life were made apparent to him. Some of his biographers see a parallel between the Custer who burned farmhouses when Mosby humiliated him and the Custer who tried to kill his troops when the hostile Plains riders eluded him. That could be; at any rate, after stumbling around the prairie for six weeks without getting a fight, he ordered his column to march from the Republican to the Platte, a sixty-five-mile waterless jornada, in a single day.

The weather was hot, the sun was high. The men marched, the horses stumbled. Troopers dropped down and led; then the men stumbled and had to mount up on the exhausted troop horses again. At eleven o'clock at night Custer apparently had had enough of it; he turned his command over to Major Joel Elliott, took his orderly, the doctor, and Lieutenant Myles Moylan, and rode ahead to water, leaving the bulky command to come along behind him.

At the Platte he and his three companions drank, drove their sabers into the sand for picket pins – the only reason for carrying sabers on the Plains – and slept. When they woke up the column was on the river, three miles below them; some of the men had not gotten in till dawn. Also, Custer learned, he had slept through an Indian attack on a stage station only a mile from his sandy bed. Three men had been killed. Custer had slept through his first real chance to fight; and now he got orders from Fort Sedgwick; a lieutenant and squad of the 2nd Cavalry was searching for him back on the Republican to order him to come in to Fort Wallace for supplies. If the dispatch from Sedgwick didn't end with the Army word forthwith, it implied it. But Custer was on the Platte with an exhausted column.

That night the desertion movement changed from a dribble to a torrent. Custer later said that forty troopers and non-coms went over the hill; he exaggerated, but enough men left that night of July 7 to panic the fame-seeking colonel.

The next day twelve more men started out of noon camp. Custer ordered his officers to go after them and "bring in none alive." Elliott and Cook went after the deserters; the seven troopers who were mounted got away; of five dismounted fugitives two feigned death and escaped and three were shot down. One of them died ten days later.

Custer got into Fort Wallace a week after the shooting of the enlisted men. On the way there he found the body of Lieutenant Kidder of the 2nd and his escort who had been sent out to find Custer; they had been killed by Indians, but no part of the blame for that could be laid at Colonel Custer's door; the greenhorn lieutenant had followed the wrong set of tracks.

Fort Wallace, garrisoned by two understrength companies of the 7th was in bad shape; Captain Barnitz reported to his colonel that he had repeatedly been attacked and there was cholera in the camp. Hancock had ordered A.J. Smith to order Custer to work out of Fort Wallace for the time being. But if there was cholera at Wallace, there might be cholera at Riley; and Libby Custer was at Riley. Custer deserted his command and rode for Riley. He took with him all of his soldiers who had operative horses, seventy-five troopers, Cook, Hamilton, and Tom Custer, his brother.

Custer had started the ride with worn-out men; he wore them out worse on his way through Hays and Harker to Riley. Twenty more men deserted, and finally he deserted the escort, too, and went ahead with only Tom Custer, Cook, and two orderlies. By then hostile skirmishers had killed two of his rearguard; he didn't stop to fight, but left orders at the next infantry post for the foot soldiers to go out and bury bis dead.

Colonel Smith was at Fort Harker. Andrew Jackson Smith, class of 1838, U.S.M.A., was not a young man in 1867. Aroused from his sleep he listened to Custer's rather garbled account of the death of Lieutenant Kidder, 2nd Cavalry, the desertions, the cholera, all told in a jumble of words, and told Custer to go on to Riley if he wanted to. The next day Smith was more wide-awake. He wired Custer to return to his post of duty at the head of his command.

Custer found no cholera at Riley. If he had the court-martial that sat on his case at Hancock's orders might have been easier on him. He was tried for destroying government horses, failing to fight Indians who had attacked his command, and ordering his officers to shoot the deserters, one of whom had died as a result of those orders. He was found guilty and sentenced to suspension of rank, command, and pay for one year. The court also recommended that he be turned over to a civilian court to be tried for murder but left this part of their findings up to the President for review. Johnson never did anything about it. General of the Army Grant reviewed and confirmed the military punishment and marked it as lenient.

The Army used to talk about Custer's Luck. He had plenty of it; now a large and concrete portion of it descended over him. He was tried in mid-September. In the same month Hancock and Phil Sheridan were ordered to exchange commands; the ambulance rider went south to govern Reconstruction territory, the little black general came northwest to Leavenworth, to take over the Department of the Missouri, headquartered at St. Louis. But Leavenworth was his forward post, and quarters suitable for a general had been made ready for him. He turned them over to Libby and Autie Custer as a mark of personal favor, even if Custer was on the suspended basis. They lived in them all winter, then went back to the house she had inherited in Monroe, Michigan. They passed a "delightful" summer there; the adjective is Custer's.

Things were not delightful on the Plains. The Indian Bureau had issued arms – for hunting – to the Cheyennes and Arapahoes. They weren't very good arms; the legend that the Plains Indians always had better guns than the Army was exposed at the time by George Bird Grinnell, and subsequent research confirms his careful findings. But the guns were good enough for raids on little white settlements in Kansas. The 7th Cavalry and some of the 3rd Infantry took the field under another ambulance-riding commander, Brevet Brigadier General Sully, lieutenant colonel of infantry.

Major Joel Elliott commanded the eleven companies of the 7th; he seems to have been the only officer of field grade left with the regiment.

The hostiles ran Bully's column back to Fort Dodge.

Phil Sheridan decided that the Indians could not be licked on the Plains while the grass was up; he laid out a winter campaign, and he persuaded Sherman that Custer was needed to fight in it. Sherman endorsed the plea for suspension of sentence by saying that Custer was "very brave, even to rashness, a good trait in a cavalry officer."

Custer joined Sheridan at Fort Hays and was given orders to go on to Fort Dodge. The expedition would be under the command of Sully; Custer would lead eleven companies of the 7th, and Kansas would supply a regiment of Volunteer Cavalry.

The 7th was on Bluff Creek, about thirty miles out from Dodge. It was in worse shape than when Custer had ridden it to death before deserting it. Joel Elliott, commanding, was a major by mistake; he had been a captain of Volunteers in the Civil War, and then superintendent of schools in Toledo. Then he had taken an examination for the Regular Army, hoping to get a lieutenant's commission; but his schoolmaster's experience with examinations had caused him to turn in a perfect paper, and the board had commissioned him a full major.

Custer started hazing the 7th into some sort of military fitness. It was no easy task. The hostiles had seen how the 7th did not turn to avenge or even bury its dead on Custer's march; on Sully's the Indians had been able to kidnap two rearguards with impunity.

Now young braves studying war rode constantly around the camp on Bluff Creek, whooping and deriding the blue-coated pony soldiers. It was the thing to do, like street kids stealing fruit or taunting cops. Custer sent four companies out to try and find the village of the derisive raiders, but he picked a highly picturesque man, self-called California Joe, as chief of scouts. Unfortunately, Joe got drunk and charged his own column and was demoted, and the expedition got nowhere near the hostiles.

Custer kept the 7th on the move, trying to harden it, trying to make soldiers of men who were determined not to be soldiers. He ordered target practice, for which he might have had to pay out of his own pocket; the expenditure of cartridges on the range was not usually authorized for another ten years or more. He sorted the regimental troop horses by color, and assigned each color to a company, often a good morale builder and always a good tool for rallying in a battle or skirmish. The band – always of Custer importance – rode gray horses. Cold weather came on, and Custer drew winter uniforms for the men. He ended up with a regiment that looked and moved like a fighting outfit. Then he moved out, early in November. But he moved toward the lodges and villages of the Indians who had settled where the government told them to; against the friendly Sioux-Cheyenne-Kiowas-Arapahoes, instead of against the hostiles.

The fault was Sheridan's, not Custer's; the 7th rode where the lieutenant general told them to. The fault may have been – quite probably was – even higher up, in Washington. Total annihilation of the Plains Indians seems to have been a tacit policy of the government for a while, though no written record of it can be found. Crook was not yet on the Plains.

Sully was in command. That had been clear all along. But as soon as the column was out of reach of Sheridan, Custer disputed the chain of seniority. He and Sully had both been made lieutenant colonels on the same day; Sully's highest brevet was that of brigadier general, Custer's was a rank higher.

While the two highest officers in the expedition were bickering, Sheridan rode out to see how his men were doing. Custer talked to Sheridan and Sheridan sent Sully back to Fort Dodge. Then Custer's band serenaded Sheridan, and Sheridan and his staff presented Custer with a winter outfit – fur cap, buffalo vest, buffalo shoes.

After a few days Sheridan turned back; Custer was in command, Elliott second-in-command; the Kansas Volunteers had not showed up, except for two companies which Sheridan used for a personal escort.

Now Custer showed what he could do: move men. His column rode toward the Washita hard and well; he had made a regiment out of the 7th at last. It was discouraging when the valves on the musical instruments froze and they couldn't have band music, but they kept going anyway.

Custer dropped his wagon train on the Canadian River and shoved on, Osage scouts ahead of him. Elliott was out to the south with three companies, following an Indian trail in the snow. The main column cut across the arc of Elliott's trail. At sundown the slower moving main body was right on Elliott's track; they kept going, there was moonlight. What they were riding up on was Fort Cobb, an Army Indian post where General William B. Hazen, who had been one of Custer's instructors when Custer was a cadet, was feeding Indians who wanted peace with the white man.

Specifically – though Custer didn't know whether he was about to attack Sioux or Kiowa Apaches or whatever – the people below were Black Kettle's Cheyennes, and Black Kettle was as peace-loving a Cheyenne as existed; he had talked his people into giving up vengeance for Chivington's slaughter at Sand Creek.

Custer split his command into three parts, two to attack from the rear of the village, he to take the front. It was not a battle, it was a slaughter; a massacre, though the nineteenth century reserved that term for encounters in which the whites lost. The three columns hit the sleeping village and poured fire into it from their repeating carbines. Men, women, children, it didn't matter. Black Kettle was killed in the door of his lodge.

But there had been a gap between the two columns that hit the rear of the village and Indians streamed out through it. Major Elliott pursued, followed by the sergeant major and eighteen troopers.

Custer went on with the main job, which was killing Indians. He killed over a hundred braves; dead women and children weren't counted, but fifty-three of them were taken prisoner; most had wounds. Captain Hamilton was killed, Barnitz badly wounded, and thirteen other men were hurt, including Tom Custer.

As was the custom in winter fighting, the troopers had slipped their overcoats and knapsacks before charging; they had left them under guard. Now the guards were driven in, saying that the sacks and coats had been taken by Indians and one of Custer's pet dogs had been killed.

The Osage scouts, who had advised Custer against attacking, now reported that the valley of the Washita was alive with Indian villages, and that hostiles were massing on the bluffs above Black Kettle's village. If they hadn't been hostiles yesterday, they were today.

Godfrey, sent out to round up the Cheyenne pony herd, reported that he had heard firing: obviously Elliott and his nineteen men were engaged across the valley. Custer put two companies to charging the gathering Indians, while the rest of his command gathered up the Indians' goods – tepees, blankets, winter supplies, the usual plunder of a winter village – and burned them. Then he killed the Cheyenne ponies, and the band – perhaps the fire had thawed the valves – played the 7th out of the village and away.

Custer had made no effort to find his second-in-command, his sergeant major, his eighteen troopers. He was never tried for this desertion. The fog of battle – which should be written "battle (?)"– covered the whole thing. He just reported to Sheridan that Elliott and six – not nineteen – men had been killed. Excuses were given for him by others, not by himself.

Excuse One: He had to get off the Washita because his men had lost their coats and would freeze. But he had captured more buffalo robes than he had men.

Excuse Two: He was surrounded by hostiles who outnumbered him. But he had marched out with band playing, not the act of a surrounded, outnumbered commander.

Excuse Three: With the country turned hostile, he had to get back to his supply train or his column would starve. But he had captured great supplies in the village, his wagon train was firmly planted by him, and anyway, any trooper who fought on the Plains had to learn to eat horseflesh sooner or later; Custer had killed and abandoned hundreds of Cheyenne ponies.

Charles King, the officer of Crook's who later turned fiction writer, felt that the 7th never trusted Custer after he abandoned Elliott, that most of the trouble in that regiment arose from the slaughter on the Washita.

There doesn't seem to be much evidence that this is so; King was probably imagining how he would have felt if a superior officer had behaved as Custer did.

Custer admirers have never been able to explain why he did what he did; and only the most bitter of Custer haters say he was a coward. There is simply no explanation for what happened.

And there is no record of what Brevet Brigadier General Lieutenant Colonel Sully thought about the incident. Sheridan could well have sent him as Custer's second-in-command.

Custer was back at the Washita a couple of weeks later. This time the 7th Cavalry had the Kansas Volunteers along. Custer also had an elderly Irish cook – female – along to fix his meals; a correspondent from the New York *Herald*, De B.R. Keim, to sing his praises; and a civilian, Daniel A. Brewster, who was looking for a sister captured by the Cheyennes back in the summer.

They found, without difficulty, the stripped, coyote-gnawed bodies of Elliott and all but four of his men, two miles from the Black Kettle Village. Captain Benteen of the 7th was so indignant about the desertion of Elliott that he wrote a long and florid letter about it to a friend in St. Louis, and the friend gave the document to a newspaper, which published it over a pseudonym. The details were too accurate for it to have been written from hearsay; Custer called his officers together and said he would whip the one who had written it. He had a dogwhip ready in his hand.

Benteen told him to start whipping. Custer said he would see him later and dropped the whole matter. But, again, this could not be cowardice; Captain Frederick W. Benteen, a Brevet Brigadier General, was older than Custer, shorter, and fatter.

Sheridan was with Custer on this second trip to the Washita. They found General Hazen annoyed; Sherman had put him out there to pacify the Indians, he had done so, and now it was all undone. But he doesn't seem to have argued with Sheridan, who was a lieutenant general – Hazen was a substantive colonel who had commanded a corps under Sherman in the War.

There weren't any hostiles to shoot; they had scattered too far. Custer took the 7th down near the Texas border of Indian Territory and set them to building. The result was called Fort Sill. While this was going on he took forty sharpshooters from his command and set out to help Daniel Brewster to recover his sister.

That wasn't to happen yet; but Custer did find Little Raven's band of Arapahoes, a group of warriors who far outnumbered Custer's sharpshooters. The colonel suddenly behaved sensibly; he talked to Little Raven and his chiefs calmly, and when he left them they were headed for Fort Sill and surrender.

Back at the Washita Sheridan, too, had had a streak of the hard sense he had shown so often in the Civil War and so seldom since; he made peace with the Kiowas.

Now only the Southern Cheyennes were on the warpath south of the Platte. Custer returned to Sheridan; the lieutenant general went East, and Custer was left with his regiment and the Kansas Volunteers. He dismounted the latter to use as infantry; altogether he had about fifteen hundred men, half of them cavalry. He also had his band along as he hunted Cheyennes. The Kansans reported that band music was no substitute for food, which was in short supply.

Custer found a Cheyenne trail and stuck to it with a persistence that would have done Crook credit. When he caught up with the Indians, he was almost alone, his column far behind him; he sent Cook riding back to bring the troops up, and calmly rode in, followed by a single orderly, to parley with Stone Forehead, whom the whites called Medicine Arrow because he was the keeper of the Cheyennes' traditional bundle of sacred arrows.

The Custer who had never exhibited anything worthwhile except courage suddenly was intelligent and diplomatic. Perhaps the long, long trail that led to Stone Forehead's village had calmed him down, given him time to think. But diplomacy, tact, patience did no good. Next to Chivington, Custer was the most hated name in the Cheyenne language. Grinnell, who was with Custer in the Black Hills a few years later, and who remains, after all these years, the leading authority on the Cheyenne Indians, says that the sachem put his most powerful curse on Custer, speaking in a mild and welcoming voice, seated him in the place of dishonor – on his host's right – and told him he was a traitor, and a murderer.

Custer, who knew no Cheyenne, unconsciously confirms the story. He thought the seat he was given was that of high honor; and he noted that while he was handed a pipe, none of the Indians smoked with him.

Custer was maneuvering for time, to get his troops into position; Stone Forehead was maneuvering for position, to get the troops bivouacked out of sight of the village, so his people could flee before the treacherous might of Custer hit them as it had hit Black Kettle's people. The troop column was carrying a Washita squaw as interpreter; she found out that Brewster's sister, Mrs. Morgan, and another young white woman were indeed in the Cheyenne camp.

Custer accepted the campsite Stone Forehead had assigned to him, but he put sentries on a hill where they could watch the Cheyennes. Stone Forehead sent men over to dance for the yellow-haired colonel, a distraction he hoped would keep Custer from knowing that the people were getting away; but the sentries reported that the ponies had been brought into the village from their grazing grounds, and Custer seized the dancers as hostages; he sent one of them back to the village with word that he would attack if the white women weren't released and the rest of the village marched to the reservation.

Stone Forehead made a mistake; he dragged the negotiations out too long. If he had known Custer better, he would have known that nothing could engage that dashing soldier's attention very long. Custer wanted to free the white girls, he wanted to show that he could pacify as well as murder Indians, but not if it meant too many days of inactivity.

Finally, he snapped an ultimatum at Stone Forehead. The Indians had till sunset to deliver the white women to Custer; as the sun went down, the three hostages Custer held would go up – on ropes strung around their necks.

The women were released. Custer's Irish cook lent them civilized clothing, and Custer broke camp, taking the hostages with him; he left word with Stone Forehead that the three men would be released when the band came into the reservation. Stone Forehead said that would be as soon as the grass was high enough for the ponies to travel.

Why Custer behaved so well that one time may be explained by passages in a letter he sent ahead to his wife from the Washita, where he tarried:

> And now my most bitter enemies cannot say that I am either blood-thirsty or possessed of an unworthy ambition … Many have come to me and confessed their error.

That summer Kiowas, Arapahoes, and Cheyennes went on the reservation; the 7th had nothing to do but ride out showing the flag. Colonel A.J. Smith completed the thirty years necessary for his pension, and resigned; S.D. Sturgis became colonel, but the 7th was known as Custer's regiment. It was a good one, everyone admitted. Best disciplined on the Plains.

How it got that way – and why it had such a high rate of desertions – may be explained by a statement of Captain (Brevet Brigadier General) Benteen made after he retired: "(That) summer of '69 General Custer had in use a hole deeply dug in the ground about 30 x 30 feet, by about 15 feet deep, entrance by ladder, hole boarded over: this was the guard house and a man even absent from roll call was let down."

Don Rickey, Jr., whose study of enlisted men covers the years from the Civil War to the end of the century, found that the 7th was known as one of the harshest commands.

With the Cheyennes on the reservation, the hostages were to be released. But two of them were killed in the process – Big Head and Dull Knife – and two soldiers were also knifed to death. This doesn't seem to have been Custer's fault.

Evenings, that summer of '69, were gay for the Custers. Though the colonel didn't drink – he had taken the pledge at his half-sister's request – liquor was served in the Custer quarters, and the romping was of the childish sort to be expected. The officers of the 7th were split apart; there was the Custer clique – Tom, Moylan, Cook, etc. – and then there were what have been called the more reliable and responsible officers.

In October the outfit was moved back to Leavenworth. Custer started writing the story of his life; he was then almost thirty years old. He never finished the book, though he later wrote *My Life on the Plains.*

The next summer was again quiet; Custer took winter leave. He and Libby were lionized in New York, and in the house Libby had inherited in Monroe, Michigan. Then the 7th was given Reconstruction duty in Kentucky, Tennessee, and South Carolina. No glory there; Custer tried to transfer to another regiment, without success. He got back to the Plains once before the regiment went there for a tour of duty in March '73. The interim trip was on orders; he accompanied a grand duke of Russia on a hunting trip.

By March 1873 the Plains were beginning to seethe again. The government, consistently, had broken all its pledges to the Sioux and Cheyenne, and they were beginning to listen to Sitting Bull who had never believed the white man's promises in the first place.

Crook was still in Arizona. Sheridan sent Custer and the 7th out toward the Yellowstone. One squadron was detached under a new major, Marcus A. Reno, to guard a party of surveyors who were surveying the western Canadian border; Colonel Sturgis was called to St. Paul for staff duty; the golden-haired lieutenant colonel was in charge of the rest of the regiment. The purpose of the march was to guard the men laying out the Northern Pacific Railroad and to show the flag both to the Indians and to the white settlers who had been complaining that they were in jeopardy from hostiles.

The ten companies of the 7th were not to go alone; as many companies of the 8th and 9th and five of the 22nd, one of the 6th, all infantry outfits, herded beef cattle for subsistence and the soldiers were further provided for by civilian wagoners and guides, one civilian for every five soldiers. There were two fieldpieces, too, and a few Arikara scouts. The Arikaras were a branch of the Pawnee nation, and sworn enemies of the Sioux.

It was a big outfit, and commanded by Colonel David S. Stanley, formerly a full army Commander in the war. Custer tried to take over, and Stanley, who found him "cold-blooded, untruthful, and unprincipled," snapped him to attention. Custer respected men stronger than he; he started behaving properly.

Three companies, two of them 7th Cavalry, were dropped off on the Yellowstone to build a fort – plenty of evidence to the Sioux that the white man was there to stay.

Custer was riding advance guard with Tom Custer's and Myles Moylan's troops on August 4; up till now no hostiles had been seen. The troopers were unsaddling for noon when a half-dozen Sioux rode down, trying to stampede the horses, some of whom were already stripped and rolling. The pickets drove them off with carbine fire, and the stampede failed; the two Custers took off after the hostiles with all the men able to go; Moylan waited behind while the rest of the troopers threw their saddles and bridles back on. It was a trap; the stampede had only been a feint. The handful of Sioux rode through a body that Custer estimated at three hundred hostiles, and a fire fight started.

It went on for hours with hardly any results at all. An Arikara shot a Sioux off his horse, and perhaps killed him. Then Custer ordered his trumpeter to blow To Horse and charged the hostiles. They split and fled; two more Sioux were killed, a couple of troopers wounded, and the thing was over. But the hostiles circled and caught two Army men between Custer and the main body of Stanley's column; they killed the men, one a veterinary, the other a trader or sutler named Baliran.

Four days later the trail of a big party of Sioux was cut; Custer, who had the only cavalry with the column, was sent out after them. He led the 7th from ten o'clock at night till sunup, about five o'clock, let them rest three hours, and took up the trail again until noon. Then he camped, planning to hit the village at dawn, as he had hit on the Washita. But the Indians got away, and the 7th found itself unable to cross the fast, deep Yellowstone.

The Sioux found out about this and began peppering the troopers from the south bank; Custer's orderly was shot through the head. The Sioux braves started swimming back to surround Custer; their light horses, lightly accoutered, had no trouble with the river. Surrounded, Custer ordered the band to play and the troopers to charge. The Sioux on the north bank scattered and recrossed the river and vanished as Stanley's heavy column came up with its artillery and its infantry long rifles. Four of the cavalrymen had been killed, and four more wounded, but Custer counted it a victory by claiming that forty Sioux were dead; maybe they were. At any rate, no heavy harassment of the column was tried again; the 7th got back to Fort Lincoln late in September, and summer maneuvers were over.

Custer spent the winter at Fort Abraham Lincoln, hunting with his huge pack of hounds, bickering with the civilians of Bismarck, muttering, not too softly, about the sutler and trader appointments of Secretary of War Belknap, an appointee and personal friend of President Grant.

In the spring Sioux ran off the fort's mule herd and Custer left the post unguarded and took every man out after the hostiles. The hard-chased Sioux abandoned the mules, which Custer sent back to Lincoln with a tiny escort, not nearly enough to defend the women there – and the ammunition and supplies – if the hostiles circled or another body of them appeared.

The 7th chased the Sioux till the troop horses played out; they captured a few Indian ponies but did no damage to the hostile riders. On the second day of July the grass was high enough for the 7th to move out toward the Black Hills; they took with them two companies of infantry, a fieldpiece and three Catlings, and were off to penetrate to the very heart of Sioux country, the sacred, tree-covered hills where the Sioux went to worship their god in their own way; the land that had been most solemnly promised to them for ever and ever, without the intrusion of a single white man.

The march was completely without incident. There was no glory in this; Custer had to do something to call attention to himself. He issued a statement that the Black Hills were paved with gold; that miners with his column had shaken the heavy dust "out of the grass roots."

This was 1874. Custer had signed his death warrant. The Sioux could never leave the warpath while miners were pouring into the sacred pine forests of the Black Hills to pan the sacred creeks. The Indians could be beaten off the warpath, they could be taught there was no use fighting, but they could not, out of their religious conviction, quit and remain true Sioux.

The Battle of the Little Big Horn was now inevitable. But Custer had gotten his name in the papers. And all over the country men read the news – or had it read to them – and headed for the Black Hills and the chance of a possible fortune in a nation going through a cycle of depression.

Custer started the winter by arresting Rain-in-the-Face, a Sioux who was boasting that he had killed the trader Baliran and the veterinary doctor, Honsinger, on the Yellowstone foray. The lieutenant colonel threw him in the guardhouse and turned detective.

Grain had been disappearing from the Fort Lincoln stores. Custer got a trooper to confess he had stolen it and sold it to civilian traders in Bismarck.

Custer marched on Bismarck, seized the stolen grain, and arrested the civilians who had it in their possession. He threw his prisoners in with his lone Sioux captive; one of them cut a hole in the rear of the guardhouse, and whites and Indian all ran away.

All through the summer of '75 prospectors poured into the Black Hills, thousands of them. The Sioux stayed quiet; perhaps they thought the miners would pan the gold out of the streams and go away again.

There wasn't much gold in the grass roots. But unfortunately, there were vast deposits of low grade quartz ore, no good to the pan and blanket prospector, but fine for organized exploitation by machinery owned by stock companies. These were founded, and they are still in the Black Hills. The Homestake mine is the largest producer of gold in the United States today.

One explanation for the Sioux's failure to attack in that summer of 1875 is the very nature of the Black Hills. They are so sacred to Sioux minds, so holy that it might have seemed certain that the gods who dwelt there would run the white men out. Whatever the reason, the Sioux waited through the summer for the Army to keep its word and run the miners out of the Hills. Crook and Richard Dodge and Custer did turn out and evict the trespassers; but it was easy to go back into the mountains where the troops were not; the soldiers were well aware that they were bailing a sinking boat with sieves.

Custer spent the winter of 1875-76 getting himself into as serious trouble as he had ever before managed. The Indian Bureau spent that same winter committing as great idiocies as it had ever managed.

Custer, first.

On leave in New York he continued to berate Secretary of War William W. Belknap. When a committee was formed under Representative Hiester Clymer of Pennsylvania to investigate the matter of Army sutlers, Custer promptly offered his testimony. Belknap had already resigned and was under arrest; Custer's testimony wasn't needed; and when he finally got on the stand, it turned out he had known nothing except by hearsay. Desperate, he dragged the President's brother, Orville Grant, into the mess, and then had to admit that he was again going on hearsay.

Sheridan had married, and unless Mrs. Sheridan was different from any other woman in the world, she probably was tired of hearing of the virtues of Libby Custer, who had known her husband before she did. Sheridan was still pro-Custer, but his fervor cooled a bit. And Grant was not only President and Commander-in-Chief, he had been the general who had given Sherman and Sheridan fame and rank and power.

The Clymer committee listened to Custer's stumbling testimony – there was one matter of five thousand sacks of grain that seemed to have some substance to it – and ordered him to stand by for further questioning.

But the troops were moving out against the Sioux and the Cheyennes; Custer had to go West. It was up to President Grant. Not surprisingly, the President was not interested in granting Custer an interview.

Custer had to go West, or all his post-war career was without a climax. For this was to be the big Plains War, that would forever still the Sioux and the Cheyenne. The warpath had never been so crowded.

The quiet summer of 1875 had been followed by the heaviest snows of years. The Indian agents wired East that they would need extra money to feed their charges. Congress acted slowly; they finally passed the appropriation in the spring, when it was too late. The agents, seeing peaceful Indians starve, gave them permission to go off the reservation where game was plentiful.

Early in December the Indian Bureau issued an order; all Plains Indians must be on the reservations by the end of January or be declared hostile and subject to being hunted down by the Army. Runners were sent out to take the word to the hunting villages. The snow was so bad that few runners got through; most of these couldn't get back to their bases before the deadline had passed. The villages would not be able to move – hampered by valuable ponies and by women and children – until the snows melted and the grass came up.

The order simply couldn't be executed. On February 7 Sheridan was told that dominion over the Plains Indians had passed from the Indian Bureau to the Army. As soon as he could he was to take the field. Crook made his winter campaign, ruined by Reynolds' failure to consolidate a victory over Crazy Horse. Blizzards came on and held Terry up while Custer in Washington fretted; Terry had told him that he could head the expedition against the Sioux. Terry picked another leader for the war column, Colonel Hazen, who had been agent to the Sioux and Cheyenne. But Custer – this could be coincidence, not a plan – involved Hazen in his testimony, and Hazen was summoned to Washington, too.

The Clymer committee released Custer, but Grant would not let him leave Washington. Sherman, as General of the Army, issued a statement: Custer was not the only officer in the Army capable of leading the expedition on the Plains; the Army had "hundreds" of men capable of the job.

Custer left Washington without permission. Sherman wired Sheridan in Chicago to stop the runagate colonel there and to order Terry to get moving out without Custer. Sheridan did so. He bawled Custer out with all the fury of his well-known Irish tongue, but he did grant the colonel the right to wire Sherman appealing for a reversal of the General of the Army's decision. Terry was at his headquarters in St. Paul. Sherman's orders to Sheridan had seemed to include that place as not forbidden to Custer; Custer went to St. Paul.

Alfred Howe Terry was not a West Pointer; he had entered the Army in the Civil War; before that he had been a lawyer in Connecticut. Now he used his attorney's training to write a series of telegrams for Custer to sign, and he proposed to Grant a compromise, the great lawyer's weapon: Terry would command the war against the Sioux-Cheyennes, but Custer would command his own regiment. Grant must have been heartily sick of the whole thing by then. He consented.

Sherman passed the consent along, with a little advice; and advice from the General of the Army was, of course, an order; be prudent, and don't take any newspapermen along, they always make trouble. Terry had saved Custer; had given him one more chance at glory; had probably kept him from being thrown out of the Army. Custer walked out of Terry's office and told every officer he met – at least four remembered and later told – that he had no intention of serving under Terry in the field. His words were that he would "cut loose and swing clear" of his benefactor-general.

The rest is history, and much hashed-over history. Terry tried too large a combination, and combinations seldom work. Crook marched successfully and fought successfully without ever knowing where Terry was or if he was in the field at all.

Custer broke his orders and did his best to keep an independent command; Custer refused re-enforcements from Terry because he wanted all the glory for the 7th, which he had boasted could lick all the Indians on the Plains.

Custer refused to believe his Indian scouts when they pointed out the huge army of hostiles waiting in the valley of the Little Big Horn; refused to believe them when the hostiles were raising such a cloud of dust in the air that the Arikaras had to be right.

Custer split his command, and sent Marcus Reno off to fight, promising to re-enforce him, and then never again seems to have given Reno any more thought than he had given Elliott on the Washita.

On June 25, 1876, Custer and two hundred and sixty men of the 7th Cavalry died at the Little Big Horn. And Custer became the most widely known cavalryman the United States has ever had – on the same day he became a corpse.

Historically speaking one of the most famous horses that ever served in the U.S. Cavalry was Comanche, the only living thing found on the battlefield after the Battle of the Little Big Horn. Although the horse was suffering from seven wounds, he was brought back to Fort Riley where he recovered and lived out his remaining years in retirement, dying November 6, 1891. For many years Comanche appeared in all 7th Cavalry parades, decked out in mourning and led by a trooper from I Troop.

Chapter 27

They Danced in their Shirts

It can be said that Custer did not die in vain. He called attention to the stalemate on the Plains. Sheridan re-enforced Terry and Crook, and the Sioux-Cheyennes were dismounted, disarmed and forcibly put at peace, all but Sitting Bull and a small band who fled to Canada.

There was peace on the Plains, then, and there was more cavalry. Congress decreed that a tenth of the whole Army, twenty-five hundred men, be mounted. The artillery had to be stripped of ten companies to make up the loss to the infantry.

Enlistments rose; young men wanted to avenge Custer. But by the time they could be trained, Crook had done their work for them with the old Regulars. Reno, with what was left of the 7th, helped him.

The Army enlisting program, for the first time in peace, could invoke patriotism, if being anti-American Indian can be called being patriotic. Young men calling themselves Custer Avengers all wanted to join the 7th; but the survivors of Custer's discipline were a tough bunch of mercenaries, and the recruits were sent where they were needed; many of them were quickly disillusioned and deserted. Officers and professional non-coms let them go, usually; the wartime type of volunteer simply didn't fit into the social ranks of men to whom the thirteen dollars a month looked like high living, or even a human way of life.

The 7th Cavalry, famous because it had suffered the worst defeat ever given by Indians to a Regular regiment, was one of the last cavalry outfits to fight Indians; parts of it were in two small engagements in Arizona in 1896.

Before that, however, the regiment, in toto, had been the chief Army weapon at the Battle of Wounded Knee, as it is called by the Army, or the Massacre at Wounded Knee, as the Sioux still remember it, the incident near the Pine Ridge Indian Agency on the south edge of South Dakota in the last month of 1890.

This really marks the end of the Indian Wars; there were sporadic incidents after it, but they almost all involved one or two Indians, and the so-called hostiles were usually drunk.

Wounded Knee is unique not only because it was the last major Indian-Army engagement but because it was also part of the first national Indian movement, really the only national Indian movement if it is regarded – as it should be – as the forerunner of the Native American Church, the peyote cult.

Indians are not united today. The Navajos have little use for their Apache cousins, the Apaches despise their Maricopa and Pima neighbors and there are disagreements among such cooperative and peaceful people as the Pueblo villages and the Mission bands of Southern California. But something that started in 1870 far, far away from South Dakota and the Sioux country has really not ended yet and was the direct cause of the Wounded Knee trouble in 1890.

It was called the Ghost Dance, more properly the Ghost Shirt Dance. Curiously it was first conceived by a Northern Paiute, ordinarily a tribe looked down upon by other Indians.

Paiute means Water Ute, and the regular Utes and the Shoshone (Snakes) and other tribes who speak a language similar to the Paiutes usually translate it fish-eating Ute; like other and completely unrelated people, such as the Navajo, they hold the theory that when an Indian stops hunting for his meat and starts eating the undramatically caught water flesh, he degenerates into less than a man.

The Paiute was a man named Tavibo, who went to bed one night in his village in Nevada sorely distressed by the number of white men who had settled in his country. He had a dream that if he made a special shirt and did a special dance in it, not only would the white men go away, but the buffalo would come back and all would be as it once had been.

Tavibo was an old man, and he had an old man's illusion about how fine his youth and the times of his youth had been. He died shortly after he had his vision, but he had made a few converts among his people; they looked to his son or nephew Wowoka to take up the old shaman's evangelistic torch.

But Wowoka had turned Christian. He called himself Jack Wilson, after the farming couple who had employed and converted him. After a while Wowoka left the farm and became an itinerant fruit picker, working through the Northwest coast states. There were a lot of Indians in the crop-following gangs: Yakimas, Skokomish, people from all the tribes of the Northwest. They weren't any happier than the Okies of the Dust Bowl days or the wetbacks today; traveling fruit pickers are always poorly paid, poorly housed, and overly attended by the police, who move them on when they are no longer needed. Indians were a little worse off than other fruit pickers. There has always been a tendency in Indian country to pay the tribesman slightly less than his white competitor.

It was the decade of peace in the Indian wars, the 1880s. It was also a decade of disillusionment; cooperation with the Indian Bureau had not brought any great prosperity for any tribe of Indians.

Jack Wilson went home to Mason Valley. Jack Wilson went back to being Wowoka (or Wovoka). Wowoka invented a religion partly based on his father's old vision, partly on Christianity, partly on several rather strange little cults he had encountered among other Indian crop followers.

There is no doubt that Wowoka was a good evangelist; and the time was exactly ripe for something like his preaching. The Indians had learned that they couldn't lick the Army and couldn't trust the Indian Bureau, and blind faith was the only thing left to them. If putting on a Ghost Shirt and doing a dance in it would bring back the buffalo and exterminate the white man, they would try it.

The movement spread through the Mason Valley; most of the Paiutes joined it. That was in 1886; by '88 Ghost Shirt dancing had died down again as the dancers looked around and saw more white men than ever, and no buffaloes.

Wowoka used something he had learned about when he was Jack Wilson: an almanac. It said there would be an eclipse in January '89. He was ill at the time – it is usually believed that he had scarlet fever, always bad in an adult, worse in an Indian without inherited immunity – and he timed a death and a rebirth to coincide with the eclipse or death and rebirth of the sun.

It worked wonderfully. The Mason Valley Paiutes were reconverted, and other members of the tribe, across Nevada and into Utah, heard and believed. Many of the Utes, in Utah, had become Mormons, and Wowoka's predictions seemed to coincide with those the Angel Moroni had disclosed to Joseph Smith about the second coming of Christ and the raising up of the Lamanites, as Mormons call Indians.

Other Shoshoneans were converted: Gosiutes, Bannocks, the various tribes of the Northwest coast. The Yuman tribes down in Arizona heard about the movement, probably through their neighbors the Pimas and Papagos.

Then a party of Plains Shoshones came across the mountains to look into this new message of hope in what had seemed a hopeless world. They brought with them an Arapahoe friend, Nakash, who – this is legend – was said to have been with the Sioux and Cheyennes at the Battle of the Little Big Horn. Nakash was impressed. Wowoka was no longer vague. The time for the resurrection of the buffalo and an Indian messiah and the disappearance of the white man was set: the fall of 1891.

Nakash was impressed, and Nakash was impressive. When he returned to the Plains he converted the Arapahoes almost at once. He also converted an Oglala Sioux named Spoonhunter who lived with the Arapahoes as husband of one of their women.

Spoonhunter got word to his nephew Kicking Bear to come learn about this wonderful new thing. Kicking Bear was chief of the Cheyenne River Sioux, who were Minneconjou Sioux. He came west, saw, listened, danced and was converted, and went home again. On his way back to Cheyenne River he stopped off at Pine Ridge Reservation. The Oglalas there had already heard about the prophet Wowoka. The news was spreading. The Cheyennes were definitely interested; and, probably for the good of the movement, the old enemies of the Sioux-Cheyenne-Arapahoe alliance, the Crows, were not interested.

Women started making Ghost Shirts, medicine men started revising old tribal dances to conform with the new method of dancing in a large circle of men and women holding each other's hands.

All kinds of miracles happened. The Plains Indians, though they did not know a word of Paiute, had understood Wowoka when he addressed them; dancing Indians fell "dead" in trances and saw the faces of their beloved dead, even spoke to them; sometimes a man came out of a trance with pemmican that tasted like buffalo in his hand, though the buffalo were gone.

The belief became prevalent that the Ghost Shirt – a beautifully painted white garment covered with crosses, half moons and other symbols – was bulletproof.

At first the Indian agents in the Sioux country paid little attention to the dances. A few of them sent out their Indian policemen to stop them, with more or less success. At Lame Deer Agency, two Ghost dancers killed a white rancher, and then announced that they were coming into the agency armored in their dance shirts. There was a troop of 1st Cavalry on hand; the agent asked for help, and Lieutenant Robertson lined his men up with the agency police. The troopers fired round after round into the young braves, and finally killed them, but it did not seem to stop the word going across the Plains: white men's bullets cannot go through a Ghost Shirt.

Sitting Bull had come back from Canada a few years after Little Big Horn, promised amnesty by General Nelson A. Miles. He had gone on tour with Buffalo Bill Cody's Wild West Show – as had a great many other Sioux – and then settled down near Standing Rock Agency. He had seen the Ghost Shirt Dance but had not been converted; he said he was perhaps too old to dream, now that he was in his middle fifties.

But there was another Sitting Bull among the Arapahoes, a very prominent dancer. The national press got hold of this fact, confused the

Arapahoe with the Hunkpapa Sioux, and made a terrific furor; the Indians were going to rise under the chief who killed Custer, and drive the white man into the sea.

There were less than a third of a million Indians in the United States in 1890. There were sixty-seven million Americans altogether. But news was scarce, and particularly in demand from the Dakotas, which had just been admitted into the Union as full, sovereign states, the fortieth and forty-first ones. Here and there a paper advocated that the troops go into the Plains and kill a thousand or so Indians and end the matter. Other papers advocated love and kindness as antidotes to possible Indian trouble.

The Sioux, as usual, were on half rations. They might as well dance as sit around holding their empty bellies; the few trail-starved cattle that were driven up from Texas wouldn't feed them. They had just lost nine million acres of good grazing land to the government to be opened up for homesteading. If they had kept it, they didn't have cattle to graze on it; animals given them for that purpose had proved to be too old to breed.

From the East, it looked as though the Plains Indians had enough land for each family to have a prosperous farm, but a short, dry growing season was not favorable to anything but grazing; the large scale grain raising methods of today were not practical then, especially for Indians.

The Army was still tiny; desertions always kept ahead of enlistments. The Indians were now under straight Department of Interior rule, and the administration had changed from Democratic to Republican the year before, with the usual throwing out of experienced Indian agents and the appointment of men who, often, had never seen an Indian before getting the job.

The agent at Pine Ridge was named Royer. The Sioux called him Young Man Afraid of the People, and the whites around the country made a point of telling him that everything had been nice and quiet back in the days of Agent Dr. McGillicuddy.

Royer kept wiring the Indian Bureau in Washington for help; the Indian Bureau kept asking President Benjamin Harrison for troops. But the President was a calm sort of man; he replied that the Army was already investigating the Sioux matter, and would, in due course, report.

Finally, when two hundred Ghost Shirt Dancers had swarmed into Royer's office and run him out, troops were ordered to the forts on the edge of the Sioux country – Robinson at the Red Cloud Agency, and so on. A couple of infantry regiments and elements of the 1st, 2nd, 3rd, 5th, and 9th Cavalry moved into the area or were alerted to move in. Most of them had been scattered around the Southwest, on border patrol. Some came down from Fort Keogh in Montana. There were little detachments all over the country; most posts were one company in strength, and that a small company, plagued by desertion.

In the middle of November Royer made a beef issue to his Oglalas, many of whom were Ghost Dancers. This was always an exciting moment. As each steer was turned loose a young man's name was called, and the called man rode the beef animal down with his horse and killed it with bullet or arrow.

Before the last animal was dead, the Indians had eaten every scrap of meat and guts and were chewing on the bare bones, sucking the marrow. Horns and hoofs were left – and also left were empty Indian stomachs. It would be another sixty years before a reflective La Joya Luiseño Indian was to say: "When you chaw gov'mint beef all you get is wind in your belly," but the Sioux were learning it the hard way.

A Sioux named Changing Hawk, a Ghost Dancer, started haranguing the hungry Oglalas. The Indian police tried to stop him, and only the intervention of Chief American Horse prevented a fight between the Sioux Ghost Dancers and the Sioux police.

Dr. Charles Eastman, a Boston-educated Santee Sioux physician, was at the agency. American Horse and the police officers conferred with him. Then they advised Royer to send for troops.

The agent already had. He had taken another precaution; he had driven out of Pine Ridge in a horse-killing rush that took him clear to Fort Robinson. When he returned the troops were with him. Dr. Eastman, American Horse, the Sioux police officers, and Royer had all been wrong; the sight of the Army uniforms only inflamed the Indians.

Up on Grand River, the Unkpapas were in as much of a turmoil as the Oglalas at Pine Ridge. Agent McLaughlin kept being about to arrest Sitting Bull. There was trouble at Rosebud; all the Sioux nation, except the Santees to the east, seemed about to break out; the Brûlés and the Two Kettles were moving west, the Minneconjous were reported dancing with bandoliers over their Ghost Shirts, Big Road and a band of insurgents were about to rendezvous with the Brûlés at Wounded Knee above Pine Ridge.

Actually, David Humphreys Miller, who has made one of the deepest studies of the Ghost Dance, feels that the real danger at that time was not from the Dancers themselves, but from the hungry Indians who did not believe that it was only a short time till the earth covered the white man and his works, and left a new surface for the Indians and the buffalo. Riders were out scrubbing the reservations for stray cattle, no matter how old, no matter how scrawny; men, seeing their children's bellies puff up with hunger were feeling the slow, fierce anger of desperation. The Ghost Dancers, with their hope of heavenly intervention, would have been considerably less worried than the non-believers.

On November 19 General John R. Brooke marched into Pine Ridge, set up a headquarters and sent patrols of the 2nd, 9th, and 1st Cavalry out showing the flag. He kept a battalion of the 9th at the agency for headquarters guard, together with a large part of the 2nd Infantry and some fieldpieces. Three troops of the 3rd and 8th Cavalry worked the ranges west of Pine Ridge under the command of a captain.

The Sioux at Rosebud Agency feared their country would come under the troops next and went out and into the Ghost Dancer camp. Most of the Pine Ridge Sioux began moving uneasily away from the agency, trying to keep from contacting the troopers. General Brooke increased the beef ration, officially confining it to "friendly" Indians but actually, of course, unable to tell a friendly from an unfriendly Sioux.

Word came to the reservation country that General George Crook's body had been moved to Arlington National Cemetery, and this confirmed the story that he had been dead since last March; apparently some of the old chiefs had hoped that he was alive and would come to lead the Army; Red Cloud cried and said at least Crook had never lied to them.

General Nelson A. Miles came to South Dakota to take charge. He made his headquarters in Rapid City in the Black Hills, to which alarmed ranchers and miners were fleeing. Dr. McGillicuddy, who had been a success as Pine Ridge agent, was commissioned by the Governor of South Dakota to return to that agency and find out what was really happening there.

The ex-Army surgeon counciled with the Sioux chiefs, and told General Brooke that the Indians were sick of war and were more afraid of the troops than they were angry at the government. Brooke resented the surgeon's interference; he wired Washington that McGillicuddy was there "doing me dirt" in the general's remarkably slangy words. The reverse seems undoubtedly true. McGillicuddy was a sincere man and unusually versatile; having been a doctor, an Army officer, and an Indian agent, he was now interested in banking and building and other investment work in Rapid City.

Brooke had come into the Army as a volunteer in the Pennsylvania infantry early in the Civil War and had a fine war record. He had recently been made a brigadier general of the Regulars, so he had a good post-war record too, but he knew little or nothing of the Sioux. Instead of listening to McGillicuddy, he kept his troops out on the Plains, and every sight of them frightened the Indians more.

The Ghost Dancers asked that McGillicuddy come out to parley. Instead Brooke sent an interpreter with the name of Frank Merrivale. McGillicuddy went to Brooke and pointed out that the general had one of his howitzers pointed dead at the camp of one of the few friendly Sioux chiefs; the general shrugged.

The next day the storekeeper gave a wine luncheon for the Army brass, and for McGillicuddy. Royer was there, too, but more as floor show than as guest; he was doing a mock Ghost Dance when an Indian police officer arrived with the news that the Dancers had refused to parley with Merrivale; they had run him off by shooting over his head. Other police reports had the "tame" Sioux from Medicine Root out joining the other Sioux at the Dance camp.

Finally, a rancher who understood the Dakota (Sioux) language rode in to say he had slept in a Sioux lodge and overheard a plan to trap Brooke and his troops with a small group of Dancers, sucking them into an ambush that would be as fatal as that of Custer.

The Minneconjous, Sansarcs, Brûlés, and Oglalas came together in a place in the Bad Lands called The Stronghold; it was a completely undesirable camp except for one thing: it was safe, a watered and grassed mesa rising out of the horrid alkali jumble of the Bad Lands. It was not a place to foray out of, but a retreat from impending danger. The choice of it by the Sioux confirmed McGillicuddy's analysis: the Sioux were more scared than belligerent, but General Brooke couldn't or wouldn't read the signs.

Miles sent out a warrant for Sitting Bull, who seems to have never had anything at all to do with the Ghost Dance. Buffalo Bill Cody showed up with a bevy of newspapermen to prevent the arrest of his old employee and star.

The officers at Fort Yates tried drinking Cody into such a state that he couldn't continue traveling toward Standing Rock. There is no solid evidence that this unconventional tactic was under orders from Miles; at any event, it failed; the old showman outdrank the Army and kept moving.

McLaughlin, the Unkpapas' agent, sent riders after Cody, telling him that the arrest order had been rescinded; Cody and his newspapermen turned back.

The scare boiled up, quieted down. Miles told Washington he figured there were about six thousand braves involved, if it came to a fight; against them he had about two thousand troopers. The infantry, he said, would be useless in a Sioux war.

A familiar name had come into the country with the 8th Cavalry; Lieutenant Colonel Edwin V. Sumner, who did not have to put a Junior or a Second after his name; old Bull Sumner, who had hurried south with Cooke for fear they would miss the Mexican War had died in 1863 while on his way to take over the Department of the Missouri.

The infantry was posted along the Cheyenne River and some of it backed up a detachment of the 9th Cavalry at Rosebud. The 6th Cavalry took over the guarding of the railroad between Rapid City and Hermosa. There was cavalry all around Pine Ridge with infantry and artillery at the agency.

Then, early in December, an old familiar strain was heard in the Sioux country. The 7th Cavalry, now under Colonel James Forsyth, came into Pine

Ridge with the band still playing *Garryowen*. This was jam for the thickly populated press table at Pine Ridge. Custer was about to be avenged.

A "war" that was about to fade was fanned up into flame. The 7th and Sioux camped together! Copy was certain to come out of this, and the correspondents, bored with writing stories about what happened when they fed liquor to the Indians, decided to stay around awhile.

Old Red Cloud was copy; the reporters decided he was really chief of all the Sioux and the prime mover in the Ghost Dance movement. McGillicuddy told them to keep an eye on Kicking Bear instead.

A Catholic priest persuaded the Sioux chiefs to come in and talk to General Brooke. A horde of Ghost Shirt Dancers accompanied their chiefs into Pine Ridge, all armed and mounted, except for Chief Two Strike, who rode in the priest's buggy.

The usual hogwash that was exchanged at non-George Crook parleys went on. Brooke declaimed about the purity of the Army's intentions and invited the Sioux to come camp near Pine Ridge where they could see the general frequently, a privilege they should have been honored to accept. He even suggested that he might use some of the Dancers as scouts, though he made no firm offers of employment, as Crook would have. It took him two hours to say that.

A Sioux answered that there wasn't enough water and grass around the agency for the ponies; and he didn't understand how employment for scouts was going to come about if there were no hostiles to scout.

Brooke issued some rations to the councilors, and an Indian dance was mounted. In the middle of it a Ghost Shirt Dancer named Porcupine invited several of his friends to shoot at him, so that all could see the armor-like qualities of his shirt. He was at once wounded in the thigh, and carried away, claiming all the time that it didn't hurt a bit. This and the willingness of the chiefs to parley were both indications that the power of the Ghost Shirt movement was waning.

McLaughlin, at Standing Rock, took action; the agent's motto had always been: "When in doubt arrest Sitting Bull," and he sent out his policemen to do this, at the same time asking for troopers to back his Sioux officers up.

Colonel Drum at Fort Yates sent two troops of the 8th Cavalry. They arrived at Sitting Bull's camp on the Grand River as a small battle raged between the policemen and Sitting Bull's followers; they put the camp under heavy volleying and the Unkpapas retreated without returning the fire; Sitting Bull had long preached that there was no resisting the United States Army.

A party of Sioux came out and dickered with the government men; another party of braves tried to get the old chief out the back of the camp. An Indian policeman detected them and fired, and Sitting Bull fell, dead.

Then the purpose of the expedition was fulfilled; the Sioux made no further resistance to the bluecoats entering their camp. The policemen hoisted a white flag and came out, and the troops took over the village. The policemen looted it; perhaps the troopers got their share, too. One officer bought a portrait of Sitting Bull from his widows; it had been painted by a white woman admirer of the old chief.

The Ghost Dancers, led by Kicking Bear, went on the rampage. Colonel E.A. Carr of the 6th Cavalry had to send a hundred-man detachment to rescue settlers holed up on Spring Creek and surrounded by hostiles. The next day the Sioux attacked an Army supply wagon; again, it was a 6th outfit that made the rescue and, in pursuit of the hostiles rode close enough to the Stronghold to pinpoint it and make an estimate of its strength. Including the infantry, half of the tiny United States Army was now in Sioux country.

The day of Sitting Bull's death, December 15, 1890, Sumner and a battalion of his 8th had rounded up the large Sioux band of Big Foot. But the chief explained that he and his people were on their way to Fort Bennett to collect rations and goods promised them by treaty. They told the truth and Sumner believed them; he let them go on. But before they could get to the Cheyenne Agency the word reached them of the Sitting Bull massacre. The peaceful Indians began grumbling.

The 9th detachments at Pine Ridge had to be turned out on December 22 to head back fleeing Sioux who feared they were about to suffer Sitting Bull's fate. The 9th Cavalry troopers held them in. That night there was firing west of the agency, but it proved to have been caused by the Messiah-like claims of one of the several crackpots who had poured into Indian country looking for fame; an Indian patrolman had fired at the Messiah, who claimed to be President pro-tem of the Pansy Society of America.

Sumner reported to Miles that he had had Big Foot surrounded and then let him and his band go again. Miles ordered him to ride back out and hold the Sioux until Miles could decide what to do with them.

Sumner overtook Big Foot, who still seemed friendly; but there were Sitting Bull survivors now with the village, and this worried the 8th's lieutenant colonel.

Big Foot said he could not turn away naked and hungry kinsmen; this seemed logical to Sumner, who issued one day's rations to each of Big Foot's people and guests, and then they all settled down to await Nelson Miles' decision as to Big Foot's fate. The next day troopers and Indians together moved slowly toward the original home of the village. The trip to Cheyenne Agency for rations had been abandoned; the women and children were now too cold and hungry for the journey.

Back at their home on Deep Creek, the Sioux prepared to make do; then Miles' rider came to Sumner with orders; make Big Foot and his people go to Fort Bennett, where they had wanted to go in the first place.

Sumner passed the order along to Big Foot and made it clear that it was an order that neither the colonel nor the Indian chief could argue with. Then Sumner moved his battalion upstream a few miles to keep his troopers apart from the Indians.

However, Miles had ordered Colonel Merriam of the 7th Infantry to go upriver toward Deep Creek. In the night Big Foot realized he was between two bodies of troops, and he and his village fled toward the Bad Lands.

Sumner's scouts reported the flight. Sumner sent word to Miles and waited till morning to go after the fugitives. Meanwhile, Miles ordered a battalion of the 7th out to head straight for the Stronghold, certainly Big Foot's destination. The whole 6th Cavalry also took the field in the Bad Lands; the battalion of the 7th was attached to them under Colonel Carr of the 6th. Possibly Miles had heard that Forsyth of the 7th and his officers and men had all boasted that they would show no quarter to any Sioux they caught far enough out on the range.

Custer was not forgotten; only his self-destructive foolishness had faded from the minds of the regiment. Actually, there were survivors of Reno's and Benteen's Little Big Horn battalions in the Pine Ridge command, including Myles Moylan, still a captain.

Big Foot was not headed for The Stronghold, but for Pine Ridge. Red Cloud, Crook's stalwart friend, had asked him to come and parley. On the way, the people nearly starved; Big Foot would not let them steal the cattle that they passed; he wanted to get under Red Cloud's protection without any crimes against him. Some of his people quietly broke away and tried to get to the Stronghold but failed to make it and were taken in to Pine Ridge by Oglala scouts without incident.

Big Foot fed his people as he could on pony meat, against Sioux taste and principle. The Ghost Shirt Dancers at The Stronghold were eating horse, too; on December 27 they had had enough of it, and The Stronghold was abandoned.

Brooke still had four troops of the 7th at Pine Ridge. He ordered Major Whiteside to Wounded Knee, twenty miles northeast of Pine Ridge. To Whiteside's troopers in their heated tents came some of the Oglala Army scouts. They had found Big Foot and his people and would escort them into the Wounded Knee camp.

But Whiteside ordered his men to horse and rode out to surround the starving, freezing Sioux who, when they saw it was the 7th, started waving flour sacks and anything else white that they had. Big Foot wanted to parley, but Whiteside demanded unconditional surrender. Big Foot gave it, and the troopers escorted the Indian wagons back to the Wounded Knee camp.

Captain Moylan and two companies of dismounted troopers stood night guard. Orders were that no Indian men could come out of the alloted campsite; the ponies had to be watered by small boys. Hotchkiss guns (early forms of machine guns) were set up and trained on the Sioux camp.

Whiteside did send rations: a wagonload of bacon, hardtack and sugar. The Sioux sent their women to get it; the guns staring down into their camp had them nervous, and they didn't want any chance of provoking an incident.

Accounts of what happened that night differ. There seems little doubt that the troopers of the 7th had brought Christmas cheer with them; there seems no doubt at all that most of their officers took a few drinks, at least. Moylan, with the night guard duty, restrained himself; he didn't get along well with the other officers, anyway.

The worst thing that happened that night was the attempt of a dozen soldiers to take Big Foot out of his tent. Old Myles Moylan broke that up.

Colonel Forsyth arrived in the morning with his battalion of the 7th and took over from Whiteside. With them came three more Hotchkiss guns and Lieutenant Taylor, 9th Cavalry, commanding Indian scouts. Orders were simple; the Sioux were to be disarmed and taken to the railroad and shipped out of Sioux territory altogether until things got quiet.

In the meantime, more hardtack was issued to the Indians, and the 7th was deployed around them, about half of the troopers mounted, the others on foot. All the Hotchkisses were trained on the Indians.

A Ghost Shirt Dancer named Yellow Bird attended a meeting of all the Sioux braves in Big Foot's lodge. He took the floor at once, saying that everyone should put on his Ghost Shirt and let the soldiers fire if they wanted; the shirts would turn the bullets. Big Foot seemed to put more faith in the white flag that flew above his tent.

Now soldiers came into the camp with an interpreter and ordered the braves to surrender their guns, twenty men at a time; the interpreter, a half-breed, named the men.

The first twenty men surrendered two very old smoothbore guns and said that was all they had. Forsyth told the interpreter he didn't believe this. He ordered the carnp searched.

The soldiers found weapons, in a way: crowbars, firewood axes, cooking and skinning knives, and twelve guns that looked as though they would blow up if they were fired. A few braves had good Winchesters; they turned them in.

Yellow Bird started dancing the Ghost Shirt Dance all by himself; at intervals he would stop and snatch up handsful of dust and throw them at the troopers. Colonel Forsyth ordered him to sit down and be quiet. The dancer paid no attention, but another Sioux said that he would sit down when he finished the circle he was describing.

Several more rifles were surrendered, and one was snatched from under a brave's blanket. Indians unstrapped their cartridge belts and turned them in, too. Somehow or other somebody fired a gun.

Nobody now is certain who it was, or what the circumstances were. About twenty years ago little Sioux children were taught that one of the officers tried to rape a Sioux girl, and she fired in self-defense; this is much too pat, and no eyewitness backs it up, though there are tales of soldiers searching the Indian girls' bodies "looking for rifles."

Another Sioux version is that Sitting Bull's deaf adopted son was carrying a gun toward the surrender pile when he disregarded an order he couldn't hear, and in a panic a soldier grabbed the rifle and it went off.

Whoever fired the shot, it was a signal to the 7th to avenge Custer. Almost at once a mounted soldier shot Big Foot through the forehead. Dozens of other Sioux men were shot down at once, point-blank.

After a while the braves pulled themselves together and tried to run. Then the Hotchkisses opened up. They raked the camp, cutting through the frightened women and children and through a few soldiers, too; twenty-nine soldiers were killed and an equal number wounded, few by Sioux fire.

The noise was terrific. It was heard all over the Pine Ridge country. Sioux went for their horses to ride to the defense of their betrayed kin – everyone seemed to know that Big Foot had been coming in to surrender.

Yellow Bird had had a rifle cached; he ran for it and got off a few shots before an explosive shell hit the lodge where he had sheltered. He was full of bullet holes when his body was found; the Ghost Shirt had not worked.

The Indians take credit for only one military death at Sioux hands: Captain George Wallace who had been a lieutenant at Little Big Horn was brained by a brave's stone club. It is probable that some of the other Army casualties were Sioux-inflicted, but there is no proper proof of this.

The surviving Sioux fled over a cutbank and into a ravine. The corporal running one of the Hotchkiss guns enfiladed them and poured fire into the knotted Indians; he couldn't, of course, tell the sex or age of the people he was hitting.

The Sioux scouts did their best to shelter their kinsmen; and then the riders from Pine Ridge came up, about forty Oglala riders. They said later that they had decided to die with their tribesmen, but the 7th actually retreated from the galloping tribesmen, and the survivors of Wounded Knee got away.

Then the soldiers got the Hotchkiss turned around and took command of the field again.

How many Sioux were killed will never be known. The Army tried – and tries – to minimize the figure, the Indians to expand it. The estimates run as low as a hundred and fifty and as high as three hundred. Nobody is very proud of the incident. It was a mistake. The Army shared in the error; to boost recruiting and attempt to get larger appropriations from Congress, the military had kept the Custer incident alive, allowing it to grow, really.

Many of the 7th cavalrymen were the rawest of recruits, filled with the importance of being in the regiment that Custer had led; most of them had never seen violent death before, had little chance to learn that Indians were human.

Yellow Bird, the Ghost Dancer, should be given some of the blame; his antics had made the young troopers nervous.

Myles Moylan, veteran of Little Big Horn, and a particular protege of Custer's, seems to have behaved himself impeccably.

Moylan's unvarnished service record reads queerly. A Massachusetts man, he was Regular Army; enlisted in the 2nd Dragoons in 1857, he had risen to first sergeant by 1863. Then he was transferred to the 5th Cavalry and given a commission on the 19th of February, second lieutenant in an outfit that hadn't known him when he was a non-com. By October 20 he had done something bad enough to get him dismissed from the service, a discharge "other than honorable" but not a straight dishonorable discharge or a cashiering. Under a false name he enlisted in the 4th Massachusetts Cavalry, a Volunteer regiment, of course, was commissioned a month later, and rose to be a captain and brevet major.

After the war he enlisted in the "mounted service" as a private, which meant that he was an unassigned cavalryman; this time he was under his own name again, the name under which he had been dismissed from the Regulars. When the 7th Cavalry was formed he was assigned to it and almost at once became sergeant major, the top enlisted man of the regiment.

Then, in '67, he was given a first lieutenant's commission. But the officers refused to share a mess with him; Custer's biographers say that this is because he had been in the ranks, but how about that earlier dismissal? The Regular Army was small, the officers of the 7th would have known about that, and anything that got an officer dismissed in wartime must have certainly been "unbecoming an officer and gentleman."

In any event, Colonel and Mrs. Custer invited him to eat in their quarters, and along with Tom Custer and one or two other officers – Calhoun, Custer's brother-in-law, for instance – Moylan became a "Custer" officer rather than a "Benteen" officer, the two parties in the 7th.

Moylan's thirty years seem to have dated from his first commissioning; he served his last couple of years as a major in the 10th Cavalry and retired in '93.

The fighting was not over. The 9th Cavalry was out in the Bad Lands; the 7th was still at Wounded Knee, and probably General Brooke thought them too unreliable to bring back to Pine Ridge. He threw a line of Sioux police around the agency and prepared to be besieged.

Kicking Bear and another Ghost Dancer named Turning Bear were urging the Sioux to attack. The old Sioux war cry, "This is a good day to die," was sounding over the country.

Up at Wounded Knee troopers and officers were peeling bloody Ghost Shirts off the corpses for souvenirs; the legend of the armorproof cloth was gone. When Dr. Eastman, the educated Santee Sioux, got the Indian policemen to stop firing, the insurgents let their own fire trickle away.

The hostiles had something more personal to do; the 7th had split into small parties and was riding south toward Pine Ridge. The Sioux hit one of these columns and made the soldiers give up their Sioux prisoners; the Dancers with Kicking Bear fired the prairie and were about to wipe out a number of 7th cavalrymen when night ended the skirmish.

The 7th got into the Agency without anyone even whistling *Garryowen*. The next day Colonel Forsyth led them out again, on the patrol for Kicking Bear and his hostiles; but the Sioux Black Elk saw them first and trapped them in the low ground along a creek; here the Hotchkisses were no good, because the enemy could get natural defilade from the fall of the land.

Forsyth would have been as famous as Custer, but the 9th Cavalry got back from fighting Kicking Bear and charged down on the besiegers, trumpets blaring the charge and carbines barking.

Black Elk's men broke and fled, the 7th was saved, and, in effect, the Sioux wars were over at last.

This was in January of 1891; the regiment was twenty-five years old, and Little Big Horn and Wounded Knee were its outstanding engagements. In the Cuban intervention of 1898, the 7th didn't get to go overseas, but they were used in the Philippine Insurgence, and did well.

The story of this most famous of American horse outfits ends on an upnote; when Pershing was sent into Mexico in 1916 to chase Pancho Villa under orders that made it impossible for him ever to capture the Mexican rebel general, the 7th was the only one of the regiments that reached Villa and fought him; General John J. Pershing commended them highly, and *Garryowen* was again a march of honor.

Chapter 28

The Buffalo Troopers

The 9th Cavalry had done well at Pine Ridge; they had saved the 7th's lives. There is an ironic note to this; the 9th was the regiment that Custer, after the Civil War, refused the colonelcy of; he eventually accepted a lieutenant colonel's commission with the 7th instead.

For the 9th, like the 10th, Cavalry were Negro troops; in the official roster of the day they were called 9th and 10th (Colored) Cavalry. The two regiments were authorized by Congress and formed in 1866. It took a good officer to accept a commission with either; the officers were to be all white and the enlisted personnel all Negro – often still called Freedmen – and everyone predicted trouble. It is now hard to see why. Opportunities in civilian life for Negroes were practically non-existent in those post-war days. Employers who had jobs to give out had returning relatives or friends to give them to; and there were virtually no Negro employers.

The new regiments – the infantry had Negro troops, too – offered real opportunities to Negroes, where they offered only abjection to white Americans. The white enlisted men would be, largely, illiterate immigrants, with a sprinkling of men escaping the law, uncongenial wives, or the miseries of the congenital drunkard. Against this unhappy mess of potential deserters and troublemakers, the recruiting officers for the 9th and 10th could draw on the cream of the Negro population. Thirteen dollars a month, all found, was as good as a Negro man could expect in the Northern cities and a lot better than anything the ravaged South offered.

If Custer wouldn't lead the 9th, the 10th got a perfect prize of a lieutenant colonel: Wesley Merritt, '60, U.S.M.A. and not the bottom man in his class by any means. Merritt had been major general of Volunteers and brevet brigadier general, U.S.A.; he had commanded a cavalry corps under Sheridan, a grade higher than Custer's command of a division.

Merritt was thirty in 1866, old for one of Sheridan's boy generals, but younger than Crook or Sheridan himself. He'd had a brilliant career in the

402

six years since he'd gotten out of the Point; now he saw that he had it all to do over again. Like Crook, another Sheridan corps commander, he was commissioned lieutenant colonel, the real commander of the 9th; Brevet Major General Edward Hatch was nominal colonel.

There were some illustrious majors with the 9th; J.F. Wade, G.A. Forsyth, A.P. Morrow. The first was brevet brigadier, the other two brevet colonels, but G.A. Forsyth – there was a Major J.W. Forsyth on the rolls of the 10th – got his brevet brigadier general's grade two years after he joined the new regiment and got it for peacetime service: fighting the Arikara on the Republican River. Peacetime brevets were rare and highly sought after; an officer had to have good men under him to earn the honor. The troopers of the new and suspiciously regarded 10th had proved themselves almost as soon as they had taken the field.

The 10th did not start out with quite so illustrious a staff. B.H. Grierson was colonel, brevet major general and major general of Volunteers; a man named Walcutt held the crucial post of lieutenant colonel for six months; then the job was given to Brevet Major General, Brigadier General of Volunteers J.W. Davidson, who held it down for thirteen years. Probably because of this shift, the 10th didn't get into action as soon as the 9th did. Company F of the 9th was in a fight on Prairie Dog Creek, Kansas in August of '67, and a detachment from Company G skirmished against the hostiles at Pawnee Bluff Fork in the same state in September. The next month found a detachment of I of the 10th finally firing their guns in the service of their country; this was at Howard's Wells, Texas.

Note the size of the U.S. forces; a full company once, mere detachments in the other two engagements. This would be the rule for the 9th and 10th for years. Except on the Plains, the mass striking rule of the war years simply didn't apply in Indian fighting. The Plains Indians – Sioux, Cheyenne, Shoshone, and others – were actually cavalry, maneuvered like cavalry, even practiced right or left into line and other tactics. But in Texas and Kansas the Southern Cheyennes were the only Indians who could be attacked in mass; the 9th and 10th had to learn to operate in small patrols, under lieutenants or even sergeants, and fight on a hit-and-run basis.

The 10th did go to Indian Territory – Oklahoma – in 1870, where several companies, backed up by infantry, could find a fight all at one time. Usually this was at or near Indian Agencies – the Wichita, the Cheyenne and Fort Sill, later the Field Artillery School but founded as a Kiowa and Comanche agency.

The 9th stayed in Kansas until the spring of '69; then they were moved to Texas, where the 10th had been all along. This must have been rough duty; besides the Comanches and other hostiles, there were wildly unreconstructed Rebels in the Lone Star State, sure to resent Negro soldiers even more than they did the other Union troops in their former republic.

Both regiments missed serving under George Crook, who would have appreciated them; the 10th took over San Carlos Agency of the Apaches after Crook had asked to be relieved, and Miles had been given command of the Department of Arizona.

The 9th, of course, kept the 7th from being annihilated all over again in Dakota in '91. Neither 9th nor 10th had served against the Sioux until that winter of Wounded Knee, and up on those Plains the Sioux claim to have given the Negro troopers their name of "buffalo soldiers" because when they first saw the 9th, the soldiers were dressed in buffalo coats – after the buffalo had been virtually wiped out – and when the troopers took their hats off, their "hair, was made of buffalo skin, too."

Other versions of the origin of the name are available. The favorite – and possibly true one – is that Negro scalps were particularly prized by the Indians, because they were almost certain to have come from military rather than civilian heads. An enterprising Indian – most accounts say he was a Ute – figured out how to cut up buffalo hide so that it looked like Negro skin with Negro hair attached to it. He was doing a brisk trade with the braves who wanted to promote themselves by returning from dry runs with scalps, when he was discovered – and scalped. Whatever the origin of the name, the 9th and 10th troopers seem to have borne it proudly.

The 9th first fought in New Mexico in 1876; the 10th was not far away at the time, over the Texas line on the Pecos. But at hardly any time was all of one regiment together; the Army was too small for that. Usually the detachment or company or occasionally the squadron that fought under the guidons of the 9th or 10th was the only cavalry engaged; troopers were expensive to maintain and were usually used to hold the hostiles while infantry came up to re-enforce.

Once in 1876 a detachment of Company B, 10th, crossed the line into Mexico in pursuit of hostiles; the fight was at Zaragosa, in Coahuila state, not too far below the Rio Grande. The next year it was Company C's turn to go foreign; first a detachment and then a few months later the whole company ran the river in hot pursuit, caught up with Indian renegades, and fought them.

The regiments got their share of medals. It must be explained that until 1874 the now rare – and usually posthumous – Medal of Honor was the only award the United States ever gave. After that time there was a Certificate of Merit, which was later converted to the Distinguished Service Cross, but these were very rare; about ten Medals of Honor were given for each Certificate. The 9th got several more medals than the 10th, but this was made up for later; five 10th soldiers were decorated in the

Cuban War, largely for aiding – some say rescuing – the Rough Riders on San Juan Hill.

Medals of Honor were given for various things; in the Civil War most often for capturing an enemy flag; young Tom Custer got *two* medals that way, one of only five men in the hundred year history of the Medal of Honor ever to win two. His older brother never won the medal, by the way.

Since the Indians did not have battle flags, nobody in the 10th or 9th ever got one that way. Sergeant George Jordan got his for organizing and leading twenty-four troopers in the defense of Tularosa, New Mexico, when that town was attacked by Victorio and over a hundred of his hostile Apaches. This was in May 1880; the year before First Sergeant Henry Johnson won his medal at the Battle of Milk River.

This was against the Utes up in Colorado. The citation reads that the sergeant "voluntarily left a sheltered position … under heavy fire to instruct the guards … The next night he fought his way to the river and back to bring water to the wounded."

Bringing water to the wounded was about as heroic as you could be; Indian wars in the last half of the nineteenth century were almost invariably fought in dry country, and the side that ran out of water lost.

Neither regiment ever had a writer like St. George Cooke or John Gregory Bourke or Basil Duke to chronicle its doings, but the 10th had an officer with the unusual name of Powhatan Clarke who wrote well enough to appear in the popular magazines.

Clarke seems to have been a crusty sort of fellow; his narrative of A Hot Trail (of Apaches) is interrupted steadily by lectures about young officers who bawl unnecessary commands and European cavalry experts who advocate riding with short stirrups and posting, instead of letting the leathers out and standing to the trot, U.S. Cavalry style.

The pursuit was routine; the Apaches had murdered a freighter between Fort Thomas and San Carlos. Clarke led his troopers out of Fort Thomas at dusk, the horses trotting eight miles to the hour. They found the body, wrapped it in a tarp, put it up in a tree safe from coyotes, and rode on.

But the Indian villages were all deserted; it was bitterly cold in March in the Arizona night, and once they had to ford a stream up to their saddles.

Finally, eighteen miles out from Thomas, they found a man at a stage relay station who told them that the news of the murder had come ahead of them, and all the Apaches were hurrying into San Carlos away from the hostiles.

Clarke and his troopers made camp at the stage station; the men made a huge fire, very un-Apache, but very comforting. They were joined there by a number of Apache scouts, under an officer of the 4th Cavalry. At daybreak the combined outfit moved out again, back toward Thomas; the scouts were sure the renegades would be in that direction.

The Indians had returned; their chief told the soldiers that only five men were involved and that they had fled after the murder and probably joined the renegade gang of the Kid, a former scout first sergeant who had killed another Apache, shot Al Sieber and an officer, and then, when caught and sentenced, had killed the sheriff and deputies who were taking him to prison in Fort Yuma.

The scouts, with this information, picked up the hostile trail, which led straight to the Gilas; Clarke gave the "old, heartless, dreary command that deadens the spirit of the American cavalryman, and has made his feats the marvel of the European – 'Dismount!' "

Apparently, however, the horses were not left behind but led up into the rocky, steep Apache mountains. At noon the troopers found a breastwork thrown up and filled with sweet grass; the hostiles – whom Clarke calls bronchos – had slept there the night before.

The column camped for the night under oak trees, where there was grass for the horses; no grain had been taken on the saddles, for once. The men cooked their bacon and softened their hardtack in the grease and called it supper.

The sweat of the hard climb was hardly dry before the sun went down and the abysmal cold of the Arizona mountains hit them; the men rolled in their blankets and put their heads on the saddles and shivered to sleep.

The trail didn't stay up in the mountains; it came down, out the San Carlos road, and went out across the mesa. For supper the next night there were a few tablespoons of beans per man, but they had again found grass; the horses could keep on.

They moved out at dawn, breakfastless, but at noon they sidetracked to a mine where they bought flour and a yearling beef; one of the troopers shot the animal and they ate well.

The third day they were provisioned; a sergeant of I Troop, the 10th, rode them down with a packtrain; he had gone all night without stopping to catch up with the starving troopers. Unfortunately, Clarke doesn't give his name, but says that the non-com had been in the 10th since the day it was formed in '67; the story was published in 1894, but there is no way of knowing when the pursuit actually took place.

They came to the Salt River country; the renegades had abandoned their ponies there and gone over the river. The scouts moved out on foot, directly after the murderers; the troopers brought the horses around by a longer way. Leading the Apache scouts' ponies held the soldiers up, but the trail doubled back and saved them from getting completely separated from the foot scouts.

The horse troops got across the river, but horses and men were nearly played out when a shot was heard. This time they stayed in the saddle and buckjumped the horses over the shale and through the chaparral to where the scouts had finally pinned the outlaw down.

Rowdy, the Apache (possibly Apache-Yuma) sergeant of scouts, showed the men from the 10th where the outlaws were forted up in the rocks; they were nearly invisible to a non-Indian eye. But then Rowdy and his men stood back; their job was done when they found the quarry, it was up to the troopers to finish them off; Clarke says this was the rule, which did not, in Clarke's opinion, make the Apache scouts cowards, just sensible. Sergeant Rowdy, by the way, was another Medal of Honor man.

As at the big Battle of the Cave, the hostiles had to be fired at by ricochet. When one of them was wounded he yelled to his companions to surrender, and asked Clarke if they could be promised their lives if they did.

Clarke took them in; one of them was a former scout for the 10th. This was the wounded man who was also leader of the renegades. They took them down the mountains; the troopers had to help the wounded man, who kept asking that he be shot and put out of his misery. One of the troopers told the Indian he was sorry for him, but glad it wasn't a trooper who had been wounded.

The renegade chief died that night, and Clarke says everyone was glad of it; his tortures had apparently not been endured in the traditional Apache silence.

The next day the column rode into Globe, camped, and then it was back to Fort Thomas and the barracks.

This was routine for the 10th; taking San Juan Hill in Cuba must have seemed like a holiday to them.

Chapter 29

The Last Chapter

P. St. George Cooke died in 1895 in Detroit; this was sixty-three years after he had been sent out to recruit for the 1st Dragoons. Three years later the United States was at war with Cuba, and Theodore Roosevelt, ex-Assistant Secretary of the Navy, was raising a cavalry regiment of Volunteers.

Most of what is popularly remembered of the Spanish-American War is that cavalry regiment, usually called Teddy Roosevelt's Rough Riders. Roosevelt, a very aristocratic New Yorker, had been a rancher on the Plains; he recruited the regiment from the West and from Long Island; almost every man in it was either a cowboy or a polo player.

Leonard Wood, who had entered the Army as a surgeon, was colonel of the regiment; Roosevelt was its lieutenant colonel. So, the outfit was really Wood's Rough Riders; and they never really rode, except in practice and on parade. No troop horses were taken to Cuba; only high-ranking officers – including Roosevelt – rode; the cavalry fought dismounted, so the war is really no concern of a cavalry history. But one cavalry officer came out of it with distinction and fame, not of the public kind, but where it counted – within the Army. He was a captain in the 10th, and his name was John Joseph Pershing. He had not been on duty with his regiment for the past year; instead he had been at West Point as a tactical instructor. When the war started, he threatened to resign from the Army and join either the Rough Riders or the New York National Guard if he wasn't allowed to go to war with the 10th. The War Department finally returned him to his regiment, where he was appointed quartermaster, since there were no troop commands open.

The recently deceased St. George Cooke had been one of the youngest men ever to graduate from the Academy; Jack Pershing was one of the oldest. He had been just a few days under the top age of twenty-two when he was admitted as cadet in 1882, after taking a competitive examination.

Pershing had been a schoolteacher before he was a cadet, and even had a college degree, the rather startling one of Bachelor of Scientific Didactics, granted by the Missouri State Normal School at Kirksville after two years of study. He did well at the Point, possibly because of his age; the youngest cadet in his class was nearly six years younger than he, most of the class were at least four years younger. Pershing got the highest cadet rank there is, Cadet Captain. His first duty was under Miles with the 6th Cavalry, chasing Apaches, first at Fort Bayard and then at Fort Stanton. He was in on the final surrender of Geronimo.

Then Colonel Eugene A. Carr of the 6th sent him up to Fort Wingate, near Gallup in northwestern New Mexico, where the normally peaceful Zunis had surrounded three white men in a barn and were threatening to kill them; the three had stolen Zuni horses and killed Zuni horseguards. Pershing spoke Apache, which was absolutely no use when talking to a Zuni; but he somehow managed to persuade the Indians that the white men would be punished if he was allowed to take them into Wingate. The Zunis – there were about a hundred and fifty of them – pulled back, and Pershing kicked the barn door in and went in alone, pointing a pistol at the murderers. They surrendered, and he led them into the fort for trial.

The 6th went up to Dakota for the Ghost Dance trouble; Pershing was relieved of his troop and handed a command of Sioux scouts. He got along with them fine, he reported; born earlier he might have been another Crook.

Then he taught – as what would now be called an ROTC officer – Military Science and Tactics at the University of Nebraska. This course, required at land grant colleges, was unpopular, and so, usually, was its teacher. Pershing placated the faculty by offering to teach mathematics on the side, organized a Cadet Corps that became popular with the young men students, and took a law degree in his spare time. One of the most humorless men in the history of an often humorless profession, Pershing later said drily that he taught math to both Willa Cather and Dorothy Canfield Fisher but doubted that he gave "either of them a taste for literature."

In 1895 Pershing went to the 10th, at Fort Assiniboine, Montana, and spent a year rounding up Canadian Cree Indians and shoving them across the International Border, where they were wanted for murder. Then he went back to West Point, and then the Spanish-American War started.

He guided the 2nd Squadron of the 10th up San Juan Hill and got one of the new Silver Stars for it. He also got a brevet as major of Volunteers; that empty system of military rewards was still in force.

Though Pershing was only a junior captain, he was ordered back to Washington from Cuba to become Chief Ordnance Officer; then he was transferred again, to organize a Bureau of Insular Affairs – in other words the military government for the islands taken from Spain in the war.

Regulars with law degrees were rare. There was no way for him to be made a major or colonel; promotion below the rank of brigadier was strictly by seniority.

Pershing had made powerful friends: Theodore Roosevelt; Charles G. Dawes, who was to be Vice-President under Calvin Coolidge; and Elihu Root, Secretary of War under William McKinley and later Secretary of State under Teddy Roosevelt. But the captain applied for field duty again and was shipped to the Philippines. As the year ended and 1900 began, Pershing turned forty – unmarried, still company grade, though assigned to staff work, which he hated. He was Adjutant General of the Department of Mindanao and Jolo, a job that called for a full colonel's pay, at least. Without the rank, Pershing could do very little about the way the Army was putting down the Insurrection. The United States had freed the Filipinos from the Spaniards, only to find that the Filipinos wanted to be freed from the United States, too. Pershing had fought Apaches and seen how necessary it was to understand the enemy before you could pacify him; he had led Sioux scouts and grown fond of them. But the Army was working on the European theory in the Philippines: it doesn't matter what the enemy is thinking about except on military subjects.

The elderly captain had always had a flair for languages. Now he started studying the main dialogue of the southern islands, Moro. As he did, he found that they were spoken by people who hardly resembled the northern Filipino at all; the Moro was a fanatic Mohammedan, believing sincerely that being killed while trying to kill an unbeliever was a sure way of getting to Paradise; the Tagalog were Catholic, with a Christian ethic that made killing anyone at all sit uneasily on their conscience. A captain doesn't tell a general things like this; he talks about polo and drill, perhaps liquor and sex, or he keeps his mouth shut.

General Jacob Smith had the nickname of Hell Roaring. When insurgents wiped out an infantry company on Samar, he gave orders to his infantrymen to wipe out all the inhabitants of the islands, make it "a howling wilderness," take no prisoners. The attempt to do this took years, when small cavalry patrols, patiently working the barrios, as the Filipinos call their villages, could have quickly learned who was friendly, who was insurgent, and which mayors, priests, and sultans really had power. But Smith was using mass, as though the Civil War had started all over again; it simply wouldn't work against unorganized natives any more than it had against the Apaches.

Pershing, however, was south of Samar, on Mindanao, which was lucky for him. There were two distinct Philippine Insurrections, the real one and the Moro; in the north, particularly on Luzon, where Manila is, the Tagalogs led the other Christian people in a bitter war against the Americans who

410

had been their allies in throwing out Spain. The Filipinos, under Emilio Aguinaldo, felt they had been betrayed by their liberators, and history seems to back them up.

Cavalry around Manila mostly fought dismounted; nearly every regiment was in on the trouble up there. There were now fifteen cavalry regiments, and moreover each company in them was authorized to have a hundred to a hundred and fifty men in it; twice or three times the Plains' era number.

Down south in Mindanao the Moros had never been subdued by Spain, and the Filipinos asking for freedom on Luzon really didn't want to take over the job of managing the wild Muslims of the southern islands. So, Pershing finally got off the desk – after he was adjutant general he was chief engineer, ordnance, and signal officer all at once – and into the saddle. His department commander, Brigadier General William A. Kobbé, sent him as an observer with what was to be a punitive expedition up the Rio Grande de Cagayan on Mindanao. It was a column in force, and too unwieldy. The Moros waited till the cavalrymen – troopers of the 4th Cavalry – were watering their horses, and then hit.

The cavalry took cover, the infantry split into two parties and settled down for a fire fight. The chief observer somehow or other got one of the two fighting parties, about fifteen footsoldiers of the 40th Infantry, and the insurgents were beaten off – or simply retired, Apache fashion, to harass the next day. Probably they were in the village of Mocajambos when the column prepared to besiege and assault it.

The assault was never necessary. Adjutant General Chief Engineer Chief Ordnance Officer Chief Signalman Captain Brevet Major Pershing had taken charge of the mountain howitzers that accompanied the column; when he started lobbing shells into the nipa-hut barrio, the natives fled.

A month later Pershing sent a dispatch to his general; the insurgents were willing to come in and talk surrender; keep up show-the-flag patrols, Pershing advised, but warn the troopers not to molest anyone heading for headquarters; such travelers meant peace.

The Insurrection had turned into a cavalry war. But this was the cavalry of the West; small patrols, led by a lieutenant or even a sergeant, showing the flag, arresting individual miscreants instead of shooting natives indiscriminately. But the Army did not yet realize this. Having pacified Cagayan – this is the province on Mindanao, not the one on Luzon – Pershing dropped down to Ilican, the next province south, and started dealing with the sultans and priests – pandits – and tribal chiefs around there.

While he was doing this, Colonel Frank Baldwin was sent to the south of the island with a column of a thousand men, largely infantry, to pacify the

Moros there. Pershing kept busily telling his neighbors that Baldwin knew the difference between them and the southern Moros; whether the captain believed this or not is not now known. Pershing was now officially part of the new 15th Cavalry.

Baldwin stormed the Sultan of Bayan's headquarters with his heavy column, killed about three hundred Moros, and set up a permanent camp. He asked for Pershing to be his intelligence officer, a job Pershing didn't want. The captain seemed to think that Baldwin was going about things in the wrong order; he was later heard to comment that Baldwin should have offered peace before shooting, instead of afterward.

On June 30, 1902, Captain Pershing was given command of Baldwin's camp near Bayan; Baldwin was made a brigadier and moved; and majors, lieutenant colonels, and full colonels all over the islands screamed with anguish as the company officer was jumped over their heads. One of the most frequent charges seems to have been that it was unfair and unmilitary of Pershing to have learned Moro and Tagalog when he could have been – say – playing poker, a suitable occupation for an officer and a gentleman. General Adna R. Chaffee was commandant in the Philippines; he was an old 9th Cavalry officer; the appointment stuck.

Another occupation that would have been suitable was reading Rudyard Kipling, then as popular a writer as was working in English. His descriptions of life in the officers' corps of the British Army in India filled American officers with envy; shoulder straps and a white skin were all that was needed to be treated like royalty.

The dour, sombre ex-schoolteacher from Missouri seems to have missed being indoctrinated by Kipling altogether. Like Crook, he could always tell one native from another, and he showed as consistent curiosity about the Filipinos as he had about the Sioux and Apaches. This was – and is – very uncommon in a West Pointer. As this is written, United States troops are fighting in Southwest Asia, and complaining how hard it is to tell hostiles from allies.

But gradually resistance to Pershing's rule from Camp Vicars built up among the neighboring sultans, who saw their people regarding Pershing as a sort of super-sultan.

Pershing called the sultans together and threatened to spatter them with hog's blood – sure barrier to Paradise – if they did not sign a peace treaty written by him. They signed; the incident is one of the most frequently repeated and distorted bits of Pershing lore.

But as peace reigned in Lanao Province, sniping began to break out; Camp Vicars was fired on nearly every night. Pershing recognized this for what it was; the religiously warlike Moros were losing respect for a non-fighting occupying force. He reported to his superiors that he would have to take the field or lose the respect and allegiance of his friendly Moros. Early in the fall he took five companies of the 15th, with a battalion of infantry and a battery of fieldpieces, and set out to attack the Sultan of Maciu, on the south shore of the lake.

He also took newspapermen along. As his troops went into position around the sultan's stronghold, one of the correspondents hopefully asked if there'd be a charge. Pershing shook his head. His plan was to bombard the stockade, then form a tight perimeter around it and take the Moros one by one as they sneaked out to get away from the shelling.

It worked perfectly. The infantrymen in the front line and the dismounted troopers backing them up had only to kill about fifty of the sultan's forces before the stronghold surrendered and Pershing's prestige was re-established in southern Mindanao.

He took his whole column around the country afterward, showing the flag as carried by the men who had conquered the tough Peninsula of Maciu. Then he went back to Camp Vicars and his own particular brand of diplomacy, which was hardly the velvet glove on the hand of iron; Pershing's iron always showed; he was as grim as Phil Sheridan. He showed iron to his men, too; in some way he achieved the almost impossible task of keeping his troopers away from the Moro women. The first sultan he had beaten died, and the new Sultan of Bayan armed for war. Leaving his troopers to patrol, Pershing marched on the sultan with a small infantry escort guarding his field artillery battery. After he had fired a twenty-one gun salute in the sultan's honor, that impressed head of state kissed Pershing on both cheeks, made him honorary father of the chief sultana and of four little Moros, and then told him he was now a datu and prince of the Moslem church.

Bored war correspondents made a big thing of this in the Stateside press; good news from the Philippines was rare; up on Luzon the Army was trying to impose censorship to cover the betrayal of Aguinaldo and his government. Pershing became famous. The Sultan of Bacolod, way over in the western reaches of the Pershing area, decided that his personal fame as a warrior-ruler depended on defying the datu-captain. Pershing marched on Bacolod.

He dismounted his troopers there and put them with his infantry to cover the engineers while they bridged the sultan's moat. At the same time, he put together his mountain howitzers – jackass artillery, carried disassembled on muleback – and aimed it at the center of the palace-fort. It took half an hour to carry and completely occupy the fort. Three of Pershing's men were wounded; none killed. But cholera struck the column as it continued to push west; seven soldiers died.

For quite a ways past Bacolod the news of that engagement preceded Pershing, and he was feted and honored by people to whom fighting was the normal way of life, and a good fighter to be honored rather than hated.

413

But then the Americans entered country where the Spanish were only a rumor, the North Americans not even that. There was a fight at the Taraca River and Pershing hit the stronghold of the Datu Ampuan at Taraca and fought a twenty-four hour engagement. The infantry assaulted the fort by day, and the cavalry (dismounted) by night, and they killed over a hundred Moros, captured about half that number, and took an amazing amount of artillery, some of it quite large and all of it very antique.

Only one sultan still held out. Pershing conquered him and returned to Camp Vicars in triumph. Correspondents had accompanied him, and though he really never got along very well with the press, they built him into an international hero.

Nelson A. Miles was about to retire as General of the Army; he went all the way to Mindanao to visit Captain Pershing as one of his last acts in office. Elihu Root, the Secretary of War, was heard to remark – perhaps just casually – that his friend Captain Pershing ought to be made a brigadier general. It was still the only promotion possible; the Army was rigidly bound by seniority below general rank. William McKinley, George Crook's old aide, was President; Secretary Root was a friend of Theodore Roosevelt's and Pershing's; but nothing came of the idea. Root was busy reorganizing the whole Army; there would now be a General Staff of three generals, twenty-two field officers, and twenty captains.

Root brought Pershing back to Washington and made him a General Staff captain. McKinley was assassinated, and Theodore Roosevelt became the youngest President in the country's history. In addressing Congress about the need for breaking the strict seniority rule in the Army, he cited Pershing by name as an officer who had rendered service far above his rank. Nothing came of this, either.

Duty in Washington was social; Pershing met, danced with, and proceeded to court Helen Francis Warren of Cheyenne, Wyoming, whose father happened to be Senator Francis E. Warren, who was chairman of the Military Affairs Committee and one of the most powerful men in the Senate.

In January 1905, Pershing and Miss Warren were married. At once they left for the Far East, where the aging captain had been detailed as an observer in the Russo-Japanese War. He left his young wife – two years out of college – in Tokyo; when the war ended he joined her there as military attaché. In the fall of 1906, the Pershings were recalled to the States, and while they were en route, Teddy Roosevelt made Pershing a brigadier general.

Similiar promotions had been handed a handful of other company and field grade officers, but the fact that Senator Warren was the new general's father-in-law may have had something to do with the jump in grade.

414

Certainly, a great many of the more than eight hundred officers over whom Pershing jumped thought so.

The promotion got him command of Fort McKinley in Luzon, and Pershing went back to the Philippines. It was easy duty; except for a trip to Europe to pick up new military ideas, and a short tour Stateside to be cured of a tropical disease, the Pershings lived in Luzon until 1910; then he was given the (military) governorship of his old island of Mindanao, plus the Sulu Islands south of it. He was back with the Moros.

The Moros were never quiet. Pershing ruled them in the Crook tradition: employ hostiles as scouts, break up captured villages and scatter the warriors among pacified barrios – which he usually called *rancherías*, in the Southwestern style – and teach agriculture.

On the whole he was successful. But the island of Jolo, in the Sulus, flared when he issued an order forbidding the carrying of weapons by civilians in his territory. Pershing took eight troops of the 2nd Cavalry, an infantry regiment, and six companies of native troops and moved to Jolo.

Four of his native companies were Philippine Scouts, natives with Army officers; two were Philippine Constabulary, a queer outfit, also native, but officered by youngsters out of military schools in the States, old non-coms, almost any American who wanted a commission and wasn't really entitled to one.

Pershing cut his force into five columns and sent them combing the jungles. Opposition died here and there and finally crystallized into one strong force of Moro holdouts, who took their families and forted up in the crater of the extinct Bud Dajo volcano. This had happened once before, when Leonard Wood was governor of the Moro country. Wood's troops had had to storm the crater with heavy losses to themselves and horrible slaughter of women and children among the defenders.

Pershing was determined not to repeat the incident; he brought in about a thousand of his troops and put them all around the crater, with barbed wire to close the gaps. Eventually the defenders were starved out of their fort without loss of non-combatants; but, in February 1913, the Moros on Jolo repeated themselves; this time the fort was the extinct crater on Mount Bagsak.

Pershing was luckier at Bagsak than he had been at Bud Dajo; his Philippine Scouts cut between the Moro warriors and the non-combatant villages following them to the crater. Pershing and his men took the fort with bayonets and were able to slaughter the defenders without worrying about women and children being killed. Queerly, the earlier slaughter under Wood's command was to cling to Pershing in the popular mind; the men he commanded in France used it against him continually.

But the bloody slaughter of the Moro braves at Mount Bagsak broke the Moro resistance forever; the Moros – who do not think like Christians –

promoted Datu Pershing to Sultan Pershing, and a Medal of Honor was proposed for the Brigadier. He refused the medal; his letter doing so is on file in the Defense Department, taken over from the old War Department files.

Through 1913 the Moro peace was watched anxiously; by the end of the year it was deemed permanent, and Governor Pershing was relieved of his command and replaced with a civilian.

The Pershings reached San Francisco early in 1914; the general was given an infantry command, the 8th Brigade. In April trouble broke out on the Mexican border and the 8th was ordered to El Paso. Pershing got himself an automobile in which to lead his footsoldiers.

The Mexican flame flickered up and down. Pershing realized he was going to be on the border a long time. He was looking for a home in El Paso to bring his family to in 1915 when he received a wire; Mrs. Pershing and his three daughters had been burned to death in their ramshackle quarters in San Francisco. His only son, Warren, had been saved. He took the bodies to Cheyenne, his wife's home, and buried them and returned to the border. He had never been a chummy man or a jolly one; now he had plenty of reason for his grim sombreness.

For two years the Army patrolled the border. Washington backed first one Mexican party, then another; Woodrow Wilson was now President, and he seemed to have little idea of Mexican affairs. The First World War, of course, had started in Europe and the country, dominated by the heavily populated Eastern seaboard, was much more interested in what was happening in the Old Countries. But, almost two years after Pershing had taken his infantry brigade to El Paso, Francisco "Pancho" Villa – Mexican folk hero, Mexican bandit, looter or benefactor of the poor, as you will – attacked the headquarters town of the 13th Cavalry, Columbus, New Mexico, about fifty miles east of El Paso on the Southern Pacific Railroad.

Columbus is a tiny town, about three miles north of the border; just below the border lies Las Palomas, Chihuahua. The 13th had been there five years and were bored. There still isn't any direct road to El Paso from Columbus – you drive up to Deming, thirty miles to the north, then go east to the Texas city. If any of the officers had a car, it probably took a full day to make the round trip, but in those pre-automobile days, train service was more frequent and accommodating than it is now.

There was a Drunkard's Special – not the official name – that got in from El Paso at midnight with anyone who'd spent an evening on the city. On the night of March 8, 1916, the Officer of the Day strolled down to the station to meet the regimental polo team, which had been playing over at Fort Bliss. When he got them bedded down, ponies and men, the officer – a Lieutenant Castleman – was the only one awake in the 13th Headquarters.

The whole regiment wasn't there; just four troops, one of them the machine-gun troop for the regiment. Three more troops were on the railroad line about fourteen miles west of town, and one was down opposite Las Palomas, at the border gate.

Villa was probably infiltrating the border while Castleman was tucking the polo team into its beds and boxstalls. The Mexicans hit an hour before dawn by killing two sentries. Officer of the Day Castleman rushed out of his office, had his hat knocked off with a bullet, and shot the hat-molester dead at point-blank.

Most of the officers slept in town; Troop F was on standby and rolled out, and with Lieutenant Castleman's guard, started fighting back. It is estimated that Villa had from four hundred to fifteen hundred horsemen – the last is the Army's figure – riding behind him, including his famous Dorado bodyguard, marksmen (mostly Yaqui Indians) who wore gold-colored sombreros and carried excellent Winchester rifles, as well as two sidearms each.

The sergeants organized the other headquarters troops, but altogether there weren't enough 13th men to stop the Villistas, who shot out most of the glass in town and set fire to the hotel.

Lieutenant Lucas, who was one of the polo team, was also commander of the machine guns. He and his men set up one of the guns, but it jammed. He deployed his remaining guns and his troopers as dismounted rifles and posted them so that the Villistas were between them and the burning building; the silhouettes made perfect targets.

The raid didn't last long; shortly after dawn Villa pulled south again, leaving more than two hundred of his men dead behind him. The 13th lost seven dead and eight wounded; civilian losses were about the same.

Why Villa made the raid is hard to figure out. He probably believed that there was a trainload of ammunition in Columbus which the United States was going to send south to Venustiano Carranza whom the Colossus of the North had recognized as President of Mexico. Or he may have simply wanted to show the people of Mexico that Pancho Villa was not frightened of the United States Army.

Southwestern old-timers swear that Villa never made the raid at all; that Carranza had dressed up some of his men as Villistas, including Dorados, and that Germany had paid him to do it, since it would mean intervention by the United States, which was threatening to come to the aid of the allies in Europe. But Carranza's mayors and commandants later acted as though intervention was the last thing they wanted, and it is certain that they did so on that President's orders.

In any event, Villa got more out of the raid than Carranza did; the former's prestige boomed as he outwitted the American Army – with

Carranza's aid; the latter got nothing at all but trouble which eventually led to his downfall.

Major Frank Tompkins took about thirty troopers and went after Villa in hot pursuit. At Las Palomas he was held up by Villa's rearguard. The gringos drove the rearguard back into the main body with their sidearms, by which time two more troops had caught up with Tompkins.

The 13th was mad. They harassed the Villistas for fifteen miles below the border, sniping stragglers and rearguardsmen; Tompkins' report estimated that they killed seventy-five to a hundred Mexicans before the troop horses played out, and the pursuit was called off.

The next day President Wilson issued orders: the Army was to go into Mexico and take Villa, but it must do it with *"scrupulous regard for the sovereignty of Mexico."*

If we do not now know what Villa was thinking about, we are equally in doubt as to Wilson's thoughts. The order was impossible to execute; anybody who knew Mexico and Mexicans could have seen that at once. Unless Pershing – who got the command of the expedition – or one of his men actually saw Villa, in person, give an order to a Mexican, that Mexican was not a Villista, and Pershing was bound not to make war on anybody but Villistas.

And how about that scrupulous regard, etc., etc.? Every Mexican town of any size at all had a garrison, perhaps a tiny one, but it was disregard of Mexican sovereignty for the United States troops to enter a place which the Mexican commander said was in order and was not hiding Villa.

Pershing took off a week after Villa rode out of Columbus. He split his command into two columns and went wih the west column himself. In his immediate command was his old outfit, the buffalo soldiers of the 10th Cavalry, the 7th, an infantry regiment, and a battery of three-inch fieldpieces, 6th Field Artillery. The west column went south from Columbus; the 13th, of course, rode with it, backed up by two infantry regiments and another battery of the 6th Field Artillery.

The rest of the Army moved down on the border, leaving the coast artillery to protect the seaboard. Wilson federalized seventy-five thousand of the National Guard and they went to the border, too. However no National Guardsmen ever entered Mexico, while eventually most of the Regulars did.

It was the last ride of the horse-troopers but, of course, they didn't know that. Pershing did not ride, despite the widely published picture of him leading his headquarters party out of the Santa Maria River – completely dry. Pershing and his headquarters traveled by automobile, in what are always called four Dodge touring cars, though the one used by Pershing looks suspiciously like a Buick in the photographs.

No carbines were carried by the troopers; the sidearm – .45 Colt Automatics – was their only weapon. Pershing was forbidden to use the Mexican railroads – though Villa was adept at loading horses, fighters, and the camp-following families on flatcars – or to enter the Mexican cities.

Carranza sided with Villa, whom he hated and who was his archrival, against the *norteamericanos*. To have expected him to do anything else would be to expect the Republicans to side with a Mexican invasion during a Democratic regime.

There were foreboding elements in the expedition. Pershing was given eight airplanes out of the thirteen that constituted the Aero Squadron of the Signal Corps, the whole United States air force of the time. Six of what were then called aëroplanes broke down almost at once. Pershing had field telephones, though the wires kept breaking. Pershing had radios – Morse code, of course – though their range was less than twenty-five miles.

The troopers got to fight. The 7th contacted Villa at Guerrerro, west of the city of Chihuahua, and routed him. Colonel Dodd took his troopers around the city and Villa got away with the 7th in pursuit. They chased him for seventeen hours and then found his army had just evaporated; probably handfuls of his men were in all the little towns the gringo forces weren't allowed to enter.

Pershing had studied his tactics; he knew what Crook would have done. But Villa was not Geronimo, and his Yaquis were not Apaches; they were Mexican patriots, and the Mexicans sheltered them. Still, Pershing detached Tompkins and his squadron of the 13th and told them to go after Villa and stay on the trail till they caught up. Tompkins believed Villa was in the mountains around Parral; he had always headed there when in trouble before.

Tompkins took off, with his squadron and a packtrain from the 11th Cavalry. He cut Villa's trail and tailed him right into the city of Parral itself. The mayor ordered the troopers out of the city; the people threw stones; the Carranzista troops leveled their guns at the men who had come to wipe out their rival in the Mexican civil war.

Tompkins kept his men in hand, the troopers kept their .45s on their hips, and the squadron pulled out of town to camp where the major had told them to. The Carranzistas attacked their packtrain, and Tompkins retreated, still not fighting, until the Mexican Army tried to cut off his retreat.

Major Tompkins simply could not start a battle; he was outnumbered beyond any outfit's ability to survive. He told off one squad of troopers to fight rearguard, and marched away, his other men still keeping their guns bolstered. The Mexican soldiers pursued them for fifteen miles, and the rearguard reported killing at least forty of the followers.

Pershing was furious. He found out that the mayor of Parral had invited Tompkins in, and had then tried to close the trap with the Carranzistas.

But there wasn't much he could do. Washington sent him more troops but without using the railroads it was almost impossible to supply them. Civilian truck convoys were gotten up, and finally began to work.

Villa broke his command up into tiny bands and scattered them all over the country. Pershing did the same, organizing his command into five separate districts, each with orders to run its own intelligence and to enlist local "agents." This, again, was Crook's old tactic of using hostiles as scouts; but the Mexicans were patriots, not members of dissident Indian bands.

There were more skirmishes. Major Robert L. Howze whipped the bands of Acosta and Dominguez, two of Villa's known lieutenants. Then a rumor reached Washington that Germany was backing Carranza and that the Mexican general was going to move in his army between Pershing and the border and effectively keep the United States Regular Army out of the European war. The government added more National Guard to the border forces, ready to strike south at the back of any Mexican force that moved north of Pershing.

Three months after the raid on Columbus there were U.S. Army troops all over Mexico, and there were dozens of rumors that Villa was dead – Carranza said he was – and that the Yanquis had no more business in Mexico.

Around the middle of June two troops of the 10th were riding toward Ahumada when they came to the town of Carrizal, square across their track. The town commandant refused them permission to ride through; the senior captain, commanding the ninety troopers, decided to go through anyway. The troopers were outnumbered more than four to one, and the Mexican soldiers had machine guns. It was a short, bitter battle; the 10th troopers showed more courage than their commander had sense; he was killed, the junior captain was severely wounded, eleven troopers were killed outright, several more wounded, and twenty-three prisoners were taken by the Mexicans. The prisoners were later turned back to the United States at El Paso, and both the United States and Mexico realized that they had almost been in a war that neither wanted.

Diplomatic negotiations were started, but it was January 1917 before all the troops were out of Mexico.

Pershing returned to the States a hero, despite his failure to capture Pancho Villa. When the United States entered the European War in April, he was the natural choice to head the American Expeditionary Force; he was the general best known to the American people.

The horse soldiers were through. No troop horses were taken to France; some of the cavalry rode patrol in the Philippines during the war; some were dismounted and used in France for military police and similar duties. No horses went to the Second World War, either, though the troopers drilled on horseback daily until they went overseas, and saber charges were practiced.

The screening and intelligence functions of the horse soldiers had been taken over by aviation; the ride to the battle to fight dismounted is now done in a truck, tank, half-track, glider, or helicopter.

Fitzhugh Lee had shown up in the Cuban War as Consul General in Cuba. He was made Military Governor of that island when it surrendered, with the rank of Brigadier General, USA, a Regular. The next year Fitzhugh Lee, Jr., reported from West Point to the Cavalry. Today there is a Fitzhugh Lee in the armed services; he is a flier, Vice Admiral (Aviation) in the Navy. Light-Horse Harry would be Fighter-Plane Harry nowadays.

The Cavalry name is carried on. In World War II light armored or tank outfits bore the old horse designations; in the current Vietnam struggle the cavalry are airborne infantry.

The horses didn't leave the Army all at once; in the late 1940s the last of them were mustered into retirement up in Colorado, and the last of the artillery horses went with them.

The horse soldier was no more. But before the troopers climbed out of their saddles, they had gained a continent for the country they served, they had helped that country gain independence, and they had given the new mechanized Army its first Commander-in-Chief.

They will not be forgotten.

A Few Useful Books

Formal bibliographies by career historians mean less and less each year; to the principal books read have been added all the books read, and then all the books quoted in all the books read.

For an informal history like this, the technique has been to read several books on each subject, usually the biographies of the leading figure in each war, campaign, or period. Then the best book was selected and used as a guide, checking it against all the others, foreground and background, until as approximate a truth as possible could be reached.

Of course, contemporary magazines and often newspapers were read. Figures – usually number of troops – were taken from official War Department, now Department of Army, records. In a surprising number of cases they do not agree with those given in diaries and regimental histories and autobiographies.

For Light-Horse Harry Lee, the best book to read is his own, *The Memoirs of the War in the Southern Department*. It should be reprinted in one of the fine modern editions; at present it has to be consulted out of the locked cases in the larger libraries. For bibliophiles it is a curiosity, in that the 1812, or first edition is less valuable than the 1869, or second; this is because Harry's son, Robert E., wrote an introduction for the second edition.

An amazing amount of legend has been published about Francis Marion, the Swamp Fox, but he never wrote an autobiography. His story here was synthesized from a half dozen books, especially the *Life of Francis Marion* which W.G. Simms published in 1844. State histories of South Carolina usually have a good deal of material on the partisan leader.

For the Revolution in general, *The War of the Revolution*, by Christopher Ward was found to be most useful and reliable.

Official Army records filled in the period before, during, and after the War of 1812. For the casual reader, the *American Military History, ROTCM 145-20* issued by the Department of the Army – the edition used here was

July 1959 – is accurate, readable, and can be purchased and taken home. Library research sometimes gets difficult; to track down the true story of Richard Mentor Johnson and his Kentucky cavalry at the Battle of the Thames, for instance, it was necessary to have a librarian take Richard Johnson's own autobiography out of a locked case or vault; the reader then researched while an armed guard watched him closely. The names of the library and its city remain behind lips locked as closely as the case.

As the cavalry scene moved west, H.H. Bancroft's monumental work was, of course, consulted steadily. The various volumes will not be cited here as used; anyone interested in the part of our country that lies past 100 degrees west needs a set of Bancroft as a prime tool.

Dwight L. Clarke's *Stephen Watts Kearny, Soldier of the West*, was published in 1961, and fills a long-felt need.

For more knowledge of P. St. George Cooke, by all means read his *The Conquest of New Mexico and California*, republished in 1964 by Horn and Wallace of Albuquerque. Unfortunately, Cooke's equally delightful *Scenes and Adventures in the Army, or Romance of Military Life*, is another locked case item at the moment. However, Miss Ruth Rambo, of the Library of the Museum of New Mexico, did not cover me with a gun while I reread it.

In telling the story of the Mormon Battalion, Cooke's narrative was followed, with exceptions from memory. For the purposes of a novel published in 1960, I read as many of the Mormon diaries as possible, and in giving the present account, did not make the journeys necessary to reread.

The 2nd Dragoons have a book all to themselves, *From Everglade to Cañon with the 2nd U.S. Cavalry*, by T.F. Rodenbough. To know more about the Seminole War – lightly covered in this book, because it was really not a cavalry matter, though the 2nd fought all through it – it is necessary to consult Bureau of Ethnology, Chronicles of Oklahoma and Florida State records.

Like his uncle, Phil Kearny has his own book, *Kearny the Magnificent*, by Irving Werstein. It is entertaining and pretty well researched.

The trouble between Kearny and Cooke on one side and Frémont on the other was mostly taken from the Congressional Records; all through the budget troubles of the cavalry, the Record and its predecessor, the Globe, were used.

The amount written on the Civil War – or War between the States – is, as any researcher knows, appalling. The works of Bruce Catton and Henry Steele Commager do not need endorsement here.

John W. Thomason, Jr.'s biography of J.E.B. Stuart is the most readable of all the volumes written about the Cavalier. Thomason was a captain in the Marine Corps at the time he wrote the book, and a colonel before he died in the service. He was also a novelist, short story writer, illustrator,

423

and portrait painter, and remarkably good at everything he tried. For source material, one of Stuart's aides, H.B. McClellan, wrote a biography; and almost any Southern library of size has a memoir by one of Stuart's riders.

Phil Sheridan wrote his own *Personal Memoirs*. Richard O'Connor, Pershing's biographer, also wrote a good book on Sheridan. The Encyclopedia Brittanica article on the Shenandoah Valley campaigns is a masterful thing.

Mosby, the raider-lawyer, wrote his *Reminiscences*; he also wrote *Stuart's Cavalry Campaigns*, but the former is more interesting; the character of the writer-protagonist comes through clearly. Again, it is not difficult to find reminiscences and memoirs, published and unpublished, by Mosby men.

Basil W. Duke, John Morgan's brother-in-law, second-in-command and successor as Commanding General, was such an excellent observer and writer that there is little necessity to read any later evaluations. The name of the book is *History of Morgan's Cavalry*. Allan Keller's *Morgans Raid* is fine reading, and covers the period when Duke was absent in the South as a union prisoner-for-exchange. It is also more explicit as to Morgan's escape from prison.

Nathan Bedford Forrest could hardly have been expected to write an autobiography. The late nineteenth- and early twentieth-century biographies by Wyeth and Mathes and others are prejudiced in the raider's favor, but accurate enough as to his cavalry activities. *First with the Most Forrest* by Ralph Selph Henry is good reading, and believable.

The story of the Iowa cavalry on the Plains is pretty much a condensation of Captain Eugene Ware's *The Indian War of 1864*, with obvious annotations and comments from official records and other sources.

The description of the McClellan saddle is from an 1863 War Department book of specifications for suppliers to the military.

The material on the Civil War in the Southwest is synthesized from a myriad of sources, collected for the writing of this book and other work.

George Crook never finished his memoirs; the fragment he did write has been published but is not very illuminating. His officer, Captain John G. Bourke wrote *On the Border with Crook* and *An Apache Campaign*, both excellent books, and John F. Finerty of the Chicago *Times* went along on the Sioux-Cheyenne Campaign – as well as on the later 1879 campaign up to the Canadian border, and wrote a fine book called *War-Path and Bivouac*, very well worth reading.

The material on the "small" Indian wars was mostly taken from State Historic sources.

A small, elegant library could be filled with all that has been written about George Armstrong Custer. If there is an afterlife and a purgatory, no more fitting fate could be imagined than making Custer read everything written about Frémont, and vice versa. Custer himself wrote several books, and so did his wife, Elizabeth. Colonel W.A. Graham, USA retired, has written, compiled, or published at least seven books on the various phases of the Little Big Horn and the subsequent Court of Inquiry on Marcus Reno. Those who wish to read about Custer may do so where they will.

David Lavender, that expert and devoted chronicler of Western matters, has written *Ghost Dance*. There is more material in the Bureau of Ethnology records for those who want it. The opinion that the Ghost Shirt Dance movement segued into the peyote or Native American Church movement is personal with me, based on observation and conversation and research, as was the Sioux version of the Massacre at Wounded Knee.

Richard O'Connor's book on Pershing I found the most interesting and most easily reconcilable with the pro-Pershing and anti-Pershing newspaper and magazine accounts of that soldier's life. It is called *Black Jack Pershing*, a name given Pershing because he served with Negro troops, a touch of West Point humor not worth commenting on.

The University of Oklahoma, which has published or republished so many of the books used in the preparation of this present volume, brought out Don Rickey Jr.'s *Forty Miles a Day on Beans and Hay* in 1963. In it can be found detailed accounts of the life of a trooper in the post Civil War West; I have borrowed from it unblushingly.

Santa Fe, New Mexico, 1965-66.

Index